· T H E ·
GREAT BOOK OF
BASEBALL
KNOWLEDGE

The Ultimate Test for
the Ultimate Fan

DAVID NEMEC

MASTERS PRESS

NTC/Contemporary Publishing Group

Library of Congress Cataloging-in-Publication Data

Nemec, David.
    The great book of baseball knowledge: the ultimate test for
the ultimate fan / David Nemec.
        p.   cm.
    ISBN 0-8092-2659-6
    1. Baseball—United States—Miscellanea. I. Title.
GV867.3.N467 1999
796.357'0973—dc21

98-45461
                                            CIP

Photos on pages 1, 13, 15, 31, 56, 71, 88, 98, 118, 125, 148, 151, 173, 184,
200, 210, 226, 252, 254, 265, 274, 287, 301, 330, 353, 368, 371, 373, 383, 390,
392, 406, 418, 431, 451, 454, 472, 481, 484, 501, 508, 511, 525, 529, 535, 547,
555, 560, 580, 592, and 597 courtesy of Transcedental Graphics, Boulder, CO.
Photo on page 138 courtesy of Joe Santry. Photos on pages 177, 292, 320, and
539 courtesy of the author. Photos on pages 8, 50, 415, 436, 445, 467, 570,
and 582 courtesy of the National Baseball Library, Cooperstown, NY.

Cover design by Scott Rattray
Interior Design by Point West, Inc.

Published by Masters Press
A division of NTC/Contemporary Publishing Group, Inc.
4255 West Touhy Avenue, Lincolnwood (Chicago), Illinois 60646-1975 U.S.A.
Printed in the United States of America
International Standard Book Number: 0-8092-2659-6

99 00 01 02 03 04 VL 18 17 16 15 14 13 12 11 10 9 8 7 6 5 4 3 2 1

To Barney McCosky: line-drive hitter, tough out (1917–96)

Contents

Postseason and All-Star Action

The Teams

Honors and Awards

Historian's Corner

Miscellaneous

FOREWORD

The Great Book of Baseball Knowledge is a product of a lifetime of exhaustive research and record keeping by David Nemec. In it, Nemec combines the most compelling features of his many baseball quiz and history books as well as his bestselling *Great Baseball Feats, Facts, & Firsts*. The result is a book that is absolutely original, an illustrated treasure of questions, answers, lore, and information that serves as both an invaluable reference work and an enormously entertaining learning tool.

In *The Great Book of Baseball Knowledge*, Nemec divides the game into nine eras much as he does in *Great Baseball Feats, Facts, & Firsts* and then takes the reader on a journey through time, covering more than 125 years of baseball history. But the main difference here is that unlike other reference works, which consider 1901 or, less commonly, 1876 as the dawn of big league ball, *The Great Book of Baseball Knowledge* guides readers back to the National Association (1871–75), baseball's fledgling "major league," to embrace a much ignored period.

This collection engages the reader with more than a thousand probing questions and insights about baseball's legendary teams, players, and events. Accompanying the questions are hordes of fascinating lists of season and career record holders. Simply flip through the chapters, stop at a page at random, and luxuriate in charts on topics that have never appeared in any other volume. Nemec has created "Top 10" leader lists covering previously untapped categories ranging from the most losses by a Hall of Famer in his rookie year to the fewest combined runs and RBI produced in a season by a player who led the major leagues in hits.

However, what truly separates this work from trivia or "challenge" books is Nemec's unique format. Most question/answer books test recall of facts already learned—the reader will either know the answer or not. They do not provide a way of directly accessing the answer and learning in the process. Nemec's questions have a different aim. They are designed to help readers at all levels of baseball knowledge, from novice to expert, to expand their understanding of the game and lead them through the wondrous maze of facts and figures in order to solve his puzzlers. The clues to each question are crafted to steer the reader gradually to the correct player or team while providing tantalizing information and added questions along the way that are often as much fun as the original teaser.

Here is an example of how Nemec's questions are constructed, from the "Hallowed Hitsmiths" chapter:

The 1920–41 era was the most hitter friendly in history. Name the only big leaguer to play 1,000 games in that era and compile a sub-.240 career batting average.

- A) He was a middle infielder.
- B) Babe Ruth rated his the best AL shortstop glove in the early 1930s.
- C) He debuted with the 1930 Red Sox and finished with the 1940 Cubs.
- D) His real first name was Harold, but he was known by the same nickname as another middle infielder who was born George Nill.
- E) He also had the same nickname as another light-hitting middle infielder of the same period who made the Hall of Fame.

Here, clue (A) reveals the player's general position. Clue (B) pinpoints his exact position and also the league where he achieved most of his success. Clue (C) frames his career, or you might say "bookends" it, and reveals two of his teams. Clue (D) reveals his first name and also telegraphs his nickname to readers aware of George "Rabbit" Nill. Clue (E) will help steer many knowledgeable readers to Rabbit Maranville and then ultimately to the answer. Nemec links and extends the question with a chart of 1,000-gamers with the lowest batting average in each era.

Readers will quickly notice and appreciate that the many questions within questions as well as the "stumpers" that can be devised from the bounty of charts and lists swell the total number of possible puzzlers in this book to literally hundreds of thousands. For trivia buffs, Nemec's book is a feast of thought-provoking questions and answers on all facets of the game. Even the most casual reader is guaranteed to win an endless supply of free drinks at his or her favorite sports bar and stump the neighborhood expert. For historians and fans looking for a handy compendium of record holders, single-season and career leaders, and dozens of Top10 batting, pitching, and fielding lists, in one volume, *The Great Book of Baseball Knowledge* is a must. It is also a great teaching tool for young fans and those who have only a basic knowledge of the game.

So, sit back, kick back, and turn the pages. Get ready to learn and enjoy.

Scott Flatow
The Macmillan
Baseball Quiz Book

ACKNOWLEDGMENTS

In a sense, I began this book when I was about 11 years old and first wondered who had the second-most career home runs of anyone who made his major league debut as a pitcher. My question to myself drove me to seek out the answer, and it slowly grew into a "Top 10" list. Others like it soon followed.

At the time, back in the 1950s, I worked totally alone and assumed that I always would. Who else could be so crazy as to spend his Saturday nights poring through *The Baseball Encyclopedia* in search of all the pitchers with at least 10 years of major league service who never had a winning season?

Now, happily, I'm in almost daily contact with several dozen minds every bit as crazy, and many of them were of extraordinary help to me in putting together this book.

Three I especially want to cite are Scott Flatow, Tom Ruane, and Dave Zeman. Their combined age is less than the present age of Lou Polli (the oldest living ex–major leaguer as of this writing), but their combined knowledge is priceless. Scott and Dave are writers and baseball historians destined to treat you again and again to their personal treasures in the years ahead. Tom is in a world of his own at the moment, in part because he alone knows how he creates the research tools he has at his fingertips, but it's a world full of discoveries that he will gladly and unstintingly share with any and all who care.

Once again, I thank Mark Rucker for sharing several more jewels from his seemingly bottomless storehouse of vintage baseball photographs. Mark and I have worked together before, always to my infinite gain.

I also want to thank Ken Samelson for his supportive and helpful editing, Fran Collin for once again representing my interest in the publishing world, and the following fellow writers, researchers, and general mavens: Tony Salin, Pete Palmer, Sean Lahman, Phil Von Borries, Ray Nemec, Dick Thompson, Joe Santry, Rich Topp, Al Blumkin, and Tom Zocco.

Finally, I want to thank the many readers who have written to apprise me of inaccuracies they've found in my other books. There may be one or two in this one too, so continue to let me know. Your help is invaluable and deeply appreciated.

THE HITTERS

The Elite 3,000

1. **Three career milestones assure baseball immortality and eventual Hall of Fame entry— collecting 3,000 hits, hitting 500 home runs, and winning 300 games. But not all members of these elite lists have uniformly impeccable Hall of Fame credentials. Examine the following list of career leaders in 11 major offensive departments among the 21 men with 3,000 hits and then name the *Elite* 3,000 tailenders in the same 11 departments.**

Highest Batting Average...Ty Cobb .366
Highest Slugging Average ....Stan Musial .559
Most Total Bases...Hank Aaron 6856
Most Home Runs ....Hank Aaron 755
Highest On-Base Percentage ....Ty Cobb .432
Most RBI ....Hank Aaron 2297
Most Runs ....Ty Cobb 2245
Most Triples ....Ty Cobb 295
Most Walks...Carl Yastrzemski 1845
Fewest Strikeouts...Cap Anson 302
Most Stolen Bases..Lou Brock 938

Note: Anson's 1897 strikeout total is unavailable, as are the totals for several of Tris Speaker's and Nap Lajoie's seasons. All three almost certainly had fewer careers Ks than Paul Waner (376), who has the lowest total among *Elite 3,000* members with complete career data.

2. **Who are the only four members of the *Elite* 3,000 whose hits all came before age 40?**
   A) All four achieved *Elite* 3,000 membership since expansion.
   B) All but one of the four won at least one batting title.
   C) Three of the four collected some of their hits as DHs.
   D) Three of the four played with just one team for their entire careers.
   E) Three of the four retired prior to age 40, and the fourth died while active.

3. **Name the only *Elite* 3,000 member who never played in a postseason game.**
   A) He and Rod Carew are the only 3,000-hit men who never played in a World Series, but Carew played in several LCSes.
   B) Both he and Carew won multiple batting titles.
   C) He and Carew saw regular duty at the same two positions during their careers.
   D) He began the 1902 season with the AL pennant winner that year.
   E) The club with which he finished the 1902 season was nicknamed for him after he became its player-manager.

Elite 3,000—Postseason Hits

NAME	DIV.	LCS	WS	TOTAL
Pete Rose	6	45	35	86
George Brett	2	35	19	56
Paul Molitor	5	15	23	43
Eddie Collins	—	—	42	42
Eddie Murray	11	19	11	41
Lou Brock	—	—	34	34
Roberto Clemente	—	13	21	34
Hank Aaron	—	5	20	25
Carl Yastrzemski	—	5	19	24
Stan Musial	—	—	22	22
Tris Speaker	—	—	22	22
Willie Mays	—	5	17	22
Robin Yount	6	4	12	22
Dave Winfield	7	8	6	21
Ty Cobb	—	—	17	17
Cap Anson	—	—	16	16
Al Kaline	—	5	11	16
Honus Wagner	—	—	14	14
Rod Carew	—	11	—	11
Paul Waner	—	—	5	5
Nap Lajoie	—	—	—	—

4. **Name the six Elite 3,000 members who spent their entire careers with just one team.**
    A) Two did it with NL teams, and four with AL teams.
    B) Two of the six did it with expansion teams.
    C) Only one of the six collected the bulk of his career hits prior to expansion.
    D) Only one of the six played the same position his entire career.
    E) The only one of the six who never won a batting title bagged two MVP Awards, each while playing a different position.

5. **Three Elite 3,000 members never had a 200-hit season. Two of them are Eddie Murray and Dave Winfield. Who is the third?**
    A) His high of 191 hits came his sophomore year.
    B) He won a bat title one year despite collecting just 162 hits.
    C) Even though he never had a 200-hit season, he twice paced the AL in hits.
    D) Just once in his 23 seasons did he collect fewer than 100 hits.
    E) His hit total is second only to Stan Musial's among players who spent their entire careers with just one team.

Most Hits, Career, All Hits with One Team

RANK	NAME	YEARS	TEAM	HITS
1	Stan Musial	1941–63	StL, NL	3630
2	Carl Yastrzemski	1961–83	Bos, AL	3419
3	George Brett	1973–93	KC, AL	3154
4	Robin Yount	1974–93	Mil, AL	3142
5	Al Kaline	1953–74	Det, AL	3007
6	Roberto Clemente	1955–72	Pit, NL	3000
7	Mel Ott	1925–47	NY, NL	2876
8	Brooks Robinson	1955–77	Bal, AL	2848
9	Charlie Gehringer	1924–42	Det, AL	2839
10	Luke Appling	1930–50	Chi, AL	2749

Note: Active players excluded; Cal Ripken and Tony Gwynn otherwise would both be on this list.

6. **Name the five Elite 3,000 members who never won a batting title.**
   A) Only one of the five posted a .300+ career BA.
   B) The .300 hitter collected 3,315 career hits.
   C) The other four all played after expansion.
   D) The .300 hitter died before any of the other four logged his first hit.
   E) Three of the five were still active in 1993.

7. **Who is the only Elite 3,000 member to appear in a box score with just one other Elite 3,000 member in either a regular-season, a postseason, or an All-Star game?**
   A) He played against another Elite 3,000 member only in regular-season action.
   B) He is the only Elite 3,000 man whose last hit came with the Yankees.
   C) He made his 3,000th hit with the Boston Braves.
   D) He and his brother hold the season record for the most combined hits by two sibling teammates.
   E) The only fellow Elite 3,000 member ever in a box score with him was Stan Musial.

8. **Name the first two Elite 3,000 members to face each other in a major league game.**
   A) Both played the same position the first time they faced each other.
   B) They were more than 20 years apart in age at the time.
   C) Both were player-managers during much of their careers.
   D) The nicknames by which both are best remembered rhyme.
   E) Their respective teams when they first faced each other were the Chicago Colts and the Philadelphia Phillies.

9. **Who were the first Elite 3,000 members to be teammates?**
   A) They first became teammates after each had collected his 3,000th hit.
   B) One of the two was back with his original team that season after playing a dozen years in another AL city.
   C) They were joined the following year by a third Elite 3,000 member.
   D) The trio were the first three lefty hitters to collect 3,000 hits.
   E) The 1927–28 A's enjoyed the services of the three immortals.

10. Whose 40 career pinch hits led all *Elite* 3,000 members in pinch bingles prior to 1985 when Rod Carew tied him for the top spot?

   A)   Third to him and Carew with 37 pinch bingles is Al Kaline.
   B)   Stan Musial had the second-most pinch hits (35) of any *Elite* 3,000 member at the time he retired.
   C)   He was 10-for-21 as a pinch hitter with Brooklyn in 1943.
   D)   He walked as a pinch hitter in his final big league at bat in 1945.
   E)   He was "poison" with a bat long before he collected his first pinch hit.

Elite 3,000—Most Pinch Hits, Career

RANK	NAME	ABS	BA	PHS
1	Rod Carew	124	.323	40
	Paul Waner	164	.244	40
3	Al Kaline	115	.322	37
4	Stan Musial	126	.278	35
5	Lou Brock	125	.264	33
6	Dave Winfield	101	.317	32
7	Eddie Collins	105	.257	27
8	Willie Mays	94	.245	23
9	Pete Rose	84	.250	21
10	Tris Speaker	60	.333	20

11. Who was the first *Elite* 3,000 member to slap a hit in a 20th century World Series?

   A)   His first postseason bingle came 18 years after Cap Anson became the first future *Elite* 3,000 member to hit safely in a 19th century World Series.
   B)   He garnered hits in two different World Series.
   C)   His two Series appearances came six years apart.
   D)   His first postseason at bat came against Cy Young.
   E)   He is the lone *Elite* 3,000 member to compile a hit with a Louisville ML franchise.

12. Who was the first *Elite* 3,000 member to spread his safeties among four different ML teams?

   A)   All four teams were in the same league.
   B)   He collected World Series hits with two of the teams.
   C)   He is the lone *Elite* 3,000 member to log a hit in a Washington uniform.
   D)   He won his lone batting title while with Cleveland.
   E)   He was the first southpaw to notch 3,000 hits.

13. Bob Feller almost surely would have won 300 games had his career not been curtailed by World War II. What two Hall of Famers almost definitely would have collected 3,000 hits if their careers hadn't been shortened by military service?

   A)   One had 2,749 career hits and lost almost two full seasons to World War II, and the other finished with 2,654 hits and missed all or part of five seasons.
   B)   Each was a multiple batting title winner.
   C)   Between them, they played on just one pennant winner, that in 1946.
   D)   Each holds his team's record for the highest BA in a season.
   E)   One of the pair is the only shortstop to win two AL batting titles.

14. Cap Anson is the only 19th century star to amass 3,000 hits, but not all authorities credit him with that distinction because he had more than 400 hits in the National Association, which is not universally recognized as a major league. In any event, Anson leads all players active between 1876 and 1900 in hits, with 2,995. Who is second to him in career hits among post-1876 players who retired before the turn of the century?

    A) He collected the last of his 2,467 career hits with the 1897 St. Louis Browns.

    B) His first hit came as a member of the 1880 Troy Trojans.

    C) He is the only lefty thrower in the Hall of Fame who was a regular at three different positions, none of which was an outfield post.

    D) He played 17 years in the NL without ever winning a senior loop homer crown.

    E) He nonetheless holds the record for the most career homers by anyone active prior to Babe Ruth.

15. In 1980, Pete Rose became only the second man to play in a World Series after he'd collected his 3,000th hit. Who was the first to do it?

    A) He collected his first hit when he was 20 and his last at age 42.

    B) He is the only *Elite* 3,000 member whose last plate appearance came in a Series game.

    C) He has the most career home runs of anyone who was never an RBI leader.

    D) He is the lone *Elite* 3,000 member to collect the majority of his hits for a team based on the West Coast.

    E) He alone has seen Series action for two different New York NL franchises.

The Elite 3,000

	NAME	YEARS	HITS	3,000TH	TEAM
1	Pete Rose	1963–86	4526	1977	Cin, NL
2	Ty Cobb	1905–28	4189	1921	Det, AL
3	Hank Aaron	1954–76	3771	1970	Atl, NL
4	Stan Musial	1941–63	3630	1958	StL, NL
5	Tris Speaker	1907–28	3514	1925	Cle, AL
6	Carl Yastrzemski	1961–83	3419	1979	Bos, AL
7	Honus Wagner	1897–1917	3415	1914	Pit, NL
8	Cap Anson	1871–97	3414	1894	Chi, NL
9	Paul Molitor	1978–98	3319	1996	Min, AL
10	Eddie Collins	1906–30	3315	1925	Chi, AL
11	Willie Mays	1951–73	3283	1970	SF, NL
12	Eddie Murray	1977–97	3255	1995	Cle, AL
13	Nap Lajoie	1896–1916	3242	1914	Cle, AL
14	George Brett	1973–93	3154	1992	KC, AL
15	Paul Waner	1926–45	3152	1942	Bos, NL
16	Robin Yount	1974–93	3142	1992	Mil, AL
17	Dave Winfield	1973–95	3110	1993	Min, AL
18	Rod Carew	1967–85	3053	1985	Cal, AL
19	Lou Brock	1961–79	3023	1979	StL, NL
20	Al Kaline	1953–74	3007	1974	Det, AL
21	Roberto Clemente	1955–72	3000	1972	Pit, NL

Toward the end of the 1916 season, Nap Lajoie became the first man to collect 2,500 hits in the AL. His 3,000th career hit came two years earlier. Lajoie is the only Elite 3,000 member who never appeared in a postseason game.

The Cooperstown 500

1. **Examine the following list of leaders in 11 major offensive departments among the 15 men who have collected 500 career home runs and then try to identify the *Cooperstown* 500 tailenders in the same 11 departments.**

   Highest Batting Average ....Ted Williams .344

   Highest Slugging Average...Babe Ruth .690

   Most Total Bases ....Hank Aaron 6856

   Highest Home Run Ratio ....Babe Ruth 8.5

   Highest On-Base Percentage...Ted Williams .483

   Most Hits...Hank Aaron 3771

   Most RBI..Hank Aaron 2297

   Most Runs..Babe Ruth 2174

   Most Walks ....Babe Ruth 2056

   Fewest Strikeouts ....Ted Williams 709

   Most Stolen Bases ....Willie Mays 338

2. **After clubbing his 299th career home run, Gary Carter went a record 66 games and 225 at bats before belting his 300th. Most 500-homer men, in contrast, quickly reached the coveted pinnacle after tagging their 499th. What *Cooperstown* 500 member suffered the longest drought (14 games and 66 at bats) before garnering his 500th blast?**

   A) Les Tietje surrendered his 300th homer.

   B) He was the first *Cooperstown* 500 member to stroke his final homer as a Phil.

   C) George Caster was his victim when he got his 500th.

   D) He was the first *Cooperstown* 500 member to homer under the lights.

   E) He and a gardener named Piersall had the same first name but spelled it differently.

3. **Mickey Mantle hit all of his 536 dingers in a Yankees uniform. Eddie Murray currently holds the record for wearing the uniform of the most different franchises of any *Cooperstown* 500 member. Who shared the record with Murray prior to Murray's appearance with Anaheim in 1997?**

   A) He had the most four-baggers as a rookie of any 500-homer man.

   B) He was the first 500-homer man to wear the uniform of an Ohio-based team.

   C) He is additionally the only *Cooperstown* 500 member to wear the uniform of **both** Ohio-based teams.

   D) He is the only *Cooperstown* 500 member to homer in his first AB as a player-manager.

   E) He was the first man to win an MVP Award in both the NL and the AL.

4. **Which 3 of the 16 franchises in existence since 1901 have yet to have a *Cooperstown* 500 member wear their uniforms while an active player?**
    A) Two are in the NL.
    B) The AL franchise waited the longest of the clubs extant in 1901 before it had its first home run leader.
    C) One NL franchise recently had its first loop tater king in more than half a century.
    D) The other NL franchise once had a player who won seven home run crowns in his first seven seasons in its uniform.
    E) The three franchises last saw World Series action in 1959, 1979, and 1987.

5. **Who is the only *Cooperstown* 500 member to make his ML debut as a second baseman?**
    A) He has the most career homers of anyone who played 150 games in a season at 3B.
    B) He has the most career homers of anyone who played 150 games in a season at 1B.
    C) He has the most career homers of anyone who played exclusively in the AL.
    D) He has the most career home runs by a Bonus Baby.
    E) He broke Ralph Kiner's record for the most career home runs by anyone whose last name begins with the letter K.

6. **Babe Ruth was the first *Cooperstown* 500 member to homer while serving as a pitcher. Who is the only *Cooperstown* 500 member to connect for a four-bagger while in the lineup as a catcher?**
    A) In his first ML season, he was 6-for-9, all as a pinch hitter.
    B) He caught 109 games in his career.
    C) He started at 3B in the 1935 All-Star Game.
    D) He is the only *Cooperstown* 500 member to play in three straight World Series for a team other than the New York Yankees.
    E) He played 1,919 games at first base.

Most Games at Each Position—Cooperstown 500 Member

POSITION	NAME	GAMES
C	Jimmie Foxx	109
P	Babe Ruth	163
1B	Eddie Murray	2413
2B	Harmon Killebrew	11
3B	Mike Schmidt	2212
SS	Ernie Banks	1125
OF	Willie Mays	2843

7. **Three pairs of *Cooperstown* 500 members were teammates at some point in their careers. Name them.**
    A) Only one pair were teammates on a World Championship team.
    B) One pair of teammates each won at least one Triple Crown.
    C) The third pair of teammates played together on the last team that had to triumph in a three-game pennant playoff to win a flag.
    D) Only one of the three teams involved is still in the same city where it was originally located.
    E) None of the six players involved hit a homer in the majors after 1980.

8. Who was the first *Cooperstown* 500 member to manage in the majors?
- A) He hit his last four-bagger while a player-manager.
- B) He is the only *Cooperstown* 500 member to hit his first ML blast before he turned 20.
- C) He was the first *Cooperstown* 500 member to hit all his taters with the same team.
- D) He once held the NL record for the most career home runs.
- E) He currently owns the record for the most career home runs by a player whose last name begins with the letter O.

9. Who was the last *Cooperstown* 500 member to bat against a pitcher legally allowed to throw a spitball?
- A) Another *Cooperstown* 500 member also faced the same spitballer earlier in the last season it was done.
- B) Babe Ruth faced the last spitballer two years earlier in a World Series game.
- C) Ruth was a teammate of the last spitballer during the spitballer's final days in the majors.
- D) The spitballer's final 10 games were as a Yankees reliever in 1934.
- E) The *Cooperstown* 500 member in question played for the A's in 1934.

10. Ernie Banks failed to hit a four-bagger in a World Series for the simple reason that he never played in one. What two *Cooperstown* 500 members who did see Series action also failed to connect in a fall classic?
- A) One of the pair played in two World Series.
- B) The other member of the pair was the first *Cooperstown* 500 member to retire without hitting a Series four-bagger.
- C) The two opposed each other several times in All-Star play.
- D) One of the two is the only 500-homer man to hit four dingers in a game.
- E) The other is the only *Cooperstown* 500 member to homer in his final ML at bat.

Cooperstown 500—Postseason Homers

NAME	DIV.	LCS	WS	TOTAL HRs
Mickey Mantle	—	—	18	18
Reggie Jackson	2	6	10	18
Babe Ruth	—	—	15	15
Frank Robinson	—	2	8	10
Eddie Murray	1	3	4	8
Hank Aaron	—	3	3	6
Jimmie Foxx	—	—	4	4
Mel Ott	—	—	4	4
Harmon Killebrew	—	2	1	3
Mike Schmidt	—	1	2	3
Willie McCovey	—	2	1	3
Willie Mays	—	1	0	1
Eddie Mathews	—	—	1	1
Ted Williams	—	—	0	0
Ernie Banks	—	—	—	—

11. **Prior to Babe Ruth, the notion that anyone could hit 500 career homers seemed absurd. But then, no one had ever before averaged anywhere near Ruth's 8.5 home runs per 100 at bats. Who was the only slugger prior to 1920 to average as many as three career home runs per 100 at bats?**

    A)   He averaged 3.01 dingers per 100 ABs in his 11-year career.

    B)   He won his last homer crown with the fewest ABs of any tater leader since 1876.

    C)   At age 31 he owned just 2 career blasts, but he retired with 119.

    D)   He held the NL 20th century season home run record prior to 1922.

    E)   His last dinger crown came in 1919 while he was the Phillies' player-manager.

12. **Who was the first *Cooperstown* 500 member to have a future 300-game winner for a teammate when he reached his coveted 500th?**

    A)   Earlier in their careers, the pair had been teammates on another team in the same league.

    B)   The *Cooperstown* 500 member had exactly 500 dingers at the close of the season in which he reached the magic mark.

    C)   The 300-game winner had exactly 300 wins at the close of the season in which he reached the magic mark.

    D)   The years the two ascended to their respective pinnacles were 1940 and 1941.

    E)   Between them, the pair won 301 games in the majors.

13. **Who was the first member of the *Cooperstown* 500 club to smack his pinnacle blast with an expansion team?**

    A)   His final 11 career blasts are the only homers hit by a *Cooperstown* 500 member in the uniform of a certain AL franchise.

    B)   His seventh career homer broke Babe Ruth's record for the most career dingers hit by a *Cooperstown* 500 member wearing the uniform of a certain big league team.

    C)   His first 490 homers came with his original NL franchise.

    D)   He is the only *Cooperstown* 500 member to find the seats while wearing the uniform of teams in three different cities that were all part of the same franchise.

    E)   His 500th homer came as a teammate of Rusty Staub the year Staub became the first member of an expansion team to lead the NL in doubles.

14. **Apart from Babe Ruth, who is the only *Cooperstown* 500 member to log a decision in the majors as a pitcher?**

    A)   His only big league decision—a win—came when he was 37.

    B)   His last ML homer came in 1945, the same year he earned his lone hill decision.

    C)   He was the first right-handed hitter to top 500 home runs.

    D)   He and Mark McGwire are the only two men to enjoy two 50-homer seasons while wearing the uniforms of two different franchises.

    E)   Prior to 1998 he, Hank Greenberg, and Mark McGwire shared the season record for both the most homers by a righty hitter and the most homers by a first baseman.

The Cooperstown 500

RANK	NAME	YEARS	HRS	500TH	TEAM	VICTIM
1	Hank Aaron	1954–76	755	1968	Atl, NL	Mike McCormick
2	Babe Ruth	1914–35	714	1929	NY, AL	Willis Hudlin
3	Willie Mays	1951–73	660	1965	SF, NL	Don Nottebart
4	Frank Robinson	1956–76	586	1971	Bal, AL	Fred Scherman
5	Harmon Killebrew	1954–75	573	1971	Min, AL	Mike Cuellar
6	Reggie Jackson	1967–87	563	1984	Cal, AL	Bud Black
7	Mike Schmidt	1972–89	548	1987	Phi, NL	Don Robinson
8	Mickey Mantle	1951–68	536	1967	NY, AL	Stu Miller
9	Jimmie Foxx	1925–45	534	1940	Bos, AL	George Caster
10	Ted Williams	1939–60	521	1960	Bos, AL	Wynn Hawkins
	Willie McCovey	1959–80	521	1978	SF, NL	Jamie Easterly
12	Eddie Mathews	1952–68	512	1967	Hou, NL	Juan Marichal
	Ernie Banks	1953–71	512	1970	Chi, NL	Pat Jarvis
14	Mel Ott	1926–47	511	1945	NY, NL	John Hutchings
15	Eddie Murray	1977–97	507	1996	Bal, AL	Felipe Lira

Frank Robinson owns a multitude of records and honors. Among them is the distinction of being the only Cooperstown 500 *member thus far to collect more career regular-season managerial wins (680) than home runs (586).*

Hallowed Hitsmiths

1. **George Sisler and Pete Rose, the respective owners of the records for the most hits in a season and in a career, are household names. Not so well known are some hitsmiths whose feats are nearly as noteworthy. For instance, Rose is one of the only three players to compile 2,000 hits in a specific decade. Do you know who the other two are?**

   A) Rose is the only one of the three to collect 3,000 career hits.

   B) Rose is the only one of the three not yet in the Hall of Fame.

   C) Rose is the only one of the three who didn't do it during the 1920s.

   D) One of the other two began as a pitcher and the other as a shortstop, but both are best remembered at other positions.

   E) One of the duo holds the record for the most career triples after age 30, and the other for the highest career BA by a middle infielder.

2. **Ross Barnes concluded the inaugural NL season in 1876 with a .392 career batting average, including his five seasons in the National Association. Who are the only other two men to debut since 1871 and sport career batting averages of .380+ in as many as their first two full seasons in the majors?**

   A) Neither is in the Hall of Fame.

   B) One would now be in Cooperstown if not for a fall from grace.

   C) Both hit over .400 in their first full ML seasons.

   D) One was the first switch-hitter to bat .400, albeit in fewer than 400 ABs.

   E) The first and last initials of both these hitsmiths are like Mickey Mantle's—i.e., they are alliterative.

3. **At the end of the 1931 season, three active ML'ers with at least 1,000 career at bats flaunted batting averages of at least .360. Who are they?**

   A) Two of the three were right-handed hitters.

   B) All three won bat crowns, but only one did so after 1931.

   C) All saw World Series action with NL teams between 1929 and 1939.

   D) Two of the trio won Triple Crowns.

   E) Two of the three concluded their careers in 1944 as they had begun them—with rival Philadelphia teams.

4. **The 1920–41 era was the most hitter friendly in history. Name the only big leaguer to play 1,000 games in that era and compile a sub-.240 career BA.**

   A) He was a middle infielder.

   B) Babe Ruth rated his the best AL shortstop glove in the early 1930s.

   C) He debuted with the 1930 Red Sox and finished with the 1940 Cubs.

   D) His real first name was Harold, but he was known by the same nickname as another middle infielder who was born George Nill.

   E) He also had the same nickname as another light-hitting middle infielder of the same period who made the Hall of Fame.

Lowest Career BA in Each Era (1,000 Games During Era)

ERA	NAME	YEARS	ABS	HITS	BA
1876–92	Pop Smith	1880–91	4238	941	.222
1893–1900	Tommy Corcoran	1890–1907	8804	2252	.256
1901–19	Billy Sullivan	1899–1916	3647	777	.213
1920–41	Rabbit Warstler	1930–40	4088	935	.229
1942–60	Jim Hegan	1941–60	4772	1087	.228
1961–76	Bobby Wine	1960–72	3172	682	.215
1977–93	Rob Deer	1984–96	3881	853	.220

Note: No one as yet has played 1,000 games in the post-1993 era.

Total Baseball *credits "Good-Field No-Hit" Rabbit Warstler with –243 career-adjusted batting runs. Warstler's high-water mark was 1935, when he hit .250 for the Philadelphia A's, which was still some 30 points below the AL average.*

5. **The only man prior to Rudy Pemberton in 1996 to hit .500 in a season with at least 40 at bats went 21-for-42 in 1947. Who is he?**

    A)   He arrived in 1946 as probably the most vaunted rookie in Washington Senators history and promptly hit .209.
    B)   He was an outfielder.
    C)   Even including his .500 season, at the close of his first four years in the majors, he sported a meager .236 career BA.
    D)   In 1948 his 23 steals were second in the AL.
    E)   His initials match those of the first sacker on the 1961 NL champs.

Highest BA, Season (Minimum 40 ABs)

RANK	NAME	TEAM	YEAR	ABS	HITS	BA
1	Rudy Pemberton	Bos, AL	1996	41	21	.512
2	Gil Coan	Was, AL	1947	42	21	.500
3	Levi Meyerle	Ath, NA	1871	130	64	.492
4	Craig Wilson	Chi, AL	1998	47	22	.468
5	Gary Ward	Min, AL	1980	41	19	.463
6	Monte Cross	Pit, NL	1894	43	19	.442
7	Hugh Duffy	Bos, NL	1894	539	237	.440
8	Babe Ganzel	Was, AL	1927	48	21	.438
9	Tip O'Neill	StL, AA	1887	517	225	.435
10	Walter Johnson	Was, AL	1925	97	42	.433

6. **The most recent man to slap 200 hits in a season while collecting fewer than 10 strikeouts also set the all-time record that year for the most hits by a batter while fanning fewer than 10 times. Who is he?**

    A)   He was the third and, to date, the last 20th century performer to compile 200 hits in a season with fewer than 10 KS.
    B)   His first taste of World Series action came in 1948.
    C)   He was in the Yankees chain early in his career but never played in the AL.
    D)   Amazingly, he also led the NL in homers the year he notched the most hits ever by a batter with fewer than 10 KS.
    E)   Denizens of "The Jury Box" at Braves Field loved him.

Most Hits, Season, Fewer than 10 Ks

RANK	NAME	TEAM	YEAR	Ks	HITS
1	Tommy Holmes	Bos, NL	1945	9	224
2	Willie Keeler	Bal, NL	1894	6	219
3	Willie Keeler	Bal, NL	1896	9	210
	Steve Brodie	Bal, NL	1894	8	210
5	Joe Sewell	Cle, AL	1925	4	204
	Lave Cross	Phi, NL	1894	7	204
7	Charlie Hollocher	Chi, NL	1922	5	201
8	Sam Rice	Was, AL	1929	9	199
	Lou Boudreau	Cle, AL	1948	9	199
10	Monte Ward	NY, NL	1893	5	193
	Ed McKean	Cle, NL	1896	9	193

7. **The 20th century record for the most career runs by a player with fewer than 2,000 hits belongs to what former shortstop who notched 1,280 tallies on 1,804 bingles?**

   A)   He led the AL in walks five times.

   B)   In 1916 he set an AL record when he had just five doubles in 550 ABs.

   C)   He began his ML career as a teammate of Sam Crawford and finished as a teammate of Bucky Harris.

   D)   He left with the AL record (since broken) for the most career runs by a switch-hitter.

   E)   He piloted the 1927 World Series loser.

Most Runs with Fewer than 2,000 Hits, Career, Since 1901

RANK	NAME	YEARS	HITS	RUNS
1	Donie Bush	1908–23	1804	1280
2	Bobby Bonds	1968–81	1886	1258
3	Eddie Yost	1944–62	1863	1215
4	Earle Combs	1924–35	1866	1186
5	Fielder Jones	1896–1915	1920	1180
6	Jim Gilliam	1953–66	1889	1163
7	Lu Blue	1921–33	1696	1151
8	Ben Chapman	1930–46	1958	1144
9	Minnie Minoso	1949–80	1963	1136
10	Jack Clark	1975–92	1826	1118

Note: Retired players only; among active players, Tony Phillips has the most runs (1,215) with fewer than 2,000 hits (1,924). Fielder Jones, the lone list member active prior to 1901, is here because the bulk of his career came in the 20th century.

8. **Who owns the career record for the most runs by anyone with fewer than 2,000 hits?**
    A) Second to his 1,571 runs is Arlie Latham with 1,478.
    B) He died in 1927 in Washington, his last ML stop and the only place he ever managed in the bigs.
    C) He was probably the first batter to compile 1,000 career strikeouts.
    D) He was the only 19th century player to collect 150 or more ABs with 10 different teams.
    E) He and the title character of a novel about an English schoolboy share the same name.

9. **Excluding pitchers who played a significant number of games at other positions, thereby eliminating just about every pre-1893 hurler, who holds the record for the most career hits by a moundsman maintaining at least a .250 batting average?**
    A) He collected 521 hits in 22 years with three different AL teams.
    B) Even after his 58 career pinch hits are deducted from his total, he still has the record by a huge margin.
    C) His first career hit came with the 1924 Boston Red Sox.
    D) His last career hit came with the 1947 Chicago White Sox.
    E) All but 5 of his 36 career homers came in a Yankees uniform.

Most Career Hits by a Pitcher (Minimum .250 BA)

RANK	NAME	YEARS	BA	HITS
1	Red Ruffing	1924–47	.269	521
2	Red Lucas	1923–38	.281	404
3	George Mullin	1902–15	.263	401
4	George Uhle	1919–36	.288	393
5	Brickyard Kennedy	1892–1903	.261	333
6	Wes Ferrell	1927–41	.280	329
7	Joe Bush	1912–28	.253	313
8	Carl Mays	1915–29	.268	291
9	Dutch Ruether	1917–27	.258	250
10	Schoolboy Rowe	1933–49	.263	239

Note: Maximum 25 games at other positions; among the post-1892 pitchers eliminated by this restriction are Al Orth, Clarence Mitchell, and Jesse Tannehill.

10. **Whose .345 career batting average is the highest of any Hall of Famer or HOF-eligible player who never hit .400 in a season?**
    A) His high mark was .389 in 1925.
    B) He last played with the star-studded 1928 A's.
    C) He has the highest career BA of any man who wore a Washington uniform for a full season.
    D) He was the second outfielder to act as player-manager for an AL flag winner.
    E) He was noted more for his defense than his hitting!

	Highest BA with No .400 Seasons, Career				
RANK	**NAME**	**YEARS**	**ABS**	**HITS**	**BA**
1	Tris Speaker	1907–28	10,195	3514	.345
2	Dan Brouthers	1879–1904	6711	2296	.34212
	Babe Ruth	1914–35	8399	2873	.34206
4	Lou Gehrig	1923–39	8001	2721	.340
5	Riggs Stephenson	1921–34	4508	1515	.336
6	Tony Gwynn	1982–	8517	2856	.335
7	Al Simmons	1924–44	8759	2927	.334
8	Paul Waner	1926–45	9459	3152	.3332
9	Eddie Collins	1906–30	9949	3312	.3329
10	Stan Musial	1941–63	10,972	3630	.331

Note: BAs are carried out to four or five decimal points where ties would otherwise exist.

11. Tony Oliva is the most recent man to top the AL in hits three straight years (1964–66). Who is the most recent man to do the same in the NL?

A)   He did it with Cinci, but his name was not Pete Rose.

B)   He once played 138 consecutive errorless games at first base, then a record.

C)   His record errorless skein came with the Phils in 1946.

D)   He was last seen in the 1948 World Series.

E)   He led the NL in RBI in 1939 and won the MVP Award.

12. In 1982 who became the first man to amass as many as 1,500 career hits without as yet having played at least 750 games in the field?

A)   He broke in with the 1968 Reds.

B)   He once lost a bat title by a single point in a very controversial manner.

C)   In 1985 he became the first man to collect 2,000 career hits without as yet having played at least 750 games in the field.

D)   He lost the AL bat title by a single point in 1976 to teammate George Brett.

E)   In 1994 he managed his son in the majors.

13. Whose .397 career batting average leads all men who appeared in at least 500 big league games?

A)   He was hitless in 10 of his 16 ML seasons.

B)   Eleven of his 31 career hits came in the AL prior to the DH rule.

C)   He led the AL in saves in 1974.

D)   He appeared in five World Series games with the Dodgers without ever getting to swing a bat.

E)   He has the same initials as the pre-1996 record holder for the most hits in a season by a shortstop.

RANK	NAME	YEARS	GAMES	ABS	HITS	BA
	Highest BA, Career (Minimum 500 Games)					
1	Terry Forster	1971–86	614	78	31	.397
2	Ty Cobb	1905–28	3035	11,434	4189	.366
3	Rogers Hornsby	1915–37	2259	8173	2930	.359
4	Joe Jackson	1908–20	1332	4981	1772	.356
5	Lefty O'Doul	1919–34	970	3264	1140	.349
6	Ed Delahanty	1888–1903	1835	7505	2597	.346
7	Tris Speaker	1907–28	2789	10,195	3514	.345
8	Ted Williams	1939–60	2292	7706	2654	.3444
9	Billy Hamilton	1888–1901	1591	6268	2158	.3443
10	Dan Brouthers	1879–1904	1673	6711	2296	.342

Note: BAs are carried out to four decimal points where ties would otherwise exist.

14. **Although he never led a loop in hits, he was the first hitsmith in the 20th century to lead the majors in total bases two years in a row. Who is he?**
   A) Many sluggers have played in both the NL and the AL, but he was the first to lead each in home runs.
   B) It was his mark for the most consecutive innings played that Ripken broke.
   C) He participated in the first 20th century World Series.
   D) His 25 homers in 1899 marked the season record for a lefty hitter until 1919.
   E) His initials match those of the owner of the highest career FA by a catcher.

15. **What outfielder compiled 2,705 hits without fanfare but is well known for pacing the majors in at bats for a record six seasons while wearing four different uniforms?**
   A) He never played in the NL.
   B) He first led in at bats as a member of the 1933 A's.
   C) He played last with the 1948 Tigers.
   D) He tied for the AL lead in hits in 1940 with the Red Sox.
   E) His nickname was "Doc."

16. **Name the season record holder for the most hits with a sub-.300 batting average.**
   A) The AL record belongs to Bill Buckner, .299 on 201 hits for the 1985 Red Sox.
   B) In 1955, his fifth season in organized baseball, the all-time record holder hit .202 for Fort Worth in the Texas League.
   C) He hit .299 on 208 hits in 695 ABs in his record season.
   D) A switch-hitter, he batted .302 the following year for a world champ and led the NL in steals.
   E) In his record year, teammate Tommy Davis was the NL batting titlist.

Evolution of Record for Most Hits, Season, BA Under .300

NAME	TEAM	YEAR	BA	HITS
Davy Force	Was, NA	1871	.278	45
John Radcliff	Bal, NA	1872	.290	86
Doug Allison	NY, NA	1874	.283	90
Tom York	Har, NA	1875	.296	111
Abner Dalrymple	Chi, NL	1882	.295	117
Paul Hines	Pro, NL	1883	.299	132
Dave Rowe	StL, UA	1884	.293	142
Long John Reilly	Cin, AA	1885	.297	143
Bill Phillips	Bro, AA	1886	.274	160
Bill Gleason	StL, AA	1887	.288	172
Dick Johnston	Bos, NL	1888	.296	173
Tommy McCarthy	StL, AA	1889	.291	176
Herman Long	Bos, NL	1892	.280	181
George Stone	StL, AL	1905	.296	187
Rabbit Maranville	Pit, NL	1922	.295	198
Jo-Jo Moore	NY, NL	1935	.295	201
Maury Wills	LA, NL	1962	.299	208

Note: George Wright (107 for Providence in 1879) held the NL record prior to 1882.

17. **Who holds the season record for both the fewest hits and the lowest batting average by a player with at least 600 at bats?**
    A) He died in 1995 at age 79.
    B) In 4 of his 11 big league seasons, he had more walks than hits.
    C) He had a poor .231 career BA but a fine .366 OBP.
    D) He compiled just 127 hits in 1947 when he hit a meek .211.
    E) He formed a keystone combo for Detroit in 1947 with a second sacker who had the same first name.

Fewest Hits, Season (Minimum 600 ABs)

RANK	NAME	TEAM	YEAR	ABS	BA	HITS
1	Eddie Lake	Det, AL	1947	602	.211	127
2	Duke Farrell	Pit, NL	1892	605	.215	130
3	Ray Powell	Bos, NL	1920	609	.225	137
	Ron Santo	Chi, NL	1962	604	.227	137
5	Vince Coleman	StL, NL	1986	600	.232	139
6	Ozzie Smith	SD, NL	1980	609	.230	140
7	Sam Jethroe	Bos, NL	1952	608	.232	141
	Freddy Parent	Bos, AL	1905	602	.234	141
	Chris Speier	SF, NL	1971	601	.235	141
	Freddy Parent	Bos, AL	1906	600	.235	141

18. **Who once tied for the ML lead in hits with 210 but had only 57 RBI and 72 runs for a combined total of 129, the lowest such combined total ever by a major league hit leader in at least 100 games?**
    A) He played center field that season between a former NL batting champ and one of the first Hawaiian-born ML'ers.
    B) He first topped the majors in hits with 218 in 1966.
    C) He later managed his son in the majors.
    D) He was one of three brothers who starred in the majors.
    E) He managed the team that owned the best record in the majors when the strike shut down the 1994 season.

ML Leaders in Hits with the Fewest Combined Runs and RBI, Season

RANK	NAME	TEAM	YEAR	HITS	RUNS	RBI	TOTAL
1	Felipe Alou	Atl, NL	1968	210	72	57	129
2	Richie Ashburn	Phi, NL	1958	215	98	33	131
	George Burns	Phi, AL	1918	178	61	70	131
4	Tony Gwynn	SD, NL	1994	165	79	64	143
5	Johnny Pesky	Bos, AL	1947	207	106	39	145
6	Matty Alou	Pit, NL	1969	231	105	48	153
7	Richie Ashburn	Phi, NL	1951	221	92	63	155
8	Johnny Pesky	Bos, AL	1942	205	105	51	156
	Red Schoendienst	NY/Mil, NL	1957	200	91	65	156
10	Tony Gwynn	SD, NL	1984	213	88	71	159

Note: Beginning in 1884, the first year the schedule called for at least 100 games; 1981 strike season excepted. Burns's 1918 season and Gwynn's 1994 season were abbreviated by World War I and a player strike, respectively.

19. **In 1988, Wade Boggs became the first major leaguer since Al Simmons in 1931 to hit .350 four years in a row. In 1996, Tony Gwynn became the first NL'er since 1925 to accomplish the same feat. Prior to Gwynn's skein, who had been the most recent NL'er to hit as high as .330 four years in a row?**
    A) He won a bat crown during his four-year run.
    B) In 1970 he collected 201 hits but just 241 total bases.
    C) He saw World Series action with two teams that play in parks located less than 10 miles apart.
    D) The Bay Bridge is the best conduit between the two parks.
    E) In 1963 he led the NL in pinch-hit ABs but was better known for being part of the only all-brother outfield in ML history.

20. **Who put the ball in play with the highest degree of frequency of any man in ML history with at least 4,000 career plate appearances?**
    A) In 1,380 ML games and 4,345 ABs, he collected just 138 walks and 267 strikeouts.
    B) In 1970 he walked a personal-high 21 times while hitting .306 in 458 ABs.
    C) He K'd a personal-high 40 times for the 1965 Giants in 543 ABs.
    D) His initials are the same as those of Boston's second sacker in the 1967 World Series.
    E) In 1963 he and his two brothers combined for just 29 walks in 665 ABs while performing for the same NL team.

Evolution of Season Record for Most Hits, Each Position

19th Century

	NAME	HITS	YEAR	TEAM	LEAGUE
1B	Joe Start	58	1871	New York	NA
	Everett Mills	79	1872	Baltimore	NA
	Cap Anson	101	1873	Athletics	NA
	Jim O'Rourke	104	1874	Boston	NA
	Cal McVey	138	1875	Boston	NA
	Dan Brouthers	159	1883	Buffalo	NL
	Dave Orr	162	1884	New York	AA
	Roger Connor	169	1885	New York	NL
	Dave Orr	193	1886	New York	AA
	Tommy Tucker	196	1889	Baltimore	AA
	Dan Brouthers	197	1892	Brooklyn	NL
	Nap Lajoie	197	1897	Philadelphia	NL
	Fred Tenney	209	1899	Boston	NL
2B	Ross Barnes	63	1871	Boston	NA
	Ross Barnes	99	1872	Boston	NA
	Ross Barnes	137	1873	Boston	NA
	Ross Barnes	143	1875	Boston	NA
	Fred Dunlap	185	1884	St. Louis	UA*
	Roger Connor	151	1884	New York	NL
	Bill McClellan	152	1886	Brooklyn	AA
	Hardy Richardson	178	1887	Detroit	NL
	Monte Ward	193	1893	New York	NL
	Bobby Lowe	212	1894	Boston	NL
3B	Levi Meyerle	64	1871	Athletics	NA
	Davy Force	94	1872	Troy/Baltimore	NA
	Jim Holdsworth	97	1874	Philadelphia Whites	NA
	Ezra Sutton	116	1875	Athletics	NA
	King Kelly	120	1879	Cincinnati	NL
	Hick Carpenter	120	1882	Cincinnati	AA
	Ezra Sutton	134	1883	Boston	NL
	Ezra Sutton	162	1884	Boston	NL
	Arlie Latham	174	1886	St. Louis	AA
	Denny Lyons	209	1887	Philadelphia	AA
	Jimmy Williams	219	1899	Pittsburgh	NL

	NAME	HITS	YEAR	TEAM	LEAGUE
SS	John Radcliff	47	1871	Athletics	NA
	John Radcliff	86	1872	Baltimore	NA
	George Wright	86	1872	Boston	NA
	George Wright	126	1873	Boston	NA
	George Wright	136	1875	Boston	NA
	Jack Glasscock	142	1884	Cleveland/Cincinnati	NL/UA
	Jack Glasscock	158	1886	St. Louis	NL
	Oyster Burns	188	1887	Baltimore	AA
	Jack Glasscock	205	1889	Indianapolis	NL
	Hughie Jennings	209	1896	Baltimore	NL
OF	Steve King	57	1871	Troy	NA
	Dave Eggler	98	1872	New York	NA
	Cal McVey	123	1874	Boston	NA
	Andy Leonard	127	1875	Boston	NA
	Paul Hines	146	1879	Providence	NL
	Orator Shaffer	168	1884	St. Louis	UA*
	Jim O'Rourke	162	1884	Buffalo	NL
	Pete Browning	174	1885	Louisville	AA
	Tip O'Neill	190	1886	St. Louis	AA
	Tip O'Neill	225	1887	St. Louis	AA
	Hugh Duffy	237	1894	Boston	NL
	Jesse Burkett	240	1896	Cleveland	NL
C	Cal McVey	66	1871	Boston	NA
	Nat Hicks	82	1872	New York	NA
	Deacon White	121	1873	Boston	NA
	Deacon White	136	1875	Boston	NA
	Fred Carroll	140	1886	Pittsburgh	AA
	King Kelly	140	1888	Boston	NL
	Jack O'Connor	148	1890	Columbus	AA
	Doggie Miller	156	1891	Pittsburgh	NL**
	Deacon McGuire	179	1895	Washington	NL

* Not all authorities recognize Dunlap's and Shaffer's UA feats as 19th century records; therefore, alternate record holders are provided.

** Miller played more games at catcher than anywhere else in 1891, but only 41 of his 135 games were served behind the plate.

20th Century

	NAME	HITS	YEAR	TEAM
1B	*American League*			
	John Anderson	190	1901	Milwaukee
	Charlie Hickman	193	1902	Boston/Cleveland
	Hal Chase	193	1906	New York
	George Sisler	257	1920	St. Louis
	National League			
	Jake Beckley	177	1901	Cincinnati
	Jake Beckley	179	1904	St. Louis
	Shad Barry	182	1905	Chicago/Cincinnati
	Hal Chase	184	1916	Cincinnati
	Jack Fournier	197	1921	St. Louis
	Jake Daubert	205	1922	Cincinnati
	Jim Bottomley	227	1925	St. Louis
	Bill Terry	254	1930	New York
2B	*American League*			
	Nap Lajoie	232	1901	Philadelphia
	National League			
	Gene DeMontreville	174	1901	Boston
	Bill Sweeney	204	1912	Boston
	Rogers Hornsby	218	1920	St. Louis
	Rogers Hornsby	235	1921	St. Louis
	Rogers Hornsby	250	1922	St. Louis
3B	*American League*			
	Jimmy Collins	187	1901	Boston
	Lave Cross	191	1902	Philadelphia
	Frank Baker	198	1911	Philadelphia
	Frank Baker	200	1912	Philadelphia
	Buck Weaver	208	1920	Chicago
	Buddy Lewis	210	1937	Washington
	Red Rolfe	213	1939	New York
	George Kell	218	1950	Detroit
	Wade Boggs	240	1985	Boston

NAME	HITS	YEAR	TEAM
National League			
Otto Krueger	143	1901	St. Louis
Tommy Leach	143	1902	Pittsburgh
Harry Wolverton	152	1903	Philadelphia
Ernie Courtney	165	1905	Philadelphia
Harry Steinfeldt	176	1906	Chicago
Bobby Byrne	178	1910	Pittsburgh
Heinie Zimmerman	207	1912	Chicago
Frankie Frisch	211	1921	New York
Freddy Lindstrom	231	1928	New York
Freddy Lindstrom	231	1930	New York

SS

NAME	HITS	YEAR	TEAM
American League			
Freddy Parent	158	1901	Boston
Freddy Parent	170	1903	Boston
Freddy Parent	172	1904	Boston
Joe Sewell	182	1921	Cleveland
Chick Galloway	185	1922	Philadelphia
Joe Sewell	195	1923	Cleveland
Joe Sewell	204	1925	Cleveland
Luke Appling	204	1936	Chicago
Johnny Pesky	205	1942	Boston
Johnny Pesky	208	1946	Boston
Harvey Kuenn	209	1953	Detroit
Robin Yount	210	1982	Milwaukee
Cal Ripken	211	1983	Baltimore
Tony Fernandez	213	1986	Toronto
Alex Rodriguez	215	1996	Seattle*

NAME	HITS	YEAR	TEAM
National League			
Honus Wagner	196	1901	Pittsburgh**
Bobby Wallace	179	1901	St. Louis
Honus Wagner	182	1903	Pittsburgh
Honus Wagner	199	1905	Pittsburgh
Honus Wagner	201	1908	Pittsburgh
Dave Bancroft	209	1922	New York
Garry Templeton	211	1979	St. Louis

* Cecil Travis had 218 hits in 1941 for Washington but played too many games at third base to be considered the AL record holder.

** Wagner played more games at shortstop than any other position, but fewer than half of his 140 games were at short; as a result, many authorities start with Wallace's 1901 figure, and the record then progresses as shown.

	NAME	HITS	YEAR	TEAM
OF	**American League**			
	Irv Waldron	186	1901	Milwaukee/Washington
	Patsy Dougherty	195	1903	Boston
	George Stone	208	1906	St. Louis
	Ty Cobb	212	1907	Detroit
	Ty Cobb	216	1909	Detroit
	Ty Cobb	248	1911	Detroit
	Al Simmons	253	1925	Philadelphia
	National League			
	Jesse Burkett	226	1901	St. Louis
	Paul Waner	237	1927	Pittsburgh
	Lefty O'Doul	254	1929	Philadelphia
C	**American League**			
	Boileryard Clarke	118	1901	Washington
	Oscar Stanage	133	1911	Detroit
	Hank Severeid	133	1917	St. Louis
	Steve O'Neill	157	1920	Cleveland
	Hank Severeid	166	1922	St. Louis
	Mickey Cochrane	170	1929	Philadelphia
	Mickey Cochrane	174	1930	Philadelphia
	Bill Dickey	176	1937	New York
	Yogi Berra	192	1950	New York
	Ivan Rodriguez	192	1996	Texas
	National League			
	Mal Kittridge	96	1901	Boston
	Johnny Kling	124	1902	Chicago
	Johnny Kling	146	1903	Chicago*
	Gabby Hartnett	172	1930	Chicago
	Spud Davis	173	1933	Philadelphia
	Ted Simmons	193	1975	St. Louis
	Mike Piazza	201	1997	Los Angeles**

* Ted Easterly, with 146 hits for Kansas City of the Federal League in 1914, shared the pre-1920 catchers' record with Kling.

** Joe Torre collected 203 hits for St. Louis in 1970 but played 73 games at third base, too many at another position besides catcher to be considered the record holder.

On the Double

1. The extra-base-hit totals of even the game's giants usually decline dramatically toward the end of their careers. Babe Ruth, for one, averaged just slightly more than 20 doubles per season during his last three campaigns as a regular. In contrast, Kirby Puckett stroked a total of 148 two-baggers, or an average of 37 per year, in his final four campaigns before an eye ailment forced his premature retirement. Who is the only other man to slap 30 or more doubles in each of his last four seasons?

    A) For 20 consecutive seasons, he racked up between 18 and 45 doubles per year.
    B) He holds the record for the most career intentional walks by an AL'er (229).
    C) Fifth in career doubles, he fell just one two-bagger short of tying Tris Speaker's record of 152 doubles during the last four seasons of his career.
    D) He and Jeff Heath are the only two men in AL history to collect 20 or more doubles, triples, and homers in the same season.
    E) He is the only member of the 3,000-hit club who both won a batting title and played his entire career with an expansion team.

Most Doubles in Last Four Seasons of Career

RANK	NAME	YEARS	2BS	AVE.
1	Tris Speaker	1925–28	152	38
2	George Brett	1990–93	151	37.8
3	Kirby Puckett	1992–95	148	37
4	Bob Meusel	1927–30	137	34.3
5	Ed Delahanty	1900–03	134	33.5
6	Harry Heilmann	1928–30/32	124	31
	Bob Johnson	1942–45	124	31
8	Dale Alexander	1930–33	121	30.3
9	Don Mattingly	1992–95	119	29.8
10	Harry Hooper	1922–25	117	29.3

Note: Jim O'Rourke had a pre-1901 record 115 doubles in his last four seasons (1890–93) before returning in 1904 for a token one-game appearance.

2. The only man since 1879 to collect 30 doubles and fewer than 100 hits in a season did it quite recently. Do you remember his feat?

    A) Even though he had 34 doubles in 1981 in fewer than 400 ABs, his SA was only .370.
    B) His 34 doubles in 1981 generated a mere 39 RBI for the Padres.
    C) In 1979 he became the first Mariner to score 100 runs in a season.
    D) He was the regular right fielder on the Angels' most recent postseason entry.
    E) He is the only Yankees player to date whose first name is the same as the last name of the Yankees owner responsible for Babe Ruth's wearing pinstripes.

Most Doubles, Season, Fewer than 100 Hits

RANK	NAME	TEAM	YEAR	HITS	2BS
1	Ruppert Jones	SD, NL	1981	99	34
2	Charlie Eden	Cle, NL	1879	96	31
3	Tim Teufel	NY, NL	1987	92	29
	Bill Phillips	Cle, NL	1883	94	29
	Billy Taylor	StL, UA/Phi, AA	1884	96	29
	Tom York	Cle, NL	1883	99	29
7	Tommy Henrich	NY, NL	1940	90	28
	Mike McFarlane	KC, AL	1992	94	28
	Moises Alou	Mon, NL	1992	96	28
	Earl Averill	Cle/Det, AL	1939	96	28
	Jimmy Dykes	Phi, AL	1931	97	28

3. **Men with high extra-base-hit totals usually also score lots of runs, which makes Mark Grudzielanek's feat all the more amazing. In 1997, Grudzielanek set a new NL record by a wide margin when he tallied just 76 runs on 54 doubles. Who previously had been the only man to pound 50 doubles in a season and tally fewer than 80 runs?**

    A)   He was part of the only outfield trio who each hit .300 five years in a row.

    B)   He totaled just 62 runs for two AL teams in 1926 on 51 two-baggers.

    C)   In 1926 he split the season between the Browns and the Red Sox.

    D)   In 1922 his team lost the AL pennant by just one game as he hit .317.

    E)   His nickname was "Baby Doll."

50 Doubles, Season, Fewer than 100 Runs

RANK	NAME	TEAM	YEAR	2BS	RUNS
1	Baby Doll Jacobson	StL/Bos, AL	1926	51	62
2	Mark Grudzielanek	Mon, NL	1997	54	76
3	Beau Bell	StL, AL	1938	51	82
4	Stan Spence	Was, AL	1946	51	83
5	George Burns	Cle, AL	1927	51	84
6	Mickey Vernon	Was, AL	1946	51	88
7	Al Simmons	Phi, AL	1926	53	90
8	Nap Lajoie	Cle, AL	1910	51	94
9	Enos Slaughter	StL, NL	1939	52	95
10	Tris Speaker	Cle, AL	1926	52	96
	Earl Webb	Bos, AL	1931	67	96
12	George Burns	Cle, AL	1926	64	97
	Mark Grace	Chi, NL	1995	51	97
14	Joe Vosmik	Bos, AL	1938	51	98

Note: Burns and Speaker in 1926 became the only pair of teammates to each rip 50 doubles and score fewer than 100 runs in a season.

4. **Prior to the end of the Deadball Era, it was not unusual for a regular position player to compile fewer than 10 doubles in a season. Roy Thomas averaged just 4.3 doubles a year for the Phillies during 1900–02, and Donie Bush in 1916 rapped a mere five doubles in 550 ABs for the Tigers. Since 1920, however, only one ML'er collected fewer than seven doubles in a season with as many as 500 ABs. Who is he?**
   A) In 1966, his first full season, he batted .292 but had only a .334 SA when his 174 bingles included only six doubles.
   B) He broke in as a shortstop.
   C) His only postseason action came as a defensive replacement in the 1969 NLCS.
   D) He and Robin Yount are the only two ML'ers since WW II to play regularly for a full season at both shortstop and center field.
   E) He and the only player with a .350+ career BA not in the Hall of Fame have the same last name.

5. **Is it possible to crack 40 doubles in a season and yet score fewer than 50 runs? You bet it is. Brad Fullmer almost did it in 1998. Who actually did do it?**
   A) His career runs-per-at-bat ratio of .077 is the poorest in history of any player with 4,000 ABs.
   B) In 1979 he tallied just 42 runs on 41 two-baggers.
   C) He was a third baseman.
   D) In 1981, his last season as a regular, he scored just 10 runs for the Cubs.
   E) He and the season record holder for the most triples by a second sacker share the same last name.

Fewest Runs, Season, 40 or More Doubles

RANK	NAME	TEAM	YEAR	2BS	RUNS
1	Ken Reitz	StL, NL	1979	41	42
2	John Valentin	Bos, AL	1993	40	50
3	Brad Fullmer	Mon, NL	1998	44	58
4	Pedro Guerrero	StL, NL	1989	42	60
5	Brian Harper	Min, AL	1990	42	61
	Gino Cimoli	StL, NL	1959	40	61
7	Baby Doll Jacobson	StL, AL	1926	51	62
8	Vince DiMaggio	Pit, NL	1943	41	64
	Warren Cromartie	Mon, NL	1977	41	64
10	Bert Niehoff	Phi, NL	1916	42	65
	Joe Dugan	Bos, AL	1920	40	65

6. **His seven doubles in 1898 are the fewest ever by a 200-hit man.**
   A) He's the only man to play for New York Giants teams managed by both Monte Ward and John McGraw.
   B) He had a .410 SA in 1898.
   C) A teammate of his in 1898 tallied a record 143 runs on fewer than 10 doubles.
   D) He won his second of two NL batting crowns in 1898.
   E) He collected 200 hits a record eight years in a row between 1894 and 1901.

100 Runs, Season, Fewer than 10 Doubles

RANK	NAME	TEAM	YEAR	2BS	RUNS
1	John McGraw	Bal, NL	1898	8	143
2	Roy Thomas	Phi, NL	1900	4	132
3	Willie Keeler	Bal, NL	1898	7	126
4	John McGraw	Bal, NL	1893	9	123
5	Shorty Fuller	StL, AA	1890	9	118
6	Harry Taylor	Lou, AA	1890	7	115
7	Patsy Donovan	Pit, NL	1893	5	114
8	Bid McPhee	Cin, AA	1884	8	107
9	Duff Cooley	Phi, NL	1895	9	106
10	Ned Hanlon	Det, NL	1886	6	105
11	Roy Thomas	Phi, NL	1901	5	102

Note: The record since 1920 is 87 runs, held jointly by Donie Bush (1921) with seven doubles, and Charlie Neal (1958) with nine.

John McGraw (seen here) and Willie Keeler combined in 1898 to score 269 runs for the Baltimore Orioles despite compiling just 15 doubles between them. McGraw's 143 tallies that year are the most ever by anyone who collected fewer than 10 two-baggers.

7. **In his second big league season, he hit .191 in 127 games and had just 14 RBI and 7 doubles; two years later, his 43 doubles led the NL. Who is he?**

    A) His 14 RBI in 1907 are a record low by a third baseman with 400 ABs.

    B) In 1915 he collected just six doubles for the Phillies in 105 games and was benched in the World Series in favor of Milt Stock.

    C) He played on the 1909 world champs.

    D) He and the owner of the first Brooklyn entry to win a major league pennant have the same last name.

    E) His initials match those of the 1993 NL MVP.

8. **Albert Belle currently owns the record for the most doubles in a season with 50 homers. In 1961, Mickey Mantle and Roger Maris jointly set a new record for the fewest doubles with 50 home runs when each rapped just 16 two-baggers. Whose old record of 18 doubles did they break?**

    A) Prior to him the record low was 19.

    B) He is one of the few men to log 20 doubles, 20 triples, and 20 homers in a season.

    C) Prior to 1996 he was the only 50-homer club member who never led in RBI.

    D) Ralph Kiner held the record when it stood at 19 doubles.

    E) Prior to 1996 he was the last NL'er to collect 20 triples in a season.

9. **Who holds the record for the fewest doubles (11) with 40 homers in a season?**

    A) He also holds the record for the fewest combined doubles and triples (18) by a league leader in SA.

    B) Only in 1954, his ML debut, did he amass more doubles than home runs.

    C) In 1959 he became the first man to compile 40 home runs and bat under .250.

    D) In 1966 he hit a career-high 27 doubles for the defending AL champs.

    E) In 1964, 49 of his 60 extra-base hits with the Twins were home runs.

10. **In 1939 what three NL teammates finished 1-2-3 in doubles with a total of 144?**

    A) One was the NL batting champ that year.

    B) All three are in the Hall of Fame.

    C) One holds the NL record for the most doubles in a season.

    D) The NL two-bagger leader in 1939 was a World Series hero seven years later.

    E) Two of the three played on championship teams with the Yankees in the 1950s, and the third played on the Gas House Gang.

11. **What duo owns the season record for the most combined doubles by two teammates?**

    A) In 1936, Charlie Gehringer (60) and Gee Walker (55) of the Tigers fell one double short of their record of 116.

    B) Their record was set 10 years earlier in 1926.

    C) Both men collected at least one double for the winner of the 1920 Series.

    D) In 1926 one of the duo set a new ML record for doubles (64) that's since been eclipsed.

    E) The other member of the duo currently has the record for most career doubles.

Most Combined Doubles, Season, Two Teammates

RANK	DUO	TEAM	YEAR	TOTAL 2Bs
1	George Burns (64) & Tris Speaker (52)	Cle, AL	1926	116
2	Charlie Gehringer (60) & Gee Walker (55)	Det, AL	1936	115
3	Hank Greenberg (63) & Charlie Gehringer (50)	Det, AL	1934	113
4	Alex Rodriguez (54) & Edgar Martinez (52)	Sea, AL	1996	106
5	Joe Medwick (64) & Terry Moore (39)	StL, NL	1936	103
6	Mickey Vernon (51) & Stan Spence (50)	Was, AL	1946	101
7	Tris Speaker (59) & Joe Sewell (41)	Cle, AL	1923	100
	Chuck Klein (59) & Pinky Whitney (41)	Phi, NL	1930	100
	Enos Slaughter (52) & Joe Medwick (48)	StL, NL	1939	100
10	Lou Gehrig (52) & Bob Meusel (47)	NY, AL	1927	99
	Mark Grudzielanek (54) & Mike Lansing (45)	Mon, NL	1977	99

12. In 1886 the New York Mets became the last ML team in a season when a full schedule was played to total fewer than 110 doubles when they finished with 108. The record low since is 115, held by the 1910 White Sox. What rookie outfielder tied for the Pale Hose club lead that year with just 10 two-baggers?

A) He and his coleader, Lee Tannehill, share the post-1886 record for the fewest doubles by a team leader in two-baggers.

B) He also had one home run, and his club-high 29 bases on extra-base hits were 6 more than runner-up Patsy Dougherty's 23.

C) He had only 91 TBs, a post-1893 low for a team leader in extra-base hits.

D) His .197 BA in 1910 is an all-time low for a team leader in extra-base hits.

E) He and a teammate on his last flag-winning club in 1919 share the same last name.

Fewest Doubles, Season, Club Leader (Since 1886)

RANK	NAME	TEAM	YEAR	TEAM 2Bs	LEADER
1	Shano Collins/Lee Tannehill	Chi, AL	1910	115	10
2	Harry Lord	Bos, AL	1908	116	15
	George Cutshaw	Pit, NL	1919	130	15
4	Walt Wilmot	Was, NL	1888	98	16
	Tom Brown/Hughie Jennings/John Grim	Lou, NL	1892	133	16
	Jake Beckley/Pug Bennett	StL, NL	1906	137	16
	George McBride	Was, AL	1909	148	16
	George Cutshaw	Pit, NL	1918	107	16
9	Bill Grey	Pit, NL	1898	140	17
	Joe Tinker	Chi, NL	1902	131	17
	John Anderson	Chi, AL	1908	145	17
	Hans Lobert	Cin, NL	1908	129	17

Note: In 1918–19, World War I shortened the schedule; Pittsburgh's 107 doubles in 126 games in 1918 are therefore not considered a 20th century team record low.

13. **Since the pitching mound was established at its present distance from home plate in 1893, what is the longest span that a major league has gone without a player who collected at least 40 doubles in a season?**
    A) The record drought ended when a rookie led the league with 47 doubles.
    B) The drought began the year after an MVP shortstop tied for the loop lead with 45 doubles.
    C) The NL high during the AL's drought was Wes Parker's 47 doubles in 1970.
    D) The rookie who ended the drought when he led the AL with 47 doubles set the current junior-loop frosh mark for two-baggers.
    E) Baltimore saw postseason action in both the first and the last years of the drought.

14. **Morrie Rath played regularly at second base for three years and averaged just seven doubles per 400 at bats during his career. The only other man to average as few as seven doubles per 400 at bats in a major league career lasting at least three full seasons as a regular remarkably was a first baseman who collected just 30 two-baggers in 440 games. Who is he?**
    A) He was later a judge.
    B) He played on a flag winner in his rookie year and in the same infield with John McGraw and Hughie Jennings in his final season.
    C) In 1892 he garnered 128 hits but just 137 total bases for Louisville.
    D) His initials match those of the current record holder for the most total bases in a season by a rookie.
    E) He and a 1947 Dodgers pitcher share the same first and last names.

Fewest Doubles per 400 ABs, Career, Regular at Least Three Seasons

RANK	NAME	YEARS	ABS	2BS	AVE./400
1	Harry Taylor	1890–93	1762	30	7
	Morrie Rath	1909–20	2048	36	7
	Harry Lyons	1887–93	1713	31	7
4	Roy Thomas	1899–1911	5296	100	8
	Spike Shannon	1904–08	2613	49	8
	Phil Lewis	1905–08	1775	33	8
	Amby McConnell	1908–11	1506	30	8
	Dick Harley	1897–1903	2879	59	8
	Ed Hahn	1905–10	2045	42	8
	Rodney Scott	1975–82	2132	43	8

15. **A certain rookie in his lone ML season set a record for the fewest doubles by a bat title qualifier when he poked just three two-baggers in 413 at bats. Yet, he also set many positive offensive records despite hitting just .206 and collecting a mere 93 total bases. Who is he?**
    A) His 27 steals are the post-1898 record among men who played just one ML season.
    B) His 80 walks are the all-time record among men who played just one ML season.
    C) He manned right field for Pittsburgh in 1907.
    D) He has the same last name as the first man to win a major league slugging crown with a sub-.300 BA.
    E) They called him "Goat."

Fewer than 130 TBs in Only ML Season (Minimum 400 ABs)

RANK	NAME	TEAM	YEAR	ABS	TBS
1	Ben Conroy	Phi, AA	1890	404	84
2	Goat Anderson	Pit, NL	1907	413	93
3	Milt Whitehead	StL/KC, UA	1884	415	106
4	Gair Allie	Pit, NL	1954	418	112
5	Sparky Anderson	Phi, NL	1959	477	119
6	Hector Rodriguez	Chi, AL	1952	407	125
7	Ham Schulte	Phi, NL	1940	436	128

16. **In 1889, Jerry Denny became the first man in ML history to collect more than 20 doubles in a season without hitting any triples. The record for the most doubles in a season without any triples has gradually increased ever since. Who currently holds the mark with 52 two-baggers?**

    A) He broke Jody Reed's old record of 45, set in 1990 with Boston.
    B) Tim Wallach is currently the NL record holder with 42 in 1989.
    C) The year after setting the current record, he again stroked 52 doubles but failed to lead his league in two-baggers.
    D) His extra-inning double in 1995 won Seattle's most important postseason victory to date.
    E) He won a batting title the year he set the record.

Evolution of Season Record for Most Doubles, No Triples

NAME	TEAM	YEAR	BA	2BS
Bob Addy	Roc, NA	1871	.271	6
Dave Eggler	NY, NA	1872	.338	20
Jerry Denny	Ind, NL	1889	.282	24
Chief Roseman	StL/Lou, AA	1890	.339	26
Jimmy Collins	Bos/Phi, AL	1907	.278	29
Morrie Arnovich	Phi, NL	1938	.275	29
Mel Ott	NY, NL	1941	.286	29
Frank McCormick	Cin, NL	1945	.276	33
Ted Kluszewski	Cin, NL	1950	.307	37
Orlando Cepeda	StL, NL	1965	.325	37
Jim Morrison	Chi, AL	1980	.283	40
Tim Wallach	Mon, NL	1989	.277	42
Jody Reed	Bos, AL	1990	.289	45
Edgar Martinez	Sea, AL	1995	.356	52

17. **George Burns's season record of 64 doubles in 1926 was later surpassed by Earl Webb, but when Burns added 51 two-baggers in 1927, he set a mark of 115 over a two-year period that still stands. Who has come the closest to breaking Burns's two-season mark in the years since?**

A) He fell one short of Burns's record but set the NL mark of 114.

B) He also set the NL season mark for second basemen in the process.

C) The year after setting the NL second-base mark, he tied his own record.

D) His 486th and final career double came in 1947 while he was serving as Pittsburgh's player-manager.

E) He and Johnny Evers are the only two second sackers in this century to play in three World Series for a Chicago-based team.

Evolution of Season Record for Doubles, Each Position

19th Century

	NAME	2BS	YEAR	TEAM	LEAGUE
1B	Charlie Gould	9	1871	Boston	NA
	Everett Mills	14	1872	Baltimore	NA
	Everett Mills	19	1873	Baltimore	NA
	Cal McVey	36	1875	Boston	NA
	Dan Brouthers	41	1883	Buffalo	NL
2B	Jimmy Wood	10	1871	Chicago	NA
	Ross Barnes	10	1871	Boston	NA
	Ross Barnes	28	1872	Boston	NA
	Ross Barnes	29	1873	Boston	NA
	Fred Dunlap	34	1883	Cleveland	NL
	Hardy Richardson	34	1883	Buffalo	NL
	Sam Barkley	39	1884	Toledo	AA
	Fred Dunlap	39	1884	St. Louis	UA
	Nap Lajoie	43	1898	Philadelphia	NL
3B	Cap Anson	11	1871	Rockford	NA
	Davy Force	11	1872	Troy	NA
	Levi Meyerle	14	1873	Philadelphia Whites	NA
	Cap Anson	19	1877	Chicago	NL
	Ned Williamson	20	1879	Chicago	NL
	King Kelly	20	1879	Cincinnati	NL
	Ned Williamson	20	1880	Chicago	NL
	Jim O'Rourke	21	1881	Buffalo	NL
	Ned Williamson	27	1882	Chicago	NL
	Ned Williamson	49	1883	Chicago	NL*
	Jack Gleason	30	1884	St. Louis	UA
	Denny Lyons	43	1887	Philadelphia	AA

	NAME	2BS	YEAR	TEAM	LEAGUE
SS	Davy Force	9	1871	Olympics	NA
	George Wright	16	1872	Boston	NA
	George Wright	19	1873	Boston	NA
	George Wright	20	1875	Boston	NA
	Tom Burns	20	1881	Chicago	NL
	King Kelly	37	1882	Chicago	NL
	Tom Burns	37	1883	Chicago	NA
	Jack Glasscock	40	1889	Indianapolis	NL
	Hughie Jennings	41	1895	Baltimore	NL
OF	Steve King	10	1871	Troy	NA
	Lip Pike	10	1871	Troy	NA
	Dave Eggler	20	1872	New York	NA
	Lip Pike	22	1874	Hartford	NA
	Lip Pike	22	1875	St. Louis Browns	NA
	Dick Higham	22	1878	Providence	NL
	Charlie Eden	31	1879	Cleveland	NL
	Paul Hines	32	1883	Providence	NL
	Orator Shaffer	40	1884	St. Louis	UA
	Tip O'Neill	52	1887	St. Louis	AA
	Ed Delahanty	55	1899	Philadelphia	NL
C	Doug Allison	10	1871	Olympics	NA
	Nat Hicks	12	1872	New York	NA
	Deacon White	15	1873	Boston	NA
	Deacon White	23	1875	Boston	NA
	Charlie Bennett	34	1883	Detroit	NL
	Jocko Milligan	35	1891	Philadelphia	AA

* Specious record aided by extremely short fences in Williamson's home park and an 1883 rule that balls hit over them counted as ground-rule doubles. Lyons's 1887 figure is considered the true 19th century record by most authorities.

20th Century

	NAME	2BS	YEAR	TEAM
1B	**American League**			
	John Anderson	46	1901	Milwaukee
	Harry Davis	47	1905	Philadelphia
	George Sisler	49	1920	St. Louis
	George Burns	64	1926	Cleveland

NAME	2BS	YEAR	TEAM
National League			
Jake Beckley	36	1901	Cincinnati
Ed Konetchy	38	1911	St. Louis
George Kelly	42	1921	New York
Ray Grimes	45	1922	Chicago
George Kelly	45	1929	Cincinnati
Stan Musial	50	1946	St. Louis*
Wes Parker	47	1970	Los Angeles
Keith Hernandez	48	1979	St. Louis
Mark Grace	51	1995	Chicago

* Not recognized as NL record because Musial played 42 outfield games in 1946.

	NAME	2BS	YEAR	TEAM
2B	**American League**			
	Nap Lajoie	48	1901	Philadelphia
	Nap Lajoie	49	1904	Cleveland
	Nap Lajoie	51	1910	Cleveland
	Johnny Hodapp	51	1930	Cleveland
	Charlie Gehringer	60	1936	Detroit
	National League			
	Tom Daly	38	1901	Brooklyn
	Larry Doyle	40	1915	New York
	Bert Niehoff	42	1916	Philadelphia
	Rogers Hornsby	44	1920	St. Louis
	Rogers Hornsby	44	1921	St. Louis
	Rogers Hornsby	46	1922	St. Louis
	Rogers Hornsby	47	1929	Chicago
	Billy Herman	57	1935	Chicago
	Billy Herman	57	1936	Chicago
3B	**American League**			
	Jimmy Collins	42	1901	Boston
	Frank Baker	42	1911	Philadelphia
	Red Kress	46	1931	St. Louis
	Odell Hale	50	1936	Cleveland
	George Kell	56	1950	Detroit

NAME	2BS	YEAR	TEAM
National League			
Charlie Irwin	25	1901	Cincinnati/Brooklyn
Harry Steinfeldt	32	1903	Cincinnati
Bobby Byrne	43	1910	Pittsburgh
Pinky Whitney	43	1929	Philadelphia
Sparky Adams	46	1931	St. Louis
Pete Rose	51	1978	Cincinnati*

* Rose also hit 47 doubles in 1975 when he played 137 games at 3B and 35 in the outfield.

SS

NAME	2BS	YEAR	TEAM
American League			
Freddy Parent	23	1901	Boston
Bobby Wallace	32	1902	St. Louis
Joe Sewell	36	1921	Cleveland
Joe Sewell	41	1923	Cleveland
Joe Sewell	45	1925	Cleveland
Joe Sewell	48	1927	Cleveland
Joe Cronin	51	1938	Boston
Alex Rodriguez	54	1996	Seattle
National League			
Honus Wagner	37	1901	Pittsburgh*
Bobby Wallace	34	1901	St. Louis
Honus Wagner	44	1904	Pittsburgh
Dick Bartell	48	1932	Philadelphia
Mark Grudzielanek	54	1997	Montreal

* Wagner played more games at shortstop than any other position, but fewer than half of his 140 games were at short; as a result, many authorities start with Wallace's 1901 figure, and the record then progresses as shown.

OF

NAME	2BS	YEAR	TEAM
American League			
Ducky Holmes	28	1901	Detroit
Dummy Hoy	28	1901	Chicago
Ed Delahanty	43	1902	Washington
Socks Seybold	45	1903	Philadelphia
Ty Cobb	47	1911	Detroit
Tris Speaker	53	1912	Boston
Tris Speaker	59	1923	Cleveland
Earl Webb	67	1931	Boston

NAME	2BS	YEAR	TEAM
National League			
Ed Delahanty	38	1901	Philadelphia
Cy Seymour	40	1905	Cincinnati
Pat Duncan	44	1922	Cincinnati
Riggs Stephenson	46	1927	Chicago
Paul Waner	50	1928	Pittsburgh
Johnny Frederick	52	1929	Brooklyn
Chuck Klein	59	1930	Philadelphia
Paul Waner	62	1932	Pittsburgh
Joe Medwick	64	1936	St. Louis
American League			
Mike Powers	26	1901	Philadelphia
Steve O'Neill	35	1919	Cleveland
Steve O'Neill	39	1920	Cleveland
Mickey Cochrane	42	1930	Philadelphia
Lance Parrish	42	1983	Detroit*
Brian Harper	42	1990	Minnesota
Ivan Rodriguez	47	1996	Texas

C

* Parrish was not recognized as tying the then-existing ML record because he DH'd in 27 games.

NAME	2BS	YEAR	TEAM
National League			
Deacon McGuire	16	1901	Brooklyn
Johnny Kling	19	1902	Chicago
Johnny Kling	29	1903	Chicago
Bob O'Farrell	30	1926	St. Louis
Gabby Hartnett	32	1927	Chicago
Gabby Hartnett	32	1931	Chicago
Spud Davis	32	1931	Philadelphia
Gabby Hartnett	32	1935	Chicago
Babe Phelps	37	1937	Brooklyn
Johnny Bench	40	1968	Cincinnati
Ted Simmons	40	1978	St. Louis
Terry Kennedy	42	1982	San Diego

Triple Threats

1. **When Lance Johnson led the National League with 21 triples in 1996—11 more than runner-up Marquis Grissom—it marked the first time that anyone other than Babe Ruth had led an extra-base-hit department with a total more than double the amount his runner-up achieved. In 1996, Johnson also became only the sixth man to lead two different major leagues in triples. The first to do it? The typical knee-jerk answer is Sam Crawford, but it's wrong. What's the correct answer?**

   A) His 174 career triples brought him four three-bagger crowns.
   B) He led the NL in triples as a rookie in 1880.
   C) He was also the first man to lead two different major leagues in home runs.
   D) His name at birth was Harry Duffield Stowe.
   E) He was the first man to amass 100 career home runs in ML play.

Players Leading More than One ML in Triples

NAME	1ST LEAGUE	2ND LEAGUE
Harry Stovey	NL, 1880/91	AA, 1884/88
Perry Werden	AA, 1890	NL, 1893
Jimmy Williams	NL, 1899	AL, 1901–02
Sam Crawford	NL, 1902	AL, 1903/10/13–15
Brett Butler	NL, 1983/94	AL, 1986
Lance Johnson	AL, 1991–94	NL, 1996

2. **The old soap-opera classic *The Romance of Helen Trent* touted the premise that a woman could still find true happiness after age 35. What Hall of Famer found so much happiness in the twilight of his ML career that he set an almost unbreakable record for the most triples after age 35?**

   A) Amazingly, 98 of his 184 career triples came after his 35th birthday.
   B) He led the AL with 18 triples in 1923 when he was 33.
   C) All but one of his career triples came with Washington.
   D) He quit just 13 hits short of 3,000.
   E) His real first name was Edgar, but he preferred Sam.

3. **Name the owner of the post–Deadball Era record for the most triples in a season.**

   A) He hit 26 triples in his second full ML season.
   B) He narrowly missed setting a record for the highest BA by a rookie in 400 ABs when he slammed .354 as a frosh in 1924.
   C) He played on a world champ the year he hit 26 triples.
   D) His 26 triples helped him produce 86 extra-base hits in 1925.
   E) His real first name was Hazen.

4. In 1899, Hughie Jennings set a post-1876 record when he knocked 12 triples in just 224 at bats. What fellow Hall of Famer had the fewest at bats of any man since 1899 to tag 10 or more triples in a season?

   A)   He hit the first postseason inside-the-park home run in Yankee Stadium.

   B)   He also hit the first out-of-the-park postseason home run in Yankee Stadium.

   C)   He stroked .368 for the 1922 Giants with 10 triples in 250 ABs.

   D)   He was present, in uniform, for the most postseason home runs in Yankee Stadium of any man who ever played in the majors.

   E)   He was the first manager the present-day New York Mets ever had.

Fewest ABs, Season, 10 or More Triples

RANK	NAME	TEAM	YEAR	3BS	HITS	ABS
1	John Bass	Cle, NA	1871	10	27	89
2	Hughie Jennings	Bal/Bro, NL	1899	12	67	224
3	Charley Jones	Chi/Cin, NL	1877	10	75	240
4	Bill Joyce	Bos, AA	1891	15	75	243
5	Jack Rowe	Buf, NL	1881	11	82	246
	Tom Kinslow	Bro, NL	1892	11	75	246
7	Casey Stengel	NY, NL	1922	10	92	250
8	Fred Corey	Wor, NL	1882	12	63	255
9	Taffy Wright	Was, AL	1938	10	92	263
10	Luis Alicea	StL, NL	1992	11	65	265

5. Chief Wilson amassed 62 triples over a three-year period owing largely to his record 36 three-baggers in 1912. Only one other 20th century NL performer has averaged as many as 19 triples per season over a three-year span. Who is he?

   A)   He averaged exactly 19 triples per season during 1909–11.

   B)   He hit .292 with 12 triples as a Cinci frosh in 1907, then fell prey to the sophomore jinx, slipping to .222 in 1908 with just 111 total bases in 406 ABs.

   C)   During his eight-year career spanning 1907–14, only Sam Crawford, Ty Cobb, and Chief Wilson collected more triples than he did.

   D)   His career year was 1909, when he led the NL in triples and finished second in both batting and slugging.

   E)   He and the record holder for the most triples in a season since World War II share the same last name.

6. Who has the most career triples of anyone who was exclusively a middle infielder?

   A)   Eddie Collins ranks second to him.

   B)   In 1890 he collected more triples (22) than he had doubles and home runs combined.

   C)   All of his 188 career triples came for teams based in the same city.

   D)   He holds almost all the 19th century fielding records for second sackers.

   E)   He was Cincinnati's only regular second baseman from 1882 through 1899.

7. **Milt May and Jody Davis share the record for the fewest career triples (11) by anyone who caught 1,000 games in the majors. Who is the only man to catch 1,000 ML games and compile as many as 100 career triples?**
    A) He became mainly a catcher after he hit .215 as a third baseman in 1892.
    B) His last of 123 career triples came with Boston of the AL in 1904.
    C) He was the first switch-hitter to catch 1,000 games in the majors.
    D) He held the career record for pinch hits (23) when he retired in 1905.
    E) He is the only man in ML history to collect 100 hits six years in a row for six different teams.

Most Triples, Career, 1,000 Games as Catcher

RANK	NAME	YEARS	G/C	3BS
1	Duke Farrell	1888–1905	1003	123
2	Wally Schang	1913–31	1435	90
3	Deacon McGuire	1884–1912	1611	79
4	Chief Zimmer	1884–1903	1239	76
5	Bill Dickey	1928–46	1708	72
6	Charlie Bennett	1878–93	954	67
7	Mickey Cochrane	1925–37	1451	64
	Gabby Hartnett	1922–41	1793	64
9	Johnny Kling	1900–13	1168	61
10	Jack Clements	1884–1900	1073	60

Note: Bennett is excepted because he played only 1,062 total games; Buck Ewing, on the other hand, had 178 triples but appeared as a catcher in only 636 of his 1,315 total games. Tim McCarver, the most recent catcher to be an NL loop leader in triples, is 12th on the list with 57 three-baggers.

8. **Among men who won three or more bat titles, who has the fewest career triples?**
    A) He hit only one triple in his last five ML seasons.
    B) Fifteen of his 34 career triples came in his first three seasons.
    C) The season he won his fourth and last NL bat title, he had no triples.
    D) He is the only bat titlist in this century to be awarded the crown in a season when he collected fewer than 300 ABs.
    E) He's the only right-handed hitter since expansion to win as many as four bat titles.

9. **Who is currently the only man in ML history with 400 career doubles and fewer than 20 career triples?**
    A) After banging four triples in just 279 ABs in his rookie year, he never again collected more than three triples in a season.
    B) He led the AL in batting in his sophomore season.
    C) He currently holds the Yankees' franchise record for the most doubles in a season, with 53.
    D) He was last active in 1995.
    E) He currently holds the record for the highest career FA by a first baseman.

10. The record for the most career triples among men who were never league leaders in three-baggers is 194. Who owns it?

A) In 1906 he had 11 triples for Cincinnati even though he hit just .228.

B) 1906 was the 10th and last season he reached double digits in triples.

C) His first and last triples came 17 years apart for the Boston NL franchise.

D) Between 1893 and 1896, he hammered 74 of his 194 career triples for Baltimore.

E) He spelled his last name with two *e*'s, but a two-time NL batting champ in the 1880s with the same last name spelled it with only one *e*.

Most Career Triples, Never Leading in Triples

RANK	NAME	YEARS	TOP YEAR	3BS
1	Joe Kelley	1891–1908	20—1894	194
2	Eddie Collins	1908–30	17—1916	186
3	Jesse Burkett	1890–1905	16—1896	182
4	Ed Konetchy	1907–21	18—1915	181
5	Rabbit Maranville	1912–35	20—1924	177
6	Zack Wheat	1909–27	15—1910	172
7	Sherry Magee	1904–19	17—1905/10	166
8	George Davis	1890–1909	27—1893	163
	Bill Dahlen	1891–1911	19—1892/96	163
	Nap Lajoie	1896–1916	23—1897	163

11. In 1889 what third sacker set a record that stood until 1943 when he compiled 578 at bats without hitting any triples?

A) He was the first of some 55 ML'ers to date who attended St. Mary's College in northern California.

B) His last name at birth was Eldridge, but he played under a name that was derived from his middle name.

C) His 1,286 career hits are the most of any man with the first name of Jeremiah.

D) His 76 career home runs are a 19th century record for third sackers.

E) His initials are the same as those of another third baseman of the same period who's the only man to hit .201 or less with a minimum of 400 ABs three seasons in a row.

Evolution of Season Record for Most ABs, No Triples

NAME	TEAM	YEAR	BA	ABS
Dickey Pearce	NY, NA	1871	.270	162
Dave Eggler	NY, NA	1872	.338	290
Davy Force	Chi, NA	1874	.313	294
Tim Murnane	Phi Pearls, NA	1875	.272	313
Orator Shaffer	Chi, NL	1879	.304	316
John Peters	Pro, NL	1880	.228	359
Joe Ellick	CP/KC/Bal, UA	1884	.226	429
Jerry Denny	Ind, NL	1889	.282	578
Mickey Witek	NY, NL	1943	.314	622
Cal Ripken	Bal, AL	1989	.257	646

12. **In the 19th century, it was common for a hitter to accumulate more triples than doubles in a season. Nowadays it is extremely rare. Name the most recent batsman to notch more than 20 triples and fewer than 20 doubles in a season.**
    A) The year he did it, he amassed 23 triples and just 42 extra-base hits.
    B) He also led the AL in hits that year.
    C) His last triple came as a pinch hitter with the 1955 Indians.
    D) His next-to-last career AB was a famous strikeout in the 1956 World Series.
    E) He batted leadoff for the Tribe from 1947 through 1953.

20th Century Players Compiling 20 Triples and Fewer than 20 Doubles, Season

NAME	TEAM	YEAR	2BS	3BS
Dale Mitchell	Cle, AL	1949	16	23
Jake Daubert	Cin, NL	1922	15	22
Vic Saier	Chi, NL	1913	15	21
Chief Wilson	Pit, NL	1912	19	36
Tommy Leach	Pit, NL	1902	14	22
Sam Crawford	Cin, NL	1902	18	22

Note: Players are listed in reverse chronological order.

13. **In the strike-shortened 1981 season, Craig Reynolds topped the NL with 12 triples while hitting just 10 two-baggers. Who is the most recent three-bagger king to post more triples than doubles in a season when a full schedule was played?**
    A) He led the NL twice in triples.
    B) He is the only man to be a loop leader twice in an extra-base-hit department despite posting a sub-.300 career SA.
    C) His career was shortened by a severe hand injury.
    D) As Craig Reynolds was Houston's shortstop during most of the 1980s, our man was the 'Stros shortstop during most of the 1970s.
    E) He and a National League co–Rookie of the Year in 1976 share the same last name.

14. **When Chief Wilson stroked an all-time record 36 triples in 1912, he had 17 more triples than doubles and narrowly missed equaling what slugger's all-time season record of 18 more triples than doubles?**
    A) It was accomplished in 1897 by the NL leader that year in triples.
    B) In his first five seasons, he had 63 triples and 42 doubles.
    C) He played under Connie Mack on both of the only two ML teams Connie managed.
    D) He led the AL in doubles three times in the first decade of the 20th century.
    E) He was the first man in ML history to win four straight home run crowns.

15. Which of the 16 franchises extant in 1901 went the deepest into the 20th century before it had a league leader in triples?

    A)   The team's first three-bagger king had just one home run that season.

    B)   The team's first three-bagger leader had 28 doubles that season while wearing its uniform but 29 doubles total.

    C)   The team's first three-bagger leader also won the NL bat crown that season.

    D)   The team's first three-bagger leader had a brother who'd led the AL in triples exactly 10 years earlier.

    E)   He was nicknamed "The Hat" and his brother was called "Dixie."

16. Gaylord Perry retired in 1983 with the record for the most career at bats (1,076) without hitting a triple. Who has since broken his record?

    A)   He eclipsed Perry's mark in 1991.

    B)   He extended his own record to 1,234 in his last AB in 1996.

    C)   He logged 38 extra-base hits for the Orioles in 1989, but no three-baggers.

    D)   He could be labeled a three-baggerless third sacker.

    E)   He has the same last name as the Twins hurler who led the AL in saves in 1968.

Evolution of Career Record for Most ABs, No Triples

NAME	YEARS	BA	ABS
Gene Kimball	1871	.191	131
Asa Brainard	1871–74	.248	467
Walter Hackett	1884–85	.230	540
George Winter	1901–08	.194	589
Joe Oeschger	1914–25	.165	599
Flint Rhem	1924–36	.144	610
Pat Malone	1928–37	.188	688
Lefty Gomez	1930–43	.147	904
Earl Averill	1956–63	.242	1031
Gaylord Perry	1962–83	.131	1076
Craig Worthington	1988–96	.230	1234

17. Babe Ruth easily holds the record for the most home runs per 100 at bats among players with 4,000 career at bats. Who holds the equivalent mark for triples?

    A)   He broke Buck Ewing's old mark of .0331 triples per 100 ABs.

    B)   His .0337 triples per 100 ABs ratio trails only George Treadway's .0359 among players with a minimum of 1,000 career ABs.

    C)   In all nine of the seasons in which he had 400 ABs, he collected at least 13 triples.

    D)   He holds a share of the AL record for the most triples (26) in a season.

    E)   His last three-bagger came in 1920, the year he was banned for life.

Evolution of Season Record for Triples, Each Position

19th Century

	NAME	3BS	YEAR	TEAM	LEAGUE
1B	Everett Mills	4	1871	Olympics	NA
	Charlie Gould	8	1872	Boston	NA
	Everett Mills	9	1873	Baltimore	NA
	Cal McVey	9	1875	Boston	NA
	Deacon White	11	1877	Boston	NL
	Roger Connor	18	1882	Troy	NL
	Harry Stovey	23	1884	Philadelphia	AA
	Dave Orr	31	1886	New York	AA
2B	Ross Barnes	9	1871	Boston	NA
	Bill Craver	11	1874	Philadelphia Whites	NA
	Bill Craver	13	1875	Athletics/Centennials	NA
	Ross Barnes	14	1876	Chicago	NL
	Pop Smith	17	1883	Columbus	AA
	Bid McPhee	19	1887	Cincinnati	AA
	Bid McPhee	22	1890	Cincinnati	NL
	Heinie Reitz	31	1894	Baltimore	NL
3B	Ezra Sutton	7	1871	Cleveland	NA
	Cap Anson	7	1872	Athletics	NA
	Jim Holdsworth	9	1874	Philadelphia Whites	NA
	Ned Williamson	13	1879	Chicago	NL
	Ezra Sutton	15	1883	Boston	NL
	Willie Kuehne	16	1884	Columbus	AA
	Fred Corey	16	1884	Philadelphia	AA
	Willie Kuehne	19	1885	Pittsburgh	AA
	Jumbo Davis	19	1887	Baltimore	AA
	George Davis	27	1893	New York	NL
	Jimmy Williams	27	1899	Pittsburgh	NL
SS	John Bass	10	1871	Cleveland	NA
	George Wright	10	1879	Providence	NL
	Fred Corey	12	1882	Worcester	NL
	Sadie Houck	12	1883	Detroit	NL
	Frank Fennelly	15	1884	Washington/Cincinnati	AA
	Frank Fennelly	17	1885	Cincinnati	AA
	Frank Fennelly	17	1886	Cincinnati	AA
	Oyster Burns	19	1887	Baltimore	AA
	Billy Shindle	21	1890	Philadelphia	PL
	Ed McKean	24	1893	Cleveland	NL

	NAME	3Bs	YEAR	TEAM	LEAGUE
OF	Lip Pike	7	1871	Troy	NA
	Lip Pike	8	1873	Baltimore	NA
	George Hall	8	1874	Boston	NA
	Dave Eggler	8	1874	Philadelphia Whites	NA
	Lip Pike	12	1875	St. Louis Browns	NA
	George Hall	12	1875	Athletics	NA
	George Hall	13	1876	Philadelphia	NL
	Buttercup Dickerson	14	1879	Cincinnati	NL
	Harry Stovey	14	1880	Worcester	NL
	Mike Mansell	16	1882	Pittsburgh	AA
	Fred Mann	18	1884	Columbus	AA
	Sam Thompson	23	1887	Detroit	NL
	Elmer Smith	23	1893	Pittsburgh	NL
	Sam Thompson	27	1894	Philadelphia	NL
C	Cal McVey	5	1871	Boston	NA
	Deacon White	5	1871	Cleveland	NA
	Deacon White	6	1873	Boston	NA
	Deacon White	7	1874	Boston	NA
	John Clapp	7	1875	Athletics	NA
	Lew Brown	8	1877	Boston	NL
	Jack Rowe	11	1881	Buffalo	NL
	Billy Taylor	13	1882	Pittsburgh	AA*
	Buck Ewing	13	1883	New York	NL
	Buck Ewing	20	1884	New York	NL

* Taylor played mostly catcher but also played many games at other positions.

20th Century

	NAME	3Bs	YEAR	TEAM
1B	**American League**			
	Buck Freeman	15	1901	Boston
	Charlie Hickman	16	1904	Cleveland/Detroit*
	Jake Stahl	16	1908	New York/Boston
	Jake Stahl	16	1910	Boston
	Jack Fournier	18	1915	Chicago
	George Sisler	18	1920	St. Louis
	George Sisler	18	1921	St. Louis
	George Sisler	18	1922	St. Louis
	Wally Pipp	19	1924	New York
	Lou Gehrig	20	1926	New York

* Hickman played 79 games at 1B and 45 games at 2B.

	NAME	3BS	YEAR	TEAM
	National League			
	Kitty Bransfield	16	1901	Pittsburgh
	John Ganzel	16	1907	Cincinnati
	Ed Konetchy	16	1910	St. Louis
	Jake Daubert	16	1912	Brooklyn
	Vic Saier	21	1913	Chicago
	Jake Daubert	22	1922	Cincinnati
2B	*American League*			
	Jimmy Williams	21	1901	Baltimore
	Jimmy Williams	21	1902	Baltimore
	Snuffy Stirnweiss	22	1945	New York
	National League			
	Tom Daly	10	1901	Brooklyn
	Claude Ritchey	10	1903	Pittsburgh
	Claude Ritchey	12	1904	Pittsburgh
	Whitey Alperman	16	1907	Brooklyn
	Larry Doyle	25	1911	New York
3B	*American League*			
	Jimmy Collins	16	1901	Boston
	Bill Bradley	22	1902	Cleveland
	National League			
	Tommy Leach	13	1901	Pittsburgh
	Tommy Leach	22	1902	Pittsburgh
SS	*American League*			
	Bill Keister	21	1901	Baltimore
	National League			
	Bobby Wallace	15	1901	St. Louis
	Honus Wagner	19	1903	Pittsburgh
	Honus Wagner	19	1908	Pittsburgh
	Honus Wagner	20	1912	Pittsburgh
OF	*American League*			
	Chick Stahl	16	1901	Boston
	Buck Freeman	19	1902	Boston
	Sam Crawford	25	1903	Detroit
	Joe Jackson	26	1912	Cleveland
	Sam Crawford	26	1914	Detroit

NAME	3Bs	YEAR	TEAM
National League			
Jimmy Sheckard	19	1901	Brooklyn
Sam Crawford	22	1902	Cincinnati
Mike Mitchell	22	1911	Cincinnati
Chief Wilson	36	1912	Pittsburgh

C   **American League**

NAME	3Bs	YEAR	TEAM
Roger Bresnahan	9	1901	Baltimore
Lou Criger	10	1902	Boston
Ted Easterly	10	1909	Cleveland*
Eddie Ainsmith	12	1919	Detroit
Mickey Cochrane	12	1928	Philadelphia

* Easterly also hit 12 triples for Kansas City of the Federal League in 1914, making him the only catcher in this century to achieve double figures twice in triples.

National League

NAME	3Bs	YEAR	TEAM
Duke Farrell	6	1901	Brooklyn
Frank Bowerman	6	1902	New York
Johnny Kling	13	1903	Chicago
Tim McCarver	13	1966	St. Louis*

* McCarver tied for the NL lead in triples in 1966.

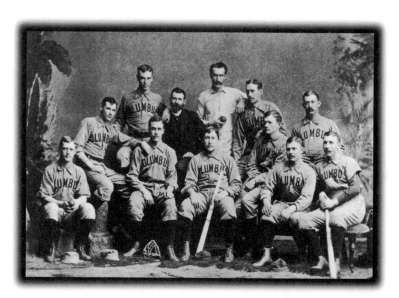

The 1884 Columbus Buckeyes. Jim Field and Frank Mountain stand, Field with his hand on manager Gus Schmelz's right shoulder and Mountain with his hand on Pop Smith's right shoulder. Seated are Ed Morris, Tom Brown, Fred Carroll, Rudy Kemmler, Dummy Dundon, Willie Kuehne, and Fred Mann. Shortstop John Richmond stands between Kuehne and Mann. In his first four seasons in the majors, Kuehne collected just 374 hits, but 66 of them were three-baggers. One of the greatest low-average high-production batsmen in history, Kuehne complied a mere 140 total bases in 1885 despite tagging 19 triples.

Tater Titans

1. **Just once in history have two men been teammates for a full season after both had won home run titles the previous year in different major leagues. For what team did these two reigning tater kings combine their crowns?**

   A)   They played together just one year and hit 76 dingers between them.

   B)   Their team finished last despite their mammoth power contributions.

   C)   One of the pair the previous year had become the first player to hammer 40 home runs on a sub-.300 BA.

   D)   The other member of the pair the previous year had become the first player since Fred Odwell in 1905 to win a tater crown with a sub-.250 BA.

   E)   In 1946, the year that one of the pair won his first of seven homer crowns and the other won his last of four crowns, a Cleveland outfielder became the first slugger ever to collect 20 home runs on a sub-.230 BA.

Evolution of Record for Lowest BA, Season, 20 HRs

NAME	TEAM	YEAR	HRS	BA
Ned Williamson	Chi, NL	1884	27	.278
Cy Williams	Phi, NL	1927	30	.274
Dolph Camilli	Phi, NL	1935	25	.261
Dolph Camilli	Phi, NL	1938	24	.251
Pat Seerey	Cle, AL	1946	26	.225
Roy Cullenbine	Det, AL	1947	24	.224
Wes Westrum	NY, NL	1951	20	.219
Daryl Spencer	NY, NL	1953	20	.208
Willie Kirkland	Cle, AL	1962	21	.200
Rob Deer	Det, AL	1991	25	.179

2. **Who is the only slugger to clout 25 or more homers in three separate seasons and yet finish with fewer than 100 career blasts?**

   A)   His big league coda consisted of six pinch-hit appearances in 1954.

   B)   His booming bat kept him active in the high minors until his late 40s.

   C)   He was slain in 1979 during an attempted holdup in the city where he played his entire ML career.

   D)   It later emerged that this ex–Negro Leaguer was 35 when he played his first full ML season with Cleveland.

   E)   His first name is remarkably similar to a Hall of Fame shortstop's, and his middle name is identical to that shortstop's nickname.

3. **The only man to homer in both his first and his last ML at bats amazingly hit just two career homers. Who is he?**

   A) His two homers came three years apart, with the second and last coming off Jim Merritt.

   B) The second dinger, in 1969, came with the Dodgers.

   C) His first ML dinger made him the first Yankee ever to homer in his first AB.

   D) His initials match those of the NL's last Triple Crown winner.

   E) He has the same last name as the AL leader in pinch hits in both 1934 and 1935, who was nicknamed "Bing."

4. **Who is the only man to win a home run crown in the same season that he posted his loop's lowest batting average by a bat-title qualifier?**

   A) Of his 109 hits that year, 37 were four-baggers.

   B) His .204 mark broke a 100-year-old record for the lowest BA by a home run king.

   C) His .204 BA in 1982 is the poorest ever among first basemen with 500 ABs.

   D) His ill-advised presentation of a live rat to a female reporter hastened his departure from the bigs.

   E) His 35 homers in 1986 are the most by anyone in his final ML season.

Evolution of Record for Lowest BA, Season, League HR Leader

NAME	YEAR	TEAM	HRS	BA
Fred Treacey	1871	Chi, NA	4	.339
Lip Pike	1872	Bal, NA	6	.292
Harry Stovey	1880	Wor, NL	6	.265
Oscar Walker	1882	StL, AA	7	.239
Dave Kingman	1982	NY, NL	37	.204

5. **Who broke Babe Ruth's record for the most career home runs by a BoSox player and held the mark until Jimmie Foxx surpassed him?**

   A) He was Foxx's backup on the 1931 A's in his ML finale.

   B) He was the first man to total more than 50 homers in Red Sox garb.

   C) His top home run season came in 1928 when he banged 12 of his 52 career taters with the Crimson Hose.

   D) His .258 career BA is the lowest of any first baseman with 2,000 ABs active between 1920 and expansion.

   E) He and the Spiders player-manager in the 1890s share the same initials.

Evolution of Red Sox Career HR Record

NAME	YEARS	HRS
Buck Freeman	1901–07	48
Babe Ruth	1914–19	49
Phil Todt	1924–30	52
Jimmie Foxx	1936–42	222
Ted Williams	1939–60	521

6. Whose 184 homers in pinstripes are the most by any Yankees player who retired before Mickey Mantle did and to date has failed to make the Hall of Fame?

A) Roger Maris retired in 1968, the same year Mantle did.

B) Tommy Henrich just missed the mark when he retired with 183 homers.

C) The last five of our man's 189 career homers came with Detroit.

D) He batted .438 in his first World Series in 1939.

E) He and the Brooklyn reliever who led the NL with 13 bullpen wins in 1951 share the same initials.

Most Career HRs with Yankees by a Non–Hall of Famer

RANK	NAME	TOTAL HRs	HRS/NYY
1	Graig Nettles	390	250
2	Roger Maris	275	203
3	Charlie Keller	189	184
4	Tommy Henrich	183	183
5	Bobby Murcer	252	175
6	Joe Pepitone	219	166
7	Bill Skowron	211	165
8	Elston Howard	167	161
9	Roy White	160	160
10	Hank Bauer	164	158

Note: Limited to retired players eligible for the Hall of Fame.

7. In 1992, despite banging 43 homers, Juan Gonzalez scored only 77 runs to set a new record for the fewest tallies on 40 or more dingers. Gonzalez's mark was topped in 1994 when Matt Williams garnered just 74 runs on 43 four-baggers before the strike ended the campaign. Prior to Gonzalez, only one other slugger had totaled at least 40 round-trippers in a season while scoring fewer than 80 runs. Who is he?

A) He was NL Rookie of the Year after slugging 23 homers and scoring just 55 runs.

B) He finished with 382 career homers and 865 runs.

C) In 1968 he clubbed 44 homers but crossed the plate just 79 times.

D) He was an All-American cager at Ohio State.

E) He led the AL in home runs and RBI in 1970 for Washington.

Evolution of Season Record for Fewest Runs, 40 or more HRs

NAME	TEAM	YEAR	HRS	RUNS
Babe Ruth	NY, AL	1920	54	158
Rogers Hornsby	StL, NL	1922	42	141
Cy Williams	Phi, NL	1923	41	98
Hank Greenberg	Det, AL	1946	44	91
Gus Zernial	Phi, AL	1953	42	85
Rocky Colavito	Cle, AL	1958	41	80
Frank Howard	Was, AL	1968	44	79
Juan Gonzalez	Tex, AL	1992	43	77
Matt Williams	SF, NL	1994	43	74

8. When they hit a 20th-century-low three homers in 1908, the White Sox received just one tater from an outfielder. What team's gardeners 10 years earlier formed the last outer-perimeter corps to date that failed to hit a single home run?

   A) The team's shortstop accounted for 9 of its 18 home runs.
   B) The team's left fielder finished fifth in the NL in batting at .341.
   C) The previous year, a rookie right fielder for the team had clipped three home runs and hit .338 in just 278 ABs.
   D) One of the team's pitchers collected more career wins than all of the team's other staff members combined.
   E) The team's rookie right fielder in 1897 was a Penobscot Indian.

Homerless Outer Perimeters

TEAM	YEAR	REGULAR OUTFIELDERS
StL, NL	1877	J. Blong, J. Remsen & M. Dorgan
Chi, NL	1877	P. Hines, D. Eggler & J. Glenn
Mil, NL	1878	B. Holbert, A. Dalrymple & M. Golden
Buf, NL	1879	B. Crowley, D. Eggler & J. Hornung
Chi, NL	1879	O. Shaffer, G. Gore & A. Dalrymple
Tro, NL	1879	J. Evans, A. Hall & T. Mansell
Cle, NL	1880	O. Shaffer, P. Hotaling & N. Hanlon
Phi, AA	1882	B. Blakiston, J. Mansell & J. Birchall
Cle, NL	1898	J. Burkett, J. McAleer & H. Blake

Note: Teams since 1876 that played a full schedule. Several other 19th century teams also got no homers from outfield regulars but are omitted because sub outfielders homered. Pre-1876 teams are omitted because of short schedules.

9. **In 1884 no fewer than five members of the Chicago White Stockings homered in double digits, but the team played in a tiny park that rendered its homer totals specious. Name the first two teammates who produced at least 10 home runs apiece for a team other than the 1884 Chicagos.**

   A) The pair tied for the NL home run crown that year with 11 each.

   B) In 1887 both took part in the longest World Series in history—15 games.

   C) In 1887 the pair joined with Sam Thompson to make Detroit the first team other than the 1884 Chicagos to feature three double-digit home run hitters.

   D) One of the two had the highest career BA in the game prior to the adoption of the 60'6" pitching distance, and the other led the PL in RBI.

   E) Their first names at birth were Daniel and Abram.

Evolution of Season Record for Most HRs by Two Teammates

TEAM	YEAR	DUO	TOTAL HRS
Phi, NA	1871	Levi Meyerle (4) & Ned Cuthbert (3)	7
Bal, NA	1872	Lip Pike (6) & Dick Higham/Tom Carey (2)	8
Bos, NA	1874	Jim O'Rourke (5) & Cal McVey/Deacon White (3)	8
Bos, NA	1875	Jim O'Rourke (6) & Cal McVey (3)	9
Bos, NL	1879	Charley Jones (9) & John O'Rourke (6)	15
Cin, AA	1883	Charley Jones (11) & John Reilly (9)	20
Buf, NL	1884	Dan Brouthers (14) & Hardy Richardson (6)	20
Phi, AA	1885	Harry Stovey (13) & Henry Larkin (8)	21
Det, NL	1886	Dan Brouthers (11) & Hardy Richardson (11)	22
Was, NL	1887	Billy O'Brien (19) & Paul Hines (10)	29
Chi, NL	1889	Jimmy Ryan (17) & Hugh Duffy (12)	29
Phi, NL	1893	Ed Delahanty (19) & Jack Clements (17)	36
Phi, NL	1913	Gavvy Cravath (19) & Fred Luderus (18)	37
NY, AL	1920	Babe Ruth (54) & three with (11)	65
NY, AL	1921	Babe Ruth (59) & Bob Meusel (24)	83
NY, AL	1927	Babe Ruth (60) & Lou Gehrig (47)	107
NY, AL	1961	Roger Maris (61) & Mickey Mantle (54)	115

Note: Ned Williamson (27) and Fred Pfeffer (25) hit 52 home runs between them for the 1884 Chicago White Stockings, NL, but are excluded because the outfield fences in their tiny home park were less than regulation distance.

10. **When he hit 11 dingers as a rookie in just half a season, he ranked only fourth on his team in homers; 10 years later, he led that same team in home runs with a mere 8. Who perpetrated this peculiar feat?**

   A) The team suffered a big drop in homer production after it moved to a new park in midseason the year he led it with eight taters.

   B) His eight home runs were one-fifth of his team's total in 1938.

   C) He and the Yankees' tater leader in 1946 share the same initials.

   D) In 1933 he led the NL in homers and was the only member of his team to homer in double digits.

   E) In 1936 he hit four homers in a game at Forbes Field.

Fewest HRs, Season, Team Leader

RANK	NAME	TEAM	YEAR	HRS
1	Guy Curtright & John Dickshot	Chi, AL	1945	4
2	Babe Phelps	Bro, NL	1936	5[1]
3	Jack Rothrock	Bos, AL	1929	6
	Jake Powell	Was, AL	1935	6[2]
5	Curt Walker	Cin, NL	1929	7
6	Paul Waner & Earl Grace	Pit, NL	1932	8
	Chuck Klein	Phi, NL	1938	8
	Bobby Estalella	Phi, AL	1945	8[3]
	Danny Litwhiler	Bos, NL	1946	8[4]
	Phil Cavarretta & Bill Nicholson	Chi, NL	1946	8
	Vern Stephens	Bal, AL	1954	8[5]
12	Jose Cruz	Hou, NL	1979	9
13	Bobby Bonds	Cal, AL	1976	10
	John Stone	Det, AL	1931	10
15	Earl Averill	Cle, AL	1933	11
	Larry Parrish	Mon, NL	1976	11
	Todd Zeile	StL, NL	1991	11
18	Gary Mathews	SF, NL	1975	12[6]
19	Dave Winfield	SD, NL	1976	13
20	Tommie Agee, Cleon Jones & Ed Kranepool	NY, NL	1971	14
	Ted Ford	Tex, AL	1972	14[7]
22	Amos Otis	KC, AL	1971	15
	Tom Paciorek	Sea, AL	1980	15
24	Robin Yount	Mil, AL	1984	16[8]
25	Roy White	NY, AL	1968	17
26	Ron Fairly	Tor, AL	1977	19
27	Orestes Destrade	Fla, NL	1993	20
28	Charlie Hayes	Col, NL	1993	25

Note: Record low for each ML franchise since 1929, the first year the ML home run total topped 1,200, an average of 75 per team; 1981, 1994, and 1995 strike seasons excepted. Insufficent data as yet for Tampa Bay and Arizona.

[1] Los Angeles club record: Len Gabrielson, 10 in 1968.

[2] Minnesota club record: John Castino, 13 in 1980.

[3] Kansas City A's club record: Rick Monday, 14 in 1967.
   Oakland A's club record: Mitchell Page, 17 in 1978; Davey Lopes & Dwayne Murphy, 17 in 1983.

[4] Milwaukee club record: Hank Aaron, 24 in 1964.
   Atlanta club record: Jim Wynn, 17 in 1976.

[5] St. Louis Browns club record: Red Kress, 9 in 1929.

[6] New York club record: Mel Ott, 18 in 1943.

[7] Washington club record: Harry Bright & Chuck Hinton, 17 in 1962.

[8] Seattle club record: Don Mincher, 25 in 1969.

The 1898 Cleveland Spiders. In 1898 the Spiders tagged just 18 home runs. Shortstop Ed McKean accounted for half of the team's total, and pitcher Cy Young was third on the club with two dingers. The Spiders' entire outer perimeter of Jesse Burkett, Harry Blake, Jimmy McAleer and subs Emmett Heidrick, Louis Sockalexis, Fred Frank, and Ed Beecher went homerless.

11. **In 1998 not just one but two teammate combos—Mark McGwire and Ray Lankford of the Cards and Sammy Sosa and Henry Rodriguez of the Cubs—smashed the former NL record for the most home runs by a pair of teammates. What dynamite duo's long-standing senior-circuit mark thereupon became another of the many four-bagger-record casualties in 1998?**

   A) They finished 1st and 4th in the NL home run derby that year.
   B) A rookie that same year set a still-existing loop frosh home run mark.
   C) One of the dynamite duo cracked the 50-homer barrier that year.
   D) The duo helped their team set an all-time senior-loop SA record of .489.
   E) The 50-homer man saw his NL season dinger record fall in 1998.

Most HRs by Two Teammates, Season

RANK	TEAM	YEAR	DUO	TOTAL HRs
1	NY, AL	1961	Roger Maris (61) & Mickey Mantle (54)	115
2	NY, AL	1927	Babe Ruth (60) & Lou Gehrig (47)	107
3	StL, NL	1998	Mark McGwire (70) & Ray Lankford (31)	101
4	Sea, AL	1998	Ken Griffey Jr. (56) & Alex Rodriguez (42)	98
5	Chi, NL	1998	Sammy Sosa (66) & Henry Rodriguez (31)	97
6	Sea, AL	1997	Ken Griffey Jr. (56) & Jay Buhner (40)	96
7	Chi, NL	1930	Hack Wilson (56) & Gabby Hartnett (37)	93
	Phi, AL	1932	Jimmie Foxx (58) & Al Simmons (35)	93
	Sea, AL	1993	Ken Griffey Jr. (49) & Jay Buhner (44)	93
10	NY, AL	1931	Babe Ruth (46) & Lou Gehrig (46)	92

12. **Power numbers plummeted in the mid-1940s, owing chiefly to the poor quality of rubber used in wartime baseballs. Who was the only big leaguer to hit as many as 15 homers in every season between 1942 and 1947?**

   A)   In 1945 he was the only AL'er to hit two homers in Washington's Griffith Stadium, but he didn't play for Washington.
   B)   He is the only man in ML history to hammer as many as 30 homers in under 400 ABS as a rookie.
   C)   He hit his last homer with the 1947 White Sox.
   D)   He was the only man to play in both the 1945 and 1946 World Series.
   E)   He led the AL in homers in 1943.

Highest HR Percentage, Rookie Year (Minimum 100 Games)

RANK	NAME	TEAM	YEAR	HRs	ABS	PER 100 ABS
1	Rudy York	Det, AL	1937	35	375	9.3
2	Mark McGwire	Oak, AL	1987	49	557	8.8
3	Bob Hamelin	KC, AL	1994	24	312	7.7
4	Matt Nokes	Det, AL	1987	32	461	6.9
5	Wally Berger	Bos, NL	1930	38	555	6.8
6	Ron Kittle	Chi, AL	1983	35	520	6.7
7	Frank Robinson	Cin, NL	1956	38	572	6.643
8	Jimmie Hall	Min, AL	1963	33	497	6.639
	Earl Williams	Atl, NL	1971	33	497	6.639
10	Mike Piazza	LA, NL	1993	35	547	6.3

Note: Limited to undisputed rookie seasons.

13. **What free-swinger led the AL in homers the year after he set the all-time AL record for the lowest OBP (.258) by an outfielder with 500 at bats?**

   A)   He collected 250 career home runs and just 260 career walks.
   B)   In 1982 he set a personal high when he got 33 free passes.
   C)   With the sole exception of Tim Jordan, who played only four full seasons in the majors, he has the fewest career walks of any two-time home run champ since 1889, when walks were first granted on four balls.
   D)   In 1982 he hit just .218 with a .258 OBP in 574 at bats for the Red Sox.
   E)   He and the brother of the current career tater leader have the same initials.

14. **The NL record for the most home runs in a season by a batting champion belongs to what Hall of Famer?**

   A)   Willie Mays fell one short of the record in 1954.
   B)   He broke his own record the year he set the present mark of 42.
   C)   His previous record of 21 was only a year old when he broke it.
   D)   The AL mark at the time was jointly held by George Sisler and Harry Heilmann.
   E)   He currently holds the record for the most career homers by a second baseman.

Most HRs by a League Batting Champion, Season

RANK	NAME	TEAM	YEAR	BA	HRS
1	Mickey Mantle	NY, AL	1956	.353	52
2	Jimmie Foxx	Bos, AL	1936	.349	50
3	Lou Gehrig	NY, AL	1934	.363	49
	Frank Robinson	Bal, AL	1966	.316	49
5	Jimmie Foxx	Phi, AL	1933	.356	48
6	Babe Ruth	NY, AL	1924	.378	46
7	Carl Yastrzemski	Bos, AL	1967	.326	44
8	Rogers Hornsby	StL, NL	1922	.401	42
9	Norm Cash	Det, AL	1961	.361	41
	Willie Mays	NY, NL	1954	.345	41

15. **The same year in which Babe Ruth set a new record when he hit 29 homers, what slugger won his last NL homer crown?**
    A) He debuted with the Red Sox and later faced the Sox in his only World Series.
    B) He won the most home run crowns of any player forenamed Clifford.
    C) He won six NL homer crowns altogether.
    D) His last crown came in a year when he collected only 214 ABs.
    E) "Gavvy" was his most popularly used nickname.

16. **Numerous sluggers in recent years have amassed 350 career homers on sub-.270 batting averages, but only three did it without ever fanning 100 times in a season. Two of them are Carlton Fisk and Graig Nettles; the third has the most career homers of any non–Hall of Famer who never served as a DH. Who is he?**
    A) He was never on a pennant winner.
    B) All but 3 of his 374 career home runs came in the AL.
    C) He is the only non–Hall of Famer to put together a five-year skein (1958–62) when he hit at least 35 homers each season.
    D) He is the most recent position player to bag a win as a pitcher.
    E) Fans in his original big league port of call were begged not to "knock" him.

350 or More Career HRs, Never Fanning 100 Times in a Season

RANK	NAME	YEARS	TOP K YEAR	HRS
1	Hank Aaron	1954–76	96	755
2	Ted Williams	1939–60	64	521
3	Mel Ott	1926–47	69	511
4	Lou Gehrig	1923–39	84	493
5	Stan Musial	1941–63	46	475
6	Carl Yastrzemski	1961–83	96	452
7	Billy Williams	1959–76	84	426
8	Al Kaline	1953–74	75	399
9	Graig Nettles	1967–88	94	390
10	Carlton Fisk	1969–93	99	376
11	Rocky Colavito	1955–68	89	374
12	Gil Hodges	1943–63	99	370
13	Joe DiMaggio	1936–51	39	361
14	Johnny Mize	1936–53	57	359
15	Yogi Berra	1946–65	38	358

17. **Although he had just 139 career homers, 28 came as his team's leadoff batter in a game, a record until Bobby Bonds broke it. Who is he?**

A) He played his first ML game in 1944 when he was just 17.

B) He's the only man among the Top 10 in career walks who didn't collect 2,000 hits.

C) He's the only man with at least 125 career homers whose career OBP is higher than his SA.

D) They called him "The Walking Man."

E) He held down the Senators third base job seemingly forever.

18. **What park witnessed the most homers by one player in a season?**

A) It was not Yankee Stadium.

B) It sat empty on the final weekend of the season as the man who'd clubbed a record 39 four-baggers in it that summer finished the campaign on the road.

C) The park was named after its owner at the time but has since been renamed.

D) The park was home in 1938 to a slugger who collected just 19 of his 58 home runs on the road.

E) In 1996 the park was home to the first team to lose 100 games despite hitting 200 home runs.

19. **In 1897, Willie Keeler set a record unlikely ever to be surpassed when he logged 304 total bases while going homerless. In the more than 100 seasons since, the closest challenger to his mark has been Nap Lajoie with 280 total bases in 1906. Who owns the post–Deadball Era season mark for the most total bases without hitting a tater?**

A) His 254 TBs are tied for the third spot on the all-time list.

B) The year he set the post–Deadball Era mark, he played shortstop.

C) He also served as a regular second baseman later in his career.

D) He has the lowest career BA of any Hall of Fame shortstop.

E) In 1922 he set not only the post–Deadball Era season record for the most TBs without a home run but also the all-time record for the most ABs while going homerless.

Most TBs, Season, No HRs

RANK	NAME	TEAM	YEAR	BA	TBS
1	Willie Keeler	Bal, NL	1897	.424	304
2	Nap Lajoie	Cle, AL	1906	.355	280
3	Hughie Jennings	Bal, NL	1896	.401	254
	Rabbit Maranville	Pit, NL	1922	.295	254
5	Doc Cramer	Bos, AL	1938	.301	250
	Luke Appling	Chi, AL	1940	.348	250
	Johnny Pesky	Bos, AL	1947	.324	250
8	Jesse Burkett	Cle, NL	1898	.341	249
9	Lave Cross	Phi, AL	1902	.342	246
10	Milt Stock	StL, NL	1920	.319	244
	Dave Cash	Phi, NL	1977	.289	244

20. **Name the lone player in ML history to collect 50 home runs and fewer than 50 Ks in the same season.**
    A) He K'd just 524 times in 6,443 career ABs.
    B) He led the AL in pinch hits three years in a row.
    C) He led the NL in triples before he ever led it in home runs.
    D) He missed the Triple Crown in 1939 when he finished second in RBI.
    E) Prior to 1998 he owned the NL season record for the most homers by a first sacker.

21. **When Roger Maris went deep 61 times in 1961, his 366 total bases broke Ernie Banks's 1955 mark for the most total bases (355) by a player with a sub-.300 batting average. Maris's record endured for 35 years until Brady Anderson broke it in 1996. Who held the mark for some three decades prior to Banks?**
    A) He collected 338 TBs on a .290 BA the year he won his only loop homer crown.
    B) His record stood for exactly 30 years before Banks broke it.
    C) He also led the AL in RBI the year he won his lone homer crown.
    D) He was the first player from a team that finished as low as seventh to top the AL in both homers and RBI.
    E) The team he played for did not finish in the second division again—let alone seventh—for 40 years.

Evolution of Record for Most TBs, Season, Sub-.300 BA

NAME	TEAM	YEAR	BA	TBS
Ned Cuthbert	Ath, NA	1871	.247	63
Lip Pike	Bal, NA	1872	.288	127
George Hall	Ath, NA	1875	.299	153
Buttercup Dickerson	Cin, NL	1879	.291	154
Harry Stovey	Wor, NL	1880	.265	161
Abner Dalrymple	Chi, NL	1882	.295	167
Joe Hornung	Bos, NL	1883	.278	199
Fred Pfeffer	Chi, NL	1884	.289	240
Roger Connor	NY, NL	1887	.285	255
Dick Johnston	Bos, NL	1888	.296	276
Buck Freeman	Bos, AL	1903	.288	281
Tillie Walker	Phi, AL	1922	.283	310
Bob Meusel	NY, AL	1925	.290	338
Ernie Banks	Chi, NL	1955	.295	355
Roger Maris	NY, AL	1961	.269	366
Brady Anderson	Bal, AL	1996	.297	369
Ken Griffey Jr.	Sea, AL	1998	.284	387

Evolution of Season Record for HRs, Each Position

19th Century

	NAME	HRS	YEAR	TEAM	LEAGUE
1B	Charlie Gould	2	1871	Boston	NA
	Jim O'Rourke	5	1874	Boston	NA
	Dan Brouthers	6	1882	Buffalo	NL
	Harry Stovey	14	1883	Philadelphia	AA
	Dan Brouthers	14	1884	Buffalo	NL
	Cap Anson	21	1884	Chicago	NL*
	Billy O'Brien	19	1887	Washington	NL
2B	Jimmy Wood	1	1871	Chicago	NA
	Jimmy Wood	2	1872	Troy	NA
	Ross Barnes	2	1873	Boston	NA
	Jack Burdock	2	1873	Atlantics	NA
	Bill Craver	2	1875	Athletics/Centennials	NA
	Fred Dunlap	4	1880	Cleveland	NL
	Jack Farrell	5	1881	Providence	NL
	Pete Browning	5	1882	Louisville	NL
	Jack Burdock	5	1883	Boston	NL
	Fred Dunlap	13	1884	St. Louis	UA
	Fred Pfeffer	25	1884	Chicago	NL*

	NAME	HRS	YEAR	TEAM	LEAGUE
	Fred Pfeffer	16	1887	Chicago	NL
	Bobby Lowe	17	1894	Boston	NL
3B	Levi Meyerle	4	1871	Athletics	NA
	Mike Muldoon	6	1882	Cleveland	NL
	Jerry Denny	8	1883	Providence	NL
	Ned Williamson	27	1884	Chicago	NL*
	Jerry Denny	9	1886	St. Louis	NL
	Jerry Denny	11	1887	Indianapolis	NL
	Jerry Denny	12	1888	Indianapolis	NL
	Jerry Denny	18	1889	Indianapolis	NL
SS	John Bass	3	1871	Cleveland	NA
	George Wright	3	1873	Boston	NA
	Jimmy Hallinan	3	1875	New York	NA
	Tom Burns	4	1881	Chicago	NL
	Sam Wise	4	1882	Boston	NL
	Jack Glasscock	4	1882	Cleveland	NL
	Chick Fulmer	5	1883	Cincinnati	AA
	Frank Meinke	6	1884	Detroit	NL
	Tom Burns	7	1884	Chicago	NL*
	Frank Fennelly	10	1885	Cincinnati	AA
	Billy Shindle	10	1890	Philadelphia	PL
	Jim Canavan	10	1891	Cincinnati/Milwaukee	AA
	Bill Dahlen	15	1894	Chicago	NL
OF	Fred Treacey	4	1871	Chicago	NA
	Lip Pike	4	1871	Troy	NA
	Lip Pike	6	1872	Baltimore	NA
	Jim O'Rourke	6	1875	Boston	NA
	Charley Jones	9	1879	Boston	NL
	Charley Jones	10	1883	Cincinnati	AA
	Cannonball Crane	12	1884	Boston	UA
	Abner Dalrymple	22	1884	Chicago	NL*
	George Wood	14	1887	Philadelphia	NL
	Tip O'Neill	14	1887	St. Louis	AA
	Jimmy Ryan	16	1888	Chicago	NL
	Sam Thompson	20	1889	Philadelphia	NL
	Buck Freeman	25	1899	Washington	NL
C	Doug Allison	2	1871	Olympics	NA
	Charlie Hodes	2	1871	Chicago	NA
	Cal McVey	2	1873	Baltimore	NA
	Deacon White	3	1874	Boston	NA
	John Clapp	3	1874	Athletics	NA

NAME	HRS	YEAR	TEAM	LEAGUE
Charlie Bennett	7	1881	Detroit	NL
Buck Ewing	10	1883	New York	NL
Jocko Milligan	12	1889	St. Louis	AA
Jack Clements	17	1893	Philadelphia	NL

* Specious record because Chicago played in a substandard park in 1884.

20th Century

	NAME	HRS	YEAR	TEAM
1B	**American League**			
	Buck Freeman	12	1901	Boston
	Charlie Hickman	12	1903	Cleveland
	Harry Davis	12	1906	Philadelphia
	Wally Pipp	12	1916	New York
	George Sisler	19	1920	St. Louis
	Joe Hauser	27	1924	Philadelphia
	Lou Gehrig	47	1927	New York
	Jimmie Foxx	58	1932	Philadelphia
	Hank Greenberg	58	1938	Detroit
	National League			
	Dan McGann	6	1901	St. Louis
	Dan McGann	6	1904	New York
	Frank Chance	6	1904	Chicago
	Tim Jordan	12	1906	Brooklyn
	Tim Jordan	12	1908	Brooklyn
	Fred Luderus	16	1911	Philadelphia
	Fred Luderus	18	1913	Philadelphia
	Vic Saier	18	1914	Chicago
	George Kelly	23	1921	New York
	Jack Fournier	27	1924	Brooklyn
	Jim Bottomley	31	1928	St. Louis
	Don Hurst	31	1929	Philadelphia
	Rip Collins	35	1934	St. Louis
	Johnny Mize	43	1940	St. Louis
	Johnny Mize	51	1947	New York
	Mark McGwire	70	1998	St. Louis
2B	**American League**			
	Nap Lajoie	14	1901	Philadelphia
	Jimmy Dykes	16	1921	Philadelphia
	Tony Lazzeri	18	1926	New York
	Tony Lazzeri	18	1927	New York

NAME	HRS	YEAR	TEAM
Tony Lazzeri	18	1929	New York
Charlie Gehringer	19	1933	Detroit
Charlie Gehringer	19	1935	Detroit
Joe Gordon	25	1938	New York
Joe Gordon	28	1939	New York
Joe Gordon	30	1940	New York
Joe Gordon	32	1948	Cleveland

National League

NAME	HRS	YEAR	TEAM
Gene Demontreville	5	1901	Boston
Larry Doyle	6	1909	New York
Larry Doyle	8	1910	New York
Larry Doyle	13	1911	New York*
Rogers Hornsby	21	1921	St. Louis
Rogers Hornsby	42	1922	St. Louis
Davey Johnson	43	1973	Atlanta**

* Duke Kenworthy with 15 homers for Kansas City of the Federal League in 1914 held the post-1901 mark for second basemen prior to 1921.

** Including one home run as a pinch hitter; hence the current record is officially shared by Hornsby and Johnson with 42.

3B   American League

NAME	HRS	YEAR	TEAM
Bill Coughlin	6	1901	Washington
Jimmy Collins	6	1901	Boston
Bill Bradley	11	1902	Cleveland
Frank Baker	11	1911	Philadelphia
Frank Baker	12	1913	Philadelphia
Jimmy Dykes	12	1922	Philadelphia
Gene Robertson	14	1925	New York
Marty McManus	18	1929	Detroit*
Pinky Higgins	23	1935	Philadelphia
Harlond Clift	29	1937	St. Louis
Harlond Clift	34	1938	St. Louis
Al Rosen	37	1950	Cleveland
Al Rosen	43	1953	Cleveland
Harmon Killebrew	49	1969	Minnesota**

National League

NAME	HRS	YEAR	TEAM
Harry Steinfeldt	6	1901	Cincinnati
Tommy Leach	6	1902	Pittsburgh
Tommy Leach	7	1903	Pittsburgh
Dave Brain	10	1907	Boston
Heinie Zimmerman	14	1912	Chicago

NAME	HRs	YEAR	TEAM
Les Bell	17	1926	St. Louis
Freddy Lindstrom	22	1930	New York
Mel Ott	36	1938	New York
Eddie Mathews	47	1953	Milwaukee
Mike Schmidt	48	1980	Philadelphia

* McManus's 91 homers during 1920–29 were second among infielders (first basemen excepted) only to Rogers Hornsby.

** Killebrew played too many games at other positions to be considered the all-time record holder; the mark instead belongs to Schmidt with 48.

SS *American League*

Wid Conroy	5	1901	Milwaukee
Freddy Parent	6	1904	Boston
Roger Peckinpaugh	7	1919	New York
Roger Peckinpaugh	8	1920	New York
Roger Peckinpaugh	8	1921	New York
Jimmy Dykes	13	1929	Philadelphia*
Red Kress	16	1930	St. Louis
Eric McNair	18	1932	Philadelphia
Joe Cronin	18	1937	Boston
Joe Cronin	19	1939	Boston
Joe Cronin	24	1940	Boston
Vern Stephens	24	1945	St. Louis
Vern Stephens	29	1948	Boston
Vern Stephens	39	1949	Boston
Rico Petrocelli	40	1969	Boston
Alex Rodriguez	42	1998	Seattle

* Of Dykes's 119 games, 60 were at SS and 48 at 3B.

National League

George Davis	7	1901	New York
Dave Brain	7	1904	St. Louis
Bill Dahlen	7	1905	New York
Honus Wagner	10	1908	Pittsburgh
Travis Jackson	11	1924	New York
Glenn Wright	18	1925	Pittsburgh
Travis Jackson	21	1927	New York
Glenn Wright	22	1930	Brooklyn
Alvin Dark	23	1953	New York
Ernie Banks	44	1955	Chicago
Ernie Banks	47	1958	Chicago

	NAME	HRS	YEAR	TEAM
OF	**American League**			
	Socks Seybold	8	1901	Philadelphia
	Socks Seybold	16	1902	Philadelphia
	Babe Ruth	29	1919	Boston
	Babe Ruth	54	1920	New York
	Babe Ruth	59	1921	New York
	Babe Ruth	60	1927	New York
	Roger Maris	61	1961	New York
	National League			
	Sam Crawford	16	1901	Cincinnati
	Wildfire Schulte	21	1911	Chicago
	Gavvy Cravath	24	1915	Philadelphia
	Cy Williams	26	1922	Philadelphia
	Cy Williams	41	1923	Philadelphia
	Chuck Klein	43	1929	Philadelphia
	Hack Wilson	56	1930	Chicago
	Sammy Sosa	66	1998	Chicago
C	**American League**			
	Billy Sullivan	4	1901	Chicago
	Boileryard Clarke	6	1902	Washington
	Cy Perkins	12	1921	Philadelphia
	Mickey Cochrane	12	1927	Philadelphia
	Mickey Cochrane	17	1931	Philadelphia
	Mickey Cochrane	23	1932	Philadelphia
	Bill Dickey	29	1937	New York
	Rudy York	33	1938	Detroit*
	Yogi Berra	30	1952	New York
	Yogi Berra	30	1956	New York
	Gus Triandos	30	1958	Baltimore
	Lance Parrish	32	1982	Detroit
	Lance Parrish	33	1984	Detroit*
	Carlton Fisk	37	1985	Chicago*
	Terry Steinbach	35	1996	Oakland
	National League			
	Mal Kittridge	2	1901	Boston
	Pat Moran	2	1901	Boston
	Mal Kittridge	2	1902	Boston
	Pat Moran	7	1903	Boston
	Tex Erwin	7	1911	Brooklyn
	Earl Smith	10	1921	New York
	Butch Henline	14	1922	Philadelphia

NAME	HRs	YEAR	TEAM
Gabby Hartnett	16	1924	Chicago
Gabby Hartnett	24	1925	Chicago
Gabby Hartnett	37	1930	Chicago
Roy Campanella	41	1953	Brooklyn
Todd Hundley	42	1996	New York**

* Because York played 15 games at other positions in 1938, Berra and Triandos were considered the AL co-record-holders prior to 1982; Parrish, in 1984, was similarly disqualified for DH'ing in 22 games, as was Fisk in 1985 for DH'ing in 28 games.

** Johnny Bench hit 45 homers for Cincinnati in 1970 but played too many games at other positions to be considered the present NL record holder.

Brilliant Bat Titlists

1. **Ty Cobb, the owner of the highest career batting average (.366), naturally won the most batting titles. The owner of the lowest career batting average of anyone to win a major league bat title ranks almost 100 points behind Cobb at .268. Who is he?**

   A)   The year he won his lone bat crown, he set a post-1920 record for the lowest SA by a league leader (.476).
   B)   He finished with Cleveland in 1952.
   C)   He won his bat crown by .00009 points, the narrowest margin in history.
   D)   He played beside the "Scooter" in the 1947 World Series.
   E)   He was "snuffed" in 1958 when his commuter train plunged into the Hudson.

RANK	NAME	YEARS	TITLE	BA

Lowest Career BA, Bat Title Winner				
RANK	**NAME**	**YEARS**	**TITLE**	**BA**
1	Snuffy Stirnweiss	1943–52	1945	.268
2	Terry Pendleton	1984–	1991	.270
3	Norm Cash	1958–74	1961	.271
4	Bobby Avila	1949–59	1954	.281
5	Guy Hecker	1882–90	1886	.283
6	Carl Yastrzemski	1961–83	1963/67/68	.2852
7	Willie Wilson	1976–94	1982	.2855
8	Dick Groat	1952–67	1960	.2857
9	Mickey Vernon	1939–60	1946/53	.2858
10	Alex Johnson	1964–76	1970	.288

Note: Includes active players' career BAs through 1998; Hecker's bat crown is disputed.
BAs are carried out to four decimal points where ties would otherwise exist.

2. **Bat title winners traditionally lapse the following season, sometimes by more than 100 points. The few who hike their averages almost always are repeat winners. The largest increase in batting average by a defending bat title winner who failed to repeat is a mere 12 points. What Hall of Famer set the mark the year after he copped his lone bat crown?**

   A)   When he followed his bat crown with a career-high .365, he became the most recent defending bat titlist to hike his average and fail to repeat.
   B)   He broke Jimmie Foxx's old record hike of 11 points.
   C)   He has the record for the most home runs by a batting title winner.
   D)   He also currently holds the record for the highest career SA by the owner of a sub-.300 BA.
   E)   He was the first switch-hitter since 1889 to win a batting title.

Largest Increase in BA, Bat Title Winner Failing to Repeat

RANK	NAME	TEAM	YEARS	1ST	2ND	GAIN
1	Mickey Mantle	NY, AL	1956–57	.353	.365	12
2	Jimmie Foxx	Bos, AL	1938–39	.349	.360	11
3	Joe DiMaggio	NY, AL	1940–41	.352	.357	5
4	Elmer Flick	Cle, AL	1905–06	.308	.311	3
5	Ty Cobb	Det, AL	1915–16	.369	.371	2
6	Stan Musial	StL, NL	1952–53	.336	.337	1
	Tip O'Neill	StL, AA	1888–89	.3346	.3352	1

Note: Dan Brouthers, the 1892 NL bat crown winner, hiked his average two points in 1893 but was held by injuries to only 287 ABs.

3. In 1989, Kirby Puckett won the AL bat title despite suffering a 17-point drop from his 1988 average. Who previously had held the 20th century record for the largest dip (15 points) by a bat titlist who was only an also-ran a year earlier?

    A)   His lone bat crown was the first by a member of his AL franchise.

    B)   His first and last ML hits came 21 years apart.

    C)   He is the only 20th century performer to notch both a pitching shutout and a multiple home run game as a batter with teams in two different leagues representing the same city.

    D)   He was the first in ML history to compile a season SA more than twice his BA.

    E)   His career BA leads all men with 500 home runs.

Largest Drop in BA, Bat Titlist Not Winning the Previous Year

RANK	NAME	TEAM	YEARS	1ST	2ND	DROP
1	Kirby Puckett	Min, AL	1988–89	.356	.339	17
2	Jack Glasscock	Ind/NY, NL	1889–90	.352	.336	16
3	Babe Ruth	NY, AL	1923–24	.393	.378	15
4	Edd Roush	Cin, AL	1918–19	.333	.321	12
5	Snuffy Stirnweiss	NY, AL	1944–45	.319	.309	10
6	Jimmie Foxx	Phi, AL	1932–33	.364	.356	8
7	Cap Anson	Chi, NL	1887–88	.347	.344	3
	Larry Walker	Col, NL	1997–98	.366	.363	3

4. Norm Cash shattered all 20th century records for the largest dip in batting average by a defending bat crown winner when he tumbled 118 points from .361 in 1961 to .243 the following year. Not surprisingly, Cash wasn't a repeat winner. What defending bat titlist did repeat despite suffering a 100-point drop in his batting average?

    A)   He saw action in four straight World Series.

    B)   He was the first man in history to collect 400 hits over a two-year span.

    C)   He won his first bat title the only year batters received more than three strikes.

    D)   In 1887 he became the first foreign-born player to win a major league bat crown.

    E)   He and a former Speaker of the House share the same name.

Largest Drop in BA, Defending Bat Titlist

RANK	NAME	TEAM	YEARS	1ST	2ND	DROP
1	Levi Meyerle	Ath, NA	1871–72	.492	.329	163
2	Fred Dunlap	StL, UA/StL, NL	1884–85	.412	.270	142
3	Norm Cash	Det, AL	1961–62	.361	.243	118
4	Chicken Wolf	Lou, AA	1890–91	.363	.253	110
5	Tip O'Neill	StL, AA	1887–88	.435	.335	100
6	Willie McGee	StL, NL	1985–86	.353	.256	97
7	Jack Glasscock	NY, NL	1890–91	.336	.241	95
8	Cy Seymour	Cin/NY, NL	1905–06	.377	.286	91
	Goose Goslin	Was, AL	1928–29	.379	.288	91
	Debs Garms	Pit, NL	1940–41	.355	.264	91

Note: Excluding bat titlists who failed to qualify for a crown the following year owing to injury or illness; among the affected are Ross Barnes, Babe Ruth, George Sisler, Lew Fonseca, Rico Carty, Julio Franco, and Edgar Martinez.

Norm Cash led the AL in batting in 1961 with a .361 BA. His career BA was only .271. The 90-point differential between his winning mark and his career BA is the largest in the 20th century for a bat titlist.

5. **E. V. Parish was the official scorer in a season-ending doubleheader with crucial bearing on an AL batting title race that is still shrouded in controversy. In what park was Parish acting as scorer that day?**

   A) Cleveland was the visiting club.

   B) The home club's manager was unofficially banned from ever working again in the majors for his part in the events that unfolded that day.

   C) The park was later shared by another ML club.

   D) The two bat crown contenders who were affected by Parish's scoring decisions were Ty Cobb and Nap Lajoie.

   E) The park's predecessor had been home to the only St. Louis team to win four consecutive pennants.

6. **Prior to Edgar Martinez in 1995, the only AL batting champ to collect 400 at bats but play fewer than 100 games in the field the year he won his crown unlike Martinez was not a DH. Who is he?**

   A) He won with a .354 BA.

   B) He played every position but pitcher and catcher during his career.

   C) He's one of the few men to play 100 games in a season at three different positions—first base, second base, and third base.

   D) He saw postseason action in 1959 for the only time.

   E) He filled in for two months in left field for an injured Ted Williams the year he won his bat title.

7. **Who won an AL bat crown at age 27 after topping .300 for the third consecutive year but finished in 1976 at age 33 without ever again hitting higher than .291?**

   A) He hit .239 for the 1972 Indians.

   B) He debuted with the 1964 Phillies.

   C) In his 13-year career, he played with eight different franchises and was never with the same team more than two years in a row.

   D) His brother rushed for 1,000 yards one year in the NFL.

   E) He beat out Yaz by a hair the year he won his lone bat title.

8. **What Hall of Famer holds the record for the fewest combined runs and RBI by a bat titlist with at least 400 at bats in a year when a full schedule was played?**

   A) His 112 combined runs and RBI are second among bat crown winners with 400 ABs only to Zack Wheat's combined total of 90 in the war-shortened 1918 season.

   B) He broke Matty Alou's old record of 113 combined runs and RBI, set in 1966.

   C) The previous year, a Twins teammate of his set the all-time season record for the lowest slugging average (.368) by anyone who batted .300 with 200 hits.

   D) He won hitting titles while playing two different positions.

   E) His .388 BA in 1977 is the highest since 1930 by a loop leader with 200 hits.

Fewest Combined Runs and RBI, Season, Bat Crown Winner

RANK	NAME	TEAM	YEAR	RUNS	RBI	TOTAL
1	Rod Carew	Min, AL	1972	61	51	112
2	Matty Alou	Pit, NL	1966	86	27	113
3	Pete Runnels	Bos, AL	1960	80	35	115
4	Tony Gwynn	SD, NL	1996	67	50	117
5	Ferris Fain	Phi, AL	1951	63	57	120
6	Harry Walker	StL/Phi, NL	1947	81	41	122
7	Jake Daubert	Bro, NL	1913	76	52	128
8	Richie Ashburn	Phi, NL	1958	98	33	131
9	Richie Ashburn	Phi, NL	1955	91	42	133
	Willie Wilson	KC, AL	1982	87	46	133

Note: Minimum 400 ABs; 1918, 1919, 1981, and 1994 seasons excluded because of abbreviated schedules.

9. **The Boston Red Sox were the next-to-last of the 16 teams extant in 1901 to produce a bat titlist. Who was the first member of the Crimson Hose to cop an AL bat crown?**
   A) He debuted with the Tigers.
   B) He was the first member of a last-place team to win an AL bat crown.
   C) He played the same position as Jimmie Foxx, the Red Sox's second batting champ.
   D) He was the first bat titlist to play for two different teams the year he won.
   E) His initials and last name are the same as those of the Blue Jays right-hander whose .739 winning percentage in 1984 on a neat 17–6 topped the AL.

Each Team's First Batting Crown Winner

TEAM	YEAR	WINNER
Philadelphia A's	1901	Nap Lajoie
St. Louis Cardinals	1901	Jesse Burkett
Washington Senators	1902	Ed Delahanty
Pittsburgh Pirates	1902	Ginger Beaumont
Cleveland Indians	1903	Nap Lajoie
Cincinnati Reds	1905	Cy Seymour
St. Louis Browns	1906	George Stone
Detroit Tigers	1907	Ty Cobb
Philadelphia Phillies	1910	Sherry Magee
Chicago Cubs	1912	Heinie Zimmerman
Brooklyn Dodgers	1913	Jake Daubert
New York Giants	1915	Larry Doyle
New York Yankees	1923	Babe Ruth
Boston Braves	1928	Rogers Hornsby
Boston Red Sox	1932	Dale Alexander
Chicago White Sox	1936	Luke Appling

Note: The 16 teams extant in 1901.

10. **When Elmer Flick paced the AL in 1905 with .308, the lowest mark prior to 1968 to win a loop bat crown, who was the junior loop runner-up at .302?**
    A) Like Flick, the runner-up is in the Hall of Fame.
    B) The runner-up had previously been a National League bat titlist.
    C) In 1904 the runner-up hit .343 and finished second in the AL to Nap Lajoie.
    D) The runner-up posted a .343 career BA in 19 seasons.
    E) The runner-up coined the phrase "Hit 'em where they ain't."

Leagues with Fewest .300 Hitters, Season

RANK	LEAGUE	YEAR	NO.	.300 HITTERS
1	AL	1968	1	Yastrzemski
2	AL	1966	2	F. Robinson, Oliva
3	AL	1905	3	Flick, Keeler, Bay
	AL	1908	3	Cobb, Crawford, Gessler
	AL	1945	3	Stirnweiss, Cuccinello, Dickshot
	AL	1965	3	Oliva, Yastrzemski, Davalillo
7	AA	1882	4	Browning, Carpenter, Swartwood, O'Brien
	NL	1907	4	Wagner, Magee, Beaumont, Leach
	NL	1909	4	Wagner, Mitchell, Hoblitzel, Doyle
	AL	1943	4	Appling, Wakefield, Hodgin, Cramer
	AL	1963	4	Yastrzemski, Kaline, Rollins, Pearson
	AL	1967	4	Yastrzemski, F. Robinson, Kaline, Scott

11. **Since 1901 no one has won a bat title in both the AL and the NL. John Olerud came close in 1998 when he was the NL runner-up after winning the AL crown in 1993. Who is the only man in this century to be a bat title runner-up in both leagues?**
    A) He never won a big league batting crown.
    B) He logged a .334 career mark in 12 seasons.
    C) He married the actress Mabel Hite.
    D) His runner-up seasons were 1901 in the AL and 1904–05 in the NL.
    E) Known as "Turkey Mike," he played under McGraw in both the AL and the NL.

12. **Prior to expansion in 1961, just three 20th century performers won back-to-back bat titles and failed to make the Hall of Fame. One was Federal League star Benny Kauff. Who are the other two?**
    A) Both played the same position.
    B) Both were left-handed all the way.
    C) Both had only one season in which their homer totals reached double figures.
    D) Both were rarities at their position in that they were under 6'0".
    E) The first to do it played in the 1919 World Series, and the second was the first multiple bat titlist to retire with a sub-.300 career BA.

Non–Hall of Famers Winning Back-to-Back Batting Titles

NAME	TEAM	YEARS WON
Ross Barnes	Bos, NA	1872–73
Paul Hines	Pro, NL	1878–79
Pete Browning	Lou, AA	1885–86
Tip O'Neill	StL, AA	1887–88
Jake Daubert	Bro, NL	1913–14
Benny Kauff	Ind/Nwk, FL	1914–15
Ferris Fain	Phi, AL	1951–52
Tommy Davis	LA, NL	1962–63
Tony Oliva	Min, AL	1964–65
Bill Madlock	Chi, NL	1975–76
Dave Parker	Pit, NL	1977–78

Note: Includes only players eligible for the Hall of Fame. Browning's 1886 crown is disputed.

13. Name the only two multiple bat leaders in big league history who never had a year when they averaged one hit per every three at bats (.333).
- A) One is among the elite few players in this century to play 100 games in a season at three different positions.
- B) The same man is also one of the elite few players to win batting crowns while playing two or more different positions.
- C) He broke in as a shortstop with Washington in 1951.
- D) The other man also was a regular at two different positions and served as a regular DH late in his career.
- E) The two were teammates in 1961–62 and won all of their bat crowns with the same AL team.

14. The Pittsburgh Pirates have won a franchise-record 24 batting crowns, including three club members who collected back-to-back bat titles. Who are the three?
- A) The first to do it bagged four crowns in a row, the second took two in a row more than 40 years later, and the third garnered his two titles after both of the others were dead.
- B) The first two are in the Hall of Fame, but the third is not and may never be.
- C) Only the third man was not a shortstop.
- D) The third man finished his career in 1991 as a DH.
- E) The three played on Pittsburgh World Series winners in 1909, 1960, and 1979.

Batting Crown Winners, Pittsburgh Pirates Franchise

NAME	NO.	YEARS
Honus Wagner	8	1900/03–04/06–09/11
Roberto Clemente	4	1961/64–65/67
Paul Waner	3	1927/34/36
Dave Parker	2	1977–78
Bill Madlock	2	1981/83
Ed Swartwood	1	1883
Ginger Beaumont	1	1902
Arky Vaughan	1	1935
Debs Garms	1	1940
Dick Groat	1	1960

15. Prior to Frank Thomas in 1997, the Chicago White Sox last owned a bat titlist in 1943. In the 53 intervening seasons, who came the closest to replacing Luke Appling as the last Pale Hose bat titlist?

A) He once lost the AL bat crown by .00009, the narrowest margin in history.

B) That season also marked the last time the Sox had two of the AL's top three hitters.

C) The unlucky loser never played another ML game after that season.

D) The unlucky loser hit .30845 to the winner's .30854.

E) The unlucky loser's initials and first name are the same as those of the unlucky Red Sox slugger whose career was all but wrecked by a 1967 beaning.

16. The Giants moved to San Francisco in 1958, and the A's arrived in Oakland in 1968. Whether it's the Bay Area weather, the way their ballparks are designed, or a combination of these and other factors, neither team has had a batting titlist since relocating to the Bay Area. Who came the closest to being the first Bay Area bat king when he lost his bid for a crown on the last day of the season?

A) He finished at .333, three points off the pace, after the winner went 3-for-4 in his finale while he had an 0-for day.

B) He led all hitters in both leagues that year in LCS action.

C) He homered off Nolan Ryan in his first major league at bat.

D) The year he just missed making a Bay Area breakthrough nearly saw a Bay Area double when an Oakland A's third sacker also had a shot at the AL bat crown on the final day of the season.

E) His nickname is "Will the Thrill."

Bat King Runners-Up from Bay Area Teams

NAME	TEAM	YEAR	BA	WINNER
Willie Mays	San Francisco	1958	.347	Richie Ashburn, .350
Danny Cater	Oakland	1968	.290	Carl Yastrzemski, .301
Will Clark	San Francisco	1989	.333	Tony Gwynn, .336
Carney Lansford	Oakland	1989	.336	Kirby Puckett, .339
Rickey Henderson	Oakland	1990	.325	George Brett, .329

Note: Mays got three hits on the final day of the 1958 season but gained no ground because Ashburn also made three hits. In 1958, the Giants played in Seals Stadium, home to several PCL batting champions, including Joe DiMaggio.

17. **When Albert Belle and Kenny Lofton finished second and fourth in the 1994 AL bat race, it marked the first year since when that the Indians had two of the AL's top four hitters?**

    A) Prior to 1994 the last time the Tribe had two hitters in the top five was 1965, when Vic Davalillo finished third and Leon Wagner fifth.

    B) When Bobby Avila, Cleveland's last bat titlist to date, won the crown in 1954, the Tribe had no one else among the top five.

    C) Ted Williams, Al Zarilla, and Barney McCosky rounded out the top five when Cleveland last put two hitters among the top four.

    D) It was the last season to date that the Tribe won it all.

    E) The Tribe's manager and leadoff-hitting left fielder were the pair who ranked in the top four.

18. **King Kelly caught a lot of games in the two years when he won NL bat crowns, but he was not primarily a catcher either season. Who was the only pure catcher to finish among the top five in a major league batting race more than once in the 19th century?**

    A) He ranked among the top five three times in a six-year period.

    B) He debuted with the Keystones in the Union Association.

    C) In 1891 he and Billy Hamilton made the Phils the only NL team with two .300 hitters.

    D) He was the first man to catch 1,000 games in the majors.

    E) He holds the record for the highest season BA by a catcher in enough games to qualify for a batting title.

19. **Who was the first simon-pure rookie to win an undisputed bat crown?**

    A) He also led his loop in slugging and was second in hits and home runs.

    B) He played second base as a rookie but is better known as an outfielder.

    C) He played most of his career for his hometown team.

    D) He was the first man to win batting titles in two different major leagues.

    E) His real first name was Louis, but he preferred "Pete," and sportswriters of his day called him "The Gladiator."

20. **In 1881, Cap Anson became the first player-manager to win a batting crown. He was also the second in 1888. Who is the only man in all the years since 1888 to match Anson's feat while serving as a player-manager for the entire season?**

    A) He was the third player-manager from his team to make the Hall of Fame.

    B) His bat crown marked the only time in history that two different players at his position won consecutive hitting titles in the same major league.

    C) Four years later, he was a bat title runner-up when he enjoyed his career year.

    D) Even in the season in which he won a bat title, he was better known for his fielding.

    E) He was the last player-manager to pilot a world champion.

Player-Managers Who Won Batting Crowns

NAME	TEAM	LEAGUE	YEAR	BA
Cap Anson	Chicago	NL	1881	.399
Fred Dunlap	St. Louis	UA	1884	.412
Cap Anson	Chicago	NL	1888	.344
Rogers Hornsby	Boston	NL	1928	.387
Lou Boudreau	Cleveland	AL	1944	.327

Note: Dunlap and Hornsby managed their teams only part of the season.

21. What Hall of Famer was the first man to win a bat title with a mark that turned out to be lower than his career batting average?

A) It was done for the second time the following year by another Hall of Famer.

B) Elmer Flick was both the third player and the first AL'er to do it.

C) His .340 BA the year he won his first of two NL bat crowns was four points below his career mark.

D) He retired with 915 career stolen bases, a record at the time.

E) He did it in 1891 as a member of the Phillies.

22. Who is the only batting leader to pitch against his runner-up on the final day of the season?

A) It was his only mound outing in the majors.

B) The runner-up was formerly a pro basketball player with the Cleveland Rebels.

C) The bat titlist began his pro career as a pitcher.

D) The runner-up didn't have enough plate appearances to qualify for a bat title under today's rules.

E) The titlist played for the Cards and the runner-up for the Cubs that year.

23. Name the only leadoff hitter to pace his league in batting and walks in the same season.

A) Although he had the top BA in the majors by 22 points the year of his double win, the AL bat leader's OBP was 21 points higher than his.

B) He also led all gardeners in the majors in total chances the year of his double win.

C) His unprecedented double win came with a last-place team.

D) Five of the Top 10 seasons in total chances by an outfielder belong to him.

E) After a long wait, he made the Hall of Fame in 1995.

Position Record Holders for the Most Batting Titles

	RANK	NAME	TITLES	YEARS
1B	1	Dan Brouthers	5	1882, 1883, 1889, 1891–92
	2	Many with 2		
2B	1	Rogers Hornsby	7	1920–25, 1928
	2	Rod Carew	5	1969, 1972–75
3B	1	Wade Boggs	5	1983, 1985–88
	2	Bill Madlock	4	1975–76, 1981, 1983
SS	1	Honus Wagner	7	1903–04, 1906–09, 1911
	2	Luke Appling	2	1936, 1943
OF	1	Ty Cobb	12	1907–15, 1917–19
	2	Tony Gwynn	8	1984, 1987–89, 1994–97
	3	Ted Williams	6	1941–42, 1947–48, 1957–58
	4	Stan Musial	5	1943, 1948, 1950, 1951–52
	5	Roberto Clemente	4	1961, 1964–65, 1967
		Harry Heilmann	4	1921, 1923, 1925, 1927
C	1	Ernie Lombardi	2	1938, 1942
	2	Bubbles Hargrave	1	1926
P	1	Guy Hecker	1	1886
	2	None		

Note: Carew also won two batting titles while playing first base, Musial won one batting title as a first baseman, and Wagner won one as an outfielder. Hecker's crown is disputed.

RBI Rulers

1. **Runs batted in did not become an official statistic until Babe Ruth sprang to prominence in 1920. Nevertheless, researchers have succeeded in reconstructing reasonably accurate RBI data for almost every major league season prior to then. We now know that only five players since 1871 have bagged 100 or more RBI in a season despite compiling fewer than 120 hits. Can you mine the clues to name them all?**

   A) For more than 40 years, the record for the fewest hits with at least 100 RBI belonged to Heinie Reitz, who had 106 RBI on 133 hits in 1896.

   B) One of the five did it as a rookie. Another was a Rookie of the Year. A third did it in his first year as a regular. The most recent NL'er to do it set a new record for the fewest hits in a season by a 100-RBI man. The most recent addition to the list did it for a defending world champ in a strike season.

   C) The years the five did it were 1937, 1953, 1954, 1993, and 1994, respectively.

   D) The first did it with Detroit and still holds the AL record for the fewest hits in a season with 100 RBI. The second did it with Pittsburgh. The third with the Senators. The fourth with the Pads; and the most recent with the Jays.

   E) The first three were right-handed hitters who played first base among other positions, the fourth as yet has never played anywhere but in the outfield, and the most recent has been both a regular outfielder and a regular first baseman.

Evolution of AL Record for Fewest Hits with 100 RBI, Season

NAME	TEAM	YEAR	RBI	HITS
Buck Freeman	Boston	1901	114	166
Buck Freeman	Boston	1903	104	163
Del Pratt	St. Louis	1916	103	159
Babe Ruth	Boston	1919	114	139
Ken Williams	St. Louis	1925	105	136
Rudy York	Detroit	1937	103	115

2. **Jay Buhner set a new season record in 1995 for a 100-RBI man when he snagged 121 ribbies on just 123 hits for a phenomenal RBI-to-hit ratio of 98.4. Who held the record prior to Buhner?**

   A) In a nine-year career (1957–66) he had 549 RBI on just 759 hits.

   B) His first AB came with the last team to play in Brooklyn.

   C) It was his club homer record of 46 that Frank Robinson broke in 1966.

   D) It was recently discovered that he tied Maris for the 1961 AL RBI crown.

   E) In 1961, his career year, he amassed 141 RBI on just 147 hits for the O's.

AL Best RBI/Hits Ratio, Season (Minimum 100 RBI)

RANK	NAME	TEAM	YEAR	HITS	RBI	RATIO
1	Jay Buhner	Seattle	1995	123	121	98.4
2	Jim Gentile	Baltimore	1961	147	141	95.9
3	Harmon Killebrew	Minnesota	1962	134	126	94.0
4	Harmon Killebrew	Minnesota	1971	127	119	93.7
5	Rudy York	Detroit	1938	138	127	92.0
6	Hank Greenberg	Detroit	1937	200	183	91.5
	Harmon Killebrew	Minnesota	1969	153	140	91.5
8	Gorman Thomas	Milwaukee	1979	136	123	90.4
9	Jay Buhner	Seattle	1996	153	138	90.2
10	Vern Stephens	Boston	1949	177	159	89.8

3. **The all-time NL season record for the best ratio of RBI to hits by a player who compiled at least 100 RBI was shattered in 1998 by Mark McGwire. Who had previously held the 20th century NL mark?**
   A) He had a 91.8 RBI-to-hits ratio when he won his second and last NL RBI crown.
   B) He finished with just 1,063 career RBI, even though he had six 100-RBI seasons.
   C) His 1,000th career RBI came in Brooklyn garb.
   D) He collected 350 RBI in 1929–30.
   E) He has been credited by SABR researchers with a previously undiscovered RBI in 1930, which would swell his already record total to 191.

NL Best RBI/Hits Ratio, Season (Minimum 100 RBI)

RANK	NAME	TEAM	YEAR	HITS	RBI	RATIO
1	Mark McGwire	St. Louis	1998	152	147	96.7
2	Oyster Burns	Brooklyn	1890	134	128	95.5
3	Hack Wilson	Chicago	1930	208	190	91.3
4	Phil Plantier	San Diego	1993	111	100	90.1
5	Jack Clark	St. Louis	1987	120	106	88.3
6	Willie McCovey	San Francisco	1970	143	126	88.1
7	Frank Thomas	Pittsburgh	1953	116	102	87.9
8	Roy Campanella	Brooklyn	1953	162	142	87.7
9	Billy Nash	Boston	1893	141	123	87.2
10	Johnny Bench	Cincinnati	1972	145	125	86.2

4. **In 1995 two sluggers who played the same position but were on different teams combined to produce an incredible 169 RBI on just 163 hits. Who are they?**
   A) One set a new record for the most RBI on fewer than 80 hits when he drove home 79 teammates on just 76 bingles.
   B) The other shattered the record for the most RBI by a player with fewer than 100 hits when his 87 bingles helped lead to 90 ribbies.
   C) Both played first base and also DH'd on occasion in 1995.
   D) Both played for AL teams.
   E) In 1996 the two were the regular first sackers for the second- and third-place finishers in the AL West.

Most RBI per Fewest Hits, Season

	NAME	TEAM	YEAR	HITS	RBI
Zero Hits					
AL	Hi Jasper	Chicago	1914	(0–for–5)	4
Fewer than 10 Hits					
AL	Rogers Hornsby	St. Louis	1934	7	11
	Smoky Burgess	Chicago	1967	8	11
	Joe Becker	Cleveland	1936	9	11
	Vic Raschi	New York	1953	9	11
NL	Mule Watson	New York	1924	9	11
	Joe Niekro	Chicago	1967	9	11
Fewer than 20 Hits					
NL	Pat Crawford	New York	1929	17	24
AL	Ron Northey	Chicago	1956	17	23
Fewer than 30 Hits					
NL	Bobby Hofman	New York	1954	28	30
AL	Frank Fernandez	New York	1968	23	30
Fewer than 40 Hits					
AL	Eddie Robinson	New York	1955	36	42
NL	Harry Truby	Chicago/Pittsburgh	1896	33	34
Fewer than 50 Hits					
AL	Johnny Blanchard	New York	1963	49	45
NL	Scott Servais	Houston	1994	49	41
AA	Ed Herr	St. Louis	1888	46	43
Fewer than 60 Hits					
NL	Dusty Rhodes	New York	1954	56	50
	Vince Barton	Chicago	1931	57	50
	Jerry Lynch	Cincinnati	1961	57	50
	Matt Williams	San Francisco	1989	59	50
AL	Oscar Gamble	New York	1980	54	50
Fewer than 70 Hits					
AL	Jim Leyritz	New York	1994	66	58
NL	Brian Hunter	Pittsburgh/Cincinnati	1994	60	57
Fewer than 80 Hits					
AL	Paul Sorrento	Cleveland	1995	76	79
NL	Wes Westrum	New York	1951	79	70

	NAME	TEAM	YEAR	HITS	RBI
Fewer than 90 Hits					
AL	Mark McGwire	Oakland	1995	87	90
NL	Charlie Ferguson	Philadelphia	1887	85	85
Fewer than 100 Hits					
AL	Mark McGwire	Oakland	1995	87	90
NL	Charlie Ferguson	Philadelphia	1887	85	85

5. **Six teams have finished in the cellar despite having two players who collected 100 RBI. What was the first team to achieve this unhappy distinction?**
   A) The team also received 97 RBI from its left fielder, who hit .383.
   B) Every player on the team with 250 or more ABs hit at least .280.
   C) The team set a new record for the most runs (944) by a cellar dweller.
   D) The team's right fielder tallied a 20th century NL-record 158 runs.
   E) The team also set an all-time record for the highest staff ERA.

Cellar Dwellers with Two 100-RBI Men

YEAR	TEAM	DUO
1930	Phi, NL	Chuck Klein (170) & Pinky Whitney (117)
1934	Chi, AL	Zeke Bonura (112) & Al Simmons (104)
1935	Phi, AL	Jimmie Foxx (115) & Bob Johnson (109)
1937	StL, AL	Harlond Clift (118) & Beau Bell (117)
1941	Phi, AL	Bob Johnson (107) & Sam Chapman (106)
1959	Was, AL	Harmon Killebrew (105) & Jim Lemon (100)

6. **Just twice in ML history have hitsmiths compiled 100 RBI while scoring fewer than 60 runs in a season. Who are these two lefty sluggers?**
   A) They did it a year apart for teams playing a 154-game schedule.
   B) The NL'er collected 115 RBI with just 59 runs the year before an AL slugger scored a mere 45 times while driving home 103 runs.
   C) Four years earlier, in 1956, the AL'er had 106 RBI but scored just 65 runs.
   D) The NL'er drove in 100 runs four times during the 1950s with Cincinnati.
   E) One man had the same first name as the Philadelphia A's last AL home run leader, and the other had the same first name as the A's first black regular.

Fewest Runs, Season, 100 or More RBI

RANK	NAME	TEAM	YEAR	RBI	RUNS
1	Vic Wertz	Bos, AL	1960	103	45
2	Gus Bell	Cin, NL	1959	115	59
3	Pedro Guerrero	LA, NL	1989	117	60
	Smead Jolley	Bos, AL	1932	106	60
	Ernie Banks	Chi, NL	1969	106	60
6	Harmon Killebrew	Min, AL	1969	119	61
	Ray Boone	Det, AL	1955	116	61
	Lee May	Bal, AL	1976	109	61
	Del Ennis	StL, NL	1957	105	61
	Heinie Zimmerman	NY, NL	1917	102	61
	Willie Montanez	Phi/SF, NL	1975	101	61

7. **The worst run-producer of all time? Here's our leading candidate: the only big leaguer to compile 500 at bats and fewer than 30 RBI in three straight seasons.**

   A) He began his career as a southpaw catcher.

   B) He ended his career the holder of the all-time record for the fewest RBI (26) in a season by a first baseman in 500 ABs.

   C) He collected 2,200+ hits and 1,200+ runs, played in the last Temple Cup Series, and was in uniform, but not in action, the day Merkle failed to touch second.

   D) He played in the same infield with Bobby Lowe, Herman Long, and Jimmy Collins.

   E) He and the first pitcher in ML history to win 200 games before he made his initial plate appearance share the same initials.

Evolution of Record for Fewest RBI, Season, First Baseman, 500 ABs

NAME	TEAM	YEAR	AB	RBI
Bill Phillips	Bro, AA	1886	585	72
Sid Farrar	Phi, NL	1888	508	53
Harry Taylor	Lou, AA	1890	553	53
Mickey Lehane	Col, AA	1891	511	52
Klondike Douglass	Phi, NL	1898	582	48
Pop Dillon	Bro, NL	1904	511	31
Fred Tenney	Bos, NL	1905	549	28
Fred Tenney	Bos, NL	1906	544	28
Fred Tenney	Bos, NL	1907	554	26

8. **What was the first keystone combo to compile 100 or more RBI each in a season?**

   A) The second baseman collected 55 extra-base hits that year but only 22 doubles and two home runs.

   B) The shortstop hit .222 in 594 ABs just two years earlier.

   C) The shortstop holds the season record for the most RBI (121) by anyone who failed to homer.

   D) The pair did it in 1894 and again in 1896.

   E) Their real first names were Henry and Hugh.

Keystone Combos with 100 RBI Apiece, Season

DUO	TEAM	YEAR
Hughie Jennings (109) & Heinie Reitz (105)	Bal, NL	1894
Hughie Jennings (121) & Heinie Reitz (106)	Bal, NL	1896
Ed McKean (112) & Cupid Childs (106)	Cle, NL	1896
George Davis (134) & Kid Gleason (106)	NY, NL	1897
Charlie Gehringer (127) & Billy Rogell (100)	Det, AL	1934
Joe Cronin (111) & Bobby Doerr (105)	Bos, AL	1940
Joe Gordon (124) & Lou Boudreau (106)	Cle, AL	1948
Vern Stephens (137) & Bobby Doerr (111)	Bos, AL	1948
Vern Stephens (159) & Bobby Doerr (109)	Bos, AL	1949
Vern Stephens (144) & Bobby Doerr (120)	Bos, AL	1950

9. **In 1996, Chipper Jones bagged 110 RBI and filled in at short while Jeff Blauser was hurt. But Jones played third most of the way for Atlanta. Who is the only NL'er since expansion to enjoy a 100-RBI campaign while playing short all season?**
   - A) He had 100 ribbies on the nose in his first season at shortstop.
   - B) He played 100 or more games in a season at three different positions.
   - C) A right-handed hitter, he was last active as a DH with Kansas City.
   - D) He broke in with the Mets in 1980.
   - E) His 100-ribby season as a shortstop came with the 1985 Expos.

Most RBI, Season, NL Shortstop, Since 1961

RANK	NAME	TEAM	YEAR	BA	RBI
1	Hubie Brooks	Montreal	1985	.269	100
2	Denis Menke	Houston	1970	.304	92
3	Denis Menke	Houston	1969	.269	90
4	Barry Larkin	Cincinnati	1996	.298	89
5	Dave Concepcion	Cincinnati	1979	.281	84
6	Dave Concepcion	Cincinnati	1974	.281	82
7	Leo Cardenas	Cincinnati	1966	.255	81
8	Ernie Banks	Chicago	1961	.278	80
9	Garry Templeton	St. Louis	1977	.322	79
	Dickie Thon	Houston	1983	.286	79

10. **In 1997, Joe Carter became only the second man to collect 100 RBI on a sub-.250 batting average three times in his career when he knocked home 102 runs for Toronto while hitting .234. Who is the only man to match Carter's feat?**
    - A) In 1979 he fell just three RBI short of Harmon Killebrew's record of 126 RBI on a sub-.250 BA.
    - B) Even though he had three 100-RBI seasons, he collected only 782 RBI in his 13-year career between 1973 and 1986.
    - C) He led the AL in homers twice with a sub-.250 BA.
    - D) In 1983 he was traded to Cleveland by his original team for Rick Manning.
    - E) In 1982 he and Ben Oglivie became the only two teammates both to attain 100 RBI on a sub-.250 BA.

Evolution of Record for Most RBI, Season, Sub-.250 BA

NAME	TEAM	YEAR	BA	RBI
Ned Cuthbert	Ath, NA	1871	.247	30
Cherokee Fisher	Bal, NA	1872	.231	36
George Bechtel	Phi, NA	1873	.244	40
Bob Ferguson	Har, NA	1875	.240	43
John Morrill	Bos, NL	1880	.237	44
Monte Ward	Pro, NL	1881	.244	53
Jerry Denny	Pro, NL	1884	.248	59
Fred Pfeffer	Chi, NL	1885	.241	73
Reddy Mack	Bal, AA	1889	.241	87
Jim Canavan	Cin/Mil, AA	1891	.238	87
Jake Beckley	Pit, NL	1892	.236	96
Eddie Robinson	Phi, AL	1953	.247	102
Roy Sievers	Was, AL	1954	.232	102
Harmon Killebrew	Was, AL	1959	.242	105
Bob Allison	Min, AL	1961	.245	105
Harmon Killebrew	Min, AL	1962	.243	126

Note: In 1887, Blondie Purcell, Baltimore, AA, had 96 RBI on a .250 BA.

11. **Who is the only man to rack up both 100-run and 100-RBI seasons and play his last game in the majors before he reached his 25th birthday?**
    A)   He was born in Amesbury, Massachusetts, as was his brother who also played up top.
    B)   He had a .320 career BA in four seasons after debuting with St. Louis in 1893.
    C)   He played in the same outfield with "The Heavenly Twins" in 1894.
    D)   His nickname was "Foxy Grandpa."
    E)   He and the Yankees slugger who compiled 21 homers and 54 RBI on just 243 ABs in 1961 share the same initials.

12. **To date, three men who amassed 2,000 career hits never registered as many as 50 RBI in a season. Who are these three anemic run-producers?**
    A)   One won a bat title, one set a new season mark in a baserunning department, and the third was known best for his glove, even though he rapped 2,191 hits.
    B)   All three were switch-hitters.
    C)   Two of the three opposed each other in the 1980 World Series.
    D)   The third played in four World Series with the same team between 1959 and the beginning of division play.
    E)   Two of the three were shortstops, and the third was a centerfielder.

13. **In 1929 who became the only man ever to total as many as 90 RBI and 90 walks in fewer than 350 at bats?**
    A)   As a rookie with the 1923 Cubs, he led all NL batters in Ks.
    B)   He played in two Series in the 1920s with another NL team besides the Cubs.
    C)   He played first base in the 1925 Series and second base in the 1927 Series.
    D)   He set a new 20th century Pittsburgh team record when he collected 93 walks in 1929.
    E)   He and the third sacker who hit his 300th career home run in a Cards uniform in 1996 share the same initials.

14. Who was the first member of a cellar team to lead a major league in RBI?

A) That same year, he also led his loop in homers.
B) He had his top home run season as a rookie.
C) He was the first rookie to clout more than 30 homers.
D) He was a teammate of Babe Ruth in the Babe's last season.
E) He was the only member of the Braves to lead the NL in RBI in this century while the franchise was in Boston.

RBI Leaders on Cellar Dwellers

NAME	TEAM	RBI	YEAR
Wally Berger	Bos, NL	130	1935
Roy Sievers	Was, AL	114	1957
Frank Howard	Was, AL	126	1970
Andre Dawson	Chi, NL	137	1987
Darren Daulton	Phi, NL	109	1992

Note: Berger and Sievers are the only true RBI kings on cellar dwellers. Howard, Dawson, and Daulton won crowns with teams that finished last only in their divisions, not the entire league.

15. Babe Ruth and Jimmie Foxx were the first two AL'ers to win RBI crowns with two different teams. Who was the third and last AL'er to date to do it?

A) His first RBI crown came with a pennant winner, and his second with a club that finished one game off the pace.
B) He is the only man to tie for an RBI crown twice in his career.
C) He is furthermore the only man to tie for RBI crowns in back-to-back seasons.
D) He holds the all-time season record for the most RBI by a shortstop.
E) He compiled 303 RBI for the 1949–50 Red Sox.

RBI Leaders with Two Different Teams

NAME	1ST TEAM	2ND TEAM
Dan Brouthers	Buf, NL 1883	Bro, NL 1892
Sam Thompson	Det, NL 1887	Phi, NL 1895
Nap Lajoie	Phi, NL 1898	Phi, AL 1901
Babe Ruth	Bos, AL 1919	NY, AL 1920
Jimmie Foxx	Phi, AL 1932	Bos, AL 1938
Johnny Mize	StL, NL 1940	NY, NL 1942
Vern Stephens	StL, AL 1944	Bos, AL 1949
Orlando Cepeda	SF, NL 1961	StL, NL 1967

16. The record for the fewest RBI by a .350 hitter with at least 400 at bats is 27. To whom does it belong?

    A)   He set the mark in his rookie year.

    B)   The only other player to hit .340 or better with as few as 27 RBI did it with the same team as he did, albeit 39 years later.

    C)   He collected a record 678 hits in his first three seasons.

    D)   He also holds the all-time season record for the largest differential (106) between runs scored (133) and RBI (27).

    E)   He and his brother hold many sibling batting records.

Highest BA, Season, Less than 50 RBI (Minimum 400 ABs)

RANK	NAME	TEAM	YEAR	RBI	BA
1	Willie Keeler	Bal, NL	1898	44	.385
2	Harry Walker	StL/Phi, NL	1947	41	.371
3	Lloyd Waner	Pit, NL	1927	27	.355
4	Ginger Beaumont	Pit, NL	1899	38	.352
5	Richie Ashburn	Phi, NL	1958	33	.350
6	Max Carey	Pit, NL	1925	44	.34317
7	Ralph Garr	Atl, NL	1971	44	.34272
8	Willie Keeler	NY, AL	1904	40	.34254
9	Patsy Dougherty	Bos, AL	1902	34	.34247
10	Matty Alou	Pit, NL	1966	27	.34206

Note: BAs are carried out to five decimal points where ties would otherwise exist.

17. His real first name was David, but he used his middle name and is the only player in *The Baseball Encyclopedia* to go by that name. He is also the only player in this century to lead his team in total bases and home runs one year despite compiling fewer than 25 RBI. Who is he?

    A)   After leaving the majors, he was a minor league star in the late teens in the American Association.

    B)   In 1909 he led Boston, NL, with six homers and 183 TBs but had just 24 RBI.

    C)   He played in two straight World Series with the New York Giants in 1911–12.

    D)   He was the runner-up for the NL bat crown in 1914.

    E)   His initials are the same as those of the NL Manager of the Year in 1998.

Most TBs, Season, Fewer than 25 RBI

RANK	NAME	TEAM	YEAR	RBI	TBS
1	Don Blasingame	StL, NL	1959	24	221
2	Harry Bay	Cle, AL	1905	22	204
3	Donie Bush	Det, AL	1917	24	187
4	Beals Becker	Bos, NL	1909	24	183
5	Jigger Statz	Bro, NL	1927	21	180
6	Morrie Rath	Chi, AL	1912	19	178
	Bill Virdon	Pit, NL	1965	24	178
8	Clyde Milan	Was, AL	1910	16	177
9	Richie Ashburn	Phi, NL	1959	20	173
	Sparky Adams	StL/Cin, NL	1933	22	173

Beals Becker slugged 45 home runs between 1908 and 1915, a relatively high number for the Deadball Era. Becker netted only 292 career RBI, however. Among men who completed their careers prior to 1920 and had at least 20 home runs, only Billy O'Brien (6.44) collected fewer RBI per home run than Becker's ratio of 6.49.

18. As a rookie in 1942, this outfielder collected a mere 31 RBI in 402 at bats; 14 years later, he netted 23 RBI in 48 at bats, the all-time season record high by anyone with fewer than 50 at bats. Who is he?

A) In 1948 he hit .321 in 96 games for the Cardinals and was 11-for-25 as a pinch hitter.

B) He debuted with the 1942 Phillies.

C) His son played with the Royals in 1969.

D) He topped the White Sox and the AL with 15 pinch hits in 1956.

E) He was nicknamed "The Round Man."

Most RBI, Season, Fewer than 50 ABs

RANK	NAME	TEAM	YEAR	ABS	RBI
1	Ron Northey	Chi, AL	1956	48	23
2	Buck Ewing	NY, NL	1891	49	18
3	Hank Greenberg	Det, AL	1936	46	16
4	Ken McMullen	LA, NL	1975	46	14
	Jimmy Sheckard	Bal, NL	1897	49	14
6	Monte Cross	Pit, NL	1894	43	13
	Al Orth	Phi, NL	1895	45	13
	Babe Ganzel	Was, AL	1927	48	13
	Don Larsen	NY, AL	1958	49	13
	Nelson Mathews	Chi, NL	1962	49	13
	Jerry Martin	KC, AL	1983	44	13
	Paul Sorrento	Min, AL	1991	47	13

19. Four infield trios have driven in 100 runs each in the same season. Only one of the four did not include a first baseman. Who were the members of the only second base, shortstop, and third base trio to each collect 100 RBI in a season?

A) None of the three ever again drove in 100 runs in a season.

B) The first sacker in the infield unit later drove in 100 runs three years in a row.

C) The trio finished fourth, sixth, and eighth in the AL in RBI that year, and the eighth-place finisher won the MVP Award.

D) Two years later, another AL infield trio became the most recent to collect 100 RBI apiece in the same season.

E) The trio helped catapult their team to its last World Championship to date.

100-RBI Infield Trios

YEAR	TEAM	TRIO
1934	Det, AL	Billy Rogell, Charlie Gehringer & Hank Greenberg
1940	Bos, AL	Joe Cronin, Bobby Doerr & Jimmie Foxx
1948	Cle, AL	Ken Keltner, Lou Boudreau & Joe Gordon
1950	Bos, AL	Vern Stephens, Bobby Doerr & Walt Dropo

20. Who was the most recent man to knock in 100 runs with fewer than 10 whiffs?

 A) He won the AL MVP Award the year he did it.
 B) He caught a game for the third and last time in his career in 1948.
 C) He was the last player-manager to take his team to a World Championship.
 D) Prior to 1996 he was the most recent shortstop to bat over .350.
 E) He logged all of these achievements in the same season.

Most RBI, Season, Fewer than 10 Ks

RANK	NAME	TEAM	YEAR	Ks	RBI
1	Lave Cross	Phi, NL	1894	7	125
2	Tommy Holmes	Bos, NL	1945	9	117
3	Ed McKean	Cle, NL	1896	9	112
4	Pie Traynor	Pit, NL	1929	7	108
5	Lou Boudreau	Cle, AL	1948	9	106
6	Lave Cross	Phi, NL	1895	8	101
7	Jack Glasscock	StL/Pit, NL	1893	7	100
	Jack Doyle	NY, NL	1894	3	100
9	Joe Sewell	Cle, AL	1925	4	98
10	Mickey Cochrane	Phi, AL	1929	8	95

Note: Since 1884, when overhand pitching was legalized and strikeout totals jumped accordingly.

21. The most recent performer to compile 100 RBI on fewer than 10 home runs twice in his career also is the most recent to collect more than 120 RBI in a season on fewer than 10 home runs. Who is he?

 A) He had back-to-back seasons in which he totaled 240 RBI on just 17 home runs.
 B) His big RBI years followed a season when he won a batting title.
 C) His 15 dingers as a Yankees rookie in 1933 turned out to be his career high.
 D) He was the lone Dodgers player to homer in the 1947 World Series.
 E) His brother won the 1947 NL batting title.

Players with 120 RBI and Fewer than 10 HRs (Post-1920)

RANK	NAME	TEAM	YEAR	HRS	RBI
1	Paul Waner	Pit, NL	1927	9	131
2	Luke Appling	Chi, AL	1936	6	128
3	Bobby Veach	Det, AL	1922	9	126
4	Dixie Walker	Bro, NL	1945	8	124
	Pie Traynor	Pit, NL	1928	3	124
6	Baby Doll Jacobson	StL, AL	1920	9	122
7	Johnny Hodapp	Cle, AL	1930	9	121
	Tony Lazzeri	NY, AL	1930	9	121
9	Larry Gardner	Cle, AL	1921	3	120

22. Who are the only two catchers to log 100 RBI in a season prior to Gabby Hartnett in 1930?

   A)   The first man to do it also collected 76 RBI in just 72 games in 1889.

   B)   The second man to do it broke in with Cincinnati in 1886 and finished with Cincinnati in 1899.

   C)   Prior to 1930 it was last done by a catcher in 1893.

   D)   It was first done in 1891 by the Philadelphia A's regular backstopper, who also led the AA that year in triples.

   E)   The two who did it prior to Hartnett were nicknamed "Jocko" and "Farmer."

Evolution of Season Record for Most RBI, Each Position

19th Century

	NAME	RBI	YEAR	TEAM	LEAGUE
1B	Joe Start	34	1871	New York	NA
	Joe Start	50	1872	New York	NA
	Everett Mills	57	1873	Baltimore	NA
	Jim O'Rourke	71	1874	Boston	NA
	Cal McVey	87	1875	Boston	NA
	Dan Brouthers	97	1883	Buffalo	NL
	Cap Anson	102	1884	Chicago	NL
	Cap Anson	108	1885	Chicago	NL
	Cap Anson	147	1886	Chicago	NL
2B	Al Reach	34	1871	Athletics	NA
	Ross Barnes	34	1871	Boston	NA
	Wes Fisler	48	1872	Athletics	NA
	Ross Barnes	62	1873	Boston	NA
	Jack Burdock	88	1883	Boston	NL
	Fred Pfeffer	101	1884	Chicago	NL
	Lou Bierbauer	105	1889	Philadelphia	AA
	Bobby Lowe	115	1894	Boston	NL
	Nap Lajoie	127	1898	Philadelphia	NL
3B	Levi Meyerle	40	1871	Athletics	NA
	Cap Anson	50	1872	Athletics	NA
	Levi Meyerle	58	1873	White Stockings	NA
	Ezra Sutton	59	1875	Athletics	NA
	Cap Anson	59	1876	Chicago	NL
	Ned Williamson	60	1882	Chicago	NL
	Ezra Sutton	73	1883	Boston	NL
	Ned Williamson	84	1884	Chicago	NL
	Jumbo Davis	109	1887	Baltimore	AA
	Jerry Denny	112	1889	Indianapolis	NL
	Billy Nash	123	1893	Boston	NL
	Lave Cross	125	1894	Philadelphia	NL
	Jimmy Collins	132	1897	Boston	NL

	NAME	RBI	YEAR	TEAM	LEAGUE
SS	Davy Force	29	1871	Olympics	NA
	John Radcliff	44	1872	Baltimore	NA
	George Wright	50	1873	Boston	NA
	George Wright	61	1875	Boston	NA
	Tom Burns	67	1883	Chicago	NL
	Tom Burns	71	1885	Chicago	NL
	Jack Rowe	87	1886	Detroit	NL
	Oyster Burns	99	1887	Baltimore	AA
	Ed McKean	133	1893	Cleveland	NL
	George Davis	136	1897	New York	NL
OF	Lip Pike	39	1871	Troy	NA
	Lip Pike	60	1872	Baltimore	NA
	Andy Leonard	61	1873	Boston	NA
	Cal McVey	71	1874	Boston	NA
	Andy Leonard	74	1875	Boston	NA
	King Kelly	95	1884	Chicago	NL
	Sam Thompson	166	1887	Detroit	NL
C	Cal McVey	43	1871	Boston	NA
	Deacon White	66	1873	Boston	NA
	King Kelly	71	1888	Boston	NL
	Buck Ewing	87	1889	New York	NL
	Jocko Milligan	106	1891	Philadelphia	AA
	Farmer Vaughn	108	1893	Cincinnati	NL

20th Century

	NAME	RBI	YEAR	TEAM
1B	**American League**			
	Buck Freeman	114	1901	Boston
	George Sisler	122	1920	St. Louis
	Lou Gehrig	175	1927	New York
	Lou Gehrig	184	1931	New York
	National League			
	Kitty Bransfield	91	1901	Pittsburgh
	Jack Doyle	91	1903	Brooklyn
	Fred Luderus	99	1911	Philadelphia
	George Kelly	122	1921	New York
	George Kelly	136	1924	New York
	Jim Bottomley	136	1928	St. Louis
	Jim Bottomley	137	1929	St. Louis
	Don Hurst	143	1932	Philadelphia
	Andres Galarraga	150	1996	Colorado

	NAME	RBI	YEAR	TEAM
2B	*American League*			
	Nap Lajoie	125	1901	Philadelphia
	Charlie Gehringer	127	1934	Detroit
	National League			
	Tom Daly	90	1901	Brooklyn
	Bill Sweeney	100	1912	Boston
	Rogers Hornsby	126	1921	St. Louis
	Rogers Hornsby	152	1922	St. Louis
3B	*American League*			
	Jimmy Collins	94	1901	Boston
	Lave Cross	108	1902	Philadelphia
	Frank Baker	115	1911	Philadelphia
	Frank Baker	130	1912	Philadelphia
	Al Rosen	145	1953	Cleveland
	National League			
	Otto Krueger	79	1901	St. Louis
	Tommy Leach	85	1902	Pittsburgh
	Tommy Leach	87	1903	Pittsburgh
	Heinie Zimmerman	99	1912	Chicago
	Heinie Zimmerman	102	1917	New York
	Pie Traynor	106	1925	Pittsburgh
	Pie Traynor	106	1927	Pittsburgh
	Pie Traynor	124	1928	Pittsburgh
	Pinky Whitney	124	1932	Philadelphia
	Eddie Mathews	135	1953	Milwaukee
	Joe Torre	137	1971	St. Louis
	Vinny Castilla	144	1998	Colorado
SS	*American League*			
	Bill Keister	93	1901	Baltimore
	George Davis	93	1902	Chicago
	Joe Sewell	93	1921	Cleveland
	Joe Sewell	109	1923	Cleveland
	Joe Cronin	126	1930	Washington
	Joe Cronin	126	1931	Washington
	Luke Appling	128	1936	Chicago
	Vern Stephens	137	1948	Boston
	Vern Stephens	159	1949	Boston

NAME	RBI	YEAR	TEAM
National League			
Honus Wagner	126	1901	Pittsburgh*
Bobby Wallace	91	1901	St. Louis
Honus Wagner	101	1903	Pittsburgh
Honus Wagner	101	1905	Pittsburgh
Honus Wagner	109	1908	Pittsburgh
Glenn Wright	111	1924	Pittsburgh
Glenn Wright	121	1925	Pittsburgh
Glenn Wright	126	1930	Brooklyn
Ernie Banks	129	1958	Chicago
Ernie Banks	143	1959	Chicago

* Fewer than half of Wagner's games were at short; as a result, many consider Wallace's 1901 figure a better starting point, and the record then progresses as shown.

	NAME	RBI	YEAR	TEAM
OF	**American League**			
	Socks Seybold	90	1901	Philadelphia
	Buck Freeman	121	1902	Boston
	Ty Cobb	127	1911	Detroit
	Babe Ruth	137	1920	New York
	Babe Ruth	171	1921	New York
	National League			
	Ed Delahanty	108	1901	Philadelphia
	Cy Seymour	121	1905	Cincinnati
	Sherry Magee	123	1910	Philadelphia
	Gavvy Cravath	128	1913	Philadelphia
	Irish Meusel	132	1922	New York
	Hack Wilson	159	1929	Chicago
	Hack Wilson	190	1930	Chicago
C	**American League**			
	Billy Sullivan	56	1901	Chicago
	Wilbert Robinson	57	1902	Baltimore
	Hank Severeid	57	1917	St. Louis
	Ray Schalk	61	1920	Chicago
	Hank Severeid	78	1921	St. Louis
	Hank Severeid	78	1922	St. Louis
	Mickey Cochrane	80	1927	Philadelphia
	Mickey Cochrane	95	1929	Philadelphia
	Mickey Cochrane	112	1932	Philadelphia
	Bill Dickey	133	1937	New York

NAME	RBI	YEAR	TEAM
National League			
Deacon McGuire	40	1901	Brooklyn
Mal Kittridge	40	1901	Boston
Johnny Kling	57	1902	Chicago
Johnny Kling	68	1903	Chicago
Larry McLean	71	1910	Cincinnati
Bob O'Farrell	84	1923	St. Louis
Gabby Hartnett	122	1930	Chicago
Walker Cooper	122	1947	New York
Roy Campanella	142	1953	Brooklyn
Johnny Bench	148	1970	Cincinnati*

* Bench played a significant number of games at other positions.

Silver Sluggers

1. The American League almost surely would have become the first loop to average more than 500 extra-base hits per team in 1994 if a strike had not truncated the season. In 1995 the power surge continued, and then in 1996 slugging records toppled everywhere as Seattle became the first team in history to collect more than 600 extra-base blows (607) and Baltimore, with 585, also surpassed the 1936 Yankees' old mark of 580. The recent power explosion excepted, slugging averages have plummeted dramatically since expansion. What former Silver Slugger Award winner's .534 career slugging average is currently the highest of any retired performer with at least 3,000 at bats who debuted after 1960?

   A) He is among the elite few post–World War II sluggers who accumulated nearly as many career runs (1,099) as RBI (1,119).
   B) He paced the NL in runs as a rookie.
   C) He won a Silver Slugger Award in both loops.
   D) He's not in the Hall of Fame, though long eligible.
   E) He is currently the only White Sox performer to win two SA crowns.

Highest Career SA, Players Debuting After 1960

RANK	NAME	YEARS	BA	SA
1	Dick Allen	1963–77	.292	.534
2	Willie Stargell	1962–82	.282	.529
3	Mike Schmidt	1972–89	.267	.527
4	Jim Rice	1974–89	.298	.502
5	Bob Horner	1978–88	.277	.499
6	Reggie Jackson	1967–87	.262	.490
7	Reggie Smith	1966–82	.287	.489
8	George Brett	1973–93	.306	.487
9	Fred Lynn	1974–90	.283	.484
10	Andre Dawson	1976–96	.279	.483

Note: Limited to retired players with 3,000 career ABs. The only postexpansion slugger affected by both the post-1960 and AB qualifiers is Jim Gentile (1957–66), with a .486 SA in 2,922 ABs.

2. **Prior to Frank Thomas's arrival, the White Sox traditionally had the least pop of any team in the majors. Between 1901 and Thomas's debut in 1991, only 22 Pale Hosers posted season slugging averages as high as .500, led by Dick Allen's AL-best .603 in 1972. Allen's Silver Slugger Award win was only the second by a White Sox player. Who was the only ChiSoxer prior to 1972 to bag an AL slugging crown?**

   A) His .491 SA was 46 points better than teammate Joe Jackson's.
   B) He and teammate Eddie Collins finished second and third that year in batting.
   C) It was Pants Rowland's first year at the White Sox helm.
   D) He led the NL in homers in 1924.
   E) His big year with the ChiSox came in 1915.

Evolution of White Sox Season Record for Highest SA

NAME	YEAR	TBS	BA	SA
Fred Hartman	1901	204	.309	.431
Harry Lord	1911	243	.321	.433
Jack Fournier	1915	207	.322	.491
Joe Jackson	1916	293	.341	.495
Joe Jackson	1919	261	.351	.506
Joe Jackson	1920	336	.382	.590
Dick Allen	1972	305	.308	.603
Frank Thomas	1993	333	.317	.607
Frank Thomas	1994	291	.353	.729

Note: Thomas had only 399 ABs in the strike-abbreviated 1994 season, but 109 walks swelled his total plate appearances to well over 500.

3. **The season record for the highest slugging average by a bat title qualifier with fewer than 10 home runs belongs to Ty Cobb—.621 on eight dingers in 1911. Only one other bat title qualifier has slugged .600 with fewer than 10 taters. Who is he?**

   A) His .602 SA was achieved on 74 extra-base hits but just six four-baggers.
   B) In his second season as a full-time player, he rapped a career-high .393, slugged .602, and scored 165 runs.
   C) He is the only Hall of Famer who played both his first and his last seasons with a franchise for which he never played at any other point in his career.
   D) His 194 career triples are the most by anyone who was never a league leader in three-baggers.
   E) He played on five pennant winners between 1894 and 1900.

The greatest hitting team ever—the 1894 Philadelphia Phillies. Top: Nixey Callahan, Bob Allen, Ed Delahanty, Jack Boyle, Sam Thompson, Jack Taylor, and Charlie Reilly. Middle: Jack Clements, Gus Weyhing, Bill Hallman, manager Arthur Irwin, Kid Carsey, Billy Hamilton, and George Haddock. Bottom: Fred Hartman, Jack Sharrott, Tuck Turner, and Mike Grady. After his first four ML seasons, Ed Delahanty had just a .265 career BA. Over the next dozen seasons, he hit a heady .368 to hike his overall mark to .346. In 1894, Delahanty posted the highest SA ever (.585) by anyone with 400 at bats and fewer than five home runs.

Highest SA, Season, Fewer than 10 HRs

RANK	NAME	TEAM	YEAR	HRS	SA
1	Ty Cobb	Det, AL	1911	8	.621
2	Joe Kelley	Bal, NL	1894	6	.602
3	George Sisler	StL, AL	1922	8	.594
4	Joe Jackson	Cle, AL	1911	7	.590
5	Ed Delahanty	Phi, NL	1894	4	.585
6	Ty Cobb	Det, AL	1912	7	.584
7	Ed Delahanty	Phi, NL	1899	9	.582
8	Joe Jackson	Cle, AL	1912	3	.579
9	Honus Wagner	Pit, NL	1900	4	.573
10	Dan Brouthers	Buf, NL	1883	3	.572

Note: Minimum 400 ABs; the only potential list qualifier excluded by the minimum is Ross Barnes with a .590 SA in 1876 and just one home run in 322 ABs.

4. **The converse of Ty Cobb's 1911 slugging mark arguably is the lowest season slugging average accompanied by 40 or more home runs. Prior to Ralph Kiner in 1948, no one had ever hit 40 dingers and slugged under .575. Kiner's .533 mark remained the record low for only a short time, however. By the end of the 1950s, the record belonged to Rocky Colavito—.512 in 1959. Who later broke Colavito's mark, reducing the record low to .507?**

   A) He won three AL Silver Slugger crowns.

   B) Among men who had 450 career homers, his .462 career SA is the lowest.

   C) His .285 career BA is the lowest among men who won more than two bat titles.

   D) He has the lowest career SA of any 20th century Triple Crown winner.

   E) His 3,419 career hits are the most by any AL'er who spent his entire career with the same team.

Evolution of Record for Lowest SA, Season, 40 HRs

NAME	TEAM	YEAR	HRs	BA	SA
Babe Ruth	NY, AL	1920	54	.376	.847
Babe Ruth	NY, AL	1921	59	.378	.846
Rogers Hornsby	StL, NL	1922	42	.401	.722
Cy Williams	Phi, NL	1923	41	.293	.576
Ralph Kiner	Pit, NL	1948	40	.265	.533
Gil Hodges	Bro, NL	1951	40	.268	.527
Rocky Colavito	Cle, AL	1959	42	.257	.512
Carl Yastrzemski	Bos, AL	1969	40	.255	.507
Jay Buhner	Sea, AL	1997	40	.243	.506

5. **Whose .355 career slugging average is easily the lowest of anyone with at least 2,000 hits and a .300 career batting average?**

   A) In 1904 he had just 106 total bases in 436 ABs for Washington.

   B) He was born in Queenstown, Ireland, in 1865.

   C) In 1894 he became the first man to lead a major league in sacrifice hits.

   D) His top years came with Pittsburgh during the 1890s.

   E) He was once erroneously believed to be the brother of a Tigers pitching star in the early 1900s who was nicknamed "Wild Bill."

Lowest Career SA (Minimum 2,000 Hits & .300 Career BA)

RANK	NAME	YEARS	HITS	BA	SA
1	Patsy Donovan	1890–1907	2253	.301	.355
2	Stuffy McInnis	1909–27	2405	.307	.381
3	Richie Ashburn	1948–62	2574	.308	.382
4	Lloyd Waner	1927–45	2459	.316	.393
5	Stan Hack	1932–47	2193	.301	.397
6	Luke Appling	1930–50	2749	.310	.398
7	Jake Daubert	1910–24	2326	.303	.401
8	Buddy Myer	1925–47	2131	.303	.406
9	Billy Herman	1931–47	2345	.301	.407
10	Harvey Kuenn	1952–66	2092	.303	.408

6. **Name the first man to win a loop slugging crown with a sub-.300 batting average.**

    A) He had 338 career steals, the most of anyone born in Europe.
    B) Bob Bescher broke his record for the most career thefts by a switch-hitter.
    C) His .330 BA in 1901 stood as the pre–Mickey Mantle AL season record by a switch-hitter with 400 ABs.
    D) In 1898 he accomplished a feat that became commonplace after expansion when he became the first SA leader to bat under .300.
    E) He and the Orioles centerfielder in 1998 share the same last name.

SA Leaders with a Sub-.300 BA Prior to Expansion

NAME	TEAM	YEAR	SA	BA
John Anderson	Bro/Was, NL	1898	.494	.294
Gavvy Cravath	Phi, NL	1915	.510	.285
Rudy York	Det, AL	1943	.527	.271
Larry Doby	Cle, AL	1952	.541	.276
Duke Snider	Bro, NL	1956	.598	.292
Roger Maris	NY, AL	1960	.581	.283
Frank Robinson	Cin, NL	1960	.595	.297

Note: After expansion, slugging leaders with sub-.300 batting averages proliferated; Reggie Jackson alone won three such crowns.

7. **Mike Tiernan copped back-to-back Silver Slugger honors for the New York Giants in 1890–91. Who was the next Giant to top the NL in slugging average?**

    A) Willie Mays was the only New York Giant besides Tiernan to win more than one NL slugging crown.
    B) The Giants' first SA leader in the 20th century never won a bat crown.
    C) He won the SA crown in the final year of an eight-year run in which he had 100 or more RBI each season.
    D) He won his slugging crown the year Paul Waner took his last batting crown.
    E) He was the first *Cooperstown* 500 member to hit all his career home runs while playing for just one team.

8. **After Gavvy Cravath posted a .510 slugging average in 1915, no NL'er broke .500 again until 1920. What shortstop registered the top senior loop slugging mark (.484) during the intervening four years (1916–19)?**

    A) He also had the top senior loop SA between 1916 and 1919 by a third baseman.
    B) He played beside Dots Miller the year he compiled the NL's top SA in 1916–19.
    C) His .484 SA for the Cardinals in 1917 was the best on his team by 85 points.
    D) He has the highest career BA of anyone who saw regular duty at three different positions.
    E) His .756 SA in 1925 is the highest ever by a second baseman.

9. **In 1997, Mark McGwire set a new season record for the highest slugging average by a batting title qualifier with a sub-.300 batting average. McGwire then broke his own mark in 1998. Who held the record prior to McGwire?**

    A) He broke his own old mark of .628 when he set the "pre-McGwire" record of .646.
    B) Prior to 1997 his record had last been seriously threatened by Kevin Mitchell in 1989.
    C) He hit his 475th and last career home run in 1982.
    D) He spent his entire 21-year career with the same team.
    E) He won his only MVP Award when he was 39 years old.

Evolution of Record for Highest SA, Season, Sub-.300 BA

NAME	TEAM	YEAR	BA	SA
Ed Pinkham	Chi, NA	1871	.263	.453
Charley Jones	Cin, AA	1883	.294	.471
Ned Williamson	Chi, NL	1884	.278	.554
Cy Williams	Phi, NL	1923	.293	.576
Rudy York	Det, AL	1938	.298	.579
Jimmie Foxx	Bos, AL	1940	.297	.581
Hank Greenberg	Det, AL	1946	.277	.604
Roger Maris	NY, AL	1961	.269	.620
Willie Stargell	Pit, NL	1971	.295	.628
Willie Stargell	Pit, NL	1973	.299	.6456
Mark McGwire	Oak, AL/StL, NL	1997	.274	.6463
Mark McGwire	StL, NL	1998	.299	.752

Note: Limited to batting title qualifiers.

10. **Name the first man to play 10 full seasons in the majors and finish with a .500 career slugging average on a sub-.300 career batting average.**

   A) He finished in 1945 with a .506 career SA.

   B) His brother led the AL at various times in both doubles and triples; he led the AL only in OBP, that in 1944.

   C) He was the last man to compile 200 home runs in a Philadelphia A's uniform.

   D) He was the last man to play 10 full seasons as a regular under Connie Mack.

   E) He was nicknamed "Indian Bob."

Highest Career SA, Sub-.300 BA

RANK	NAME	YEARS	BA	SA
1	Mickey Mantle	1951–68	.298	.557
2	Ralph Kiner	1946–55	.279	.548
3	Frank Robinson	1956–76	.294	.537
4	Dick Allen	1963–77	.292	.534
5	Willie Stargell	1962–82	.282	.529
6	Mike Schmidt	1972–89	.267	.528
7	Willie McCovey	1959–80	.270	.515
8	Eddie Mathews	1952–68	.271	.50943
9	Jeff Heath	1936–49	.293	.50881
10	Harmon Killebrew	1954–75	.256	.50853

Note: Minimum 4,000 ABs; retired players only. SAs are carried out to five decimal points where ties would otherwise exist.

11. **When Babe Ruth led the AL in slugging average seven years in a row (1918–24), he broke a record for the most consecutive slugging crowns (six) that was shared at the time by Ty Cobb and what 19th century star?**

   A)   His first of six straight slugging crowns came in his first full season.

   B)   After copping six consecutive slugging crowns in his first six full seasons in the majors, he led only once more in SA.

   C)   His .519 career SA was a record when he retired.

   D)   He is one of the only two men who won slugging crowns in two different major leagues prior to the NL-AA consolidation in 1892.

   E)   His .342 career BA is the highest of any man active primarily before 1893.

Most Consecutive Seasons Leading League in SA

RANK	NAME	LEAGUE	SPAN	TOTAL
1	Babe Ruth	AL	1918–24	7
2	Dan Brouthers	NL	1881–86	6
	Ty Cobb	AL	1907–12	6
	Rogers Hornsby	NL	1920–25	6
	Babe Ruth	AL	1926–31	6
	Ted Williams	AL	1941–49	6
7	Honus Wagner	NL	1907–09	3
	Chuck Klein	NL	1931–33	3
	Johnny Mize	NL	1938–40	3
	Frank Robinson	NL	1960–62	3
	Willie McCovey	NL	1968–70	3
	Mike Schmidt	NL	1980–82	3

Note: Williams's career was interrupted by military service in 1943–45; he led in 1941–42 and again in 1946–49.

12. **Who is the only man to be a slugging leader in a season when he also would have led his league in batting if he had not been ruled ineligible for the crown?**

   A)   His .613 SA was 78 points higher than the runner-up in his loop, resulting in his being awarded the crown although he lacked the required number of ABs.

   B)   He also led his league in OBP that year.

   C)   The previous year, he had compiled a .901 SA, the highest in history by anyone with more than 100 plate appearances.

   D)   Jackie Jensen's .472 SA was second on the team that year to the leader's .613 mark.

   E)   He lost the AL batting crown in 1954 to Bobby Avila, even though he had more than enough plate appearances to qualify for the title by the current rule.

13. **Who set the current NL record for the lowest slugging average by a batting crown winner just two years after he led the senior loop in slugging?**

   A)   His .386 SA the year he won his bat crown included only 18 extra-base hits.

   B)   He was second on his team in total bases that year to Jimmy Johnston.

   C)   He and Ginger Beaumont (1902) are the only two NL bat crown winners to go homerless for the entire season.

   D)   His .461 SA topped the NL in 1916.

   E)   He saw action in both the 1916 and the 1920 World Series.

Lowest SA, Season, Batting Crown Winner

RANK	NAME	TEAM	YEAR	BA	SA
1	Rod Carew	Min, AL	1972	.318	.379
2	Zack Wheat	Bro, NL	1918	.335	.386
3	Dick Groat	Pit, NL	1960	.325	.39442
4	Pete Runnels	Bos, AL	1960	.320	.39394
5	Luke Appling	Chi, AL	1943	.328	.407
6	Willie Keeler	Bal, NL	1898	.385	.410
7	Tony Gwynn	SD, NL	1988	.313	.415
8	Ginger Beaumont	Pit, NL	1902	.357	.418
9	Billy Hamilton	Phi, NL	1891	.340	.42125
10	Matty Alou	Pit, NL	1966	.342	.42056

Note: Groat and Runnels made 1960 the only year that both loop batting leaders slugged less than .400. SAs are carried out to five decimal points where ties would otherwise exist.

14. Whose .239 slugging average in 1968 is the lowest since World War II by a batting title qualifier?
   A)   As a rookie in 1964, he slugged .347, but he departed in 1973 with a .275 SA.
   B)   He never played in a World Series, but his father was in three in the 1940s.
   C)   He and the first shortstop to win a home run crown share the same initials.
   D)   In his rookie year, he and Jose Pagan were the Giants' keystone combo.
   E)   He managed the Astros in the late 1980s.

Lowest SA, Season, Each Position (Minimum 400 ABs)

POS.	NAME	TEAM	YEAR	BA	SA
LF	Jim Lillie	KC, NL	1886	.175	.206
2B	Pete Childs	Phi, NL	1902	.194	.206
3B	Bobby Byrne	StL, NL	1908	.191	.212
RF	Goat Anderson	Pit, NL	1907	.206	.225
C	Billy Sullivan	Chi, AL	1908	.191	.228
SS	Germany Smith	Bro, NL	1890	.191	.231
CF	Mike Slattery	Bos, UA	1884	.208	.232
1B	Milt Scott	Bal, AA	1886	.190	.242

15. Who is the only shortstop to pace the AL in slugging average?
   A)   Despite his landmark season, he failed to break Rico Petrocelli's then-existing record for the highest season SA by an AL shortstop.
   B)   He played in his lone World Series the year he led in SA.
   C)   His 367 total bases were an AL record for shortstops prior to 1991.
   D)   He won MVP Awards at two different positions.
   E)   He collected all of his 3,000+ hits in the same AL uniform.

16. **No catcher has ever led his loop in slugging average. Mike Piazza came close when he was second to NL leader Larry Walker in 1997. Who was the most recent backstopper prior to Piazza to finish as high as second in slugging?**
    A) His .538 SA was 65 points behind the leader.
    B) His .538 SA is still his loop's rookie record for catchers and included a league-leading nine triples.
    C) Johnny Bench never finished higher than third in SA or led in triples.
    D) He and Bench once were opposing catchers in a famous World Series.
    E) His extra-inning home run extended that World Series to a seventh game.

Highest SA, Season, Rookie Catcher (Minimum 400 ABs)

RANK	NAME	TEAM	YEAR	BA	SA
1	Mike Piazza	LA, NL	1993	.318	.561
2	Carlton Fisk	Bos, AL	1972	.293	.538
3	Matt Nokes	Det, AL	1987	.289	.536
4	Earl Williams	Atl, NL	1971	.260	.491
5	Bill Dickey	NY, AL	1929	.324	.485
6	Benito Santiago	SD, NL	1987	.300	.467
7	Mickey Cochrane	Phi, AL	1925	.331	.448
8	Johnny Bench	Cin, NL	1968	.275	.433
9	Joe Torre	Mil, NL	1961	.278	.424
10	Al Lopez	Bro, NL	1930	.309	.418

Note: In 1937, Rudy York slugged .651 but appeared in just 54 games as a catcher and had only 375 ABs. Earl Williams played only 72 games as a backstop in 1971, but catcher was still his primary position.

17. **What is the only season since 1901 that middle infielders have copped both ML slugging crowns?**
    A) Both of that season's winners are in the Hall of Fame.
    B) The NL leader's closest pursuer was Mike Grady.
    C) The AL leader also won the batting and RBI crowns that year.
    D) The two opposed each other often in the 19th century but never in the 20th.
    E) There was no World Series the year that both these middle infielders won slugging crowns.

18. **Prior to 1996 when Marquis Grissom set a new all-time record and Lance Johnson narrowly missed tying Grissom's mark, whose 327 total bases had been the most in a season by anyone with a sub-.500 slugging average?**
    A) In 1921, the year he set a new mark, he broke Mike Donlin's 1905 record of 300 total bases on a sub-.500 SA.
    B) His .352 BA in 1921 was a career high, as were his 236 hits.
    C) He was the last member of the FL St. Louis Terriers active in the majors.
    D) He was part of the only outfield trio that all hit .300 four years in a row.
    E) He and the only 20th century pitcher to hammer three homers in a game share the same initials and last name.

Most TBs, Season, Sub-.500 SA

RANK	NAME	TEAM	YEAR	BA	SA	TBS
1	Marquis Grissom	Atl, NL	1996	.308	.489	328
2	John Tobin	StL, AL	1921	.352	.487	327
	Lance Johnson	NY, NL	1996	.333	.479	327
4	Lou Brock	StL, NL	1967	.299	.472	325
	Paul Molitor	Mil, AL	1991	.325	.489	325
6	Vada Pinson	Cin, NL	1965	.305	.484	324
7	Bill White	StL, NL	1963	.304	.491	323
8	Johnny Callison	Phi, NL	1964	.274	.492	322
	Steve Garvey	LA, NL	1977	.297	.499	322
	Steve Garvey	LA, NL	1979	.315	.497	322

19. **Ted Williams is the most recent hitsmith to post a .600 slugging average six seasons in a row with enough plate appearances to be a batting title qualifier. Who is the most recent NL'er to have as many as three consecutive .600 slugging averages in seasons when a full schedule was played?**

   A) Barry Bonds might have done it if a full schedule had been played in 1994.

   B) In his first full season in the AL, he had a .595 SA, even though he hit just .277 and had no triples.

   C) He led the NL four times in SA, last in 1942.

   D) He holds the record for hitting three or more homers in the most games.

   E) His three consecutive seasons when he slugged .600 were 1938–40.

20. **Who is the only man with a .500+ career slugging average to play with 10 or more different major league teams?**

   A) He won slugging crowns with three different teams.

   B) The only year he played regularly and his SA fell below .460, he was on a flag winner that had to sit on the sidelines during the World Series that season.

   C) He never hit more than 14 homers in a season.

   D) Even though he was a loop leader in triples just once, he stands eighth on the all-time three-bagger list with 205.

   E) His first slugging crown in 1881 was also the first by a member of a Buffalo ML team, and his last 10 years later was also the last by an AA performer.

Evolution of Season SA Record, Each Position (Since 1876)

19th Century

	NAME	SA	YEAR	TEAM	LEAGUE
1B	Cal McVey	.406	1876	Chicago	NL
	Deacon White	.545	1877	Boston	NL
	Dan Brouthers	.547	1882	Buffalo	NL
	Dan Brouthers	.572	1883	Buffalo	NL
	Dan Brouthers	.581	1886	Detroit	NL

	NAME	SA	YEAR	TEAM	LEAGUE
2B	Ross Barnes	.590	1876	Chicago	NL
	Fred Dunlap	.621	1884	St. Louis	UA*

* Not all authorities recognize Dunlap's UA feats as major league records.

	NAME	SA	YEAR	TEAM	LEAGUE
3B	Cap Anson	.440	1876	Chicago	NL
	King Kelly	.493	1879	Cincinnati	NL
	Ned Williamson	.554	1884	Chicago	NL*
	Denny Lyons	.523	1887	Philadelphia	AA
	Denny Lyons	.531	1890	Philadelphia	AA
	George Davis	.554	1893	New York	NL
	Bill Joyce	.648	1894	Washington	NL**

* Williamson's mark was compiled largely on 27 homers in a substandard park.

** Joyce had fewer than 400 at bats, but many authorities nevertheless consider the mark a record.

	NAME	SA	YEAR	TEAM	LEAGUE
SS	John Peters	.418	1876	Chicago	NL
	Jack Glasscock	.450	1882	Cleveland	NL
	Frank Fennelly	.480	1884	Washington-Cincinnati	AA
	Sam Wise	.522	1887	Boston	NL
	Bill Dahlen	.566	1894	Chicago	NL
OF	George Hall	.545	1876	Philadelphia	NL
	Tip O'Neill	.691	1887	St. Louis	AA
C	Deacon White	.419	1876	Chicago	NL
	Cal McVey	.455	1877	Chicago	NL
	Jack Rowe	.480	1881	Buffalo	NL
	Buck Ewing	.481	1883	New York	NL
	Buck Ewing	.545	1890	New York	PL
	Jocko Milligan	.505	1891	Philadelphia	AA*
	Jack Clements	.612	1895	Philadelphia	NL

* Milligan holds the 19th century record by a catcher with 400 at bats.

Note: NA records excluded because abbreviated and uneven schedules created too many unrepresentative performances; in 1871, for example, several all-time position SA records were established, led by Levi Meyerle's .700 mark for third basemen.

20th Century

	NAME	SA	YEAR	TEAM
1B	*American League*			
	Buck Freeman	.520	1901	Boston
	Charlie Hickman	.539	1902	Boston/Cleveland
	George Sisler	.632	1920	St. Louis
	Lou Gehrig	.765	1927	New York

NAME	SA	YEAR	TEAM
National League			
Jake Beckley	.429	1901	Cincinnati
Jake Beckley	.447	1903	Cincinnati
Fred Luderus	.472	1911	Philadelphia
Vic Saier	.477	1913	Chicago
George Kelly	.528	1921	New York
Ray Grimes	.572	1922	Chicago
Jack Fournier	.588	1923	Brooklyn
Jim Bottomley	.628	1928	St. Louis
Johnny Mize	.636	1940	St. Louis
Ted Kluszewski	.642	1954	Cincinnati
Willie McCovey	.656	1969	San Francisco
Hank Aaron	.669	1971	Atlanta*
Jeff Bagwell	.750	1994	Houston
Mark McGwire	.752	1998	St. Louis

* Aaron played 71 games at 1B and 60 games in the outfield.

2B   **American League**

NAME	SA	YEAR	TEAM
Nap Lajoie	.643	1901	Philadelphia*
Nap Lajoie	.533	1903	Cleveland
Nap Lajoie	.554	1904	Cleveland
Charlie Gehringer	.555	1936	Detroit

* Many authorities view all of Lajoie's 1901 AL achievements as suspect. If his 1901 mark is rejected, his 1903 season saw the first .500 SA by an AL second baseman, and the record then progresses as shown.

National League

NAME	SA	YEAR	TEAM
Tom Daly	.444	1901	Brooklyn
Larry Doyle	.527	1911	New York
Rogers Hornsby	.559	1920	St. Louis
Rogers Hornsby	.639	1921	St. Louis
Rogers Hornsby	.722	1922	St. Louis
Rogers Hornsby	.756	1925	St. Louis

3B   **American League**

NAME	SA	YEAR	TEAM
Jimmy Collins	.495	1901	Boston
Bill Bradley	.515	1902	Cleveland
Frank Baker	.541	1912	Philadelphia
Jimmie Foxx	.548	1928	Philadelphia*
Harlond Clift	.554	1938	St. Louis
Al Rosen	.613	1953	Cleveland
George Brett	.664	1980	Kansas City

* Only 60 of Foxx's 119 games were at 3B.

NAME	SA	YEAR	TEAM
National League			
Tommy Leach	.411	1901	Pittsburgh
Tommy Leach	.426	1902	Pittsburgh
Harry Steinfeldt	.481	1903	Cincinnati
Heinie Zimmerman	.571	1912	Chicago
Freddy Lindstrom	.575	1930	New York
Mel Ott	.583	1938	New York
Eddie Mathews	.627	1953	Milwaukee
Dick Allen	.632	1966	Philadelphia
Mike Schmidt	.644	1981	Philadelphia

SS

NAME	SA	YEAR	TEAM
American League			
Bill Keister	.482	1901	Baltimore
Joe Cronin	.513	1930	Washington*
Joe Cronin	.536	1938	Boston
Vern Stephens	.539	1949	Boston
Rico Petrocelli	.589	1969	Boston
Alex Rodriguez	.631	1996	Seattle

* In 1929, Jimmy Dykes of Philadelphia had a .539 SA in 119 games, but only 60 were at SS.

NAME	SA	YEAR	TEAM
National League			
Honus Wagner	.491	1901	Pittsburgh*
Bobby Wallace	.451	1901	St. Louis
Honus Wagner	.518	1903	Pittsburgh
Honus Wagner	.520	1904	Pittsburgh
Honus Wagner	.542	1908	Pittsburgh
Glenn Wright	.543	1930	Brooklyn
Arky Vaughan	.607	1935	Pittsburgh
Ernie Banks	.614	1958	Chicago

* Wagner played more games at SS than any other position, but because fewer than half of his 140 games were at SS, many consider Wallace's 1901 figure the starting point.

OF

NAME	SA	YEAR	TEAM
American League			
Socks Seybold	.503	1901	Philadelphia
Ed Delahanty	.590	1902	Washington
Ty Cobb	.621	1911	Detroit
Babe Ruth	.657	1919	Boston
Babe Ruth	.847	1920	New York

NAME	SA	YEAR	TEAM
National League			
Jimmy Sheckard	.534	1901	Brooklyn
Cy Seymour	.559	1905	Cincinnati
Gavvy Cravath	.568	1913	Philadelphia
Cy Williams	.576	1923	Philadelphia
Kiki Cuyler	.598	1925	Pittsburgh
Chick Hafey	.604	1928	St. Louis
Chuck Klein	.657	1929	Philadelphia
Hack Wilson	.723	1930	Chicago

C   **American League**

Bob Wood	.384	1901	Cleveland
Ossee Schreckengost	.402	1902	Cleveland/Philadelphia
Steve O'Neill	.427	1919	Cleveland
Wally Schang	.450	1920	New York
Patsy Gharrity	.455	1921	Washington
Glenn Myatt	.518	1924	Cleveland
Mickey Cochrane	.526	1930	Philadelphia
Mickey Cochrane	.553	1931	Philadelphia
Bill Dickey	.617	1936	New York

National League

Deacon McGuire	.375	1901	Brooklyn
Johnny Kling	.428	1903	Chicago
Mike Grady	.474	1904	St. Louis
Chief Meyers	.477	1912	New York
Bubbles Hargrave	.513	1922	Cincinnati
Bubbles Hargrave	.521	1923	Cincinnati
Gabby Hartnett	.523	1924	Chicago
Gabby Hartnett	.555	1925	Chicago
Gabby Hartnett	.630	1930	Chicago
Mike Piazza	.638	1997	Los Angeles

Speed Merchants

1. **A third baseman who can hit with power and also steal bases is so rare that Howard Johnson is the lone hot corner operative who has compiled both 200 career homers and 200 thefts. But Frank Baker, who played in a very different era, may have actually been the best third sacker to date at providing both power and artful baserunning. Certainly Baker won his share of home run crowns—four in a row at one point. However, only one third sacker has ever won as many as three consecutive stolen base crowns. Who is he?**

A) His 106 career steals are less than Vince Coleman compiled as a rookie.

B) He led the AL in hits in 1948.

C) Even though he was the lone St. Louis Brownie to sweep three straight theft crowns, he ranks far down on the list of career thefts by a third baseman.

D) He was the first bespectacled stolen base champ in major league history.

E) He and a notorious Depression Era bank robber share the same last name.

Most Stolen Bases by a Third Baseman, Career (Since 1898)

RANK	NAME	YEARS	HRS	SBS
1	Hans Lobert	1903–17	32	316
2	Art Devlin	1904–13	10	285
3	Wid Conroy	1901–11	22	262
4	George Moriarty	1903–16	5	248
5	Jimmy Austin	1909–29	13	244
6	Toby Harrah	1969–86	195	238
7	Frank Baker	1908–22	96	235
8	Howard Johnson	1982–95	228	231
9	Carney Lansford	1978–92	151	224
10	Billy Werber	1930–42	78	215

Note: Minimum 1,000 games at third base, except Johnson, who fell just three games short. Paul Molitor has the most steals of any man who was a regular third baseman for a significant period of time, but he served as a DH in more games than he did at third. 1898 was the year the modern rule for what constitutes a stolen base was first in effect. Arlie Latham and John McGraw, both of whom played mostly before 1898, were far and away the two most prolific base thieves ever to play third base.

2. The first third baseman to win a National League theft crown after 1900 still holds the 20th century NL record for the most thefts in a season by a third sacker. Who is he?

    A) He was on a pennant winner as a rookie in 1904.

    B) He is the only third sacker in the 20th century to log back-to-back seasons when he swiped 50 bases.

    C) He played on a world champ the year he set the theft mark for third sackers.

    D) He tied Billy Maloney for the NL theft crown in 1905 with 59 steals.

    E) He and the only 30-game winner to be banned for life for dumping games share the same last name.

3. What rookie was in just 85 games and hit a weak .219, yet topped his league in steals— albeit with the lowest batting average to date by a post-1898 theft king?

    A) He won his lone stolen base crown subsequent to the end of the Deadball Era.

    B) The year before he debuted with the Phils, Art Mahan led the Phils in thefts with just four.

    C) He last played with the same NL team that he later piloted to two World Series wins.

    D) He died in 1976 of heart trouble some 10 months short of his 60th birthday.

    E) He is the only man to pilot Pittsburgh to more than one world title.

Lowest BA, Season, League Leader in Stolen Bases

RANK	NAME	TEAM	YEAR	SBS	BA
1	Hugh Nicol	Cin, AA	1887	138	.215
2	Danny Murtaugh	Phi, NL	1941	18	.219
3	George Case	Cle, AL	1946	28	.225
4	Vince Coleman	StL, NL	1986	107	.232
5	Tommy Harper	Sea, AL	1969	73	.235
	Omar Moreno	Pit, NL	1978	71	.235
7	Rickey Henderson	Oak, AL	1998	66	.236
8	Bob Bescher	Cin, NL	1909	54	.2399
9	Bert Campaneris	Oak, AL	1972	52	.2400
10	Tom Brown	Lou, NL	1893	66	.2401

Note: BAs are carried out to four decimal points where ties would otherwise exist.

4. The first AL'er to steal 250 bases held the junior circuit career theft mark prior to Ty Cobb. Who is he?

    A) The first 3 of his 253 career steals came with the 1899 Chicago Colts.

    B) He swiped 23 bases in 1909, his final major league season.

    C) He stole 37 bases as the second sacker for the 1906 world champs.

    D) He holds the AL season record for the most thefts by a first baseman.

    E) He holds the record for the most career thefts by a player whose last name begins with the only vowel in the word *inning*.

5. Who is the only man to be a loop leader in steals in both the AL and the NL?

- A) He surrendered his NL theft crown to teammate Tim Raines.
- B) His last big league theft came with the 1982 White Sox.
- C) He led the AL in both runs and thefts in 1978.
- D) His most productive years were spent with the Tigers.
- E) He had a teammate in his final season who shares his initials and is the most recent member of the White Sox to steal more than 70 bases in a season.

6. Though 6'1" and weighing 200 pounds, what speed merchant made his mark as one of the top leadoff hitters and base thieves of the Deadball Era?

- A) The first switch-hitter in the 20th century to be a loop leader in steals, he finished in 1918 with 428 career thefts, second at the time only to Honus Wagner among players weighing 200 pounds.
- B) He led the NL in runs and steals in 1912.
- C) Most of his career was spent with the Reds.
- D) Prior to 1962 he held the 20th century NL season record for thefts with 70 in 1910.
- E) He and the first NL'er to join the 40/40 club share the same initials.

Most Stolen Bases by a 200-Pounder, Career

RANK	NAME	YEARS	WGT.	SBS
1	Honus Wagner	1898–1917	200	703
2	Ron LeFlore	1974–82	200	455
3	Bob Bescher	1908–18	200	428
4	Tony Gwynn	1982–	200	296
5	Kirk Gibson	1979–95	215	284
6	Lloyd Moseby	1980–91	200	280
7	Reggie Jackson	1967–87	200	228
8	Dave Winfield	1973–94	220	223
9	Cy Seymour	1898–1913	200	219
10	Terry Puhl	1977–91	200	217

Note: Since 1898, the year the modern rule for what constitutes a stolen base was first put into effect, thereby excluding Cap Anson, Jake Beckley, and Sam Thompson, 200-pounders active prior to 1898 who had more than 200 career steals. Honus Wagner also had 19 stolen bases prior to 1898, bringing his career total to 722.

7. What speed merchant is the only big leaguer to break up two extra-inning no-hitters with singles?

- A) They were the first two extra-inning no-no's in the 20th century.
- B) He played for the ChiSox and the Giants in the two games in which he acted the spoiler.
- C) His 52 steals and 108 RBI in 1905 tied him with Honus Wagner for the honor of being the first man since 1898 to compile 50 thefts and 100 RBI in the same year.
- D) He topped the NL in RBI in 1903.
- E) He and the most recent Cleveland hurler to collect 300 Ks in a season share the same initials and the same first name.

Most Stolen Bases, Season, Minimum 100 RBI

RANK	NAME	TEAM	YEAR	RBI	SBS
1	Ty Cobb	Det, AL	1911	127	83
2	Ty Cobb	Det, AL	1909	107	76
3	Ben Chapman	NY, AL	1931	122	61
4	Honus Wagner	Pit, NL	1905	101	57
	Cesar Cedeno	Hou, NL	1974	102	57
6	Ty Cobb	Det, AL	1917	102	55
7	Honus Wagner	Pit, NL	1908	109	53
8	Sam Mertes	NY, NL	1905	108	52
	Barry Bonds	Pit, NL	1990	114	52
10	George Sisler	StL, AL	1922	105	51

Note: Since 1898, the year the modern stolen base rule was devised.

8. **When Cecil Fielder stole his first base in 1995, what backstopper's records did he restore for the most career runs (215) and the most career at bats (2,504) in the majors without ever stealing a base?**
   A) He and his twin brother Roy were both signed by Cleveland, but Roy never made the show.
   B) Though never successful, he was caught stealing seven times, with a high of three in 1958.
   C) In 1958, the only season in which he played 100 or more games in the field, he hit .301 for the Tribe.
   D) He started the season at the helm of the most recent Atlanta cellar dweller.
   E) Anthony Hopkins starred in a recent film whose title character shared his last name.

Evolution of Record for Most ABs, Career, No Stolen Bases

NAME	YEARS	POS.	ABS
John Kirby	1886–88	P	256
Henry Gruber	1887–91	P	489
Tully Sparks	1897–1910	P	798
Lefty Tyler	1910–21	P	870
Bob Shawkey	1913–27	P	1049
Stan Coveleski	1912–28	P	1058
Lee Meadows	1915–29	P	1117
Herb Pennock	1912–34	P	1214
Waite Hoyt	1918–38	P	1287
Ted Lyons	1923–46	P	1563
Aaron Robinson	1943–51	C	1839
Russ Nixon	1957–68	C	2504

Note: Since 1886; stolen base stats prior to 1886 are unavailable for most seasons.

9. Who holds the record for the most at bats in a season without any stolen bases?

A) The year he had a record 677 ABs with no thefts, he led the AL in hits.

B) He stole just one base the year he won his only batting title.

C) He had 145 RBI the year he won an MVP Award.

D) He currently has the record for the highest career FA by a first baseman.

E) He was the most recent Yankees player to cop an MVP prize.

Evolution of Season Record for Most ABs, No Stolen Bases

NAME	TEAM	YEAR	ABS
Fatty Briody	KC, NL	1886	215
Joe Gunson	StL/Cle, NL	1893	224
Pop Schriver	Pit, NL	1898	315
Lee Tannehill	Chi, AL	1911	516
Mule Haas	Phi, AL	1929	578
Mule Haas	Chi, AL	1933	585
Bill Terry	NY, NL	1934	602
Hank Lieber	NY, NL	1935	613
Joe Vosmik	Bos, AL	1938	621
Jerry Lumpe	KC, AL	1962	641
Pete Rose	Cin, NL	1975	662
Cal Ripken	Bal, AL	1983	663
Don Mattingly	NY, AL	1986	677

Note: Since 1886; stolen base stats prior to 1886 are unavailable for most seasons.

10. What speed merchant racked up 31 thefts and 33 runs in the majors without ever once coming to bat in a regular season or postseason game?

A) He spent his entire two-year ML career with the same AL team.

B) He appeared in the 1974 World Series.

C) He was a world-class sprinter before playing ML baseball.

D) One of Charlie Finley's more interesting experiments, early in his 1974 rookie season, he broke the record for most career stolen bases with no ABs (2), held jointly by Charlie Faust and Dutch Schirick.

E) In 1975 an A's teammate of his with the same last name stole 40 bases to his 2.

11. The Boston Braves franchise originated in 1871. Three years later, two Boston outfielders, Jim O'Rourke and Andy Leonard, tied for the National Association theft crown with 11 steals each. Name the lone other member of the Braves franchise to win a stolen base crown before the club left Boston prior to the 1953 season.

A) He won two consecutive theft crowns with the Braves.

B) He was the first switch-hitter since 1925 to win back-to-back theft crowns.

C) His last major league appearance came with the 1954 Pirates.

D) He was the NL Rookie of the Year the season he won his first theft title.

E) He was the Braves' first black player to qualify for a batting crown.

12. **Who was the first man in the 20th century to win stolen base titles with two different teams?**
    A) Frankie Frisch became the second man to do it in 1927.
    B) Prior to Rickey Henderson's arrival, he held the A's franchise record for the most thefts in a season.
    C) His second stolen base crown came with the 1919 AL champs.
    D) He played the same position as Frankie Frisch.
    E) He compiled the fewest career homers of any member of the 3,000-hit club.

13. **After Paul Richards rebuilt the painfully slow Chicago AL team into the Go-Go White Sox in 1951, who was the only member of another AL team to lead the junior loop in thefts in the 1950s?**
    A) He is the most recent theft king in either major league who also won an RBI crown during his career.
    B) He is the only man in big league history to have a season when he compiled 100 RBI, scored 100 runs, and stole 20 bases without hitting a triple.
    C) Married at one time to Olympic swimming star Zoe Ann Olson, in 1959 he tied Sparky Adams's post–Deadball Era record for the most stolen bases in a season without hitting a triple.
    D) He won three RBI crowns during the 1950s.
    E) He quit the game while in his prime because he hated plane travel.

Evolution of Post-1920 Record for Most Stolen Bases, Season, No Triples

NAME	TEAM	YEAR	ABS	SBS
Burt Shotton	StL, NL	1920	180	5
Sam Crane	Cin, NL	1920	144	5
Sparky Adams	Chi, NL	1923	311	20
Jackie Jensen	Bos, AL	1959	548	20
Horace Clarke	NY, AL	1967	588	21
Carl Yastrzemski	Bos, AL	1970	566	23
Tommie Agee	NY, NL	1971	425	28
Herb Washington	Oak, AL	1974	0	29
Larry Lintz	Oak, AL	1976	1	31
Miguel Dilone	Oak, AL	1978	258	50

14. **The year before the Go-Go White Sox were spawned, the Pale Hose ranked last in the AL in stolen bases with just 19. Who led them with six thefts?**
    A) He played every one of the club's 156 games.
    B) In 1947 he was second in the AL with 21 thefts.
    C) He stole just two bases as the regular right fielder for the 1954 AL champs.
    D) He finished with 102 career stolen bases and 93 career pinch hits.
    E) Prior to Jerry Hairston, he held the record for the most career pinch hits by a switch-hitter.

Fewest Stolen Bases, Season, Team Leader in Thefts

RANK	NAME	TEAM	YEAR	TEAM SBs	LEADER(S)
1	Buck Jordan, Les Mallon, Bill Urbanski & Wally Berger	Bos, NL	1935	20	3
	Julio Becquer	Was, AL	1957	13	3
3	Buck Jordan & Bill Urbanski	Bos, NL	1933	25	4
	Lonnie Frey	Cin, NL	1938	19	4
	Art Mahan	Phi, NL	1940	25	4
	Lenny Merullo & Andy Pafko	Chi, NL	1947	22	4
	Johnny Lipon	Det, AL	1948	22	4
	Pete Reiser, George Strickland & Joe Garagiola	Pit, NL	1951	29	4
	Pat Mullin	Det, AL	1952	27	4
	Enos Slaughter	StL, NL	1953	18	4
	Ed Kranepool & Joe Christopher	NY, NL	1965	28	4

15. Who is the only man to win back-to-back steal crowns with fewer than 20 thefts both years?

A) His 33 steals over a two-year period earned him one stolen base crown outright and a share of a second.

B) He is the only third sacker to win back-to-back steal crowns in the NL.

C) He won his first stolen base crown the last time a Chicago team opposed a New York team in a fall classic.

D) He has the fewest career RBI (642) of any third sacker with 2,000 hits.

E) He played in the most recent World Series game that involved the Chicago Cubs.

16. Since Ty Cobb stole 96 bases in 1916, who is the only U.S.-born Caucasian player to swipe as many as 75 bases in a season?

A) He bagged 24 steals as a rookie with the 1975 Angels.

B) He hit .216 in 102 games for Cincinnati in 1978 while leading the NL in pinch-hit at bats.

C) He led the AL in triples in 1984.

D) His 79 steals in 1979 are the most since 1916 by a Caucasian player.

E) He and the man with the second-most career thefts by a Caucasian player share the same last name.

17. Lou Brock is of course the St. Louis Cardinals' all-time theft leader. Who was the only Cardinal prior to Lou Brock to win more than one NL theft crown?

A) He won three theft titles, even though he stole fewer than 150 career bases.

B) He spent his entire 13-year career with the Cards.

C) One year, 5 of his 21 steals came in postseason play.

D) His 122 runs in 1933 were the most by a National League third sacker in the 1920–41 era.

E) He was nicknamed "The Wild Horse of the Osage."

18. Who has the most career steals of any player who never swiped 30 bases in a season?

A) Lave Cross held the record of 301 thefts without a 30-steal season when he retired in 1907, but his mark was later broken.

B) The current mark of 380 belongs to a Hall of Famer.

C) He and Lave Cross were teammates in his first two seasons, 1896–97.

D) In 1998, Ricky Henderson tied his record for the most consecutive seasons (20) with 10 or more stolen bases.

E) His career high of 29 steals came with Cleveland in 1904.

Stolen Base Season Bests and Worsts

Highest BA, 0 Stolen Bases
AL .388 Ted Williams, Boston, 1957
NL .354 Bill Terry, New York, 1934

Highest SA, 0 Stolen Bases
AL .731 Ted Williams, Boston, 1957
NL .656 Willie McCovey, San Francisco, 1969

Most Hits, 0 Stolen Bases
AL 238 Don Mattingly, New York, 1986
NL 213 Bill Terry, New York, 1934

Most Runs, 0 Stolen Bases
AL 142 Ted Williams, Boston, 1946
NL 119 Mel Ott, New York, 1934

Most RBI, 0 Stolen Bases
AL 144 Walt Dropo, Boston, 1950
NL 141 Ted Kluszewski, Cincinnati, 1954

Most Total Bases, 0 Stolen Bases
AL 388 Don Mattingly, New York, 1986
NL 368 Ted Kluszewski, Cincinnati, 1954

Most Doubles, 0 Stolen Bases
AL 54 John Olerud, Toronto, 1993
NL 47 Pete Rose, Cincinnati, 1975

Most Triples, 0 Stolen Bases
NL 16 Johnny Mize, St. Louis, 1938
AL 11 Jim Bottomley, St. Louis, 1936

Most Home Runs, 0 Stolen Bases
AL 61 Roger Maris, New York, 1961
NL 49 Ted Kluszewski, Cincinnati, 1954

Most Stolen Bases, BA Below .250
NL 107 Vince Coleman, St. Louis, 1986 (.232)
AL 74 Fritz Maisel, New York, 1914 (.239)

Most Stolen Bases, BA Below .200
All-time 33, Jim Canavan, Chicago, 1892 (.166)
AL 29 Fritz Maisel, New York, 1917 (.198)
NL 24 Monte Cross, Philadelphia, 1901 (.197)

Most Stolen Bases, 0 Runs
NL 3 Jerry White, Montreal, 1974
AL 2 Done by many

Most Stolen Bases, 0 Hits
NL 31 Larry Lintz, Montreal, 1976
AL 29 Herb Washington, Oakland, 1974

Most Stolen Bases, 0 Triples (Minimum 400 ABs)
AL 40 Jose Canseco, Oakland, 1988
NL 37 Billy Gilbert, New York, 1903

Most Stolen Bases, 0 Home Runs
NL 107 Vince Coleman, St. Louis, 1986
AL 63 Eddie Collins, Philadelphia, 1912

First Season with 400 At Bats and 0 Stolen Bases
AL 516 ABs Lee Tannehill, Chicago, 1911
NL 482 ABs Tommy Griffith, Brooklyn, 1924

First Season with 500 At Bats and 0 Stolen Bases
AL 516 ABs Lee Tannehill, Chicago, 1911
NL 602 ABs Bill Terry, New York, 1934

First Season with 600 At Bats and 0 Stolen Bases
NL 602 ABs Bill Terry, New York, 1934
AL 621 ABs Joe Vosmik, Boston, 1938

Hall of Famer Bill Terry, the first ML'er to come to bat 600 times in a season without stealing a base. Terry still holds the NL record for the top BA by anyone who was blanked in the theft column.

Super Scorers

1. **The team that scores the most runs wins the game. That's always been the first principle in baseball. Yet, men who excel in crossing the plate have never received their due. The first team to log 1,000 runs in a season featured a teammate duo who combined to post 330 tallies, the most by a brace of teammates in every year except the run-happy 1894 season. Who are they?**

   A) Neither player is in the Hall of Fame.
   B) One super scorer was a third baseman, and the other a left fielder.
   C) Their team also showcased the first trio of 25-game winners in history.
   D) Their team lost to Detroit in the longest World Series in history.
   E) Their nicknames were "Tip" and "Arlie."

300 Runs Combined by Two Teammates, Season

RANK	DUO	TEAM	YEAR	TOTAL RUNS
1	Billy Hamilton (192) & Ed Delahanty (147)	Phi, NL	1894	339
2	Tip O'Neill (167) & Arlie Latham (163)	StL, AA	1887	330
	Willie Keeler (165) & Joe Kelley (165)	Bal, NL	1894	330
4	Willie Keeler (162) & Hughie Jennings (159)	Bal, NL	1895	321
5	Hugh Duffy (160) & Bobby Lowe (158)	Bos, NL	1894	318
6	Billy Hamilton (166) & Ed Delahanty (149)	Phi, NL	1895	315
7	Lou Gehrig (163) & Babe Ruth (149)	NY, AL	1931	312
8	Tom Brown (177) & Hugh Duffy (134)	Bos, AA	1891	311
9	Babe Ruth (158) & Lou Gehrig (149)	NY, AL	1927	307
	Kiki Cuyler (155) & Woody English (152)	Chi, NL	1930	307
11	King Kelly (155) & George Gore (150)	Chi, NL	1886	305
	Babe Ruth (177) & Roger Peckinpaugh (128)	NY, AL	1921	305
13	Willie Keeler (153) & Joe Kelley (148)	Bal, NL	1896	301

2. **By scoring at least one run in 18 consecutive games in 1939, what infielder set a 20th century ML record?**
   A) In 1939 he led the AL in hits, doubles, and runs.
   B) He hit .400 in the 1936 World Series.
   C) He nearly piloted the 1950 Tigers to a pennant.
   D) He spent his entire career with the Yankees.
   E) In 1937 he tallied the second-most runs in this century by a third baseman.

3. Who is the only member of a last-place team to lead his loop in runs scored?

    A) Prior to 1997 he was also the most recent NL'er to score as many as 145 runs in a season.

    B) Amazingly, he scored well over 145 runs for a last-place team.

    C) His first and last homers came in a Phillies uniform.

    D) He once won a Triple Crown.

    E) His big year came in 1930, when he tallied a 20th century NL-record 158 runs.

Most Runs by a Player on a Last-Place Team, Season

RANK	NAME	TEAM	YEAR	RUNS
1	Chuck Klein	Phi, NL	1930	158
2	Cub Stricker	Cle, AA	1887	122
	Tom Brown	Lou, NL	1894	122
	Lefty O'Doul	Phi, NL	1930	122
5	Lu Blue	Chi, AL	1931	119
	Tony Gwynn	SD, NL	1987	119
7	Jimmie Foxx	Phi, AL	1935	118
	Ralph Kiner	Pit, NL	1947	118
9	George Van Haltren	NY, NL	1900	114
	Bob Johnson	Phi, AL	1938	114

Note: Remarkably, no fewer than six cellar dwellers have had two players who scored 100 runs; besides the 1930 Phils, they are: 1887 Cleveland, AA, 1892 Baltimore, NL, 1924 Chicago, AL, 1935 Philadelphia, AL, and 1947 Pittsburgh, NL. Kiner is one of four players who scored 100 runs with a doormat on two occasions. The others are Dummy Hoy, George Van Haltren, and Bob Johnson; Hoy and Van Haltren did it with two different franchises.

4. Though Frank Thomas was on a course to set a new mark prior to the strike in 1994, who still holds the White Sox franchise record for the most runs in a season?

    A) He led the AL in walks and steals the year he tallied a Sox-record 135 runs.

    B) Two years later, his career was nearly ended by a suicide attempt.

    C) He first surfaced as a second baseman in 1918 but was an outfielder when he next appeared in 1921.

    D) In 1925, his super-scorer season, he became the only preexpansion record holder in team runs to hit below .300 the year he set the mark.

    E) He and the most recent NL'er to win a Triple Crown share the same initials.

5. What two men are tied for the most seasons leading in runs scored by anyone who never won a batting title?

    A) One tied the mark in 1990 when he led the AL for the fifth time in runs.

    B) The other led the NL in runs five times, all with the same team.

    C) One will make the Hall of Fame, the other almost certainly never will, even though he retired with more than 2,000 hits and nearly 400 stolen bases.

    D) The NL'er was in three World Series with the Giants, last in 1921.

    E) The NL'er and the current record holder for the most doubles in a season by a first baseman share the same name.

6. **Name the all-time record holder for the most runs (97) in a season by anyone who compiled fewer than 100 hits.**

   A)   The 20th century mark belongs to Jo-Jo White with 82 runs on 99 hits in 1935.

   B)   The all-time record was set in 1889 by a second baseman.

   C)   Also in 1889, the NL mark of 93 runs was set by a Boston outfielder who holds the record for the most career runs (1,521) by anyone with fewer than 2,000 hits.

   D)   The man who scored 97 runs on 94 hits in 1889 played in four 19th century World Series.

   E)   He also held the record prior to 1889 (the first year four balls instead of five became a walk) for the most walks in a season, with 116 for the St. Louis Browns in 1888.

Most Runs, Season, Fewer than 100 Hits

RANK	NAME	TEAM	YEAR	HITS	RUNS
1	Yank Robinson	StL, AA	1889	94	97
2	Dave Eggler	NY, NA	1872	98	94
3	Tom Brown	Bos, NL	1889	89	93
4	Bill Joyce	Bro, NL	1892	91	89
5	George Wright	Bos, NA	1872	86	87
	Ned Williamson	Chi, NL	1885	97	87
	Billy Hulen	Phi, NL	1896	90	87
8	George Gore	Chi, NL	1881	92	86
9	Andy Leonard	Bos, NA	1873	95	85
10	Ned Cuthbert	Ath, NA	1872	88	83
	Buck Ewing	NY, NL	1887	97	83

Note: The 20th century NL record belongs to Bip Roberts with 81 runs on 99 hits for San Diego in 1989.

7. **The 20th century record holder for the fewest hits by anyone scoring 100 runs compiled 102 tallies on just 110 hits. Who is he?**

   A)   A second baseman, he batted .232 that year for a world champ.

   B)   The following year, he scored a phenomenal 117 runs on just 111 hits.

   C)   As you may have already guessed, he walked a lot.

   D)   He played most of his career behind the 300-game winner with the fewest career losses and under the helmsman who lost more games than any other manager.

   E)   His nickname was "Camera Eye."

8. **In 1945, Tommy Holmes set a 20th century Boston Braves record when he posted 125 tallies, but the lone Braves player since 1901 to lead the NL in runs before the club moved to Milwaukee is not Holmes. Who is he?**

   A)   He gave Holmes's record a close chase before finishing with 120 markers the year he broke the 20th century scoring-leader drought for the Braves.

   B)   He was a member of the last Boston Braves World Series entrant.

   C)   He also was a member of the most recent Chicago Series entrant.

   D)   His loop-leading 120 runs in 1950 were the most by a National League first baseman during the 1942–60 era.

   E)   He had the same first name and hailed from the same Washington town that produced a Hall of Famer.

9. **In 1997, Nomar Garciaparra fell just three runs short of becoming only the second shortstop to lead the AL in both runs and hits in the same season. Whose unique feat did he narrowly miss matching?**

   A)   He won the MVP Award that year.
   B)   His team won the World Championship that year.
   C)   Lou Boudreau, Phil Rizzuto, and Luke Appling were all long retired before this shortstop became the first to lead the AL in runs and hits.
   D)   He was the third member of the Baltimore Orioles to top the AL in runs.
   E)   He and his brother later formed a keystone combo with the Orioles.

Shortstops Leading the AL in Runs

NAME	TEAM	YEAR	RUNS
Donie Bush	Detroit	1917	112
Ray Chapman	Cleveland	1918	84
Zoilo Versalles	Minnesota	1965	126
Cal Ripken	Baltimore	1983	121
Derek Jeter	New York	1998	127

10. **Name the only loop leader in runs who batted under .250.**

   A)   His BA the year he led was 14 points above his team's average of .235.
   B)   He played for a world champ the year he won his only AL run crown.
   C)   A second baseman that year, he played in an era when no AL second sackers scored as many as 100 runs in a season.
   D)   His 95 runs topped the AL in 1968.
   E)   In 1968, the year he led, he played beside a shortstop who scored just 13 runs in 111 games.

Lowest BA, Season, Leader in Runs

RANK	NAME	TEAM	YEAR	RUNS	BA
1	Dick McAuliffe	Det, AL	1968	95	.249
2	Fred Tenney	NY, NL	1908	101	.256
3	Tommy Harper	Cin, NL	1965	126	.257
4	Jim McTamany	Col, AA	1890	140	.2575
5	Eddie Stanky	Bro, NL	1945	128	.2576
6	Bobby Bonds	SF, NL	1969	120	.259
7	Albie Pearson	LA, AL	1962	115	.2606
8	Tommy Leach	Pit, NL	1909	126	.2607
9	Spike Shannon	NY, NL	1907	104	.265
10	Ray Chapman	Cle, AL	1918	84	.267

Note: BAs are carried out to four decimal points where ties would otherwise exist.

11. **No catcher has ever been a league leader in runs scored. Who came the closest when he ranked fourth in the AL one year with 116 tallies?**
    A) He fell just 2 short of Mickey Cochrane's record 118 tallies by a catcher.
    B) He is currently the only catcher to lead his team in ABs more than once.
    C) He caught 148 games in his super 116-run season and hit .322.
    D) He was a multiple MVP Award winner.
    E) He played in a record 75 World Series games, all with the Yankees.

12. **Who was the only league leader in runs later to be formally banned from baseball?**
    A) He was not involved in the Black Sox scandal.
    B) He was not banned for anything he did as a player.
    C) He topped the NL in runs four years prior to his banishment.
    D) His loop-leading season came with Providence in 1878.
    E) He is currently the only umpire ever to be formally barred from the game.

13. **Among players with 200 career home runs, who tallied the fewest runs (506)?**
    A) Prior to him the record holder was Gus Zernial with 572 runs on 237 homers.
    B) He topped the AL in RBI in his first season in the junior circuit.
    C) His last home run came with the 1969 Angels after a stint in Japan.
    D) In 1956 he slugged more than 60 home runs for Lincoln in the Western League.
    E) He was called "Dr. Strangeglove."

Fewest Runs, Career, Minimum 200 HRs

RANK	NAME	YEARS	HRS	RUNS
1	Dick Stuart	1958–69	228	506
2	Don Mincher	1960–72	200	530
3	Bob Horner	1978–88	218	560
4	Rob Deer	1984–96	230	568
5	Gus Zernial	1949–59	237	572
6	Wally Post	1949–64	210	594
7	Joe Pepitone	1962–73	219	606
8	Tony Armas	1976–89	251	614
9	Roy Campanella	1948–57	242	627
10	Leon Wagner	1958–69	211	636

Note: Armas currently holds the record for the fewest career runs with 250 homers.

14. **Excluding pitchers and catchers, who holds the record for participating in the most big league seasons without ever scoring 100 runs in a season?**
    A) He accumulated 1,232 career runs, with a single-season high of 91.
    B) For five seasons in the 1960s, he and the record holder for the most career runs without ever scoring 100 runs in a season were teammates.
    C) He tallied 82 runs the year he won an AL MVP Award.
    D) He spent his entire 23-year career with the same team.
    E) He received the most Gold Glove Awards of any third baseman to date.

Most Runs, Career, Never Scoring 100 Runs in a Season

RANK	NAME	YEARS	HIGH	TOTAL
1	Luis Aparicio	1956–73	98	1335
2	Willie Randolph	1975–92	99	1239
3	Brooks Robinson	1955–77	91	1232
4	Al Oliver	1968–85	96	1189
	Rusty Staub	1963–85	98	1189
6	Buddy Bell	1972–89	89	1151
7	Steve Garvey	1969–87	96	1143
8	Deacon White	1871–90	82	1141
9	Jack Clark	1975–92	93	1118
10	Jimmy Dykes	1918–39	93	1108

Note: Retired players only; several active players such as Chili Davis and Harold Baines may one day join this list.

15. **Excluding players active too recently to be eligible for enshrinement, who compiled the most career runs of any ML performer not currently in the Hall of Fame?**

    A) He has not been an active player for nearly a century.
    B) He scored all 1,678 of his runs playing for teams based in the same city.
    C) Prior to the mid-1970s, he also held the record for the most runs scored by a player with a sub-.300 career BA.
    D) His last at bat came in 1899 against Cincinnati cigar-store clerk Eddie Kolb.
    E) He was Cincinnati's greatest second baseman prior to Joe Morgan.

Most Runs, Career, Non-Hall of Famer

RANK	NAME	YEARS	RUNS
1	Bid McPhee	1882–99	1678
2	Jimmy Ryan	1885–1903	1642
3	George Van Haltren	1887–1903	1639
4	Bill Dahlen	1891–1911	1589
5	Tom Brown	1882–98	1521
6	Harry Stovey	1880–93	1492
7	Arlie Latham	1880–1909	1478
8	Dwight Evans	1972–91	1470
9	Herman Long	1889–1904	1455
10	Dummy Hoy	1888–1902	1426

Note: Limited to players eligible for enshrinement.

OLD JUDGE CIGARETTES Goodwin & Co., New York.

Bid McPhee, considered by many authorities to be the best all-around player not in the Hall of Fame. McPhee's 1,678 career runs are the most by anyone without a plaque in Cooperstown.

16. **Who won the most batting titles without ever scoring 100 runs in a season?**
    A)   He once scored just 35 runs in a season when he won a bat title.
    B)   Although he collected more than 2,000 hits, he finished with fewer than 1,000 career runs and fewer than 1,000 career RBI.
    C)   His last ML appearance came in the 1987 ALCS as a DH for Detroit.
    D)   Two of his four batting titles were back-to-back wins with the Cubs.
    E)   Prior to Wade Boggs, he held the record for the most bat crowns won by a third baseman.

17. **The 1968 season is the only time in ML history that a full schedule calling for at least 100 games was played and no one scored as many as 100 runs. The 1894 season was the opposite: no fewer than 45 men scored 100 runs that year. What is the last season in history when there were two major leagues and the leader in each averaged more than one run scored per each game played by his team?**
    A)   Both ML loops that year played a 140-game schedule.
    B)   The NL runs leader that year also won the batting title and paced the majors with 111 stolen bases.
    C)   The runs leader in the AA crossed the plate a pre-1893-record 177 times for a pennant winner based in Boston.
    D)   It was the last season that the AA, the NL's chief rival for supremacy in the 19th century, existed.
    E)   The previous year, there had been three major leagues.

18. **Who set a post–Deadball Era record when he scored 19.6 percent of his team's runs the first time he led the NL in tallies?**
    A)   His team trailed the division-champ Phils by eight games the year he did it.
    B)   He was the first switch-hitter from an expansion team to lead the NL in batting.
    C)   In 1983 a teammate of his tallied 104 runs, meaning that the pair scored 35 percent of their club's runs.
    D)   He made his first World Series appearance in 1996.
    E)   His high-scoring teammate in 1983 was Andre Dawson.

19. **In 1913, when Burt Shotton scored 105 of last-place St. Louis's 528 runs for an all-time high of 19.9 percent, what Brownie was second to Shotton that year with 72 runs?**
    A)   The runner-up led the Browns in homers in 1913 with five.
    B)   In 1914, Shotton's runner-up set a new big league record by K'ing 120 times.
    C)   The runner-up's initials match those of the Yankees GM in the 1950s.
    D)   The runner-up's nickname was "Gloomy Gus."
    E)   The runner-up and the most recent player to score 150 runs in a season share the same last name.

20. **In 1901, Jesse Burkett of the Cardinals led the NL with 142 runs. The Cards then proceeded to become one of the most inept-scoring teams in the majors. Who was the next Card to score 100 runs in a season?**
    A)   He scored 101 runs for a seventh-place team managed by Roger Bresnahan.
    B)   The following year, he trailed loop-leader Jimmy Sheckard by 15 when he tallied 106 runs.
    C)   He later managed the Cards.
    D)   In 1905 he tallied 117 runs for Cincinnati to set a 20th century season record for NL second basemen that lasted until Rogers Hornsby came along.
    E)   He was the first former second baseman to win a pennant as an AL manager.

21. **Name the only Cleveland Indian to score 100 runs in a season between the inception of expansion and Toby Harrah's arrival in 1980.**
    A)   He also scored 100 runs as a rookie with another AL club.
    B)   He tallied 101 runs in 1964, his lone season as a Tribe regular.
    C)   In 1965 he collected just six RBI in 307 at bats for Cleveland.
    D)   Many authorities rate him and not Don Schwall the true top AL rookie in 1961.
    E)   He died less than two years after piloting an AL club to a world title.

22. **Who was the only member of either the original or the expansion Washington Senators franchise to pace the AL in runs?**
    A)   He scored 100 runs four times with the Senators and led the AL the last time he did it.
    B)   He was a member of the last Washington team to finish as high as second.
    C)   He spent all but one of his 11 ML seasons in Washington garb.
    D)   His final season was 1946 with Cleveland.
    E)   He led the AL in steals five years in a row while with the Senators.

23. **Between 1941 and Walter O'Malley's move to Los Angeles in 1958, Brooklyn showcased the NL leader in runs seven times. Between the Spanish-American War and 1941, only once did a Brooklyn performer pace the NL in runs. Who was he?**
    A)   He was the NL coleader in runs for a Brooklyn flag winner.
    B)   He's in the Hall of Fame.
    C)   He played for all three New York ML franchises in the first decade of the 20th century.
    D)   He debuted as a left-handed third sacker with the 1892 Giants, two years after Hub Collins became the first man from a Brooklyn team to lead the NL in runs.
    E)   He's best known for his feats with the Baltimore Orioles.

24. **In 1952 he topped the NL in runs with 105, even though he hit a mere .268 and swiped just one base in six tries to set a new loop record that still stands for the fewest thefts by a runs leader. Whom are we describing?**

    A) He managed the Cardinals for two and a half seasons in 1959–61.

    B) As a rookie in 1951, he replaced Marty Marion.

    C) He was named after a biblical solon.

    D) His nickname and initials are the same as those of an outfielder on the most recent Cubs team to win a World Championship.

    E) His initials are the same as those of the Cubs third sacker in the three most recent World Series that involved the Bruins.

Fewest Stolen Bases by a Leader in Runs, Season

RANK	NAME	TEAM	YEAR	RUNS	SBS
1	Ted Williams	Bos, AL	1946	142	0
	Roger Maris	NY, AL	1961	132	0
	Ted Williams	Bos, AL	1947	125	0
	Cal Ripken	Bal, AL	1983	121	0
5	Ted Williams	Bos, AL	1949	150	1
	Stan Musial	StL, NL	1954	120	1
	Solly Hemus	StL, NL	1952	105	1
8	Nine with two SBs, last done by Frank Thomas, Chi, AL, in 1994				

25. **Who set the current 20th century season record for the most runs (145) scored by anyone at his position while playing for a seventh-place team that won just 57 games?**

    A) He broke the former 20th century mark by a comfortable margin of 16 runs.

    B) The following year, another player in his league at the same position fell just two runs short of his record with 143 tallies.

    C) The same season he set his mark, Lou Gehrig established a new all-time record for the most runs by a first baseman.

    D) He was managed in 1936, the year he set his record, by the current 20th century season record holder for the most runs scored by a second baseman.

    E) He and the only ML bat titlist to date who batted right and threw left share the same initials.

Evolution of Season Record for Most Runs, Each Position

19th Century

	NAME	RUNS	YEAR	TEAM	LEAGUE
1B	Clipper Flynn	43	1871	Troy	NA
	Denny Mack	68	1872	Athletics	NA
	Jim O'Rourke	79	1873	Boston	NA
	Jim O'Rourke	82	1874	Boston	NA
	Cal McVey	89	1875	Boston	NA
	Harry Stovey	90	1882	Worcester	NL
	Harry Stovey	110	1883	Philadelphia	AA

	NAME	RUNS	YEAR	TEAM	LEAGUE
	Harry Stovey	124	1884	Philadelphia	AA
	Harry Stovey	130	1885	Philadelphia	AA
	Dan Brouthers	139	1886	Detroit	NL
	Dan Brouthers	153	1887	Detroit	NL
2B	Ross Barnes	66	1871	Boston	NA
	Ross Barnes	81	1872	Boston	NA
	Ross Barnes	125	1873	Boston	NA
	Ross Barnes	126	1876	Chicago	NL
	Fred Dunlap	160	1884	St. Louis	UA*
	Bid McPhee	139	1886	Cincinnati	AA
	Hub Collins	139	1889	Brooklyn	AA
	Hub Collins	148	1890	Brooklyn	NL
	Bobby Lowe	158	1894	Boston	NL

* Not all authorities recognize Dunlap's UA feats as major league records; if you don't, McPhee was the first second baseman to top Barnes's 126 runs.

	NAME	RUNS	YEAR	TEAM	LEAGUE
3B	Fred Waterman	46	1871	Olympics	NA
	Davy Force	69	1872	Baltimore/Troy	NA
	Davy Force	77	1873	Baltimore	NA
	Ezra Sutton	83	1875	Athletics	NA
	Ezra Sutton	101	1883	Boston	NL
	Arlie Latham	115	1884	St. Louis	AA
	Arlie Latham	152	1886	St. Louis	AA
	Arlie Latham	163	1887	St. Louis	AA
SS	John Radcliff	47	1871	Athletics	NA
	George Wright	87	1872	Boston	NA
	George Wright	99	1873	Boston	NA
	George Wright	106	1875	Boston	NA
	Candy Nelson	114	1884	New York	AA
	Jack Rowe	135	1887	Detroit	NL
	Bill Gleason	135	1887	St. Louis	AA
	Herman Long	137	1889	Kansas City	AA
	Herman Long	149	1893	Boston	NL
	Bill Dahlen	149	1894	Chicago	NL*
	Hughie Jennings	159	1895	Baltimore	NL

* Dahlen played 66 games at SS and 55 at 3B.

	NAME	RUNS	YEAR	TEAM	LEAGUE
OF	Dave Birdsall	51	1871	Boston	NA
	Dave Eggler	94	1872	New York	NA
	George Gore	99	1882	Chicago	NL
	Joe Hornung	107	1883	Boston	NL
	King Kelly	120	1884	Chicago	NL

NAME	RUNS	YEAR	TEAM	LEAGUE
Orator Shaffer	130	1884	St. Louis	UA*
King Kelly	155	1886	Chicago	NL
Tip O'Neill	167	1887	St. Louis	AA
Tom Brown	177	1891	Boston	AA
Billy Hamilton	192	1894	Philadelphia	NL

* Not all authorities recognize UA feats; Kelly's 120 runs in 1884 is the alternate record.

	NAME	RUNS	YEAR	TEAM	LEAGUE
C	Cal McVey	43	1871	Boston	NA
	Cal McVey	56	1872	Boston	NA
	Deacon White	79	1873	Boston	NA
	Buck Ewing	90	1883	New York	NL
	Buck Ewing	90	1884	New York	NL
	Buck Ewing	91	1889	New York	NL*
	Buck Ewing	98	1890	New York	PL

* John Kerins of Louisville, AA, scored 113 runs in 1886 while catching 65 games and playing 55 games at other positions.

20th Century

	NAME	RUNS	YEAR	TEAM
1B	**American League**			
	Frank Isbell	93	1901	Chicago
	Harry Davis	93	1905	Philadelphia
	Harry Davis	94	1906	Philadelphia
	George Sisler	96	1919	St. Louis
	George Sisler	137	1920	St. Louis
	Lou Gehrig	149	1927	New York
	Lou Gehrig	163	1931	New York
	Lou Gehrig	167	1936	New York
	National League			
	Kitty Bransfield	92	1901	Pittsburgh
	Shad Barry	100	1905	Chicago/Cincinnati
	Frank Chance	103	1906	Chicago
	Jack Fournier	103	1921	St. Louis
	Jake Daubert	114	1922	Cincinnati
	Jim Bottomley	123	1928	St. Louis
	Bill Terry	139	1930	New York

	NAME	RUNS	YEAR	TEAM
2B	*American League*			
	Nap Lajoie	145	1901	Philadelphia*
	Eddie Collins	104	1909	Philadelphia
	Eddie Collins	137	1912	Philadelphia
	Charlie Gehringer	144	1930	Detroit
	Charlie Gehringer	144	1936	Detroit

* Many authorities view Lajoie's 1901 AL achievements as suspect. If his mark isn't accepted, Collins was the first AL second baseman to score as many as 100 runs in a season, and the record then progresses as shown.

	NAME	RUNS	YEAR	TEAM
	National League			
	Tom Daly	88	1901	Brooklyn
	Miller Huggins	96	1904	Cincinnati
	Miller Huggins	117	1905	Cincinnati
	Rogers Hornsby	131	1921	St. Louis
	Rogers Hornsby	141	1922	St. Louis
	Rogers Hornsby	156	1929	Chicago
3B	*American League*			
	Jimmy Collins	108	1901	Boston
	Sammy Strang	108	1902	Chicago
	Frank Baker	116	1912	Philadelphia
	Frank Baker	116	1913	Philadelphia
	Ossie Vitt	116	1915	Detroit
	Billy Werber	129	1934	Boston
	Harlond Clift	145	1936	St. Louis
	National League			
	Otto Krueger	77	1901	St. Louis
	Tommy Leach	97	1902	Pittsburgh
	Sammy Strang	101	1903	Brooklyn
	Bobby Byrne	101	1910	Pittsburgh
	Frankie Frisch	121	1921	New York
	Woody English	152	1930	Chicago*
	Pepper Martin	122	1933	St. Louis
	Dick Allen	125	1964	Philadelphia
	Pete Rose	130	1976	Cincinnati

* Since English played 83 games at 3B and 78 games at SS in 1930, he can be rated the record holder at either, both, or neither position, depending on your viewpoint.

	NAME	RUNS	YEAR	TEAM
SS	*American League*			
	Freddy Parent	87	1901	Boston
	Freddy Parent	91	1902	Boston
	Germany Schaefer	96	1908	Detroit

NAME	RUNS	YEAR	TEAM
Donie Bush	114	1909	Detroit
Donie Bush	126	1911	Detroit
Roger Peckinpaugh	128	1921	New York
Frankie Crosetti	137	1936	New York
Alex Rodriguez	141	1996	Seattle
National League			
Honus Wagner	101	1901	Pittsburgh*
George Davis	69	1901	New York
Bill Dahlen	69	1901	Brooklyn
Bobby Wallace	69	1901	St. Louis
Honus Wagner	97	1903	Pittsburgh
Honus Wagner	97	1904	Pittsburgh
Honus Wagner	114	1905	Pittsburgh
Dave Bancroft	121	1921	New York
Woody English	131	1929	Chicago
Pee Wee Reese	132	1949	Brooklyn

* Wagner played more games at shortstop than any other position, but fewer than half of his 140 games were at short; as a result, many consider Davis's, Dahlen's, and Wallace's 1901 figures of 69 a better starting point, and the record then progresses as shown.

OF **American League**

NAME	RUNS	YEAR	TEAM
Fielder Jones	120	1901	Chicago
Ty Cobb	147	1911	Detroit
Babe Ruth	158	1920	New York
Babe Ruth	177	1921	New York

National League

NAME	RUNS	YEAR	TEAM
Jesse Burkett	142	1901	St. Louis
Kiki Cuyler	144	1925	Pittsburgh
Lefty O'Doul	152	1929	Philadelphia
Chuck Klein	158	1930	Philadelphia

C **American League**

NAME	RUNS	YEAR	TEAM
Boileryard Clarke	58	1901	Washington
Ray Schalk	64	1920	Chicago
Wally Schang	77	1921	New York
Mickey Cochrane	80	1927	Philadelphia
Mickey Cochrane	92	1928	Philadelphia
Mickey Cochrane	113	1929	Philadelphia
Mickey Cochrane	118	1932	Philadelphia

NAME	RUNS	YEAR	TEAM
National League			
Art Nichols	50	1901	St. Louis
Johnny Kling	67	1903	Chicago
Roger Bresnahan	69	1906	New York
Roger Bresnahan	70	1908	New York
Bob O'Farrell	73	1923	Chicago
Gabby Hartnett	84	1930	Chicago*
Roy Campanella	103	1954	Brooklyn
Johnny Bench	108	1974	Cincinnati**

* Prior to 1930, the 20th century catchers' record belonged to Art Wilson of Chicago in the Federal League, with 78 runs in 1914.

** Bench played a significant number of games at other positions.

Walk Wizards

1. **Eddie Stanky had just a .268 career batting average, but his on-base percentage was .410. Billy Herman's career OBP was only .367 even though he hit .304. It's great food for debate which of these second sackers was more valuable on offense. Herman made the Hall of Fame. Stanky never will, despite being among an elite few players with more than one season when they had 400 plate appearances and compiled more walks than hits. Just three Hall of Famers had even one such season. Who are they?**

   A) Two of the trio did it in their finales, and one did it twice in his career.
   B) The third is the only man ever to compile more than 130 hits and 130 walks in a season when he had fewer than 400 ABs.
   C) Two of the three clubbed 500 career home runs.
   D) The non-500-homer man was the first defending AL home run champ to play in the NL the following season.
   E) All three won AL home run crowns between 1946 and 1956.

2. **In 1950, Eddie Stanky reached base safely a phenomenal 314 times with 158 hits, 144 walks, and 12 hit-by-pitches. Stanky's performance is technically the NL record for the most times reaching base safely on a sub-.300 batting average, since he hit .2998. The ML mark, however, for a sub-.300 batting average is 318. Who owns it?**

   A) He hit a career-high .295 the year he set the mark.
   B) In his 10th full ML season, he hit .231, the lowest season batting mark ever by a player who walked 150 times.
   C) He set the ML record for the most times reaching base safely on a sub-.300 BA the same year Stanky set the NL mark.
   D) In 1960, his second year with Detroit, he became the first third baseman ever to lead his league in OBP two years in a row.
   E) His .440 OBP in 1950 is the second highest in Washington Senators history, trailing only Goose Goslin's .442 in 1928.

3. **Ted Williams reached base safely 300 times a record six straight seasons during 1941–49, excluding a three-year armed services interruption. Who is the only other man to have as many as five such consecutive seasons?**

   A) He won four batting titles during his five-year skein.
   B) He led the AL in OBP all five years during his skein.
   C) His six career OBP titles are the most ever by a third baseman.
   D) He is the only third sacker in history to hit .350 four years in a row.
   E) Only Ted Williams won more bat crowns than he while playing for the Red Sox.

4. Ted Williams walked an all-time record 20.8 percent of his plate appearances. The only other man to play 10 years and walk more than 20 percent of the time he came to bat played under the same manager in his final season that Williams did as a rookie. Can you name him?

    A)   He is the only 20th century batting title qualifier to tally more runs than hits in a season.

    B)   His .423 career OBP is a record 152 points higher than his career BA.

    C)   The 1928 season was his lone .300 campaign and the only time between 1926 and 1933 that he bagged fewer than 100 walks.

    D)   He played beside such shortstops as Joe Boley and Eric McNair.

    E)   He and baseball's famed "Super Spy" share the same initials.

Greatest Difference Between Career BA and OBP (Minimum 3000 ABs)

RANK	NAME	YEARS	ABS	BA	OBP	DIFF.
1	Max Bishop	1924–35	4494	.271	.423	152
2	Gene Tenace	1969–83	4390	.241	.391	150
3	Eddie Stanky	1943–53	4301	.268	.410	142
4	Eddie Yost	1944–62	7346	.254	.395	141
5	Ted Williams	1939–60	7706	.344	.483	139
6	Ferris Fain	1947–55	3930	.290	.425	135
7	Yank Robinson	1882–92	3428	.241	.375	134
8	Roy Cullenbine	1938–47	3879	.276	.408	132
	Babe Ruth	1914–35	8399	.342	.474	132
	John McGraw	1891–1906	3924	.334	.466	132

Note: Retired players only.

5. As of 1999, only one man with at least 3,000 career at bats has retired with an OBP of .400 or better since the inception of the DH rule in 1973. Who is he?

    A)   His real first name is Dudley, and his career OBP is .400 on the nose.

    B)   He is the lone Cleveland player since 1950 to lead the AL in OBP.

    C)   Prior to 1996 he held the Tribe's record for the most walks in a season.

    D)   He was nicknamed "The Human Rain Delay."

    E)   He piloted the 1997 World Series loser.

6. What catcher had a dismal .217 career batting average in 11 big league seasons but posted a fine .357 OBP owing to 489 walks as against just 503 hits?

    A)   He also had 96 home runs and a .373 career SA.

    B)   In 1951 he hit just .219 but had a .400 OBP, thanks to his 104 walks.

    C)   In the 1951 World Series, he collected five walks in six games.

    D)   He replaced Casey as the Mets' pilot.

    E)   He and the record holder for the most career homers (131) by a man who was never a batting title qualifier share the same first name.

7. **In 1922 he led his team with 89 walks, 5 more than the runner-up had; the next year, he was second on his team with 67 walks but trailed the club leader by the whopping margin of 103 free passes. Who is he, and who was the club leader?**

   A) The club leader that year led his league in walks by the largest margin ever.

   B) The club runner-up's real first name was Ladislaw.

   C) The 1922 season was his first as the Yankees' center fielder.

   D) His initials are the same as those of the 1982 AL batting champ.

   E) He and the only hurler to throw a perfect game on the final day of a season share the same last name.

Widest Margin Between League Leader and Runner-Up in Walks

RANK	YEAR	LEAGUE	LEADER	WALKS	RUNNER-UP	WALKS	MARGIN
1	1923	AL	Babe Ruth	170	Joe Sewell	98	72
2	1920	AL	Babe Ruth	148	Tris Speaker	97	51
3	1905	AL	Topsy Hartsel	121	Fielder Jones	73	48
4	1888	AA	Yank Robinson	116	Frank Fennelly	72	44
	1911	NL	Jimmy Sheckard	147	Johnny Bates	103	44
6	1946	AL	Ted Williams	156	Charlie Keller	113	43
	1963	NL	Eddie Mathews	124	Frank Robinson	81	43
8	1921	AL	Babe Ruth	144	Lu Blue	103	41
9	1924	AL	Babe Ruth	142	Topper Rigney	102	40
	1959	AL	Eddie Yost	135	Pete Runnels	95	40

8. **Rickey Henderson joined the top 10 list in career walks in 1996. Name the only other leadoff hitter in ML history to rank among the top 10.**

   A) He alone among the career top 10 in walks had fewer than 2,000 hits.

   B) He once held Henderson's current record for the most career home runs by a player serving as the leadoff hitter in a game for his team.

   C) He notched his first career walk in 1944 when he was just 17 years old.

   D) He led the AL in walks six times, last in 1960.

   E) He has the record for the most walks in a season by a third baseman.

9. **Whose .248 batting average is the lowest among players who rank among the top 20 in career free passes?**

   A) Second to him is Harmon Killebrew at .256.

   B) He currently ranks eighth in career walks with 1,605.

   C) In 1988 he hit just .208 for the Tigers but snagged 84 walks.

   D) He holds the current major league record for the most home runs (34) in a season by a 40-year-old performer.

   E) He was part of the first teammate trio who hit 40 homers apiece in a season.

Most Career Walks, Sub-.250 BA

RANK	NAME	YEARS	BA	WALKS
1	Darrell Evans	1969–89	.248	1605
2	Graig Nettles	1967–88	.248	1088
3	Eddie Joost	1936–55	.239	1043
4	Gene Tenace	1969–83	.241	984
5	Mickey Tettleton	1984–	.241	949
6	Darrell Porter	1971–87	.247	905
7	Dick McAuliffe	1960–75	.247	882
8	Chris Speier	1971–89	.246	847
9	Frankie Crosetti	1932–48	.245	792
10	Paul Radford	1883–94	.242	790

10. **Eddie Collins once held the record for the most career walks by a middle infielder, with 1,499. Who broke his mark and became the first middle infielder to top 1,500 free passes?**

    A)   The current record holder was playing for Houston when he set the mark.
    B)   He played for San Francisco when he broke Mel Ott's record for the most career walks in the NL.
    C)   He led the NL in walks as a rookie in 1965.
    D)   He won back-to-back MVP awards in 1975–76.
    E)   He is considered Cincinnati's all-time-greatest second baseman.

11. **Babe Ruth collected 100 walks for the first time in 1919; Lou Gehrig had his first 100-walk season in 1926. Who was the only major leaguer besides Ruth to walk 100 times in a season twice between 1919 and 1926?**

    A)   He collected just 377 career walks.
    B)   He hit .300 as a rookie shortstop with the Tigers in 1922 and set a frosh record for the most sacrifice hits with 39.
    C)   In 1926, his last season as a regular, he walked 108 times for the Red Sox.
    D)   His first name was Emory, but they called him "Topper."
    E)   He and the first man to manage a big league team nicknamed the Angels share the same last name.

12. **Between 1914, when Miller Huggins paced the NL with 104 walks, and 1928, which saw Rogers Hornsby lead with 107 walks, only one senior loop performer walked 100 times in a season. Who is he?**

    A)   Even though he walked more than 89 times just once in his career, he paced the NL in walks on five occasions.
    B)   In 1923 he walked 101 times as Cincinnati's leadoff hitter.
    C)   In 1919 he led the NL in both walks and steals.
    D)   He spent the first 11 of his 15 big-time seasons with the Giants.
    E)   He and the first man to collect 60 doubles in a season share the same name.

13. **What team won three straight pennants despite using as its leadoff hitter an outfielder who garnered just 60 walks over the three-year span and, in the second year of that span, set a record for the fewest walks by a leadoff hitter on a World Championship team?**
    A)   Though a leadoff hitter much of his career, the outfielder compiled just a .329 career OBP as against a .295 BA.
    B)   In 1980, his career year, he batted .333 with 210 hits but just 20 walks.
    C)   He led the AL in triples and stolen bases in 1975.
    D)   He was replaced as leadoff hitter on the three-time flag winner by a second baseman who topped the AL with 119 walks in 1980.
    E)   He played center field for the next-to-last team to win two consecutive World Championships.

Fewest Walks, Season, Leadoff Hitter on a World Champion

RANK	NAME	TEAM	YEAR	OBP	WALKS
1	Mickey Rivers	NY, AL	1977	.351	18
2	Jo-Jo Moore	NY, NL	1933	.323	21
3	Lou Brock	StL, NL	1967	.324	28
	Willie Wilson	KC, AL	1980	.357	28
5	Mickey Rivers	NY, AL	1978	.305	29
6	Skeeter Webb	Det, AL	1945	.254	30
	Bobby Richardson	NY, AL	1961	.295	30
8	Pepper Martin	StL, NL	1934	.337	32
	Bert Campaneris	Oak, AL	1972	.279	32
10	Patsy Dougherty	Bos, AL	1903	.372	33
	Red Schoendienst	Mil, NL	1957	.345	33
	Luis Aparicio	Bal, AL	1966	.312	33

Note: Since 1903, the first modern World Series; war-abbreviated and strike seasons excluded; limited to leadoff hitters with a minimum of 400 ABs. Ten of Schoendienst's 33 walks came with New York prior to his midseason trade to Milwaukee.

14. **Babe Ruth has held the record for the most walks in a season continuously since 1920 when he bagged 148 free passes. Whose mark did the Babe break?**
    A)   Prior to 1945 he held the NL record for the most walks in a season.
    B)   His 73 stolen bases in 1899 topped the NL.
    C)   He led the NL in SA in 1901 and homers in 1903.
    D)   His 147 walks in 1911 were one-quarter of his team's total of 585.
    E)   He was named after the loser in the 1876 presidential race.

15. **Who holds the 19th century record for the most walks in a season?**
    A)   As a rookie in 1890, he walked 96 times for Columbus of the AA.
    B)   He hit .213 the year he compiled a 19th-century-high 136 walks.
    C)   He once held the season record for the highest fielding average by a second baseman.
    D)   His last name suggests that he had larceny in his heart each time he stepped to the plate.
    E)   His initials are the same as those of the man who piloted the first 20th century World Series winner.

16. After Billy Hamilton led the NL in walks two years in a row in 1896–97, only two other members of the Boston franchise paced the senior loop in free passes before it relocated to Milwaukee. One is Rogers Hornsby in 1928. Who is the other?

A) He holds the all-time Braves season franchise record for most walks with 131.
B) He won the NL MVP Award the year before he broke the Braves' walk record.
C) The year he collected 131 walks, Ralph Kiner was the only other NL'er to top 100.
D) His MVP prize came the first season a black American was voted Rookie of the Year.
E) He was the third sacker on the last Boston NL World Series entry.

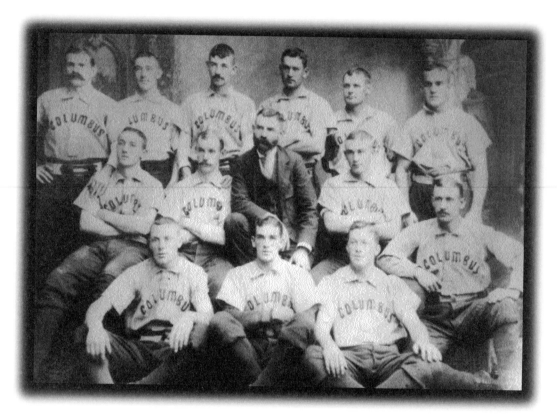

The 1890 Columbus Solons. Standing: Jim McTamany, Frank Knauss, Mike Lehane, Hank Gastright, Spud Johnson, and Jack Crooks. Seated: Jack Doyle, Bill Widner, manager Gus Schmelz, and Icebox Chamberlain. Front: Jack O'Connor, Bobby Wheelock, Jack Easton, and John Sneed. A year later, McTamany became the only man to date to notch both 100 runs and 100 walks in his last ML season. Two years later, Crooks set a 19th century season record for walks.

17. Whose .408 career OBP included a .401 finale in which he hit just .224 and totaled 33 more walks than hits?

A) He was the first switch-hitter in AL history to average better than one hit in every three at bats (.333) in a season when he compiled at least 100 hits.
B) His 24 homers in his 1947 finale were a career high.
C) His 137 walks in 1947 are the most by a player in his last ML season.
D) His final World Series game saw him oppose a shortstop with the same first name in the last World Series game to date played by the Cubs.
E) His first name and initials are the same as those of the ML record holder for the most RBI in a season by a catcher.

Most Walks by a Player in His Last ML Season

RANK	NAME	TEAM	YEAR	BA	WALKS
1	Roy Cullenbine	Det, AL	1947	.224	137
2	Mickey Mantle	NY, AL	1968	.237	106
3	Hank Greenberg	Pit, NL	1947	.249	104
4	Jim McTamany	Col/Phi, AA	1891	.239	101
5	Ferris Fain	Det/Cle, AL	1955	.260	94
6	Elbie Fletcher	Bos, NL	1949	.262	84
7	Marty Berghammer	Pit, FL	1915	.243	83
8	Jack Burns	StL/Det, AL	1936	.281	82
9	Goat Anderson	Pit, NL	1907	.206	80
10	Ted Scheffler	Roc, AA	1890	.245	78

Note: Fain had only 258 ABs in 1955, making for a phenomenal .459 OBP.

18. Who holds the all-time record for the lowest batting average by a loop walk leader?
A) He broke Yank Robinson's old mark of .208 by one percentage point.
B) The year after he set the record, he lost his walk title to a .233 hitter.
C) In 1974 he had 108 walks and 108 RBI for the NL champs.
D) Prior to 1996 he shared the NL record for the most walks in a season.
E) He was nicknamed "The Toy Cannon."

Lowest BA, Season, Leader in Walks

RANK	NAME	TEAM	YEAR	WALKS	BA
1	Jim Wynn	Atl, NL	1976	127	.207
2	Yank Robinson	StL, AA	1889	118	.208
3	Gene Tenace	Oak, AL	1974	110	.211
4	Jack Crooks	StL, NL	1892	136	.213
5	Herman Dehlman	StL, NA	1875	11	.224
6	Jack Graney	Cle, AL	1917	94	.228
7	Yank Robinson	StL, AA	1888	116	.2308
8	Donie Bush	Det, AL	1912	117	.2309
9	Eddie Yost	Was, AL	1956	151	.2311
10	Max Bishop	Phi, AL	1929	128	.232

Note: Bishop's .2316 BA (officially .232) is slightly lower than the marks of Jack Remsen (1878) and Donie Bush (1911), who also led in walks while hitting .2321 and .2317, respectfully. BAs are carried out to four decimal points where ties would otherwise exist.

19. What major league franchise was in existence for 54 years before one of its players collected as many as 100 walks in a season?

A)   The team leader in the franchise's maiden ML season had just 21 walks.

B)   In 1893, Denny Lyons collected 97 walks to set a franchise record that lasted until 1936.

C)   In 1907 the team walk leader with 80 was Goat Anderson, a rookie outfielder who hit just .206.

D)   George Grantham was the first member of this team to collect as many as 90 walks in a season in the 20th century.

E)   Arky Vaughan broke the ice in 1936 when he set a new team record with 118 walks.

Evolution of Record for Most Walks, Season, Pittsburgh Franchise

NAME	YEAR	BA	WALKS
Ed Swartwood	1882	.329	21
Ed Swartwood	1883	.357	25
Mike Mansell	1883	.257	25
Ed Swartwood	1884	.288	33
Tom Brown	1885	.307	34
Sam Barkley	1886	.266	58
Fred Carroll	1889	.330	85
Denny Lyons	1893	.306	97
Arky Vaughan	1935	.385	97
Arky Vaughan	1936	.335	118
Elbie Fletcher	1940	.273	119
Ralph Kiner	1950	.272	122
Ralph Kiner	1951	.309	137

Note: Carroll, Vaughan (both years), Fletcher, and Kiner (1951) led the league in OBP.

20. Name the only performer since 1889 (the first year four balls earned a walk) to lead his loop in walks, runs, hits, and at bats in the same season.

A)   The year he did it, his 129 walks, 194 hits, and 637 ABs were all career highs.

B)   He twice led the NL in hits.

C)   His 143 runs the lone year he topped the NL in tallies have been exceeded by only one other player on his team in the 20th century.

D)   He leads all performers with at least 50 World Series at bats in homers per 100 at bats (12.0).

E)   His 143 runs in 1993 were the most by a National League player since Chuck Klein's 152 in 1932.

21. Who was the first batting title qualifier in major league history to finish the season with more walks than hits?

A)   He had 116 walks and 105 hits while playing beside a shortstop who hit just .175 for a pennant winner.

B)   In his last five ML seasons (1888–92), he had 441 walks and 369 hits.

C)   He played in four 19th century World Series.

D)   He held the St. Louis Browns' second-base job from 1886 to 1889.

E)   In 1888 he set the all-time record for the lowest BA (.231) by a loop leader in on-base percentage.

Seasons with More Walks than Hits (Minimum 100 Walks)

NAME	TEAM	LEAGUE	YEAR	WALKS	HITS	DIFF.
Jack Crooks	St. Louis	NL	1892	136	95	41
Jim Wynn	Atlanta	NL	1976	127	93	34
Roy Cullenbine	Detroit	AL	1947	137	104	33
Eddie Yost	Washington	AL	1956	151	119	32
Yank Robinson	Pittsburgh	PL	1890	101	70	31
Wes Westrum	New York	NL	1951	104	79	25
Yank Robinson	St. Louis	AA	1889	118	94	24
Gene Tenace	San Diego	NL	1977	125	102	23
Jack Clark	San Diego	NL	1989	132	110	22
Max Bishop	Philadelphia	AL	1929	128	110	18
Max Bishop	Philadelphia	AL	1930	128	111	17
Jack Clark	St. Louis	NL	1987	136	120	16
Jim Wynn	Houston	NL	1969	148	133	15
Jack Crooks	St. Louis	NL	1893	121	106	15
Jack Clark	San Diego	NL	1990	104	89	15
Rickey Henderson	San Diego	NL	1996	125	112	13
Eddie Joost	Philadelphia	AL	1949	149	138	11
Yank Robinson	St. Louis	AA	1888	116	105	11
Gene Tenace	San Diego	NL	1978	101	90	11
Mark McGwire	St. Louis	NL	1998	162	152	10
Max Bishop	Philadelphia	AL	1926	116	106	10
Gene Tenace	Oakland	AL	1974	110	102	8
Jim Wynn	Los Angeles	NL	1975	110	102	8
Mickey Tettleton	Baltimore	AL	1990	106	99	7
Toby Harrah	Texas	AL	1985	113	107	6
Max Bishop	Philadelphia	AL	1932	110	104	6
Eddie Stanky	Brooklyn	NL	1945	148	143	5
Eddie Stanky	Brooklyn	NL	1946	137	132	5
Mickey Tettleton	Texas	AL	1995	107	102	5
Hank Greenberg	Pittsburgh	NL	1947	104	100	4
Ted Williams	Boston	AL	1954	136	133	3
Eddie Joost	Philadelphia	AL	1947	114	111	3
Mickey Mantle	New York	AL	1968	106	103	3
Willie McCovey	San Francisco	NL	1973	105	102	3
Max Bishop	Philadelphia	AL	1927	105	103	2
Mickey Mantle	New York	AL	1962	122	121	1

BothWay Bammers

1. **Until recent years, switch-hitters were fairly rare. As a result, almost all the current season and career bothway batting marks have been set since World War II. Some go back a ways, though—for instance, the all-time record for the most runs scored in a season by a switch-hitter. Do you know what Hall of Famer owns this mark?**

   A) His record 140 runs came in 1922 on 207 hits and 10 homers, both career highs.
   B) He never played any position but the outfield in the majors.
   C) He hit a career-high .343 in 1925 when he played in his only World Series.
   D) Not long ago, Tim Raines eclipsed his record for the most career steals by a switch-hitter.
   E) His birth name was Maximillian Carnarius.

Most Runs, Season, Switch-Hitter

RANK	NAME	TEAM	YEAR	POS.	RUNS
1	Max Carey	Pit, NL	1922	OF	140
2	Tom Daly	Bro, NL	1894	2B	135
3	Walt Wilmot	Chi, NL	1894	OF	134
	Cliff Carroll	Chi, NL	1890	OF	134
5	Augie Galan	Chi, NL	1935	OF	133
	Willie Wilson	KC, AL	1980	OF	133
	Tim Raines	Mon, NL	1983	OF	133
8	Mickey Mantle	NY, AL	1956	OF	132
	Mickey Mantle	NY, AL	1961	OF	132
10	Lu Blue	Det, AL	1922	1B	131

2. **The first switch-sticker to compile 100 RBI in a season in the NL broke through in 1893 and is also a Hall of Famer. Can you name him?**

   A) Had he played five more games at second base in 1908, he would have become the first man in ML history to play 100 games in a season at four different positions.
   B) In 1897 he and a New York Giants teammate set the all-time season record for the most runs produced by switch-hitting keystone partners.
   C) He once held the season record for the highest fielding average by a shortstop.
   D) He once held the record for the most career hits by a switch-hitter.
   E) He still holds the record for the most RBI (136) in a season by a switch-hitter.

Most RBI, Season, Switch-Hitter

RANK	NAME	TEAM	YEAR	RBI
1	George Davis	NY, NL	1897	136
2	Walt Wilmot	Chi, NL	1894	130
	Mickey Mantle	NY, AL	1956	130
	Ken Caminiti	SD, NL	1996	130
5	Ripper Collins	StL, NL	1934	128
	Mickey Mantle	NY, AL	1961	128
7	Eddie Murray	Bal, AL	1985	124
8	Ripper Collins	StL, NL	1935	122
9	Bobby Bonilla	Pit, NL	1990	120
10	George Davis	NY, NL	1893	119
	Ruben Sierra	Tex, AL	1989	119

3. **We were fairly deep into the 20th century before the AL produced its first 100-RBI season by a switch-hitter. What Springfield, Illinois, native achieved this landmark first?**

   A) He was half of the first AL keystone pair who each cracked the 100-RBI barrier.

   B) He was on the most recent world champ that had a catcher as its player-manager.

   C) He was the Tigers shortstop when Hank Greenberg debuted.

   D) In 1934 he and Charlie Gehringer, his keystone partner in his 100-RBI season, set the all-time mark for the most runs produced by a keystone combo.

   E) He and the Yankees record holder for most hits in a season prior to Don Mattingly share the same initials.

Most Runs Produced by Keystone Partners, Season

RANK	NAMES	TEAM	YEAR	TOTAL
1	Charlie Gehringer (250) & Billy Rogell (211)	Det, AL	1934	461
2	Rogers Hornsby (266) & Woody English (182)	Chi, NL	1929	448
3	Bobby Lowe (253) & Herman Long (193)	Bos, NL	1894	446
4	Bid McPhee (222) & Frank Fennelly (222)	Cin, AA	1887	444
5	Jack Rowe (225) & Hardy Richardson (217)	Det, NL	1887	442
6	Ed McKean (232) & Cupid Childs (207)	Cle, NL	1893	439
7	Vern Stephens (239) & Bobby Doerr (196)	Bos, AL	1950	435
8	Ed McKean (236) & Cupid Childs (193)	Cle, NL	1894	429
9	Hughie Jennings (239) & Heinie Reitz (189)	Bal, NL	1894	428
	George Davis (238) & Kid Gleason (190)	NY, NL	1897	428

4. **A certain switch-hitter's 85 RBI paced the first St. Louis AL entry in 1902, but he's better known as the first bothway bammer to win a slugging average crown. Who is he?**
   A) He was the first man to win a major league SA crown with a BA below .300.
   B) His .330 BA for Milwaukee in 1901 was the highest by an AL switch-hitter prior to the end of the Deadball Era.
   C) He still holds the AL record for the most hits in a season by a first baseman who hit both ways.
   D) His 1,841 career hits are the most by anyone born in Scandinavia.
   E) He and a 1980 presidential candidate share the same name.

5. **Beaver, Pennsylvania, produced the first switch-hitter to clout three homers in a game. Who is he?**
   A) He was also the lone Louisville NL player to go "yard" three times in a game.
   B) He hit only 26 homers in his nine NL seasons.
   C) In 1896, his first full big league season, he led the NL with 21 triples.
   D) In 1896 he also became the only man to hit .350+ and lead the majors in Ks.
   E) His initials are the same as those of the Cards center fielder in the late '30s.

6. **The only all-switch-hitting infield in ML history performed as a unit for two seasons. Can you name this quartet?**
   A) In their second season together, the quartet played in a World Series.
   B) The left side of the infield was Afro-American and the right side Caucasian.
   C) Their team was swept in the World Series after sweeping the Yankees in a World Series three years earlier.
   D) Their two seasons as a unit came with the 1965–66 Dodgers.
   E) Two of the four were named Jim, and both won a National League Rookie of the Year Award.

7. **What was the first team to have an infield unit that featured as many as three switch-hitters?**
   A) The second baseman was one of the very few middle infielders in ML history who began his career as a catcher.
   B) The third sacker later tied Duke Farrell's record for the most pinch hits in a season by a switch-hitter.
   C) The shortstop retired with many career switch-hitting records.
   D) The first baseman, Frank Isbell, batted lefty.
   E) The second baseman was the only man to play on all of Brooklyn's 19th century NL pennant winners.

8. **The first switch-hitter to lead his league in a major offensive department six years earlier had led all third basemen in errors with 62. Who is he?**
   A) He topped the NL in on-base percentage in 1878.
   B) He was the first switch-hitter to collect as many as 1,000 career hits.
   C) He is the only man ever to be president of a major league while an active player (the National Association in 1872).
   D) He umped in several 19th century World Series and called himself "The King of Umpires."
   E) His other nickname was "Death to Flying Things."

9. **Who owns the records for both the most hits and the highest batting average by a switch-hitter in his final ML season?**
   A) He had 208 hits and batted .331 in his finale.
   B) Prior to 1956 he held the AL record for the highest BA in a season by a switch-hitter with 400 or more ABs.
   C) He became a switch-hitter in 1917 and eventually hiked his career BA to .272 after being a sub-.250 hitter while batting only righty in his first five seasons.
   D) His 208 hits in 1920 set a new 20th century record for third basemen.
   E) He did not leave the game voluntarily after serving as the White Sox third sacker in his 1920 finale.

10. **When Mickey Mantle led the AL in 1955 with 37 dingers, whose record for the most home runs in a season by a switch-hitter did he break?**

   A) The old record was 35.
   B) The previous record holder led the NL in homers the year he set the mark.
   C) At 5'9", he was one of the smallest first basemen in the 20th century.
   D) He was a member of the Gas House Gang.
   E) He held the NL record for the most home runs by a switch-hitter until 1987, when Howard Johnson broke it.

Evolution of Record for Most HRs, Season, Switch-Hitter

NAME	TEAM	YEAR	HRS
Bob Ferguson	Tro, NL	1881	1
Cliff Carroll	Pro, NL	1883	1
Bill Greenwood	Bro, AA	1884	3
Cliff Carroll	Pro, NL	1884	3
Jim Manning	Bos/Det, NL	1885	3
Tommy Tucker	Bal, AA	1887	6
Tommy Tucker	Bal, AA	1888	6
Duke Farrell	Chi, NL	1889	11
Walt Wilmot	Chi, NL	1890	13
Lu Blue	StL, AL	1928	14
Buzz Arlett	Phi, NL	1931	18
Ripper Collins	StL, NL	1932	21
Ripper Collins	StL, NL	1934	35
Mickey Mantle	NY, AL	1955	37
Mickey Mantle	NY, AL	1956	52
Mickey Mantle	NY, AL	1961	54

11. **Who is the only switch-hitter besides Pete Rose to win more than one bat title?**

   A) He came to the team where he won his two bat titles in a swap for Bob Sykes.
   B) He holds the NL record for the biggest drop in BA (97 points) by a defending batting titlist.
   C) He has the 20th century NL record for the highest BA by a switch-hitter.
   D) He played on the losing side in the 1996 NLCS.
   E) He is the only man to win a ML batting title in absentia (while no longer playing in the league where he won).

12. **In 1991, Mickey Tettleton broke the 20th century record for the most whiffs by a switch-hitter when he K'd 160 times. Who has the converse 20th century mark—the fewest Ks by a switch-hitter with enough plate appearances to be a bat title qualifier?**

   A) He tied George Davis's 19th century mark when he fanned just 10 times in 1927.
   B) He also fanned just 10 times while playing with a flag winner in 1934.
   C) He had 2,880 career hits and just 272 Ks.
   D) He was traded even up for Rogers Hornsby prior to the 1927 season.
   E) Being a three-sport star at Fordham University earned him the nickname "The Fordham Flash."

13. **Who was the only AL switch-hitter prior to Mickey Mantle in 1956 to collect at least 100 hits in a season and average better than a hit in every three at bats?**

    A)   Mantle broke his record for the most walks in a season by a switch-hitter.

    B)   In postseason action, he played against the first world champ managed by Billy Southworth and later played for the only world champ managed by Steve O'Neill.

    C)   He currently holds the record for the most walks by a player in his final ML season.

    D)   Prior to 1956 his .335 BA on 110 hits for the Tigers in 1946 was the AL's best mark by a switch-hitter in 100 or more games.

    E)   In his 1947 finale, he notched 137 walks and just 104 hits to set an all-time record for the largest differential between walks and hits by a player who had at least 100 of each.

Highest BA by an AL Switch-Hitter, Season (Prior to 1956)

RANK	NAME	TEAM	YEAR	ABS	HITS	BA
1	Roy Cullenbine	Detroit	1946	328	110	.335
2	Buck Weaver	Chicago	1920	629	208	.331
3	John Anderson	Milwaukee	1901	576	190	.330
4	Mark Koenig	New York	1928	533	170	.3189
5	Wally Schang	New York	1922	408	130	.3186
6	Roy Cullenbine	St. Louis	1941	501	159	.317
7	Wally Schang	New York	1921	424	134	.316
8	Mickey Mantle	New York	1952	549	171	.31147
9	Lu Blue	Detroit	1924	395	123	.31139
10	Lu Blue	Detroit	1921	585	180	.308

Note: Minimum 100 games. BAs are carried out to four or five decimal points where ties would otherwise exist.

14. **Who is the only switch-hitter to score 1,000 runs and win 100 games in the majors?**

    A)   He won a career-high 38 games for the 1890 Phillies.

    B)   He tallied a career-high 95 runs for the 1905 Phillies.

    C)   He played on the first Baltimore ML flag winner and the first Detroit ML team in the AL.

    D)   With the Giants in 1897, he was part of the only switch-hitting keystone combo to date each to collect 100 RBI in a season.

    E)   He was no longer a "kid" when he managed the Black Sox.

15. **Who was the first documented switch-hitter to fan 100 times in a season?**

    A)   He debuted with Pittsburgh in 1907 and finished with Cleveland in 1916.

    B)   He was an outfielder with Washington the year he K'd 103 times.

    C)   That same year, he also became the first documented AL'er to fan 100 times.

    D)   In 1913 his 62 steals ranked second in the AL and were the most by any player prior to expansion who fanned 100 times in a season.

    E)   His initials are the same as those of the current ML record holder for the highest fielding average in a season by a third baseman in at least 100 games.

16. Who held the Yankees record for the most hits in a season by a switch-batter prior to Mickey Mantle?

A)   Ask yourself, too, who held the equivalent Cincinnati Reds record prior to Pete Rose?

B)   He was a Yankees regular for four seasons.

C)   He was the only switch-hitter on the 1927 Yankees.

D)   At the time of his death, he was the last living member of the 1927 Yankees.

E)   Knowing his name can save you time working on the Cincinnati question because he's the answer to both.

Evolution of Season Record for Most Hits by a Switch-Hitter

NAME	YEAR	TEAM	LEAGUE	HITS
Bob Ferguson	1871	New York	NA	38
Bob Ferguson	1872	Atlantics	NA	45
Bob Ferguson	1873	Atlantics	NA	59
Bob Ferguson	1874	Atlantics	NA	63
Bob Ferguson	1875	Hartford	NA	88
Bob Ferguson	1878	Chicago	NL	91
Bob Ferguson	1881	Troy	NL	96
Cliff Carroll	1884	Providence	NL	118
Tommy Tucker	1887	Baltimore	AA	144
Tommy Tucker	1888	Baltimore	AA	149
Tommy Tucker	1889	Baltimore	AA	196
Walt Wilmot	1894	Chicago	NL	197
Buck Weaver	1920	Chicago	AL	208
Frankie Frisch	1921	New York	NL	211
Frankie Frisch	1923	New York	NL	223
Pete Rose	1973	Cincinnati	NL	230
Willie Wilson	1980	Kansas City	AL	230

Note: Some sources contend that Fred Lewis, who collected 106 hits in 1884, was a switch-hitter, but the preponderance of evidence is that he batted lefty just a few times as an experiment; Monte Ward did the same thing in 1888 from the right side. Prior to Wilmot, the NL record belonged to George Davis, with 195 hits for New York in 1893. The AL record prior to Wilson belonged not to Mickey Mantle, as most would expect, but to John Anderson, who set the mark way back in 1901 with 190 hits for Milwaukee.

Most Hits by a Switch-Hitter, Season, Each Position

	NAME	TEAM	YEAR	HITS	NAME	TEAM	YEAR	HITS
	National League				*American League*			
1B	Pete Rose	Philadelphia	1979	208	John Anderson	Milwaukee	1901	190
2B	Frankie Frisch	New York	1923	223	Carlos Baerga	Cleveland	1992	205
3B	Pete Rose	Cincinnati	1976	215	Buck Weaver	Chicago	1920	208
SS	Garry Templeton	St. Louis	1979	211	Tony Fernandez	Toronto	1986	213
LF	Pete Rose	Cincinnati	1973	230	Roy White	New York	1970	180
					Miguel Dilone	Cleveland	1980	180
CF	Willie McGee	St. Louis	1985	216	Willie Wilson	Kansas City	1980	230
RF	Pete Rose	Cincinnati	1969	218	Ruben Sierra	Texas	1991	203
C	Ted Simmons	St. Louis	1975	193	Ted Simmons	Milwaukee	1983	185
P	Kid Nichols	Boston	1894	50	Jack Coombs	Philadelphia	1911	45

Tommy Tucker, the first switch-hitter to win a batting title. He copped the AA bat crown in 1889. Tucker also at one point held the season records for both the most hits and the most home runs by a bothway bammer.

In a Pinch

1. **The game's foremost pinch hitters generally also used to be decent position players—at least early in their careers. Now some pinch-hitting specialists hardly even need to own a glove. Chip Hale, for one, by trade a second baseman, in 1997 completed his seventh season in the majors with 575 career at bats in 333 games, just 64 of which saw him at the keystone sack. What deluxe pinch hitter played in 733 games over a 12-year period from 1973 to 1984 but took the field in only 104 contests?**

   A)   The closest he came to a regular job was in 1980 when he DH'd in 86 games.

   B)   He was Cleveland's hitting coach when Albert Belle was a rookie.

   C)   He led both major leagues at various times in pinch hits.

   D)   He ranks fourth on the list for most career pinch hits.

   E)   Prior to 1995 he held the record for the most pinch hits in a season.

2. **What lefty swinger's .284 career PH batting average leads all pitchers with at least 100 career pinch at bats?**

   A)   He's in the Hall of Fame.

   B)   He's the most recent player to be an opening-game starter for the same team at two different positions, one of which was pitcher.

   C)   He hit 37 career home runs.

   D)   He made his big league debut in 1941 as a third baseman.

   E)   His entire career was spent with Cleveland.

Highest Career Pinch-Hit BA, Pitcher (Minimum 100 Pinch ABs)

RANK	NAME	YEARS	PH ABS	HITS	BA
1	Bob Lemon	1941–58	109	31	.284
2	Schoolboy Rowe	1933–49	101	28	.277
3	Red Lucas	1923–38	437	114	.261
4	George Uhle	1919–36	169	44	.260
5	Chubby Dean	1936–43	191	49	.257
6	Red Ruffing	1924–47	228	58	.254
7	Dode Criss	1908–11	147	35	.238
8	Dutch Ruether	1917–27	145	34	.2344
	Ray Caldwell	1910–21	154	36	.2337
10	Clarence Mitchell	1911–32	145	31	.214

Note: BAs are carried out to four decimal points where ties would otherwise exist.

3. **Ty Cobb was hit for three times during his career. Each instance came in 1906, and all three times his sub delivered. The last occasion, on September 17, resulted in a triple by the first pitcher to collect 100 career pinch at bats. Who is this five-time 20-game winner?**
   - A) He tied for the AL lead in pinch hits in 1904.
   - B) He was 0-for-2 as a pinch hitter in the 1909 World Series.
   - C) He threw a no-hitter in 1912 on his birthday.
   - D) At the time he retired, he held the Tigers record for the most career victories.
   - E) He is the only 20th century hurler to lose 20 games for a pennant winner.

4. **At age 36, he was a putrid 9-for-51 (.176) in pinch roles after the 1956 season, but he finished six years later with 93 career pinch hits and a PH average just a shade below .300. Can you name him?**
   - A) As a White Sox rookie in 1941, he was 0-for-4 in pinch roles.
   - B) His only taste of World Series action came in 1954.
   - C) He retired with 1,700 career hits.
   - D) He holds the record for the most consecutive pinch hits.
   - E) He and the Kansas City catcher who led the AL in 1979 with 121 walks share the same initials.

5. **The first man to parlay a knack for pinch hitting into a substantial career, he put in seven seasons between 1909 and 1918, seldom getting more than one at bat a game. Name this outfielder–first baseman.**
   - A) His initials match those of a Hall of Fame gardener of the same era.
   - B) In 1918, his final season, he topped the AL in PH ABs.
   - C) As a rookie in 1909, he led the NL in pinch hits and played in his only Series.
   - D) His 57 career pinch hits and 240 pinch ABs were both record highs when he departed in 1918.
   - E) He and the Tigers outfielder who won four AL batting crowns in the 1920s also share the same initials.

6. **Duke Farrell, the finest pinch hitter of his day, played in the first 20th century World Series in 1903, but he was not the first to garner a pinch hit in a Series game. Do you know who was?**
   - A) He delivered while batting for Charlie O'Leary in Game One of the 1908 classic.
   - B) Although only in the third season of a 10-year ML career in 1908, he never collected another pinch hit.
   - C) Two days after rapping the first Series pinch hit, he went the whole way behind the plate in Game Three.
   - D) He also went the whole way behind the plate for a different AL team in Game One of the 1910 World Series.
   - E) Even nonbaseball people think of his first name every April 15.

7. **What batsman notched the first pinch hit in All-Star play some four years after he became the first future Hall of Famer to homer in his initial big league at bat?**
   - A) He notched the AL's fourth and final RBI in the first All-Star clash when he singled to center off Lon Warneke to score Joe Cronin.
   - B) His lone taste of World Series action consisted of three pinch-hit appearances for the loser of the 1940 fray.
   - C) He was the most important batter Dizzy Dean faced in All-Star competition.
   - D) He hailed from Snohomish, Washington.
   - E) Some 26 years after he rapped two pinch hits for Cleveland in 1930, his son and namesake garnered two pinch hits in his rookie season with the Tribe.

8. **Among players with 200 career PH at bats, to date he alone retired with a career pinch batting average of .300+.**

   A)   In pinch roles he was 76-for-253 to finish at .300 on the nose.

   B)   He died of a heart attack at age 40 in 1938.

   C)   In 1927 he hit .359 and had 114 RBI.

   D)   He had a .325 career BA in 12 seasons with three AL teams.

   E)   A chronic weight problem, plus the presence of Cobb, Heilmann, and Manush, relegated him to part-time outfield duty during most of his tenure with the Tigers.

Highest Career BA, Pinch Hitter (Minimum 200 PH ABs)

RANK	NAME	YEARS	PH ABS	HITS	BA
1	Bob Fothergill	1922–33	253	76	.300
2	Dave Philley	1941–62	311	93	.299
3	Manny Mota	1962–82	505	150	.297
4	Rance Mulliniks	1977–92	202	59	.292
5	Terry Puhl	1977–91	211	61	.289
6	Smoky Burgess	1949–67	507	145	.286
7	Ken Griffey Sr.	1973–91	252	71	.282
8	Steve Braun	1971–85	402	113	.281
9	Kevin Bass	1982–95	289	81	.280
10	Rusty Staub	1963–85	358	100	.279

Bob Fothergill, the second man to collect 50 career pinch hits. In 1932 he became the first to compile 60. He was passed shortly thereafter on the career leaders list by pitcher Red Lucas.

9. **Until quite recently, men who made a living as pinch hitters usually maintained respectable batting averages. Who was the first man to collect 200 PH at bats and retire with a sub-.200 pinch batting average?**
   A) He was 40-for-208 (.192) as a pinch hitter.
   B) He spent his entire 10-year career with the same AL team.
   C) In 1948, his only season with 400 ABs, he hit 23 homers for Detroit.
   D) His initials match those of the 1993 World Series MVP.
   E) He and the first man to bag 200 wins in Tigers livery share the same last name.

10. **Name the only man to log at least 10 pinch hits and 100 RBI in the same season.**
   A) He led the AL in pinch hits with 17 two years later.
   B) He had five 100-RBI seasons, all in the AL.
   C) His first pinch hit came with the 1947 Tigers, his last with the 1963 Twins.
   D) His .938 slugging average led all performers on both teams in his lone postseason appearance.
   E) The same year he collected 10 pinch hits and 103 RBI he set the all-time record for the fewest runs scored by anyone with 100 RBI.

11. **In 1996, Willie McGee took over the top BA spot among all players with at least 100 career pinch at bats while Harold Baines pulled into second place. The two swapped slots in 1997 when Baines went 8-for-14 in pinch roles, but McGee then fell out of the top 10 in 1998 with a poor 7-for-39 season. Prior to 1996, the all-time leader was the only retired performer with 100 career pinch at bats to average at least one hit for every three at bats (.333). Who is he?**
   A) He finished exactly at .333 (40-for-120).
   B) All but 2 of his 40 career pinch hits came with Cincinnati.
   C) He came to the Reds after the 1959 season in a trade for Johnny Temple.
   D) He was the Reds' regular first sacker the year they lost the World Series to the Yankees in five games.
   E) His initials are the same as those of the NL leader in pinch hits in 1959 who at one time held the record for most career pinch homers.

Highest Career BA, Pinch Hitter (Minimum 100 PH ABs)

RANK	NAME	YEARS	PH ABS	PHS	BA
1	Harold Baines	1988–	149	50	.336
2	Gordy Coleman	1959–67	120	40	.333
3	Luis Polonia	1987–	127	42	.331
4	Ward Miller	1909–17	110	36	.327
5	Doc Miller	1910–14	120	39	.325
6	Rod Carew	1967–85	124	40	.323
7	Al Kaline	1953–74	115	37	.322
8	Tommy Davis	1959–76	197	63	.320
9	Estel Crabtree	1929–44	116	37	.319
10	Earl Smith	1919–30	129	41	.318

12. **What former Bonus Baby was a weak 27-for-144 (.188) as a pinch hitter after his first 12 seasons but retired with a career .277 pinch batting average when he hit a torrid .348 in his last 181 PH at bats?**
    - A) His 90 career pinch hits all came with the same team.
    - B) He had the best five-year stretch ever by a pinch hitter when he rapped .396 (57-for-144) between 1974 and 1978.
    - C) Prior to 1974 he played on two flag winners.
    - D) His .486 BA in 1974 is a season record among players with at least 30 pinch ABs.
    - E) He garnered his first career pinch hit for the Mets when he was just 18.

13. **Although never a league leader in pinch hits, he owned the most dangerous bat coming off the bench from 1989 through 1992, when he hit .420 (34-for-81) over that span. Name this native New Yorker who once played for the Yankees.**
    - A) He was with the same AL team (not the Yankees) from 1988 until the middle of 1992.
    - B) Never seeing enough action to be a batting title qualifier, he logged 100 hits only in 1988 with Seattle.
    - C) A fine defensive center fielder with excellent speed, he was one of the most underrated players in the majors before he fled to Japan.
    - D) He was traded to Florida for Dave Magadan prior to the 1993 season.
    - E) He has the same initials as the center fielder on the first Cincinnati team to win back-to-back pennants.

14. **The first man in big league history to tag 100 career pinch hits played only 907 games in the majors. Name him.**
    - A) He led the NL four times in pinch hits.
    - B) He was 0-for-17 as a pinch hitter in his finale in 1938 for Pittsburgh.
    - C) Control was his forte—he unleashed just seven wild pitches in 2,542 innings.
    - D) He was nicknamed "Red."
    - E) With Cinci in 1931, he led the NL in both pinch hits and complete games.

Evolution of Career Record for Pinch Hits

NAME	YEARS	R/Y	PHs
Duke Farrell	1888–1905	1904	23
Dode Criss	1908–11	1910	35
Ted Easterly	1909–15	1913	45
Ham Hyatt	1909–18	1914	57
Bob Fothergill	1922–33	1931	76
Red Lucas	1923–38	1933	114
Smoky Burgess	1949–67	1965	145
Manny Mota	1962–82	1979	150

Note: Beginning with Farrell, the first documented player to attain 10 pinch hits. R/Y denotes year set new record; Farrell's year is the last year he collected a pinch hit.

15. **The only player to collect 30 or more PH at bats for 10 consecutive seasons unsurprisingly also holds the record for the most career PH at bats. Who is he?**
    A) What is surprising is that not once during his 17 seasons in the NL did he lead the senior loop in pinch ABs.
    B) Both his first and his last pinch bingles came with Houston.
    C) He played in two World Series with the Phils and also led the NL in pinch hits while a Phil.
    D) His 143 career pinch hits currently rank third on the all-time list.
    E) He has the same initials as a current coholder of the season record for the most RBI by a player with fewer than 350 ABs.

16. **Whose entire postseason career is captured herein: struck out batting for Labine; homered batting for Podres; walked batting for Wills; homered batting for Snider?**
    A) He hit 21 homers for Cleveland in 1961.
    B) He was a running back at Stanford.
    C) He is one of the only two men to bang two pinch homers in a World Series.
    D) He is of Armenian descent.
    E) He and the Rangers' center fielder in 1989 have the same initials.

17. **Among retired players with 10 career pinch hits, Jimmy Reese (15-for-33) has the top batting average at .455; among players with 20 career pinch hits, Duke Farrell (23-for-59) leads at .390. Who is the leader among players with 30 career pinch hits?**
    A) He was 32-for-86 (.372).
    B) Like Farrell, he was a catcher.
    C) He debuted with the Cards in 1912 and finished with the Cards 15 years later.
    D) He was the main backstopper on the first team to participate in four straight 20th century World Series.
    E) He and the first man to catch at least one ML game in 15 consecutive seasons have the same last name.

Highest Career BA, Pinch Hitter (Minimum 30 Pinch Hits)

RANK	NAME	YEARS	ABS	HITS	BA
1	Frank Snyder	1912–27	86	32	.372
2	Duffy Dyer	1968–81	81	30	.370
3	Charlie Moore	1973–87	91	32	.352
4	Tony Oliva	1962–76	86	30	.349
5	Herschel Bennett	1923–27	95	32	.337
6	Harold Baines	1988–	149	50	.336
7	Gordy Coleman	1959–67	120	40	.333
8	Luis Polonia	1987–	127	42	.331
9	Ward Miller	1909–17	110	36	.327
10	Doc Miller	1910–14	120	39	.325

18. **Who has the highest career PH batting average among catchers with 150 pinch plate appearances?**
   A)   He hit .313 (46-for-147).
   B)   His top season in pinch duty was 1957 when he was 11-for-27 for Washington.
   C)   As a rook in 1952, he grabbed the Browns catching job and hit .286 in 119 games.
   D)   His nickname was "Scrap Iron."
   E)   He was the first bespectacled big league catcher.

Highest Career Pinch-Hit BA, Catcher (Minimum 100 Pinch ABs)

RANK	NAME	YEARS	PH ABS	PHS	BA
1	Earl Smith	1919–30	129	41	.318
2	Clint Courtney	1951–61	147	46	.313
3	Spud Davis	1928–45	146	45	.308
4	Jack Hiatt	1964–72	101	30	.297
5	Joe Torre	1960–77	124	36	.290
6	Manny Sanguillen	1967–80	160	46	.288
7	Smoky Burgess	1949–67	507	145	.2857
8	Terry Kennedy	1978–91	112	32	.286
9	Johnny Edwards	1961–74	104	29	.27885
10	Ron Hassey	1978–91	165	46	.27879

Note: Torre also played other positions. BAs are carried out to four or five decimal points where ties would otherwise exist.

19. **Solly Hemus, with a .164 batting average (31-for-189), is the only preexpansion player to post a sub-.175 career average off the bench with at least 150 at bats. Who subsequently broke Hemus's record when he hit just .117 in 180 career PH at bats?**
   A)   His 5-for-30 (.167) in his 1974 finale proved to be his top pinch performance.
   B)   San Diego fans groaned when they saw him deliver just two pinch hits in 35 ABs for their Pads in 1973.
   C)   In 1970, his lone year as a regular, he hit .245 for the Pads with 12 homers but had just 35 RBI.
   D)   An outfielder and sometimes first baseman, he was born in Panama and debuted with the 1963 Astros.
   E)   He had the same first name as the first pitcher to toil 10 consecutive seasons with the Red Sox.

20. **Among players with 200 career PH at bats, whose .176 mark is the lowest?**
   A)   He was 49-for-278, all in the AL.
   B)   In 1953, his first pro season, he hit an astounding .432 for McAlester in the Sooner State League.
   C)   He hit .303 in 117 games for the 1966 world champs.
   D)   His initials match those of the man with the highest career BA of any righty hitter in the 20th century eligible for the Hall of Fame but not as yet enshrined.
   E)   He and the owner of the top BA among players with at least 85 career pinch ABs have the same last name.

Players with a Sub-.200 Career Pinch-Hit BA (Minimum 200 Pinch ABs)

RANK	NAME	YEARS	PH ABS	PHS	BA
1	Russ Snyder	1959–70	278	49	.176
2	Bill Robinson	1966–83	222	40	.180
3	Jim Hickman	1962–74	241	45	.187
4	Don Mincher	1960–72	221	42	.1900
5	Hawk Taylor	1957–70	205	39	.1902
6	Pat Mullin	1940–53	208	40	.1916
7	Cap Peterson	1962–69	240	46	.1923
8	Marty Keough	1956–66	243	47	.193
9	Rick Monday	1966–84	227	44	.194
10	Carl Sawatski	1948–63	209	41	.196
11	Dick Schofield	1953–71	247	49	.198

Note: BAs are carried out to four decimal points where ties would otherwise exist.

21. **What pre–World War II slugger was the first man to amass at least 10 pinch home runs?**
    A) He either won or shared four NL home run crowns.
    B) At one time he held the NL career record for the most homers by a lefty hitter.
    C) In 1930, his final season, he was 8-for-16 as a pinch hitter with the Phils.
    D) He is the oldest player in NL history to win a home run crown.
    E) He and the 1922 AL home run king had the same last name.

22. **Gates Brown currently holds the record for the most career pinch home runs in AL competition with 16. Whose record did he break?**
    A) Brown's predecessor had 12 pinch blasts.
    B) Prior to him the AL record holder was Gus Zernial with 10.
    C) He and Zernial were teammates in 1957 on the Kansas City A's.
    D) His first pinch hit came in 1952 with the Yankees.
    E) In 1958 he set the Kansas City A's club record when he creamed 38 home runs.

23. **The current record for the most career pinch home runs belongs to Cliff Johnson with 20. Who did Johnson surmount to claim the top spot?**
    A) Of his 116 career pinch hits, 18 were circuit clouts.
    B) In the only season he had 400 ABs, he hit .312 for the 1958 Reds.
    C) When he left the majors at the close of the 1966 season, he was second only to Smoky Burgess in career pinch hits.
    D) His initials are the same as those of the second sacker on the only NL team to lose three straight LCSes.
    E) He and one half of an 1884 pitching tandem that was the first to feature two 30-game winners have the same last name.

Leaders in Career Pinch HRs

RANK	NAME	YEARS	PHS	PH/HRS
1	Cliff Johnson	1972–86	68	20
2	Jerry Lynch	1954–66	116	18
3	Willie McCovey	1959–80	66	16
	Gates Brown	1963–75	107	16
	Smoky Burgess	1949–67	145	16
6	George Crowe	1952–61	76	14
7	Joe Adcock	1950–66	39	12
	Bob Cerv	1951–62	55	12
	Jose Morales	1973–84	123	12
	Graig Nettles	1967–88	48	12

Season Pinch-Hitting Leaders, 1891–1998

Documented season league leaders in pinch hits, pinch hit at bats, and pinch hit batting average, beginning with 1891, the first year a manager was permitted to use a pinch hitter at any point in a game and for any player, not just for a player who had been injured. The hit leader is listed first, followed by the batting average leader and at bats leader, with the leading totals designated in **bold**. A batting average leader must have at least half the number of pinch hits compiled by the leader in pinch hits to qualify; whenever the leader in pinch hits had more than twice as many hits as the runner-up, he is also deemed the batting leader. Pinch hitters who played in both major leagues are listed only when their aggregate totals exceed those of either league leader that year.

		NAME	TEAM	PHS	ABS	BA
1891	National League	Bobby Lowe	Boston	0	1	.000
		Bob Caruthers	Brooklyn	0	1	.000
		Amos Rusie	New York	0	1	.000
		Piggy Ward	Pittsburgh	0	1	.000
	American Association	Jack Stivetts	St. Louis	1	**3**	**.333**
1892	National League	Jack Doyle	Cleveland	1	1	**1.000**
		Connie Mack	Pittsburgh	1	1	**1.000**
		Tom Daly	Brooklyn	1	1	**1.000**
		Charlie Reilly	Philadelphia	1	2	.500
		Frank Killen	Pittsburgh	1	**4**	.250
1893		John Sharrott	Philadelphia	2	4	**.500**
		Jake Stenzel	Pittsburgh	1	**6**	.167

		NAME	TEAM	PHS	ABS	BA
1894		Frank Connaughton	Boston	2	2	**1.000**
		Tom Parrott	Cincinnati	2	3	.667
		Mike Grady	Philadelphia	2	3	.667
		Kid Gleason	St. Louis/Baltimore	2	4	.500
		Jack Stivetts	Boston	2	5	.400
1895		Tuck Turner	Philadelphia	2	4	**.500**
		Win Mercer	Washington	2	5	.400
		Varney Anderson	Washington	1	5	.200
1896		Doggie Miller	Louisville	6	9	.667
		Jack Stivetts	Boston	4	5	**.800**
		Duke Farrell	New York/Washington	4	10	.400
		Ducky Holmes	Louisville	3	10	.300
1897		Duke Farrell	Washington	8	14	**.571**
1898		Duke Farrell	Washington	5	10	.500
		Farmer Vaughn	Cincinnati	4	6	**.667**
		Jack Clements	St. Louis	1	12	.083
1899		Bid McPhee	Cincinnati	3	5	**.600**
		Ginger Beaumont	Pittsburgh	3	6	.500
		Art Madison	Pittsburgh	3	6	.500
		Pearce Chiles	Philadelphia	2	10	.200
1900		Mike Donlin	St. Louis	4	10	**.400**
		Shad Barry	Boston	3	14	.214
1901		Duke Farrell	Brooklyn	3	4	**.750**
		Bill Dinneen	Boston	2	11	.182
	American League	Nixey Callahan	Chicago	3	10	.300
		Ossee Schreckengost	Boston	3	9	.333
		Tom Leahy	Milwaukee/Philadelphia	2	3	**.667**
		Billy Friel	Milwaukee	2	3	**.667**
1902	National League	Frank Kitson	Brooklyn	3	7	**.429**
		Mike O'Neill	St. Louis	1	12	.083
	American League	Harry Gleason	Boston	3	8	.375
		Ollie Pickering	Cleveland	2	2	**1.000**
		Nixey Callahan	Chicago	2	12	.167

		NAME	TEAM	PHS	ABS	BA
1903	National League	Jack Dunleavy	St. Louis	4	9	.444
		Tom McCreery	Brooklyn/Boston	2	2	**1.000**
	American League	Jake Stahl	Boston	5	11	.455
		Danny Hoffman	Philadelphia	5	11	.455
		Nixey Callahan	Chicago	3	5	**.600**
1904	National League	Frank Roth	Philadelphia	4	12	.333
		Watty Lee	Pittsburgh	2	3	**.667**
		Doc Gessler	Brooklyn	2	12	.167
	American League	Jesse Tannehill	New York	2	10	.200
		Deacon McGuire	New York	2	2	**1.000**
		John Ganzel	New York	2	4	.500
1905	National League	Sammy Strang	New York	8	14	**.571**
		Otto Krueger	Philadelphia	3	16	.188
	American League	Ed McFarland	Chicago	4	9	.444
		Ike Van Zandt	St. Louis	4	18	.222
		Ducky Holmes	Chicago	2	3	**.667**
1906	National League	Fred Clarke	Pittsburgh	5	7	**.714**
		Johnny Lush	Philadelphia	1	14	.071
	American League	Howard Wakefield	Washington	9	16	**.563**
		Joe Yeager	New York	3	18	.167
1907	National League	Fred Osborn	Philadelphia	7	19	**.368**
		Sammy Strang	New York	4	19	.211
	American League	John Hoey	Boston	8	18	**.444**
		Charlie Hickman	Washington/Chicago	4	22	.182
1908	National League	Ed Phelps	Pittsburgh	7	12	**.583**
		Ernie Courtney	Philadelphia	3	17	.176
	American League	Dode Criss	St. Louis	12	41	**.293**
1909	National League	Ham Hyatt	Pittsburgh	9	37	.243
		Ginger Beaumont	Boston	5	14	**.357**
	American League	Dode Criss	St. Louis	7	24	.292
		Al Orth	New York	5	13	**.385**
		Charlie Hemphill	New York	6	24	.250
1910	National League	Ward Miller	Cincinnati	11	40	.275
		Al Burch	Brooklyn	7	18	**.389**
	American League	Dode Criss	St. Louis	7	44	.159
		Earl Gardner	New York	4	14	**.286**

		NAME	TEAM	PHS	ABS	BA
1911	National League	Patsy Flaherty	Boston	6	17	**.353**
		Beals Becker	New York	3	**26**	.115
	American League	Dode Criss	St. Louis	9	**38**	.237
		Frank Lange	Chicago	8	19	**.421**
1912	National League	Moose McCormick	New York	11	**30**	.367
		Roger Bresnahan	St. Louis	7	14	**.500**
	American League	Ted Easterly	Cleveland/Chicago	13	**30**	**.433**
1913	National League	Doc Miller	Philadelphia	20	**56**	.357
	American League	Jack Lelivelt	New York/Cleveland	12	35	.343
		Germany Schaefer	Washington	11	21	**.524**
		Ted Easterly	Chicago	8	**37**	.216
1914	National League	Ham Hyatt	Pittsburgh	14	**58**	.241
		Josh Devore	Philadelphia/Boston	11	25	**.440**
	American League	Wally Rehg	Boston	10	**36**	.278
		Ernie Walker	St. Louis	10	29	**.345**
	Federal League	Grover Hartley	St. Louis	8	24	.333
		Skipper Roberts	Pittsburgh/Chicago	8	29	.276
		Al Shaw	Brooklyn	5	7	**.714**
		Del Young	Buffalo	7	**37**	.189
1915	National League	Dan Costello	Pittsburgh	14	**46**	.304
		Red Murray	New York/Chicago	8	17	**.471**
	American League	Marty Kavanagh	Detroit	10	20	**.500**
		Ray Caldwell	New York	9	**33**	.273
	Federal League	Ed Lennox	Pittsburgh	14	**45**	.311
		Ted Easterly	Kansas City	8	20	**.400**
1916	National League	Art Butler	St. Louis	13	**54**	**.241**
	American League	Sam Crawford	Detroit	8	15	.533
		Les Nunamaker	New York	6	11	**.545**
		Marty Kavanagh	Detroit/Cleveland	7	**46**	.152
1917	National League	Tommy Clarke	Cincinnati	9	**27**	.333
		Harry Wolter	Chicago	7	16	**.438**
	American League	Bill Rumler	St. Louis	16	**71**	.225
		Eddie Murphy	Chicago	12	32	**.375**
1918	National League	Mike Fitzgerald	Philadelphia	8	**30**	.267
		Bill Hinchman	Pittsburgh	6	19	**.316**
	American League	Jack Graney	Cleveland	7	18	**.389**
		Ham Hyatt	New York	4	**21**	.190

		NAME	TEAM	PHS	ABS	BA
1919	National League	Joe Schultz	St. Louis	8	**31**	.258
		Vern Clemons	St. Louis	5	10	**.500**
	American League	Eddie Murphy	Chicago	8	21	.381
		Fred McMullin	Chicago	4	8	**.500**
		Ray Demmitt	St. Louis	6	**27**	.222
1920	National League	Gavvy Cravath	Philadelphia	12	34	**.353**
		Fred Nicholson	Pittsburgh	12	**38**	.316
	American League	Sammy Hale	Detroit	17	**52**	.327
		Josh Billings	St. Louis	9	22	**.409**
1921	National League	Babe Twombley	Chicago	15	**38**	.395
		Bevo LeBourveau	Philadelphia	9	16	**.563**
	American League	Chick Shorten	Detroit	9	**37**	.243
		Paul Johnson	Philadelphia	7	14	**.500**
1922	National League	Rube Bressler	Cincinnati	13	**43**	.302
		Lew Fonseca	Cincinnati	8	18	**.444**
	American League	Tris Speaker	Cleveland	9	17	**.529**
		Danny Clark	Detroit	8	**36**	.222
1923	National League	Jack Bentley	New York	10	20	**.500**
		Frank Snyder	New York	5	8	**.625**
		Earl Smith	New York/Boston	6	**35**	.171
	American League	Amos Strunk	Chicago	12	**39**	.308
		Bobby Veach	Detroit	8	22	**.364**
1924	National League	Earl Smith	Boston/Pittsburgh	10	21	**.476**
		Bill Terry	New York	9	**38**	.237
	American League	George Uhle	Cleveland	11	26	.423
		Joe Bush	New York	8	16	**.500**
		Phil Todt	Boston	4	**30**	.133
1925	National League	Jack Bentley	New York	9	**28**	.321
		Russ Wrightstone	Philadelphia	6	7	**.857**
		Cotton Tierney	Brooklyn	7	**28**	.250
	American League	Walt French	Philadelphia	13	37	.324
		Herschel Bennett	St. Louis	9	16	**.563**
		Tex Vache	Boston	10	**49**	.204

		NAME	TEAM	PHS	ABS	BA
1926	National League	Chick Tolson	Chicago	14	40	.350
		Mel Ott	New York	9	24	.375
		Joe Kelly	Chicago	9	24	.375
	American League	Herschel Bennett	St. Louis	12	28	.429
		Johnny Neun	Detroit	12	42	.286
1927	National League	Danny Clark	St. Louis	12	40	.300
		Jack Fournier	Boston	8	19	.421
		Mel Ott	New York	11	46	.239
	American League	Eddie Collins	Philadelphia	12	34	.353
		Chick Galloway	Philadelphia	6	9	.667
1928	National League	Joe Harris	Pittsburgh/Brooklyn	9	42	.214
		Jack Smith	Boston	9	25	.360
		Pid Purdy	Cincinnati	6	8	.750
	American League	Guy Sturdy	St. Louis	10	44	.227
		Carl Reynolds	Chicago	6	10	.600
1929	National League	Red Lucas	Cincinnati	13	42	.310
		Harvey Hendrick	Brooklyn	7	13	.538
		Pat Crawford	New York	10	44	.227
	American League	Bob Fothergill	Detroit	19	53	.283
		Ken Williams	Boston	10	30	.333
1930	National League	Red Lucas	Cincinnati	14	39	.359
		Cy Williams	Philadelphia	8	16	.500
		Danny Taylor	Chicago	7	14	.500
	American League	Bibb Falk	Cleveland	13	34	.382
		Jimmy Reese	New York	10	20	.500
1931	National League	Red Lucas	Cincinnati	15	60	.250
		Ethan Allen	New York	8	14	.571
	American League	Bibb Falk	Cleveland	14	43	.326
		Smead Jolley	Chicago	14	30	.467
		Tom Winsett	Boston	11	52	.212
1932	National League	Sam Leslie	New York	22	72	.306
	American League	Dave Harris	Washington	14	43	.326
		Billy Rhiel	Detroit	13	27	.481
1933	National League	Harry McCurdy	Philadelphia	15	52	.288
		Red Lucas	Cincinnati	13	41	.317
	American League	Jo-Jo White	Detroit	10	26	.385
		Bing Miller	Philadelphia	7	30	.233

		NAME	TEAM	PHS	ABS	BA
1934	National League	Pat Crawford	St. Louis	11	43	.256
		Harry Danning	New York	8	16	.500
	American League	Bing Miller	Philadelphia	10	33	.303
		Frenchy Bordagaray	Chicago	8	12	.667
1935	National League	Joe Mowry	Boston	10	30	.333
		Babe Phelps	Brooklyn	6	12	.500
		Jim Bottomley	Cincinnati	5	10	.500
		Ernie Lombardi	Cincinnati	8	36	.222
	American League	Bing Miller	Boston	13	43	.302
		Gee Walker	Detroit	7	14	.500
1936	National League	Sid Gautreaux	Brooklyn	16	55	.291
		Jimmy Ripple	New York	9	19	.474
	American League	Ed Coleman	St. Louis	20	62	.323
		Chubby Dean	Philadelphia	13	34	.382
1937	National League	Red Lucas	Pittsburgh	9	37	.243
		Les Scarsella	Cincinnati	9	27	.333
		Johnny Moore	Philadelphia	7	20	.350
	American League	Goose Goslin	Detroit	9	29	.310
		Larry Rosenthal	Chicago	9	29	.310
		Lynn Nelson	Philadelphia	9	38	.237
		Ethan Allen	St. Louis	8	23	.348
		Jim Bottomley	St. Louis	7	38	.184
1938	National League	Frenchy Bordagaray	St. Louis	20	43	.465
		Harl Maggert	Boston	10	43	.233
	American League	Taffy Wright	Washington	13	39	.333
1939	National League	Chuck Klein	Philadelphia/Pittsburgh	11	25	.440
		Jimmy Ripple	New York/Brooklyn	9	38	.237
	American League	Lou Finney	Philadelphia/Boston	13	40	.325
		Chubby Dean	Philadelphia	10	26	.385
1940	National League	Johnny McCarthy	New York	11	43	.256
		Johnny Rucker	New York	8	20	.400
	American League	Chet Laabs	St. Louis	14	35	.400
		Al Simmons	Philadelphia	8	16	.500
		Odell Hale	Cleveland	8	40	.200
	Both	Joe Gallagher	Browns/Dodgers	12	42	.286

		NAME	TEAM	PHS	ABS	BA
1941	National League	Debs Garms	Pittsburgh	10	31	.323
		Lew Riggs	Brooklyn	10	29	.345
		Bud Stewart	Pittsburgh	10	25	**.400**
		Ken O'Dea	New York	9	**42**	.214
	American League	Dee Miles	Philadelphia	15	**45**	**.333**
1942	National League	Dom Dallesandro	Chicago	9	26	.346
		Max Macon	Brooklyn	5	11	**.444**
		Rip Russell	Chicago	5	**31**	.161
	American League	Charlie Gehringer	Detroit	11	**38**	.289
		Bob Harris	Detroit	6	15	**.400**
1943	National League	Schoolboy Rowe	Philadelphia	15	**49**	.306
		Paul Waner	Brooklyn	10	21	**.476**
	American League	Joe Cronin	Boston	18	42	**.429**
		Rip Radcliff	Detroit	11	**44**	.250
1944	National League	Lou Novikoff	Chicago	12	39	.308
		Spud Davis	Pittsburgh	8	17	**.471**
		Al Rubeling	Pittsburgh	9	**41**	.220
	American League	Bill LeFebvre	Washington	10	29	.345
		Russ Derry	New York	5	7	**.714**
		Jimmy Grant	Cleveland	5	**32**	.156
	Both	Paul Waner	Dodgers/Yankees	13	**45**	.289
1945	National League	Rene Monteagudo	Philadelphia	18	**52**	.346
		Debs Garms	St. Louis	10	26	**.385**
	American League	Joe Schultz Jr.	St. Louis	11	**35**	.314
1946	National League	Jimmy Brown	Pittsburgh	7	20	.350
		Chuck Workman	Boston/Pittsburgh	7	24	.292
		Bob Scheffing	Chicago	7	19	**.368**
		Babe Young	New York	5	**32**	.156
	American League	Joe Schultz Jr.	St. Louis	10	23	.435
		Bob Dillinger	St. Louis	8	18	**.444**
		George Binks	Washington	7	**35**	.200
	Both	Jimmy Wasdell	Philadelphia/Cleveland	10	**36**	.278

		NAME	TEAM	PHS	ABS	BA
1947	National League	Frank McCormick	Boston/Philadelphia	13	36	.361
		Arky Vaughn	Brooklyn	10	26	**.385**
		Charlie Gilbert	Philadelphia	9	**40**	.225
	American League	Bobby Brown	New York	9	27	.333
		Doc Cramer	Detroit	9	33	.273
		Rusty Peters	St. Louis	6	11	**.545**
		Joe Schultz Jr.	St. Louis	7	**38**	.184
1948	National League	Johnny McCarthy	New York	13	**45**	.289
		Johnny Hopp	Pittsburgh	7	14	**.500**
	American League	Hal Peck	Cleveland	8	30	.267
		Bob Kennedy	Chicago/Cleveland	6	12	**.500**
		Yogi Berra	New York	5	10	**.500**
		Joe Schultz Jr.	St. Louis	7	**37**	.189
1949	National League	Dixie Walker	Pittsburgh	13	40	.325
		Jimmy Bloodworth	Cincinnati	8	14	**.571**
		Don Mueller	New York	7	**42**	.167
	American League	Buddy Lewis	Washington	9	24	**.375**
		Whitey Platt	St. Louis	7	**34**	.206
1950	National League	Dick Whitman	Philadelphia	12	39	.308
		Walker Cooper	Cincinnati/Boston	6	12	**.500**
		Nanny Fernandez	Pittsburgh	6	12	**.500**
		Eddie Kazak	St. Louis	10	**42**	.238
	American League	Gordy Goldsberry	Chicago	12	**39**	.308
		Jim Delsing	New York/St. Louis	8	24	**.333**
1951	National League	Bob Addis	Boston	12	36	.333
		Phil Cavarretta	Chicago	12	33	**.364**
		Hank Edwards	Brooklyn/Cincinnati	8	**37**	.216
	American League	Charlie Keller	Detroit	9	**38**	.237
		Bud Stewart	Chicago	9	31	.290
		Johnny Mize	New York	9	21	.429
		Floyd Baker	Chicago	9	33	.273
		Mike McCormick	Washington	7	15	**.467**
1952	National League	Peanuts Lowrey	St. Louis	13	27	**.481**
	American League	Johnny Mize	New York	10	48	.208
		Tom Wright	St. Louis/Chicago	10	34	.294
		Earl Rapp	St. Louis/Washington	10	**54**	.185
		Gene Bearden	St. Louis	7	11	**.636**
	Both	Ted Wilson	ChiSox/Giants	12	**48**	.250*

* Wilson led the NL in pinch-hit ABS.

		NAME	TEAM	PHS	ABS	BA
1953	National League	Peanuts Lowrey	St. Louis	22	59	.373
		Bobby Hofman	New York	13	34	**.382**
	American League	Johnny Mize	New York	19	61	.311
		Johnny Pesky	Detroit	12	30	**.400**
1954	National League	Joe Frazier	St. Louis	20	62	.323
		Dusty Rhodes	New York	15	45	**.333**
	American League	Eddie Robinson	New York	15	49	.306
		Enos Slaughter	New York	11	31	**.355**
1955	National League	Frank Baumholtz	Chicago	15	37	**.405**
		Bill Taylor	New York	15	60	.250
	American League	Enos Slaughter	New York/Kansas City	16	42	.381
		Elmer Valo	Kansas City	14	31	**.457**
		Dale Mitchell	Cleveland	13	45	.289
1956	National League	Frank Baumholtz	Philadelphia	14	52	.269
		Ed Bailey	Cincinnati	8	13	**.615**
		Bob Skinner	Pittsburgh	9	54	.167
	American League	Ron Northey	Chicago	15	39	**.385**
		Ernie Oravetz	Washington	11	49	.224
1957	National League	Jim Bolger	Chicago	17	48	.354
		Joe Cunningham	St. Louis	11	29	**.379**
	American League	Julio Becquer	Washington	18	65	.277
		Dave Philley	Chicago/Detroit	12	29	**.414**
1958	National League	Dave Philley	Philadelphia	18	44	.409
		Bob Bowman	Philadelphia	13	31	**.419**
		Chuck Tanner	Chicago	12	53	.226
	American League	Gus Zernial	Detroit	15	38	**.395**
		Enos Slaughter	New York	13	48	.271
1959	National League	George Crowe	Cincinnati	17	63	.270
		Earl Averill	Chicago	10	25	**.400**
	American League	Julio Becquer	Washington	12	56	.214
		John Romano	Chicago	8	13	**.615**
1960	National League	Jerry Lynch	Cincinnati	19	66	.288
		Willie Jones	Cincinnati	10	27	**.370**
	American League	Bob Hale	Cleveland	19	63	.302
		Vic Wertz	Boston	10	18	**.556**

		NAME	TEAM	PHS	ABS	BA
1961	National League	Jerry Lynch	Cincinnati	19	47	**.404**
		Bob Will	Chicago	11	**52**	.212
	American League	Dave Philley	Baltimore	24	**72**	.333
		Don Dillard	Cleveland	15	35	**.429**
	Both	Elmer Valo	Minneapolis/Philadelphia	13	72	.181
1962	National League	Red Schoendienst	St. Louis	22	**72**	.306
		Lee Walls	Los Angeles	13	27	**.481**
	American League	Vic Wertz	Detroit	17	53	.321
		Dick Williams	Baltimore	13	31	**.419**
		Joe Hicks	Washington	9	**61**	.148
1963	National League	Merritt Ranew	Chicago	17	41	.415
		Charlie James	St. Louis	10	18	**.556**
		Matty Alou	San Francisco	8	**45**	.178
	American League	Dick Williams	Boston	16	48	.333
		George Alusik	Kansas City	9	19	**.474**
		Bob Sadowski	Los Angeles	12	**50**	.240
1964	National League	Ty Cline	Milwaukee	14	40	.350
		Donn Clendenon	Pittsburgh	7	15	**.467**
		Cap Peterson	San Francisco	12	**55**	.218
	American League	Bob Johnson	Baltimore	15	45	.333
		Willie Smith	Los Angeles	10	23	**.435**
1965	National League	Bob Skinner	St. Louis	15	47	.319
		Manny Mota	Pittsburgh	11	32	**.344**
		Jesse Gonder	New York/Milwaukee	13	**52**	.250
	American League	Smoky Burgess	Chicago	20	65	**.308**
	Both	Gene Freese	Pittsburgh/ChiSox	12	31	**.387**
1966	National League	Chuck Hiller	New York	15	45	.333
		Ron Swoboda	New York	8	19	**.421**
		Doug Clemens	Philadelphia	12	**49**	.245
		Jerry Lynch	Pittsburgh	10	**49**	.204
	American League	Smoky Burgess	Chicago	21	66	.318
		Tim Talton	Kansas City	10	25	**.400**

		NAME	TEAM	PHS	ABS	BA
1967	National League	Manny Jiminez	Pittsburgh	12	42	.286
		Bob Johnson	New York	12	31	.387*
		Doug Clemens	Philadelphia	11	54	.204
	American League	Dalton Jones	Boston	13	47	.277
		Rich Reese	Minnesota	13	41	.317
		Jimmie Hall	California	8	14	.571
		Smoky Burgess	Chicago	8	60	.133

* Johnson was also 1-for-3 in 1967 as a pinch hitter with Baltimore, AL, giving him a composite .382 pinch average (13-for-34) and a tie for the ML lead in pinch hits with 13.

		NAME	TEAM	PHS	ABS	BA
1968	National League	Fred Whitfield	Cincinnati	11	46	.239
		Rick Auerbach	Cincinnati	7	13	.538
		Manny Jiminez	Pittsburgh	10	53	.189
	American League	Gates Brown	Detroit	18	39	.462
		Leon Wagner	Cleveland/Chicago	11	46	.239
1969	National League	Jose Pagan	Pittsburgh	19	42	.452
		Fred Whitfield	Cincinnati	8	51	.157
	American League	Pete Ward	Chicago	17	46	.370
		Richie Scheinblum	Cleveland	14	54	.259
1970	National League	Vic Davalillo	St. Louis	24	73	.329
		Jim Fairey	Montreal	14	37	.378
	American League	Tito Francona	Oakland/Milwaukee	15	64	.234
		Dalton Jones	Detroit	11	29	.379
1971	National League	Bob Burda	St. Louis	14	48	.292
		Willie Crawford	Los Angeles	8	19	.421
		Jimmy Stewart	Cincinnati	11	48	.229
	American League	Gomer Hodge	Cleveland	16	68	.235
		Rich McKinney	Chicago	11	21	.524
1972	National League	Jim Howarth	San Francisco	13	39	.333
		Tom Hutton	Philadelphia	8	19	.421
		Jim Fairey	Montreal	10	55	.182
	American League	Felipe Alou	New York	10	29	.345
		Al Kaline	Detroit	10	24	.417
		Gonzalo Marquez	Oakland	7	16	.438
		Steve Hovley	Kansas City	9	37	.243

		NAME	TEAM	PHS	ABS	BA
1973	National League	Mike Rogodzinski	Philadelphia	16	47	.340
		Dave Winfield	San Diego	8	17	**.471**
		Ken Boswell	New York	12	**51**	.235
	American League	Wilson Llenas	California	16	**56**	**.286**
1974	National League	Ed Kranepool	New York	17	35	**.486**
		Manny Mota	Los Angeles	15	**53**	.283
	American League	Gates Brown	Detroit	16	**53**	.302
		Bob Hansen	Milwaukee	14	34	**.412**
1975	National League	Jose Morales	Montreal	15	51	.294
		Jay Johnstone	Philadelphia	10	25	**.400**
		Rod Gilbreath	Atlanta	10	25	**.400**
		Tony Taylor	Philadelphia	12	**54**	.222
	American League	Jim Holt	Oakland	10	**43**	.233
		Walt Williams	New York	10	31	.323
		Rico Carty	Cleveland	6	8	**.750**
1976	National League	Jose Morales	Montreal	25	**78**	.321
		Bruce Boisclair	New York	12	21	**.571**
	American League	Ken McMullen	Oakland	9	31	.290
		Ben Oglivie	Detroit	9	**38**	.237
		Steve Braun	Minnesota	5	9	**.556**
1977	National League	Merv Rettenmund	San Diego	21	**67**	.313
		Ed Kranepool	New York	13	29	**.448**
	American League	Tim Corcoran	Detroit	10	32	.313
		Lamar Johnson	Chicago	10	26	.385
		Craig Kusick	Minnesota	10	**38**	.263
		Jim Norris	Cleveland	5	10	**.500**
1978	National League	Jerry Turner	San Diego	20	49	**.408**
		Dave Collins	Cincinnati	14	**64**	.219
	American League	Jose Morales	Minnesota	14	**46**	.304
		Otto Velez	Toronto	8	20	**.400**
1979	National League	Mike Lum	Atlanta	17	**52**	.327
		Mike Ivie	San Francisco	9	23	**.391**
	American League	Larry Milbourne	Seattle	12	30	.400
		Bill Nahorodny	Chicago	6	11	**.545**
		Jose Morales	Minnesota	9	**42**	.214

		NAME	TEAM	PHS	ABS	BA
1980	National League	Kurt Bevacqua	San Diego/Pittsburgh	17	**56**	.304
		Pedro Guerrero	Los Angeles	11	17	**.647**
	American League	Jose Morales	Minnesota	13	36	.361
		Pat Kelly	Baltimore	11	23	**.478**
		Terry Crowley	Baltimore	11	**37**	.297
1981	National League	Mike Cubbage	New York	12	**44**	.273
		Rusty Staub	New York	9	24	**.375**
	American League	Bob Molinaro	Chicago	9	**35**	.257
		Bill Stein	Texas	9	20	**.450**
1982	National League	Greg Gross	Philadelphia	19	53	.358
		Broderick Perkins	San Diego	11	29	**.379**
		Bob Molinaro	Chicago/Philadelphia	14	**67**	.209
	American League	Bill Stein	Texas	12	34	.353
		Jerry Hairston	Chicago	11	**47**	.234
		Reggie Jackson	California	6	11	**.545**
	Both	Wayne Nordhagen	Toronto/Pittsburgh	11	26	.423
1983	National League	Rusty Staub	New York	24	**81**	.296
		Kurt Bevacqua	San Diego	14	34	**.412**
	American League	Jerry Hairston	Chicago	17	**62**	.274
		Rick Miller	Boston	16	35	**.457**
1984	National League	Rusty Staub	New York	18	**66**	.273
		Len Matuszek	Philadelphia	10	24	**.417**
	American League	Jerry Hairston	Chicago	18	**59**	.305
1985	National League	Thad Bosley	Chicago	20	60	.333
		Milt Thompson	Atlanta	13	30	**.433**
		Scot Thompson	San Francisco/Montreal	9	**62**	.145
	American League	Jerry Hairston	Chicago	14	**54**	.259
		Bill Stein	Texas	10	24	**.417**
1986	National League	Chris Chambliss	Atlanta	20	**68**	.294
		Terry Kennedy	San Diego	11	23	**.478**
		Kal Daniels	Cincinnati	11	23	**.478**
		Dane Iorg	San Diego	13	**70**	.186
	American League	Hal McRae	Kansas City	15	**47**	.319
		Ron Hassey	New York/Chicago	10	18	**.556**
	Both	Harry Spilman	Detroit/San Francisco	16	42	.381

		NAME	TEAM	PHS	ABS	BA
1987	National League	Wallace Johnson	Montreal	17	61	.279
		Lee Mazzilli	New York	17	55	.309
		Ken Griffey Sr.	Atlanta	11	18	**.611**
		Graig Nettles	Atlanta	13	**72**	.181
	American League	Thad Bosley	Kansas City	12	**42**	.286
		Gary Ward	New York	8	12	**.667**
1988	National League	Wallace Johnson	Montreal	22	**64**	.344
		Gary Varsho	Chicago	11	28	**.393**
	American League	Jim Eppard	California	8	26	.308
		George Hendrick	California	8	**29**	.276
		Bill Buckner	California/Kansas City	8	28	.286
		Luis Salazar	Detroit	5	9	**.556**
1989	National League	Ken Oberkfell	Pittsburgh/San Francisco	18	50	.360
		Curtis Wilkerson	Chicago	11	28	**.393**
		John Cangelosi	Pittsburgh	12	**68**	.176
	American League	Ken Phelps	New York/Oakland	11	**38**	**.289**
		Bill Buckner	Kansas City	10	**38**	.263
1990	National League	Tommy Gregg	Atlanta	18	51	.353
		Dave Magadan	New York	9	22	**.409**
		Chris Gwynn	Los Angeles	13	**56**	.232
	American League	Kevin Reimer	Texas	12	**40**	.300
		Carlos Baerga	Cleveland	11	31	**.355**
1991	National League	Junior Noboa	Montreal	14	46	.304
		Chico Walker	Chicago	13	32	**.406**
		Chris Gwynn	Los Angeles	13	**56**	.232
	American League	Randy Bush	Minnesota	13	34	.382
		Henry Cotto	Seattle	10	15	**.667**
		Matt Merullo	Chicago	7	**41**	.171
1992	National League	Mitch Webster	Los Angeles	17	47	.362
		Willie McGee	San Francisco	11	21	**.524**
		Jeff Grotewold	Philadelphia	13	**61**	.213
	American League	Herm Winningham	Boston	12	38	.316
		Alvin Davis	California	6	11	**.545**
		Randy Bush	Minnesota	9	**48**	.188

		NAME	TEAM	PHS	ABS	BA
1993	National League	Gerald Perry	St. Louis	24	70	.349
		Deion Sanders	Atlanta	12	28	.429
	American League	Hubie Brooks	Kansas City	10	33	.303
		Brian Harper	Minnesota	5	8	.625
		Ernest Riles	Boston	8	47	.170
1994	National League	John Vander Wal	Colorado	14	58	.241
		Gerald Perry	St. Louis	12	40	.300
	American League	Chip Hale	Minnesota	11	31	.355
1995	National League	John Vander Wal	Colorado	28	72	.389
	American League	Chip Hale	Minnesota	14	47	.298
		Mike Aldrete	Oakland/California	11	31	.355
1996	National League	Scott Livingstone	San Diego	19	61	.311
		Mark Johnson	Pittsburgh	14	31	.452
		Dwight Smith	Atlanta	16	69	.232
	American League	Chip Hale	Minnesota	19	65	.292
		Ron Coomer	Minnesota	10	27	.370
1997	National League	Mark Sweeney	St. Louis/San Diego	22	60	.367
		Bill Spiers	Houston	15	33	.455
		Dave Clark	Chicago	20	65	.313
	American League	Dave Magadan	Oakland	13	45	.289
		Mike Stanley	Boston/New York	10	28	.357
		Jesse Levis	Milwaukee	11	45	.244
1998	National League	Dave Clark	Houston	17	64	.266
		Greg Colbrunn	Colorado/Atlanta	15	42	.357
		John Vander Wal	Colorado/San Diego	14	66	.212
	American League	Mike McFarlane	Kansas City/Oakland	7	11	.636
		Midre Cummings	Boston	7	20	.350
		Frank Catalanotto	Detroit	7	30	.233

THE PITCHERS

- ◆ THE CHOICE 300
- ◆ STRIKEOUT STORIES
- ◆ KINGS OF THE HILL:
  1871—1919
- ◆ KINGS OF THE HILL:
  1920—98

- ◆ PRECIOUS PEN MEN
- ◆ NO-NO'S AND PERFECTOS
- ◆ WONDROUS WILD MEN

The Choice 300

1. Examine the following list of career leaders in 10 major pitching departments among the 20 men who have collected 300 wins and then try to identify the *Choice* 300 tailenders in the same 10 departments.

Lowest ERA.. Christy Mathewson 2.13
Fewest Walks... Pud Galvin 744
Most Strikeouts .... Nolan Ryan 5714
Fewest Hits per 9 Innings .... Nolan Ryan 6.56
Highest Winning Percentage...................................... Lefty Grove .680
Most Shutouts .... Walter Johnson 110
Most Complete Games.. Cy Young 749
Fewest Losses .... Lefty Grove 141
Most 20-Win Seasons .... Cy Young 15
Lowest Opponents' OBP .... Christy Mathewson .273

2. Who is the only *Choice* 300 member never to throw a pitch in a World Series, a Temple Cup Series, or a League Championship Series game?
    A) He topped the NL in Ks in four of his first five full seasons in the majors—but it was in Ks by a batter!
    B) He never was a league leader in pitching Ks.
    C) He pitched on Pittsburgh teams in three different major leagues.
    D) Although among the top 10 in all-time wins and the top five in all-time losses, he never was a league leader in either wins or losses.
    E) In 1888 he became the first boxman to achieve 300 career wins.

3. Name the only two 300-game winners who earned all their victories in the 20th century and never appeared in a World Series game.
    A) Both pitched for the Yankees during their careers.
    B) Both were 20-game winners in the NL.
    C) Both appeared in NLCS games within three years of the first NLCS.
    D) One debuted with a 1962 flag winner, and the other with the Milwaukee Braves.
    E) Both had brothers who also won more than 200 games.

4. What *Choice* 300 member played on no fewer than five World Series entrants during his prime but was given the ball in only seven postseason contests?
    A) He nevertheless ranks second in Series losses with five.
    B) Although among the top 10 in career wins, he never was a loop leader in wins.
    C) He's the only 300-game winner who wore a St. Louis Browns uniform.
    D) He was verging on age 26 when he garnered his first win, making him the oldest future 300-game winner to embark on joining the select circle.
    E) He once held the record for the most career wins by a lefty.

5. **Only two *Choice* 300 members ever played for the Yankees, but no fewer than six played with a Cleveland ML team. Can you name all six?**

   A) Two were teammates from 1892 to 1894 on the Spiders.
   B) Two were teammates on a postexpansion Cleveland cellar dweller.
   C) Two had brothers who also won more than 200 games.
   D) One is the Tribe's only Cy Young winner to date.
   E) The sixth is the only one of the sextet to play on a Cleveland flag winner as well as the only one of the six to win his 300th game in a Cleveland uniform.

6. **Nolan Ryan won 300 games while serving two separate stints in both the NL and the AL. Who was the most recent *Choice* 300 member to enter the select circle with all of his wins coming in one major league?**

   A) His wins were spread among three different teams.
   B) He saw World Series action with two different teams.
   C) He posted his last win against the Kansas City A's.
   D) His first win came with the Washington Senators.
   E) His final win in 1963 gave him an even 300 victories.

Choice 300—All Wins in One League

NAME	YEARS	LEAGUE	300TH
Mickey Welch	1880–92	NL	1890
John Clarkson	1882–94	NL	1892
Kid Nichols	1890–1906	NL	1900
Christy Mathewson	1900–16	NL	1912
Walter Johnson	1907–27	AL	1920
Pete Alexander	1911–30	NL	1924
Lefty Grove	1925–41	AL	1941
Warren Spahn	1942–65	NL	1961
Early Wynn	1939–63	AL	1963

7. **Only one *Choice* 300 member, Don Sutton, ever pitched for the Dodgers franchise, going all the way back to its inception in 1884, but the Braves franchise remarkably has owned seven 300-game winners, including the much traveled Gaylord Perry. Who are the other six?**

   A) One was the most recent Braves hurler to lose 20 games in a season.
   B) One was the only member of the sextet to play on more than three pennant winners with the Braves franchise.
   C) Two were teammates in 1888–89.
   D) Two are the all-time-winningest right-hander and left-hander, respectively.
   E) One holds the season record for the most wins, and another has the mark for the second-most wins, but neither did it in a Braves uniform.

8. Of the 16 ML franchises extant in 1901, what is the only one that has never had a *Choice* 300 member throw a pitch in live competition wearing its uniform?

    A)   The Reds aren't it because Radbourn, Matty, and Seaver all pitched for them.

    B)   The White Sox aren't it because Carlton and Wynn both pitched for them.

    C)   The franchise has had several 200-game winners who collared all of their victories wearing its uniform.

    D)   The franchise represents a city that had a National League team in the last century that never had a 300-game winner either.

    E)   Jack Morris collected 198 of his 254 career wins while with this franchise.

9. Robin Roberts was the first hurler subsequent to expansion in 1961 to win as many as 280 games and not achieve 300. Prior to 1961, what man had the most post-1876 wins of anyone who fell short of gaining membership in the *Choice* 300 club?

    A)   In each of his first four full ML seasons, he toiled 400+ innings with four different teams.

    B)   Had he not been suspended for a full season in his prime, he almost certainly would have won more than 300 games.

    C)   He was the first 200-game winner to have an African American batterymate at one point in his career.

    D)   The first of his 285 career wins came with Detroit in 1881, and the last with Cleveland in 1894.

    E)   Nicknamed "Count," he began the 1894 season with Baltimore and would have been on his only pennant winner if the Orioles had not dumped him in midseason.

Tony Mullane. His suspension for a full season in 1885 after repeated contract-jumping offenses cost him almost certain membership in the Choice 300 *club and a spot in Cooperstown.*

10. **What *Choice* 300 member had to wait the longest to make the Hall of Fame after nailing his 300th victory?**
    A) He was elected to the Hall 83 years after posting his 300th.
    B) He won 34 games as a rookie.
    C) He won his last game in 1891 when he was 32.
    D) He was part of the only longtime pitching tandem in ML history to include two future *Choice* 300 members.
    E) He and the most recent hurler to win more than 25 games in a season share the same last name.

11. **What *Choice* 300 member posted his first and last victories with the same team 22 years apart?**
    A) Walter Johnson is a terrific guess, but he played only 21 years.
    B) He's the lone *Choice* 300 member to start LCS games for three different teams.
    C) At the start of his seventh season, his career winning percentage was below .500.
    D) He is currently the oldest pitcher to start a postseason game.
    E) He has the fewest 20-win seasons of any *Choice* 300 member.

12. **The record for posting the highest winning percentage by an ERA qualifier on a last-place team belongs to what *Choice* 300 member?**
    A) He broke Camilo Pascual's 13-year-old record for the highest winning percentage by a pitcher on a doormat.
    B) He is the only *Choice* 300 member to win a game with both the Minnesota Twins and the San Francisco Giants.
    C) In 1997 a pitcher on the same NL franchise for which he played in his record-shattering season became only the 12th ERA qualifier in history to notch a .600 winning percentage with a doormat.
    D) In 1972 he broke Ned Garver's mark for the highest winning percentage by a 20-game winner on a doormat.
    E) He holds the record for the most career Ks by a southpaw.

RANK	NAME	TEAM	YEAR	TEAM W–L	W–L	PCT.
\multicolumn{7}{l}{**.600 Winning Percentage, Pitcher on a Doormat**}

RANK	NAME	TEAM	YEAR	TEAM W–L	W–L	PCT.
1	Steve Carlton	Phi, NL	1972	59–97	27–10	.730
2	Rick Reuschel	Pit, NL	1985	57–104	14–8	.636
	Tom Glavine	Atl, NL	1989	63–97	14–8	.636
4	Camilo Pascual	Was, AL	1959	63–91	17–10	.630
	Dave Fleming	Sea, AL	1992	64–98	17–10	.630
6	Ned Garver	StL, AL	1951	52–102	20–12	.625
7	Denny Neagle	Pit, NL	1995	58–86	13–8	.619
8	Bob Friend	Pit, NL	1955	60–94	14–9	.609
9	Wilbur Cooper	Pit, NL	1917	51–103	17–11	.607
	Curt Schilling	Phi, NL	1997	68–94	17–11	.607
11	Bob Hooper	Phi, AL	1950	52–102	15–10	.600
	Bill Doak	StL, NL	1916	60–93	12–8	.600

Note: Includes only ERA qualifiers; in 1983, Jesse Orosco was an amazing 13–7 (.650) in relief for the last-place Mets but hurled just 110 innings.

13. **Who is the only *Choice* 300 member to compile 20-win seasons with three different teams in the same league?**
    A) After his first six seasons, he had 63 shutouts.
    B) He saw World Series action with two different teams and would have appeared in a Series with a third if he had not lost much of one season to military duty.
    C) In 1928, at age 41, he hit .291 in 86 at bats.
    D) He led the NL six times in wins, last in 1920.
    E) He is the only *Choice* 300 member named after a former president.

14. **Which of the 20 *Choice* 300 members won the most games after his 30th birthday?**
    A) He won more games after turning 30 than Lefty Grove won total.
    B) He won his first game at age 23 and his last at 44.
    C) He lost to Eddie Dent of Brooklyn in his last big league outing.
    D) He faced Cap Anson in his first ML game.
    E) He also won the most games after his 20th birthday of any *Choice* 300 member.

15. **Who was the only *Choice* 300 member to lose 30 games in his rookie year?**
    A) He was also a 30-game winner as a rookie.
    B) He won his first 69 games for a team based in a city that has not had a major league franchise in more than a century.
    C) He was the first *Choice* 300 member to collect all his wins in the same ML.
    D) He won his 300th in 1890 for the New York Giants.
    E) They called him "Smiling Mickey."

Most Losses, Rookie Season, *Choice 300* Member

RANK	NAME	TEAM	YEAR	W	L
1	Mickey Welch	Tro, NL	1880	34	30
2	Pud Galvin	Buf, NL	1879	37	27
3	Kid Nichols	Bos, NL	1890	27	19
4	Christy Mathewson	NY, NL	1901	20	17
5	Eddie Plank	Phi, AL	1901	17	13
	Tom Seaver	NY, NL	1967	16	13
	Pete Alexander	Phi, NL	1911	28	13
8	Don Sutton	LA, NL	1966	12	12
	Lefty Grove	Phi, AL	1925	10	12
10	Walter Johnson	Was, AL	1907	5	9

16. **Name the first hurler to win 300 games before he registered 150 losses.**
    A) He was the first *Choice* 300 member to wear a Cleveland uniform.
    B) He is the lone *Choice* 300 member to wear a Worcester big league uniform.
    C) He was the first *Choice* 300 member who never played in a ML game when the pitching distance was still only 45 feet from home plate.
    D) He is the only *Choice* 300 member to achieve his 300th win in less than 10 full ML seasons.
    E) He was the last hurler to win 50 games in a season.

17. What two moundsmen had 259 and 258 career wins, respectively, at the close of the 1942 season and would almost surely have each won 300 games if their careers had not been interrupted at that point by military service?

A) Between them, they were 7–2 in World Series action.

B) Between them, they pitched on seven pennant winners.

C) Only one of the pair played on a pennant winner or in a postseason game.

D) One of the pair holds the AL record for the most career pinch hits by a pitcher, and the other is the most recent hurler to make at least 20 starts in a season and complete them all.

E) The 7–2 hurler in postseason play was managed in his final ML season by the other potential 300-game winner whose career was shortened by military service.

Choice 300—Postseason Wins

NAME	DIV.	TC	LCS	WS	TOTAL
Christy Mathewson	—	—	—	8	8
Steve Carlton	0	—	4	2	6
Don Sutton	—	—	4	2	6
Cy Young	—	3	0	2	5
Tim Keefe	—	—	—	4	4
Warren Spahn	—	—	—	4	4
Lefty Grove	—	—	—	4	4
Hoss Radbourn	—	—	—	3	3
Walter Johnson	—	—	—	3	3
Pete Alexander	—	—	—	3	3
Tom Seaver	—	—	2	1	3
John Clarkson	—	—	0	2	2
Kid Nichols	—	0	2	0	2
Eddie Plank	—	—	—	2	2
Nolan Ryan	1	—	1	0	2
Mickey Welch	—	—	—	1	1
Early Wynn	—	—	—	1	1
Gaylord Perry	—	—	1	—	1
Phil Niekro	—	—	0	—	0
Pud Galvin	—	—	—	—	—

Note: TC denotes Temple Cup Series; the 1892 postseason series between first- and second-half season winners is included under LCS wins.

18. Phil Niekro was 46 before he attained his 300th win. Who was the first *Choice* 300 member to enter the club after his 40th birthday?

A) Eddie Plank won his 300th just before he turned 40.

B) Like Plank, our man was 25 when he collected his first big league win.

C) His only losing season came in his rookie year.

D) He led the AL in ERA for the ninth and last time when he was 39.

E) His 30 starts in 1931 are the fewest in a season by a 30-game winner.

RANK	NAME	YEARS	W	300TH	TEAM
	The Choice 300				
1	Cy Young	1890–1911	511	1901	Bos, AL
2	Walter Johnson	1907–27	417	1920	Was, AL
3	Pete Alexander	1911–30	373	1924	Chi, NL
	Christy Mathewson	1900–16	373	1912	NY, NL
5	Warren Spahn	1942–65	363	1961	Mil, NL
6	Kid Nichols	1890–1906	361	1900	Bos, NL
7	Pud Galvin	1875–92	360	1888	Pit, NL
8	Tim Keefe	1880–93	342	1890	NY, PL
9	Steve Carlton	1965–88	329	1983	Phi, NL
10	John Clarkson	1882–94	326	1892	Bos, NL
	Eddie Plank	1901–17	326	1915	StL, FL
12	Don Sutton	1966–88	324	1986	Cal, AL
	Nolan Ryan	1966–93	324	1990	Tex, AL
14	Phil Niekro	1964–87	318	1985	NY, AL
15	Gaylord Perry	1962–83	314	1982	Sea, AL
16	Tom Seaver	1967–86	311	1985	Chi, AL
	Hoss Radbourn	1881–91	311	1890	Bos, PL
18	Mickey Welch	1880–92	307	1890	NY, NL
19	Early Wynn	1939–63	300	1963	Cle, AL
	Lefty Grove	1925–41	300	1941	Bos, AL

Strikeout Stories

1. **When Bob Feller fanned 346 hitters in 1946 to inspire *Strikeout Story*, his initial biography, he was the lone Cleveland Indian to finish among the top eight AL hurlers in strikeouts. His performance was typical. Just once in history has a team boasted a trio of pitchers who were 1-2-3 in their league in Ks. Awesome as that seems, the club failed to win the pennant. What team is it?**

   A) The top two K finishers are in the Hall of Fame.
   B) The third-place K finisher was a longtime major league pitching coach.
   C) The third-placer led the AL in relief wins in 1970 with 10 for the Twins.
   D) The team finished second to the only flag winner managed by Fred Hutchinson.
   E) The team also finished second the next season after losing the pennant in a three-game playoff.

2. **The first team with three pitchers who notched 200 Ks also did not garner a pennant. What club is it?**

   A) Two years later, for the second and last time to date, the Houston Astros had three 200-K men.
   B) The original threesome got most of their relief help from Al Worthington and Ron Kline.
   C) The only one of the trio who finished among the AL's top five in Ks that year was third to Jim Lonborg's leading total of 246.
   D) One of the trio was the only AL hurler to win a Cy Young Award between 1962 and 1966.
   E) The trio's team lost the pennant on the last day of the season.

3. **Since Bob Feller debuted in 1936, who is the only right-hander apart from Feller and Nolan Ryan to lead either major league in Ks three years in a row?**

   A) A late-season trade to Toronto in the AL caused David Cone to miss doing it in 1992 when he finished one K behind John Smoltz after leading the NL the previous two seasons.
   B) Dwight Gooden was a loop leader only in his first two big league seasons.
   C) The righty we're looking for did it the first three seasons his team was based in a new sector.
   D) His older brother won his first ML start at age 19 in 1951 and never won another game in the bigs.
   E) He failed to record a single K in his lone World Series start for the Twins in 1965.

4. **When Bob Turley paced the AL in Ks the first year the St. Louis Browns were based in Baltimore, he was only the second hurler in the franchise's history to be a loop leader in Ks. Who was the only Brownie to top the AL in hill whiffs?**

   A) His 149 Ks were the most in the AL between 1918 and 1924.
   B) He K'd just 35 batters in 200 innings in 1927, his final full season in the majors.
   C) He died near the end of the 1928 campaign of a heart ailment.
   D) He collected a St. Louis Browns' club record 126 career wins.
   E) His name should not come as a "shock."

Top Strikeout Seasons by St. Louis Browns Pitchers (1902–53)

RANK	NAME	YEAR	KS
1	Rube Waddell	1908	232
2	Bobo Newsom	1938	226
3	Harry Howell	1905	198
4	Jack Powell	1903	169
5	Fred Glade	1904	156
6	Urban Shocker	1922	149
	Bump Hadley	1933	149
8	Rube Waddell	1909	141
	Joe Lake	1910	141
10	Harry Howell	1906	140

Note: Waddell's 232 Ks were second in the AL in 1908; Shocker, in 1922, was the Browns' lone AL K leader.

5. **Who was the first pitcher to be a K leader in each league after the AL achieved major league status in 1901?**
    A) All his K crowns came after interleague trading was legalized.
    B) He failed to play on a pennant winner in either major league.
    C) He is one of the handful of hurlers who won 100 games in each major league.
    D) He also hurled a no-hitter in each major league.
    E) He made the Hall of Fame in 1996.

6. **Rube Waddell won six straight AL strikeout crowns in 1902–07. Who is the only other southpaw to cop as many as two consecutive league K crowns between 1901 and 1919, the end of the Deadball Era?**
    A) Both of his crowns came in seasons when the schedule was abbreviated.
    B) The first 23 of his 178 career wins came with the Yankees.
    C) He led the NL in innings pitched in both 1918 and 1919.
    D) He won the pitching Triple Crown for the 1918 World Series loser.
    E) He was the loser in the only double no-hit game in major league history.

7. **Who is the only pitcher to win three or more K crowns even though he logged fewer than 1,000 career whiffs?**
    A) All three of his K crowns came as a member of a National League team.
    B) His last 17 career Ks came as a member of the Yankees while they were still known as the Highlanders.
    C) His three K crowns all came in a row.
    D) He was the first southpaw in NL history to win a K crown as a rookie.
    E) If you've used your noodle, you know by now that he's the only hurler to win consecutive K crowns in two different centuries.

RANK	NAME	CROWN YEARS	CROWNS	SEASON HIGH Ks	CAREER Ks
		Fewest Career Ks, Multiple Strikeout Crown Winner			
1	Herb Score	1955–56 AL	2	263	837
2	Bill Hallahan	1930–31 NL	2	177	856
3	Tommy Bond	1877–78 NL	2	182	860
4	Noodles Hahn	1899–1901 NL	3	239	912
5	Len Barker	1980–81 AL	2	187	975
6	Dizzy Dean	1932–35 NL	4	199	1163
7	Johnny Vander Meer	1941–43 NL	3	202	1294
8	Mark Baldwin	1889 AA & 1890 PL	2	368	1354
9	Sam Jones	1955–56 NL & 1958 NL	3	225	1376
10	Hippo Vaughn	1918–19 NL	2	195	1416

Herb Score topped the AL in Ks in each of his first two ML seasons. A near-fatal injury forced him to change his delivery. Score finished with just 837 career Ks, the fewest in history by a multiple strikeout crown winner.

8. What hurler never logged another inning in the majors after posting a club-best 71 whiffs with the most recent hill staff to total fewer than 400 Ks?

A) A fine hitter, in 1944 he topped the Red Sox with seven pinch hits.

B) He lost 20 games for the Phils in 1936 while reaching his career high in Ks with 80.

C) His team in 1945, his finale, was absent a hurler who was occupied elsewhere after winning three straight loop K crowns earlier in the decade.

D) His initials are the same as those of the Yankees hurler who led the AL in starts in 1964 and notched two wins in the World Series.

E) He was not affiliated with the baseball card company that bore his last name.

9. **Connie Mack's 1941 Philadelphia A's had the most recent AL hill staff to compile fewer than 400 Ks. What rookie led the Mackmen that year in strikeouts with 74?**
   A) In 1942 and again in 1947, he led the AL in walks.
   B) In 1946 he tied for the AL lead in losses.
   C) He and the Cubs lefty who topped the NL with 17 losses in 1951 share the same initials.
   D) He spent much of World War II in a POW camp.
   E) He was the last right-hander to win as many as 19 games in a season in a Philadelphia A's uniform.

10. **What 20th century world champ received only 67 strikeouts from its staff K leader?**
   A) The staff K leader was also the team's only 20-game winner.
   B) Rosy Ryan was the team's lone frontline pitcher to average more than three strikeouts per nine innings.
   C) The following year, the team won its second straight World Championship when Ryan led it in Ks with 72.
   D) Two years later, the team won its fourth straight flag, with the lefty who'd led its first champion in Ks again the leader with 72.
   E) The team's fourth straight flag was also the last one claimed by John McGraw.

Fewest Pitcher Ks, Season, Pennant Winner (Since 1903)

RANK	TEAM	LEAGUE	YEAR	TEAM LEADER	TEAM Ks
1	New York Giants	NL	1921	Art Nehf, 67	357
2	St. Louis Cardinals	NL	1926	Flint Rhem, 72	365
3	Pittsburgh Pirates	NL	1925	Vic Aldridge, 88	386
4	New York Giants	NL	1922	Rosy Ryan, 75	388
5	New York Giants	NL	1924	Art Nehf, 72	406
6	St. Louis Cardinals	NL	1928	Jesse Haines, 77	422
7	New York Yankees	AL	1927	Waite Hoyt, 86	431
8	Pittsburgh Pirates	NL	1927	Carmen Hill, 95	435
9	Chicago Cubs	NL	1906	Jack Pfeister, 153	446
10	Washington Senators	AL	1933	General Crowder, 110	447

Note: 1903 was the first year foul balls became strikes in both major leagues; 1918–19 war seasons and 1981, 1994, and 1995 strike seasons excepted. The 1927 Yankees set many team records; the mark for the fewest Ks of any AL flag winner since 1903 that played a full schedule may be their least-publicized accomplishment.

11. **In 1998, Mike Sirotka led the White Sox in Ks with just 128, an unusually low total for a staff leader in this day and age. Name the only pitcher since 1893, when the current pitching distance was established, to top his team in Ks with a total fewer than 50.**
   A) Rube Waddell led the AL that year with 210 Ks.
   B) After notching 45 Ks to lead one AL club, our man was sold to the Boston Pilgrims, for whom he collected 15 more Ks.
   C) He played under John McGraw the only year he led an AL club in Ks.
   D) He won 20 for the first AL World Series entrant but lost his only fall start.
   E) He and the Red Sox righty who in 1942 was an AL coleader in Ks with just 113 share the same initials.

Fewest Ks, Season, Team Strikeout Leader (Since 1893)

RANK	NAME	TEAM	YEAR	TEAM Ks	Ks
1	Tom Hughes	Bal, AL	1902	258	45
2	Gus Weyhing	Phi, NL	1895	245	53
	Red Lucas	Cin, NL	1930	361	53
4	Jim Hughey	Cle, NL	1899	215	54
5	Ed Stein	Bro, NL	1895	216	55
	Sarge Connally	Chi, AL	1924	360	55
	Hal Carlson	Phi, NL	1926	331	55
8	Icebox Chamberlain	Cin, NL	1893	258	59
	Bill Hutchison	Chi, NL	1894	281	59
	Hal Wiltse	Bos, AL	1926	336	59
	Win Ballou	StL, AL	1926	337	59

12. **In 1903 a foul ball became a strike for the first time in both major leagues, resulting in a sharp hike in strikeout totals. What four teammates hurled 596 innings among them in 1933 and combined for only 90 Ks to help their club set the post-1903 record for the fewest Ks per game—310 in 153 contests?**

   A) One of the four is in the Hall of Fame; one once held the career record for pinch hits; one later committed suicide; and the fourth man was the staff relief ace.

   B) In the process of setting a negative K record, the team also set the NL mark for the fewest walks issued in a season (257) but nevertheless finished last.

   C) The team was the last to be managed in the majors by the man who'd piloted the NL pennant-winner six years earlier.

   D) A dozen years later, the team became the last to notch fewer than 400 Ks in a season.

   E) Six years later, the team won its first of two consecutive pennants.

13. **Who posted the fewest Ks of any 20th century hurler who worked enough innings to qualify for an ERA crown by today's rule (one inning pitched for every game played by his team)?**

   A) He collected just 20 Ks in 155.1 innings as a rookie with a Philadelphia A's club that was led in wins by Lynn "Line Drive" Nelson.

   B) In 1940 he was the lone A's hurler to have a winning record (8–4).

   C) His last major league appearance came with the only team to knock off Joe McCarthy's Yankees in a World Series.

   D) His initials are the same as those of the flaky southpaw who married Mamie Van Doren.

   E) The first syllable of his last name matches the last name of the Giants season save record holder with 48.

		Fewest Ks, ERA Qualifier, Season (Since 1893)			
RANK	**NAME**	**TEAM**	**YEAR**	**IP**	**KS**
1	Frank Bates	StL/Cle, NL	1899	161.2	13
2	Les German	NY, NL	1894	134	17
3	Edgar McNabb	Bal, NL	1893	142	18
	Jack Dunn	Bro/Phi, NL	1900	143	18
5	Duke Esper	Bal, NL	1896	155.2	19
	Dan Daub	Bro, NL	1897	137.2	19
7	Les German	NY/Was, NL	1896	169.1	20
	Bill Beckman	Phi, AL	1939	155.1	20
9	Walt Woods	Lou, NL	1899	186.1	21
10	Bill Rhodes	Lou, NL	1893	151.2	22
	Bill Kissinger	StL, NL	1896	136	22

14. Since the mound was established at its present distance in 1893, who collected the fewest strikeouts while fashioning a 20-win season?

A) He had 21 wins, 24 Ks, and just 20 walks in 227.2 innings for a world champ.

B) He labored most of his career for weak Cardinals teams in the decade of the 1910s.

C) His manager in his lone 20-win season was Pat Moran.

D) They called him "Slim."

E) His name follows Roger Salkeld's in baseball encyclopedias.

15. Who owns the major league record for the most Ks in a season by a pitcher with fewer than five wins?

A) He broke Tom Hall's record of four wins on 137 Ks, set in 1971.

B) He was 3–15 with 160 Ks after suffering 20 losses the previous year.

C) Seven years later, his record was nearly broken by a National League hurler who clocked 149 Ks on just two wins.

D) He won 222 games in the majors.

E) He still holds the Mets record for the most wins by a rookie—19 in 1968.

16. When Tom Henke fanned 128 hitters in 1987 without posting a win, whose mark did he break for the most Ks in a season by a winless hurler?

A) The old mark was also set in the 1980s.

B) The former record holder also holds the current mark for the most career Ks (108) by a pitcher who never garnered a win in the majors.

C) Of his 108 career Ks, 92 came with the Twins in 1982.

D) He also holds the mark for the most career losses (16) by a hurler who never posted a win in the majors.

E) He and the Chicago reliever who led the AL in saves in 1974 share the same initials and first name.

Evolution of Season Record for Most Ks, No Wins

NAME	TEAM	YEAR	IP	KS
Denny Mack	Roc, NA	1871	13	1
Bill Stearns	Oly, NA	1872	99	2
Deacon White	Chi, NL	1876	2	3
Jack Manning	Cin, NL	1877	44	6
Mike Dorgan	Syr, NL	1879	12	8
Stump Weidman	Buf, NL	1880	113.2	25
Bones Ely	Lou, AA	1886	44	28
John Malarkey	Was, NL	1895	100.2	32
Gene Dale	StL, NL	1912	61.2	37
Roy Moore	Phi/Det, AL	1922	70.1	38
Jim Suchecki	StL, AL	1951	89.2	47
Gene Conley	Mil, NL	1958	72	53
Bob Moorhead	NY, NL	1962	105.1	63
Jose Santiago	KC, AL	1964	83.2	64
Dick Radatz	Bos/Cle, AL	1966	75.2	68
Orlando Pena	Det/Cle, AL	1967	90.1	74
Bill Laxton	Det, AL	1976	94.2	74
Diego Segui	Sea, AL	1977	111	91
Terry Felton	Min, AL	1982	117.1	92
Tom Henke	Tor, AL	1987	94	128

17. A certain hill staff had two 200-game winners, including a Hall of Famer and one of the best-hitting pitchers ever, plus a lefty with arguably the best control of any southpaw in history and a fourth hurler who won 20 games that year. And yet the staff somehow contrived to post just 312 Ks in 153 games, the fewest of any AL team since 1903. What team's pitchers are we talking about?

A) The 20-game winner was an AL coleader in losses that year with 17.

B) The southpaw control artist also had perhaps the best pickoff move ever to first base.

C) The Hall of Famer won 20 games the following year for Bucky Harris's second straight flag winner.

D) The hurler who could hit holds the record for the highest career BA by a 200-game winner.

E) The team was managed by a Hall of Fame center fielder.

18. Pete Alexander was the first hurler subsequent to 1901 to win NL strikeout crowns with two different teams. Who was the first to perform the same feat in the AL?

A) He paced the AL with 151 Ks as a rookie.

B) He had something important in common with Chief Bender and Moses Yellowhorse.

C) The year he bagged his second K crown, he won 20 games, topped the AL with a 2.06 ERA, and notched his fifth and sixth World Series wins.

D) He was traded prior to the 1947 season for Joe Gordon.

E) Of his 182 career wins, 131 came with the Yankees between 1947 and 1954.

19. **In 1900, Rube Waddell became the first Pittsburgh hurler to lead the NL in Ks. Some 45 years later, Preacher Roe became the second Corsairs K champ when he paced the NL with just 148 whiffs. Who is the lone Pirate to top the senior loop in whiffs since Roe's triumph at the close of World War II?**
    A) He threw with the same arm as Waddell and Roe.
    B) He is the lone Pirates hurler since 1893 to fan 200 batters in a season.
    C) Sandy Koufax sandwiched two of his K titles around the only K title since 1945 won by a Pittsburgh hurler.
    D) His left arm won exactly 100 games for the Pirates during the 1960s.
    E) He and the Corsairs manager in 1972, his final season with Pittsburgh, share the same initials.

Top Strikeout Seasons by Pirates Pitchers Other than Bob Veale (Since 1893)

RANK	NAME	YEAR	KS
1	Larry McWilliams	1983	199
2	Bob Friend	1960	183
3	Bert Blyleven	1978	182
4	Doug Drabek	1972	177
5	Claude Hendrix	1912	176
6	Dock Ellis	1969	173
7	Bert Blyleven	1979	172
8	Bert Blyleven	1980	168
9	Don Robinson	1982	165
	Bob Moose	1969	165

20. **Walter Johnson won a record eight straight K crowns between 1912 and 1919. No hurler has equaled his record in the years since, but two teams have had the individual K leader in their loop eight years in a row. Who are the teams and players?**
    A) In each case, one hurler won seven of the eight consecutive crowns.
    B) In the first instance, one hurler took the last seven of the eight crowns bagged by a member of his team.
    C) In the second instance, an injury-riddled year allowed a teammate of a famous strikeout king to interrupt a skein that might otherwise have tied Johnson's record.
    D) Burleigh Grimes is one of the four hurlers involved.
    E) Both of the teams that have had eight consecutive winners since 1919 are now based in the same metropolitan area.

21. **Dwight Gooden and Herb Score both won K crowns in each of their first two big league seasons, but neither ever won another. Who is the only hurler since 1901 to launch his career by winning more than two consecutive K crowns?**
    A) He led his league in Ks in each of his first seven seasons.
    B) As a rookie, he notched just 116 Ks and had a 4.75 ERA.
    C) He won pitching Triple Crowns in both of the last two years that he led in Ks.
    D) His 2,266 career Ks were second only to Rube Waddell's 2,316 among southpaws when he retired.
    E) His 300th win came in his final big league start.

22. Between 1947 and 1961, only three AL pitchers achieved as many as 200 Ks in a season. Two of them were Hall of Famer Jim Bunning and the ill-fated Herb Score. Who was the third?

   A)   He was an AL K leader during that period but not the year he bagged 200.

   B)   The year he hit the 200 mark, he trailed Score by 35 Ks, but he nevertheless compiled the most Ks of any pitcher on his team since 1904.

   C)   The last previous pitcher on his team to notch 200 Ks was also the last 200-K hurler in major league history to average at least one win for every six Ks.

   D)   His mark for the most Ks by a pitcher on his team since the end of the Deadball Era was broken by Al Downing in 1964.

   E)   They called him "Bullet Bob."

23. Who is the only hurler to win a league K crown with a total greater than the combined K total achieved by any other two pitchers in his loop that year?

   A)   One of his teammates was second to him that year, with 135 Ks.

   B)   Third in his loop that season was a Cincinnati Reds hurler with 86 Ks.

   C)   His 262 Ks that season were nearly 8 percent of the NL total of 3,383.

   D)   The NL batting leader that season hit .424.

   E)   He was the Dodgers' most famous K king prior to Koufax.

League Leaders in Ks by a Margin of 100 or More

RANK	NAME	TEAM	YEAR	Ks	2ND MOST	MARGIN
1	Tim Keefe	NY, AA	1883	359	203	156
2	Mark Baldwin	Col, AA	1889	368	217	151
3	Toad Ramsey	Lou, AA	1887	355	217	138
4	Dazzy Vance	Bro, NL	1924	262	135	127
5	Nolan Ryan	Cal, AL	1973	383	258	125
6	Nolan Ryan	Cal, AL	1974	367	249	118
7	Rube Waddell	Phi, AL	1903	302	187	115
8	Tim Keefe	NY, NL	1888	335	223	112
	Randy Johnson	Sea, AL	1993	308	196	112
10	Rube Waddell	Phi, AL	1904	349	239	110
11	One Arm Daily	CP/Was, UA	1884	483	374	109
12	Sandy Koufax	LA, NL	1965	382	276	106
13	Amos Rusie	NY, NL	1893	208	107	101
14	J. R. Richard	Hou, NL	1979	313	213	100

24. Among the many odd and contradictory records that Nolan Ryan collected in 1987 was a share of the mark for the fewest wins by a pitcher with 200 strikeouts. Prior to expansion in 1961, the post-1893 record belonged to what rookie right-hander with just 10 wins and more than 200 Ks in 308.1 innings?

   A)   His 225 Ks in 1901 were the post-1893 rookie mark prior to Pete Alexander.

   B)   He was the first man ever to play as many as nine seasons for a Washington major league entry.

   C)   He holds the post-1893 record for the fewest whiffs by a staff leader in Ks.

   D)   He won 20 games for the first 20th century world champ.

   E)   He was called "Long Tom" in part to distinguish him from another pitcher of his era who had the same name.

Evolution of Season Record for Fewest Wins with 200 Ks

NAME	TEAM	YEAR	KS	W
Will White	Cin, NL	1879	232	43
Lee Richmond	Wor, NL	1880	243	32
George Derby	Det, NL	1881	212	29
Bob Barr	Was/Ind, AA	1884	207	12
Toad Ramsey	Lou, AA	1888	228	8
Bob Johnson	KC, AL	1970	206	8
Nolan Ryan	Hou, NL	1987	270	8

25. Prior to Herb Score, who was the only 20th century hurler to collect 200 Ks in a season twice in his career and fail to make the Hall of Fame?

A)   He was never a loop leader in Ks.

B)   He fanned 200 or more hitters in back-to-back seasons.

C)   He is the only 20th century hurler not in the Hall of Fame despite having a season in which he won 30 games and fanned 200 hitters.

D)   He logged 21 Ks and three wins in his first World Series.

E)   He hit .200 in the four games he played as an outfielder in his second and last World Series in 1920.

26. After his 20-K gem with the Cubs in 1998, Kerry Wood currently owns the NL record, the rookie record, and a share of the major league record for the most strikeouts in a nine-inning game. He also, of course, now owns the single-game record for the most Ks by a member of the Chicago NL franchise. Whose mark did he break?

A)   The old record was 16, set by a Hall of Famer.

B)   The Hall of Famer still owns the record for the most wins in a season by a Chicago NL hurler.

C)   He also owns the record for the most wins in a season by a member of the Boston-Milwaukee-Atlanta Braves franchise.

D)   His last win came in a Cleveland Spiders uniform in 1894.

E)   His 16-K game occurred in 1886, two years before he was sold to Boston.

Top Five Strikeout Kings in Each Era (Minimum 1,000 Innings)

RANK	NAME	YEARS	IP	KS	KS/9 INN.
1871–75					
1	Bobby Mathews	1871–75	2221.2	322	1.30
2	Candy Cummings	1872–75	1778	220	1.11
3	Cherokee Fisher	1871–75	1087.2	87	0.72
4	Al Spalding	1871–75	2347.2	186	0.71
5	Dick McBride	1871–75	2016	145	0.65

RANK	NAME	YEARS	IP	KS	KS/9 INN.
1876–92					
1	Toad Ramsey	1885–90	2100.2	1515	6.49
2	One Arm Daily	1882–87	1415	846	5.38
3	Amos Rusie	1889–92	1806	1075	5.36
4	Dupee Shaw	1883–88	1762	950	4.85
5	Matt Kilroy	1886–92	2263.1	1157	4.60
1893–1900					
1	Cy Seymour	1896–1900	1026	582	5.11
2	Amos Rusie	1893–98	1941.2	853	3.95
3	Doc McJames	1895–99	1270.1	551	3.91
4	Kid Nichols	1893–1900	2914.2	875	2.702
5	Jouett Meekin	1893–1900	2107	631	2.695
1901–19					
1	Rube Waddell	1901–10	2659.2	2137	7.23
2	Joe Wood	1908–19	1434.1	988	6.20
3	Walter Johnson	1907–19	4091	2614	5.75
4	Orval Overall	1905–13	1535.1	935	5.48
5	Ed Walsh	1904–17	2964.1	1736	5.27
1920–41					
1	Bob Feller	1936–41	1448.1	1233	7.66
2	Dazzy Vance	1922–35	2933.2	2027	6.22
3	Van Lingle Mungo	1931–41	1739.1	1031	5.34
4	Dizzy Dean	1930–41	1963.1	1163	5.33
5	Bobo Newsom	1929–41	2213.1	1308	5.32
1942–60					
1	Sam Jones	1951–60	1412.1	1184	7.55
2	Don Drysdale	1956–60	1071.1	822	6.91
3	Jim Bunning	1955–60	1093	832	6.85
4	Camilo Pascual	1954–60	1180.1	891	6.80
5	Bob Turley	1951–60	1443	1070	6.67
1961–76					
1	Nolan Ryan	1966–76	1935	2085	9.70
2	Sandy Koufax	1961–66	1632.2	1713	9.45
3	Sam McDowell	1961–75	2492.1	2453	8.86
4	Bob Veale	1962–74	1925.2	1703	7.96
5	Jim Maloney	1961–71	1785.1	1557	7.85

RANK	NAME	YEARS	IP	Ks	Ks/9 INN.
1977–93					
1	Nolan Ryan	1977–93	3451	3629	9.46
2	Randy Johnson	1988–93	1073.1	1126	9.44
3	Lee Smith	1980–93	1125.2	1110	8.88
4	David Cone	1986–93	1521	1418	8.39
5	Sid Fernandez	1983–93	1590.2	1458	8.25

Note: Too few pitchers as yet have pitched 1,000 innings in the post-1993 era.

Kings of the Hill: 1871–1919

1. **Many fine early-day pitchers languish in obscurity because they played for poor teams. Henry Boyle is a prime example. Boyle was typical of his luckless breed; his career was mercifully short because pitchers in the last century who lost big rarely lasted long unless they also won big. In truth, only one 19th century hurler who finished with 200 losses collected fewer than 200 wins. Can you name him?**

   A) Stationed in the outfield between pitching assignments on June 9, 1883, he became the first NL'er to score six runs in a nine-inning game.
   B) He was the first to top his loop in both wins and losses in the same season.
   C) In 1883 he became the first hurler to lose 20 games for a pennant winner.
   D) He finished third in the NL in SA and fifth in batting in 1882.
   E) They called him "Grasshopper."

Most Losses, Career, Fewer than 200 Wins

RANK	NAME	YEARS	WIN. PCT.	W	L
1	Bob Friend	1951–66	.461	197	230
2	Chick Fraser	1896–1909	.452	175	212
3	Jim Whitney	1881–90	.484	191	204
4	Claude Osteen	1957–75	.501	196	195
5	Tom Zachary	1918–36	.493	186	191
6	Curt Simmons	1947–67	.513	193	183
	Larry Jackson	1955–68	.515	194	183
	Joe Bush	1912–28	.516	195	183
9	Danny Darwin	1978–98	.484	171	182
10	Murry Dickson	1939–59	.487	172	181
	Rick Wise	1964–82	.509	188	181
	Dutch Leonard	1933–53	.513	191	181

Note: Retired pitchers only.

2. **The first team to flaunt three 20-game winners was a 19th century club—no surprise. But amazingly, it didn't win the pennant. What team is it?**

   A) One of the trio also won 19 games that season in another major league.
   B) The trio beat such teams as the St. Paul Apostles and the Pittsburgh Stogies.
   C) The trio's team finished second to the St. Louis Maroons.
   D) The trio's team made a certain city the first in Ohio to have two ML teams in the same season.
   E) Prior to that season the team pirated the Cincinnati AA team's ballpark.

3. The first team to have three 20-game losers was also a 19th century club. And amazingly enough, it didn't finish last in its league. Name it.

A) Only the weakest-hitting team in history to play a schedule of at least 100 games kept this club from finishing last.

B) Two of the club's three big losers were Al Mays and Ed Cushman.

C) Two years earlier, the third 20-game loser had been one half of the first mound tandem to feature two 30-game winners.

D) The team played most of its home games on Staten Island.

E) In 1884 the team had been the first ML flag winner from the Big Apple.

4. Early-day pitchers' won–lost records generally mirrored their team's winning percentage. Who was the first chucker in history with at least 20 decisions to post a losing record for a flag winner?

A) He was 9–15 for the Players League champion Boston Reds.

B) He had a brother who also pitched briefly in the majors.

C) He had previously pitched in the AA.

D) He holds a major season pitching record, which he achieved as a rookie.

E) He also holds the all-time season record for the most wins (47) by a southpaw.

Lowest Winning Percentage, Season, Pitcher on a Pennant Winner

RANK	NAME	TEAM	YEAR	W–L	PCT.
1	Dennis Martinez	Bal, AL	1983	7–16	.304
2	Larry French	Chi, NL	1938	10–19	.345
3	Bill Bevens	NY, AL	1947	7–13	.350
	Steve Avery	Atl, NL	1995	7–13	.350
5	Matt Kilroy	Bos, PL	1890	9–15	.375
6	Bill Hallahan	StL, NL	1934	8–12	.400
	Bud Black	KC, AL	1985	10–15	.400
8	Larry Jaster	StL, NL	1968	9–13	.409
9	Tom Zachary	Was, AL	1925	12–15	.444
10	Don Drysdale	LA, NL	1966	13–16	.448

Note: Minimum 20 decisions. Because Martinez hurled only 153 innings, 9 short of qualification for the ERA crown in 1983, some authorities do not consider him the record holder for the worst winning percentage on a flag winner. But Martinez is unquestionably the only pitcher with at least 20 decisions to post a sub-.500 winning percentage for two pennant winners; he was also 15–16 for the 1979 Orioles. In 1966, Don Sutton went just 12–12 for Los Angeles, making the 1966 Dodgers the only pennant winner except for the 1973 Mets with two regular starters at or below .500.

5. In 1997 no pitcher on either the pennant-winning Marlins or Indians lost more than 12 games, even though neither club had an extraordinary winning percentage. Actually, only one hurler on a flag winner in the present decade—Mike Moore of Oakland in 1990—has lost as many as 14 games. However, a certain 20th century hurler was on three consecutive pennant winners, led his league in winning percentage in one of those three seasons, and yet dropped 41 decisions, or nearly 14 per season, during that span! Who is he?

A) In 1914 he was a perfect 8–0 in relief for the first Federal League champion.

B) He was a member of the only AL team to lose three consecutive World Series.

C) All but 19 of his 228 career wins came with his original AL club.

D) He is the lone 20th century hurler to lose 20 games for a pennant winner.

E) He died in Wabash, Indiana, explaining his nickname of "Wabash George."

Most Losses by a Pitcher on a Pennant Winner, Season

RANK	NAME	TEAM	YEAR	L
1	Jim Whitney	Bos, NL	1883	21
	Silver King	StL, AA	1888	21
3	George Mullin	Det, AL	1907	20
4	Larry French	Chi, NL	1938	19
5	Earl Mosely	Ind, FL	1914	18
6	Pat Malone	Chi, NL	1932	17
	Don Drysdale	LA, NL	1963	17
	Ken Holtzman	Oak, AL	1974	17
9	Roy Patterson	Chi, AL	1901	16
	Cy Young	Bos, AL	1904	16
	Cy Falkenberg	Ind, FL	1914	16
	Don Drysdale	LA, NL	1966	16
	Jon Matlack	NY, NL	1973	16
	Dennis Martinez	Bal, AL	1979	16
	Steve Carlton	Phi, NL	1983	16
	Dennis Martinez	Bal, AL	1983	16

Note: The 1914 FL Indianapolis Hoosiers are the only post-1893 flag winner with two pitchers who each lost more than 15 games.

6. In "Hypothetical Cy Young Winners" later in the book, we highlight five 19th century hurlers whose arms gave out by the time they were 30. Whose face should adorn the opposite side of the coin, for logging the most wins after age 30 of any pitcher in the 19th century?

A) He won only 17 games before he turned 30.

B) Second to his 167 wins after age 30 is Tim Keefe with 149.

C) He was the last pitcher in ML history to collect more than half of his team's wins in a season.

D) He was the last pitcher to win 40 games two years in a row.

E) Between ages 30 and 32, he won 123 games for Chicago.

Pitchers with 100 Career Wins After Age 30 (Prior to 1901)

RANK	NAME	YEARS	YEAR/30	POST-30 W
1	Bill Hutchison	1884–97	1889	167
2	Tim Keefe	1880–93	1887	149
3	Hoss Radbourn	1881–91	1884	146
4	Bobby Mathews	1871–87	1881	125
5	Pud Galvin	1875–92	1886	110

7. The only pitcher prior to 1893 to compile a 30-win season despite working fewer than 350 innings is the near opposite of the five men on the preceeding list in that he won only 13 games after his 30th birthday. Who is he?

    A) He was 31–11 in 347.2 innings for a flag winner.

    B) He is one of the select few pitchers who were both 40-game winners and 40-game losers during their careers.

    C) He had 252 wins before he hit 30 and looked certain to become the first 300-game winner, but he finished with only 265.

    D) In 1885–86 he was 51–15 for the Chicago White Stockings.

    E) His initials match those of the 1993 AL Cy Young winner.

8. What longtime Hall of Famer pitched in a time when most staff aces made more than 40 starts a year while he was fashioning a career that made him the first hurler to compile 200 wins without ever working as many as 300 innings in a season?

    A) His peak workload was 33 starts and 270 innings as a 19-year-old rookie.

    B) In the last year in which he worked enough to be an ERA qualifier, he was 4–16 in 178.1 innings.

    C) In the next-to-last year he worked enough to be an ERA qualifier, he was 17–3 in 179 innings.

    D) In 1913 he won 21 games in just 21 starts for the world champs and led the AL with 13 saves.

    E) He has the most career wins of any pitcher of American Indian extraction.

200-Game Winners with No 300-Inning Seasons (Prior to 1961)

RANK	NAME	YEARS	WINS	MAXIMUM IP
1	Lefty Grove	1925–41	300	291.2 (1932)
2	Red Ruffing	1924–47	273	289.1 (1928)
3	Herb Pennock	1912–34	240	286.1 (1924)
4	Waite Hoyt	1918–38	237	282.1 (1921)
5	Sam Jones	1914–35	229	298.2 (1921)
6	Mel Harder	1928–47	223	287.1 (1935)
7	Earl Whitehill	1923–39	218	279.1 (1935)
8	Freddie Fitzsimmons	1925–43	217	263.1 (1934)
9	Chief Bender	1903–25	212	270 (1903)
10	Rube Marquard	1908–25	201	294.2 (1912)

9. **Pedro Martinez gave up just 66 walks in 1997 when he became the most recent pitcher to post an ERA below 2.00. His antithesis is Mickey Welch, who ceded 131 walks in 1885, the most ever by a hurler with a sub-2.00 ERA. What Deadball Era chucker holds the 20th century record for the most walks issued on a sub-2.00 ERA?**

   A)   As a rookie he ceded 130 walks while posting a 1.80 ERA.

   B)   As a rookie he played on a National League flag winner that lost to the A's in fall play.

   C)   As a rookie he set a National League frosh record with an .833 winning percentage.

   D)   He and the Indians rookie outfielder who stole 40 bases in just 63 games in 1990 share the same last name.

   E)   Despite his name, he was never a merry old soul, if only because he died before his 30th birthday.

Most Walks Issued with an ERA Under 2.00, Season

RANK	NAME	TEAM	YEAR	ERA	BBS
1	Mickey Welch	NY, NL	1885	1.66	131
2	King Cole	Chi, NL	1910	1.80	130
3	Babe Ruth	Bos, AL	1916	1.75	118
	Bill James	Bos, NL	1914	1.90	118
	Cy Young	Cle, NL	1892	1.93	118
6	Cy Morgan	Phi, AL	1910	1.55	117
7	Jack Coombs	Phi, AL	1910	1.30	115
8	Billy Rhines	Cin, NL	1890	1.95	113
9	Scott Perry	Phi, AL	1918	1.98	111
10	Hal Newhouser	Det, AL	1945	1.81	110
	Sam McDowell	Cle, AL	1968	1.81	110

Note: The only teammates besides Morgan and Coombs to issue 100 walks with sub-2.00 ERAs were Mickey Welch and Tim Keefe (1.58 with 102 walks), New York, NL, 1885; Morgan is the only hurler to issue 100 walks two years in a row with a sub-2.00 ERA.

10. **The first hurler on a cellar dweller to win 20 games without also suffering 20 defeats was also only the second moundsman in history to post a winning record with a basement finisher. Use your bean to think of him.**

   A)   He topped the NL in innings and strikeouts that year.

   B)   His .537 winning percentage broke Pud Galvin's .519 mark—set 10 years earlier—for the best winning percentage by a pitcher on a last-place team.

   C)   He has the fewest wins after his 26th birthday of any hurler since 1893 who compiled at least 125 career wins.

   D)   The cellar team he won 20 for was managed by Bid McPhee.

   E)   He got his nickname as a boy by carrying soup to his father for lunch.

First 10 Pitchers on Cellar Dwellers to Win More than They Lost

RANK	NAME	TEAM	YEAR	TEAM W–L	W–L	PCT.
1	Pud Galvin	Pit, NL	1891	55–80	14–13	.519
2	Noodles Hahn	Cin, NL	1901	52–87	22–19	.537
3	Joe McGinnity	Bal, AL	1902	50–88	13–10	.565
4	Doc Scanlan	Bro, NL	1905	48–104	14–12	.538
5	Jesse Tannehill	Bos, AL	1906	49–105	13–11	.542
6	Slim Sallee	StL, NL	1913	51–99	18–15	.545
7	Earl Hamilton	StL, AL	1913	57–96	13–12	.520
8	Doc Crandall	StL, FL	1914	62–89	13–9	.591
9	Jeff Tesreau	NY, NL	1915	65–83	19–16	.543
10	Sailor Stroud	NY, NL	1915	65–83	11–9	.550

Note: Minimum 20 decisions. Galvin was the lone 19th century hurler to top .500 with a cellar dweller, but two others (Alex Ferson, 17–17, Washington, NL, 1889 and Pink Hawley, 18–18, New York, NL, 1900) finished at .500 exactly. Three Finger Brown (12–6) made the 1914 FL Terriers the first doormat with two .500+ pitchers. The 1915 Giants not only were the first doormats with two .500+ hurlers in at least 20 decisions, but they also had Rube Marquard, who was 9–8.

11. **Nowadays there's so much stigma attached to a pitcher who loses 20 games that we might never see it happen again. Yet no fewer than 12 teams in history have had not just one but three and in some cases as many as four 20-game losers. What was the last team to date with three 20-game losers?**

    A) Two members of the luckless trio won 29 of the team's 36 victories.
    B) The team finished last in an eight-team loop, a record 40 games behind the seventh-place team.
    C) The team's keystone combo was Nap Lajoie and Whitey Witt.
    D) One of the 20-game losers had just one win that year.
    E) Two years earlier, the team had won the AL flag.

Teams with Three 20-Game Losers

TEAM	YEAR	PITCHERS
NY, AA	1886	Lynch (30), Mays (28), Cushman (20)
Pit, NL	1887	McCormick (23), Morris (22), Galvin (21)
Was, NL	1887	Whitney (21), O'Day (20), Gilmore (20)
Ind, NL	1888	Healy (24), Shreve (24), Boyle (22)
StL, NL	1896	Hart (29), Breitenstein (26), Donahue (24)
Bro, NL	1898	Yeager (22), Kennedy (22), Dunn (21)
StL, NL	1898	Taylor (29), Sudhoff (27), Hughey (24)
Was, AL	1904	Townsend (26), Jacobson (23), Patten (23)
StL, AL	1905	Glade (25), Howell (22), Sudhoff (20)
Bos, NL	1905	Willis (29), Fraser (22), Wilhelm (22), Young (21)
Bos, NL	1906	Young (25), Dorner (25), Lindaman (23), Pfeffer (22)
Phi, AL	1916	Bush (24), Myers (23), Nabors (20)

BROOKLYN BASEBALL TEAM.

Brickyard Kennedy, seen here (bottom right) as a rookie with the 1892 Brooklyn Bridegrooms. In 1898, Kennedy joined Jack Dunn and Joe Yeager to give Brooklyn a trio of 20-game losers. A year later, he, Dunn, and Jim Highes gave the Brooklyns a 20-game-winning trio that would have become a foursome, the first such quartet in history, if 19-game-winner Doc McJames had posted just one more win.

12. **The 1877 Cincinnati Red Stockings were the first doormat without at least one 20-game loser, largely owing to the fact that the team logged only 57 decisions. What was the first cellar dweller that played a schedule of at least 100 games and escaped having a 20-game loser?**

   A) The team was also the first doormat with a pitcher who posted a break-even (.500) winning percentage in at least 20 decisions.

   B) Walt Wilmot led the club in homers with nine.

   C) Connie Mack's .293 BA led all team members who had at least 350 at bats.

   D) George Haddock led the team in losses with 19.

   E) The following year, Mack and Haddock were batterymates on the Players League doormat Buffalo Bisons.

13. **The only two pitchers to lose 40 games in their rookie seasons did it a year apart. Can you name these two heavily battered 19th century freshmen?**

   A) Each man had yet to turn 21 when he had his record-loss season.

   B) Each man set a loop record for losses the year he dropped 40 decisions.

   C) One hurler debuted with his hometown Indianapolis team.

   D) The other man became an outfielder two years after being saddled with an all-time-record 48 defeats.

   E) The two seasons were 1883 and 1884.

Most Losses, Season, Rookie—Pre-1893

RANK	NAME	TEAM	YEAR	L
1	John Coleman	Phi, NL	1883	48
2	Larry McKeon	Ind, AA	1884	41
3	Kid Carsey	Was, AA	1891	37
	George Cobb	Bal, NL	1892	37
5	Fleury Sullivan	Pit, AA	1884	35
6	Matt Kilroy	Bal, AA	1886	34
7	Hardie Henderson	Phi, NL/Bal, AA	1883	33
	Harry McCormick	Syr, NL	1879	33
	Jim Whitney	Bos, NL	1881	33
10	John Harkins	Cle, NL	1884	32

14. **What rookie tied the post-1893 record for the most losses (23) by a pitcher on a team with a winning record and then went 172–78 (.688) over the next 11 seasons to finish with the eighth-highest career winning percentage of all-time at .658?**

   A)   His team went 76–73 in his rookie season to finish seventh in a 12-team loop.

   B)   All his 194 career wins came with the same team.

   C)   He never pitched against a major league team from Detroit in either a regular or a postseason game.

   D)   He was a member of a team that beat Detroit in a World Series but saw no action in the affair.

   E)   His first ML manager was Bill Watkins, but for the last 11 years of his career, he played under Fred Clarke.

Most Losses, Season, Rookie—Post-1893

RANK	NAME	TEAM	YEAR	L
1	Still Bill Hill	Lou, NL	1896	28
2	Chick Fraser	Lou, NL	1896	27
	Bill Carrick	NY, NL	1899	27
4	Bob Groom	Was, AL	1909	26
5	Patsy Flaherty	Chi, AL	1903	25
	Harry McIntyre	Bro, NL	1905	25
	Stoney McGlynn	StL, AL	1907	25
8	Sam Leever	Pit, NL	1899	23
	Beany Jacobson	Was, AL	1904	23
	Vive Lindaman	Bos, NL	1906	23
	Elmer Myers	Phi, AL	1916	23

15. **Six pitchers in history have won 20 games in a season while making fewer than 25 starts. What man became the first to do it five years after he made his ML debut as a second baseman for his hometown New Haven club?**
    A) He umpired in the American Association in the late 1880s.
    B) He won 21 of his 24 starts in his first full ML season.
    C) He was one-half of the first pitching staff to feature two 20-game winners.
    D) His initials and first name are the same as those of the NL save leader in 1969.
    E) He was the first hurler to play on a flag winner in each of his first three full ML seasons.

Fewest Starts, Season, 20-Game Winner

RANK	NAME	TEAM	YEAR	W	GS
1	Bob Grim	NY, AL	1954	20	20
2	Chief Bender	Phi, AL	1913	21	22
3	Johnny Beazley	StL, NL	1942	21	23
4	Fred Goldsmith	Chi, NL	1880	21	24
	Jesse Tannehill	Pit, NL	1902	20	24
	Ernie Broglio	StL, NL	1960	21	24
7	Jerry Nops	Bal, NL	1897	20	25
	Wes Ferrell	Cle, AL	1929	21	25
9	Ray Kremer	Pit, NL	1926	20	26
	Lefty Gomez	NY, AL	1921	21	26

16. **During his long career, he was a 20-game winner, a 20-game loser, a major league ERA leader one year, a winning-percentage runner-up another year, and was also once a loop leader in relief wins. He pitched in the Union Association and the Players League as well as in the National League both before and after 1900. He was a teammate of Cannonball Morris, Charlie Ferguson, Joe McGinnity, and Christy Mathewson and played nearly as many games as an outfielder as he did as a pitcher. Given all that, you'd think he was surely a major contributor to the game. Yet he had fewer than 100 career wins and a sub-.250 career batting average. Who is he?**
    A) His lone 20-win season in 1898 followed a year when he'd posted no wins.
    B) He lost 21 games on a 5.30 ERA for Washington in 1893, two years before he led the NL in ERA.
    C) He died at 92 in Philly, where he debuted with the UA Keystones in 1884.
    D) His nickname was "Smiling Al."
    E) He and the Dodgers 20-game winner in 1974 who became one of the game's first free agents two years later share the same initials.

17. **Anthony Young broke Cliff Curtis's mark for the most consecutive losses in 1993. The record holder prior to Curtis also owns a significant negative career record and pitched for a team that set several major negative records in its own right. Who is he?**
    A) Prior to Curtis, the record was 16 straight losses.
    B) The previous record holder suffered 30 defeats the year he set the mark.
    C) He had a 4–30 record that year and led his team in both wins and losses.
    D) He has the career record for the most complete games without logging a shutout.
    E) His team lost an all-time-record 134 games in 1899.

18. **After winning 29 games for Brooklyn in 1900, Joe McGinnity jumped to the American League the following year and put up 26 wins with Baltimore. Name the only pitcher since McGinnity in 1901 to be a 25-game winner in back-to-back seasons in two different major leagues.**

    A) Not Jack Chesbro, who won just 21 his first year in the AL.
    B) Our man compiled only 94 career victories, the fewest of any 20th century hurler with two 25-win seasons.
    C) His first 16 wins came with the 1912 Phillies.
    D) He never won a game in the AL.
    E) He and the only hurler ever to win 25 games for an expansion team share the same first name and the same initials.

19. **The only 20th century pitcher to lose 10 games for two different teams in the same season debuted in the Deadball Era and got his last win in 1928. Who is he?**

    A) He was traded in midseason in 1919.
    B) The two teams involved in the deal were the Cards and the Phils.
    C) He toiled for the 1927 World Series loser.
    D) His 180 career losses are the most of any 20th century hurler prior to World War II who failed to win 200 games.
    E) He was the first 20th century performer to wear glasses.

Pitchers Losing 10 Games in One Season with Two Different Teams

NAME	YEAR	TEAMS	TOTAL L
Bob Barr	1884	Was, AA (23)/Ind, AA (11)	34
Dupee Shaw	1884	Det, NL (18)/Bos, UA (15)	33
Jouett Meekin	1892	Lou, NL (10)/Was, NL (10)	20
Lee Meadows	1919	StL, NL (10)/Phi, NL (10)	20

20. **What luckless moundsman set a post-1893 record in 1904 when he compiled 26 more complete games than he did wins?**

    A) He also holds the 20th century record for the lowest career winning percentage by anyone involved in at least 100 decisions.
    B) He spent the bulk of his career with dismal Washington teams.
    C) He shares the AL record for the most losses in a season, with 26.
    D) In 1904 he completed 31 of 34 starts but had just a 5–26 record.
    E) His nickname of "Happy" must have been ironic.

Worst Career Winning Percentage (Minimum 100 Decisions)

RANK	NAME	YEARS	W	L	PCT.
1	Jim Hughey	1891–1900	29	80	.266
2	Happy Townsend	1901–06	35	82	.299
3	Jesse Jefferson	1973–81	39	81	.325
4	Buster Brown	1905–13	51	103	.331
5	Bob Barr	1883–91	49	98	.333
	Bill Bailey	1907–22	38	76	.333
7	Hugh Mulcahy	1935–47	45	89	.336
	Rollie Naylor	1917–24	42	83	.336
	George Smith	1916–23	41	81	.336
10	Steve Arlin	1969–74	34	67	.337

21. **Jim Abbott's 2–18 mark in 1996 is not the poorest by a starting pitcher. It's not even in the top 10. Whose ghastly 0–17 performance in 20 starts with the 1910 Browns is the worst ever by a starter?**

    A) Three relief wins brought his overall 1910 mark to 3–18.

    B) He was a stellar 4–1 as an 18-year-old rookie with the 1907 Browns, but it was his lone winning season.

    C) He and Chief Bender were a combined 10–35 in 1915 for the FL Baltimore Terrapins.

    D) Unlike his namesake, the hero of a famous song, he was rarely invited by teams to return.

    E) He and the Reds record holder prior to Johnny Bench for the most homers in a season by a catcher share the same last name.

Worst Winning Percentage as a Starter, Season (Minimum 20 Starts)

RANK	NAME	TEAM	YEAR	GS	W–L	PCT.
1	Bill Bailey	StL, AL	1910	20	0–17	.000
	Bob Miller	NY, NL	1962	20	0–11	.000
3	Jack Nabors	Phi, AL	1916	30	1–20	.048
4	Les German	NY/Was, NL	1896	20	1–17	.056
5	Walt Dickson	Bos, NL	1912	20	1–15	.063
6	Art Houtteman	Det, AL	1948	20	1–14	.067
7	Pascual Perez	Atl, NL	1985	22	1–13	.071
	Charlie Bishop	Phi, AL	1953	20	1–13	.071
9	Joe Harris	Bos, AL	1906	24	2–21	.087
10	Kirtley Baker	Pit, NL	1890	21	2–19	.095

Note: Frank Bates made only 19 starts when he went 1–18 in 1899 for Cleveland, NL.

22. In his only full season as a pitcher, he won 43 games, split between two major leagues; in his first season as a regular, he had the third-best slugging average in the American Association; in his final game as a catcher, he tied an all-time record when he committed seven errors. Who is he?

A) His finale behind the plate came with Baltimore on May 29, 1886.

B) One of the more renowned head cases of his time, he was dropped by Pittsburgh after the 1883 season when he was accused of robbing a local dignitary.

C) In 1884 he set the all-time record for the most wins in a season by a pitcher twirling in two different major leagues.

D) He was called "Bollicky Billy."

E) He and the Cardinals righty whose 16–5 mark led the NL in winning percentage in 1992 share the same initials.

Most Wins Pitching in Two Different Leagues, Season

RANK	NAME	YEAR	LEAGUES	TOTAL W
1	Billy Taylor	1884	UA (25)/AA (18)	43
2	Charlie Sweeney	1884	NL (17)/UA (24)	41
3	Jim McCormick	1884	NL (19)/UA (21)	40
4	Dupee Shaw	1884	NL (9)/UA (21)	30
5	Joe McGinnity	1902	AL (13)/NL (8)	21
	Hank Borowy	1945	AL (10)/NL (11)	21
7	Al Atkinson	1884	AA (11)/UA (9)	20
	Patsy Flaherty	1904	AL (1)/NL (19)	20
	Rick Sutcliffe	1983	AL (4)/NL (16)	20
10	Randy Johnson	1998	AL (9)/NL (10)	19

23. Ben Cantwell set an all-time record for the fewest innings worked by a 25-game loser when he suffered 25 defeats for the Boston Braves in 1935 in just 210.2 frames. What 19th century hurler holds the comparable all-time record for a 20-game loser?

A) He suffered 20 defeats in just 169.1 innings, breaking Bert Inks's record of 205.1 innings set just one year earlier.

B) It was his record for the most career complete games without throwing a shutout that Jim Hughey broke in 1899.

C) A Baltimore native, he debuted in 1890 with Baltimore of the AA.

D) Despite going a miserable 2–20 for Washington in 1896 with a 6.43 ERA, he was retained the following year.

E) He and the Kansas City southpaw who topped the AL in 1983 with 18 losses share the same initials.

Fewest Innings, Season, 20-Game Loser

RANK	NAME	TEAM	YEAR	W–L	IP
1	Les German	NY/Was, NL	1896	2–20	169.1
2	Dick Barrett	Phi, NL	1945	7–20	190.2
3	Joe Oeschger	Bos, NL	1922	6–22	195.2
4	Roy Wilkinson	Chi, AL	1921	4–20	198.1
5	Don Larsen	Bal, AL	1954	3–21	201.2
6	Joe Bowman	Phi, NL	1936	9–20	203.2
7	Harry Kelley	Phi, AL	1936	13–21	205
8	Bert Inks	Lou, NL	1895	7–20	205.1
	Al Jackson	NY, NL	1965	8–20	205.1
10	Mal Eason	Bro, NL	1905	5–21	207

24. **Whose 1,702 career Ks are the most any hurler achieved during the Deadball Era without making the Hall of Fame?**
    A) He collected 183 career wins, all in the NL.
    B) His lone 20-win season came with McGraw's only world champ.
    C) In 1914 he led the NL in both losses and saves.
    D) His real first name was Leon, but they called him "Red."
    E) His initials match those of the Twins closer throughout most of the 1990s.

Most Career Ks, Non–Hall of Famer, Each Era

ERA	NAME	YEARS	KS
1871–75	Bobby Mathews	1871–87	322
1876–92	Tony Mullane	1881–94	1803
1893–1900	Ted Breitenstein	1891–1901	876
1901–19	Red Ames	1903–19	1702
1920–41	Bobo Newsom	1929–53	2082
1942–60	Billy Pierce	1945–64	1999
1961–76	Mickey Lolich	1963–79	2832
1977–93	Frank Tanana	1973–93	2773

25. **Since the 60'6" pitching distance was established in 1893, only one man has reaped a 20-win season and never won a game in the majors after his 23rd birthday. Who is he?**
    A) He debuted in 1914 at age 19.
    B) He led the NL in losses at age 20.
    C) Christy Mathewson managed him the year he won 20.
    D) He once hit five home runs in a game in the PCL.
    E) He and the Royals career leader in both wins and innings pitched share the same initials.

26. Name the lone post-1893 pitcher to post five double-digit win seasons before he turned 25 and never appear in a major league game after his 25th birthday.

    A)   He is also the youngest man to qualify for a National League bat title in the 20th century.

    B)   He threw a no-hitter when he was 20.

    C)   In 1910, his final season, he led the Cardinals in wins with 14.

    D)   His 1906 no-hitter was the last by a Phillie prior to expansion.

    E)   He and the only man in this century to be a loop leader in triples and a major pitching department (albeit not in the same season) share the same initials.

Most Career Wins, None After 25th Birthday

RANK	NAME	YEARS	LAST W (AGE)	W
1	Monte Ward	1878–84	24	165
2	Jumbo McGinnis	1882–87	23	102
3	Charlie Ferguson	1884–87	24	99
4	Elmer Smith	1886–92	24	75
5	Willie McGill	1890–96	22	71
6	Johnny Lush	1904–10	24	66
7	Charlie Sweeney	1883–87	23	64
8	Pete Conway	1885–89	22	61
9	Darby O'Brien	1888–91	24	59
	Pete Schneider	1914–19	23	59

27. Who is the only post-1893 hillman to lose 20 games three years in a row for three different teams?

    A)   He holds the career record for the most hit batsmen (219) at the 60'6" distance.

    B)   His 175 career wins are the fewest of any pitcher who incurred 200 or more career losses.

    C)   He was the first 20-game winner for a Philadelphia AL entry.

    D)   His three consecutive 20-loss seasons came in the NL with Philadelphia, Boston, and Cincinnati.

    E)   He and the Angels current record holder for the most career wins by a lefty share the same initials.

28. Dick McBride, a National Association bulwark, has the record for the most career wins by a pitcher who never won a game in either the NL or the AL. Who holds the post-NA record for the same achievement?

    A)   All of his 114 wins came in the American Association.

    B)   He's among the handful of hurlers who were 20-game winners in their final ML seasons.

    C)   In his first full ML season, he fanned 499 hitters.

    D)   His 38 wins in 1886 are the fifth-most in history by a southpaw.

    E)   His nickname was "Toad."

Most Career Wins with None in the NL or AL

RANK	NAME	YEARS	LEAGUE	W
1	Dick McBride	1871–75	NA	149
2	Toad Ramsey	1885–90	AA	114
3	Jumbo McGinnis	1882–87	AA	102
4	Henry Porter	1884–89	UA & AA	96
5	Al Mays	1885–90	AA	53
6	Al Atkinson	1884–87	AA & UA	51
7	Billy Taylor	1882–87	AA & UA	50
8	Nat Hudson	1886–89	AA	48
9	Larry McKeon	1884–86	AA	46
10	Bob Emslie	1883–85	AA	44

Note: McBride had four losses in the NL in 1876. Taylor had one loss in the NL in 1881. McKeon had two losses in the NL in 1886.

Kings of the Hill: 1920–98

1. **The Yankees were so dominant in the 1940s and 1950s that pitchers in that era prayed to wear pinstripes. As but one illustration of the Yanks' superiority, only one pinstripes-wearer suffered more than 12 losses in a season during the 15-year span between 1948–62. Name him.**

    A) He came to the Yankees in a mammoth trade with another AL club.
    B) Toiling for Baltimore in 1954, he led the AL with 185 Ks.
    C) In 1958 he won 21 games for the Yankees and was the Series hero that fall.
    D) He was the first AL hurler to win a Cy Young Award.
    E) His nickname was "Bullet Bob."

Most Losses Each Season by a Yankee, 1948–62

YEAR	NAME	L
1948	Ed Lopat	11
1949	Vic Raschi & Ed Lopat	10
1950	Allie Reynolds	12
1951	Vic Raschi	10
1952	Allie Reynolds	8
1953	Johnny Sain, Allie Reynolds & Jim McDonald	7
1954	Whitey Ford	8
1955	Bob Turley	13
1956	Johnny Kucks	9
1957	Johnny Kucks	10
1958	Art Ditmar & Johnny Kucks	10
1959	Bob Turley	11
1960	Art Ditmar & Whitey Ford	9
1961	Buddy Daley & Bill Stafford	9
1962	Ralph Terry	12

2. **When Dennis Martinez dropped 16 games in just 153 innings for the 1983 Orioles, he set a new mark for the most losses by a non-ERA qualifier on a flag winner. He also fell just one short of the all-time record for the most losses in a season by a non-ERA qualifier, which is shared by five pitchers, the most recent being Lew Krausse of the Kansas City A's in 1967. Who is the most recent NL hurler to claim a share of the record by suffering 17 losses in fewer than 162 innings?**

    A) Two years earlier, he earned immortality for a home run he surrendered.
    B) His 17-loss season followed on the heels of another 17-loss season by a non-ERA qualifier on the same team the previous year.
    C) The team owned the last two hurlers to lose as many as 24 games in a season.
    D) As a frosh in 1961, he logged 109 Ks but just two wins in 132.2 innings.
    E) He gave up Roger's 61st in '61 while pitching for the Red Sox.

Most Losses, Season, Non-ERA Qualifier

RANK	NAME	TEAM	YEAR	IP	L
1	Craig Anderson	NY, NL	1962	131.1	17
2	Crazy Schmit	Cle, NL	1899	138.1	17
3	Claude Willoughby	Phi, NL	1930	153	17
4	Tracy Stallard	NY, NL	1963	154.2	17
5	Lew Krausse	KC, AL	1967	160	17
6	Mike Parrott	Sea, AL	1980	94	16
7	Anthony Young	NY, NL	1993	100.1	16
8	Gene Garber	Atl, NL	1979	106	16
9	Bill Greif	SD, NL	1972	125.1	16
10	Hal Woodeschick	Hou, NL	1962	139.1	16
	Rick Honeycutt	Tex, AL	1987	139.1	16

Note: Ranked according to fewest innings pitched; other non-ERA qualifiers, including Dennis Martinez in 1983, also suffered 16 losses but in more than 139.1 innings.

New York Yankees ace Allie Reynolds lost just 41 games in the five years between 1949 and 1953, an average of 8.2 a season. The big right-hander nevertheless led the powerful Bombers three times in losses during that span.

3. **In 1997, Hideo Nomo became only the 13th pitcher to notch 200 Ks despite posting a 4.00+ ERA. What southpaw who was still around in 1997 once logged a 4.85 ERA, the second highest in history by a pitcher with 200 strikeouts in a season?**

   A) He led his loop in both Ks and walks as a rookie.

   B) He achieved his 2,000th career K in 1993.

   C) He led the AL in Ks three times as a member of the Mariners.

   D) He swapped uniforms with Randy Johnson in 1989.

   E) He won 19 games for the Angels in 1991, his top season to date.

Pitchers with a 4.00 ERA and 200 Ks, Season

RANK	NAME	TEAM	YEAR	KS	ERA
1	Bobo Newsom	StL, AL	1938	226	5.08
2	Mark Langston	Sea, AL	1986	245	4.85
3	Mike Mussina	Bal, AL	1996	204	4.81
4	Todd Stottlemyre	Oak, AL	1995	205	4.55
5	Hideo Nomo	LA, NL	1997	233	4.25
6	Darryl Kile	Hou, NL	1996	219	4.19
7	Chuck Finley	Cal, AL	1996	215	4.16
8	Mickey Lolich	Det, AL	1974	202	4.15
9	Bob Feller	Cle, AL	1938	240	4.08
	Don Sutton	LA, NL	1970	201	4.08
11	Phil Niekro	Atl, NL	1977	262	4.03
12	Bert Blyleven	Min, AL	1986	215	4.01
13	Don Wilson	Hou, NL	1969	235	4.00

4. **A monumental event in his career might suggest to you that a certain pitcher threw hard, but his overall record suggests quite the opposite. His 862 career Ks are the fewest since 1876 by a pitcher with 200 wins. Who is he?**

   A) In 1924 he won 20 games for the Reds while notching just 68 Ks.

   B) He led the AL and the Red Sox in hit batsmen in 1917.

   C) He led the AL in wins in 1921 with 27.

   D) He is the most recent Red Sox hurler to win the final ML game of a season.

   E) He is best remembered for "The Pitch That Killed."

5. **What fireballer's 2,453 career Ks tops all pitchers who posted fewer than 200 wins?**

   A) He also has the most career Ks of any retired hurler with fewer than 150 wins.

   B) He was a loop leader in Ks five times.

   C) He led the AL in shutouts in 1966.

   D) He is the only AL southpaw who twice notched 300 or more Ks in a season.

   E) They called him "Sudden Sam."

Pitchers with 2,000 Career Ks and Fewer than 200 Wins

RANK	NAME	YEARS	W	KS
1	Sam McDowell	1961–75	141	2453
2	Mark Langston	1984–	179	2411
3	Dennis Eckersley	1975–98	197	2401
4	Sandy Koufax	1955–66	165	2396
5	Randy Johnson	1988–	143	2329
6	Rube Waddell	1897–1910	193	2316
7	David Cone	1986–	168	2243
8	Camilo Pascual	1954–71	174	2167
9	Dwight Gooden	1984–	185	2150
10	Fernando Valenzuela	1981–97	173	2074
11	Dazzy Vance	1915–35	197	2045

6. **Except for Al Spalding, who toiled in the 1870s when strikeouts were nearly as scarce as grand slams, only one pitcher has ever won 200 games without collecting 100 Ks in a season or 1,000 Ks in his career. Who is he?**

A)   He has the record for the fewest innings pitched (94) by a shutout leader.

B)   He led the NL with an .889 winning percentage at age 39.

C)   He led the NL in starts in 1933 when he posted a career-high 78 Ks.

D)   His lost his last postseason start for the 1941 Series loser.

E)   His nickname was "Fat Freddie."

200-Game Winners with Fewer than 1,000 Career Ks

RANK	NAME	YEARS	W	100 KS	KS
1	Al Spalding	1871–78	252	0	227
2	Carl Mays	1915–29	207	2	862
3	Freddie Fitzsimmons	1925–43	217	0	870
4	Bob Caruthers	1884–92	218	4	900
5	Al Orth	1895–1909	204	2	948
6	Clark Griffith	1891–1914	237	1	955
7	Jesse Haines	1918–37	210	1	981
	Stan Coveleski	1912–28	215	3	981

7. **In the low-scoring Deadball Era, Tom Hughes shut out Cleveland four times in 1905, and Pete Alexander did the same to the 1916 Reds. What postexpansion hurler tied their record when he blanked a pennant winner four times in a season?**
   A) He achieved his four shutouts in four consecutive starts against this team.
   B) All but 3 of his 35 career wins came with the Cardinals.
   C) His shutout patsies were the 1966 Dodgers.
   D) Thanks largely to the Dodgers, he was a National League shutout coleader in 1966 and in so doing became the only shutout king to spend six weeks in the minors during the season in which he led.
   E) He and the most recent Cubs hurler to win as many as 24 games in a season share the same initials.

8. **Name the only man since 1901 to craft a 25-win season without tossing a shutout.**
   A) His 26 wins the year he did it fell 11 short of Toad Ramsey's all-time record of 37 wins in 1887 without logging a shutout.
   B) He played for the AL flag winner that year.
   C) George Uhle led the AL that season with five shutouts.
   D) He won 194 games in his career, but 1922 was his lone 20-win season.
   E) He and a Negro League mound great whose last name was Rogan share the same nickname.

9. **Randy Johnson set an AL southpaw record in 1997 when he won 20 games while working just 213 innings. Who are the only three pitchers to win 20 games in seasons when they hurled fewer than 210 innings?**
   A) One did it as a frosh when he became the only 20-game winner to log fewer than 200 innings.
   B) The other two did it while toiling for division winners.
   C) The pair who won 20 for division winners in fewer than 210 innings did it in the same season.
   D) The pair who did it in the same season both led their respective leagues in winning percentage that year.
   E) The year that two 20-game winners worked fewer than 210 innings was 1991.

Fewest Innings Pitched, Season, 20-Game Winner

RANK	NAME	TEAM	YEAR	W	IP
1	Bob Grim	NY, AL	1954	20	199
2	Scott Erickson	Min, AL	1991	20	204
3	John Smiley	Pit, NL	1991	20	207.2
4	Fred Goldsmith	Chi, NL	1880	21	210.1
5	Randy Johnson	Sea, AL	1997	20	213
6	Johnny Beazley	StL, NL	1942	21	215.1
7	Bob Forsch	StL, NL	1977	20	217.1
8	Ray Sadecki	StL, NL	1964	20	220
9	Tommy John	LA, NL	1977	20	220.1
10	Jerry Nops	Bal, NL	1897	20	220.2

10. Name the only hurler to win 19 games in a season in fewer than 170 innings.

- A) He pitched on a pennant winner that year.
- B) He completed just 1 of his 31 starts that year.
- C) The previous year, he was 0–2 in two World Series starts.
- D) His first World Series start resulted in a win for the 1983 world champs.
- E) His real first name is George, but he was known by a nickname that differs by only one letter from the last name of Johnny, the Yankees rookie first-base regular in 1941.

11. For more than half a century, Larry Corcoran's 177 career wins led all pitchers with fewer than 2,500 innings. Who finally broke his record and still owns the mark?

- A) He also has the record for the longest span between K crowns—nine years.
- B) He bagged 182 wins in 2,492.1 innings.
- C) He is currently second in career World Series saves and sixth in career Series starts.
- D) He is the lone hurler to win at least one game in five straight World Series.
- E) He came to the Yankees from Cleveland in 1947 in a deal for Joe Gordon.

Most Career Wins, Fewer than 2,500 Innings

RANK	NAME	YEARS	IP	W
1	Allie Reynolds	1942–54	2492.1	182
2	Larry Corcoran	1880–87	2392.1	177
3	Ron Guidry	1975–88	2392	170
4	General Crowder	1926–36	2344.1	167
5	Ed Lopat	1944–55	2439.1	166
6	Sandy Koufax	1955–66	2324.1	165
7	Monte Ward	1878–84	2461.2	164
8	Nig Cuppy	1892–1901	2284.1	162
9	Ed Reulbach	1905–17	2362.2	161
10	Addie Joss	1902–10	2327	160

12. The record for the most career wins by a pitcher who never had a season when he won 20 games or fanned 100 batters belongs to what southpaw?

- A) He collected his 186th and final win for the 1935 Dodgers.
- B) His first career win came under the alias of Zach Walton.
- C) He won his only three World Series starts, the last in 1928.
- D) In 1929 he was 12–0 to set a season mark for the most wins without a loss.
- E) He leads all pitchers whose last name begins with Z in career wins.

Most Wins, Career, No 20-Win or 100-K Seasons

RANK	NAME	YEARS	W
1	Tom Zachary	1918–36	186
2	Willis Hudlin	1926–44	158
3	Red Lucas	1923–38	157
4	Harry Gumbert	1935–50	143
5	Gerry Staley	1947–61	134
6	Danny MacFayden	1926–43	132
7	Eldon Auker	1933–42	130
8	Clarence Mitchell	1911–32	125
9	Bob Stanley	1977–89	115
10	Sherry Smith	1911–27	114
	Fritz Ostermueller	1934–48	114

Note: Post-1884, when overhand pitching was first legalized; prior to then, several pitchers won more than 100 games with remarkably few Ks, led by George Zettlein with 129 wins on just 142 whiffs.

13. **A certain pitcher once hit six home runs in a season, just one short of the current NL record. He's more famous, though, for another "six" achievement: namely, being the only pitcher in the 20th century to win 20 games six years in a row without ever being on a pennant winner.**

   A) He won his first game for the 1965 Phils.

   B) Although only once a loop K leader, he fanned more than 3,000 hitters.

   C) He was a win leader in both major leagues.

   D) His 284th and last win came with the 1983 Cubs.

   E) He rapped six homers for the Cubs in 1971, the year he won his only Cy Young.

14. **What preexpansion chucker's season winning percentage fell to .938 and his career mark to 85–30 (.739) when he logged his only loss of the year on closing day?**

   A) His .938 WP is the season record for a starter in at least 15 decisions.

   B) As a rookie in 1932, he started a Series game but was removed after just two-thirds of an inning upon surrendering five runs.

   C) He retired with a .654 winning percentage in 217 decisions.

   D) He dropped his 1937 finale 1–0 to Jake Wade of the Tigers.

   E) He is the only man to play with the Babe and against the Scooter in a Series game.

Best Winning Percentage as a Starter, Season (Minimum 15 Decisions)

RANK	NAME	TEAM	YEAR	GS	W–L	PCT.
1	Johnny Allen	Cle, AL	1937	20	15–1	.938
2	Greg Maddux	Atl, NL	1995	28	19–2	.905
3	Lefty Grove	Phi, AL	1931	30	27–3	.900
	Randy Johnson	Sea, AL	1995	30	18–2	.900
5	Ron Guidry	NY, AL	1978	35	25–3	.893
6	Freddie Fitzsimmons	Bro, NL	1940	18	15–2	.882
7	Preacher Roe	Bro, NL	1951	33	21–3	.875
	Fred Goldsmith	Chi, NL	1880	24	21–3	.875
	Tom Seaver	Cin, NL	1981	23	14–2	.875
10	Joe Wood	Bos, AL	1912	38	33–5	.868

15. **Billy Taylor won 25 games before he jumped the St. Louis UA team in 1884 to join the Philadelphia AA club, thereby setting the all-time season record for the most wins by a pitcher before he changed teams. Who holds the comparable 20th century record?**

   A) He was traded on August 19 one year for two players and $200,000.

   B) He had 14 wins at the time and went on to collect 16, his career high.

   C) After going 3–15 as a starter in 1987, he became solely a pen man with the A's.

   D) In 148 games during 1992–94, he earned just three wins and five saves.

   E) His 16 wins in 1983 were divided between the Rangers and the Dodgers.

16. **When the Indians failed to produce a pitcher who won more than seven games in 1987, seven 20th century hurlers' names were erased from the books for leading a mound staff with a record-low eight wins, including two postexpansion pairs who tied for that small honor. Who is the only pitcher on that list whose meager total of eight victories not only led his club but also all came in relief roles?**

   A) He was a staff leader just once in his six-year AL career, when he collected 8 of his 23 career victories.

   B) He was also second on his club in saves that year with seven.

   C) His first ML win came in relief with Detroit in 1950.

   D) His eight victories in 1953 made him the last St. Louis Browns win leader.

   E) He and the Twins hurler who led the AL in starts in both 1984 and 1985 share the same initials.

Staff Leaders with Fewer than Nine Wins (Minimum 154-Game Season)

RANK	NAME	TEAM	YEAR	W
1	Jim Hughey	Cle, NL	1899	4
2	Tom Candiotti, Phil Niekro & Scott Bailes	Cle, AL	1987	7
	Omar Oliveras	Det, AL	1996	7
4	Buster Brown	Bos, NL	1911	8
	Ray Benge	Phi, NL	1928	8
	Marlin Stuart	StL, AL	1953	8
	Jack Fisher & Al Jackson	NY, NL	1965	8
	Jay Ballard & Dave Schmidt	Bal, AL	1988	8
	Joe Niekro & Al Santorini	SD, NL	1969	8
	John Wasdin	Oak, AL	1996	8

17. **Roy Face (18–1 in 1959) is just one of several relievers to be winning-percentage leaders while working relatively few innings. Who is the only starting pitcher to lead his league in winning percentage even though he failed to throw enough innings to qualify for the ERA crown by today's rules?**

   A) His 16 wins in his odd season are the most by a non-ERA qualifier prior to World War II.

   B) His 11 complete games the year he went 16–2 in just 134.1 innings qualified him for the ERA crown at that time.

   C) In 1935 he tied for the NL lead in shutouts despite going 4–8 and pitching just 94 innings.

   D) He has the most career wins of any post-1876 pitcher with fewer than 1,000 Ks who never had a 100-K season.

   E) He was nicknamed "Fat Freddie."

Most Season Wins by a Starting Pitcher, Non-ERA Qualifier

RANK	NAME	TEAM	YEAR	IP	W
1	Freddie Fitzsimmons	Bro, NL	1940	134.1	16
2	Larry French	Bro, NL	1942	147.2	15
	Don Gullett	Cin, NL	1975	159.2	15
4	Al Orth	Phi, NL	1899	144.2	14
	Fritz Peterson	Cle, AL	1975	146.1	14
	Don Gullett	NY, AL	1977	158.1	14
7	11 with 13 wins, led in fewest innings by:				
	Rip Sewell	Pit, NL	1948	121.2	13

Note: Maximum two relief wins allowed; fewer than 154 innings required for 1892, 1898, and 1899 seasons and all seasons between 1904 and 1960 AL and 1961 NL; fewer than 162 innings for all seasons since 1961 AL and 1962 NL; 1981, 1994, and 1995 seasons excepted.

18. **Among pitchers who toiled in at least 100 ML games, who is the only man to retire with a career winning percentage above .800?**
    A)   In his only big league start, he hurled a shutout.
    B)   He was 6–0 in 1951 with a 1.82 ERA.
    C)   He broke in with the 1950 White Sox.
    D)   He was born in Havana in 1923.
    E)   He and the AL hurler who notched a then-record 29 saves in 1961 share the same first name and same initials.

Highest Career Winning Percentage (Minimum 100 Games)

RANK	NAME	YEARS	G	W–L	PCT.
1	Luis Aloma	1950–53	116	18–3	.857
2	Mike Wallace	1973–77	117	11–3	.786
3	Howie Krist	1937–46	128	37–11	.771
4	Tom Tellman	1979–85	112	18–7	.720
5	Spud Chandler	1937–47	211	109–43	.717
6	Joe Black	1952–57	172	30–12	.714
7	Jack Spring	1955–65	155	12–5	.706
	Bill Kelso	1964–68	119	12–5	.706
9	Bob Caruthers	1884–92	340	218–97	.692
10	Dave Foutz	1884–94	251	147–66	.690

19. **Need more evidence that the offensive surge in the last couple of years is the greatest since the mid-1890s? Then check this out: In 1996 a certain southpaw broke a 102-year-old record for the highest ERA by a leader in shutouts when he clocked in at 5.12. Who is he?**
    A)   He tied Pat Hentgen and Ken Hill for the AL shutout crown with three.
    B)   He also led the AL in walks with 116.
    C)   His 1996 team claimed him from the Pirates on waivers in 1994.
    D)   Tom Kelly gave him 31 starting assignments in 1996.
    E)   He and the only hurler to throw a perfect game between 1915 and 1956 share the same last name.

Highest Season ERA, Leader in Shutouts

RANK	NAME	TEAM	YEAR	SOS	ERA
1	Rich Robertson	Min, AL	1996	3	5.12
2	Kid Nichols	Bos, NL	1894	3	4.75
3	Nig Cuppy	Cle, NL	1894	3	4.56
4	George Earnshaw	Phi, AL	1930	3	4.44
5	Charlie Root	Chi, NL	1930	4	4.33
6	Bucky Walters	Phi, NL	1936	4	4.26
7	Hal Carlson	Phi, NL	1925	4	4.23
8	Phil Douglas	NY, NL	1921	3	4.21
9	George Blaeholder	StL, AL	1929	4	4.18
10	Ed Wells	Det, AL	1926	4	4.15

Note: All pitchers on the list except Wells tied for the league lead in shutouts.

20. The record holder for the fewest complete games by a 25-game winner went the route just twice but nevertheless received a controversial Cy Young Award in his career year. Who is he?

A) Both of his complete games were shutouts.

B) Ironically, the following year, he had seven complete games but just 12 wins.

C) He earned his 200th career win with a last-place team after bagging his 199th win with a division champ.

D) His 199th and 200th career wins came in the same uniform.

E) He debuted with the 1978 Dodgers and spent his first nine seasons in L.A.

21. Only two pitchers have set loop records for both wins and losses in the same era. One is in the Hall of Fame, the other in the "Hall of Shame." Name both.

A) Both were right-handers.

B) One set a National League era record for both wins and losses five years apart while pitching for the same team.

C) The other hurler set a comparable AL record three years apart while toiling for two different teams.

D) The NL hurler faced the Yankees in his lone World Series appearance, and the AL'er opposed the Cardinals in his lone Series 18 years later.

E) Both hurlers hold the post–World War II season mark for the most wins in their respective leagues.

Season Records by Era

	National League			American League		
	RECORD	NAME	YEAR	RECORD	NAME	YEAR
Innings						
1871–75	625.2	Bobby Mathews	1875—NA			
1876–92	**680**	**Will White**	**1879**	670.2	Guy Hecker	1882
1893–1900	482	Amos Rusie	1893	447.1	Ted Breitenstein	1894
1901–19	434	Joe McGinnity	1903	454.2	Jack Chesbro	1904
1920–41	363.1	Pete Alexander	1920	357.2	George Uhle	1923
1942–60	371.1	Bob Feller	1946	346.2	Robin Roberts	1953
1961–76	346.1	Steve Carlton	1972	376.2	Wilbur Wood	1972
1977–93	342	Phil Niekro	1979	319	Jim Palmer	1977
1994–	268.2	Curt Schilling	1998	265.2	Pat Hentgen	1996
Games						
1871–75	72	Al Spalding	1875—NA			
1876–92	76	Will White	1879	75	Guy Hecker	1884
	76	Pud Galvin	1883			
	76	Hoss Radbourn	1883			
1893–1900	56	Amos Rusie	1893	56	Pink Hawley	1895
	56	Ted Breitenstein	1894			
1901–19	56	Christy Mathewson	1908	66	Ed Walsh	1908
1920–41	56	Hugh Mulcahy	1937	64	Firpo Marberry	1926
1942–60	74	Jim Konstanty	1950	70	Mike Fornieles	1960
1961–76	**106**	**Mike Marshall**	**1974**	88	Wilbur Wood	1968
1977–93	94	Kent Tekulve	1978	90	Mike Marshall	1979
1994–	84	Stan Belinda	1997	88	Mike Myers	1997
				88	Sean Runyan	1998

		National League			American League	
	RECORD	NAME	YEAR	RECORD	NAME	YEAR

Wins

	RECORD	NAME	YEAR	RECORD	NAME	YEAR
1871–75	54	Al Spalding	1875—NA			
1876–92	**60**	**Hoss Radbourn**	**1884**	52	Guy Hecker	1884
1893–1900	36	Frank Killen	1893	36	Amos Rusie	1894
1901–19	35	Joe McGinnity	1904	41	Jack Chesbro	1904
1920–41	30	Dizzy Dean	1934	31	Lefty Grove	1931
1942–60	28	Robin Roberts	1952	29	Hal Newhouser	1944
1961–76	27	Sandy Koufax	1966	31	Denny McLain	1968
	27	Steve Carlton	1972			
1977–93	24	Steve Carlton	1980	27	Bob Welch	1990
	24	Dwight Gooden	1985			
1994–	24	John Smoltz	1996	21	Andy Pettitte	1996
				21	Roger Clemens	1997

Winning Percentage (Minimum 20 Decisions)

	RECORD	NAME	YEAR	RECORD	NAME	YEAR
1871–75	**.915**	**Al Spalding**	**1875—NA**			
1876–92	.875	Fred Goldsmith	1880	.784	Bob Caruthers	1889
1893–1900	.838	Bill Hoffer	1895	.824	Jim Hughes	1899
1901–19	.833	King Cole	1910	.872	Joe Wood	1912
1920–41	.826	Elmer Riddle	1941	.886	Lefty Grove	1931
1942–60	.880	Preacher Roe	1951	.833	Spud Chandler	1943
1961–76	.833	Sandy Koufax	1963	.862	Whitey Ford	1961
1977–93	.870	David Cone	1988	.893	Ron Guidry	1978
1994–	.905	Greg Maddux	1995	.900	Randy Johnson	1995

Losses

	RECORD	NAME	YEAR	RECORD	NAME	YEAR
1871–75	38	Bobby Mathews	1875—NA			
1876–92	**48**	**John Coleman**	**1883**	41	Larry McKeon	1884
1893–1900	35	Red Donahue	1897	30	Ted Breitenstein	1895
				30	Jim Hughey	1899
1901–19	29	Vic Willis	1905	26	Pete Dowling	1901
				26	Happy Townsend	1904
				26	Bob Groom	1909
1920–41	27	Paul Derringer	1933	25	Scott Perry	1920
				25	Red Ruffing	1928
1942–60	22	Robin Roberts	1957	22	Art Ditmar	1956
1961–76	24	Jack Fisher	1965	22	Denny McLain	1971
	24	Roger Craig	1962			
1977–93	20	Phil Niekro	1977	20	Brian Kingman	1980
	20	Phil Niekro	1979			
1994–	17	Mark Leiter	1997	18	Jim Abbott	1996
	17	Darryl Kile	1998			

	National League				American League	
RECORD	**NAME**	**YEAR**	**RECORD**	**NAME**	**YEAR**

Strikeouts

1871–75	100	Bobby Mathews	1874—NA			
1876–92	441	Hoss Radbourn	1884	**513**	**Matt Kilroy**	**1886**
1893–1900	239	Cy Seymour	1898	208	Amos Rusie	1893
1901–19	267	Christy Mathewson	1903	349	Rube Waddell	1904
1920–41	262	Dazzy Vance	1924	261	Bob Feller	1940
1942–60	246	Don Drysdale	1960	348	Bob Feller	1946
1961–76	382	Sandy Koufax	1965	383	Nolan Ryan	1973
1977–93	313	J. R. Richard	1979	341	Nolan Ryan	1977
1994–	319	Curt Schilling	1997	294	Randy Johnson	1995

Walks *(1871–88 Excluded)*

1889–92	**289**	**Amos Rusie**	**1890**	274	Mark Baldwin	1889
1893–1900	218	Amos Rusie	1893	213	Cy Seymour	1898
1901–19	181	Bob Harmon	1911	168	Elmer Myers	1916
1920–41	130	Sheriff Blake	1929	208	Bob Feller	1938
1942–60	185	Sam Jones	1955	181	Bob Turley	1954
1961–76	151	J. R. Richard	1976	202	Nolan Ryan	1974
1977–93	164	Phil Niekro	1977	204	Nolan Ryan	1977
1994–	119	Al Leiter	1996	116	Rich Robertson	1996

Fewest Walks per Nine Innings *(1871–88 Excluded)*

1889–92	1.79	Scott Stratton	1892	1.27	Scott Stratton	1890
1893–1900	0.98	Cy Young	1898	1.01	Cy Young	1900
1901–19	**0.62**	**Christy Mathewson**	**1913**	0.69	Cy Young	1904
1920–41	**0.62**	**Babe Adams**	**1920**	1.15	Herb Pennock	1930
1942–60	1.09	Don Newcombe	1959	0.96	Tiny Bonham	1942
1961–76	1.02	Gary Nolan	1976	1.19	Jim Merritt	1967
1977–93	0.77	Bob Tewksbury	1992	1.07	La Marr Hoyt	1983
1994–	0.66	Bret Saberhagen	1994	1.22	David Wells	1998

ERA *(Minimum One Inning per Games Team Played)*

1871–75	1.41	Tommy Bond	1875—NA			
1876–92	**0.86**	**Tim Keefe**	**1880**	1.21	Denny Driscoll	1882
1893–1900	1.88	Clark Griffith	1898	2.10	Al Maul	1898
1901–19	1.04	Mordecai Brown	1906	0.96	Dutch Leonard	1914
1920–41	1.66	Carl Hubbell	1933	2.06	Lefty Grove	1931
1942–60	1.78	Mort Cooper	1942	1.64	Spud Chandler	1943
1961–76	1.12	Bob Gibson	1968	1.60	Luis Tiant	1968
1977–93	1.53	Dwight Gooden	1985	1.74	Ron Guidry	1978
1994–	1.58	Greg Maddux	1994	2.05	Roger Clemens	1997

	National League			American League		
	RECORD	**NAME**	**YEAR**	**RECORD**	**NAME**	**YEAR**
Games Started						
1871–75	70	Bobby Mathews	1875—NA			
1876–92	**75**	**Will White**	**1879**	73	Guy Hecker	1884
	75	**Pud Galvin**	**1883**			
1893–1900	52	Amos Rusie	1893	50	Done by five men	
1901–19	48	Joe McGinnity	1903	51	Jack Chesbro	1904
1920–41	40	Pete Alexander	1920	44	George Uhle	1923
1942–60	42	Bob Friend	1956	42	Bob Feller	1946
1961–76	42	Done by four men		49	Wilbur Wood	1972
1977–93	44	Phil Niekro	1979	40	Mike Flanagan	1978
				40	Dennis Leonard	1978
				40	Jim Clancy	1982
1994–	36	Tom Glavine	1996	36	Mike Mussina	1996
Complete Games						
1871–75	69	Bobby Mathews	1875—NA			
1876–92	**75**	**Will White**	**1879**	72	Guy Hecker	1884
1893–1900	50	Amos Rusie	1893	46	Ted Breitenstein	1894
				46	Ted Breitenstein	1895
1901–19	45	Vic Willis	1902	48	Jack Chesbro	1904
1920–41	33	Pete Alexander	1920	32	Red Faber	1921
	33	Burleigh Grimes	1923	32	George Uhle	1926
1942–60	33	Robin Roberts	1953	36	Bob Feller	1946
1961–76	30	Juan Marichal	1968	30	Fergie Jenkins	1971
	30	Steve Carlton	1972	30	Catfish Hunter	1975
1977–93	23	Phil Niekro	1979	28	Rick Langford	1980
1994–	15	Curt Schilling	1998	11	Scott Erickson	1998
Shutouts						
1871–75	7	George Zettlein	1875—NA			
	7	Candy Cummings	1875—NA			
	7	Al Spalding	1875—NA			
1876–92	**16**	**George Bradley**	**1876**	12	Ed Morris	1886
1893–1900	6	Wiley Piatt	1898	6	Jack Powell	1898
1901–19	**16**	**Pete Alexander**	**1916**	13	Jack Coombs	1910
1920–41	10	Carl Hubbell	1933	6	Done by nine men	
1942–60	10	Mort Cooper	1942	10	Bob Feller	1946
				10	Bob Lemon	1948
1961–76	13	Bob Gibson	1968	11	Dean Chance	1964
1977–93	10	John Tudor	1985	9	Ron Guidry	1978
1994–	5	Carlos Perez	1997	5	David Wells	1998
	5	Greg Maddux	1998			

		National League			American League	
	RECORD	**NAME**	**YEAR**	**RECORD**	**NAME**	**YEAR**
Saves						
1871–75	9	Al Spalding	1875—NA			
1876–92	5	Jack Manning	1876	5	Tony Mullane	1889
1893–1900	4	Tony Mullane	1894	4	Kid Nichols	1898
	4	Frank Kitson	1900			
1901–19	13	Mordecai Brown	1911	13	Chief Bender	1913
1920–41	15	Joe Quinn	1931	26	Firpo Marberry	1926
1942–60	26	Lindy McDaniel	1960	27	Joe Page	1949
				27	Ellis Kinder	1953
1961–76	37	Clay Carroll	1972	38	John Hiller	1973
1977–93	53	Randy Myers	1993	**57**	**Bobby Thigpen**	**1990**
1994–	53	Trevor Hoffman	1998	46	Jose Mesa	1995
				46	Tom Gordon	1998
Home Runs Allowed						
1871–75	15	Tommy Bond	1874—NA			
1876–92	35	Larry Corcoran	1884	21	Park Swartzel	1889
1893–1900	27	Frank Dwyer	1894	27	Jack Stivetts	1894
1901–19	13	Al Mattern	1911	18	Al Orth	1902
1920–41	32	Lon Warneke	1937	30	Bobo Newsom	1938
1942–60	46	Robin Roberts	1956	43	Pedro Ramos	1957
1961–76	40	Phil Niekro	1970	42	Denny McLain	1966
1977–93	41	Phil Niekro	1979	**50**	**Bert Blyleven**	**1986**
1994–	39	Brian Anderson	1998	40	Brad Radke	1996
	39	Pedro Astacio	1998	40	Shawn Boskie	1996

Opponents' On-Base Percentage *(Minimum One Inning per Games Team Played)*

1871–75	.216	Cherokee Fisher	1872—NA			
1876–92	.217	George Bradley	1880	**.198**	**Guy Hecker**	**1882**
1893–1900	.272	Kid Nichols	1898	.275	Al Maul	1898
1901–19	.225	Christy Mathewson	1908	.217	Walter Johnson	1913
1920–41	.259	Babe Adams	1920	.267	Garland Braxton	1928
1942–60	.247	Warren Hacker	1952	.258	Roger Wolff	1945
1961–76	.228	Sandy Koufax	1965	.233	Luis Tiant	1968
1977–93	.244	Mike Scott	1986	.250	Ron Guidry	1978
1994–	.245	Greg Maddux	1994	.265	David Wells	1998

Note: All-time leaders are in **bold**. In the 1876–92 era, men who appear under the American League column are the American Association record holders. In the 1893–1900 era, men who appear under the American League column are the runners-up to the National League record holders.

Precious Pen Men

1. **Firpo Marberry and Doc Crandall were the first two pitchers to carve their reputations mainly as relievers, but they were also often employed as starters. So were Johnny Murphy and Mace Brown, two other outstanding bullpenners who took over Marberry's mantle in the late 1930s. Name the first man to make 100 or more pitching appearances in his ML career without ever getting a starting assignment.**

   A)   In his rookie year, he became the only hurler to win both ends of a doubleheader on the final day of the season when he stopped Cleveland twice in relief to pull his team into a tie for fifth place with the Indians.
   B)   He led the AL in saves as a rookie in 1944.
   C)   He was nearing age 40 in his rookie year.
   D)   His initials are the same as those of a Braves stopper in the early 1990s.
   E)   His nickname was "Jittery Joe."

Evolution of Career Record for Most Games, No Starts

NAME	YEARS	GAMES
Joe Berry	1942–46	133
Gordon Maltzberger	1943–47	135
Frank Funk	1960–63	137
Barney Schultz	1955–65	227
Terry Fox	1960–66	248
Hal Reniff	1961–67	276
Dick Radatz	1962–69	381
Jack Baldschun	1961–70	457
Jack Aker	1964–74	495
Bob Locker	1965–75	576
Sparky Lyle	1967–82	899
Kent Tekulve	1974–89	1050

Note: Minimum 100 games. Men listed held the record at the time of their last ML appearances. In some cases, other active hurlers had more relief appearances without a start than the record holder—e.g., Radatz in 1967 and Tekulve in 1988—but were not eligible until retirement ensured they would never make a start.

2. **Born in San Diego (Texas) and died in Paris (Arkansas), he set the NL mark for the longest shutout stint by a reliever when he blanked Boston for 14 frames to give the Cubs a 22-inning 4–3 win on May 17, 1927. Name him.**

A) It was his sole relief win that season.

B) His 14-inning scoreless skein was very uncharacteristic in that he never hurled a shutout in 43 big league starts.

C) He paced the NL in relief wins with six in 1931, his big league finale.

D) In 1930 he had the distinction of being the lone pitcher in the NL whose ERA exactly matched the loop's 20th century record-high 4.97 ERA.

E) His initials and first name are the same as those of the Mets lefty who topped the NL in winning percentage in 1986.

3. **Among hurlers with at least 50 relief victories, whose .718 winning percentage (51–20) is the best bullpen mark to date?**

A) His last relief win came with the 1949 Yankees.

B) His most famous relief loss was administered by the Yankees.

C) He faced the Yankees twice in World Series action during the 1940s.

D) Despondent when a big league comeback failed, he committed suicide in 1951.

E) It was his third-strike pitch to Tommy Henrich that made Mickey Owen the goat of the 1941 World Series.

Highest Relief Winning Percentage, Career (Minimum 50 Decisions)

RANK	NAME	YEARS	W–L	PCT.
1	Doc Crandall	1908–18	37–14	.725
2	Hugh Casey	1935–49	51–20	.718
3	Bobby Bolin	1961–73	38–17	.691
4	Guy Bush	1923–45	43–20	.683
5	Doug Bird	1973–83	44–21	.677
6	Lew Burdette	1950–67	36–19	.655
7	Grant Jackson	1965–82	62–33	.653
8	Pedro Borbon	1969–80	69–37	.651
9	Al Hrabosky	1970–82	64–35	.647
10	Eddie Rommel	1920–32	51–28	.646

Note: Borbon tops all relievers with 100 career decisions; Johnny Murphy (73–42) is second with a .635 winning percentage, and Dick Hall (71–41) is third at .634.

Hugh Casey didn't mind spring training at all, particularly when it took his Dodgers to Cuba. Like many preexpansion hurlers who spent most of their time in the bullpen, Casey also was frequently used as a starter. He was a mediocre 24–22 in starting roles but 51–20 out of the pen.

4. **Firpo Marberry, the game's marquee reliever during the 1920s, was forced to share the spotlight in 1927 with what Washington teammate who led the AL in both saves and mound appearances?**
   A)   He debuted with the 1921 Braves.
   B)   In 1926 he was 5–1 in 37 games with the Yankees.
   C)   In 1928, still with Washington, he paced the AL in ERA.
   D)   His initials are the same as those of the 1902 NL bat crown winner.
   E)   His first name is the same as the last name of the hurler who led the AL in losses in 1977 after the Indians made him their first big free-agent pickup.

5. **After nine years as a starter, what southpaw went to the bullpen in 1971 and posted a perfect 6–0 record despite fashioning a dreadful 6.99 ERA in 37 outings?**
   A) He recorded 11 saves in 1973 as the Red Sox top lefty fireman.
   B) In 1964 he won 18 and led the NL in KS.
   C) His six wins in 1971 are the most ever by a bullpenner who posted a season ERA above 5.00 without suffering any losses.
   D) He led NL hurlers in walks four times as a member of the same NL team.
   E) He owns the Pirates season record for the most pitching strikeouts.

Most Wins, Season, No Losses, ERA Above 5.00

RANK	NAME	TEAM	YEAR	IP	ERA	W
1	Bob Veale	Pit, NL	1971	46.1	6.99	6
2	Pete Appleton	Chi, AL	1940	57.2	5.62	4
	Ted Wilks	StL, NL	1947	50.1	5.01	4
	Johnny Klippstein	LA, NL	1959	45.2	5.91	4
	Omar Daal	LA, NL	1995	20	7.20	4
6	Many with 3					

6. **Bob Veale's modest six wins are the most without a loss by a pitcher with an ERA above 5.00, but what pen man recently set an inauspicious season record when he snagged a bounteous total of 35 saves on a 5.00+ ERA?**
   A) He broke Mike Henneman's year-old mark of 31 saves on a 5.00+ ERA.
   B) He was 2–6 with a 5.28 ERA the year he broke Henneman's record.
   C) Wing trouble idled him for all of the 1990 and 1991 seasons.
   D) In 1996 he and his brother combined to set a season sibling save record.
   E) His 36 saves in 1986 are still the rookie record.

Evolution of Season Record for Most Saves, ERA Above 5.00

NAME	TEAM	YEAR	ERA	SAVES
Harry Wright	Bos, NA	1871	6.27	3
Bill Sowders	Bos/Pit, NL	1889	6.37	3
Tony Mullane	Bal/Cle, NL	1894	6.59	4
Jim Middleton	Det, AL	1921	5.03	7
Jess Doyle	Det, AL	1925	5.93	8
Wilcy Moore	NY, AL	1933	5.52	8
Xavier Rescigno	Pit, NL	1945	5.72	9
Joe Page	NY, AL	1950	5.04	13
Darold Knowles	Chi, NL	1975	5.81	15
Tug McGraw	Phi, NL	1979	5.14	16
Rollie Fingers	Mil, AL	1985	5.01	17
Dave Smith	Chi, NL	1991	6.00	17
Rob Dibble	Cin, NL	1993	6.48	19
Doug Jones	Bal, AL	1995	5.01	22
Mike Henneman	Tex, AL	1996	5.79	31
Todd Worrell	LA, NL	1997	5.28	35

7. Bruce Sutter amassed a remarkable total of 105 saves in his first four seasons, but he was not the first reliever to crack the 100-save mark so quickly. Who was?

   A) His last save came with the Expos, but almost all his other saves were achieved in the AL.
   B) He starred at Michigan State in the late 1950s.
   C) He finished in 1969 with 122 career saves, most of them notched in his first four seasons.
   D) He had a "monster" year in 1964 when he collected a record 181 Ks in relief.
   E) As a frosh, he led the AL with 24 saves for Boston, which won only 76 games.

8. When he logged his 17th and last career save in 1904, what Hall of Famer had the most saves in history to that point?

   A) He's the only pitcher to win 20 games after missing two full ML seasons in a row for any reason but a military service interruption.
   B) He holds the record for the most career wins by a switch-hitter.
   C) He's the only pitcher to post five 30-win seasons since the mound was established at its present distance from home plate.
   D) He led all pitchers in wins during the decade of the 1890s.
   E) His nickname proved apt when he won 27 games as a 20-year-old rookie for Boston in 1890.

Evolution of Career Record for Saves

NAME	YEARS	SAVES	SET RECORD
Kid Nichols	1890—1906	17	1891
Joe McGinnity	1899—1908	24	1907
Three Finger Brown	1903—16	48	1910
Firpo Marberry	1923—36	101	1926
Johnny Murphy	1932—47	107	1946
Roy Face	1953—69	193	1962
Hoyt Wilhelm	1952—72	227	1969
Rollie Fingers	1968—85	341	1980
Jeff Reardon	1979—94	367	1992
Lee Smith	1980—97	478	1993

Note: Since 1891, the year the substitution rule was liberalized, allowing a team to bring a pitcher into a game off the bench. Face surpassed Murphy in 1962.

9. The only hurler to make both 400 career starts and 400 relief appearances was never a league leader in saves but compiled 42 career relief wins. Who is he?

   A) He twice led the AL in starts and once led in complete games.
   B) He played in three World Series, all with the same team, and made eight postseason mound appearances altogether, all in relief.
   C) He ranks among the top 10 in career walks.
   D) He's on the elite list of 200-game winners who never had a 20-win season.
   E) He last pitched for the Marlins in 1994.

10. **Born Carlos Clolo, he was a career 29–40 as a starter, but coming out of the pen, he put up 25 wins and just five losses. By what name was he better known?**

    A)   He debuted with Cincinnati in 1906 and collected his last career save with the Cardinals in 1916 but was best known for his work in the AL.

    B)   He made two relief appearances in the 1912 World Series for the victors.

    C)   In 1912 he was 15–8 and 6–0 as a fireman to top the AL in relief wins.

    D)   His initials are the same as those of the Texas workhorse in the late 1980s.

    E)   His nickname was "Sea Lion."

Best Relief Winning Percentage, Career (Minimum 20 Relief Wins)

RANK	NAME	YEARS	W–L	PCT.
1	Deacon Phillippe	1899–1911	24–4	.857
2	Charley Hall	1906–18	25–5	.833
3	George Mullin	1902–15	23–5	.821
4	Rube Waddell	1897–1910	22–6	.786
5	Joe Black	1952–57	26–8	.765
6	Wilbur Cooper	1912–26	21–7	.750
7	Clark Griffith	1891–1914	24–9	.727
8	Lefty Leifield	1905–20	21–8	.724
9	Christy Mathewson	1900–16	26–10	.722
10	Carl Hubbell	1928–43	20–8	.714

11. **Closers nowadays generally achieve many more saves than decisions. Who is the only bullpenner with at least 150 career saves whose relief decisions outnumber his saves?**

    A)   He fell only 13 mound appearances short of 1,000 in his 21-year career.

    B)   He never appeared in a postseason game.

    C)   He amassed 207 decisions and 172 saves in relief roles.

    D)   In 1960 he was 0–2 as a starter but 12–2 in relief, with a National League–top 26 saves.

    E)   In 1957 he and his brother Von fashioned 22 wins for the Cardinals, 18 of them in starting roles.

12. **Firpo Marberry was the first man to collect both 100 wins and 100 saves. Who was the second hurler to do it?**

    A)   He celebrated his 32nd birthday in his rookie year.

    B)   He collected his last save with the White Sox at age 42.

    C)   He twice led the AL in saves during the 1950s.

    D)   In 1949 he topped the AL in winning percentage when he went 23–6.

    E)   They called him "Old Folks."

NAME	YEARS	SAVES	W
Dennis Eckersley	1975–98	354	197
Firpo Marberry	1922–36	101	148
Ron Reed	1966–84	103	146
Hoyt Wilhelm	1952–72	227	143
Lindy McDaniel	1955–75	172	141
Goose Gossage	1972–94	310	124
Bob Stanley	1977–89	132	115
Rollie Fingers	1968–85	331	114
Ron Kline	1952–70	108	114
Stu Miller	1952–68	154	105
Roy Face	1953–69	193	104
Ellis Kinder	1946–57	102	102
Dave Giusti	1962–77	145	100

Table title: **Pitchers with 100 Wins and 100 Saves**

13. **What reliever who ranks sixth in World Series mound appearances, with 13, carved a shutout in his lone fall starting assignment?**
   A) He led the NL in saves the same year he notched his Series whitewash.
   B) He last pitched for the 1962 Mets.
   C) He blanked the Yankees in his lone Series start.
   D) Four years after he blanked the Yankees, he was blasted by Stengel's last Bomber team in three World Series relief outings with a different NL club.
   E) The day prior to his Series shutout, his team was victim of a perfect game.

14. **Only one hurler who won three games in a World Series both began and ended his career as a fireman. Who is he?**
   A) He debuted with a team that was led in saves by Joe Page.
   B) He finished with a team that was led in saves by Minnie Rojas.
   C) In 1959 he became the only NL win leader to date whose given first name is Selva.
   D) He was a perfect 8–0 with eight saves in bullpen roles with Milwaukee's first NL representative in this century.
   E) His three-win World Series came at the expense of his original team.

15. **Name the lone pitcher who ranks among the top five in all of the following career departments: saves, relief wins, and mound appearances.**
   A) At one point, he worked in 130 or more innings four years in a row.
   B) He was the first man in ML history to appear in 1,000 games and accumulate fewer than 100 career ABs.
   C) He's the only man in ML history to appear in 1,000 games and have a season in which he surrendered more than 200 hits.
   D) He's one of the few hurlers to collect 100 saves in both the AL and the NL.
   E) In 1981 he notched 20 saves and a glittering 0.77 ERA for the AL flag winner.

16. **The first two southpaws to bag as many as 20 saves in a season both did it for the same team. Who are they?**

    A) On both occasions, the team won a World Championship.

    B) Although the pair did it 12 years apart, both were teammates of the same Hall of Fame catcher.

    C) The second lefty to do it began as a starter with the 1955 Cards the year after the first lefty had failed in a comeback attempt with the Pirates.

    D) The catcher who worked with both lefty relief aces in 1954 also handled the first pitcher to lead one major league in wins and the other in saves.

    E) One lefty was nicknamed "The Gay Reliever" and the other "Yo-Yo."

Evolution of Season Record for Saves by a Left-Hander

NAME	TEAM	YEAR	SAVES
Lee Richmond	Wor, NL	1880	3
Hooks Wiltse	NY, NL	1904	3
Case Patten	Was, AL	1904	3
Hooks Wiltse	NY, NL	1905	4
Hooks Wiltse	NY, NL	1906	6
Slim Sallee	StL, NL	1912	6
Slim Sallee	StL, NL	1914	6
Dutch Leonard	Bos, AL	1916	6
Dave Danforth	Chi, AL	1917	9
Garland Braxton	Was, AL	1927	13
Joe Page	NY, AL	1947	17
Joe Page	NY, AL	1949	27
Luis Arroyo	NY, AL	1961	29
Ron Perranoski	Min, AL	1969	31
Ron Perranoski	Min, AL	1970	34
Sparky Lyle	NY, AL	1972	35
John Hiller	Det, AL	1973	38
Dave Righetti	NY, AL	1986	46
Randy Myers	Chi, NL	1993	53

17. **Who is the only pitcher since 1893 to lead the majors one season in starts after previously topping all ML hurlers in relief appearances?**

    A) His first relief win came with the 1965 Pirates.

    B) He was a loop leader three years in a row in relief appearances.

    C) He was later a loop leader four years in a row in starts.

    D) After making 77 appearances, all in relief, in 1970, he made only 9 more relief appearances in the final nine years of his career.

    E) In 1973 he became the most recent pitcher to start both ends of a twin bill.

18. What Hall of Famer was the first pitcher to compile as many as 10 relief decisions in a season?

A) He led the AL in relief wins and losses as well as saves the year he did it.

B) He also led the AL in innings, mound appearances, and strikeouts that year.

C) In 1910 he set a record for the lowest ERA (1.27) by a league loss leader.

D) All of his 195 career wins came with the same AL team.

E) Nearly 21 percent of his career wins were achieved in a single season.

Season Relief Win and Loss Leaders, 1871–1900

WINS		NAME	TEAM	LOSSES	NAME	TEAM
National Association						
1871	1	Harry Wright	Boston	1	Charlie Pabor	Rockford
	1	Ed Pinkham	Chicago			
1872	2	Cherokee Fisher	Baltimore	2	Bobby Mathews	Baltimore
1873	1	Cherokee Fisher	Athletics	2	Cherokee Fisher	Athletics
				2	Al Spalding	Boston
1874	1	Bill Stearns	Hartford	2	Cherokee Fisher	Hartford
1875	1	Jack Manning	Boston	1	Al Spalding	Boston
	1	Jim Devlin	Chicago	1	George Wright	Boston
	1	Bill Parks	Washington			
National League						
1876	4	Jack Manning	Boston	None		
1877	2	Tricky Nichols	St. Louis	1	Cal McVey	Chicago
1878	1	Sam Weaver	Milwaukee	1	Tricky Nichols	Providence
	1	Harry Wheeler	Providence			
1879	5	Monte Ward	Providence	1	Monte Ward	Providence
				1	Cal McVey	Cincinnati
1880	3	George Bradley	Providence	2	Tommy Bond	Boston
				2	Pud Galvin	Buffalo
1881	1	Larry Corcoran	Chicago	1	The Only Nolan	Cleveland
	1	Hoss Radbourn	Providence	1	Hoss Radbourn	Providence
	1	Monte Ward	Providence	1	Curry Foley	Buffalo
	1	Jim Whitney	Boston	1	Monte Ward	Providence
1882	1	Tim Keefe	Troy	1	Fred Corey	Worcester
	1	Bobby Mathews	Boston	1	Bobby Mathews	Boston
	1	Hoss Radbourn	Providence			
	1	Lee Richmond	Worcester			
American Association						
1882	1	Ed Fusselbach	St. Louis	1	Billy Taylor	Pittsburgh
	1	Cub Stricker	Philadelphia	1	Harry Wheeler	Cincinnati
	1	Harry Wheeler	Cincinnati			

WINS		NAME	TEAM	LOSSES	NAME	TEAM
National League						
1883	4	Monte Ward	New York	2	Hoss Radbourn	Providence
American Association						
1883	1	Tony Mullane	St. Louis	1	Bob Barr	Pittsburgh
	1	Billy Taylor	Pittsburgh	1	Fred Corey	Philadelphia
				1	Hardie Henderson	Baltimore
				1	Billy Taylor	Pittsburgh
				1	Will White	Cincinnati
National League						
1884	1	Hoss Radbourn	Providence	1	Larry Corcoran	Chicago
	1	Charlie Sweeney	Providence	1	Frank Meinke	Detroit
				1	Cyclone Miller	Providence
				1	Jim O'Rourke	Buffalo
				1	Charlie Sweeney	Providence
				1	Jim Whitney	Boston
				1	Monte Ward	New York
American Association						
1884	3	Bob Caruthers	St. Louis	1	Tom Brown	Pittsburgh
				1	Jack Lynch	New York
				1	Jim McLaughlin	Baltimore
				1	Tony Mullane	Toledo
Union Association						
1884	2	Yank Robinson	Baltimore	2	Charlie Sweeney	St. Louis
				2	Bill Wise	Washington
National League						
1885	1	Henry Boyle	St. Louis	1	Charlie Ferguson	Philadelphia
	1	Charlie Ferguson	Philadelphia	1	Pete Wood	Buffalo
	1	Fred Pfeffer	Chicago			
American Association						
1885	1	Pop Corkhill	Cincinnati	3	Pop Corkhill	Cincinnati
	1	Charlie Eden	Pittsburgh			
	1	Dave Foutz	St. Louis			
	1	Jack Lynch	New York			
	1	Gus Shallix	Cincinnati			
National League						
1886	3	Ed Daily	Philadelphia	1	Jim Fogarty	Philadelphia
	3	Hardy Richardson	Detroit			
American Association						
1886	4	Tony Mullane	Cincinnati	1	Ted Kennedy	Philadelphia
National League						
1887	2	Al Maul	Philadelphia	2	Mike Tiernan	New York

WINS	NAME	TEAM	LOSSES	NAME	TEAM
American Association					
1887 1	Myron Allen	Cleveland	2	Phenomenal Smith	Baltimore
1	Oyster Burns	Baltimore			
1	Pop Corkhill	Cincinnati			
1	Hardie Henderson	Brooklyn			
1	Silver King	St. Louis			
1	Joe Neale	Louisville			
1	Toad Ramsey	Louisville			
1	Ed Seward	Philadelphia			
National League					
1888 3	Jimmy Ryan	Chicago	2	George Van Haltren	Chicago
American Association					
1888 1	Bob Caruthers	Brooklyn	1	Oyster Burns	Baltimore
1	Nat Hudson	St. Louis	1	Mike Mattimore	Philadelphia
1	Silver King	St. Louis			
1	Tony Mullane	Cincinnati			
1	Henry Porter	Kansas City			
1	Phenomenal Smith	Baltimore			
1	Steve Toole	Kansas City			
1	Cub Stricker	Cleveland			
National League					
1889 3	Charlie Buffinton	Philadelphia	2	Bill Burdick	Indianapolis
			2	Kid Gleason	Philadelphia
			2	John Tener	Chicago
American Association					
1889 4	Bob Caruthers	Brooklyn	2	Mark Baldwin	Columbus
			2	Jesse Duryea	Cincinnati
			2	Red Ehret	Louisville
National League					
1890 2	Jesse Burkett	New York	1	Bill Hutchison	Chicago
2	Leon Viau	Cincinnati	1	Amos Rusie	New York
			1	Crazy Schmit	Pittsburgh
			1	Mickey Hughes	New York
			1	John Sharrott	New York
			1	Bill Sowders	Pittsburgh
			1	Cy Young	Cleveland
American Association					
1890 3	Hank Gastright	Columbus	2	Charlie Sprague	Toledo
3	Jack Stivetts	St. Louis	2	Jack Stivetts	St. Louis
			2	Bill Widner	Columbus
Players League					
1890 4	Bill Daley	Boston	2	Con Murphy	Brooklyn
National League					
1891 7	Bill Hutchison	Chicago	3	Cy Young	Cleveland

WINS		NAME	TEAM	LOSSES	NAME	TEAM
American Association						
1891	5	Clark Griffith	St. Louis/Boston	2	Bill Daley	Boston
				2	Red Ehret	Louisville
				2	Phil Knell	Columbus
				2	Willard Mains	Cincinnati
National League						
1892	4	Gus Weyhing	Philadelphia	3	Frank Killen	Washington
1893	5	Frank Killen	Pittsburgh	3	Ted Breitenstein	St. Louis
1894	8	Nig Cuppy	Cleveland	5	Pink Hawley	St. Louis
1895	7	Cy Young	Cleveland	4	Dad Clarke	New York
				4	Duke Esper	Baltimore
1896	3	Pink Hawley	Pittsburgh	3	Les German	New York/Washington
	3	Silver King	Washington			
	3	Mike Sullivan	New York			
1897	5	Billy Rhines	Cincinnati	4	Cy Young	Cleveland
1898	4	Bill Damman	Cincinnati	2	Nig Cuppy	Cleveland
	4	Pink Hawley	Cincinnati	2	Charlie Hastings	Pittsburgh
				2	Bill Damman	Cincinnati
				2	Joe Yeager	Brooklyn
1899	3	Ted Lewis	Boston	5	Sam Leever	Pittsburgh
	3	Al Orth	Philadelphia			
	3	Jesse Tannehill	Pittsburgh			
	3	Joe McGinnity	Baltimore			
	3	Deacon Phillippe	Louisville			
1900	4	Ted Lewis	Boston	3	Rube Waddell	Pittsburgh

Season Relief Win and Loss Leaders, 1901–1998

WINS		NAME	TEAM	LOSSES	NAME	TEAM
National League						
1901	4	Bill Donovan	Brooklyn	2	Frank Kitson	Brooklyn
				2	Jack Powell	St. Louis
1902	2	Roy Evans	New York/Brooklyn	3	Roy Evans	New York/Brooklyn
	2	Doc Newton	Brooklyn	3	Togie Pittinger	Boston
	2	Mike O'Neill	St. Louis			
	2	Togie Pittinger	Boston			
	2	Jesse Tannehill	Pittsburgh			
1903	2	Clarence Currie	St. Louis/Chicago	2	Jack Harper	Cincinnati
	2	Joe McGinnity	New York	2	John Malarkey	Boston
	2	Togie Pittinger	Boston	2	Joe McGinnity	New York
	2	Bucky Veil	Pittsburgh			

	WINS	NAME	TEAM	LOSSES	NAME	TEAM
1904	2	Mordecai Brown	Chicago	2	Pat Carney	Boston
	2	Chick Fraser	Philadelphia			
	2	Win Kellum	Cincinnati			
	2	Christy Mathewson	New York			
	2	Joe McGinnity	New York			
	2	Jack Sutthoff	Cincinnati/Philadelphia			
1905	5	Mike Lynch	Pittsburgh	3	Charlie Chech	Cincinnati
				3	Dick Harley	Boston
1906	4	Hooks Wiltse	New York	4	Ed Karger	Pittsburgh/St. Louis
1907	4	Andy Coakley	Cincinnati	4	Joe McGinnity	New York
	4	Chick Fraser	Chicago			
1908	4	Mordecai Brown	Chicago	3	Art Fromme	St. Louis
	4	Joe McGinnity	New York	3	Jim Holmes	Brooklyn
1909	7	Howie Camnitz	Pittsburgh	5	Forrest More	St. Louis/Boston
1910	7	Doc Crandall	New York	5	Buster Brown	Boston
	7	Deacon Phillippe	Pittsburgh			
1911	7	Doc Crandall	New York	5	Frank Smith	Cincinnati
1912	6	Doc Crandall	New York	5	Doc Crandall	New York
	6	Charlie Smith	Chicago			
1913	6	Art Fromme	Cincinnati/New York	6	Bob Harmon	St. Louis
1914	5	Paul Strand	Philadelphia	5	Slim Sallee	St. Louis
1915	6	Tom Hughes	Boston	5	Hub Perdue	St. Louis
1916	9	Tom Hughes	Boston	5	Red Ames	St. Louis
				5	Elmer Knetzer	Boston/Cincinnati
				5	Poll Perritt	New York
1917	8	Red Ames	St. Louis	4	Frank Allen	Boston
				4	Burleigh Grimes	Pittsburgh
1918	7	Hod Eller	Cincinnati	4	Bill Sherdel	St. Louis
1919	6	Jean Dubuc	New York	4	Jean Dubuc	New York
1920	8	Bill Sherdel	St. Louis	8	Bill Sherdel	St. Louis
1921	6	Slim Sallee	New York	6	Bill Sherdel	St. Louis
1922	7	Rosy Ryan	New York	6	Tony Kaufmann	Chicago
1923	9	Rosy Ryan	New York	4	Jesse Barnes	New York/Boston
				4	Larry Benton	Boston
				4	Joe Genewich	Boston
				4	Lou North	St. Louis
1924	7	Art Decatur	Brooklyn	5	Huck Betts	Philadelphia

	WINS	NAME	TEAM	LOSSES	NAME	TEAM
1925	6	Johnny Morrison	Pittsburgh	5	Rosy Ryan	New York
1926	6	Guy Bush	Chicago	4	Rube Ehrhardt	Brooklyn
				4	Jakie May	Cincinnati
				4	Dutch Ulrich	Philadelphia
1927	6	Dutch Henry	New York	7	Jack Scott	Philadelphia
1928	7	Jim Faulkner	New York	8	Bob McGraw	Philadelphia
1929	10	Johnny Morrison	Brooklyn	5	Steve Swetonic	Pittsburgh
1930	7	Joe Heving	New York	5	Joe Heving	New York
				5	Glenn Spencer	Pittsburgh
1931	6	Bob Osborn	Pittsburgh	6	Joe Heving	New York
1932	12	Ben Cantwell	Boston	8	Ben Cantwell	Boston
1933	8	Dolf Luque	New York	6	Phil Collins	Philadelphia
1934	7	Waite Hoyt	Pittsburgh	6	Bob Smith	Boston
1935	5	Guy Bush	Pittsburgh	5	Ben Cantwell	Boston
	5	Waite Hoyt	Pittsburgh			
	5	Charlie Root	Chicago			
	5	Al Smith	New York			
1936	7	Mace Brown	Pittsburgh	7	Claude Passeau	Philadelphia
	7	Dick Coffman	New York			
1937	8	Dick Coffman	New York	5	Hugh Mulcahy	Philadelphia
	8	Charlie Root	Chicago			
1938	15	Mace Brown	Pittsburgh	8	Mace Brown	Pittsburgh
1939	8	Junior Thompson	Cincinnati	5	Curt Davis	St. Louis
				5	Joe Sullivan	Boston
1940	12	Joe Beggs	Cincinnati	6	Si Johnson	Philadelphia
				6	Dick Lanahan	Pittsburgh
1941	8	Hugh Casey	Brooklyn	5	Jumbo Brown	New York
				5	Ira Hutchinson	St. Louis
1942	8	Howie Krist	St. Louis	6	Johnny Sain	Boston
1943	13	Clyde Shoun	Cincinnati	7	Ace Adams	New York
1944	8	Xavier Rescigno	Pittsburgh	9	Ace Adams	New York
1945	11	Ace Adams	New York	9	Ace Adams	New York
1946	11	Hugh Casey	Brooklyn	7	Andy Karl	Philadelphia
1947	10	Hugh Casey	Brooklyn	10	Harry Gumbert	Cincinnati
	10	Harry Gumbert	Cincinnati			

	WINS	NAME	TEAM	LOSSES	NAME	TEAM
1948	10	Harry Gumbert	Cincinnati	8	Harry Gumbert	Cincinnati
1949	10	Ted Wilks	St. Louis	11	Nels Potter	Boston
1950	16	Jim Konstanty	Philadelphia	7	Jim Konstanty	Philadelphia
1951	13	Clyde King	Brooklyn	10	Jim Konstanty	Philadelphia
1952	15	Hoyt Wilhelm	New York	9	Frank Smith	Cincinnati
1953	10	Clem Labine	Brooklyn	8	Hoyt Wilhelm	New York
1954	12	Hoyt Wilhelm	New York	8	Frank Smith	Cincinnati
1955	10	Clem Labine	Brooklyn	7	Jack Meyer	Philadelphia
1956	14	Hersh Freeman	Cincinnati	12	Roy Face	Pittsburgh
1957	10	Dick Farrell	Philadelphia	7	Clem Labine	Brooklyn
				7	Turk Lown	Chicago
1958	9	Don Elston	Chicago	9	Dick Farrell	Philadelphia
1959	18	Roy Face	Pittsburgh	10	Clem Labine	Los Angeles
1960	13	Larry Sherry	Los Angeles	9	Don Elston	Chicago
	13	Lindy McDaniel	St. Louis			
1961	14	Stu Miller	San Francisco	12	Roy Face	Pittsburgh
1962	12	Jack Baldschun	Philadelphia	9	Lindy McDaniel	St. Louis
				9	Hal Woodeschick	Houston
1963	16	Ron Perranoski	Los Angeles	9	Roy Face	Pittsburgh
				9	Hal Woodeschick	Houston
1964	8	Al McBean	Pittsburgh	9	Jack Baldschun	Philadelphia
	8	Billy O'Dell	San Francisco			
	8	Ron Taylor	St. Louis			
1965	10	Billy O'Dell	San Francisco	8	Jack Baldschun	Philadelphia
				8	Bill McCool	Cincinnati
1966	14	Phil Regan	Los Angeles	11	Frank Linzy	San Francisco
1967	10	Dick Farrell	Houston/Philadelphia	8	Clay Carroll	Atlanta
				8	Dick Hall	Philadelphia
1968	12	Ron Kline	Pittsburgh	8	Clay Carroll	Atlanta/Cincinnati
	12	Phil Regan	Los Angeles/Chicago	8	Frank Linzy	San Francisco
1969	14	Frank Linzy	San Francisco	10	Dan McGinn	Montreal

	WINS	NAME	TEAM	LOSSES	NAME	TEAM
1970	9	Clay Carroll	Cincinnati	9	Phil Regan	Chicago
	9	Dave Guisti	Pittsburgh	9	Dick Selma	Philadelphia
	9	Ron Herbel	San Diego/New York			
	9	Joe Hoerner	Philadelphia			
	9	Don McMahon	San Francisco			
1971	12	Jerry Johnson	San Francisco	9	Jerry Johnson	San Francisco
				9	Bob Priddy	Atlanta
1972	14	Mike Marshall	Montreal	9	Jim Ray	Houston
1973	14	Mike Marshall	Montreal	11	Mike Marshall	Montreal
1974	15	Mike Marshall	Los Angeles	12	Mike Marshall	Los Angeles
1975	15	Dale Murray	Montreal	14	Mike Marshall	Los Angeles
1976	12	Charlie Hough	Los Angeles	9	Dale Murray	Montreal
1977	11	Goose Gossage	Pittsburgh	12	Charlie Hough	Los Angeles
1978	13	Gary Lavelle	San Francisco	13	Rollie Fingers	San Diego
				13	Skip Lockwood	New York
1979	13	Ron Reed	Philadelphia	16	Gene Garber	Atlanta
1980	11	Rollie Fingers	San Diego	12	Kent Tekulve	Pittsburgh
1981	9	Rick Camp	Atlanta	10	Gene Garber	Atlanta
	9	Tom Hume	Cincinnati	10	Dick Tidrow	Chicago
	9	Sparky Lyle	Philadelphia			
1982	12	Kent Tekulve	Pittsburgh	10	Gary Lucas	San Diego
1983	13	Jesse Orosco	New York	11	Greg Minton	San Francisco
1984	11	Bill Dawley	Houston	10	Al Holland	Philadelphia
1985	12	John Franco	Cincinnati	11	Mark Davis	San Francisco
1986	14	Roger McDowell	New York	12	Ken Howell	Los Angeles
1987	11	Scott Garrelts	San Francisco	10	Gene Garber	Atlanta
	11	Don Robinson	Pittsburgh/San Fran	10	Lance McCullers	San Diego
				10	Lee Smith	Chicago
1988	12	Jeff Parrett	Montreal	10	Mark Davis	San Diego
1989	12	Jeff Parrett	Philadelphia	11	Joe Boever	Atanta
1990	11	Bill Sampen	Montreal	9	Steve Bedrosian	San Francisco
1991	12	Mitch Williams	Philadelphia	9	John Franco	New York
				9	Barry Jones	Montreal
				9	Roger McDowell	Philadelphia/LA
1992	11	Doug Jones	Houston	10	Roger McDowell	Los Angeles

	WINS	NAME	TEAM	LOSSES	NAME	TEAM
1993	10	Pedro Martinez	Los Angeles	12	Roger Mason	San Diego/Philadelphia
1994	7	Johnny Ruffin	Cincinnati	6	Jeff Brantley	Cincinnati
	7	Mark Wohlers	Atlanta	6	Dave Burba	San Francisco
				6	Hector Carrasco	Cincinnati
				6	Greg McMichael	Atlanta
				6	John Wetteland	Montreal
1995	8	Brad Clontz	Atlanta	8	Brian Williams	San Diego
	8	Rich DeLucia	St. Louis			
	8	Jim Dougherty	Houston			
1996	9	Trevor Hoffman	San Diego	9	Rod Beck	San Francisco
	9	Antonio Osuna	Los Angeles			
1997	9	Robb Nen	Florida	10	Greg McMichael	New York
	9	Mark Wilkins	Pittsburgh			
1998	10	Dan Miceli	San Diego	9	Bob Wickman	Milwaukee

American League

	WINS	NAME	TEAM	LOSSES	NAME	TEAM
1901	3	Clark Griffith	Chicago	4	Pete Dowling	Milwaukee/Cleveland
1902	5	Rube Waddell	Philadelphia	2	Otto Hess	Cleveland
				2	Roy Patterson	Chicago
				2	Joe Yeager	Detroit
1903	2	Davey Dunkle	Chicago/Washington	2	Frank Owen	Chicago
	2	Patsy Flaherty	Chicago			
	2	Rube Kissinger	Detroit			
	2	Willie Sudhoff	St. Louis			
	2	Frank Kitson	Detroit			
	2	Cy Young	Boston			
1904	3	Jack Chesbro	New York	2	Tom Hughes	New York/Washington
				2	Ed Killian	Detroit
				2	Case Patten	Washington
1905	8	Rube Waddell	Philadelphia	3	Clark Griffith	New York
				3	Case Patten	Washington
				3	Jack Powell	New York
				3	George Winter	Boston
1906	5	Nick Altrock	Chicago	2	Jack Coombs	Philadelphia
	5	Al Orth	New York	2	Jimmy Dygert	Philadelphia
				2	Clark Griffith	New York
				2	Frank Kitson	Washington
				2	Case Patten	Washington
				2	Charlie Smith	Washington
				2	George Winter	Boston
1907	5	Ed Killian	Detroit	3	Barney Pelty	St. Louis
	5	Doc White	Chicago	3	Charlie Smith	Washington
1908	6	Rube Vickers	Philadelphia	3	Burt Keeley	Washington

	WINS	NAME	TEAM	LOSSES	NAME	TEAM
1909	5	Eddie Cicotte	Boston	3	Jack Coombs	Philadelphia
1910	6	Charley Hall	Boston	4	Elmer Koestner	Cleveland
	6	Joe Wood	Boston	4	Jim Scott	Chicago
1911	7	Ed Walsh	Chicago	5	Ed Walsh	Chicago
1912	6	Hugh Bedient	Boston	4	Joe Lake	St. Louis/Detroit
	6	Charley Hall	Boston			
1913	8	Joe Bush	Philadelphia	5	Chief Bender	Philadelphia
	8	Byron Houck	Philadelphia			
1914	6	George Baumgardner	St. Louis	5	George Baumgardner	St. Louis
				5	Hugh Bedient	Boston
1915	5	Doc Ayers	Washington	4	Doc Ayers	Washington
	5	Red Faber	Chicago	4	Red Faber	Chicago
	5	Carl Mays	Boston	4	Rube Bressler	Philadelphia
	5	Carl Weilman	St. Louis			
1916	7	Bob Shawkey	New York	6	Jim Bagby	Cleveland
1917	6	Dave Danforth	Chicago	5	Socks Seibold	Philadelphia
1918	6	Dave Danforth	Chicago	7	George Mogridge	New York
1919	7	Dickie Kerr	Chicago	4	Stan Coveleski	Cleveland
				4	Walter Johnson	Washington
1920	6	Jim Bagby	Cleveland	6	Benn Karr	Boston
	6	Bill Burwell	St. Louis			
1921	5	Bill Bayne	St. Louis	8	Jim Middleton	Detroit
	5	Benn Karr	Boston			
	5	Guy Morton	Cleveland			
1922	8	Eddie Rommel	Philadelphia	6	Slim Harriss	Philadelphia
1923	9	Allan Russell	Washington	4	Bill Piercy	Boston
				4	Eddie Rommel	Philadelphia
1924	9	Ken Holloway	Detroit	5	Joe Bush	New York
				5	Sarge Connally	Chicago
				5	Hooks Dauss	Detroit
				5	Firpo Marberry	Washington
1925	11	Elam Vangilder	St. Louis	6	Sarge Connally	Chicago
				6	Firpo Marberry	Washington
1926	11	Hooks Dauss	Detroit	5	Firpo Marberry	Washington
1927	13	Wilcy Moore	New York	7	Garland Braxton	Washington

	WINS	NAME	TEAM	LOSSES	NAME	TEAM
1928	8	Eddie Rommel	Philadelphia	9	Firpo Marberry	Washington
1929	8	Eddie Rommel	Philadelphia	5	Chad Kimsey	St. Louis
1930	9	Hank Johnson	New York	7	Chad Kimsey	St. Louis
1931	8	Bump Hadley	Washington	5	Bump Hadley	Washington
				5	Chad Kimsey	St. Louis
1932	6	Chief Hogsett	Detroit	8	Wilcy Moore	Boston/New York
1933	11	Jack Russell	Washington	9	Chief Hogsett	Detroit
1934	7	Joe Cascarella	Philadelphia	7	Jack Russell	Washington
	7	Bob Kline	Philadelphia/Washington			
	7	Jack Knott	St. Louis			
1935	6	Chief Hogsett	Detroit	6	Chief Hogsett	Detroit
	6	Johnny Murphy	New York			
	6	Leon Pettit	Washington			
	6	Russ Van Atta	St. Louis			
1936	8	Pat Malone	New York	5	Roxie Lawson	Detroit
1937	12	Johnny Murphy	New York	7	Clint Brown	Chicago
				7	Lynn Nelson	Philadelphia
1938	8	John Humphries	Cleveland	5	Harry Eisenstat	Detroit
	8	Johnny Murphy	New York	5	Denny Galehouse	Cleveland
				5	Fred Johnson	St. Louis
				5	Ed Linke	St. Louis
				5	Nels Potter	Philadelphia
				5	Eddie Smith	Philadelphia
1939	11	Clint Brown	Chicago	10	Clint Brown	Chicago
	11	Joe Heving	Boston			
1940	8	Joe Heving	Boston	10	Al Benton	Detroit
	8	Johnny Murphy	New York			
1941	8	Johnny Murphy	New York	8	Tom Ferrick	Philadelphia
1942	9	Mace Brown	Boston	10	Johnny Murphy	New York
1943	12	Johnny Murphy	New York	8	George Caster	St. Louis
1944	10	Joe Berry	Philadelphia	8	Joe Berry	Philadelphia
	10	Gordon Maltzberger	Chicago			
1945	8	Joe Berry	Philadelphia	7	Joe Berry	Philadelphia
1946	13	Earl Caldwell	Chicago	7	Joe Berry	Philadelphia/Cleveland
1947	14	Joe Page	New York	7	Russ Christopher	Philadelphia
				7	Tom Ferrick	Washington
				7	Joe Page	New York
				7	Bob Savage	Philadelphia

	WINS	NAME	TEAM	LOSSES	NAME	TEAM
1948	9	Earl Johnson	Boston	8	Joe Page	New York
1949	13	Joe Page	New York	8	Joe Page	New York
1950	9	Tom Ferrick	St. Louis/New York	9	Mickey Harris	Washington
				9	Carl Scheib	Philadelphia
1951	10	Ellis Kinder	Boston	8	Mickey Harris	Washington
1952	8	Satchel Paige	St. Louis	8	Satchel Paige	St. Louis
				8	Hal White	Detroit
1953	10	Ellis Kinder	Boston	8	Satchel Paige	St. Louis
1954	8	Sandy Consuegra	Chicago	8	Ellis Kinder	Boston
	8	Bob Grim	New York			
1955	8	Dixie Howell	Chicago	7	Ray Moore	Baltimore
	8	Tom Hurd	Boston			
	8	Ray Narleski	Cleveland			
1956	11	Ike Delock	Boston	7	Tom Morgan	New York
1957	12	Bob Grim	New York	8	Bob Grim	New York
1958	10	Dick Hyde	Washington	8	Murray Wall	Boston
1959	9	Turk Lown	Chicago	7	Ray Narleski	Detroit
				7	Billy Loes	Baltimore
1960	13	Gerry Staley	Chicago	8	Gerry Staley	Chicago
1961	15	Luis Arroyo	New York	11	Frank Funk	Cleveland
1962	9	Gary Bell	Cleveland	10	Hoyt Wilhelm	Baltimore
	9	Dick Radatz	Boston			
1963	15	Dick Radatz	Boston	8	Jim Brosnan	Chicago
				8	Ron Kline	Washington
				8	Stu Miller	Baltimore
1964	16	Dick Radatz	Boston	9	Dick Radatz	Boston
				9	Hoyt Wilhelm	Chicago
1965	15	Eddie Fischer	Chicago	11	Dick Radatz	Boston
1966	12	Jack Sanford	California	10	Ken Sanders	Boston/Kansas City
1967	12	Minnie Rojas	California	10	Stu Muller	Baltimore
1968	12	Wilbur Wood	Chicago	11	Wilbur Wood	Chicago
1969	11	Moe Drabowsky	Kansas City	11	Wilbur Wood	Chicago
1970	10	Dick Hall	Baltimore	14	Darold Knowles	Washington
	10	Stan Williams	Minnesota			
1971	10	Fred Scherman	Detroit	12	Ken Sanders	Milwaukee

	WINS	NAME	TEAM	LOSSES	NAME	TEAM
1972	11	Rollie Fingers	Oakland	9	Rollie Fingers	Oakland
				9	Ken Sanders	Milwaukee
1973	12	Lindy McDaniel	New York	9	Sparky Lyle	New York
1974	17	John Hiller	Detroit	14	John Hiller	Detroit
1975	10	Rollie Fingers	Oakland	9	Tom Murphy	Milwaukee
1976	17	Bill Campbell	Minnesota	12	Jim Willoughby	Boston
1977	16	Tom Johnson	Minnesota	10	Jim Kern	Cleveland
1978	13	Bob Stanley	Boston	12	Mike Marshall	Minnesota
1979	14	Ron Davis	New York	14	Mike Marshall	Minnesota
1980	13	Aurelio Lopez	Detroit	11	Mark Clear	California
				11	Jim Kern	Texas
1981	10	Bob Stanley	Boston	7	Bob Stanley	Boston
1982	14	Mark Clear	Boston	10	Dan Spillner	Cleveland
1983	14	Jim Slaton	Milwaukee	10	Bob Stanley	Boston
1984	10	Aurelio Lopez	Detroit	11	Ron Davis	Minnesota
1985	12	Dave Righetti	New York	10	Guillermo Hernandez	Detroit
1986	14	Mark Eichhorn	Toronto	10	Keith Atherton	Oakland/Minnesota
1987	12	Jeff Musselman	Toronto	8	Jeff Reardon	Minnesota
				8	Mark Williamson	Baltimore
1988	9	Mike Henneman	Detroit	8	Dale Mohorcic	Texas/New York
	9	Gene Nelson	Oakland	8	Mike Schooler	Seattle
	9	Duane Ward	Toronto	8	Bobby Thigpen	Chicago
1989	11	Mike Henneman	Detroit	10	Doug Jones	Cleveland
				10	Duane Ward	Toronto
1990	11	Lee Guetterman	New York	8	Duane Ward	Toronto
	11	Barry Jones	Chicago			
1991	10	Mike Henneman	Detroit	7	Paul Gibson	Detroit
	10	Joe Klink	Oakland	7	Mike Jackson	Seattle
	10	Mike Timlin	Toronto	7	Doug Jones	Cleveland
1992	10	Rusty Meacham	Kansas City	8	Greg Harris	Boston
1993	8	Scott Radinsky	Chicago	7	Todd Frohwirth	Baltimore
				7	Greg Harris	Boston
1994	9	Joe Boever	Detroit	6	Tom Henke	Texas
	9	Bill Risley	Seattle	6	Bill Risley	Seattle
				6	Jeff Russell	Boston/Cleveland

	WINS	NAME	TEAM	LOSSES	NAME	TEAM
1995	10	Julian Tavarez	Cleveland	7	John Doherty	Detroit
				7	Joe Boever	Detroit
				7	Roberto Hernandez	Chicago
1996	8	Mariano Rivera	New York	8	Bill Simas	Chicago
	8	Arthur Rhodes	Baltimore			
	8	Rafael Carmona	Seattle			
1997	10	Arthur Rhodes	Baltimore	9	Heathcliff Slocumb	Boston/Seattle
	10	Danny Patterson	Texas			
	10	Bobby Ayala	Seattle			
1998	8	Shigetoshi Hasegawa	Anaheim	10	Bobby Ayala	Seattle

Federal League

	WINS	NAME	TEAM	LOSSES	NAME	TEAM
1914	8	George Mullin	Indianapolis	5	Pete Henning	Kansas City
1915	6	Doc Crandall	St. Louis	4	Bill Bailey	Baltimore
				4	Dave Black	Chicago/Baltimore

No-No's and Perfectos

1. **Cy Young was the first pitcher to throw a winning no-hitter in both the NL and the AL, but his NL no-no came in the 19th century. Who was the first hurler to win a no-hit game in two different major leagues in the 20th century?**

   A)   Tom Hughes, the first pitcher to throw a no-no in both the NL and the AL after the turn of the century, lost his junior loop gem in extra innings.
   B)   One of our man's no-hitters was a perfecto.
   C)   He's among the elite group who won 100 games in both the NL and the AL.
   D)   Father's Day in 1964 was a gala occasion for him.
   E)   He made the Hall of Fame in 1996.

2. **What hurler authored the most no-hit games that went into extra innings?**
   A)   He's the only chucker to be involved in as many as two extra-inning no-hitters.
   B)   Both came in the same season.
   C)   His first no-hitter resulted in a loss when Johnny Lewis tagged an 11th-inning solo homer for the Mets and thus is no longer considered a no-no by ML baseball.
   D)   Leo Cardenas's solo homer decided his second gem in the 10th inning and rewarded him with his first no-no win.
   E)   He topped the Reds in wins in the 1960s with 134.

3. **What team remarkably was victimized twice in the same decade by nine-inning no-hitters that it ultimately won in overtime?**
   A)   The two games came exactly two years to the day apart.
   B)   Smoky Burgess was the losing catcher on each occasion.
   C)   The games occurred in 1956 and 1958.
   D)   Both games were played in a park that last hosted a postseason game in 1982.
   E)   The two pitchers who started the games for the opposition were Johnny Klippstein and Harvey Haddix.

4. **Who was the only man to play on the losing side in each of the first two perfect games in the majors at the 60'6" pitching distance?**
   A)   The second perfecto loss proved to be his last ML game.
   B)   He faced Cleveland's Addie Joss in his last ML at bat some nine years after he played his last game in a Cleveland ML uniform.
   C)   He caught the losing pitcher the day he first appeared in a perfecto game.
   D)   He roomed on road trips with the losing pitcher in the first perfecto game he caught and objected to his roomie's eating animal crackers in bed.
   E)   His 13-letter last name was shortened to 7 letters to fit into box scores.

5. Name the first man in history to play on the winning side in two perfectos.

A) He played against Washington and Detroit in his two perfectos.

B) He's in the Hall of Fame.

C) He was in the outfield the day Charlie Robertson retired Johnny Bassler to wrap up his perfecto.

D) Babe Ruth played on his side—albeit very briefly—the day he took part in his first perfecto.

E) He, Tris, and Duffy formed one of the greatest outfield trios in history.

6. The most recent pitcher to throw a no-hitter prior to his 21st birthday is also the only hurler to fashion a no-no for an AL or NL team in a certain city prior to 1971. Who is he?

A) Johnny Lush is a great guess, but our man did it after Lush.

B) He is also the only pitcher on a certain NL franchise to throw a no-hitter prior to 1951.

C) In 1915 two Federal League no-hit games occurred in the city where he threw his no-no at age 20 and 10 months.

D) Cliff Chambers was the second member of our man's franchise to toss a no-no.

E) In 1976, John Candelaria became the first pitcher since 1907 from our man's franchise to throw a no-hitter in his home park.

Youngest Pitchers Throwing No-Hitters

RANK	NAME	TEAM	YEAR	AGE
1	Amos Rusie	NY, NL	1891	20/3
2	Monte Ward	Pro, NL	1880	20/3.5
3	Matt Kilroy	Bal, AA	1886	20/4
4	Johnny Lush	Phi, NL	1906	20/7
5	Duck Burns	Cin, UA	1884	20/8
6	Nick Maddox	Pit, NL	1907	20/10
7	Christy Mathewson	NY, NL	1901	20/11
8	Larry Corcoran	Chi, NL	1880	21/0
9	Ed Seward	Phi, AA	1888	21/1
10	Vida Blue	Oak, AL	1970	21/2

Note: Age in years and months at time of no-hitter.

7. Don Larsen's Series perfecto made him the current record holder for tossing a hitless game falling on the latest date in the year, October 8. Who are the co-owners of the current record for a no-hitter falling on the earliest date on the calendar?

A) The date is April 7.

B) The victims of the two no-nos were the Braves in 1979 and the ChiSox in 1984.

C) The 1979 no-hitter was historical in a second very significant way because of the pitcher who threw it.

D) The 1984 no-hitter was the first by a Detroit hurler since expansion.

E) The 1979 no-no was a first that neither the Niekros nor the Perrys achieved.

8. **The two most recent perfect games were tossed by AL southpaws—Kenny Rogers and David Wells. However, when Mel Parnell flung a no-no on July 14, 1956, it was the first no-hitter by an AL lefty in nearly 25 years. Who had been the last AL portsider prior to Parnell to toss a no-hitter?**

   A) His victims were the Red Sox on August 8, 1931.

   B) All 38 of his career wins came with the same AL team.

   C) A fragile sort, he worked enough innings to be an ERA qualifier just once in his 10 ML seasons.

   D) His initials are the same as those of the White Sox southpaw who never won another game after notching 18 victories in 1986.

   E) He and the Expos rookie reliever who won nine games in 78 appearances in 1985 share the same last name.

9. **The only two Opening Day no-hitters in ML history came in 1908 and 1940. However, if the American League ever is accorded ML status for its inaugural year under its new name, it will claim the first ML Opening Day no-no. Who tossed a no-hitter on April 19, 1900, to help Ban Johnson's old Western League celebrate its first official day as the American League?**

   A) He was a southpaw with Buffalo.

   B) He never pitched a game in the majors after 1900 but won four games as a rookie with Baltimore in 1897.

   C) His real first name was Morris, but they called him "Doc."

   D) His last name and the last name of Mike, a Red Sox and Cardinals hurler in the 1930s, are anagrams.

   E) His initials are the same as those of the first man listed in the "Pitcher Register" of all current baseball encyclopedias.

10. **Joe Borden pitched the first professional no-hitter in the National Association's coda season in 1875 and followed by tossing the National League's first no-no the next year. However, the NA is not officially recognized as a major league. Who was unequivocally the first pitcher to carve no-hit games in two different major leagues?**

    A) His second gem occurred the first time two no-no's were tossed on the same day.

    B) Jim Hughes shared the spotlight with him the day he threw his second no-no.

    C) His first no-no came in the American Association.

    D) He was the first hurler to win an ERA crown at the current hill distance.

    E) He was the first hurler to throw a no-hitter in his inaugural ML start.

Pitchers Throwing No-No's in Two Different MLs

NAME	1ST LEAGUE	2ND LEAGUE
Joe Borden	1875, NA	1876, NL
Ted Breitenstein	1891, AA	1898, NL
Cy Young	1897, NL	1904, AL
Tom Hughes	1910, AL	1916, NL
Jim Bunning	1958, AL	1964, NL
Nolan Ryan	1973, AL	1981, NL

11. **Only two performers to date have made their ML debuts by appearing in the starting lineup of a team involved in a perfect game. Who are they?**

    A) Remarkably, both made their ML debuts in the same game.

    B) Even more remarkably, both debuted with the same team.

    C) Only one hit was made by either team in the game when both debuted.

    D) They manned left field and center field for the Cubs the day Sandy tossed a perfecto against the Bruins.

    E) One led the NL in batter Ks in 1966, and the other took most of the blame from Leo Durocher when the Cubs lost a critical game to the Mets in 1969.

12. **The most recent pitcher to be victimized by a no-hitter in his lone ML start was a member of the Boston Braves. Who is he?**

    A) It was his lone decision in the majors, and he lost to Pittsburgh, 3–0.

    B) It was the last triumph in a Pirates uni by his mound opponent.

    C) It was also the first no-hitter by a Pirates hurler in 44 years.

    D) The unlucky Braves hurler's initials match those of the A's top winner the year they beat Joe McCarthy's Cubs in the World Series.

    E) The unlucky hurler's last name is an anagram for where you stick a light plug.

13. **Never the site of a no-hitter, Forbes Field came the closest to hosting one on May 16, 1914, when what hurler gave up a single to Pittsburgh's Joe Kelly with two out in the ninth inning of what turned out to be a 2–0 one-hit win?**

    A) The one-hitter was one of his loop-leading eight shutouts that season.

    B) He had 102 wins after his first five seasons, but won only 17 more games.

    C) He fell one victory short of winning 20 games for a last-place team in 1915.

    D) He led the NL in ERA as a rookie in 1912.

    E) His 2.43 career ERA is among the 10 lowest of all-time.

14. **Who is the only man to play in no-hit games in three different major leagues in two different centuries?**

    A) In his first no-hit game, he played behind a pitcher making his first ML start.

    B) In his second no-hitter, he faced the first pitcher to hurl a no-no from a mound 60'6" from home plate.

    C) The last no-hitter in which he participated found him pitted against the first pitcher to throw a nine-inning no-no in the AL.

    D) He was the first outfielder in ML history to retire with 2,000 hits and a sub-.300 career BA.

    E) He participated in five no-no's altogether, easily the most ever by a player with both a hearing and speech disability.

15. **Cap Anson played in no-hit games at both the 45' and 50' pitching distances but never in one at the 60'6" distance because his Chicago team was not involved in a no-no at the current mound distance until the year after he retired. However, one man did take part in no-hit games at each of the three 19th century pitching distances. Who is he?**

    A) He was on the losing side in both his first no-hit game and Larry Corcoran's first in 1880.

    B) His last appearance in a no-hit game was at the losing end of the first no-no at the present pitching distance.

    C) He was on the winning side in no-no's thrown by Pud Galvin and Amos Rusie.

    D) He was Washington's player-manager in 1893, his final full ML season.

    E) Never bashful about speaking his piece, he was nicknamed "Orator Jim."

16. Who is the only pitcher to be on the losing end of a perfect game fewer than two weeks after he himself threw a no-hitter?

A) In 1951 Bob Feller was victimized by an Allie Reynolds no-no just 11 days after he himself threw one, but neither gem was a perfect game.

B) Our man's similar experience came in the same decade as Feller's.

C) It came in a season when he achieved another unparalleled feat—he was the runner-up for a loop MVP Award even though he had not begun the season in that loop.

D) He began the year in which he fashioned his no-no as a teammate of Bob Feller.

E) He is the lone hurler ever to come out on the short end of a no-hitter or a perfect game in postseason play.

17. What is the only team in ML history to go more than a half century between receiving no-hit efforts from its pitching staff?

A) The team's first no-hit game after the 154-game schedule was adopted was fashioned by the youngest pitcher in this century to toss a no-no.

B) Some 58 years would pass after a 20-year-old lefty no-hit the Cardinals, 1–0, before the team received another no-no.

C) The lefty was in his first full season as a pitcher at the time but two years earlier had been the team's regular first baseman.

D) The team also holds the ML record for the longest span—32 years—between 20-game winners.

E) The team's first no-no in some 58 years was the only perfecto ever tossed on Father's Day.

18. Many pitchers who lost no-hit games that went into extra innings have been removed from the record book by ML baseball because they surrendered hits in overtime. Name the only hurler who is still credited with an overtime no-hitter in the record book even though he did not emerge from the game with a victory.

A) He hurled the only no-hitter that went nine or more innings and ended in a tie.

B) His no-hitter occurred on October 4, 1884, and was the only one in ML history that involved a team from Toledo.

C) He lost 12–0 to John Hamill of Washington in his ML debut on Opening Day in 1884.

D) He started the first game in history for a Brooklyn ML team.

E) He and the only hurler ever to throw a perfect game for the franchise of which he was an original member in 1884 share the same initials.

No-Hitters Eliminated from the Record Books in 1991 by Special Decree of ML Baseball

Broken Up in Extra Innings

American League

DATE	PITCHER	TEAMS	SCORE	1ST HIT
5/9/1901	Earl Moore	Cle vs. Chi	2–4	10th
8/30/1910	Tom Hughes	NY vs. Cle	0–5	10th
5/14/1914	Jim Scott	Chi at Was	0–1	10th
9/18/1934	Bobo Newsom	StL vs. Bos	1–2	10th

National League

DATE	PITCHER	TEAMS	SCORE	1ST HIT
6/11/1904	Bob Wicker	Chi at NY	1–0	10th
8/1/1906	Harry McIntyre	Bro vs. Pit	0–1	11th
4/13/1909	Red Ames	NY vs. Bro	0–3	10th*
5/7/1917	Hippo Vaughn	Chi vs. Cin	0–1	10th**
5/26/1956	Johnny Klippstein (7) Hersh Freeman (1) Joe Black (2.1)	Cin at Mil	1–2	10th
5/26/1959	Harvey Haddix	Pit at Mil	0–1	13th***
6/14/1965	Jim Maloney	Cin vs. NY	0–1	11th
7/26/1991	Mark Gardner	Mon at LA	0–1	10th
6/3/1995	Pedro Martinez	Mon at SD	1–0	10th****

   * Opening Day game; the 1991 decree, in effect, means there has never been a no-hitter on Opening Day in NL history.

  ** Vaughn's mound opponent, Fred Toney, pitched 10 hitless innings; the 1991 decree thus retroactively expunged the only double no-hit game in major league history from the record books.

 *** Though Haddix was perfect through the first 12 innings, he too was retroactively removed from the record books in 1991.

**** Martinez was the first pitcher to be perfect for the first nine innings of a game without ever officially receiving credit for a no-hitter, let alone a perfecto.

Complete Full-Length Game Pitched, Less than Nine Innings

Players League

6/21/1890	Silver King	Chi vs. Bro	0–1

American League

7/1/1990	Andy Hawkins	NY at Chi	0–4
4/12/1992	Matt Young	Bos at Cle	1–2

Note: Players League—Though the home team, Chicago opted to bat first, depriving King of a chance at a nine-inning no-no when Chicago trailed after its last raps, eliminating the need for Brooklyn to bat in the bottom of the ninth.

American League—Walks and poor defensive work put the Yankees in an 0–4 hole; when they failed to catch up in their last raps, Hawkins, like King, received credit for a full-length complete game but not a no-hitter.

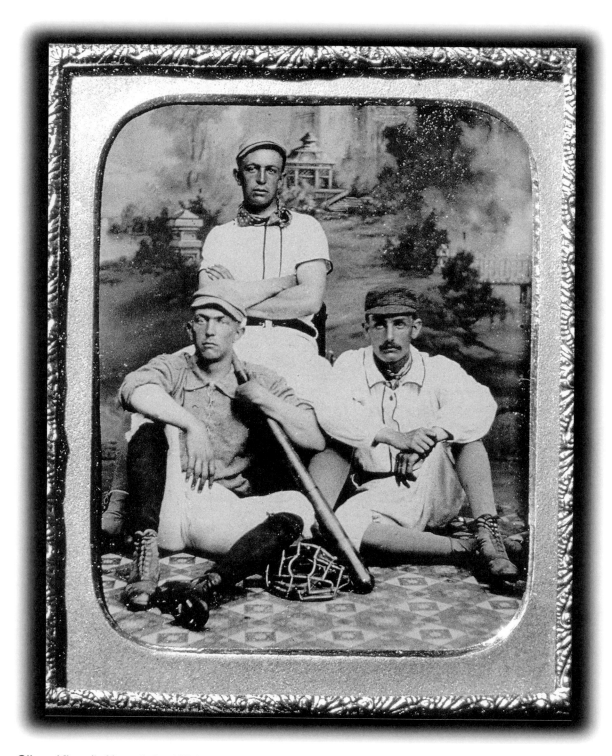

Silver King (left) and Jim Whitney (right), seated in front of an unidentified teammate on the 1886 Kansas City Cowboys. King was the first pitcher in ML *history to come out a loser despite throwing a no-hitter. With the Chicago Pirates of the Players League in 1890, he dropped a 1–0 decision in his home park to Brooklyn that has since been removed from the no-no honor roll. King hurled only eight innings after Chicago manager Charlie Comiskey chose to bat first and the Pirates went without a run in the top of the ninth.*

Wondrous Wild Men

1. Amos Rusie in his first full season heralded what kind of pitcher he would be by walking an all-time record 289 hitters. But Rusie hurled 548.2 innings in 1890, meaning he walked about one batter every two frames he worked. Only two pitchers in ML history have issued as many as 100 free passes in a season and averaged more than one walk per inning. One is the archetypal "wild man" Tommy Byrne. Who's the other?

   A) The season in which he surrendered 103 walks in 95.1 innings, a teammate with the same first name and same initials gave up 89 walks in 95.1 innings.
   B) With Chattanooga in 1948, he led the Southern Association in walks, surrendering 173 in just 132 innings.
   C) His career line between 1948 and 1954 shows 237 walks issued in 213.2 innings.
   D) He was traded to Cleveland prior to the 1950 season for Mickey Vernon.
   E) He and the Jays reliever who collected three wins in postseason play in 1992 share the same initials.

Most Walks Issued, Season, Fewer than 100 Innings

RANK	NAME	TEAM	YEAR	IP	WALKS
1	Dick Weik	Was, AL	1949	95.1	103
2	Dick Welteroth	Was, AL	1949	95.1	89
3	Steve Blass	Pit, NL	1973	88.2	84
4	Ken Wright	KC, AL	1973	80.2	82
5	Mitch Williams	Tex, AL	1986	98	79
6	Joe Sparma	Det, AL	1969	92.2	77
7	Hal Griggs	Was, AL	1956	98.2	76
8	Fred Sanford	NY/Was/StL, AL	1951	91	75
	Frank Papish	Chi, AL	1948	95.1	75
10	Bobby Witt	Tex, AL	1991	88.2	74

2. The youngest pitcher to surrender 100 walks in a season was the youngest to do a lot of things. Who is he?

   A) He hurled his 1,234th and final inning in the majors when he was just 22.
   B) A strong left arm led to his early success, and alcohol caused his early exit.
   C) When he logged a win for the Cincinnati NL Reds in 1892 at age 18, he became the youngest pitcher to post victories in three different major leagues.
   D) In 1891, the same year he became the youngest pitcher to give up 100 walks in a season, he became the youngest 20-game winner.
   E) He and the Yankees rookie 19-game winner in 1927 share the same initials.

3. Pud Galvin issued just 745 free passes in 6,003.1 innings to claim the record for the most frames worked with fewer than 1,000 walks. What legendary wild man owns the converse record for the fewest innings worked among hurlers with 1,000 career walks?

A) He's the only man to cede 1,000 career walks in under 1,500 innings.

B) In his first full year in the bigs, opponents hit .172 against him, a record 94 points below the league average among pitchers in at least 120 innings.

C) While leading the AL in walks three years in a row (1949–51), he became the most recent lefty to issue 150 walks three straight years and the season record holder for the most walks issued (179 in 1949) in fewer than 200 innings pitched.

D) Of his 85 career wins, 72 came with the Yankees.

E) He and the most recent rookie 20-game winner share the same initials.

RANK	NAME	YEARS	WALKS	IP
	Fewest Innings, Career, with 1,000 Walks			
1	Tommy Byrne	1943–57	1037	1362
2	Bob Turley	1951–63	1025	1700.2
3	Vern Kennedy	1934–45	1049	2025.2
4	Johnny Vander Meer	1937–51	1132	2104.2
5	Bobby Witt	1986–	1195	2110.1
6	Allie Reynolds	1942–54	1261	2492.1
	Sam McDowell	1961–75	1312	2492.1
8	Steve Renko	1969–83	1010	2494
9	Lefty Gomez	1930–43	1095	2503
10	Joe Coleman	1965–79	1003	2569.1

Tommy Byrne was touched for 101 walks in just 133.2 innings in 1948. His wildness masked one of the most remarkable seasons ever. In 1948, opposing hitters batted just .172 against Byrne, 94 points below the AL average, a record among pitchers with at least 120 innings.

4. **What switch-hitting southpaw set the 20th century record for the most walks issued in a major league game (16) and then did not hurl his last inning as a professional until 31 years later?**

    A) He set the record on June 28, 1915, against the Yankees, while pitching for the team that gave up the most walks in ML history.

    B) In 1921 he played NFL football after hitting .324 in 144 games for St. Paul of the American Association.

    C) He collected nearly 2,500 hits in the minors.

    D) He scouted for the last Philadelphia A's team managed by Connie Mack 36 years after Mack gave him his only big league opportunity.

    E) He and the Marlins' season record holder for saves share the same initials.

5. **Of the 16 ML franchises extant in 1901, which one was the last to have a member of its mound staff be a loop walk leader in the 20th century?**

    A) Pitchers on this franchise hold both the pre-1901 and the post-1901 record for the most walks issued in a game by a National League hurler.

    B) The post-1901 NL record holder for the most walks issued in a game is the brother of a Hall of Fame hurler.

    C) A pitcher on this franchise has the ML season mark for the most walks issued.

    D) The franchise's first 20th century walk leader was Roy Parmalee in 1935.

    E) The franchise has had only one walk leader since it relocated in 1958.

6. **Amos Rusie, the all-time record holder for the most walks issued in a season, was a right-hander. Who holds the equivalent record for a left-hander?**

    A) In 1890 he became the first 20-game winner born in the San Francisco Bay Area.

    B) His 226 walks issued in 1891 exceed the post-1893 lefty record by 13.

    C) He broke Toad Ramsey's southpaw record of 207, set in 1886.

    D) Like Ramsey, he pitched in the American Association the year he set his mark.

    E) He and the Brooklyn second sacker who was one of the runners Bill Wambsganss nailed when he performed his unassisted triple play share the same initials.

Most Walks, Season, Left-Hander

RANK	NAME	TEAM	YEAR	WALKS
1	Phil Knell	Col, AA	1891	226
2	Cy Seymour	NY, NL	1898	213
3	Toad Ramsey	Lou, AA	1886	207
4	Ted Breitenstein	StL, NL	1894	191
5	Ed Beatin	Cle, NL	1890	186
6	Matt Kilroy	Bal, AA	1886	182
	Frank Killen	Was, NL	1892	182
8	Willie McGill	Chi, NL	1893	181
9	Tommy Byrne	NY, AL	1949	179
10	Ted Breitenstein	StL, NL	1895	178

7. **In 1889 a walk came on four balls for the first time. The post-1889 record for the fewest walks issued by a loop leader in a season when a full schedule was played belongs to what recent Cy Young Award winner?**
   A) He walked 111 hitters the year he did it, but only 82 of them counted toward his loop-leading total because he switched leagues near the end of the season.
   B) Prior to leading a loop in walks, he topped the NL in Ks two years in a row.
   C) He is the only man ever to be a loop leader in a major pitching department and win a World Series game that same season for a team in another major league.
   D) He is a one-time Cy Young winner.
   E) His .870 winning percentage in 1988 is a 20th century record for a National League right-handed 20-game winner.

8. **Who holds the 20th century NL record for the most walks surrendered in a season?**
   A) He was a teammate of Rapid Robert's when he gave up his first ML walk.
   B) He was a teammate of Bob Gibson's when he collected his last big league win.
   C) He was a teammate of Bob Rush's the year he set the 20th century NL record for the most walks given up in a season.
   D) He won 21 games as a teammate of Mike McCormick's when he became the last member of the Giants prior to Shawn Estes to lead the NL in walks.
   E) He and a 200-game winner have the same name.

9. **When Howard Ehmke walked 119 hitters in 1923, he set a Red Sox club record that lasted until 1949. Who held the Crimson Hose record prior to Ehmke?**
   A) Walter Johnson walked 132 the year Ehmke's predecessor set a new BoSox record with 118 free passes.
   B) He led the AL in ERA the year he set the pre-1923 BoSox walk mark.
   C) He led the Red Sox two years in a row in both wins and walks.
   D) He still holds the record for the longest complete-game postseason win.
   E) He led the AL many times in walks received but never in walks surrendered.

10. **In 1949 something weird was going on with the AL strike zone because a record 16 junior-loop pitchers walked 100 or more hitters. That same season, only three hurlers walked as many as 100 in the NL. What flinger led the senior circuit with 117 free passes?**
    A) His team also led the NL in walks issued, with 640.
    B) Second on the club to him was Johnny Vander Meer with 85 walks.
    C) His name was often confused with that of a football star in the same era who was nicknamed "Squirmin' Herman."
    D) He led NL pitchers in walks three times between 1949 and 1952.
    E) He and the record holder for career relief wins share the same initials.

Most Walks Issued, Season, Team

RANK	TEAM	LEAGUE	YEAR	LEADER	TEAM TOTAL
1	Philadelphia	AL	1915	Weldon Wyckoff, 165	827
2	New York	AL	1949	Tommy Byrne, 179	812
3	St. Louis	AL	1951	Duane Pillette, 115	801
4	Detroit	AL	1996	Brian Williams, 85	784
5	Washington	AL	1949	Dick Weik, 103	779
6	Cleveland	AL	1971	Sam McDowell, 153	770
7	Texas	AL	1987	Bobby Witt, 140	760
8	Philadelphia	AL	1949	Alex Kellner, 129	758
9	Boston	AL	1950	Mickey McDermott, 124	748
10	St. Louis	AL	1949	Jack Kramer, 127	739

Note: This list more than suggests that something weird has been going on with the strike zone in the two leagues for quite a while. It can't be sheer coincidence that all of the top 10 walk totals belong to AL teams. Actually, it was not until 1969 that a National League team—the expansion Expos—first surrendered as many as 700 walks.

11. Who was the first pitcher in the 20th century to top his loop in both walks and Ks in the same season?

A) He did it as a rookie.

B) It was the only year he paced the AL in walks.

C) That season, Walter Johnson was the only other AL hurler to top 100 Ks.

D) He was the first post-1876 K leader to work fewer than 200 innings and also the first in AL history to give up 100 walks in fewer than 200 innings.

E) The catcher credited with the out for most of his Ks was Mickey Cochrane.

Most Walks Issued in Fewer than 200 Innings, Season

RANK	NAME	TEAM	YEAR	IP	WALKS
1	Tommy Byrne	NY, AL	1949	196	179
2	Tommy Byrne	NY/StL, AL	1951	143.2	150
3	Bobby Witt	Tex, AL	1986	157.2	143
4	Bobby Witt	Tex, AL	1987	143	140
5	Johnny Lindell	Phi/Pit, NL	1953	199	139
6	Hal Newhouser	Det, AL	1941	173	137
	Hal Gregg	Bro, NL	1944	197.2	137
8	Nolan Ryan	Cal, AL	1975	198	132
9	Lefty Grove	Phi, AL	1925	197	131
10	Roy Golden	StL, NL	1911	148.2	129

12. **In 1901, Bill Donovan became the first hurler in this century to pace the NL in both walks and wins. Who was the first AL hurler to make the same boast?**
    A) The season he did it was the second time he led the AL in wins.
    B) The season he did it, a teammate set a new AL record for doubles.
    C) In 1924 he led the AL in pinch hits.
    D) Cleveland was the beneficiary of most of his career wins.
    E) He is the only man since 1893 to retire with 200 wins and a .280+ career BA.

Pitchers Leading the League in Both Walks and Wins

NAME	TEAM	YEAR	WALKS	WINS
Jim Whitney	Bos, NL	1881	90	31
John Clarkson	Bos, NL	1889	203	49
Mark Baldwin	Chi, PL	1890	249	34
Amos Rusie	NY, NL	1894	200	36
Joe McGinnity	Bro, NL	1900	113	28
Bill Donovan	Bro, NL	1901	152	25
Tom Seaton	Phi, NL	1913	136	27
George Uhle	Cle, AL	1926	118	27
Bob Feller	Cle, AL	1939	142	24
Bob Feller	Cle, AL	1941	194	25
Bob Feller	Cle, AL	1946	153	26
Bob Turley	NY, AL	1958	128	21
Early Wynn	Chi, AL	1959	119	22
Phil Niekro	Atl, NL	1979	113	21

13. **What flinger holds both the AL record for the most hit batsmen in a season and the 20th century Boston Braves record for the most walks issued in a season?**
    A) He set the AL hit-batsmen record in his only season in the junior circuit.
    B) His last ML win came for the last Cubs team to win a World Series.
    C) He led the NL in walks as a rookie with Louisville in 1896.
    D) He was the first pitcher to have a 20-win season for both a Philadelphia NL and a Philadelphia AL team.
    E) He and the Angels lefty who led the AL in both innings pitched and starts in 1994 share the same initials.

14. **Only two pitchers among the top 20 in career walks issued failed to win 200 games. One is Bump Hadley. Who is the other?**
    A) He walked 100 hitters in a season six times with five different teams.
    B) He led the AL in winning percentage the first year he led a loop in walks.
    C) He issued his first walk in 1967 as a member of the Cardinals.
    D) He hurled two complete-game wins in the 1977 World Series.
    E) He led the AL in walks for the second time the year after he served up a famous three-run homer to Bucky Dent on the final day of the regular season.

15. When Bob Feller retired in 1956, he held the record for most career walks issued, with 1,764. Whose record of 1,732 did he break?

A) The previous record holder broke Amos Rusie's record for career walks in 1952.

B) The previous record holder's 211th and final career win came in 1953 when he was in his 46th year of life.

C) The previous record holder walked 100 or more hitters eight years in a row between 1936 and 1943.

D) The previous record holder has the 20th century mark for the highest season ERA by a 20-game winner.

E) The previous record holder holds the all-time record for the most career wins by anyone nicknamed "Bobo."

Evolution of Career Record for Most Walks Issued (Since 1889)

NAME	YEARS	WALKS
Tony Mullane	1881–94	1408
Amos Rusie	1889–1901	1704
Bobo Newsom	1929–53	1732
Bob Feller	1936–56	1764
Early Wynn	1939–63	1775
Nolan Ryan	1966–93	2795

16. Tommy Byrne had a walks-to-K ratio of 1.35 but nevertheless had a .552 career winning percentage. Who has the all-time poorest walks-to-K ratio (1.51) of any hurler that logged at least 2,000 career innings and posted a winning record?

A) George Hemming is the only other hurler with a winning record and as many as 1,500 career innings to have a worse walks-to-K ratio (1.91) than our man.

B) His rookie year and 1901 were the only seasons in which he totaled more Ks than walks.

C) His .540 career winning percentage included a 9–6 finale with a flag winner.

D) His last ML appearance came in the first 20th century World Series.

E) He collected 177 of his 187 career wins with Brooklyn between 1892 and 1901.

17. Only an elbow injury in all likelihood prevented what notorious wild man from leading his league in walks for a record seven years in a row?

A) As it was, he finished just one walk behind the loop leader the year he damaged his elbow.

B) He issued his first six career walks when he was just 19 years old.

C) He's the only hurler to give up as many as 10 grand-slam homers.

D) He issued his last 40 career walks when he was 46 years old.

E) His elbow injury in 1975 also in all likelihood stopped him from leading his league in strikeouts for a record eight years in a row.

18. The all-time award for "the Guy Nobody Dared to Dig In Against" goes to the only man ranked in the career top 10 in walks, hit batsmen, and wild pitches. Name him.

A) He's only ninth in walks, but he's tied for fourth in wild pitches.

B) His 277 career hit batsmen lead all.

C) He and his brother combined for 267 career wins.

D) He issued his 1,000th career walk in his first start in 1893.

E) He's the only man to post three straight 30-win seasons in three different major leagues.

Top Five Guys Nobody Dared to Dig In Against (Rankings/Points)

RANK	NAME	YEARS	WALKS	WPS	HB	TOTAL
1	Gus Weyhing	1887–1901	9	4	1	19
	Nolan Ryan	1966–93	1	2	—	19
3	Tony Mullane	1881–94	—	1	6	15
4	Phil Niekro	1964–87	3	6	—	13
5	Charlie Hough	1970–94	8	—	8	6

Note: Includes only pitchers ranking in the top 10 in at least two of the three "wild man" departments—Walks, Wild Pitches, and Hit Batsmen. Number in each department denotes career ranking in top 10; total equals the sum of the points for each top 10 ranking—10 points for first, 9 for second, etc.

Season Walk Leaders, 1871–1998

	WALKS	NAME	TEAM	WALKS	NAME	TEAM
National Association						
1871	75	John McMullin	Troy			
1872	52	Bobby Mathews	Baltimore			
1873	62	Bobby Mathews	New York			
1874	43	George Zettlein	Chicago			
1875	24	Dick McBride	Athletics			
National League						
1876	51	Joe Borden	Boston			
1877	53	Tricky Nichols	St. Louis			
	53	Terry Larkin	Hartford			
1878	56	The Only Nolan	Indiana			
1879	74	Jim McCormick	Cleveland			
1880	99	Larry Corcoran	Chicago			
1881	90	Jim Whitney	Boston			
American Association						
1882	103	Jim McCormick	Cleveland	78	Tony Mullane	Louisville
1883	99	One Arm Daily	Cleveland	123	Frank Mountain	Colts
1884	146	Mickey Welch	New York	116	Hardie Henderson	Baltimore
Union Association						
1884	81	Jersey Bakely	Philadelphia/Wilmington/Kansas City			

WALKS	NAME	TEAM	WALKS	NAME	TEAM

National League

	WALKS	NAME	TEAM
1885	131	Mickey Welch	New York
1886	163	Mickey Welch	New York
1887	133	Hoss Radbourn	Boston
1888	119	John Clarkson	Boston
1889*	203	John Clarkson	Boston
1890	289	Amos Rusie	New York

American Association

WALKS	NAME	TEAM
117	Hardie Henderson	Baltimore
207	Toad Ramsey	Louisville
205	Mike Morrison	Cleveland
157	Bert Cunningham	Baltimore
274	Mark Baldwin	Columbus
219	Bob Barr	Rochester

* The 1889 season was the first that four balls constituted a walk.

Players League

	WALKS	NAME	TEAM
1890	249	Mark Baldwin	Chicago

National League

	WALKS	NAME	TEAM
1891	262	Amos Rusie	New York
1892	267	Amos Rusie	New York
1893	218	Amos Rusie	New York
1894	200	Amos Rusie	New York
1895	178	Ted Breitenstein	St. Louis
1896	166	Chick Fraser	Louisville
1897	164	Cy Seymour	New York
1898	213	Cy Seymour	New York
1899	170	Cy Seymour	New York
1900	113	Joe McGinnity	Brooklyn

WALKS	NAME	TEAM
232	Jack Stivetts	St. Louis

American League

National League

	WALKS	NAME	TEAM
1901	152	Bill Donovan	Brooklyn
1902	128	Togie Pittinger	Boston
1903	143	Togie Pittinger	Boston
1904	144	Togie Pittinger	Boston
1905	149	Chick Fraser	Boston
1906	127	Doc Scanlan	Brooklyn
1907	112	Stoney McGlynn	St. Louis
1908	125	Nap Rucker	Brooklyn
1909	108	Earl Moore	Brooklyn
	108	Al Mattern	Boston
1910	133	Bob Harmon	St. Louis
1911	181	Bob Harmon	St. Louis
1912	159	Marty O'Toole	Pittsburgh
1913	136	Tom Seaton	Philadelphia
1914	140	Larry Cheney	Chicago

American League

WALKS	NAME	TEAM
132	Chick Fraser	Philadelphia
101	Earl Moore	Cleveland
106	George Mullin	Detroit
131	George Mullin	Detroit
138	George Mullin	Detroit
108	George Mullin	Detroit
108	Cy Falkenberg	Washington
111	Frank Smith	Chicago
97	Jimmy Dygert	Philadelphia
105	Bob Groom	Washington
117	Cy Morgan	Philadelphia
136	Gene Krapp	Cleveland
121	George Kahler	Cleveland
124	Vean Gregg	Cleveland
137	Jim Shaw	Washington

	WALKS	NAME	TEAM	WALKS	NAME	TEAM
Federal League						
1914	127	Ed Lafitte	Brooklyn			
1915	149	Al Schulz	Buffalo			
National League				**American League**		
1915	107	Gene Dale	Cincinnati	165	Weldon Wyckoff	Philadelphia
1916	136	Al Mamaux	Pittsburgh	168	Elmer Myers	Philadelphia
1917	117	Pete Schneider	Cincinnati	123	Jim Shaw	Washington
1918	117	Pete Schneider	Cincinnati	116	Slim Love	New York
1919	87	Jakie May	St. Louis	107	Howard Ehmke	Detroit
1920	127	Ferdie Schupp	St. Louis	149	Dixie Davis	St. Louis
1921	97	Joe Oeschger	Boston	123	Dixie Davis	St. Louis
1922	103	Jimmy Ring	Philadelphia	103	Rip Collins	Boston
1923	115	Jimmy Ring	Philadelphia	120	Elam Vangilder	St. Louis
1924	108	Jimmy Ring	Philadelphia	109	Joe Bush	New York
1925	119	Jimmy Ring	Philadelphia	131	Lefty Grove	Philadelphia
1926	92	Sheriff Blake	Chicago	118	George Uhle	Cleveland
1927	117	Charlie Root	Chicago	105	Earl Whitehill	Detroit
1928	114	Doug McWeeny	Brooklyn	104	Hank Johnson	New York
1929	108	Claude Willoughby	Philadelphia	125	George Earnshaw	Philadelphia
1930	126	Bill Hallahan	St. Louis	139	George Earnshaw	Philadelphia
1931	112	Bill Hallahan	St. Louis	130	Wes Ferrell	Cleveland
1932	115	Van Lingle Mungo	Brooklyn	171	Bump Hadley	Chi/St. Louis
1933	98	Bill Hallahan	St. Louis	141	Bump Hadley	St. Louis
1934	104	Van Lingle Mungo	Brooklyn	149	Bobo Newsom	St. Louis
1935	97	Roy Parmalee	New York	123	Sugar Cain	Phi/St. Louis
1936	118	Van Lingle Mungo	Brooklyn	147	Vern Kennedy	Chicago
1937	97	Hugh Mulcahy	Philadelphia	167	Bobo Newsom	Was/Boston
1938	125	Clay Bryant	Chicago	208	Bob Feller	Cleveland
1939	123	Kirby Higbe	Chicago/Philadelphia	142	Bob Feller	Cleveland
1940	121	Kirby Higbe	Philadelphia	143	Ken Chase	Washington
1941	132	Kirby Higbe	Brooklyn	194	Bob Feller	Cleveland
1942	114	Rube Melton	Philadelphia	140	Phil Marchildon	Philadelphia
1943	162	Johnny Vander Meer	Cincinnati	111	Hal Newhouser	Detroit
1944	137	Hal Gregg	Brooklyn	108	Rufe Gentry	Detroit
1945	120	Hal Gregg	Brooklyn	130	Allie Reynolds	Cleveland
1946	116	Monte Kennedy	New York	153	Bob Feller	Cleveland
1947	122	Kirby Higbe	Brooklyn/Pittsburgh	141	Phil Marchildon	Philadelphia
1948	124	Johnny Vander Meer	Cincinnati	135	Bill Wight	Chicago
1949	117	Herm Wehmeier	Cincinnati	179	Tommy Byrne	New York
1950	135	Herm Wehmeier	Cincinnati	160	Tommy Byrne	New York
1951	109	Warren Spahn	Boston	150	Tommy Byrne	NY/St. Louis
1952	103	Vinegar Bend Mizell	St. Louis	132	Early Wynn	Cleveland
	103	Herm Wehmeier	Cincinnati			

WALKS	NAME	TEAM	WALKS	NAME	TEAM
National League			*American League*		
1953 139	Johnny Lindell	Philadelphia/Pit	116	Mel Parnell	Boston
1954 109	Ruben Gomez	New York	181	Bob Turley	Baltimore
1955 185	Sam Jones	Chicago	177	Bob Turley	New York
1956 115	Sam Jones	Chicago	142	Paul Foytack	Detroit
1957 129	Dick Drott	Chicago	112	Ray Moore	Baltimore
1958 107	Sam Jones	St. Louis	128	Bob Turley	New York
1959 109	Sam Jones	San Francisco	119	Early Wynn	Chicago
1960 103	Bob Buhl	Milwaukee	113	Steve Barber	Baltimore
1961 119	Bob Gibson	St. Louis	132	Chuck Estrada	Baltimore
1962 107	Jack Hamilton	Philadelphia	122	Bo Belinsky	Los Angeles
1963 102	Ray Culp	Philadelphia	105	Earl Wilson	Boston
1964 124	Bob Veale	Pittsburgh	120	Al Downing	New York
1965 119	Bob Veale	Pittsburgh	132	Sam McDowell	Cleveland
119	Tony Cloninger	Atlanta			
1966 116	Tony Cloninger	Atlanta	114	Dean Chance	California
1967 119	Bob Veale	Pittsburgh	123	Sam McDowell	Cleveland
1968 94	Bob Veale	Pittsburgh	110	Sam McDowell	Cleveland
1969 123	Bill Stoneman	Montreal	129	Luis Tiant	Cleveland
1970 125	Carl Morton	Montreal	131	Sam McDowell	Cleveland
1971 146	Bill Stoneman	Montreal	153	Sam McDowell	Cleveland
1972 122	Steve Arlin	San Diego	157	Nolan Ryan	California
1973 117	Jerry Reuss	Houston	162	Nolan Ryan	California
1974 136	Steve Carlton	Philadelphia	202	Nolan Ryan	California
1975 138	J. R. Richard	Houston	133	Mike Torrez	Baltimore
1976 151	J. R. Richard	Houston	183	Nolan Ryan	California
1977 164	Phil Niekro	Atlanta	204	Nolan Ryan	California
1978 141	J. R. Richard	Houston	148	Nolan Ryan	California
1979 113	Phil Niekro	Atlanta	121	Mike Torrez	Boston
1980 98	Nolan Ryan	Houston	128	Jim Clancy	Toronto
1981 77	Bruce Berenyi	Cincinnati	78	Jack Morris	Detroit
1982 109	Nolan Ryan	Houston	108	Dave Righetti	New York
1983 113	Mike Torrez	New York	106	Richard Dotson	Chicago
1984 106	Fernando Valenzuela	Los Angeles	118	Mark Langston	Seattle
1985 114	Ron Darling	New York	120	Phil Niekro	New York
1986 118	Floyd Youmans	Montreal	143	Bobby Witt	Texas
1987 124	Fernando Valenzuela	Los Angeles	140	Bobby Witt	Texas
1988 89	Kevin Gross	Philadelphia	126	Charlie Hough	Texas
1989 99	Ken Hill	St. Louis	114	Bobby Witt	Texas
1990 90	John Smoltz	Atlanta	120	Randy Johnson	Seattle
1991 128	Jose DeJesus	Philadelphia	152	Randy Johnson	Seattle
1992 82	David Cone	New York	144	Randy Johnson	Seattle
1993 104	Ramon Martinez	Los Angeles	122	Wilson Alvarez	Chicago
1994 82	Darryl Kile	Houston	89	Todd Van Poppel	Oakland
			89	Mike Moore	Detroit

WALKS		NAME	TEAM	WALKS	NAME	TEAM
National League				*American League*		
1995	81	Ramon Martinez	Los Angeles	108	Al Leiter	Toronto
1996	119	Al Leiter	Florida	116	Rich Robertson	Minnesota
1997	100	Shawn Estes	San Francisco	95	Ken Hill	Tex/Anaheim
1998	106	Joey Hamilton	San Diego	111	Tony Saunders	Tampa Bay

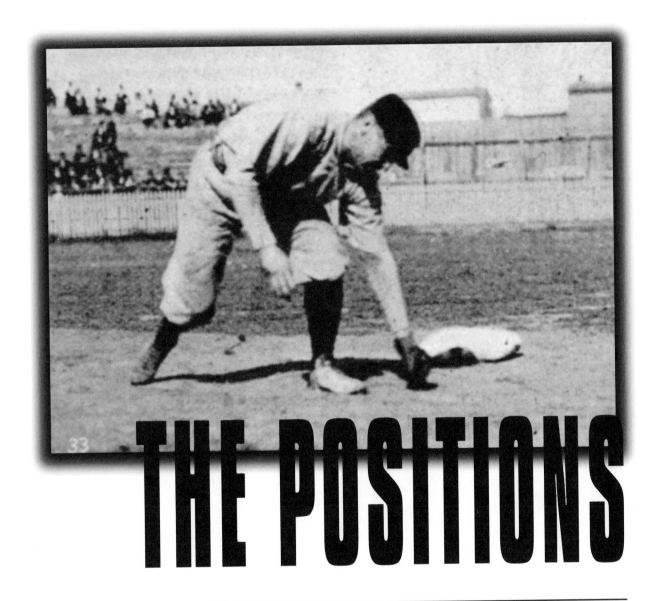

THE POSITIONS

- ◆ GOLD GLOVE GEMS
- ◆ GATEWAY GUARDIANS
- ◆ CRACKERJACK KEYSTONERS
- ◆ HOT CORNER HIGHLIGHTS
- ◆ STELLAR SHORTSTOPS
- ◆ GRAND GARDENERS
- ◆ REGAL RECEIVERS
- ◆ VERSATILE VIRTUOSOS

Gold Glove Gems

1. **The Gold Glove Award is a comparatively recent innovation, as are "Range Factor" and other artificial statistical tools invented to measure fielding prowess. Prior to 1957, when the first Gold Gloves were awarded, fielding average, putouts, assists, errors, and total chances were the staples that a player whose rep was built upon his glove cited to make a case for a salary hike. Who was the first middle infielder to be able to boast, come contract time, that he'd won as many as eight Gold Gloves?**

    A) He amassed more than 2,000 hits.
    B) He debuted in 1956 at age 19.
    C) He was the first NL'er at his position to win a Gold Glove.
    D) For all his achievements, he has never received more than token Hall of Fame consideration.
    E) His bat brought a sudden end to the 1960 World Series.

2. **What owner of the post-1900 record for the worst season fielding average at his position paradoxically led his loop in assists the year he set the negative mark?**

    A) He played for a cellar team that was managed for the last half of the season by its shortstop, who topped the NL in fielding for the second year in a row.
    B) His 92 double plays also led his loop the year he fielded a record-low .971.
    C) His 96 assists were 4 more than the number registered by Jake Beckley, who was second that year among first basemen.
    D) His initials match those of the youngest pitcher in AL history to start a game.
    E) He also has the same initials as the only man to play 100 or more games at all four infield positions wearing a Philadelphia A's uniform.

3. **Tris Speaker predictably owns the career record for the most unassisted double plays by an outfielder, but surprisingly, another man shares the mark with him. Who is he?**

    A) In 1921 he set a still-extant ML mark when he rapped seven consecutive extra-base hits in seven ABs.
    B) For several years, he and Speaker were teammates.
    C) He had the same name as a hard-hitting outfielder in the 1890s who had previously been an outstanding pitcher.
    D) Speaker and he played side by side on the 1920 world champs.
    E) He's best known for tagging the first grand-slam homer in Series history.

4. **Some sources contend this keystoner holds the record for the most consecutive years (six) leading his circuit in fielding; others give the NL fielding crown in 1904 to Fred Raymer. But in either event, our man won the most fielding crowns of any NL second sacker in the pre–Gold Glove era. Who is he?**

    A) He debuted in 1897 as a shortstop because his original team already had Bid McPhee at second base.
    B) In 1904 he set a new record for switch-hitters when he played 157 games.
    C) He hit .111 but fielded flawlessly in the first 20th century World Series.
    D) His nickname was "Little All Right."
    E) He and the first 300-game winner whose forename was Charles share the same initials.

5. What outfielder did *The Sporting News* proclaim the best all-around fly-chaser in the game in the talent-rich 1890 season because he was a better hitter than either Jim Fogarty or Curt Welch, who were rated his only defensive peers at the time?

A) Some sources make him the first man to homer in his first ML at bat.

B) He and the first switch-hitter to win a batting title broke in with the same team in the same season.

C) He tallied an all-time rookie-record 142 runs in 1887.

D) After hitting .300 for Brooklyn in 1898 and pacing all NL outfielders in FA, he quit when he was not given the club's managerial job as promised.

E) He led all NL gardeners in FA a record five times.

Most Years as a Leader in FA, Each Position (Prior to 1957)

	YEARS	NAME	FA LEADER
First Base			
NL	8	Charlie Grimm	1920, 1923–24, 1928, 1930–33
AL	6	Stuffy McInnis	1913–14, 1918, 1920–22
Second Base			
AL	9	Eddie Collins	1909–10, 1914–16, 1920–22, 1924
NL	5	Claude Ritchey	1902–03, 1905–07
Third Base			
AL	8	Willie Kamm	1924–29, 1933–34
NL	5	Heinie Groh	1917–18, 1922–24
Shortstop			
AL	8	Everett Scott	1916–23
	8	Lou Boudreau	1940–44, 1946–48
NL	5	Hughie Jennings	1894–98
	5	Joe Tinker	1906, 1908–09, 1911, 1913
	5	Eddie Miller	1940–43, 1945
Outfield			
NL	5	Mike Griffin	1891–93, 1895, 1898
AL	5	Amos Strunk	1912, 1914, 1917–18, 1920
Catcher			
AL	8	Ray Schalk	1913–17, 1920–22
NL	7	Gabby Hartnett	1925, 1928, 1930, 1934–37
Pitcher			
AL	6	Bob Lemon	1948–49, 1951–53, 1956
NL	5	Christy Mathewson	1901, 1905, 1908, 1910–11

Note: 1957 was the year the Gold Glove Award originated. For pitchers, the standard is chances accepted rather than FA.

6. **What stellar fielder won a Gold Glove the first season he collected as many as 400 at bats and then set the current NL season record for the most double plays by a shortstop the only other year he was physically able to play enough to bat 400 times?**

A) His .215 career BA is the lowest of any noncatcher with 3,000 ABs.

B) Chronic back trouble helped halt his career in 1972 while he was an Expo.

C) He won his lone Gold Glove in 1963.

D) Never on a pennant winner, he came closest in 1964 before his Phils folded.

E) In 1966–68, he played on the Phils with a first baseman and future NL president who had the same initials as his.

Evolution of Shortstops' Record for Most DPs, Season

NAME	TEAM	YEAR	DPS
George Wright	Bos, NA	1871	8
Dickey Pearce	NY, NA	1871	8
Dickie Flowers	Tro, NA	1871	8
George Wright	Bos, NA	1872	25
Davy Force	Buf, NL	1879	26
Arthur Irwin	Wor, NL	1880	27
Sadie Houck	Det, NL	1881	40
Jack Glasscock	Cle, NL	1882	40
Frank Fennelly	Cin, AA	1885	46
Frank Fennelly	Cin, AA	1886	54
Jack Glasscock	Ind, NL	1887	58
Ollie Beard	Cin, AA	1889	63
Bob Allen	Phi, NL	1890	68
Germany Smith	Cin, NL	1894	75
Bill Dahlen	Chi, NL	1898	77
Rabbit Maranville	Bos, NL	1914	92
Dave Bancroft	NY, NL	1920	95
Dave Bancroft	NY, NL	1921	105
Roger Peckinpaugh	Was, AL	1923	105
Glenn Wright	Pit, NL	1925	109
Hod Ford	Cin, NL	1928	128
Lou Boudreau	Cle, AL	1944	134
Bobby Wine	Phi, NL	1970	137
Roy Smalley Jr.	Min, AL	1979	144
Rick Burleson	Bos, AL	1980	147

7. **When Detroit Tigers outfielders Bobby Veach, Ty Cobb, and Sam Crawford ranked 1-2-3 in the AL in RBI in 1915, what AL team's garden trio unexpectedly ranked 1-4-5 in fielding average?**

   A) The left fielder and leader beat out Howie Shanks of Washington for the FA crown, .9822 to .98203.

   B) The right fielder beat out Tris Speaker for the fifth spot, .97619 to .97555.

   C) Despite having three of the AL's top five defensive gardeners in 1915, the club finished last in FA.

   D) The center fielder led the club in hits and total·bases two years after he hit just .118 for it in World Series action.

   E) The club finished last, 14 games out of seventh place.

8. **What 20th century player accomplished the following extraordinary feat in his lone ML season? He became the only man ever to lead his loop in assists even though he didn't play in enough games to qualify for the fielding-average crown!**

   A) His 83 assists are a modern low for a first-base leader in assists.

   B) His 83 assists were 3 more than runner-up Gil Hodges collared in 71 more games.

   C) In 1949 he played beside Emil Verban, who three years earlier had set the 20th century record for the fewest assists by a second-base leader in assists.

   D) He shared the Cubs gateway post in 1949 with Phil Cavarretta.

   E) His initials match those of the Seattle second sacker who led the AL in assists from 1987 through 1991.

9. **On March 31, 1998, Pokey Reese of Cincinnati became only the second shortstop to make four errors in an Opening Day game. Reese was preceded by a rookie in 1941 who rebounded to lead all NL second basemen in assists after committing four errors at short in his team's lid-lifter. His performance that day set 20th century records for both the most errors by a shortstop in his first ML game and the most errors by a shortstop on Opening Day. Can you name him?**

   A) In 1942 he led NL second sackers in errors.

   B) He finished in 1950 as a backup infielder with the Red Sox.

   C) In 1941, his frosh year, Lou Novikoff was his team's most ballyhooed rookie.

   D) His initials match those of the Hawaiian utility infielder who was the Orioles' top defensive sub in the early 1980s.

   E) He and Novikoff had the same first name.

10. **What vastly underrated shortstop narrowly missed leading the NL in fielding average a record seven straight years, 1939–45?**

   A) In 1939, although he had the NL's top FA, a broken leg kept him from playing the required number of games.

   B) After posting the top FA in 1940–43, he lost the fielding crown in 1944 to Marty Marion by a single point and then led again in 1945.

   C) In 1947 he led all ML shortstops in homers and RBI and paced the NL in doubles.

   D) He and the Red Sox regular center fielder in 1982 share the same last name.

   E) His initials are the same as those of the only switch-hitter in the *Elite* 3,000 club who never amassed 200 hits in a season.

11. **The only team since the end of the Deadball Era with eight regulars who all played at least 140 games in the field topped its loop with a .984 fielding average. Can you name that modern-day "Wall of Leather"?**
    A) The team's shortstop and second sacker both led the loop in FA.
    B) The previous year the team had won its second straight World Championship with its third baseman, left fielder, and catcher all leaders in FA.
    C) The team's center fielder and its Hall of Fame catcher were the only regulars with under 500 ABs, but the catcher nonetheless had 31 homers and 109 RBI.
    D) Fred Norman was the club's only hurler to work more than 165 innings.
    E) The previous year the team had become the only NL club since World War II to win consecutive world titles.

12. **Who are the only pair of brothers to be loop leaders in assists at their respective positions two years in a row?**
    A) One of the pair is in the Hall of Fame.
    B) They were teammates when they did it.
    C) The two seasons were 1927 and 1928.
    D) Their positions were shortstop and catcher.
    E) They set many sibling teammate records with Cleveland.

13. **Numerologists may know the only keystone combo ever to lead their loop in putouts, assists, double plays, and fielding average at their respective positions while compiling identical fielding averages. Others will need clues.**
    A) Each of them fielded at a .964 clip.
    B) That year, they played on a flag winner that lost a six-game World Series.
    C) The team featured the youngest man ever to play as many as 140 games for a flag winner.
    D) Stan Hack and a 19-year-old first sacker flanked the keystone pair.
    E) The keystone pair's team won a National League–record 19 straight games.

14. **When Ron Santo led all NL third basemen in assists seven years in a row during 1962–68 and won five straight Gold Gloves in the process, what third sacker's mark did he break for the most consecutive seasons as a loop assist leader?**
    A) His skein ended when he was moved to shortstop after a five-year rein as the hot corner assist king.
    B) He's better known for a season slugging record he set that's also since been broken.
    C) He was a member of the first infield quartet in ML history to play together as a unit for seven full seasons, albeit not at the same positions each season.
    D) His last year as a regular was 1888 when he led all NL shortstops in assists and double plays.
    E) In 1884 he hammered a 19th century season-record 27 home runs.

15. **Name the only man ever to lead his loop in outfield assists while handling at least one chance that season at every position except pitcher.**
    A) Even though he didn't handle any chances as a pitcher that year, he earned his only ML hill win.
    B) For years, several sources erroneously credited him with the AL season record for the most assists by an outfielder because he played so many positions in 1902 that it confused statisticians as to what he did at each.
    C) In 1902 he played 2B on the first AL flag winner.
    D) In 1903 he led the NL in RBI.
    E) He and the holder of the record for the most career hits by a St. Louis Cardinal share the same initials.

16. **What post–World War II performer set a new mark for the highest season fielding average by a third sacker the first year he played 100 games in the field?**
    A) His lone postseason home run came in 1954.
    B) In 1948 he bagged 120 RBI on just 12 home runs.
    C) He held the A's third-base job from mid-1946 through the 1949 season.
    D) His .988 FA in 1947 remained the standard for third sackers until 1974.
    E) He and the NL record holder for the highest season FA by a third baseman share the same nickname.

17. **Who is the only catcher in history to be behind the plate in at least 100 games in a season and average as many as two assists per game?**
    A) Three years later, he played on his first of three straight NL flag winners.
    B) He later managed two NL flag winners.
    C) The same year he broke Chief Zimmer's 13-year-old record of 188 assists, another receiver in his league, Johnny Kling, also topped Zimmer's mark by compiling 189 assists.
    D) His seven home runs the same year he set an all-time assist record for catchers were the most compiled by any AL or NL backstopper during the 1901–19 era.
    E) His 214 assists for Boston, NL, in 1903 are the all-time record for a catcher.

18. **No one has ever accepted as many as 2,000 fielding chances in a major league season. What member of a defending world champion came the closest when he was credited one season with 1,998 chances?**
    A) He topped all AL first sackers in FA for the third straight time that year.
    B) He led the AL with 609 ABs that season and also tied the then-existing ML record for the most games played by a first sacker (157).
    C) He debuted with the 1900 Pirates as a left-handed catcher.
    D) In his only World Series, he batted .333 for "The Hitless Wonders."
    E) He and the owner of the ML record for the most consecutive games hit safely share the same initials.

19. **A shortstop with a career batting average above .250 normally doesn't receive the tag "Good Field, No Hit." What outstanding glove man earned it when his .263 mark in the 1920s was the lowest of any man who played 1,000 games in that decade?**
    A) He debuted as Honus's backup shortstop in 1914.
    B) His high-water mark at the dish came in 1923 when he hit .281 while playing beside Marty McManus.
    C) Also in 1923, he set new records for the most chances accepted by a shortstop in both three consecutive and four consecutive games.
    D) He lost his only chance to see postseason action in 1922 when his team missed the AL flag by one game.
    E) He wasn't related to the baby-food maker with the same last name.

20. **The first man to win more than five consecutive Gold Gloves at any position was also the first to cop Gold Glove honors with three different teams. Who is he?**
    A) He never won a Gold Glove with his original team, the Philadelphia–Kansas City A's.
    B) Like many A's players in the mid-1950s, he was a product of the Yankees' farm system.
    C) He is the most recent man to steal home twice in the same game.
    D) His seventh and last Gold Glove came with the 1964 Angels.
    E) It was his record for the most Gold Gloves by an AL first sacker that Don Mattingly broke in 1993.

Most Gold Gloves, Career, Each Position

	GGS	NAME	YEARS
First Base			
NL	11	Keith Hernandez	1978–88
AL	9	Don Mattingly	1985–89, 1991–94
Second Base			
NL	9	Ryne Sandberg	1983–91
AL	8	Frank White	1977–82, 1986–87
Third Base			
AL	16	Brooks Robinson	1960–75
NL	10	Mike Schmidt	1976–84, 1986
Shortstop			
NL	13	Ozzie Smith	1980–92
AL	9	Luis Aparicio	1958–62, 1964, 1966, 1968, 1970
Outfielder			
NL	12	Willie Mays	1957–68
	12	Roberto Clemente	1961–72
	8	Andre Dawson	1980–85, 1987–88
	8	Barry Bonds	1990–94, 1996–98
AL	10	Al Kaline	1957–59, 1961–67
	9	Ken Griffey Jr.	1990–98
	8	Paul Blair	1967, 1969–75
	8	Dwight Evans	1976, 1978–79, 1981–85
Catcher			
NL	10	Johnny Bench	1968–77
AL	7	Ivan Rodriguez	1992–98
Pitcher			
AL	14	Jim Kaat	1962–75 (also two in the NL, 1976–77)
NL	9	Bob Gibson	1965–73
	9	Greg Maddux	1990–98

Jim Kaat, winner of a record 16 consecutive Gold Gloves between 1962 and 1977. The 1961 season was the only time Kaat pitched enough to qualify for the ERA crown without receiving a Gold Glove. The AL award that year went to Frank Lary of Detroit.

Gateway Guardians

1. First base became a bastion for outstanding hitters near the end of the 1870s, so much so that every man who made his ML debut prior to 1887 and played 1,200 or more games at first base eventually made the Hall of Fame. In sharp contrast, Jake Beckley is the lone first sacker to launch his career between 1887 and 1914, play as many as 1,000 games as a gateway guardian, and make Cooperstown. And for good reason. Only three other men besides Beckley debuted after 1886, finished their careers prior to 1928, played at least 1,000 games at first base, and compiled .300 career batting averages. One is Jack Fournier, who was active mainly in the hitter-friendly 1920s. Can you name the other two?

   A) One owns both the 1901–19 and 1920–41 era season records for the fewest Ks per at bat by an AL first baseman.

   B) He also has the career record for the most RBI (1,062) by anyone who never hit as many as five homers in a season.

   C) At one time, he also held both the career and season records for the highest FA by a first baseman.

   D) The other man won two consecutive NL bat crowns in the midteens.

   E) One was a member of "The $100,000 Infield," and the other is second only to Beckley in career hits made by men named Jake.

Highest Career BA by First Basemen Active Between 1887 and 1927 Exclusively

RANK	NAME	YEARS	G/1B	ABS	HITS	BA
1	Jack Fournier	1912–27	1313	5208	1631	.313
2	Jake Beckley	1888–1907	2377	9526	2930	.308
3	Stuffy McInnis	1909–27	1995	7822	2405	.307
4	Jake Daubert	1910–24	2002	7673	2326	.303
5	Jack Doyle	1889-1905	1043	6039	1806	.299
6	Fred Tenney	1894–1911	1810	7595	2231	.294
7	Hal Chase	1905–19	1815	7417	2158	.291
8	Tommy Tucker	1887–99	1669	6479	1882	.290
9	Walter Holke	1914–25	1193	4456	1278	.287
10	Dan McGann	1896–1908	1376	5222	1482	.284

Note: Minimum 1,000 games at first base; men active prior to 1887 or after 1927 are excluded.

2. **First base has traditionally been home to sluggers, but if Cap Anson's fluky 21 homers in his tiny Chicago home park in 1884 are discounted (as they properly should be), we were deep into the 20th century before a gateway guardian ripped as many as 20 homers in a season. Who first broke the ice?**

   A)   He and Honus were teammates in Wagner's final season.

   B)   He won the NL home run crown the year he achieved his first-sacker first.

   C)   He led the NL in RBI in 1924.

   D)   He was a member of the Giants' 1921–24 dynasty.

   E)   He had the same initials and last name as the star of *Singin' in the Rain*.

3. **Nowadays it's a rare season when a regular first sacker compiles fewer than 10 home runs. What switch-hitter had just one double-digit dinger season in a 13-year career, giving him the fewest career homers of anyone who played 1,500 games at first base since the beginning of the Lively Ball Era in 1920?**

   A)   Among men who played a minimum of 1,000 games at the first sack since 1920, only Eddie Waitkus compiled fewer career homers than his total of 44.

   B)   Only in 1932, the last year he played 100 games, did he go homerless.

   C)   In 1928, the lone season in which he punched more than 6 home runs, he set a new record for four-baggers by a switch-hitter, with 14.

   D)   In 1931 he set a record (since broken) for the most walks by a switch-hitter when he collected 127 free passes for the White Sox.

   E)   To date, he is the only ML'er whose forename was Luzerne.

Fewest Career HRs in 1,000 Games at First Base, Since 1920

RANK	NAME	YEARS	G/1B	ABS	HRS
1	Eddie Waitkus	1946–55	1046	4254	24
2	Lu Blue	1921–33	1571	5904	44
3	Earl Sheely	1921–31	1220	4471	48
	Ferris Fain	1947–55	1116	3930	48
5	Wes Parker	1964–72	1108	4157	64
6	Joe Judge	1915–34	2084	7898	71
7	George Burns	1914–29	1671	6573	72
8	Charlie Grimm	1916–36	2129	7917	79
	Elbie Fletcher	1934–49	1380	4879	79
10	Mike Hargrove	1974–85	1377	5564	80

Note: Tommy McCraw (75 homers in nearly 4,000 ABs) had only 911 games at first base. Buddy Hassett (12 homers in 3,517 ABs) had only 751 games at first base. Buck Jordan (17 homers in 2,980 ABs) had only 684 games at first base. Jack Burns (44 homers in 3,506 ABs) had only 879 games at first base.

4. **John Olerud became the most recent first sacker to top .350 in a season when a full schedule was played and not win a batting title when he slapped .354 as the NL runner-up to Larry Walker in 1998. Who is the most recent AL gateway guardian to meet the same criteria and fail to cop a batting crown?**

    A) He hit lefty unlike Frank Thomas and Jeff Bagwell, the two most recent first basemen to top .350 in strike-shortened seasons and not win batting crowns.

    B) He is the most recent AL'er at any position to hit .350 in a year when a full schedule was played and not win a batting crown.

    C) He played in two World Series seven years apart with two different AL teams.

    D) He alone had three 120-RBI seasons in the 1980s.

    E) He's the most recent lefty-hitting first sacker to post seven straight .300 seasons (1977–83), mostly with Milwaukee.

5. **When Mark McGwire hit .201 in 1991, he nearly became the first gateway guardian since John Morrill in 1888 to slip below the Mendoza line (.200) in 400 at bats. However, McGwire compiled 175 total bases and a .383 slugging average. Just twice in history has a first baseman collected fewer than 100 total bases with as many as 350 at bats. Who are these two punchless first sackers?**

    A) Both men did it after World War II, and one was a lefty all the way while the other was a righty.

    B) The lefty was later a trainer for the NL team with which he spent his only big league season in 1952.

    C) The righty set a new strikeout record for rookie batters in 1966 (since broken) and then hit .171 in 124 games two years later.

    D) The lefty hit .220 with a .265 SA as the Pirates regular first sacker in 1952, and the righty led the AL in homers and RBI in 1975.

    E) The lefty has the same first name as the 1997 NL batting champ, and the righty has the same first and last names as the star of the film *Patton*.

Fewest TBs by a Regular First Baseman, Season

RANK	NAME	TEAM	YEAR	ABS	BA	SA	TBS
1	George Scott	Bos, AL	1968	350	.171	.237	83
2	Tony Bartirome	Pit, NL	1952	355	.220	.265	94
3	Juice Latham	Lou, AA	1883	368	.250	.302	107
	Deron Johnson	Oak/Mil/Bos, AL	1974	351	.171	.305	107
5	Pat Newnam	StL, AL	1910	384	.216	.281	108
6	Charlie Comiskey	Chi, PL	1890	377	.244	.289	109
	Fred Tenney	NY, NL	1909	375	.235	.291	109
	Jim Hackett	StL, NL	1903	351	.228	.311	109
9	Ed Kranepool	NY, NL	1968	373	.231	.295	110
10	John Kerins	Ind, AA	1884	361	.216	.308	112
	Klondike Douglass	Phi, NL	1903	377	.255	.297	112

Note: Minimum 350 ABs. Johnson also DH'd in 1974. Douglass holds the all-time record for the fewest TBs by a first baseman in 400 ABs—113 in 1902.

6. **The St. Louis Maroons set many team records in 1884, the Union Association's only season as a major circuit, and several Maroons also set individual marks. Among them is the ML record for the most errors in a season by a first baseman. What 19-year-old rookie established the mark with 62 miscues?**

    A) He went on to play not only in the UA but also in the NL, the PL, and the AL.
    B) He played second base most of his career.
    C) Until the 1990s, he was the only big leaguer born in Australia.
    D) He managed and played for the worst team ever, the 1899 Cleveland Spiders.
    E) He and the oldest man to hit a home run in a major league game share the same last name.

Most Errors, Season, First Baseman

RANK	NAME	TEAM	YEAR	GAMES	FA	ERRORS
1	Joe Quinn	StL, UA	1884	100	.945	62
2	Cap Anson	Chi, NL	1884	112	.956	58
3	Dan Stearns	Bal, AA	1883	92	.947	57
	Cap Anson	Chi, NL	1885	112	.958	57
5	John Kerins	Lou, AA	1885	96	.947	56
6	Tim Murnane	Bos, NL	1876	65	.927	55
	Otto Schomberg	Ind, NL	1887	112	.958	55
	Denny Mack	Phi, NA	1874	56	.900	55
9	Mart Powell	Det, NL	1883	101	.950	54
	Dan Stearns	Bal, AA	1884	100	.949	54

7. **Jack Harshman may be the most outstanding pitcher to begin his ML career as a gateway guardian, and George Sisler is unquestionably the greatest first baseman to start out on the mound. But Sisler's top hill season delivered only four wins, and Harshman played just 13 games in the majors at first base. Only one man in big league history played 100 games at first base in a season and also had a 20-win campaign as a pitcher. Who is he?**

    A) He played 100 games at first base three years in a row.
    B) He hit .357 in 400+ ABs the last year he won 20 games.
    C) He was the Brooklyn Bridegrooms player-manager in the mid-1890s.
    D) He debuted in 1884 with the St. Louis Browns.
    E) His .690 winning percentage is second among pitchers with 200 career decisions.

8. **Jake Beckley not only leads all first sackers in career triples, but he's also the lone gateway guardian with at least 150 three-baggers who amassed nearly three times as many triples (243) as home runs (86). Who is the only other first baseman even to approach Beckley's feat by compiling 108 career triples and just 37 home runs?**

    A) He paced his loop in both triples and home runs in 1886.
    B) He was the second man to win a major league batting title in what by today's rule would have been his rookie season.
    C) By a margin of less than one percentage point, in 1890 he missed becoming the first man to lead two different major leagues in batting.
    D) In 1886, with the New York Mets, he set a record for the most triples in a season by a first baseman (31) that will probably stand forever.
    E) His .373 BA in his last season is the best coda of anyone who was not barred from the game.

Highest BA in Final ML Season (Minimum 400 ABs)

RANK	NAME	TEAM	YEAR	ABS	HITS	BA
1	Joe Jackson	Chi, AL	1920	570	218	.382
2	Dave Orr	Bro, PL	1890	464	173	.373
3	Happy Felsch	Chi, AL	1920	556	188	.338
4	Harry Moore	Was, UA	1884	461	155	.336
5	Buck Weaver	Chi, AL	1920	629	208	.331
6	Bill Lange	Chi, NL	1899	416	135	.325
7	Sam Dungan	Was, AL	1901	559	179	.3202
8	Bill Keister	Phi, NL	1903	400	128	.3200
9	Buzz Arlett	Phi, NL	1931	418	131	.313
10	Johnny Hodapp	Bos, AL	1933	413	129	.312

Note: Hodapp's .3123 exceeded Joe Knight's .3118 in 1890. BAs are carried out to four decimal points where ties would otherwise exist.

9. **Prior to the end of the Deadball Era, first basemen often were loop leaders in triples. Now it's rare. The most recent first sacker to lead in three-baggers was Rod Carew in 1977, but Carew was a latecomer to the position. So, for that matter, was the first gateway guardian in ML history to be a loop leader in triples. Who is he?**

   A) He is the only man to pitch in both the NL's inaugural season (1876) and the Players League (1890).

   B) He led the NL in three-baggers in 1877 with a total of 11.

   C) He began as a catcher and played third base most of his career.

   D) In 1877 he became the first gateway guardian to win a National League batting title.

   E) He was the catching half of the first brother battery in big league history.

Post-Deadball Era First Basemen Leading in Triples

NAME	TEAM	YEAR	BA	3BS
Jake Daubert	Cin, NL	1922	.336	22
George Sisler	StL, AL	1922	.420	18
Lou Gehrig	NY, AL	1926	.313	20
Jim Bottomley	StL, NL	1928	.325	20
Bill Terry	NY, NL	1931	.349	20
Johnny Mize	StL, NL	1938	.337	16
Stan Musial	StL, NL	1946	.365	20
Dale Long	Pit, NL	1955	.291	13
Vic Power	KC/Cle, AL	1958	.312	10
Rod Carew	Min, AL	1977	.388	16

10. **The only man to own both the NL and the AL records in the same era for the most hits by a player at his position was a first sacker. Who is he?**
    A) He holds both the NL and AL records for the most chances accepted in a doubleheader by a first baseman.
    B) His 941 RBI top all first sackers active exclusively in the Deadball Era.
    C) He and Brouthers are the only two men to win homer crowns in a Buffalo ML uni.
    D) He is the only bat crown winner who hit right and threw left.
    E) His 184 hits for the Reds in 1916 were the most by a National League first baseman during the Deadball Era, and his 193 hits for the Yankees in 1906 tied Charlie Hickman for the AL high in the same period.

11. **The first man to play 1,200 games at shortstop is not in the Hall of Fame. Nor are the first men to play 1,200 games at third or second base. As we've already noted, early-day first basemen, in contrast, are plentiful in Cooperstown. Who is the only man to play 1,200 games at first base prior to 1901 and not make the Hall of Fame?**
    A) In his rookie year he led all AA first sackers in chances.
    B) He spent 1899, his final season, with the nefarious Cleveland Spiders.
    C) His .249 BA for Boston was the lowest of any regular NL first sacker's in 1895.
    D) In 1889 he became the first switch-hitter to win a big league batting title.
    E) He and a nursery rhyme chap made to sing for his supper share the same name.

Most Games Played at First Base Prior to 1901

RANK	NAME	YEARS	G/1B
1	Cap Anson	1871–97	2156
2	Roger Connor	1880–97	1758
3	Tommy Tucker	1887–99	1669
4	Dan Brouthers	1879–96	1632
5	Jake Beckley	1888–1900	1596
6	Charlie Comiskey	1882–94	1363
7	Long John Reilly	1880–91	1075
8	Joe Start	1871–86	1070
9	Bill Phillips	1879–88	1032
10	Sid Farrar	1883–90	943

Note: In 1885, Start became the first to play 1,000 ML games at first base; Beckley also played many games at first base after 1900.

12. **The first nine men on the preceding list were of course also the first nine to play 1,000 games at the gateway post in the majors. Who was the 10th to do it?**
    A) He was the second switch-hitter to play 1,000 games at first base.
    B) In 1904 he and Claude Ritchey set a new record for switch-hitters when each played in 157 games to break Billy Clingman's old mark of 154, set in 1898.
    C) He was the regular first sacker for the last NL team to represent Baltimore.
    D) He played his 1,000th game at first base the same year he served as the regular first sacker for the first 20th century world champion.
    E) His nickname was "Candy."

13. **The first regular first sacker to go homerless for an entire season in 400 at bats is also the only man to play five full seasons in the National Association without hitting a four-bagger. Who is this seemingly powerless gateway keeper?**
    A) In his first eight seasons in the NL, he totaled just four homers.
    B) He holds a share of the ML record for the most home runs hit in two consecutive games (five).
    C) He never won a big league home run crown, but he won eight RBI crowns.
    D) No surprise—he's in the Hall of Fame.
    E) He was the first player to collect 3,000 hits.

Most ABs, No HRs, Season, First Baseman

RANK	NAME	TEAM	YEAR	BA	SA	ABS
1	Jiggs Donahue	. Chi, AL	1907	.259	.299	609
2	Hal Chase	NY, AL	1906	.323	.395	597
3	Bill Everitt	Chi, NL	1898	.319	.364	596
4	Charlie Grimm	Pit, NL	1922	.292	.383	593
5	Bill Phillips	Bro, AA	1886	.274	.369	585
6	Stuffy McInnis	Bos, AL	1921	.307	.394	584
7	Claude Rossman	Det, AL	1907	.277	.342	571
8	Stuffy McInnis	Phi, AL	1917	.303	.351	567
9	Kitty Bransfield	Pit, NL	1901	.295	.398	566
10	Jack Doyle	Phi, NL	1895	.253	.297	565

Note: Scoops Carey (.440 SA for Washington, AL, in 1902) holds the record for the highest SA by a first baseman who went homerless in at least 400 ABs.

14. **What notoriously weak-fielding first sacker in his first five seasons as a regular belied his fumble-fingered rep by leading his loop in fielding average three times and topping it in total chances per game on the other two occasions?**
    A) He set a franchise dinger record as a rookie that lasted 16 years.
    B) His last season as a regular was 1940, split between the AL and the NL.
    C) In 1938 his 22 homers set a new Washington Senators franchise record.
    D) He was the first performer to serve as a regular gateway guardian during his career with both the Cubs and the White Sox.
    E) His real first name was Henry, but he was known as "Zeke."

15. **Rare indeed are men who spend their entire careers exclusively at first base. Even Lou Gehrig on occasion played the outfield. The 1977 crop of first basemen was typical. Of the 12 regular NL first sackers in 1977, just one ended his career without playing at least one season as a regular at another position. Name him.**
    A) He won an MVP Award.
    B) He was on World Championship teams based in two different NL cities.
    C) He won a batting title but never a home run or RBI crown.
    D) He played seven games in the outfield for the Cardinals in 1980–81, preventing him from becoming only the second man in history to play as many as 2,000 career games exclusively at first base.
    E) In 1979 he and Willie Stargell became the first duo to share an MVP Award.

Most Games Played, First Base as the Only Defensive Position

RANK	NAME	YEARS	G/1B
1	Jake Daubert	1910–24	2002
2	Wally Pipp	1913–28	1819
3	George McQuinn	1936–48	1529
4	Ted Kluszewski	1947–61	1481
5	John Mayberry	1968–82	1478
6	Dolph Camilli	1933–45	1476
7	Cecil Cooper	1971–87	1475
8	Elbie Fletcher	1934–49	1380
9	Fred Luderus	1909–20	1326
10	Jason Thompson	1976–86	1314

Note: Active players excluded. Mayberry, Cooper, and Thompson also DH'd; unlike other positions, DH'ing does not exclude men from the first-base list.

16. Who is the most recent first baseman to have back-to-back seasons when he compiled 100 RBI on fewer than 10 home runs?

A) Frank McCormick in 1938 was the last NL first sacker with even one such season.

B) Our man had a three-year run in the 1920s when he totaled 303 RBI on 18 homers.

C) In 1926 he tied the current ML record for the most consecutive extra-base hits when he collected six doubles and a homer in seven ABs.

D) His son later caught for Chicago, the same AL club he served for seven seasons.

E) He and a National League co-record-holder prior to 1996 for most walks in a season have the same initials.

Most RBI with Fewer than 10 HRs by a First Baseman, Season

RANK	NAME	TEAM	YEAR	HRS	RBI
1	Dan Brouthers	Bal, NL	1894	9	128
2	Nap Lajoie	Phi, NL	1897	9	127
3	Dave Orr	Bro, PL	1890	6	124
	Dan Brouthers	Bro, NL	1892	5	124
5	Jake Beckley	Pit, PL	1890	9	120
	Cap Anson	Chi, NL	1891	8	120
	Jake Beckley	Pit, NL	1894	7	120
8	Dan Brouthers	Bos, NL	1889	7	118
9	Cap Anson	Chi, NL	1889	7	117
10	Wally Pipp	NY, AL	1924	9	114

17. In 1900 two future Hall of Famers who set 1893–1900 era records for the most doubles by any player and the most total bases by a first baseman, respectively, played side by side in the same infield. Who are they?

A) The era record holder for the most TBs by a first sacker didn't play first in 1900.

B) The era doubles record holder didn't play the infield the year he set the mark.

C) Each played at least one full season with a Cleveland ML team, but neither played for a team nicknamed the Spiders.

D) Both men set their 1893–1900 era marks with the Phillies.

E) Between them, the duo copped the first two AL batting titles.

Season Record Holders Among First Basemen for Each Era

| | | National League | | | American League | |
	RECORD	NAME	YEAR	RECORD	NAME	YEAR
At Bats						
1871–75	389	Cal McVey	1875—NA			
1876–92	614	Jake Beckley	1892	587	Charlie Comiskey	1889
1893–1900	603	Fred Tenney	1899	591	Honus Wagner	1898
1901–19	622	Dick Hoblitzel	1911	625	Tom Jones	1904
1920–41	643	Bill Terry	1932	649	George Sisler	1925
1942–60	641	Eddie Waitkus	1950	653	Mickey Rocco	1944
1961–76	666	Felipe Alou	1966	641	Chris Chambliss	1976
1977–93	673	Bill Buckner	1985	**677**	**Don Mattingly**	**1986**
1994–	628	Eric Karros	1997	635	Mo Vaughn	1996
Batting Average						
1871–75	.398	Cap Anson	1873—NA			
1876–92	.399	Cap Anson	1881	.372	Tommy Tucker	1889
1893–1900	.367	Jack Doyle	1894	.361	Nap Lajoie	1897
1901–19	.350	Jake Daubert	1913	.361	Charlie Hickman	1902
1920–41	.401	Bill Terry	1930	**.420**	*George Sisler*	**1922**
1942–60	.365	Stan Musial	1946	.353	Mickey Vernon	1946
1961–76	.327	Felipe Alou	1966	.361	Norm Cash	1961
1977–93	.370	Andres Galarraga	1993	.388	Rod Carew	1977
1994–	.367	Jeff Bagwell	1994	.353	Frank Thomas	1994
Slugging Average						
1871–75	.517	Cal McVey	1875—NA			
1876–92	.581	Dan Brouthers	1886	.551	John Reilly	1884
1893–1900	.582	Roger Connor	1894	.569	Nap Lajoie	1897
1901–19	.480	Vic Saier	1913	.539	Charlie Hickman	1902
1920–41	.636	Johnny Mize	1940	**.765**	**Lou Gehrig**	**1927**
1942–60	.642	Ted Kluszewski	1954	.604	Hank Greenberg	1946
1961–76	.656	Willie McCovey	1969	.662	Norm Cash	1961
1977–93	.602	Andres Galarraga	1993	.618	Mark McGwire	1987
1994–	.752	Mark McGwire	1998	.729	Frank Thomas	1994

		National League			American League	
	RECORD	**NAME**	**YEAR**	**RECORD**	**NAME**	**YEAR**
Hits						
1871–75	138	Cal McVey	1875—NA			
1876–92	197	Dan Brouthers	1892	196	Tommy Tucker	1889
1893–1900	209	Fred Tenney	1899	197	Nap Lajoie	1897
1901–19	184	Hal Chase	1916	193	Charlie Hickman	1902
				193	Hal Chase	1906
1920–41	254	Bill Terry	1930	**257**	**George Sisler**	**1920**
1942–60	228	Stan Musial	1946	207	Mickey Vernon	1946
1961–76	218	Felipe Alou	1966	200	Rod Carew	1976
1977–93	210	Keith Hernandez	1979	239	Rod Carew	1977
1994–	197	John Olerud	1998	207	Mo Vaughn	1996
Total Bases						
1871–75	201	Cal McVey	1875—NA			
1876–92	284	Dan Brouthers	1886	301	Dave Orr	1886
1893–1900	310	Nap Lajoie	1897	294	Dan Brouthers	1894
1901–19	260	Fred Luderus	1911	288	Charlie Hickman	1902
1920–41	392	Bill Terry	1930	**447**	**Lou Gehrig**	**1931**
1942–60	368	Ted Kluszewski	1954	326	Walt Dropo	1950
1961–76	356	Orlando Cepeda	1961	354	Norm Cash	1961
1977–93	329	Andres Galarraga	1988	388	Don Mattingly	1986
1994–	383	Mark McGwire	1998	370	Mo Vaughn	1996
Doubles						
1871–75	36	Cal McVey	1875—NA			
1876–92	41	Dan Brouthers	1883	35	John Reilly	1887
1893–1900	40	Nap Lajoie	1897	39	Dan Brouthers	1894
1900–19	38	Ed Konetchy	1911	47	Harry Davis	1905
1920–41	45	George Kelly	1929	**64**	**George Burns**	**1926**
	45	Ray Grimes	1922			
1942–60	50	Stan Musial	1946	51	Mickey Vernon	1946
1961–76	47	Wes Parker	1970	38	John Mayberry	1975
				38	Chris Chambliss	1975
1977–93	48	Keith Hernandez	1979	54	John Olerud	1993
1994–	51	Mark Grace	1995	43	Carlos Delgado	1998

		National League			American League	
	RECORD	NAME	YEAR	RECORD	NAME	YEAR
Triples						
1871–75	9	Everett Mills	1873—NA			
	9	Cal McVey	1875—NA			
1876–92	26	John Reilly	1890	**31**	**Dave Orr**	**1886**
1893–1900	29	Perry Werden	1893	28	Harry Davis	1897
1901–19	21	Vic Saier	1913	18	Jack Fournier	1915
1920–41	22	Jake Daubert	1922	20	Lou Gehrig	1926
1942–60	20	Stan Musial	1946	14	Mickey Vernon	1954
1961–76	14	Donn Clendenon	1965	12	Tommy McCraw	1968
				12	Rod Carew	1976
1977–93	11	Keith Hernandez	1979	16	Rod Carew	1977
1994–	8	Darren Daulton	1997	8	Jose Offerman	1996
Home Runs						
1871–75	5	Jim O'Rourke	1874—NA			
1876–92	21	Cap Anson	1884	19	Harry Stovey	1889
1893–1900	12	Ed Cartwright	1894	11	Roger Connor	1893
				11	Roger Connor	1896
1901–19	18	Fred Luderus	1913	12	Harry Davis	1906
	18	Vic Saier	1914	12	Charlie Hickman	1903
				12	Wally Pipp	1916
1920–41	43	Johnny Mize	1940	58	Jimmie Foxx	1932
				58	Hank Greenberg	1938
1942–60	51	Johnny Mize	1947	44	Hank Greenberg	1946
1961–76	46	Orlando Cepeda	1961	46	Harmon Killebrew	1961
				46	Jim Gentile	1961
1977–93	37	Dave Kingman	1982	51	Cecil Fielder	1990
1994–	**70**	**Mark McGwire**	**1998**	52	Mark McGwire	1996
RBI						
1871–75	87	Cal McVey	1875—NA			
1876–92	147	Cap Anson	1886	109	Dan Brouthers	1891
Other:	124	Dave Orr	1890—PL			
1893–1900	128	Dan Brouthers	1894	127	Nap Lajoie	1897
1901–19	99	Fred Luderus	1911	114	Buck Freeman	1901
1920–41	143	Don Hurst	1932	**184**	**Lou Gehrig**	**1931**
1942–60	144	Walt Dropo	1950	141	Ted Kluszewski	1954
1961–76	142	Orlando Cepeda	1961	141	Jim Gentile	1961
1977–93	117	Pedro Guerrero	1989	133	Cecil Fielder	1991
1994–	150	Andres Galarraga	1996	143	Mo Vaughn	1996

		National League			American League	
	RECORD	**NAME**	**YEAR**	**RECORD**	**NAME**	**YEAR**
Runs						
1871–75	89	Cal McVey	1875—NA			
1876–92	153	Dan Brouthers	1887	139	Charlie Comiskey	1887
1893–1900	137	Dan Brouthers	1894	125	Fred Tenney	1897
1901–19	103	Frank Chance	1906	96	George Sisler	1919
1920–41	139	Bill Terry	1930	**167**	**Lou Gehrig**	**1936**
1942–60	137	Johnny Mize	1947	102	Vic Power	1959
1961–76	122	Felipe Alou	1966	119	Norm Cash	1961
1977–93	116	Keith Hernandez	1979	128	Rod Carew	1977
1994–	130	Mark McGwire	1998	118	Mo Vaughn	1996
Walks						
1871–75	23	Denny Mack	1873—NA			
1876–92	116	Roger Connor	1892	83	Henry Larkin	1889
1893–1900	91	Roger Connor	1893	88	Bill Joyce	1898
1901–19	94	Vic Saier	1914	81	Joe Judge	1919
1920–41	119	Dolph Camilli	1938	132	Lou Gehrig	1935
	119	Elbie Fletcher	1940			
1942–60	119	Earl Torgeson	1950	137	Roy Cullenbine	1947
1961–76	137	Willie McCovey	1969	131	Harmon Killebrew	1967
1977–93	136	Jack Clark	1987	138	Frank Thomas	1991
1994–	**162**	**Mark McGwire**	**1998**	136	Frank Thomas	1995
OBP						
1871–75	.403	Cap Anson	1873—NA			
1876–92	.462	Dan Brouthers	1889	.471	Dan Brouthers	1891
1893–1900	.425	Dan Brouthers	1894	.420	Jack Doyle	1894
1901–19	.450	Frank Chance	1905	.429	Jack Fournier	1915
1920–41	.452	Bill Terry	1930	.478	Lou Gehrig	1936
1942–60	.449	Phil Cavarretta	1945	.451	Ferris Fain	1951
1961–76	.458	Willie McCovey	1969	.488	Norm Cash	1961
1977–93	.461	Jack Clark	1987	.478	John Olerud	1993
1994–	.470	Mark McGwire	1998	**.494**	**Frank Thomas**	**1994**

| | National League | | | | American League | |
	RECORD	**NAME**	**YEAR**	**RECORD**	**NAME**	**YEAR**
Stolen Bases						
1871–75	30	Tim Murnane	1875—NA			
1876–92	48	Dave Foutz	1891	**117**	**Charlie Comiskey**	**1887**
1893–1900	73	Jack Doyle	1896	62	Jack Doyle	1897
1901–19	67	Frank Chance	1903	52	Frank Isbell	1901
1920–41	26	Jack Fournier	1920	51	George Sisler	1922
1942–60	29	Jackie Robinson	1947	25	Mickey Vernon	1942
1961–76	22	Donn Clendenon	1963	24	Tommy McCraw	1967
1977–93	46	Gregg Jefferies	1993	27	Rod Carew	1978
1994–	31	Jeff Bagwell	1997	24	Jose Offerman	1996

Note: In the 1876–92 era, men who appear under the American League column are the American Association record holders. In the 1893–1900 era, men who appear under the American League column are the runners-up to the National League record holders. Players who performed at more than one position in their record season are considered the record holders at the position where they played the most games. All-time leaders among first basemen are in **bold**.

A rare action photo of Dan Brouthers, circa 1892. Considered by many authorities to be the greatest hitter in the 19th century as well as its greatest first baseman, Brouthers holds a multitude of pre-1893 batting records.

Crackerjack Keystoners

1. Second sackers are the game's most unsung performers, none more so than Bid McPhee. Among men who never played regularly anywhere but at second base, McPhee currently has the most career hits of anyone eligible for the Hall of Fame but not enshrined. There is only one other man with 2,000 career hits who was solely a second sacker and will have to be tapped by the Veterans Committee to earn a plaque in Cooperstown. Who is he?

   A) Like McPhee, he holds many career fielding records.
   B) Like McPhee, he played his entire career with the same team.
   C) His initials match those of a man who compiled more than 2,000 hits and won a batting title as a second baseman but also played regularly at third and short.
   D) He and Nellie Fox (who shared the same plight he and McPhee do prior to 1997) opposed one another on the diamond but only in All-Star play.
   E) He is best remembered for ending a World Series with one swing of his bat.

Most Career Hits, Non–Hall of Famer, 1,000 Games at Second Base

RANK	NAME	YEARS	G/2B	HITS
1	Ryne Sandberg	1981–97	1995	2386
2	Lou Whitaker	1977–95	2308	2369
3	Bid McPhee	1882–99	2125	2249
4	Willie Randolph	1975–92	2152	2210
5	Buddy Myer	1924–41	1340	2131
6	Bill Mazeroski	1956–72	2094	2016
7	Frank White	1973–90	2150	2006
8	Del Pratt	1912–24	1685	1996
9	Kid Gleason	1888–1912	1584	1944
10	Bobby Lowe	1890–1907	1313	1929

Note: Active players excluded. Myer also played other infield positions.

2. Bid McPhee played on a flag winner in his rookie year but never played on another. The first rookie in the 20th century to serve as the regular second baseman for a World Championship team had a similar fate. Who is he?

    A) Later moved to first base, he compiled 1,500+ hits in the majors.

    B) He died of tuberculosis four days before his 37th birthday.

    C) He played beside a Hall of Fame shortstop as a rookie in 1909.

    D) His nickname was "Dots."

    E) He and the current record holder for the highest season FA by a third baseman have the same initials.

First Rookie Regular, Each Position, 20th Century WS Winner

NAME	TEAM	YEAR	POS.
Norwood Gibson	Bos, AL	1903	P
Dots Miller	Pit, NL	1909	2B
Butch Schmidt	Bos, NL	1914	1B
Swede Risberg	Chi, AL	1917	SS
Joe DiMaggio	NY, AL	1936	LF
Charlie Keller	NY, AL	1939	RF
Billy Johnson	NY, AL	1943	3B
Johnny Lindell	NY, AL	1943	CF
Andy Etchebarren	Bal, AL	1966	C

3. The first second baseman to play on 20th century World Championship teams with two different franchises was a bona fide star. Who is he?

    A) He was on the first team to be the victim of a World Series sweep.

    B) In his first Series, he hit .429 to lead all players on both teams.

    C) In his final Series, he hit .226 in eight games for the losing side.

    D) His son later played 132 career games with the A's, one of his two Series teams.

    E) He has the record for the most career hits by a second baseman.

4. The only second baseman to hang up his spikes after playing on three consecutive World Championship teams is not in the Hall of Fame and never will be. Name him.

    A) His big league coda was a World Series in which he went 0-for-13.

    B) In his first Series, he hit .333 in seven games after being idled most of the season by an injury.

    C) He spent his entire 12-year career with the same franchise.

    D) The franchise changed cities early in his sojourn with them.

    E) In Game Four of the 1972 Series, he faced a Reds lefty whose initials match his.

5. What second sacker had just three career triples after his first four seasons in the majors but then tied a best-of-seven World Series record when he ripped three triples in his first fall classic?

    A) He currently has the mark for the most triples in a Series by a switch-hitter.

    B) In 1995 he hit a career-high five triples.

    C) In 1996 he hit no triples in either the regular season or the World Series.

    D) He and the Braves' top pinch hitter in 1979–80 have the same initials.

    E) A fine fielder, he led three different minor leagues in putouts and assists before joining the Braves.

6. In 1987, when a new ML home run record was set (since broken), who was the only second sacker in either league to hit 20 taters?

   A)   It was his only 20-homer season.

   B)   It was also the only season in which he had 100 RBI.

   C)   He led the NL in triples in 1987.

   D)   In 1989 the Mets tried unsuccessfully to make him a center fielder.

   E)   He set a new NL frosh record when he K'd 168 times for the 1984 Phils.

7. Who is the only AL'er to play 1,000 games at second base and average 20 home runs a season?

   A)   He reached 100 career homers in only his fourth ML season and broke Charlie Gehringer's AL record of 184 career homers by a second baseman early in his ninth campaign.

   B)   He is the only man to win an MVP Award in a season when he led his league in batter strikeouts and errors at his position.

   C)   He was part of the only second-base, shortstop, and third-base trio in history that achieved 100 RBI apiece in the same season.

   D)   He was on World Championship teams in two different AL cities in the 1940s.

   E)   He still holds the AL record for the most career homers by a second sacker.

Most Career HRs, AL Second Basemen

RANK	NAME	YEARS	GAMES	HRS
1	Joe Gordon	1938–50	1566	253
2	Lou Whitaker	1977–95	2390	244
3	Bobby Grich	1970–86	2008	224
4	Bobby Doerr	1937–51	1865	223
5	Dick McAuliffe	1960–75	1763	197
6	Charlie Gehringer	1924–42	2323	184
7	Tony Lazzeri	1926–37	1658	169
8	Frank White	1973–90	2324	160
9	Gil McDougald	1951–60	1336	112
10	Carlos Baerga	1990–	829	103

Note: Includes only men who played more than half their total career games at second base, thereby excluding Paul Molitor and Julio Franco, among others. McAuliffe also played several seasons at shortstop. Lazzeri's and Baerga's homer totals do not include blasts they hit in the NL.

8. In 1997, Tony Fernandez played second base for Cleveland in the World Series after previously playing every game of the 1993 Series at shortstop for Toronto. But Fernandez participated in only five of the seven Series games in 1997. Who is the only 20th century performer to play every game in a World Series at second base and play every game in another World Series at a different position?

   A)   He actually played every game in three different World Series; in two of them, he saw action only as an outfielder.

   B)   He lost his second-base job to a Hall of Famer.

   C)   His three World Series appearances all were with the same AL team.

   D)   He hit .329 for the A's in 1911, his last year as a regular gardener.

   E)   He has the same initials and last name as a two-time NL MVP in the 1980s.

9. **Second basemen win RBI crowns about as often as they turn unassisted triple plays. Who was the most recent second sacker to top the AL in RBI?**

   A) He played for a team based in the same city as the one that was home to the last second sacker to lead either ML in RBI.

   B) Prior to 1971 he held the AL record for the fewest runs by an RBI leader.

   C) The most recent year that a second sacker topped the AL in RBI, Tris Speaker won his only batting crown.

   D) His 966 career RBI are the most of any second sacker active exclusively prior to World War II who is not in the Hall of Fame.

   E) His initials are the same as those of a .350-hitting outfielder with Cleveland in 1930 who was called "Twitchy Dick."

	Fewest Runs, Season, Leader in RBI				
RANK	**NAME**	**TEAM**	**YEAR**	**RBI**	**RUNS**
1	Harmon Killebrew	Min, AL	1971	119	61
	Lee May	Bal, AL	1976	109	61
	Heinie Zimmerman	NY, NL	1917	102	61
4	Del Pratt	StL, AL	1916	103	64
5	Dutch Zwilling	Chi, FL	1915	94	65
6	George Kelly	NY, NL	1920	94	69
7	Bill Dahlen	NY, NL	1904	80	70
8	Chief Wilson	Pit, NL	1911	107	72
9	Sam Crawford	Det, AL	1914	104	74
10	Sherry Magee	Phi, NL	1907	85	75

Note: Since 1887, when the schedule was increased to 140 games; the abbreviated 1918, 1919, and 1981 seasons are excluded. In 1918, Bobby Veach, the AL RBI leader with 78, scored just 59 runs, but due to World War I the season ended on Labor Day.

10. **In 1929, Rogers Hornsby topped the NL in slugging average for the last time. Since then, only two second sackers have led either loop in slugging. Who are they?**

    A) No second sacker since Hornsby has won the NL slugging crown.

    B) The two AL winners since 1929 triumphed 36 years apart, and both did it in very atypical seasons.

    C) The two AL winners compiled the lowest and the second-lowest number of total bases by a junior-circuit SA leader since 1920.

    D) One of the pair won the AL batting title the same season in which he led in SA, and the other shared the AL home run crown.

    E) The bat crown winner owns the lowest career BA of any player ever to top a major league in hitting, and the home run champ rapped the fewest dingers of any home run crown winner since 1944.

Second Basemen Leading in SA

NAME	TEAM	YEAR	SA
Ross Barnes	Bos, NA	1872	.585
Ross Barnes	Bos, NA	1873	.584
Ross Barnes	Chi, NL	1876	.590
Fred Dunlap	StL, UA	1884	.621
Nap Lajoie	Phi, AL	1901	.643
Nap Lajoie	Cle, AL	1903	.533
Nap Lajoie	Cle, AL	1904	.554
Rogers Hornsby	StL, NL	1920	.559
Rogers Hornsby	StL, NL	1921	.639
Rogers Hornsby	StL, NL	1922	.722
Rogers Hornsby	StL, NL	1923	.627
Rogers Hornsby	StL, NL	1924	.696
Rogers Hornsby	StL, NL	1925	.756
Rogers Hornsby	Bos, NL	1928	.632
Rogers Hornsby	Chi, NL	1929	.679
Snuffy Stirnweiss	NY, AL	1945	.476
Bobby Grich	Cal, AL	1981	.543

Bill Greenwood, the last southpaw to serve as a regular ML second baseman. Seen here with Columbus in 1889, Greenwood finished his big league career the following year with Rochester of the AA. He also briefly held a share of the record for the most most home runs in a season by a switch-hitter when he went "yard" three times for Brooklyn in 1884.

11. **Pete Rose has the most career doubles of anyone who was ever a regular second baseman. Who has the most of anyone who was exclusively a regular at second base?**
    A) Not Nap Lajoie, who debuted as a first baseman.
    B) Not Bid McPhee, whose 303 doubles were 271 short of our man's career total.
    C) But like McPhee, our man played his entire career with the same team.
    D) He owns the record for the most doubles in a season (60) by a second sacker.
    E) He was called "The Mechanical Man."

12. **The first second sacker to lead all participants in a World Series in hits and total bases played every spot on the diamond during his 10-year career. Who is he?**
    A) He collected 12 TBs in a six-game fall fray.
    B) The 1906 season was his first as a regular second baseman.
    C) He holds the AL season record for the most stolen bases by a first sacker.
    D) At the time of his retirement, he held the record for the most career games with the White Sox as well as the most career stolen bases by an AL'er.
    E) He and Cecil, a Hall of Fame quarterback, share the same last name.

13. **No ML'er since the end of the Deadball Era has notched 100 RBI in a season on fewer than two home runs. The most recent man to do it on as few as two homers was a Hall of Fame second sacker. Who is he?**
    A) It was the only season he posted 100 RBI, but he had five seasons—all with the same NL team—when he scored 100 runs.
    B) He had just one career pinch hit, the fewest of any 20th century Hall of Famer with a .300 career BA.
    C) In his final season as a player, he managed the 1947 Pirates.
    D) Replacing a future Hall of Famer in 1932, his first full season, he garnered 206 hits for a World Series entrant.
    E) He and the goat of the "Three Men on Third" episode share the same last name.

Players with 100 RBI and Fewer than Three HRs, Season

NAME	TEAM	POS.	YEAR	HRS	RBI
Steve Brodie	Bal, NL	OF	1895	2	134
Hughie Jennings	Bal, NL	SS	1896	0	121
Joe Kelley	Bal, NL	OF	1898	2	110
Ed Delahanty	Phi, NL	OF	1900	2	109
Lave Cross	Phi, AL	3B	1902	0	108
Farmer Vaughn	Cin, NL	C	1893	1	108
Cupid Childs	Cle, NL	2B	1896	1	106
Kid Gleason	NY, NL	2B	1897	1	106
Heinie Reitz	Bal, NL	2B	1894	2	105
Pie Traynor	Pit, NL	3B	1931	2	103
Patsy Tebeau	Cle, NL	1B	1893	2	102
Jack Doyle	Phi, NL	1B	1896	1	101
Lave Cross	Phi, NL	3B	1895	2	101
Jack Glasscock	StL/Pit, NL	SS	1893	2	100
Bill Sweeney	Bos, NL	2B	1912	1	100
Billy Herman	Bro, NL	2B	1943	2	100

14. **Apart from Rogers Hornsby and the mid-1890s when hitters at all positions feasted, precious few NL second sackers have enjoyed 100-RBI seasons. Hornsby, in 1921–22, was the first senior-loop second baseman to net 100 RBI in back-to-back seasons. In 1998, Jeff Kent became only the third NL second sacker to match Hornsby's feat. Who is the lone senior loop second sacker between Hornsby in 1922 and Kent's banner campaign in 1998 to post 100 RBI in two consecutive seasons?**

    A) He collected 100 RBI on the nose in two consecutive seasons.

    B) After his 15th season, he had more than 2,200 career hits but fewer than 1,000 RBI.

    C) He compiled 54 stolen bases the first season he topped 20 homers.

    D) He debuted with the 1981 Phillies but collected only six ABs with them before moving to the NL team with which he spent the remainder of his career.

    E) He was the most recent second sacker to win a home run crown.

100 RBI, Season, NL Second Basemen

RANK	NAME	TEAM	YEAR	BA	RBI
1	Jeff Kent	San Francisco	1998	.297	128
2	Jackie Robinson	Brooklyn	1949	.342	124
3	Jeff Kent	San Francisco	1997	.250	121
4	Frankie Frisch	St. Louis	1930	.346	114
5	Frankie Frisch	New York	1923	.348	111
	Joe Morgan	Cincinnati	1976	.320	111
7	Tom Herr	St. Louis	1985	.302	110
8	Fred Pfeffer	Chicago	1884	.289	101
9	Bill Sweeney	Boston	1912	.344	100
	Billy Herman	Brooklyn	1943	.330	100
	Juan Samuel	Philadelphia	1987	.272	100
	Ryne Sandberg	Chicago	1990	.306	100
	Ryne Sandberg	Chicago	1991	.291	100

Note: Excluding Rogers Hornsby and the 1893–98 seasons.

15. **In 1884, Fred Dunlap set an all-time record for second sackers when he tallied 160 runs for St. Louis of the Union Association. Who has the season mark for the most runs by a second sacker with either a National League or American League team?**

    A) Nap Lajoie's AL record of 145, set in 1901, is 13 short of the NL record.

    B) Four of the NL record holder's 158 runs were scored in a game in which he collected 17 TBs, an all-time record for a second sacker.

    C) Icebox Chamberlain was the NL record holder's patsy the day he snared 17 TBs.

    D) In 1901, his final season with Boston, his original team, he became the ninth man in history to play 1,000 games at second base.

    E) All but 1 of his 17 TBs on his big day came via home runs.

First 10 Men to Play 1,000 Games at Second Base

RANK	NAME	YEARS	G/2B	1000TH
1	Jack Burdock	1872–91	1064	1888
2	Bid McPhee	1882–99	2126	1890
3	Fred Pfeffer	1882–97	1537	1891
4	Cub Stricker	1882–93	1145	1891
5	Lou Bierbauer	1886–98	1364	1893
6	Cupid Childs	1888–1901	1454	1897
7	Bill Hallman	1888–1903	1135	1898
8	Joe Quinn	1884–1901	1303	1898
9	Bobby Lowe	1890–1907	1313	1901
10	Kid Gleason	1888–1912	1583	1903

16. AL star Nap Lajoie amassed 200 hits on four occasions during the Deadball Era. Who was the only NL second sacker to bag 200 hits in a season even once between 1901 and 1919?

A) He was traded for a future Hall of Famer after the 1913 season.

B) His 204 hits in 1912 remained the NL 20th century record for second sackers until 1920, when Rogers Hornsby notched 218.

C) His 100 RBI in 1912 were also the most in the 20th century by a National League second baseman prior to Rogers Hornsby.

D) He left the Braves in exchange for Johnny Evers just when they were on the verge of winning their first 20th century pennant.

E) He and the only pitcher to win 40 in his final ML season share the same last name.

Most Hits, Season, NL Second Baseman, 1901–19

RANK	NAME	TEAM	YEAR	HITS
1	Bill Sweeney	Boston	1912	204
2	Larry Doyle	New York	1915	189
3	Larry Doyle	New York	1912	184
4	Gene DeMontreville	Boston	1901	173
5	Larry Doyle	New York	1909	172
6	Tom Daly	Brooklyn	1901	164
	Larry Doyle	New York	1910	164
	Bill Sweeney	Boston	1911	164
9	Larry Doyle	New York	1911	163
	Johnny Evers	Chicago	1912	163

Season Record Holders Among Second Basemen for Each Era

	RECORD	National League NAME	YEAR	RECORD	American League NAME	YEAR
At Bats						
1871–75	393	Ross Barnes	1875—NA			
1876–92	649	Lou Bierbauer	1892	595	Bill McClellan	1886
1893–1900	615	Joe Quinn	1899	613	Bobby Lowe	1894
1901–19	608	Kid Gleason	1905	602	Nap Lajoie	1906
				602	Del Pratt	1915
1920–41	666	Billy Herman	1935	650	Carl Lind	1928
1942–60	659	Red Schoendienst	1947	649	Nellie Fox	1956
1961–76	699	Dave Cash	1975	692	Bobby Richardson	1962
1977–93	**701**	**Juan Samuel**	**1984**	657	Carlos Baerga	1992
1994–	641	Mike Lansing	1996	635	Ray Durham	1998
	641	Tony Womack	1997			
Batting Average						
1871–75	**.432**	**Ross Barnes**	**1872—NA**			
1876–92	.429	Ross Barnes	1876	.345	Cupid Childs	1890
Other:	.412	Fred Dunlap	1884—UA			
1893–1900	.355	Cupid Childs	1896	.353	Cupid Childs	1894
1901–19	.344	Bill Sweeney	1912	.426	Nap Lajoie	1901
1920–41	.424	Rogers Hornsby	1924	.372	Eddie Collins	1920
1942–60	.342	Red Schoendienst	1953	.341	Bobby Avila	1954
	.342	Jackie Robinson	1949			
1961–76	.342	Glenn Beckert	1971	.364	Rod Carew	1974
1977–93	.332	Steve Sax	1986	.341	Julio Franco	1991
1994–	.325	Craig Biggio	1998	.341	Chuck Knoblauch	1996
Slugging Average						
1871–75	.584	Ross Barnes	1873—NA			
1876–92	.514	Fred Pfeffer	1884	.481	Cupid Childs	1890
Other:	.621	Fred Dunlap	1884—UA			
1893–1900	.520	Bobby Lowe	1894	.510	Nap Lajoie	1900
1901–19	.527	Larry Doyle	1911	.643	Nap Lajoie	1901
1920–41	**.756**	**Rogers Hornsby**	**1925**	.561	Tony Lazzeri	1929
1942–60	.528	Jackie Robinson	1949	.528	Bobby Doerr	1944
1961–76	.576	Joe Morgan	1976	.497	Rod Carew	1975
1977–93	.559	Ryne Sandberg	1990	.543	Bobby Grich	1981
1994–	.555	Jeff Kent	1998	.527	Roberto Alomar	1996

	RECORD	National League NAME	YEAR	RECORD	American League NAME	YEAR
Hits						
1871–75	143	Ross Barnes	1875—NA			
1876–92	178	Hardy Richardson	1887*	170	Cupid Childs	1890
Other:	185	Fred Dunlap	1884—UA			
1893–1900	212	Bobby Lowe	1894	197	Nap Lajoie	1898
1901–19	204	Bill Sweeney	1912	232	Nap Lajoie	1901
1920–41	**250**	**Rogers Hornsby**	**1922**	227	Charlie Gehringer	1936
1942–60	203	Jackie Robinson	1949	201	Nellie Fox	1954
1961–76	213	Dave Cash	1975	218	Rod Carew	1974
1977–93	210	Steve Sax	1986	206	Lou Whitaker	1983
1994–	210	Craig Biggio	1998	197	Chuck Knoblauch	1996

* Richardson played 64 games at 2B and 59 in the outfield.

	RECORD	National League NAME	YEAR	RECORD	American League NAME	YEAR
Total Bases						
1871–75	188	Ross Barnes	1873—NA			
1876–92	263	Hardy Richardson	1887	235	Cupid Childs	1890
Other:	279	Fred Dunlap	1884—UA			
1893–1900	319	Bobby Lowe	1894	280	Nap Lajoie	1898
1901–19	277	Larry Doyle	1911	350	Nap Lajoie	1901
1920–41	**450**	**Rogers Hornsby**	**1922**	356	Charlie Gehringer	1936
1942–60	313	Jackie Robinson	1949	304	Bobby Doerr	1950
1961–76	305	Davey Johnson	1973	273	Rod Carew	1973
1977–93	344	Ryne Sandberg	1990	299	Carlos Baerga	1992
1994–	325	Craig Biggio	1998	310	Roberto Alomar	1996

	RECORD	National League NAME	YEAR	RECORD	American League NAME	YEAR
Doubles						
1871–75	29	Ross Barnes	1873—NA			
1876–92	34	Hardy Richardson	1883	39	Sam Barkley	1884
	34	Fred Dunlap	1883			
Other:	39	Fred Dunlap	1884—UA			
1893–1900	43	Nap Lajoie	1898	34	Bobby Lowe	1894
1901–19	42	Bert Niehoff	1916	51	Nap Lajoie	1910
1920–41	57	Billy Herman	1935	**60**	**Charlie Gehringer**	**1936**
1942–60	43	Red Schoendienst	1950	40	Don Kolloway	1942
				40	Jerry Priddy	1948
1961–76	40	Dave Cash	1975	38	Bobby Richardson	1962
1977–93	43	Steve Sax	1986	40	Lou Whitaker	1983
1994–	51	Craig Biggio	1998	47	John Valentin	1997*

* Valentin played 79 games at 2B and 64 games at 3B.

	RECORD	National League NAME	YEAR	RECORD	American League NAME	YEAR
Triples						
1871–75	11	Bill Craver	1874—NA			
1876–92	22	Bid McPhee	1890	19	Bid McPhee	1887
1893–1900	**31**	**Heinie Reitz**	**1894**	17	Sam Wise	1893
1901–19	25	Larry Doyle	1911	21	Jimmy Williams	1901/02
1920–41	20	Rogers Hornsby	1920	19	Charlie Gehringer	1929
1942–60	17	Jim Gilliam	1953	22	George Stirnweiss	1945
1961–76	12	Joe Morgan	1965	14	Jake Wood	1961
	12	Dave Cash	1976			
	12	Phil Garner	1976			
1977–93	19	Juan Samuel	1984	13	Willie Randolph	1979
	19	Ryne Sandberg	1984			
1994–	14	Delino DeShields	1997	14	Chuck Knoblauch	1996
Home Runs						
1871–75	2	Done by several—NA				
1876–92	25	Fred Pfeffer	1884	8	Bid McPhee	1886
1893–1900	17	Bobby Lowe	1894	14	Bobby Lowe	1893
1901–19	13	Larry Doyle	1911	14	Nap Lajoie	1901
1920–41	**42**	**Rogers Hornsby**	**1922**	30	Joe Gordon	1940
1942–60	22	Charlie Neal	1958	32	Joe Gordon	1948
1961–76	**43**	**Davey Johnson**	**1973***	22	Dick McAuliffe	1967
1977–93	40	Ryne Sandberg	1990	30	Bobby Grich	1979
1994–	31	Jeff Kent	1998	27	Damion Easley	1998

* Johnson hit 42 home runs at 2B, 1 as a pinch hitter; hence, he and Hornsby share the season record for most home runs by a second baseman.

RBI						
1871–75	62	Ross Barnes	1873—NA			
1876–92	101	Fred Pfeffer	1884	105	Lou Bierbauer	1889
1893–1900	127	Nap Lajoie	1898	115	Bobby Lowe	1894
1901–19	100	Bill Sweeney	1912	125	Nap Lajoie	1901
1920–41	**152**	**Rogers Hornsby**	**1922**	127	Charlie Gehringer	1934
1942–60	124	Jackie Robinson	1949	124	Joe Gordon	1948
1961–76	111	Joe Morgan	1976	92	Felix Mantilla	1965
1977–93	110	Tom Herr	1985	114	Carlos Baerga	1993
1994–	128	Jeff Kent	1998	100	Damion Easley	1998

	National League			American League		
	RECORD	NAME	YEAR	RECORD	NAME	YEAR
Runs						
1871–75	125	Ross Barnes	1873—NA			
1876–92	148	Hub Collins	1890	139	Bid McPhee	1886
Other:	**160**	**Fred Dunlap**	**1884—UA**			
1893–1900	158	Bobby Lowe	1894	145	Cupid Childs	1893
1901–19	117	Miller Huggins	1905	145	Nap Lajoie	1901
1920–41	156	Rogers Hornsby	1929	144	Charlie Gehringer	1930/36
1942–60	128	Eddie Stanky	1945	125	Snuffy Stirnweiss	1944
1961–76	122	Joe Morgan	1972	99	Bobby Richardson	1962
1977–93	116	Ryne Sandberg	1990	110	Lou Whitaker	1987
1994–	146	Craig Biggio	1997	140	Chuck Knoblauch	1994
Walks						
1871–75	18	Ross Barnes	1873—NA			
1876–92	136	Jack Crooks	1892	118	Yank Robinson	1889
1893–1900	121	Jack Crooks	1893	120	Cupid Childs	1893
1901–19	116	Miller Huggins	1910	119	Eddie Collins	1915
1920–41	107	Rogers Hornsby	1928	128	Max Bishop	1929/30
1942–60	**148**	**Eddie Stanky**	**1945**	101	Cass Michaels	1949
1961–76	132	Joe Morgan	1975	107	Bobby Grich	1973/75
1977–93	117	Joe Morgan	1977	119	Willie Randolph	1980
1994–	84	Craig Biggio	1997	98	Chuck Knoblauch	1996
OBP						
1871–75	.456	Ross Barnes	1873—NA			
1876–92	.443	Cupid Childs	1892	.434	Cupid Childs	1890
Other:	.448	Fred Dunlap	1884—UA			
1893–1900	.475	Cupid Childs	1894	.467	Cupid Childs	1896
1901–19	.432	Miller Huggins	1913	.463	Nap Lajoie	1901
1920–41	**.507**	**Rogers Hornsby**	**1924**	.461	Eddie Collins	1925
1942–60	.460	Eddie Stanky	1950	.418	Pete Runnels	1958
1961–76	.471	Joe Morgan	1975	.435	Rod Carew	1974
1977–93	.420	Joe Morgan	1977	.429	Willie Randolph	1980
1994–	.415	Craig Biggio	1997	.448	Chuck Knoblauch	1996

	RECORD	National League NAME	YEAR	RECORD	American League NAME	YEAR
Stolen Bases						
1871–75	29	Ross Barnes	1875—NA			
1876–92	88	Monte Ward	1892	95	**Bid McPhee**	**1887**
1893–1900	51	Tom Daly	1894	49	Gene DeMontreville	1898
1901–19	49	Johnny Evers	1906	81	Eddie Collins	1910
1920–41	48	Frankie Frisch	1927	48	Eddie Collins	1923
1942–60	37	Jackie Robinson	1949	55	Snuffy Stirnweiss	1944
1961–76	77	Davey Lopes	1975	43	Dave Nelson	1973*
1977–93	72	Juan Samuel	1984	60	Harold Reynolds	1987
1994–	60	Tony Womack	1997	62	Chuck Knoblauch	1997

* Tommy Harper stole 73 bases in 1969 in 148 games, but only 59 of them were at 2B.

Note: In the 1876–92 era, men who appear under the American League column are the American Association record holders. In the 1893–1900 era, men who appear under the American League column are the runners-up to the National League record holders. Players who performed at more than one position in their record season are considered the record holders at the position where they played the most games. All-time leaders among second basemen are in **bold**.

Hot Corner Highlights

1. **Third base was the most underrepresented position in the Hall of Fame for many years. Jimmy Collins is still the only third sacker who played even a single inning in the 19th century to earn a niche in Cooperstown chiefly for his playing accomplishments. Much of the reason is that the hot corner, especially in the pre-1893 era when many fielders still played without gloves, was so hazardous that only one man who retired prior to 1893 was able to play as many as 1,000 games at third base. Who is he?**

   A) As a National League rookie with Syracuse in 1879, he saw action mostly at first base.

   B) His 1,000th game at third base came in 1889, his last full ML season.

   C) In 1882 his .342 BA was second only to Pete Browning's in the race for the first American Association bat title.

   D) He leads all left-handed throwers in ML history in games played at infield positions other than first base.

   E) His first name was Warren, but everyone knew him as "Hick."

Billy Nash in 1892. The following year, he became the fifth man to play 1,000 ML games at third base. Nash collected 400 or more at bats in 10 of his 15 ML seasons. His high mark in those 10 seasons was a .295 BA in 1887, and his low was .260 in 1892. Solid, never spectacular, Nash was arguably the most consistent performer at his position in history.

First 10 Men to Play 1,000 Games at Third Base

RANK	NAME	YEARS	G/3B	1000TH GAME
1	Hick Carpenter	1879–92	1059	1889
2	Jerry Denny	1881–94	1109	1890
3	Arlie Latham	1880–1909	1571	1891
4	George Pinkney	1884–93	1061	1893
	Billy Nash	1884–98	1464	1893
6	Denny Lyons	1885–97	1083	1896
7	Billy Shindle	1886–98	1272	1896
8	Lave Cross	1887–1907	1721	1902
9	Jimmy Collins	1895–1908	1685	1903
10	Bill Bradley	1899–1915	1388	1907

2. **Third basemen who have substantial careers generally are strong hitters. Only one man played as many as 2,000 games at third base, amassed 2,000 career hits, and never hit .300 while playing a full season. Who is he?**

   A) Eddie Yost would be a winning guess if he'd made 2,000 hits.

   B) He has the lowest career BA of anyone with 350 or more homers who never K'd 100 times in a season.

   C) His first career hit was a pinch double for the 1967 Twins.

   D) He led the AL in homers in 1976 for a flag winner.

   E) His first name is pronounced the same as but spelled differently from the first name of the only hurler to win four Cy Young trophies in a row.

Players with 2,000 Career Hits Never Batting .300 in a Season

RANK	NAME	YEARS	POS.	HITS	CAREER
1	Graig Nettles	1967–88	3B	2225	.248
2	Frank White	1973–90	2B	2006	.255
3	Harmon Killebrew	1954–75	1B/3B	2086	.256
4	Tim Wallach	1980–96	3B	2085	.257
5	Bill Mazeroski	1956–72	2B	2016	.260

Note: Darrell Evans (.248), Rabbit Maranville (.258), and Gary Carter (.262) compiled 2,000 hits without ever hitting .300 for a full season; each batted .300, though, in a partial season.

3. **No third baseman has ever won an undisputed Triple Crown. Until recently, Heinie Zimmerman was credited with a TC in 1912, but most sources now maintain he finished third that year in RBI. Assuming Zimmerman's revised 1912 RBI total is correct, who came the closest of any third baseman in history to winning a TC?**

   A) He led in homers and RBI but lost the bat crown by an eyelash when he fell a step short of beating out a ground ball in his final at bat of the season.

   B) In his near-TC season, he became only the second third sacker in history to lead the AL in runs.

   C) He was the GM of the most recent San Francisco Giants flag winner.

   D) He played in the 1954 World Series.

   E) In his near-TC season, he set the season record (since broken) for the most total bases by a third sacker, with 367.

Third Basemen Winning Two Legs of the Triple Crown

NAME	TEAM	YEAR	BA	HRS	RBI
Al Rosen	Cle, AL	1953	2	1	1
Heinie Zimmerman	Chi, NL	1912	1	1	3
Mike Schmidt	Phi, NL	1981	4	1	1
Frank Baker	Phi, AL	1913	5	1	1
Mike Schmidt	Phi, NL	1980	20	1	1
Harmon Killebrew	Min, AL	1969	25	1	1
Mike Schmidt	Phi, NL	1984	27	1	1
Howard Johnson	NY, NL	1991	40	1	1

Note: Figures under BA, HRS, and RBI indicate league rank that year.

4. **The 20th century season record for the most runs on a sub-.300 batting average belongs to the same third sacker who holds the all-time record for scoring at least one run in the most consecutive games. Who is he?**

A) In 1937 he logged 143 tallies despite hitting just .276.

B) He managed the first Detroit Tigers team to finish in last place.

C) His 143 tallies in 1937 broke the old 20th century record of 137 runs scored on a sub-.300 BA set the previous year by a teammate of his.

D) In 1939 he led the AL in runs, hits, and doubles.

E) In 28 World Series games, he hit .284, including .353 in the 1942 fall classic, which proved to be his finale.

Most Runs, Season, Sub-.300 Average

RANK	NAME	TEAM	YEAR	BA	RUNS
1	Mike Griffin	Bal, AA	1889	.279	152
2	Herman Long	Bos, NL	1893	.288	149
3	Hub Collins	Bro, NL	1890	.278	148
4	Tom Brown	Bos, PL	1890	.276	146
5	Hugh Duffy	Chi, NL	1889	.295	144
6	Red Rolfe	NY, AL	1937	.276	143
7	Harry Stovey	Bos, PL	1890	.297	142
8	Tom Poorman	Phi, AA	1887	.265	140
	Jim McTamany	Col, AA	1890	.258	140
10	Bid McPhee	Cin, AA	1886	.268	139
	Hub Collins	Bro, AA	1889	.266	139

Note: The 20th century NL record belongs to Tim Raines with 133 runs for Montreal in 1983 on a .298 BA.

5. **What third sacker will always hold the single-season record for hitting the most home runs at Braves Field?**
   A) He broke Wally Berger's old record of 18.
   B) His name is not Bob Elliott or Eddie Mathews.
   C) He set the mark the only year in the 20th century in which two Boston Braves finished 1–2 in the NL home run derby.
   D) His 25 taters (19 at home) came in his lone year as a regular third baseman and trailed leader Tommy Holmes by three homers.
   E) The year after he "worked" to set the Braves Field homer mark, Ralph Kiner won his first of a record seven straight NL home run crowns.

6. **Third basemen seldom have been pacesetters in runs. Except for John McGraw, a very atypical third baseman who began as a shortstop, and Heinie Groh in the abbreviated 1918 season, no hot corner man topped either the NL or the AL in runs until the country was in the throes of the Great Depression. Who was the first post-1901 third sacker to win a run crown in a season when a full schedule was played?**
   A) He played on a flag winner two years earlier and again two years later.
   B) He spent his entire career with the same NL team.
   C) He led in stolen bases the same year he led in runs.
   D) He was the star of the 1931 World Series.
   E) His nickname was "Pepper."

Third Basemen Leading in Runs

NAME	TEAM	YEAR	RUNS
Arlie Latham	StL, AA	1886	152
George Pinkney	Bro, AA	1888	134
John McGraw	Bal, NL	1898	143
John McGraw	Bal, NL	1899	140
Heinie Groh	Cin, NL	1918	86
Pepper Martin	StL, NL	1933	122
Mel Ott	NY, NL	1938	116
Billy Werber	Cin, NL	1939	115
Red Rolfe	NY, AL	1939	139
Al Rosen	Cle, AL	1953	115
Eddie Yost	Det, AL	1959	115
Dick Allen	Phi, NL	1964	125
Pete Rose	Cin, NL	1975	112
Pete Rose	Cin, NL	1976	130
Mike Schmidt	Phi, NL	1981	78
Paul Molitor	Mil, AL	1982	136
Wade Boggs	Bos, AL	1988	128

7. **Whose record for the most career games at third base by a switch-hitter did Terry Pendleton break in 1994?**
   A) He played his 1,433rd and last game at third in 1929.
   B) He was born in Wales.
   C) His career year was 1911, when he hit .261 and scored 84 runs in 148 games for the St. Louis Browns.
   D) His 18 seasons in the majors are the most of anyone who did not begin his ML career until he was in his 30th year of life.
   E) His last name is the same as that of a former teenage female tennis star whose first name is Tracy.

Most Games at Third Base, Career, Switch-Hitter

RANK	NAME	YEARS	G/3B
1	Terry Pendleton	1984–98	1786
2	Ken Caminiti	1987–	1481
3	Jimmy Austin	1909–29	1433
4	Doc Casey	1898–1907	1100
5	Howard Johnson	1982–96	1031
6	Bobby Bonilla	1986–	956
7	Jim Gilliam	1953–66	761
8	Pete Rose	1963–86	634
9	Bob Ferguson	1871–84	585
10	Steve Ontiveros	1973–80	569

8. **Who was the first man to play 1,000 games at third base in the AL and post a .300 career batting average?**
   A) He played on the first Yankees flag winner in his final season as a regular.
   B) He hit .363 in 25 World Series games.
   C) Prior to 1937, when Pie Traynor retired, he had the highest career BA of any retired third baseman active exclusively in the 20th century.
   D) He is the only third sacker in the 20th century to swipe 40 bases and win a league home run crown in the same season.
   E) He earned his famous nickname in the 1911 World Series.

Highest Career BA, Third Basemen Active Between 1901 and 1936 Exclusively

RANK	NAME	YEARS	G/3B	BA
1	Frank Baker	1908–22	1548	.307
2	Heinie Groh	1912–27	1299	.292
3	Milt Stock	1913–26	1349	.2890
4	Larry Gardner	1908–24	1656	.2887
5	Willie Kamm	1923–35	1674	.281
6	Hans Lobert	1903–17	1000	.274
7	Harry Steinfeldt	1901–11	1238	.270
8	Bill Bradley	1901–15	1254	.2689
9	Art Devlin	1904–13	1192	.2686
10	Eddie Foster	1910–23	1161	.264

Note: Minimum 1,000 games at 3B, eliminating Heinie Zimmerman, Tommy Leach, Freddy Lindstrom, and Andy High. Bradley and Steinfeldt were both active prior to 1901, as was Jimmy Collins (.285), but Collins didn't play 1,000 games in the 20th century. BAS are carried out to four decimal points where ties would otherwise exist.

9. **Several men have played 1,000 games at two different positions, but none on that select list has made third base one of his two 1,000-game domiciles. Who came the closest to achieving this feat?**

   A) He played 955 games at third and more than 1,000 in the outfield.

   B) He is not in the Hall of Fame.

   C) He twice led the NL in runs as an outfielder and once led the NL in homers as a third baseman.

   D) His four triples in 1903 set a World Series record that still stands.

   E) His last name rhymes with that of a sporting goods magnate who was a left-handed second baseman in the National Association.

Most Games at Third Base with 1,000 Games at Another Position

RANK	NAME	YEARS	1000 G/POS.	G/3B
1	Tommy Leach	1898–1918	OF	955
2	Jim Gilliam	1953–66	2B	761
3	Tony Perez	1964–86	1B	760
4	Joe Sewell	1920–33	SS	642
5	Pete Rose	1963–86	OF	634
6	George Davis	1890–1909	SS	530
7	Frankie Frisch	1919–37	2B	468
8	Bobby Wallace	1894–1918	SS	427
9	Cal Ripken	1981–	SS	406
10	Maury Wills	1959–72	SS	362

10. **What third sacker owns the highest career batting average of anyone who played 1,500 games in the majors (roughly 10 seasons, the minimum for Hall of Fame eligibility) and never hit .300 in either a full or partial season?**

   A)   His career BA of .275 includes a high of .295 in 1887 and a low of .199 in his rookie season three years earlier.

   B)   He is the only man born in Richmond, Virginia, to play 10 years in the majors and make his debut with a team based in his hometown.

   C)   He played on four consecutive pennant winners beginning in 1890.

   D)   In 1896 he lost his job to Jimmy Collins.

   E)   He and the only man to homer in his first two ML plate appearances share the same initials.

Highest BA, Career, Never Hitting .300

RANK	NAME	YEARS	GAMES	HIGH	BA
1	Billy Nash	1884–98	1549	.295	.275
2	Jim Gantner	1976–92	1801	.298	.274
3	Frank Howard	1958–73	1895	.296	.273
4	Ossie Bluege	1922–39	1867	.297	.272
5	Earl Torgeson	1947–61	1688	.290	.2652
6	Jim Fregosi	1961–78	1902	.291	.2646
7	Sherm Lollar	1946–63	1752	.293	.2644
8	Bill Russell	1969–86	2181	.286	.2632
9	Davey Lopes	1972–87	1812	.284	.26298
10	Dots Miller	1909–21	1589	.297	.26288
11	Manny Trillo	1973–89	1780	.296	.26252

Note: Minimum 1,500 games. BAs are carried out to four or five decimal points where ties would otherwise exist.

11. **Name the first man to play 1,000 games at third base and rap 100 career homers.**

   A)   Frank Baker had only 96 career homers.

   B)   Freddy Lindstrom had 103 home runs but played just 809 games at 3B.

   C)   He hit his 100th home run in 1936.

   D)   Though he played more than 1,000 games at 3B, many of his home runs were hit while he was playing other infield positions.

   E)   He later set a record (since broken) for the most seasons as a major league pilot without winning a pennant.

First 10 Third Basemen to Attain 100 Career HRs

RANK	NAME	YEARS	HRs	100TH
1	Jimmy Dykes	1918–39	108	1936
2	Harlond Clift	1934–45	178	1938
3	Pinky Higgins	1930–46	140	1941
4	Ken Keltner	1937–50	163	1944
5	Jim Tabor	1938–47	104	1946
6	Bob Elliott	1939–53	170	1949
7	Al Rosen	1947–56	192	1953
	Willie Jones	1947–61	190	1953
9	Eddie Mathews	1952–68	512	1954
10	Randy Jackson	1950–59	103	1958

Note: Clift was the first to hit 100 home runs while playing third base; Dykes hit some of his first 100 four-baggers while playing other positions, as did Elliott.

12. **In 1985 hot corner men dominated the AL offensive charts when Wade Boggs won the batting crown and George Brett the slugging crown. NL third sackers by and large were an especially weak crop that year, however—especially after the Phils moved Mike Schmidt to first base to make room for rookie Rich Schu, who hit .252 and had just 24 RBI in 111 games. Remarkably, just one NL hot corner operative in 1985 hit as high as .270 and had as many as 40 RBI. Who is he?**

    A) He hit .271 with 61 RBI.
    B) He played for a division cellar dweller.
    C) 1985 was his first full season, and he had only one other year as a regular.
    D) Injuries, real and imagined, helped shorten his career after he hit .317 for the Giants in 1986.
    E) He has the same last name as the Yankees hot corner man who became AL prexy.

NL Regular Third Basemen in 1985

NAME	TEAM	HRS	RBI	BA
Ken Oberkfell	Atlanta	3	35	.272
Chris Brown	San Francisco	16	61	.271
Phil Garner	Houston	6	51	.268
Graig Nettles	San Diego	15	61	.261
Tim Wallach	Montreal	22	81	.260
Rick Schu	Philadelphia	7	24	.252
Bill Madlock	Pittsburgh	10	41	.251
Howard Johnson	New York	11	46	.242
Terry Pendleton	St. Louis	5	69	.240
Ron Cey	Chicago	22	63	.232
Buddy Bell	Cincinnati	6	36	.219
Dave Anderson	Los Angeles	4	18	.199

13. In 1998, when Vinny Castilla set a new senior-loop RBI record for third basemen with 144, it marked just the 22nd time a third sacker had 120 ribbies in a season. Only one team has three different hot corner men on that select list of 22. Name the team and its three 120-RBI third sackers.

    A) One is in the Hall of Fame, and the other two never will be.

    B) Cleveland would also have three 120-RBI third sackers if Ken Keltner had bagged one more RBI in 1948.

    C) The third and last third sacker on the team in question with a 120-RBI season is also its all-time home run leader.

    D) The team's first third sacker to have a 120-RBI season later had a 100-RBI season while playing third base for the Philadelphia A's.

    E) The team's second third sacker to bag 120 RBI in a season was nicknamed "Pinky."

120 RBI, Season, Third Basemen

RANK	NAME	TEAM	YEAR	RBI
1	Al Rosen	Cle, AL	1953	145
2	Vinny Castilla	Col, NL	1998	144
3	Harmon Killebrew	Min, AL	1969	140
4	Joe Torre	StL, NL	1971	137
5	Eddie Mathews	Mil, NL	1953	135
6	Jimmy Collins	Bos, NL	1897	132
7	Frank Baker	Phi, AL	1912	130
	Deron Johnson	Cin, NL	1965	130
	Ken Caminiti	SD, NL	1996	130
10	Tony Perez	Cin, NL	1970	129
11	Lave Cross	Phi, NL	1894	125
12	Pie Traynor	Pit, NL	1928	124
	Pinky Whitney	Phi, NL	1932	124
	Eddie Mathews	Mil, NL	1960	124
15	Billy Nash	Bos, NL	1893	123
	Ron Santo	Chi, NL	1969	123
	Tim Wallach	Mon, NL	1987	123
18	Tony Perez	Cin, NL	1969	122
	Matt Williams	SF, NL	1990	122
20	Mike Schmidt	Phi, NL	1980	121
21	Larry Gardner	Cle, AL	1921	120
	Hank Majeski	Phi, AL	1948	120

Note: Killebrew also played 1B in 1969.

14. Gil McDougald is the only third sacker to win a Rookie of the Year Award outright in the AL. Who came the closest to being the second AL third sacker to do it?

A)   He hit .302 as a frosh and led the AL in putouts.

B)   His career was shortened by an injury.

C)   He played with the Twins his entire career.

D)   He tied with Alfredo Griffin for the top AL rookie prize in 1979.

E)   He has the same initials as the only third sacker active in the 19th century who made the Hall of Fame largely as a player.

Third Basemen Receiving Votes for AL Rookie of the Year

NAME	TEAM	YEAR	FINISH
Gil McDougald	New York	1951	1
Jim Finigan	Philadelphia	1954	2
Pete Ward	Chicago	1963	2
George Brett	Kansas City	1974	3
John Castino	Minnesota	1979	1
Wade Boggs	Boston	1982	3
Gary Gaetti	Minnesota	1982	5
Kevin Seitzer	Kansas City	1987	2
Travis Fryman	Detroit	1990	6
Robin Ventura	Chicago	1990	7
Leo Gomez	Baltimore	1991	8

15. Whose record for the highest career batting average by a third baseman is Wade Boggs certain to break when he retires?

A)   He is the only third baseman as yet to quit with a career BA as high as .320.

B)   He broke in as a shortstop.

C)   He played his entire career with the same NL team.

D)   Less than 50 years ago, he was voted the top third sacker in history.

E)   His first name was Harold, but they called him by a nickname that rhymes with the nickname they gave the game's all-time leading winner.

.300 Career BA, Third Basemen

RANK	NAME	YEARS	GAMES	BA
1	Wade Boggs	1981–	2350	.329
2	Pie Traynor	1920–37	1863	.320
3	Denny Lyons	1885–97	1083	.310
4	Frank Baker	1908–22	1548	.307
5	George Kell	1943–57	1692	.306
6	George Brett	1973–93	2707	.3047
7	Bill Madlock	1973–87	1440	.3045
8	Stan Hack	1932–47	1836	.301

Note: Through the 1998 season; minimum 1,000 games at 3B. Four .300 hitters who played a substantial amount of games at 3B—Deacon White (826), Freddy Lindstrom (809), Paul Molitor (791), and John McGraw (782)—failed to qualify. White is the lone performer, however, to play as many as 500 games at 3B and retire prior to 1893 with a .300 career BA.

16. **The only 20th century performer to collect 100 RBI in a season without hitting a home run played third the year he did it. Who is he?**

    A)   His 1,345 career RBI came on just 47 home runs, and he had three seasons in which he compiled 100 RBI on fewer than 10 four-baggers.

    B)   He played in his only World Series in 1905 when he was 39.

    C)   In 1902 he hit .342 and had 108 RBI with no home runs.

    D)   For many years he held the record for the most career hits by a third sacker.

    E)   His first name is the same as the last name of a French general who served on the American side in the Revolutionary War.

Most RBI, Season, No HRs

RANK	NAME	TEAM	YEAR	BA	RBI
1	Hughie Jennings	Bal, NL	1896	.401	121
2	Lave Cross	Phi, AL	1902	.342	108
3	Ed McKean	Cle, NL	1892	.262	93
4	Cap Anson	Chi, NL	1893	.314	91
	Kitty Bransfield	Pit, NL	1901	.295	91
	Jack Doyle	Bro, NL	1903	.313	91
	Nap Lajoie	Cle, AL	1906	.355	91
8	Nap Lajoie	Cle, AL	1912	.368	90
	Duffy Lewis	Bos, AL	1913	.298	90
	Harry Swacina	Bal, FL	1914	.280	90

17. **Pie Traynor owns the post-1901 record for the most seasons with 100 RBI and fewer than 10 home runs. Five of Traynor's six such seasons came in a row—1927–31. Who is the only other third sacker since 1920 (the end of the Deadball Era) to have as many as two such seasons in a row?**

    A)   His sac-fly RBI won a memorable seven-game Series that actually went eight games.

    B)   He held down the Red Sox second-base slot in 1910, his first full ML season.

    C)   He played on four AL world champs in two different cities during his career.

    D)   One of the few ML'ers to be born and die in Vermont, he lived to be 89.

    E)   In 1920–21, he totaled 233 RBI for Cleveland on just six homers.

Most Seasons, 100 RBI and Fewer than 10 HRs

RANK	NAME	YEARS	TOTAL
1	Honus Wagner	1899–1901, 1903, 1905, 1909, 1912	7
2	Hugh Duffy	1891, 1893, 1895–96, 1898–99	6
	Pie Traynor	1925, 1927–31	6
4	Cap Anson	1885, 1887, 1889–91	5
	Ty Cobb	1907–09, 1911, 1917	5
	Sam Crawford	1910–12, 1914–15	5
7	Dan Brouthers	1889, 1891–92, 1894	4
	Jake Beckley	1890, 1893–95	4
	Ed McKean	1893–96	4
	Joe Kelley	1894, 1896–98	4
	Bobby Veach	1915, 1917, 1919, 1922	4

18. **Third basemen seldom make good leadoff hitters. The rare few that do usually collect tons of walks, like Eddie Yost, and as a result compile relatively modest at-bat totals. The all-time season leader in at bats by a third sacker coaxed only 30 walks in his big year. Who is he?**

   A) Prior to his record-setting season, he was involved in a trade for a third sacker who had been the AL walk leader two years earlier.

   B) He had 200 hits to go with his record-setting 670 ABs, making for a .299 BA that put him on the short list of 200-hit men who batted under .300.

   C) He played 18 years in the bigs without ever appearing in a postseason game, but his father played in three World Series contests, all as a pinch hitter.

   D) He was the only man to make 1,000 hits in a Cleveland uniform in the 1970s.

   E) He and his dad hold the record for the most combined career hits by a father-son combo.

Season Record Holders Among Third Basemen for Each Era

	National League			American League		
	RECORD	NAME	YEAR	RECORD	NAME	YEAR
At Bats						
1871–75	366	Bob Ferguson	1875—NA			
1876–92	622	Arlie Latham	1892	627	Arlie Latham	1887
1893–1900	617	Jimmy Williams	1899	602	Lave Cross	1898
1901–19	631	Eddie Grant	1909	631	Jimmy Collins	1904
1920–41	646	Freddy Lindstrom	1928	668	Buddy Lewis	1937
1942–60	637	Bobby Adams	1952	644	Bob Dillinger	1948
1961–76	665	Pete Rose	1976	668	Brooks Robinson	1961
1977–93	660	Enos Cabell	1978	**670**	**Buddy Bell**	**1979**
1994–	645	Vinny Castilla	1998	616	Travis Fryman	1996
Batting Average						
1871–75	.492	Levi Meyerle	1871—NA			
1876–92	.346	Ezra Sutton	1884	.367	Denny Lyons	1887
1893–1900	**.391**	**John McGraw**	**1899**	.386	Lave Cross	1894
1901–19	.372	Heinie Zimmerman	1912	.347	Frank Baker	1912
1920–41	.379	Freddy Lindstrom	1930	.330	Pinky Higgins	1934
1942–60	.323	Whitey Kurowski	1945	.343	George Kell	1949
	.323	Stan Hack	1945			
1961–76	.363	Joe Torre	1971	.333	George Brett	1976
1977–93	.330	Gary Sheffield	1992	.390	George Brett	1980
1994–	.326	Ken Caminiti	1996	.325	Jeff Cirillo	1996
Slugging Average						
1871–75	.700	Levi Meyerle	1871—NA			
1876–92	.554	Ned Williamson	1884	.523	Denny Lyons	1887
1893–1900	.554	George Davis	1893	.537	George Davis	1894
1901–19	.571	Heinie Zimmerman	1912	.541	Frank Baker	1912
1920–41	.583	Mel Ott	1938	.554	Harlond Clift	1938
1942–60	.627	Eddie Mathews	1953	.613	Al Rosen	1953
1961–76	.632	Dick Allen	1966	.584	Harmon Killebrew	1969
1977–93	.624	Mike Schmidt	1980	**.664**	**George Brett**	**1980**
1994–	.621	Ken Caminiti	1996	.612	Jim Thome	1996

		National League			American League	
	RECORD	**NAME**	**YEAR**	**RECORD**	**NAME**	**YEAR**
Hits						
1871–75	116	Ezra Sutton	1875—NA			
1876–92	165	Jerry Denny	1887	209	Denny Lyons	1887
1893–1900	219	Jimmy Williams	1899	204	Lave Cross	1894
1901–19	207	Heinie Zimmerman	1912	200	Frank Baker	1912
1920–41	231	Freddy Lindstrom	1928/1930	213	Red Rolfe	1939
1942–60	193	Stan Hack	1945	218	George Kell	1950
1961–76	230	Joe Torre	1971	215	George Brett	1976
1977–93	199	Terry Pendleton	1992	**240**	**Wade Boggs**	**1985**
1994–	206	Vinny Castilla	1998	184	Jeff Cirillo	1996
Total Bases						
1871–75	144	Ezra Sutton	1875—NA			
1876–92	256	Jerry Denny	1887	298	Denny Lyons	1887
1893–1900	328	Jimmy Williams	1899	304	George Davis	1893
1901–19	318	Heinie Zimmerman	1912	312	Frank Baker	1912
1920–41	350	Freddy Lindstrom	1930	312	Harlond Clift	1937
1942–60	363	Eddie Mathews	1953	367	Al Rosen	1953
1961–76	352	Joe Torre	1971	324	Harmon Killebrew	1969
	352	Dick Allen	1964			
1977–93	342	Mike Schmidt	1980	363	George Brett	1979
1994–	**380**	**Vinny Castilla**	**1998**	309	Jim Thome	1996
Doubles						
1871–75	14	Levi Meyerle	1873—NA			
1876–92	49	Ned Williamson	1883	43	Denny Lyons	1887
1893–1900	43	Honus Wagner	1899	36	George Davis	1895
1901–19	43	Bobby Byrne	1910	42	Jimmy Collins	1901
				42	Frank Baker	1911
1920–41	43	Pinky Whitney	1929	50	Odell Hale	1936
1942–60	39	Don Hoak	1957	**56**	**George Kell**	**1950**
1961–76	38	Dick Allen	1964	38	Brooks Robinson	1961
1977–93	51	Pete Rose	1978	51	Wade Boggs	1989
1994–	45	Scott Rolen	1998	46	Jeff Cirillo	1996/1997
Triples						
1871–75	7	Ezra Sutton 1871; Cap Anson 1872; Ezra Sutton 1875—NA				
1876–92	18	Billy Shindle	1892	19	Willie Kuehne	1885
1893–1900	**27**	**George Davis**	**1893**	**27**	**Jimmy Williams**	**1899**
1901–19	22	Tommy Leach	1902	22	Bill Bradley	1903
1920–41	19	Pie Traynor	1923	18	Howie Shanks	1921
1942–60	16	Bob Elliott	1944	13	Bob Dillinger	1949
1961–76	14	Dick Allen	1965	13	George Brett	1974
1977–93	11	Mike Schmidt	1977	20	George Brett	1979
1994–	9	Joe Randa	1997	6	B. J. Surhoff	1996

		National League			American League	
	RECORD	**NAME**	**YEAR**	**RECORD**	**NAME**	**YEAR**
Home Runs						
1871–75	4	Levi Meyerle	1871—NA			
1876–92	26	Ned Williamson	1884	11	Denny Lyons	1891
1893–1900	17	Bill Joyce	1894	17	Bill Joyce	1895
1901–19	14	Heinie Zimmerman	1912	12	Frank Baker	1913
1920–41	36	Mel Ott	1938	34	Harlond Clift	1938
1942–60	47	Eddie Mathews	1953	43	Al Rosen	1953
1961–76	41	Darrell Evans	1973	**49**	**Harmon Killebrew**	**1969**
1977–93	48	Mike Schmidt	1980	37	Graig Nettles	1977
1994–	46	Vinny Castilla	1998	38	Jim Thome	1996
RBI						
1871–75	59	Ezra Sutton	1875—NA			
1876–92	112	Jerry Denny	1889	110	Duke Farrell	1891
1893–1900	132	Jimmy Collins	1897	125	Lave Cross	1894
1901–19	102	Heinie Zimmerman	1917	130	Frank Baker	1912
1920–41	124	Pie Traynor	1928	118	Harlond Clift	1937
	124	Pinky Whitney	1932	118	Harlond Clift	1938
1942–60	135	Eddie Mathews	1953	**145**	**Al Rosen**	**1953**
1961–76	137	Joe Torre	1971	140	Harmon Killebrew	1969
1977–93	123	Tim Wallach	1987	118	George Brett	1980
1994–	144	Vinny Castilla	1998	119	Dean Palmer	1998
Runs						
1871–75	83	Ezra Sutton	1875—NA			
1876–92	119	Arlie Latham	1891	**163**	**Arlie Latham**	**1887**
1893–1900	156	John McGraw	1894	143	John McGraw	1898
1901–19	101	Sammy Strang	1903	116	Frank Baker	1912/13
				116	Ossie Vitt	1915
1920–41	127	Freddy Lindstrom	1930	145	Harlond Clift	1936
	152	Woody English	1930*			
1942–60	118	Eddie Mathews	1959	125	Vern Stephens	1950
1961–76	130	Pete Rose	1976	106	Sal Bando	1969
				106	Harmon Killebrew	1969
1977–93	114	Mike Schmidt	1977	136	Paul Molitor	1982
1994–	123	Chipper Jones	1998	122	Jim Thome	1996

* English split 1930 between third and short and could be considered the era runs record holder at either position.

		National League			American League	
	RECORD	**NAME**	**YEAR**	**RECORD**	**NAME**	**YEAR**
Walks						
1871–75	18	Ed Pinkham	1871—NA			
1876–92	79	Billy Nash	1889	88	Denny Lyons	1891
Other:	123	Bill Joyce	1890—PL			
1893–1900	124	John McGraw	1899	112	John McGraw	1898
1901–19	84	Heinie Groh	1916	80	Ossie Vitt	1915
1920–41	118	Mel Ott	1938	118	Harlond Clift	1938
1942–60	131	Bob Elliott	1948	**151**	**Eddie Yost**	**1956**
1961–76	126	Darrell Evans	1974	145	Harmon Killebrew	1969
1977–93	128	Mike Schmidt	1983	125	Wade Boggs	1988
1994–	96	Chipper Jones	1998	123	Jim Thome	1996
OBP						
1871–75	.391	Davy Force	1873—NA			
1876–92	.384	Ezra Sutton	1884	.445	Denny Lyons	1891
1893–1900	**.547**	**John McGraw**	**1899**	.505	John McGraw	1900
1901–19	.418	Heinie Zimmerman	1912	.413	Frank Baker	1913
1920–41	.442	Mel Ott	1938	.424	Harlond Clift	1936
1942–60	.423	Bob Elliott	1948	.440	Eddie Yost	1950
1961–76	.424	Joe Torre	1971	.430	Harmon Killebrew	1969
1977–93	.439	Mike Schmidt	1981	.480	Wade Boggs	1988
1994–	.408	Ken Caminiti	1996	.450	Jim Thome	1996
Stolen Bases						
1871–75	19	Mike McGeary	1875—NA			
1876–92	66	Arlie Latham	1892	**129**	**Arlie Latham**	**1887**
1893–1900	78	John McGraw	1894	73	John McGraw	1899
1901–19	59	Art Devlin	1905	74	Fritz Maisel	1914
1920–41	49	Frankie Frisch	1921	40	Billy Werber	1934
1942–60	23	Jim Gilliam	1959	34	Bob Dillinger	1947
1961–76	52	Maury Wills	1968	51	Don Buford	1966
				51	Dave Nelson	1972
1977–93	46	Chris Sabo	1988	41	Paul Molitor	1982/1983/1988
1994–	20	Chipper Jones	1997	16	Dave Hollins	1997
				16	Travis Fryman	1997

Note: In the 1876–92 era, men who appear under the American League column are the American Association record holders. In the 1893–1900 era, men who appear under the American League column are the runners-up to the National League record holder. Players who performed at more than one position in their record season are considered the record holders at the position where they played the most games. All-time leaders among third basemen are in **bold**.

Stellar Shortstops

1. **Shortstop has always been the pivotal spot on the diamond. Only an extraordinary talent can maintain excellence at the position for more than a few years. Even the best shortstops generally gravitate to a less demanding post, particularly toward the end of their careers. As a result, excluding several active performers who are almost certain to play elsewhere before they retire, a phenomenally low number of men—only eight in all of major league history—have participated in as many as 250 games at shortstop without ever playing another defensive position. Who appeared in 110 or more games for 18 straight seasons without playing a single inning anywhere but at shortstop to set a durability record for the position?**

   A) Ozzie Smith had a 16-year streak in which he met the same criteria until he slipped to just 98 games in the 1994 strike season.
   B) Our man won a Rookie of the Year Award but never an MVP Award.
   C) He holds many career fielding records for shortstops.
   D) Among his career records is the mark for the most assists.
   E) He's the only man to play more games at short than Ozzie Smith.

250 Games Played, Career, Shortstop Only Defensive Position

RANK	NAME	YEARS	G/SS
1	Luis Aparicio	1956–73	2581
2	Ozzie Smith	1978–96	2511
3	Charlie Hollocher	1918–24	751
4	Jackie Tavener	1921–29	626
5	Virgil Stallcup	1947–53	556
6	Phil Lewis	1905–08	505
7	Jim Levey	1930–33	437
8	John Gochnauer	1901–03	264

Note: Shawon Dunston was third on the list after the 1996 season with 1,198 games at short; in 1997, however, he sacrificed his eligibility when he played seven games in left field.

2. **Two of the 16 ML franchises extant in 1901—Detroit and the A's—have yet to own a shortstop who made the Hall of Fame. What team has had four Hall of Fame shortstops wear its uniform in the 20th century alone?**

   A) Bones Ely was the team's shortstop when the current century dawned.
   B) No Hall of Fame shortstops have worn its uniform since World War II.
   C) One Hall of Famer played only 11 of his 1,843 games at short in its uniform.
   D) Another 'Famer played three years at short and one at second in its uniform.
   E) The other two 'Famers both won batting crowns in its uniform.

3. **In 1889, Jack Glasscock paced all NL shortstops in hits, total bases, home runs, RBI, total chances, double plays, and fielding average. Who are the only three NL performers in the 20th century to have a season when they led all shortstops in all of the same batting and fielding departments?**

   A) It was done twice between 1901 and World War II but never by Honus Wagner.

   B) The first 20th century NL shortstop to sweep did it in 1929, two years after being part of the first 20th century keystone duo to each homer in double figures.

   C) The second man swept in 1940, playing beside rookie second sacker Bama Rowell.

   D) It was last done in 1959 by a HOF'er who that year won the second of two successive MVP Awards.

   E) Rowell's keystone mate and the rookie who paced the last Braves team based in Boston in home runs share the same initials and first name.

4. **On June 20, 1892, Danny Richardson of Washington set an all-time record when he accepted 25 chances at shortstop in a doubleheader. What man became Richardson's antithesis in 1976 when he played both ends of a twin bill at short for the offspring of a Washington team without handling a single chance?**

   A) In 1977 he moved to third base and immediately led the AL in walks.

   B) A member of the 1982 All-Star squad, he failed to get into the game even though he was leading the AL in hits at the time.

   C) In 1985 he collected 113 walks and just 107 hits for the Rangers.

   D) He was fired as Cleveland's third-base coach after the 1996 season.

   E) His last name is a palindrome.

5. **Even shortstops who hit well seldom log high RBI or runs totals. Maury Wills, for one, ended in 1972 with 1,525 combined career RBI and runs, the least to that point by anyone with 2,000 hits. What fellow shortstop later broke his record?**

   A) After leading the NL in triples in 1972, he hit .211 the following year.

   B) He had more than 1,200 ABs before hitting his first ML homer.

   C) His first managerial opportunity came with San Diego.

   D) He played beside both Ron Cey and Mike Schmidt.

   E) He currently holds the record for the top career FA by a retired shortstop.

Fewest Combined RBI and Runs, Career, 2,000 Hits

RANK	NAME	YEARS	HITS	RBI	RUNS	TOTAL
1	Larry Bowa	1970–85	2192	525	987	1512
2	Maury Wills	1959–72	2134	458	1067	1525
3	Tony Taylor	1958–76	2007	598	1005	1603
4	Clyde Milan	1907–22	2100	617	1004	1621
5	Bill Mazeroski	1956–72	2016	853	769	1622
6	Dick Groat	1952–67	2138	707	829	1636
7	Wally Moses	1935–51	2138	679	1124	1703
8	Bill Madlock	1973–87	2008	860	920	1780
9	Frank White	1973–90	2006	886	912	1798
10	George Burns	1911–25	2077	611	1188	1799

6. **If shortstops as a group are notoriously weak at producing runs, they are also infrequent strikeout victims compared with other positions. The first shortstop in the 20th century to fan as many as 100 times in a season was also only the second shortstop since 1893 to lead his loop in Ks. Who is he?**

   A)   Three years after his 100-K first, he hit .194 in 145 games.
   B)   The year he led the AL with 105 Ks, he played on a world champ.
   C)   He held the record for the most World Series games at short (28) when he retired.
   D)   He was a longtime coach for the team with which he played his entire career.
   E)   He lost his job in 1941 to Phil Rizzuto.

Shortstops Leading in Ks

NAME	TEAM	KS	YEAR
Sam Wise	Bos, NL	104	1884
Charlie Bastian	Phi, NL	82	1885
Doc Lavan	StL, AL	83	1915
Frankie Crosetti	NY, AL	105	1937
Frankie Crosetti	NY, AL	97	1938
Eddie Joost	Phi, AL	110	1947
Roy Smalley Sr.	Chi, NL	114	1950
Zoilo Versalles	Min, AL	122	1965

Note: Strikeout leaders are still unavailable for the following seasons: American Association, 1882–88 and 1890; National League, 1897–1910; and American League, 1901–12.

7. **The weakest-hitting shortstop ever is open to debate, but there's no question which team got the least offensive production from its shortfielders. The club split its shortstop duties among four men—Frank Meinke, Harry Buker, Frank Cox, and Ed Santry—who hit .164, .135, .127, and .182, respectively. Can you name that team?**

   A)   The four sad-sack shortstops played under Jack Chapman.
   B)   Three years later, the team won its lone NL pennant.
   C)   Some 84 years later, a team based in the same city won a 20th century World Series with its shortstop post split between two men who hit .135 and .156, respectively.
   D)   Also on the team were Ned Hanlon, George Wood, and Charlie Bennett.
   E)   The team was nicknamed the Wolverines.

8. **When Derek Jeter crossed the plate 104 times in 1996, he was the first rookie shortstop in more than 35 years to tally 100 runs. Remarkably, Nomar Garciaparra followed in 1997 by becoming the second frosh shortstop since 1961 to post 100 tallies. Who was the last rookie shortstop prior to 1996 to score in triple digits?**

   A)   In 1963 he collected just six RBI in 307 at bats for Cleveland.
   B)   He's the only one of the six rookie shortstops in ML history who tallied 100 runs to manage a World Championship team.
   C)   The pride of Palm Beach High in West Palm Beach, Florida, he finished second in his loop's rookie balloting to Don Schwall.
   D)   He later coached for and managed the Yankees.
   E)   Still later, he managed a team in the city where he made his ML debut to its first World Championship.

Rookie Shortstops Scoring 100 Runs

NAME	TEAM	YEAR	BA	RUNS
Herman Long	KC, AA	1889	.275	137
Donie Bush	Det, AL	1909	.273	114
Johnny Pesky	Bos, AL	1942	.331	105
Dick Howser	KC, AL	1961	.280	108
Derek Jeter	NY, AL	1996	.314	104
Nomar Garciaparra	Bos, AL	1997	.306	122

9. **Remarkably, the first man to play 1,000 ML games at shortstop and compile 2,000 hits is not in the Hall of Fame. Who is he?**

   A) He debuted with Cleveland in 1879.

   B) He played all but 38 of his 1,736 games in the NL.

   C) He played with eight different NL franchises, and only his 38 games in the UA in 1884 prevented him from setting the 19th century record for playing for the most different teams while spending his entire career in the same major league.

   D) He was the first shortstop to make 200 hits in a season.

   E) In 1889 he also became the first shortstop to win a batting title.

First 10 Men to Play 1,000 Games at Shortstop

RANK	NAME	YEARS	G/SS	1000TH
1	Jack Glasscock	1879–95	1628	1889
2	Germany Smith	1884–98	1665	1893
3	Ed McKean	1887–99	1564	1895
4	Herman Long	1889–1904	1794	1897
5	Tommy Corcoran	1890–1907	2073	1898
6	Bones Ely	1884–1902	1236	1900
7	Bill Dahlen	1891–1911	2132	1901
8	Monte Cross	1892–1907	1676	1902
9	George Davis	1890–1909	1372	1905
10	Bobby Wallace	1894–1918	1826	1906

10. **Honus Wagner was the first man both to play 1,000 games at short and log 100 career homers, but many of his blasts came while he played other positions. Who was the first man to amass 100 home runs as a shortstop?**

    A) He collected his first 27 hits in the NL, but his first homer came in the AL.

    B) He was the first man to hit a pinch homer in both ends of a doubleheader.

    C) He set a new record for shortstops when he hammered 24 homers in 1940.

    D) He won a pennant for his future father-in-law as a player-manager in 1933.

    E) He has the most career homers of any shortstop who later was a league prexy.

First 10 Shortstops to Attain 100 Career HRs

RANK	NAME	YEARS	HRS	100TH
1	Honus Wagner	1897–1917	101	1915
2	Joe Cronin	1926–45	170	1939
3	Vern Stephens	1941–55	247	1947
4	Eddie Joost	1936–55	134	1951
5	Pee Wee Reese	1940–58	126	1954
6	Alvin Dark	1946–60	126	1955
7	Ernie Banks	1953–71	512	1957
8	Granny Hamner	1944–62	104	1958
9	Woodie Held	1954–69	179	1962
10	Ron Hansen	1958–72	106	1969
	Rico Petrocelli	1963–76	210	1969

Note: Wagner, Hamner, and Held all hit a number of their first 100 homers while playing other positions.

Bones Ely, the sixth man to play 1,000 games at shortstop. More notably, Ely was the first to play 1,000 games at short after his 30th birthday. He was 31 before he finally won a regular ML job.

11. He and Honus are the only two shortstops among the top 20 in career triples.

    A) He collected the last of his 177 career triples in 1933.

    B) He holds the NL record for the most at bats in a season without homering.

    C) He stood only 5'5".

    D) He was the "Miracle" Braves shortstop.

    E) He has the most career triples of any man whose real first name was Walter.

12. **Nomar Garciaparra fell just two RBI short of achieving an AL first in 1997 when he finished with 98 ribbies. As a result, there remains only one shortstop in all of big league history to compile 100 RBI as a rookie. Who is he?**
    A) In 1930 he became the first shortstop to club 20 homers in a season.
    B) Not only is he the only frosh shortstop to amass 100 RBI, but he was also the first NL'er to compile 100 RBI in each of his first two major league seasons.
    C) He topped the NL in at bats as a rookie in 1924.
    D) He was a member of the 1925 world champs.
    E) His initials and last name match those of the first "King of Shortstops."

13. **Name the only regular shortstop in the 20th century to play as many as 100 games in a season and collect more errors than he made hits.**
    A) He debuted in 1901 and was the first man to play as many as two full seasons in the majors without ever seeing action at any other position but shortstop.
    B) In his two years as a regular, he was consistent if nothing else—he hit .185 both times.
    C) He collected 98 errors in 1903 and just 81 hits.
    D) He was Cleveland's shortstop in 1902–03.
    E) His initials are the same as those of the first shortstop to win a bat title.

Highest Errors-to-Hits Ratio by a Shortstop, Season (Since 1901)

RANK	NAME	TEAM	YEAR	ERRORS	HITS	RATIO
1	John Gochnauer	Cle, AL	1903	98	81	1.21
2	Tommy McMillan	Bro/Cin, NL	1910	47	59	.7966
3	Jimmy Smith	Chi/Bal, FL	1915	70	88	.7955
4	Joe Dolan	Phi, NL/AL	1901	57	76	.75
5	Neal Ball	NY, AL	1908	80	110	.73
6	Billy Gilbert	Bal, AL	1902	78	109	.72
7	Frank Shugart	Chi, AL	1901	73	104	.70
8	Monte Cross	Phi, NL	1901	65	95	.68
9	Lee Tannehill	Chi, AL	1903	76	113	.6726
10	Doc Lavan	StL, AL	1915	75	112	.6696

Note: Minimum 100 games.

14. **The all-time leader in career errors was a shortstop—and a fine one. Who is he?**
    A) He swiped 89 bases as a rookie with the 1889 Kansas City Blues.
    B) He was the first lefty-hitting shortstop to collect 2,000 hits in the majors.
    C) In 1893 he led the NL in runs.
    D) In 1900 he became the first shortstop to lead a major league in home runs.
    E) Many consider this Boston star the best shortstop not in the Hall of Fame.

Players with the Most Career Errors

RANK	NAME	YEARS	POS.	ERRORS
1	Herman Long	1889–1904	SS	1096
2	Bill Dahlen	1891–1911	SS	1080
3	Deacon White	1871–90	3B	1018
4	Germany Smith	1884–1898	SS	1007
5	Tommy Corcoran	1890–1907	SS	991
6	Fred Pfeffer	1882–97	2B	980
7	Monte Ward	1878–94	SS	950
8	Jack Glasscock	1879–95	SS	895
9	Ed McKean	1887–99	SS	890
10	Arlie Latham	1880–1909	3B	844

15. Who was the first man to play 2,000 games at shortstop and compile 2,000 hits?

A) He didn't become a full-time shortstop until his fifth season in 1895.

B) In 1904 he led the NL in RBI with just 80, a post-1893 record low by a leader in a year when a full schedule was played.

C) In 1907, his final year under John McGraw, he became the fourth and last ML'er to make 1,000 career errors.

D) In 1894 he strung together the longest hitting streak in ML history prior to Willie Keeler.

E) Among shortstops, only Honus Wagner tallied more than his 1,590 career runs.

16. There have been so many good switch-hitting shortstops that it was almost inevitable that the first switch-hitter to slap 100 hits in a season from each side of the plate would be a shortstop. Name him.

A) He led the NL in triples in his first three seasons as a regular.

B) He's the only switch-hitting shortstop to enjoy 200-hit seasons twice.

C) He led the NL in hits in 1979, the year he banged 100 from each side of the plate.

D) He collected his 2,000th career hit with the Padres in 1990.

E) He and the slugger who has the most career home runs of anyone with a career BA of .225 or lower share the same initials.

Most Hits, Season, Switch-Hitting Shortstop

RANK	NAME	TEAM	YEAR	BA	HITS
1	Tony Fernandez	Tor, AL	1986	.310	213
2	Garry Templeton	SD, NL	1979	.314	211
3	Dave Bancroft	NY, NL	1922	.321	209
4	Maury Wills	LA, NL	1962	.299	200
	Garry Templeton	SD, NL	1977	.322	200
6	Dave Bancroft	NY, NL	1921	.318	193
7	Jimmy Brown	StL, NL	1939	.298	192
	Larry Bowa	Phi, NL	1978	.294	192
9	Maury Wills	LA, NL	1965	.286	186
	Tony Fernandez	Tor, AL	1987	.322	186
	Tony Fernandez	Tor, AL	1988	.297	186

17. In 18 big-top seasons, he never played on a pennant winner and only once hit .300—and at that just barely and in a year when his league's BA was more than .300. Nevertheless, he compiled 2,252 hits, a record at the time of his retirement for a player who performed most of his career at shortstop. He was also the first player in history to amass 1,000 RBI without ever having a 100-RBI season. Who is he?

    A) He was the first man to play 100 or more games in his first three seasons with three different teams in three different major leagues.

    B) He was the first keystoner to net 2,000 hits and live to be 90.

    C) His 619 ABs in 1898 topped all shortstops in the 1893–1900 era.

    D) His initials are the same as those of the Orioles' top pinch hitter during the late 1970s and early 1980s.

    E) He and the first pitcher to hurl three no-hitters in big league competition share the same last name.

Season Record Holders Among Shortstops for Each Era

| | National League | | | American League | | |
	RECORD	NAME	YEAR	RECORD	NAME	YEAR
At Bats						
1871–75	408	George Wright	1875—NA			
1876–92	646	Herman Long	1892	598	Bill Gleason	1887
1893–1900	619	Tommy Corcoran	1898	604	Ed McKean	1898
1901–19	605	Ed Abbaticchio	1905	602	Freddy Parent	1905
1920–41	672	Rabbit Maranville	1922	656	Frankie Crosetti	1939
1942–60	662	Granny Hamner	1949	679	Harvey Kuenn	1953
1961–76	**695**	**Maury Wills**	**1962**	666	Zoilo Versalles	1965
1977–93	680	Frank Taveras	1979	687	Tony Fernandez	1986
1994–	657	Mark Grudzielanek	1996	686	Alex Rodriguez	1998
Batting Average						
1871–75	.412	George Wright	1871—NA			
1876–92	.352	Jack Glasscock	1889	.341	Oyster Burns	1887
1893–1900	**.401**	**Hughie Jennings**	**1896**	.355	Hughie Jennings	1897
1901–19	.363	Honus Wagner	1905	.328	Bill Keister	1901
1920–41	.385	Arky Vaughan	1935	.388	Luke Appling	1936
1942–60	.322	Alvin Dark	1948	.355	Lou Boudreau	1948
1961–76	.319	Dick Groat	1963	.313	Luis Aparicio	1970
1977–93	.319	Garry Templeton	1980	.343	Alan Trammell	1987
1994–	.319	Barry Larkin	1994	.358	Alex Rodriguez	1996

		National League			American League	
	RECORD	**NAME**	**YEAR**	**RECORD**	**NAME**	**YEAR**
Slugging Average						
1871–75	.640	John Bass	1871—NA			
1876–92	.522	Sam Wise	1887	.519	Oyster Burns	1887
1893–1900	.566	Bill Dahlen	1894	.553	Bill Dahlen	1896
1901–19	.542	Honus Wagner	1908	.482	Bill Keister	1901
1920–41	.607	Arky Vaughan	1935	.536	Joe Cronin	1938
1942–60	.614	Ernie Banks	1958	.539	Vern Stephens	1949
1961–76	.507	Ernie Banks	1961	.589	Rico Petrocelli	1969
1977–93	.596	Barry Larkin	1991	.551	Alan Trammell	1987
1994–	.567	Barry Larkin	1996	**.631**	**Alex Rodriguez**	**1996**
Hits						
1871–75	136	George Wright	1875—NA			
1876–92	205	Jack Glasscock	1889	188	Oyster Burns	1887
1892–1900	209	Hughie Jennings	1896	204	Hughie Jennings	1895
1901–19	201	Honus Wagner	1908	172	Freddy Parent	1904
1920–41	209	Dave Bancroft	1921	218	Cecil Travis	1941*
1942–60	196	Alvin Dark	1951	209	Harvey Kuenn	1953
1961–76	208	Maury Wills	1962	182	Zoilo Versalles	1965
				182	Luis Aparicio	1966
1977–93	211	Garry Templeton	1979	213	Tony Fernandez	1986
1994–	201	Mark Grudzielanek	1996	**215**	**Alex Rodriguez**	**1996**

* Travis played too many games at third base in 1941 to be considered the all-time record holder.

		Total Bases				
1871–75	176	George Wright	1875—NA			
1876–92	272	Jack Glasscock	1889	286	Oyster Burns	1887
1893–1900	284	Bill Dahlen	1894	283	Ed McKean	1895
1901–19	308	Honus Wagner	1908	247	Freddy Parent	1903
1920–41	303	Arky Vaughan	1935	301	Joe Cronin	1930
1942–60	379	Ernie Banks	1958	329	Vern Stephens	1949
1961–76	284	Dick Groat	1962	315	Rico Petrocelli	1969
1977–93	308	Garry Templeton	1979	368	Cal Ripken	1991
1994–	293	Barry Larkin	1996	**384**	**Alex Rodriguez**	**1998**

		Doubles				
1871–75	20	George Wright	1875—NA			
1876–92	40	Jack Glasscock	1889	33	Oyster Burns	1887
1893–1900	41	Hughie Jennings	1895	35	Bill Dahlen	1898
1901–19	44	Honus Wagner	1904	33	Bobby Wallace	1902
1920–41	48	Dick Bartell	1932	51	Joe Cronin	1938
1942–60	45	Lou Boudreau	1944/1947	41	Alvin Dark	1951/1953
1961–76	43	Dick Groat	1963	45	Zoilo Versalles	1965
1977–93	40	Ozzie Smith	1987	49	Robin Yount	1980
1994–	**54**	**Mark Grudzielanek**	**1997**	**54**	**Alex Rodriguez**	**1996**

		National League				American League	
	RECORD	NAME	YEAR	RECORD	NAME	YEAR
Triples						
1871–75	10	John Bass	1871—NA			
1876–92	19	Bill Dahlen	1892	19	Oyster Burns	1887
1893–1900	**24**	**Ed McKean**	**1893**	20	Tommy Corcoran	1894
1901–19	20	Honus Wagner	1912	21	Bill Keister	1901
1920–41	20	Rabbit Maranville	1924	19	Cecil Travis	1941
1942–60	11	Solly Hemus	1953	15	Pete Runnels	1954
1961–76	14	Don Kessinger	1970	13	Zoilo Versalles	1963
	14	Roger Metzger	1973	13	Jim Fregosi	1968
1977–93	19	Garry Templeton	1979	17	Tony Fernandez	1990
1994–	10	Barry Larkin	1998	11	Nomar Garciaparra	1997
Home Runs						
1871–75	3	John Bass	1871—NA	3	George Wright	1873—NA
	3	Jimmy Hallinan	1875—NA			
1876–92	9	Ned Williamson	1887	10	Frank Fennelly	1885
1893–1900	15	Bill Dahlen	1894	12	Bones Ely	1894
				12	Herman Long	1894/1900
1901–19	10	Honus Wagner	1908	7	Roger Peckinpaugh	1919
1920–41	22	Glen Wright	1930	24	Joe Cronin	1940
1942–60	**47**	**Ernie Banks**	**1958**	39	Vern Stephens	1949
1961–76	29	Ernie Banks	1961	40	Rico Petrocelli	1969
1977–93	20	Dickie Thon	1983	34	Cal Ripken	1991
	20	Barry Larkin	1991			
1994–	33	Barry Larkin	1996	42	Alex Rodriguez	1998
RBI						
1871–75	61	George Wright	1875—NA			
1876–92	96	Jack Rowe	1887	97	Frank Fennelly	1887
1893–1900	136	George Davis	1897	133	Ed McKean	1893
1901–19	126	Honus Wagner	1901	93	Bill Keister	1901
				93	George Davis	1902
1920–41	126	Glenn Wright	1930	128	Luke Appling	1936
1942–60	143	Ernie Banks	1959	**159**	**Vern Stephens**	**1949**
1961–76	92	Denis Menke	1970	103	Rico Petrocelli	1970
1977–93	100	Hubie Brooks	1985	114	Robin Yount	1982
1994–	89	Barry Larkin	1996	124	Alex Rodriguez	1998

		National League				American League	
	RECORD	**NAME**	**YEAR**	**RECORD**	**NAME**	**YEAR**

Runs

1871–75	106	George Wright	1875—NA			
1876–92	135	Jack Rowe	1887	137	Herman Long	1889
1893–1900	**159**	**Hughie Jennings**	**1895**	149	Herman Long	1893
				149	Bill Dahlen	1894
1901–19	114	Honus Wagner	1905	126	Donie Bush	1911
1920–41	152	Woody English	1930*	137	Frankie Crosetti	1936
1942–60	132	Pee Wee Reese	1949	128	Eddie Joost	1948
1961–76	130	Maury Wills	1962	126	Zoilo Versalles	1965
1977–93	110	Jeff Blauser	1993	129	Robin Yount	1982
1994–	117	Barry Larkin	1996	141	Alex Rodriguez	1996

* English split 1930 between SS and 3B and can be considered the era record holder at either position.

Walks

1871–75	8	Dickey Pearce; George Wright 1873—NA				
1876–92	87	Bob Allen	1890	106	Paul Radford	1887
	87	Ed McKean	1890			
1893–1900	76	Bill Dahlen	1894	73	Herman Long	1893
				73	Bill Dahlen	1900
1901–19	82	Bill Dahlen	1903	118	Donie Bush	1915
1920–41	118	Arky Vaughan	1936	122	Luke Appling	1935
1942–60	116	Pee Wee Reese	1949	**149**	**Eddie Joost**	**1949**
1961–76	95	Bud Harrelson	1970	98	Toby Harrah	1975
1977–93	89	Ozzie Smith	1987	102	Cal Ripken	1988
				81	John Valentin	1985
1994–	96	Barry Larkin	1996			

OBP

1871–75	.453	George Wright	1871—NA			
1876–92	.401	Ed McKean	1890	.414	Oyster Burns	1887
1893–1900	.472	Hughie Jennings	1896	.463	Hughie Jennings	1897
1901–19	.423	Honus Wagner	1904/1911	.390	Ray Chapman	1918
1920–41	**.491**	**Arky Vaughan**	**1935**	.474	Luke Appling	1936
1942–60	.414	Pee Wee Reese	1947	.453	Lou Boudreau	1948
1961–76	.398	Denis Menke	1970	.406	Toby Harrah	1975
1977–93	.397	Barry Larkin	1993	.406	Alan Trammell	1987
1994–	.410	Barry Larkin	1996	.414	Alex Rodriguez	1996

	RECORD	National League NAME	YEAR	RECORD	American League NAME	YEAR
Stolen Bases						
1871–75	14	George Wright	1872—NA			
1876–92	**111**	**Monte Ward**	**1887**	89	Herman Long	1889
1893–1900	70	Hughie Jennings	1896	65	George Davis	1897
1901–19	61	Honus Wagner	1907	53	Donie Bush	1909
1920–41	25	Rabbit Maranville	1921	37	Lyn Lary	1936
1942–60	50	Maury Wills	1960	56	Luis Aparicio	1959
1961–76	104	Maury Wills	1962	62	Bert Campaneris	1968
1977–93	70	Frank Taveras	1977	53	Freddie Patek	1978
1994–	41	Edgar Renteria	1998	46	Alex Rodriguez	1998

Note: In the 1876–92 era, men who appear under the American League column are the American Association record holders. In the 1893–1900 era, men who appear under the American League column are the runners-up to the National League record holder. Players who performed at more than one position in their record season are considered the record holders at the position where they played the most games. All-time leaders among shortstops are in **bold**.

Grand Gardeners

1. **Outfielders who hit well, regardless of their defensive deficiencies, traditionally have received a disproportionate amount of recognition in comparison with players at other positions. Astonishingly, however, the first outfielder to win back-to-back batting titles not only is not in the Hall of Fame but also has never received even so much as a single vote for enshrinement! Who is he?**

    A) He was the first ML'er to play 1,000 games as an outfielder.

    B) He is the only man to play 20 seasons in the majors and both begin and end his career with Washington ML teams but never play for a Washington AL team.

    C) Some sources claim he was the first man in ML history to perform an unassisted triple play in 1878.

    D) His two batting crowns came while he was with Providence.

    E) Most authorities consider him the first Triple Crown winner in ML history.

First 10 Men to Play 1,000 Games in the Outfield

RANK	NAME	YEARS	G/OF	1000TH
1	Paul Hines	1872–91	1374	1888
2	Ned Hanlon	1880–92	1251	1889
3	George Gore	1879–92	1297	1890
4	Joe Hornung	1879–90	1054	1890
5	George Wood	1880–92	1232	1890
6	Jim O'Rourke	1872–1904	1444	1890
7	Chicken Wolf	1882–92	1042	1891
8	Tom Brown	1883–92	1783	1891
9	Curt Welch	1884–93	1075	1892
10	Pop Corkhill	1883–92	1041	1892

2. **What Hall of Famer owns the record for the most career games played by a man who never saw defensive action anywhere but in the outfield?**

    A) He broke Max Carey's record of 2,421 games solely as a gardener.

    B) He was left-handed all the way.

    C) In the Hall of Famer's final season Tony Scott played center field beside him.

    D) He's a member of the 3,000-hit club.

    E) When he retired he held the record for the most career steals.

Most Games, Career, Outfield Only Defensive Position

RANK	NAME	YEARS	G/OF
1	Lou Brock	1961–79	2507
2	Max Carey	1910–29	2421
3	Zack Wheat	1909–27	2337
4	Tony Gwynn	1982–	2069
5	Enos Slaughter	1936–59	2064
6	Duke Snider	1947–64	1918
7	Clyde Milan	1907–22	1903
8	Cy Williams	1912–30	1818
9	Patsy Donovan	1890–1907	1813
10	Kiki Cuyler	1921–38	1807

Note: Men who DH'd are excluded because they might also have played first base, especially late in their careers, had the DH slot not been available.

3. **The first man to play 2,000 ML games in the outfield has been a Hall of Famer for more than 50 years. Who is he?**
   A) He debuted as a left-handed third baseman.
   B) His final two games as an outfielder came with the 1910 Giants.
   C) At one point, he held the 20th century record for the highest season BA for both the New York AL and the Brooklyn NL franchises.
   D) He still has the mark for the highest season BA by a Baltimore ML performer.
   E) He collected 200 hits a record eight years in a row.

4. **Before expansion increased the schedule to 162 games, who held the record for the most games in a season by an outfielder?**
   A) He also held the record for the most games in a season (162) at any position prior to expansion.
   B) He topped the first Detroit AL entry in runs with 110 in 1901.
   C) He led the AL in walks in both 1903 and 1904.
   D) He and the NL leader in wins in 1945 with 23 share the same last name.
   E) He and the only currently active player both to play 1,000 games at shortstop and homer in his first ML at bat share the same initials.

5. **The Braves represented Boston in the NL for 77 seasons before moving to Milwaukee. The first 25 seasons were fun for Beantown denizens; the next half a century generally was torture. During the club's long sojourn in Beantown, only four men played as many as 700 outfield games in Boston NL garb. What Braves great holds the 1876–1952 club record for the most career games played by an outfielder (1,225)?**
   A) His last career AB came in Game Five of the 1952 World Series.
   B) He was the last Boston Brave to win a National League home run crown.
   C) He was the Boston Braves last player-manager.
   D) He has the 20th century record for the most career hits by a Boston Brave.
   E) Prior to Pete Rose, he owned the 20th century NL record for most consecutive games hit safely.

Most Games with Boston Braves, Career, Outfielder

RANK	NAME	YEARS	G/OF
1	Tommy Holmes	1942–51	1225
2	Hugh Duffy	1892–1900	1128
3	Wally Berger	1930–37	1031
4	Ray Powell	1917–24	825
5	Joe Hornung	1881–88	699
6	Billy Hamilton	1896–1901	683
7	Johnny Cooney	1921–30/1938–42	624
8	Lance Richbourg	1927–31	597
9	Gene Moore	1936–38/1940–41	550
10	Tommy McCarthy	1885/1892–95	536

6. **You'd think an infielder or a catcher would hold the all-time season record for the fewest at bats by anyone who played 100 games, but actually it's an outfielder. Name this gardener who made a career out of being a late-inning defensive replacement.**

   A) He had a record three seasons when he played 100 games with fewer than 200 ABs.

   B) In a 12-year career he played 964 games but collected just 1,913 ABs.

   C) He set the record in 1956 when he had only 63 ABs in 104 games.

   D) Sammy Byrd was called "Babe Ruth's Legs"—our man could have been called "Ted Williams's Legs."

   E) He and a BoSox shortstop who shared two RBI crowns share the same last name.

From a distance, Gene Stephens could pass for Ted Williams. Tall, willowy, a lefty hitter who threw with his right arm, Stephens actually was groomed early in his career to replace Ted. He ended as perhaps the most disappointing performer of the 1942–60 era.

Players with 100 Games and Fewer than 100 ABs, Season

RANK	NAME	TEAM	YEAR	POS.	GAMES	ABS
1	Gene Stephens	Bos, AL	1956	OF	104	63
2	Jack Reed	NY, AL	1963	OF	106	73
3	Chuck Diering	StL, NL	1947	OF	105	74
4	Tom Hutton	Phi, NL	1977	1B	107	81
5	Mike Squires	Chi, AL	1984	1B	104	82
6	Bob Gallagher	Hou, NL	1974	OF	102	87
7	Bobby Clark	Cal, AL	1982	OF	102	90
8	Otis Nixon	Cle, AL	1986	OF	105	95
9	Mick Kelleher	Chi, NL	1988	2B/3B	105	96
10	Jose Gonzalez	LA, NL	1990	OF	106	99

7. In 1904 the AL pennant winner showcased a preexpansion-record six players who participated in 155 or more games, including every regular except catcher Lou Criger and the team's left fielder. But the club's left fielder for most of the 1904 campaign was nonetheless one of the era's top performers. Who was he?

   A) He replaced Patsy Dougherty in Boston's garden after Dougherty was traded early in the 1904 campaign to New York.

   B) He was the first man to play at least one full season with both a Washington NL and a Washington AL team.

   C) He led the NL in triples in 1895.

   D) He was on the first New York NL cellar dweller in 1900, the first Baltimore AL cellar dweller in 1902, the first Washington AL cellar dweller in 1903, and the first Boston AL cellar dweller in 1906.

   E) His initials are the same as those of the last player prior to Nomar Garciaparra to collect 200 hits in his rookie season.

8. In 1994, Frank Thomas demolished the old record for the fewest at bats in a season with 100 runs, 100 RBI, and 100 walks. Observers who noted his extraordinary production in only 399 at bats thought the record must surely have previously belonged either to Babe Ruth or Ted Williams. But it didn't. It belonged to a former teammate of Ruth's. Who is he?

   A) He was born in Canada.

   B) He spent his entire nine-year career with the same AL team.

   C) The team won six pennants while he wore its uniform.

   D) His big season came in 1939 when he had to share outfield duty with Tommy Henrich and a rookie nicknamed "King Kong."

   E) His nickname was "Twinkletoes."

Fewest ABs with 100 Runs, 100 RBI, and 100 Walks, Season

RANK	NAME	TEAM	YEAR	RUNS	RBI	WALKS	ABS
1	Frank Thomas	Chi, AL	1994	106	101	109	399
2	George Selkirk	NY, AL	1939	103	101	103	418
3	Babe Ruth	Bos, AL	1919	103	114	101	432
4	Ted Williams	Bos, AL	1941	135	120	145	456
5	Babe Ruth	NY, AL	1932	120	137	130	457
6	Babe Ruth	NY, AL	1920	158	137	148	458
7	Joe Morgan	Cin, NL	1976	113	111	114	472
8	Barry Bonds	Pit, NL	1992	109	103	127	473
9	Willie McCovey	SF, NL	1969	101	126	121	491
10	Frank Thomas	Chi, AL	1995	102	111	136	493

9. What current ML team won its most recent World Championship with a trio of outfield regulars who combined to hit .230 with just three home runs and 91 RBI?

A) The center fielder has the 19th century record for most OF chances accepted by a rookie, set in 1899.

B) The left fielder formerly owned a loop record for the most walks in a season.

C) The right fielder led the NL in home runs and RBI three years later.

D) Two years earlier, the team had lost the World Championship to a club with a quartet of outfielders who batted a combined .234 with four homers and 109 RBI.

E) The center fielder was replaced by the backup gardener in all five games of the World Series that followed the season when the "Merkle Boner" occurred.

10. Who posted the all-time-lowest season batting average by an outfielder with at least 400 at bats?

A) He was a regular gardener on the last Buffalo entry in the NL.

B) He also holds the record for the lowest SA in a season (.197) by anyone with at least 400 ABs.

C) His nadir came in 1886 with Kansas City, when he hit .175 and tied the 19th century record for the fewest RBI (20) by an outfielder in 400 ABs.

D) His initials and first name match those of the St. Louis Browns shortstop who holds the 20th century record for the lowest OBP (.237) by anyone with at least 500 ABs.

E) His last name is spelled differently from but pronounced the same as that of a Dallas Cowboys Hall of Fame defensive end.

Outfielders with a Sub-.200 BA, Season (Minimum 100 Games & 350 ABs)

RANK	NAME	TEAM	YEAR	GAMES	ABS	BA
1	Jim Lillie	KC, NL	1886	114	416	.175
2	Rob Deer	Det, AL	1991	134	448	.179
3	George Wright	Tex, AL	1985	109	363	.19008
4	Ed Kennedy	NY, AA	1884	103	378	.19047
5	Reggie Jackson	Cal, AL	1983	116	397	.19395
6	Harry Lyons	StL, AA	1888	123	499	.19438
7	Billy Maloney	Bro, NL	1908	113	359	.195
8	Paul Blair	Bal, AL	1976	145	375	.197
9	Patsy Cahill	StL, NL	1886	125	463	.199

Note: BAs carried out to five decimal points where ties would otherwise exist. Jackson also DH'd in 1983.
In 1989, John Shelby hit .183 in 108 games for Los Angeles, NL, but collected just 343 ABs. In 1969, Roger Repoz hit .164 for California, AL, in 103 games but had only 219 ABs. In 1884, Paul Radford hit .197 in 355 ABs for Providence, NL, but played just 97 games.

11. Name the first team with an outfield trio who ripped 10 or more home runs apiece.

    A) The team was managed by one of its three garden regulars.

    B) That same season, another team in the same loop had an outfield trio who combined for 87 homers, but the center fielder had only 4 of them.

    C) The team with three gardeners who homered in double digits hit a loop record .316.

    D) The three garden regulars all had 2,000 career hits and .300+ BAs.

    E) The team with an outfield trio who combined for 87 homers that same year later became the only club to date to feature two gardeners who each went yard 50 or more times in the same season.

Each Team's First Outfield Trio All Homering in Double Digits

TEAM	YEAR	TRIO
Detroit Tigers	1921	Heilmann (19), Veach (16) & Cobb (12)
Philadelphia Phillies	1922	Williams (26), Lee (17) & Walker (12)
Philadelphia Athletics	1922	Walker (37), Miller (21) & Welch (11)
St. Louis Browns	1925	Williams (25), Jacobson (15) & Rice (11)
Chicago Cubs	1929	Wilson (39), Stephenson (17) & Cuyler (15)
Brooklyn Dodgers	1932	Wilson (23), O'Doul (21) & Taylor (11)
New York Giants	1935	Ott (31), Leiber (22) & Moore (15)
Cincinnati Reds	1938	Goodman (30), Berger (16) & Craft (15)
New York Yankees	1938	DiMaggio (32), Henrich (22) & Selkirk (10)
Cleveland Indians	1938	Heath (21), Averill (14) & Campbell (12)
St. Louis Cardinals	1939	Moore (17), Medwick (14) & Slaughter (12)
Boston Braves	1944	Nieman (16), Holmes (13) & Workman (11)
Pittsburgh Pirates	1949	Kiner (54), Westlake (23) & Restelli (12)
Boston Red Sox	1951	Williams (30), Vollmer (22) & DiMaggio (12)
Chicago White Sox	1953	Minoso (15), Mele (12) & Rivera (11)
Washington Senators	1959	Lemon (33), Allison (30) & Throneberry (10)

Note: Includes only frachises extant since 1901.

12. **What team set a postexpansion record for the fewest home runs by three outfield regulars with enough plate appearances to qualify for the batting title when its garden trio clubbed just 13 dingers combined?**

   A) Three years earlier the team's three most active gardeners combined for just 10 homers, including 3 by rookie Paul Dade.

   B) The year it set a new postexpansion record with just 13 homers by its regular outfielders, the team leader in homers with 23 was AL Rookie of the Year.

   C) The team's left fielder that year set a postexpansion record for the highest BA (.341) by a batting-title qualifier who failed to homer all year.

   D) The team was managed by Dave Garcia.

   E) Len Barker led both the club and the AL in strikeouts that year.

Fewest HRs by Three Regular Outfielders on a Postexpansion Team

RANK	TEAM	YEAR	TRIO	TOTAL
1	Hou, NL	1989	Bass (5), Hatcher (3), Young (0) & Puhl (0)	8
2	KC, AL	1965	Hershberger (5), Landis (3) & Reynolds (1)	9
3	StL, NL	1972	Melendez (5), Brock (3) & J. Cruz (2)	10
	StL, NL	1977	H. Cruz (6), Mumphrey (2) & Brock (2)	10
	Cle, AL	1977	Bochte (5), Dade (3) & Norris (2)	10
6	KC, AL	1966	Stahl (5), Gosger (5) & Hershberger (2)	12
7	Cle, AL	1980	Orta (10), Manning (3) & Dilone (0)	13
	KC, AL	1983	Sheridan (7), Otis (4) & Wilson (2)	13
9	StL, NL	1975	W. Davis (6), McBride (5) & Brock (3)	14
	StL, NL	1976	Crawford (9), Brock (4) & Mumphrey (1)	14

Note: Minimum 300 ABs. The 1980 Indians are the only list member with three garden regulars who all had enough plate appearances to qualify for the batting title.

13. **What grand gardener was the first man in ML history to lead his loop in both batter strikeouts and on-base percentage in the same season?**
    A) The closest anyone came to achieving this feat in the 19th century was in 1891, when Harry Stovey and Tom Brown, the NL and the AA leaders in batter strikeouts, finished tied for 10th in OBP.
    B) It's been done on only six occasions in the 20th century, three times by Babe Ruth and once apiece by three other men, including the first to do it.
    C) The first man to do it set a record that same year for the lowest OBP (.379) ever to lead a major league loop.
    D) He was a frequent home run leader in the Deadball Era.
    E) He topped both the Phillies and the NL in OBP in 1915 and again in 1916.

Players Leading in Both Batter Ks and OBP

NAME	TEAM	YEAR	KS	OBP
Gavvy Cravath	Phi, NL	1916	89	.379
Babe Ruth	NY, AL	1923	93	.545
Babe Ruth	NY, AL	1924	81	.513
Babe Ruth	NY, AL	1927	89	.487
Jimmie Foxx	Phi, AL	1929	70	.463
Mike Schmidt	Phi, NL	1983	148	.399

14. The only man to collect 100 walks in each of his first six ML seasons was an outfielder by trade. Who is he?

- A) Not Ted Williams, who had only 96 walks in his sophomore year.
- B) Our man led the NL in walks in five of his first six seasons.
- C) In 1901 he compiled the lowest SA in ML history (.334) by a .300 hitter.
- D) He walked 115 times as a rookie with the 1899 Phillies but is better known for scoring an all-time NL frosh-record 137 runs.
- E) He and the only member of the 1996 San Francisco Giants who had been a Giants teammate of Vida Blue share the same initials.

RANK	NAME	TEAM	YEAR	BA	SA
\multicolumn{6}{c}{**Lowest SA by a .300 Hitter, Season (Minimum 400 ABs)**}
1	Roy Thomas	Phi, NL	1901	.309	.334
2	Roy Thomas	Phi, NL	1900	.316	.335
3	Simon Nicholls	Phi, AL	1907	.307	.337
4	Willie Keeler	NY, AL	1904	.304	.338
5	Patsy Donovan	StL, NL	1900	.316	.342
6	Harry Taylor	Lou, AA	1890	.306	.3436
7	Ron Hunt	Mon, NL	1973	.309	.3441
8	Doc Cramer	Det, AL	1943	.300	.348
9	Tim O'Rourke	Bal/Lou, NL	1893	.304	.34908
10	Maury Wills	LA, NL	1963	.302	.34915

Note: SAs are carried out to four or five decimal points where ties would otherwise exist.

15. Sam Crawford holds the all-time record for the most career RBI (1,525) by an outfielder with fewer than 100 career homers. What gardener holds the post–Deadball Era record for the same feat with 977 RBI on 90 dingers?

- A) He reached double digits in home runs in each of his first three seasons and then never did it again in his 15-year career.
- B) He led the AL in steals in three of his first four seasons.
- C) In 1944, after being absent from the majors since 1941, he returned as a pitcher with Brooklyn.
- D) He hit .340 as a Red Sox outfield regular in 1938 but lost his job the following year to a rookie named Ted Williams.
- E) He is the only player since the close of the Deadball Era to collect 60 stolen bases and 120 RBI in the same season.

Most RBI, Career, Fewer than 100 HRs

RANK	NAME	YEARS	HRS	RBI
1	Cap Anson	1871–97	98	2076
2	Nap Lajoie	1896–1916	83	1599
3	Jake Beckley	1888–1907	86	1575
4	Sam Crawford	1899–1917	97	1525
5	George Davis	1890–1907	73	1437
6	Lave Cross	1887–1907	47	1371
7	Eddie Collins	1906–30	47	1300
8	Pie Traynor	1920–37	58	1273
9	Bill Dahlen	1891–1911	84	1233
10	Joe Kelley	1891–1908	65	1194

16. **Hack Wilson's 190 (really 191) RBI in 1930 are a record both for an outfielder and for any ML'er. What man, who was still active in 1930, 12 years earlier set an all-time season record low for an outfielder with 400 at bats when he had just 11 RBI?**

   A) He retired with 1,990 hits and a .303 BA.

   B) His 11-RBI season came with the 1918 A's, when he hit .202.

   C) In his only World Series, he hit .333 for Cleveland.

   D) In 1922 he topped the AL in hits, and then the following year he batted .359 for Cleveland with 213 hits.

   E) His initials match those of the Braves current third baseman.

Fewest RBI, Outfielder, Season (Minimum 400 ABs)

RANK	NAME	TEAM	YEAR	ABS	BA	RBI
1	Charlie Jamieson	Phi, AL	1918	416	.202	11
2	Goat Anderson	Pit, NL	1907	413	.206	12
3	Billy Sunday	Pit, NL	1888	505	.236	15
	Jack Smith	StL, NL	1919	408	.223	15
	Clyde Milan	Was, AL	1909	400	.200	15
6	Clyde Milan	Was, AL	1910	531	.279	16
	Roy Thomas	Phi, NL	1906	493	.254	16
8	George Browne	Chi, NL/Was, AL	1909	432	.271	17
	Johnny Cooney	Bos, NL	1938	432	.271	17
	Willie Keeler	NY, AL	1907	423	.234	17

Note: Thomas was the lamest outfielder ever at producing RBI; he averaged a mere 24 ribbies per 400 ABs. Even though Milan appears twice on this list, he's not on the career list for the worst run-producing gardeners; nor, for that matter, is Jamieson.

17. **Who is the only man in ML history to play 1,000 games in the outfield and collect 2,000 hits but score fewer than 900 runs?**
    A) In 1968 he scored just 30 runs for the White Sox in 132 games.
    B) Although he scored just 811 career runs, he once crossed the plate 120 times in a single season.
    C) He finished his career in 1976 as a DH.
    D) He is on the list of multiple bat crown winners with sub-.300 career BAs.
    E) Prior to 1998 he was the most recent NL'er to net more than 150 RBI in a season.

Fewest Runs, Career, 2,000 Hits

RANK	NAME	YEARS	POS.	HITS	RUNS
1	Bill Mazeroski	1956–72	2B	2016	769
2	Tommy Davis	1959–76	OF	2121	811
3	Dick Groat	1952–67	SS	2138	829
4	Stuffy McInnis	1909–27	1B	2405	872
5	George Kell	1943–57	3B	2054	881
6	Garry Templeton	1976–91	SS	2096	893
7	George Burns	1914–29	1B	2018	901
8	Charlie Grimm	1916–36	1B	2299	908
	Tim Wallach	1980–96	3B	2212	908
10	Chris Chambliss	1971–88	1B	2109	912

18. **Identify the owner of the lowest career batting average among all performers who collected 2,000 hits and whose primary defensive position was the outfield.**
    A) He ended with a .260 BA on 2,135 hits in 2,292 games.
    B) He won an MVP Award the lone year he led a major league in an offensive department (runs and RBI).
    C) In 1976 he swiped a career-high 52 bases with Oakland.
    D) In his last three seasons, he was in three World Series with three different teams.
    E) He holds the 20th century career record for the most times hit by a pitch.

Lowest Career BA, Outfielder with 2,000 Hits

RANK	NAME	YEARS	G/OF	HITS	BA
1	Don Baylor	1970–88	822	2135	.260
2	Reggie Jackson	1967–87	2102	2584	.262
3	Dale Murphy	1976–93	1853	2111	.265
4	Brian Downing	1973–92	777	2099	.267
5	Tommy Leach	1898–1918	1079	2143	.269
6	Dwight Evans	1972–91	2146	2446	.272
7	Jimmy Sheckard	1897–1913	2071	2084	.274
8	Amos Otis	1967–84	1928	2020	.277
9	Willie Davis	1960–79	2323	2561	.2792
10	Rusty Staub	1963–85	1675	2716	.2794

Note: Limited to men whose primary defensive position was the outfield, including those who also DH'd but played more games in the outfield than anywhere else.

19. **The preceeding list signals that long-term outfielders with sub-.280 career batting averages are a postexpansion phenomenon—so much so that only two preexpansion gardeners rank among the top 10. Who is the only man active primarily in the hitter-friendly 1920–41 era to play as many as 1,000 games in the outfield and post a career batting average below .280?**

   A) He debuted with the 1918 Cardinals and finished with the 1932 Phils.
   B) He was the first man to post a sub-.200 BA (.198) as a pinch hitter in at least 200 pinch plate appearances.
   C) In 1929 he hit a career-high .313 and got into his lone World Series, albeit only as a pinch hitter.
   D) He and the 1931 NL batting champ share the same initials.
   E) He and Max Flack are famed for being swapped for each other between games of a twin bill in 1922.

Lowest Career BA, Outfielder, Each Era

ERA	NAME	YEARS	G/OF	ABS	BA
1876–92	Ned Hanlon	1880–92	1251	5074	.260
1893–1900	Jimmy McAleer	1889–1907	1016	3977	.253
1901–19	Jack Graney	1908–22	1282	4705	.250
1920–41	Cliff Heathcote	1918–32	1158	4443	.275
1942–60	Bill Tuttle	1952–63	1191	4268	.259
1961–76	Mickey Stanley	1964–78	1289	5022	.247
1977–93	Gorman Thomas	1973–86	1159	4677	.225

Note: Minimum 4,000 ABs and 1,000 games as an outfielder; insufficient data for post-1994 era. McAleer's average is so much lower than any other outfielder's in the 1893–1900 era that even if he'd gotten a hit in every one of the 23 ABs he was short of 4,000, he still would have been the weakest-hitting gardener of his time. Bob Kennedy (1939–57) hit .254 in 4,624 ABs but played just 821 games in the outfield.

20. **The 1910s is the only decade (except the 1870s, when teams played much shorter schedules) when no outfielders in a major league (the NL) had a 200-hit season. Who was the only NL gardener during the 1910s to collect more than 190 hits in a season?**

   A) He was a Brave the year he led the NL with 192 hits.
   B) He once held the big league record for the most pinch hits in a season.
   C) In 1911, his big year, he missed winning the NL bat crown by a single point.
   D) They called him "Doc."
   E) He and the rookie second sacker for the 1909 world champs had the same last name and initials.

Most Hits, Season, NL Outfielder During 1910–19

RANK	NAME	TEAM	YEAR	BA	HITS
1	Doc Miller	Boston	1911	.333	192
2	Vin Campbell	Boston	1912	.296	185
3	Dave Robertson	New York	1916	.307	180
	George Burns	New York	1917	.302	180
5	Gavvy Cravath	Philadelphia	1913	.341	179
	Tommy Griffith	Cincinnati	1915	.307	179
7	Edd Roush	Cincinnati	1917	.341	178
8	Max Carey	Pittsburgh	1912	.302	177
	Bill Hinchman	Pittsburgh	1915	.307	177
	Zack Wheat	Brooklyn	1916	.312	177

21. The only man to compile at least 100 career home runs and a documented total of fewer than 200 career strikeouts was an outfielder. Who is he?

A) Both his first of 106 career home runs and his first of 199 career Ks came with the 1918 Phillies.

B) He fanned six times in 87 World Series at bats, all with the same NL team.

C) He won the NL RBI crown in 1923.

D) His brother once led the AL in batter strikeouts.

E) He and his brother opposed each other in three straight Series, 1921–23.

22. In 1896, Ed Delahanty led the NL with a slugging average of .631. Who was the next NL gardener to post a slugging average as high as .600?

A) Delahanty was the last man in the 19th century at any position to slug .600.

B) Gavvy Cravath (.568 in 1913) had the highest SA of any NL outfielder during the Deadball Era.

C) Hy Myers in 1919 was the last outfielder to lead the NL in SA until 1926.

D) Kiki Cuyler's .593 SA in 1925 stood as the 20th century record for NL outfielders until 1928.

E) The first outfielder to slug .600 in the 20th century (.604 in 1928) was the only NL'er to post a .600 SA for three straight seasons, 1928–30.

Season Record Holders Among Outfielders for Each Era

	National League			American League		
	RECORD	NAME	YEAR	RECORD	NAME	YEAR
At Bats						
1871–75	396	Andy Leonard	1875—NA			
	375	Tom York	1875—NA			
	358	Jim O'Rourke	1875—NA			
	358	Jack Remsen	1875—NA			
1876–92	660	Tom Brown	1892	604	Tommy McCarthy	1889
	623	Doggie Miller	1892	589	Tom Brown	1891
	612	Hugh Duffy	1892	585	Tom Poorman	1887
1893–1900	654	George Van Haltren	1898			
	633	Dummy Hoy	1899			
	629	Duff Cooley	1898			

	National League			American League		
	RECORD	NAME	YEAR	RECORD	NAME	YEAR
1901–19	624	Vin Campbell	1912	647	Patsy Dougherty	1904
	623	George Burns	1916	632	George Stone	1905
	622	George Burns	1915	624	Elmer Flick	1906
1920–41	696	Woody Jensen	1936	671	John Tobin	1921
	681	Lloyd Waner	1931	670	Al Simmons	1932
	681	Jo-Jo Moore	1935	661	Doc Cramer	1933/1940
1942–60	667	Carl Furillo	1951	648	Dom DiMaggio	1948
	662	Richie Ashburn	1949	640	Dale Mitchell	1949
	656	Dain Clay	1945	639	Dom DiMaggio	1951
1961–76	698	Matty Alou	1969	672	Tony Oliva	1964
	689	Lou Brock	1967	657	Cesar Tovar	1971
	680	Pete Rose	1973	650	Cesar Tovar	1970
1977–93	695	Omar Moreno	1979	**705**	**Willie Wilson**	**1980**
	676	Omar Moreno	1980	691	Kirby Puckett	1985
	659	Warren Cromartie	1979	680	Kirby Puckett	1986
1994–	682	Lance Johnson	1996	662	Kenny Lofton	1996
	678	Doug Glanville	1998	658	Brian Hunter	1997
	671	Marquis Grissom	1976	642	Johnny Damon	1998

Batting Average (280 ABs 1876–92; 400 ABs Since)

	National League			American League		
1871–75	.396	Steve King	1871—NA			
	.377	Lip Pike	1871—NA			
	.368	Lip Pike	1874—NA			
1876–92	.388	King Kelly	1886	.435	Tip O'Neill	1887
	.378	John Cassidy	1877	.402	Pete Browning	1887
	.372	Sam Thompson	1887	.378	Pete Browning	1882
1893–1900	**.440**	**Hugh Duffy**	**1894**			
	.424	Willie Keeler	1897			
	.410	Ed Delahanty	1899			
	.410	Jesse Burkett	1896			
1901–19	.377	Cy Seymour	1905	.420	Ty Cobb	1911
	.376	Jesse Burkett	1901	.410	Ty Cobb	1912
	.357	Ginger Beaumont	1902	.408	Joe Jackson	1911
1920–41	.399	Lefty O'Doul	1929	.406	Ted Williams	1941
	.393	Babe Herman	1930	.403	Harry Heilmann	1923
	.386	Chuck Klein	1930	.401	Ty Cobb	1922
1942–60	.376	Stan Musial	1948	.388	Ted Williams	1957
	.363	Harry Walker	1947	.369	Ted Williams	1948
	.357	Dixie Walker	1944	.365	Mickey Mantle	1957
	.357	Stan Musial	1943			
1961–76	.357	Roberto Clemente	1967	.337	Tony Oliva	1971
	.353	Ralph Garr	1974	.332	Hal McRae	1976*
	.351	Roberto Clemente	1961	.331	Fred Lynn	1975
				.331	Bobby Murcer	1971

	National League			American League		
	RECORD	**NAME**	**YEAR**	**RECORD**	**NAME**	**YEAR**
1977–93	.370	Tony Gwynn	1987	.356	Kirby Puckett	1988
	.358	Tony Gwynn	1993	.341	Miguel Dilone	1980
	.353	Willie McGee	1985	.340	Dave Winfield	1984
1994–	.394	Tony Gwynn	1994	.359	Paul O'Neill	1994
	.372	Tony Gwynn	1997	.357	Albert Belle	1994
	.368	Tony Gwynn	1995	.349	Kenny Lofton	1994

* McRae was primarily a DH in 1976 but played 31 games in the outfield.

Slugging Average (280 ABs 1876–92; 400 ABs Since)

1871–75	.654	Lip Pike	1871—NA			
	.573	Fred Treacey	1871—NA			
	.504	Lip Pike	1874			
1876–92	.571	Sam Thompson	1887	.691	Tip O'Neill	1887
	.545	George Hall	1876	.547	Pete Browning	1887
	.534	King Kelly	1886	.525	Harry Stovey	1889
1893–1900	.694	Hugh Duffy	1894			
	.687	Sam Thompson	1894			
	.654	Sam Thompson	1895			
1901–19	.568	Gavvy Cravath	1913	.657	Babe Ruth	1919
	.559	Cy Seymour	1905	.621	Ty Cobb	1911
	.534	Jimmy Sheckard	1901	.590	Joe Jackson	1911
				.590	Ed Delahanty	1902
1920–41	.723	Hack Wilson	1930	**.847**	**Babe Ruth**	**1920**
	.687	Chuck Klein	1930	.846	Babe Ruth	1921
	.678	Babe Herman	1930	.772	Babe Ruth	1927
1942–60	.702	Stan Musial	1948	.731	Ted Williams	1957
	.667	Willie Mays	1954	.705	Mickey Mantle	1956
	.659	Willie Mays	1955	.667	Ted Williams	1946
1961–76	.669	Hank Aaron	1971	.687	Mickey Mantle	1961
	.646	Willie Stargell	1973	.637	Frank Robinson	1966
	.645	Willie Mays	1965	.622	Carl Yastrzemski	1967
1977–93	.677	Barry Bonds	1993	.637	Fred Lynn	1979
	.635	Kevin Mitchell	1989	.633	Juan Gonzalez	1993
	.631	George Foster	1977	.617	Ken Griffey Jr.	1993
1994–	.720	Larry Walker	1997	.714	Albert Belle	1994
	.647	Barry Bonds	1994	.691	Albert Belle	1995
	.647	Sammy Sosa	1998	.674	Ken Griffey Jr.	1994

Hits

1871–75	127	Andy Leonard	1875—NA			
	123	Cal McVey	1874—NA			
	111	Tom York	1875—NA			
1876–92	203	Sam Thompson	1887	225	Tip O'Neill	1887
	189	Hardy Richardson	1886	220	Pete Browning	1887
	186	Sam Thompson	1892	197	Chicken Wolf	1890

	National League			American League		
	RECORD	NAME	YEAR	RECORD	NAME	YEAR
1893–1900	240	Jesse Burkett	1896			
	239	Willie Keeler	1897			
	238	Ed Delahanty	1899			
1901–19	226	Jesse Burkett	1901	248	Ty Cobb	1911
	219	Cy Seymour	1905	233	Joe Jackson	1911
	216	Mike Donlin	1905	226	Ty Cobb	1912
				226	Joe Jackson	1912
1920–41	**254**	**Lefty O'Doul**	**1929**	253	Al Simmons	1925
	250	Chuck Klein	1930	241	Heinie Manush	1928
	241	Babe Herman	1930	237	Harry Heilmann	1921
1942–60	230	Stan Musial	1948	204	Dale Mitchell	1948
	224	Tommy Holmes	1945	203	Stan Spence	1942
	223	Hank Aaron	1959	203	Dale Mitchell	1949
1961–76	231	Matty Alou	1969	217	Tony Oliva	1964
	230	Tommy Davis	1962	204	Tony Oliva	1970
	230	Pete Rose	1973	204	Cesar Tovar	1971
1977–93	218	Tony Gwynn	1987	234	Kirby Puckett	1988
	216	Willie McGee	1985	230	Willie Wilson	1980
	215	Dave Parker	1977	223	Kirby Puckett	1986
1994–	227	Lance Johnson	1996	210	Kenny Lofton	1996
	219	Dante Bichette	1998	200	Albert Belle	1998
	211	Ellis Burks	1996	193	Rusty Greer	1997
				193	Juan Gonzalez	1998

Total Bases

	National League			American League		
1871–75	156	Andy Leonard	1875—NA			
	154	Lip Pike	1875—NA			
	151	George Hall	1875—NA			
1876–92	311	Sam Thompson	1887	357	Tip O'Neill	1887
	287	Jimmy Ryan	1889	299	Pete Browning	1887
	283	Jimmy Ryan	1888	292	Harry Stovey	1889
1893–1900	374	Hugh Duffy	1894			
	352	Sam Thompson	1895			
	347	Ed Delahanty	1893			
1901–19	325	Cy Seymour	1905	367	Ty Cobb	1911
	308	Frank Schulte	1911	337	Joe Jackson	1911
	306	Jesse Burkett	1901	335	Ty Cobb	1917
1920–41	445	Chuck Klein	1930	**457**	**Babe Ruth**	**1921**
	423	Hack Wilson	1930	418	Joe DiMaggio	1937
	420	Chuck Klein	1932	417	Babe Ruth	1927
1942–60	429	Stan Musial	1948	376	Mickey Mantle	1956
	400	Hank Aaron	1959	368	Ted Williams	1949
	382	Stan Musial	1949	355	Joe DiMaggio	1948
	382	Willie Mays	1955			

	National League				American League	
	RECORD	**NAME**	**YEAR**	**RECORD**	**NAME**	**YEAR**
1961–76	380	Frank Robinson	1962	374	Tony Oliva	1964
	373	Billy Williams	1970	367	Frank Robinson	1966
	370	Hank Aaron	1963	366	Roger Maris	1961
1977–93	380	George Foster	1977	406	Jim Rice	1978
	365	Barry Bonds	1993	382	Jim Rice	1977
	353	Andre Dawson	1987	369	Jim Rice	1979
				369	George Bell	1987
1994–	416	Sammy Sosa	1998	399	Albert Belle	1998
	409	Larry Walker	1997	393	Ken Griffey Jr.	1997
	392	Ellis Burks	1996	387	Ken Griffey Jr.	1998

Doubles

1871–75	22	Lip Pike	1874—NA			
	22	Lip Pike	1875—NA			
	20	Dave Eggler	1872—NA			
1876–92	41	King Kelly	1889	52	Tip O'Neill	1887
	41	Sam Thompson	1890	39	Curt Welch	1889
	36	Paul Hines	1884	38	Harry Stovey	1889
	36	Jim O'Rourke	1889			
	36	Mike Griffin	1891			
1893–1900	55	Ed Delahanty	1899			
	51	Hugh Duffy	1894			
	49	Ed Delahanty	1895			
1901–19	40	Cy Seymour	1905	53	Tris Speaker	1912
	39	Sherry Magee	1910	47	Ty Cobb	1911
	39	Sherry Magee	1914	46	Tris Speaker	1914
1920–41	64	Joe Medwick	1936	**67**	**Earl Webb**	**1931**
	62	Paul Waner	1932	59	Tris Speaker	1923
	59	Chuck Klein	1930	55	Gee Walker	1936
1942–60	53	Stan Musial	1953	50	Stan Spence	1946
	51	Stan Musial	1944	44	Ted Williams	1948
	48	Stan Musial	1943	42	Tommy Henrich	1948
1961–76	51	Frank Robinson	1962	47	Fred Lynn	1975
	46	Lou Brock	1968	45	Floyd Robinson	1962
	45	Pete Rose	1974	45	Carl Yastrzemski	1965
1977–93	46	Warren Cromartie	1979	54	Hal McRae	1977
	46	Jack Clark	1978	45	Kirby Puckett	1989
	46	Von Hayes	1986	44	Chet Lemon	1979
				44	Ivan Calderon	1990
				44	Ruben Sierra	1991
1994–	49	Tony Gwynn	1997	52	Albert Belle	1995
	48	Dante Bichette	1998	50	Juan Gonzalez	1998
	48	Dmitri Young	1998	48	Albert Belle	1998

	National League				American League	
RECORD	**NAME**	**YEAR**	**RECORD**	**NAME**	**YEAR**

Triples

1871–75	12	Lip Pike	1875—NA			
	12	George Hall	1875—NA			
	8	Lip Pike	1873—NA			
	8	George Hall	1874—NA			
	8	Dave Eggler	1874—NA			
1876–92	23	Sam Thompson	1887	21	Tom Brown	1891
	21	Mike Tiernan	1890	20	Harry Stovey	1888
	21	Ed Delahanty	1892	19	Tom Poorman	1887
				19	Tip O'Neill	1887
1893–1900	27	Sam Thompson	1894			
	26	George Treadway	1894			
	25	Buck Freeman	1899			
1901–19	**36**	**Chief Wilson**	**1912**	26	Joe Jackson	1912
	25	Tom Long	1915	26	Sam Crawford	1914
	22	Sam Crawford	1902	25	Sam Crawford	1903
	22	Mike Mitchell	1911			
1920–41	26	Kiki Cuyler	1925	23	Earle Combs	1927
	23	Adam Comorsky	1930	22	Earle Combs	1930
	22	Hy Myers	1920	21	Earle Combs	1928
	22	Paul Waner	1926			
1942–60	20	Stan Musial	1943	23	Dale Mitchell	1949
	20	Willie Mays	1957	18	Minnie Minoso	1954
	19	Johnny Barrett	1944	16	Stan Spence	1944
				16	Hank Edwards	1946
				16	Jim Rivera	1953
1961–76	17	Ralph Garr	1974	15	Gino Cimoli	1962
	16	Johnny Callison	1965	13	Cesar Tovar	1970
	16	Willie Davis	1970	13	Mickey Rivers	1975
1977–93	18	Willie McGee	1985	21	Willie Wilson	1985
	15	Andy Van Slyke	1988	15	Jim Rice	1977/1978
	15	Ray Lankford	1991	15	Dave Collins	1984
				15	Willie Wilson	1980/1982/ 1987
				15	Lloyd Moseby	1984
1994–	21	Lance Johnson	1996	14	Lance Johnson	1994
	12	Dave Dellucci	1998	13	Kenny Lofton	1995
	10	Thomas Howard	1996	12	Vince Coleman	1994
	10	Marquis Grissom	1996	12	Lance Johnson	1995

	National League			American League		
	RECORD	NAME	YEAR	RECORD	NAME	YEAR
Home Runs						
1871–75	6	Lip Pike	1872—NA			
	6	Jim O'Rourke	1875—NA			
	4	Fred Treacey	1871—NA			
	4	Lip Pike	1873—NA			
	4	George Hall	1875—NA			
1876–92	22	Abner Dalrymple	1884	19	Harry Stovey	1889
	20	Sam Thompson	1889	19	Bug Holliday	1889
	17	Jimmy Ryan	1889	16	Home Run Duffee	1889
1893–1900	25	Buck Freeman	1899			
	19	Ed Delahanty	1893			
	18	Sam Thompson	1895			
	18	Hugh Duffy	1894			
1901–19	24	Gavvy Cravath	1915	29	Babe Ruth	1919
	21	Frank Schulte	1911	16	Socks Seybold	1902
	19	Gavvy Cravath	1913/1914	13	Buck Freeman	1903
1920–41	56	Hack Wilson	1930	60	Babe Ruth	1927
	43	Chuck Klein	1929	59	Babe Ruth	1921
	42	Mel Ott	1929	54	Babe Ruth	1928
1942–60	54	Ralph Kiner	1949	52	Mickey Mantle	1956
	51	Ralph Kiner	1947	43	Ted Williams	1949
	51	Willie Mays	1955	42	Roy Sievers	1957
				42	Gus Zernial	1953
				42	Rocky Colavito	1959
1961–76	52	Willie Mays	1965	61	Roger Maris	1961
	49	Willie Mays	1962	54	Mickey Mantle	1961
	48	Willie Stargell	1971	49	Frank Robinson	1966
				49	Harmon Killebrew	1964
1977–93	54	George Foster	1977	47	George Bell	1987
	49	Andre Dawson	1987	46	Jim Rice	1978
	48	Dave Kingman	1979	46	Juan Gonzalez	1993
1994–	**66**	**Sammy Sosa**	**1998**	56	Ken Griffey Jr.	1997/1998
	50	Greg Vaughn	1998	50	Albert Belle	1995
	49	Larry Walker	1997	50	Brady Anderson	1996
RBI						
1871–75	74	Andy Leonard	1875—NA			
	72	Jim O'Rourke	1875—NA			
	62	George Hall	1875—NA			
1876–92	166	Sam Thompson	1887	123	Tip O'Neill	1887
	128	Oyster Burns	1890	119	Harry Stovey	1889
	111	Sam Thompson	1889	118	Pete Browning	1887
Other:	146	Hardy Richardson	1890—PL			

	National League			American League		
	RECORD	NAME	YEAR	RECORD	NAME	YEAR
1893–1900	165	Sam Thompson	1895			
	146	Ed Delahanty	1893			
	145	Hugh Duffy	1894			
1901–19	128	Gavvy Cravath	1913	127	Ty Cobb	1911
	123	Sherry Magee	1910	121	Buck Freeman	1902
	121	Cy Seymour	1905	120	Sam Crawford	1910
1920–41	**191**	**Hack Wilson**	**1930**	171	Babe Ruth	1921
	170	Chuck Klein	1930	167	Joe DiMaggio	1937
	159	Hack Wilson	1929	165	Al Simmons	1930
1942–60	136	Duke Snider	1955	159	Ted Williams	1949
	132	Hank Aaron	1957	155	Joe DiMaggio	1948
	131	Stan Musial	1948	137	Ted Williams	1942
1961–76	153	Tommy Davis	1962	142	Roger Maris	1961
	141	Willie Mays	1962	140	Rocky Colavito	1961
	136	Frank Robinson	1962	128	Mickey Mantle	1961
1977–93	149	George Foster	1977	139	Jim Rice	1978
	137	Andre Dawson	1987	139	Don Baylor	1979
	130	Greg Luzinski	1977	134	George Bell	1987
1994–	158	Sammy Sosa	1998	157	Juan Gonzalez	1998
	141	Dante Bichette	1996	152	Albert Belle	1998
	130	Larry Walker	1997	148	Albert Belle	1996

Runs

	National League			American League		
1871–75	97	Jim O'Rourke	1875—NA			
	91	Cal McVey	1874—NA			
	87	Andy Leonard	1875—NA			
1876–92	155	King Kelly	1886	177	Tom Brown	1891
	150	George Gore	1886	167	Tip O'Neill	1887
	147	Mike Tiernan	1889	152	Mike Griffin	1889
				152	Harry Stovey	1889
1893–1900	**192**	**Billy Hamilton**	**1894**			
	166	Billy Hamilton	1895			
	165	Joe Kelley	1894			
1901–19	142	Jesse Burkett	1901	147	Ty Cobb	1911
	137	Ginger Beaumont	1903	144	Ty Cobb	1915
	126	Tommy Leach	1909	136	Tris Speaker	1912
1920–41	158	Chuck Klein	1930	177	Babe Ruth	1921
	155	Kiki Cuyler	1930	163	Babe Ruth	1928
	152	Lefty O'Doul	1929	158	Babe Ruth	1920/1927
	152	Chuck Klein	1929			
1942–60	135	Stan Musial	1948	150	Ted Williams	1949
	132	Duke Snider	1953	142	Ted Williams	1946
	131	Vada Pinson	1959	141	Ted Williams	1942

	National League				American League	
	RECORD	NAME	YEAR	RECORD	NAME	YEAR
1961–76	137	Billy Williams	1970	132	Mickey Mantle	1961
	134	Frank Robinson	1962	132	Roger Maris	1961
	134	Bobby Bonds	1970	129	Rocky Colavito	1961
1977–93	143	Lenny Dykstra	1993	146	Rickey Henderson	1985
	133	Tim Raines	1983	133	Willie Wilson	1980
	131	Dale Murphy	1983	130	Rickey Henderson	1986
1994–	143	Larry Walker	1997	132	Kenny Lofton	1996
	142	Ellis Burks	1996	125	Ken Griffey Jr.	1996
	134	Sammy Sosa	1998	125	Ken Griffey Jr.	1997

Walks

	National League				American League	
1871–75	13	Harry Wright	1871—NA			
	11	John McMullin	1872—NA			
	10	Ned Cuthbert	1871—NA			
	10	Harry Wright	1873—NA			
1876–92	102	George Gore	1886	118	Dummy Hoy	1891
	102	Billy Hamilton	1891	116	Jim McTamany	1889
	93	Tommy McCarthy	1892	112	Jim McTamany	1890
1893–1900	126	Billy Hamilton	1894			
	115	Roy Thomas	1899			
	115	Roy Thomas	1900			
1901–19	147	Jimmy Sheckard	1911	121	Topsy Hartsel	1905
	122	Jimmy Sheckard	1912	118	Burt Shotton	1915
	107	Roy Thomas	1902/1903/ 1906	118	Ty Cobb	1915
1920–41	113	Mel Ott	1929	**170**	**Babe Ruth**	**1923**
	111	Mel Ott	1936	148	Babe Ruth	1920
	105	Hack Wilson	1930	145	Ted Williams	1941
1942–60	137	Ralph Kiner	1951	162	Ted Williams	1947
	125	Richie Ashburn	1954	162	Ted Williams	1949
	122	Ralph Kiner	1950	156	Ted Williams	1946
1961–76	148	Jim Wynn	1969	132	Frank Howard	1970
	127	Jim Wynn	1976	128	Carl Yastrzemski	1970
	123	Ken Singleton	1973	126	Mickey Mantle	1961
1977–93	129	Lenny Dykstra	1993	132	Tony Phillips	1993
	127	Barry Bonds	1992	126	Rickey Henderson	1989
	126	Barry Bonds	1993	120	Rickey Henderson	1993
1994–	151	Barry Bonds	1996	125	Tony Phillips	1996
	145	Barry Bonds	1997	119	Jay Buhner	1997
	142	Gary Sheffield	1996	118	Rickey Henderson	1998

	National League				American League	
	RECORD	**NAME**	**YEAR**	**RECORD**	**NAME**	**YEAR**
OBP						
1871–75	.400	Steve King	1871—NA			
	.400	Lip Pike	1871—NA			
	.368	Lip Pike	1875—NA			
1876–92	.483	King Kelly	1886	.490	Tip O'Neill	1887
	.453	Billy Hamilton	1891	.464	Pete Browning	1887
	.447	Mike Tiernan	1889	.463	Bob Caruthers	1887
1893–1900	.523	Billy Hamilton	1894			
	.502	Joe Kelley	1894			
	.502	Hugh Duffy	1894			
1901–19	.453	Roy Thomas	1903	.486	Ty Cobb	1915
	.445	Sherry Magee	1910	.468	Joe Jackson	1911
	.440	Jesse Burkett	1901	.467	Ty Cobb	1913
1920–41	.465	Lefty O'Doul	1929	**.551**	**Ted Williams**	**1941**
	.458	Mel Ott	1930	.545	Babe Ruth	1923
	.455	Babe Herman	1930	.530	Babe Ruth	1920
1942–60	.456	Joe Cunningham	1959	.528	Ted Williams	1957
	.452	Ralph Kiner	1951	.516	Ted Williams	1954
	.450	Stan Musial	1948	.515	Mickey Mantle	1957
1961–76	.456	Rico Carty	1970	.488	Mickey Mantle	1962
	.440	Jim Wynn	1969	.453	Carl Yastrzemski	1970
	.438	Wally Moon	1961	.452	Mickey Mantle	1961
1977–93	.463	Barry Bonds	1993	.446	Tony Phillips	1993
	.461	Barry Bonds	1992	.441	Rickey Henderson	1990
	.436	Jeff Burroughs	1978	.435	Rickey Henderson	1993
1994–	.469	Gary Sheffield	1996	.464	Paul O'Neill	1994
	.465	Barry Bonds	1996	.442	Albert Belle	1994
	.458	Tony Gwynn	1994	.432	Tim Salmon	1995
Stolen Bases						
1871–75	25	Lip Pike	1875—NA			
	18	Ned Cuthbert	1875—NA			
	18	Dave Eggler	1872—NA			
1876–92	111	Billy Hamilton	1891	**138**	**Hugh Nicol**	**1887**
	102	Billy Hamilton	1890	111	Billy Hamilton	1889
	102	Jim Fogarty	1887	106	Tom Brown	1891
1893–1900	98	Billy Hamilton	1894			
	97	Billy Hamilton	1895			
	87	Joe Kelley	1896			
1901–19	81	Bob Bescher	1911	96	Ty Cobb	1915
	70	Bob Bescher	1910	88	Clyde Milan	1912
	67	Jimmy Sheckard	1903	83	Ty Cobb	1911
	67	Bob Bescher	1912			

	National League				American League		
	RECORD	**NAME**	**YEAR**	**RECORD**	**NAME**	**YEAR**
1920–41	52	Max Carey	1920	63	Sam Rice	1920
	51	Max Carey	1922	61	Ben Chapman	1931
	51	Max Carey	1923	51	George Case	1939
1942–60	40	Willie Mays	1956	61	George Case	1943
	38	Willie Mays	1957	56	Wally Moses	1943
	35	Sam Jethroe	1950/1951	49	George Case	1944
1961–76	118	Lou Brock	1974	75	Billy North	1976
	74	Lou Brock	1966	70	Mickey Rivers	1975
	70	Lou Brock	1973	58	Ron LeFlore	1976
1977–93	110	Vince Coleman	1985	130	Rickey Henderson	1982
	109	Vince Coleman	1987	108	Rickey Henderson	1983
	107	Vince Coleman	1986	100	Rickey Henderson	1980
1994–	56	Deion Sanders	1997	75	Kenny Lofton	1996
	50	Lance Johnson	1996	74	Brian Hunter	1997
	40	Barry Bonds	1996	66	Tom Goodwin	1996
				66	Rickey Henderson	1998

Note: In the 1876–92 era, men who appear under the American League column are the American Association record holders. Players who performed at more than one position in their record season are considered the record holders at the position where they played the most games. All-time leaders are in **bold**. Since there are three outfield positions, the top three outfield performances for each era are recognized.

Regal Receivers

1. Catchers in the game's early days wore only rudimentary protective gear. Consequently, the job was so grueling that for years virtually the only backstoppers who played more than half their team's games were men like Buck Ewing and Fred Carroll whose bat skills forced managers to use them elsewhere on days when their hands were too sore to catch. The first receiver to catch 100 games in a season received shamefully little acclaim at the time for his feat. He's also noted for being the only man to catch a game in the National Association and still be catching in the majors as late as 1890. Who is he?

2. The first catcher to lead his team in at bats after 1884, the initial season in which the schedule was lengthened to as many as 100 games, was also the last man for nearly half a century to perform this rare feat. Name this early-day regal receiver.

3. The first receiver to collect as many as 500 at bats in a season is in the Hall of Fame but not for his work as a player. Who is he?

4. The first man to catch 100 games in a season for a National League team is also the only man to catch for two flag winners after celebrating his 40th birthday. Name him.

First 10 Men to Catch 100 Games in a Season

RANK	NAME	TEAM	YEAR	G/C
1	Doc Bushong	StL, AA	1886	106
2	Chief Zimmer	Cle, NL	1890	125
	Connie Mack	Buf, PL	1890	112
	Jack O'Connor	Col, AA	1890	106
5	Jack Clements	Phi, NL	1891	107
	Morgan Murphy	Bos, AA	1891	104
7	Dick Buckley	StL, NL	1892	119
8	Wilbert Robinson	Bal, NL	1894	109
	Duke Farrell	NY, NL	1894	104
	Deacon McGuire	Was, NL	1894	104

Note: Several on the list caught 100 games on more than one occasion; the year listed is the first they did it.

5. The first man to catch 100 games in a season in two different major leagues did it in the 20th century but never played in the AL. Who is he?

6. In 1998, Darrin Fletcher of Toronto became the 20th man to catch 100 games in a season in both the NL and the AL. The first man to match Fletcher's feat caught both Jesse Haines and Bill Doak after previously catching Walter Johnson for many years. Who is he?

Players Who Caught 100 Games in a Season in Both the NL and AL

RANK	NAME	1ST 100-G SEASON	2ND 100-G SEASON
1	Eddie Ainsmith	Was, AL 1917	StL, NL 1922
2	Phil Masi	Bos, NL 1946	Chi, AL 1950
3	Jim Pagliaroni	Bos, AL 1961	Pit, NL 1965
4	Johnny Roseboro	LA, NL 1958	Min, AL 1968
5	Mike Ryan	Bos, AL 1966	Phi, NL 1969
6	Fred Kendall	SD, NL 1973	Cle, AL 1977
	Milt May	Hou, NL 1974	Det, AL 1977
	George Mitterwald	Min, AL 1970	Chi, NL 1977
9	Alan Ashby	Tor, AL 1977	Hou, NL 1979
10	Gene Tenace	Oak, AL 1975	SD, NL 1980
11	Ted Simmons	StL, NL 1971	Mil, AL 1982
	Darrell Porter	Mil, AL 1974	StL, NL 1982
	Bob Boone	Phi, NL 1973	Cal, AL 1982
14	Lance Parrish	Det, AL 1979	Phi, NL 1987
	Terry Kennedy	SD, NL 1981	Bal, AL 1987
16	Tony Pena	Pit, NL 1982	Bos, AL 1990
17	Don Slaught	KC, AL 1984	Pit, NL 1993
18	Joe Girardi	Chi, NL 1990	NY, AL 1996
19	John Flaherty	Det, AL 1995	SD, NL 1997
20	Darrin Fletcher	Mon, NL 1993	Tor, AL 1998

Note: Mike Matheny technically qualifies as the 21st member of the list but is excluded for the moment because his two 100-game seasons—1997 and 1998—came with the same team, Milwaukee, albeit in two different leagues owing to the fact that the Brewers switched from the AL to the NL prior to the 1998 season.

7. The first man to hit .300 and catch 100 games in the same season played his last game in the majors 20 years after his regal-receiver first. Name him.

8. The first catcher to lead his team in at bats in the 20th century also led it in homers (13) and RBI (78) that year despite hitting just .248. Who is he?

9. The only regal receiver in the past 100 years to lead his team in at bats more than once also led his club in homers, RBI, and fewest batter strikeouts the first year he performed this rare feat. Name him.

10. The first flag winner to use a rookie as its regular catcher actually had two rookie receivers. In addition, it was the first flag winner to employ a lefty receiver in more than 50 games. What team achieved these unusual multiple firsts and who were the receivers (both of whom shared the same initials)?

11. Who is the only regal receiver to work 1,000 games behind the dish, post a .300+ career batting average, and fail to make the Hall of Fame?

    A)   His 1,312th and last big league hit came with the 1945 Pirates.

    B)   Although he had a .308 career BA, he scored only 388 runs in 4,255 ABs.

    C)   In 1931 he hit .326 for the Phils in 120 games but scored just 30 runs.

    D)   He and the 1943 AL MVP had the same nickname.

    E)   He and the Cubs catcher in the Bruins' first postseason game since 1945 share the same last name.

Spud Davis owns the highest career BA of any catcher not in the Hall of Fame. One reason he's been kept waiting is that he also owns the lowest ratio of runs scored per hit (.296) of any performer eligible for the Hall of Fame who posted a .300 career BA.

Highest Career BA, Catcher

RANK	NAME	YEARS	GAMES	BA
1	Mickey Cochrane	1925–37	1451	.320
2	Bill Dickey	1928–46	1708	.313
3	Spud Davis	1928–45	1282	.308
4	Ernie Lombardi	1931–47	1544	.306
5	Joe Torre	1960–77	903	.2974
6	Gabby Hartnett	1922–41	1793	.2973
7	Manny Sanguillen	1967–80	1114	.296
8	Shanty Hogan	1925–37	908	.295
9	Thurman Munson	1969–79	1278	.292
10	Chief Meyers	1909–17	911	.291

Note: Retired players only; 800 games as catcher. The 800-game minimum eliminated three 1920s catchers: Bubbles Hargrave, Earl Smith, and Johnny Bassler. BAs are carried out to four decimal points where ties would otherwise exist.

12. Behind the dish in only 492 games in the majors and the owner of a .208 career batting average, he was nevertheless the first to catch 2,000 professional games.

    A) He caught Walter Johnson and also a ball thrown from the Washington Monument.

    B) He caught his first game in the majors in 1904 and his last in 1931.

    C) He managed the 1931 world champs.

    D) He had the same nickname as a Hall of Fame catcher who opposed his world champs in regular-season play in 1931.

    E) The abbreviation for his last name is on signs marking many roads.

13. What receiver caught more of Walter Johnson's record 110 career shutouts than any other backstopper?

    A) He was 18 when he caught his first ML game in 1910.

    B) With the Cards in 1922, he collected 13 of his 22 career home runs.

    C) Patsy Gharrity replaced him as Johnson's pet catcher in 1919.

    D) He has the same first name and initials as the last pitcher to win 30 games in a season split between the minors and the majors.

    E) He and the first Italian player in ML history have the same initials.

14. What regal receiver as a rookie shared playing time with Moses Walker and in his last ML game caught a divinity student named Al Travers?

    A) In his final contest in 1898, he became the third man to catch 1,000 ML games.

    B) In 1895 his 179 hits set a 19th century record for catchers.

    C) He was the first man to catch 100 games in the bigs after age 40.

    D) He caught at least one game in a record 25 seasons.

    E) His abstemious habits and gentlemanly demeanor accounted for his nickname.

First 10 Players to Catch 1,000 ML Games

RANK	NAME	YEARS	G/C	1000TH
1	Jack Clements	1884–1900	1073	1898
2	Wilbert Robinson	1886–1902	1316	1898
3	Deacon McGuire	1884–1912	1611	1898
4	Chief Zimmer	1884–1903	1239	1899
5	Mal Kittridge	1890–1906	1196	1903
6	Duke Farrell	1888–1905	1003	1905
7	Jack Warner	1895–1908	1032	1908
8	Billy Sullivan	1899–1916	1121	1910
9	Johnny Kling	1900–13	1168	1911
10	Red Dooin	1902–16	1195	1912

15. Who was the last catcher prior to Mike Piazza to hit .300 three years in a row with enough plate appearances to qualify for a batting title?

    A) He played on six division winners in the same city.

    B) In his only AL season, he hit .275 in 152 games at age 33.

    C) He was a member of "The Family."

    D) His .296 career BA is the best of any retired post–World War II catcher.

    E) He and the BoSox top catcher in 1996 share the same initials.

16. **What regal receiver kept both Bill Dickey and Mickey Cochrane on the bench when he went all nine behind the plate for the AL in the first All-Star Game?**
    A) He was never on a pennant winner.
    B) He broke in with the Browns in 1929 and was dealt to the Red Sox in 1933.
    C) He and his brother teamed up in 1934 to form a sibling battery in the majors.
    D) He caught in 1,805 AL games, a record when he retired.
    E) He made the Hall of Fame in 1984, but his brother, who many think is more deserving, still has no Cooperstown plaque.

17. **The first catcher in history to hit .300 four years in a row (100 or more games) played in six World Series. Who is he?**
    A) Despite his .284 career BA in 1,840 games, he never made the Hall of Fame.
    B) He had a brother who also caught in the majors.
    C) He saw Series action with the A's, the Red Sox, and the Yankees.
    D) He alone played on both of Connie Mack's A's dynasties.
    E) He was the first switch-hitter to homer from both sides in the same game.

Catchers Hitting .300 for Four or More Consecutive Seasons

RANK	NAME	SPAN	TOTAL
1	Bill Dickey	1929–34	6
	Spud Davis	1930–35	6
	Mike Piazza	1993–98	6
4	Ernie Lombardi	1934–38	5
5	Wally Schang	1919–22	4
	Hank Severeid	1921–24	4
	Shanty Hogan	1928–31	4
	Ivan Rodriguez	1995–98	4

Note: Minimum 100 games each season.

18. **With whom is Roy Campanella tied for the distinction of being the first NL catcher to hit 20 homers two years in a row?**
    A) Surprisingly, Gabby Hartnett never hit 20 two years in a row.
    B) Not Walker Cooper—he never did it, either.
    C) He and Campy had their back-to-back 20-homer years in 1949 and 1950.
    D) He and Robin Roberts were batterymates in 1950.
    E) He has the record for the most career homers by a catcher who bears the same first name as the only backstopper to date whose surname was Etchebarren.

19. **Only five times in history has a catcher led a loop in walks; one of the five topped the NL with 125 free passes despite collecting just 437 at bats. Who is he?**
    A) Two years earlier, despite hitting just .211, he became the first catcher ever to lead the AL in walks.
    B) The 1971 season was the last in which he saw no action at first base.
    C) His first name at birth was Fiore, but it was changed to Fury.
    D) In his first World Series, he hit .348 and was voted the MVP after batting just .059 in the ALCS that year.
    E) He was in three World Series with Oakland and one with the Cards.

Catchers Leading League in Walks

NAME	TEAM	YEAR	WALKS
John Clapp	Cle, NL	1881	35
Roger Bresnahan	NY, NL	1908	83
Gene Tenace	SD, NL	1977	125
Darrell Porter	KC, AL	1979	121

20. Mickey Cochrane hit .357 in 1930 to set a new AL mark for the highest batting average by a catcher in enough games to be a bat title qualifier. Who formerly held the junior-loop record?

A) He set the old mark of .346 in the same season that Glenn Myatt hit .342 as Cleveland's regular catcher.

B) He caught his first ML game in 1913 but didn't win a regular job until 1921.

C) In 2,319 ABs, mostly with Detroit, he hit just one homer.

D) The same year he hit a record .346, he was the last batter Charlie Robertson faced in his perfect game.

E) He and the author of *Ball Four* share the same initials.

21. Gabby Hartnett was the first catcher to tag 100 career homers as well as the first to crack 200. Bill Dickey was the first backstopper to attain 200 dingers in the AL. Who was the first righty-hitting catcher to rap 200 homers in the AL?

A) All his blasts came with the same team.

B) He hit .300 with 80 RBI in 1964.

C) Among catchers in more than 1,500 games, he has the highest career FA.

D) Carlton Fisk and another backstopper who played mostly with his old team have since broken his record for the most homers by a righty-hitting AL receiver.

E) He has the same initials as the Cubs' regular catcher in 1979.

First 10 Catchers to Attain 100 Career HRs

RANK	NAME	YEARS	HRS	100TH
1	Gabby Hartnett	1922–41	236	1930
2	Mickey Cochrane	1925–37	119	1933
3	Bill Dickey	1928–46	202	1937
4	Ernie Lombardi	1931–47	190	1939
5	Frankie Hayes	1933–47	119	1944
6	Walker Cooper	1940–57	173	1949
7	Yogi Berra	1946–65	358	1951
	Andy Seminick	1943–57	164	1951
9	Roy Campanella	1948–57	242	1952
10	Del Crandall	1949–66	179	1957

22. **What regal receiver caught every inning of every game for the winner of a six-game World Series without ever reaching base safely?**

    A) His sole offensive contribution was a sacrifice bunt in Game Three.

    B) He was 0-for-21 in the World Series, but so was the left fielder on the losing team that year.

    C) His team lost 1–0 in Game Four when it got only two hits off Three Finger Brown.

    D) He and his son, who also caught in the majors, were the first father and son to appear in a 20th century World Series.

    E) His .213 career BA is the lowest of any man who played 1,000 games in the majors and had 3,000 plate appearances.

World Series 0-Fors

NAME	TEAM	YEAR	ABS
Dal Maxvill	StL, NL	1968	22
Billy Sullivan	Chi, AL	1906	21
Jimmy Sheckard	Chi, NL	1906	21
Red Murray	NY, NL	1911	21
Gil Hodges	Bro, NL	1952	21
Lonnie Frey	Cin, NL	1939	17
Flea Clifton	Det, AL	1935	16
Mike Epstein	Oak, AL	1972	16
Rafael Belliard	Atl, NL	1995	16
Bill Dahlen	NY, NL	1905	15
Wally Berger	Cin, NL	1939	15

Note: Minimum 15 ABs; ranked in order of ABs.

23. **Carlton Fisk not only donned the tools of the trade in a record 2,229 games, but he also caught at least one game in 24 seasons. Fisk didn't play in the majors in 1970, however, after working his first game behind the plate in 1969. The interruption prevented him from tying what backstopper's record of catching at least one game in 24 consecutive seasons?**

    A) He and Fisk are the only two men to catch at least one game in four different decades in the 20th century.

    B) In 1986 he had 13 homers but just 29 RBI in 327 ABs.

    C) He was 39 in 1988 when he appeared in his last postseason game.

    D) He was Baltimore's regular backstopper the most recent year the O's won a World Championship.

    E) He and "The Tunney Long Count" victim share the same last name.

24. **In 1997, Mike Piazza became only the second catcher in history to post a combined batting average and slugging average of 1.000 or better with at least 100 hits when he batted .362 and slugged .638 for 1.000 on the nose. The first to crack the 1.000 mark was the greatest left-handed catcher ever, Jack Clements, in 1895. Whose .989 combined BA and SA stood as the season record prior to 1997 among righty-hitting receivers who collected at least 100 hits?**

    A) He holds an era record for the highest SA by a catcher in at least 400 ABs.

    B) Prior to 1930 he owned the season record for the most doubles by a catcher.

    C) In his lone appearance in a 19th century World Series, he opposed a Hall of Famer who held the season record for the most homers by a catcher until he broke it a year later.

    D) Born and buried in Philadelphia, he debuted with the AA Athletics in 1884.

    E) His super season—.366 BA and .623 SA—came with the 1889 St. Louis Browns.

Season Record Holders Among Catchers for Each Era

	National League				American League		
	RECORD	NAME	YEAR		RECORD	NAME	YEAR
At Bats							
1871–75	371	Deacon White	1875—NA				
1876–92	444	Chief Zimmer	1890		457	Jack O'Connor	1890
Other:	503	Connie Mack	1890—PL				
1893–1900	533	Deacon McGuire	1895		446	Marty Bergen	1898
1901–19	510	George Gibson	1909		503	Oscar Stanage	1911
1920–41	524	Harry Danning	1940		530	Bill Dickey	1937
1942–60	555	Ray Mueller	1944		597	Yogi Berra	1950
1961–76	619	Ted Simmons	1973		616	Thurman Munson	1976
1977–93	596	Gary Carter	1984		617	Thurman Munson	1978
1994–	560	Mike Piazza	1998		**638**	**Ivan Rodriguez**	**1996**
Batting Average (280 ABs Prior to 1892; 400 ABs Since)							
1871–75	.431	Cal McVey	1871—NA				
1876–92	.343	Deacon White	1876		.324	Jack O'Connor	1890
1893–1900	.353	Wilbert Robinson	1894		.336	Deacon McGuire	1895
1901–19	.298	Frank Snyder	1915		.280	Boileryard Clarke	1901
	.298	Larry McLean	1910				
Other:	.335	Ted Easterly	1914—FL				
1920–41	.349	Spud Davis	1933		**.362**	**Bill Dickey**	**1936**
1942–60	.318	Walker Cooper	1943		.322	Yogi Berra	1950
	.318	Roy Campanella	1955				
1961–76	.332	Ted Simmons	1975		.348	Elston Howard	1961
1977–93	.318	Mike Piazza	1993		.326	Brian Downing	1979
1994–	**.362**	**Mike Piazza**	**1997**		.324	Sandy Alomar	1997
Slugging Average (280 ABs Prior to 1892; 400 ABs Since)							
1871–75	.556	Cal McVey	1871—NA				
1876–92	.480	King Kelly	1888		.505	Jocko Milligan	1891
Other:	.545	Buck Ewing	1890—PL				
1893–1900	.478	Deacon McGuire	1895		.449	John Grim	1894
1901–19	.428	Johnny Kling	1903		.360	Boileryard Clarke	1901
Other:	.466	Art Wilson	1914—FL				
1920–41	.630	Gabby Hartnett	1930		.617	Bill Dickey	1936
1942–60	.611	Roy Campanella	1953		.534	Yogi Berra	1956
1961–76	.587	Johnny Bench	1970		.549	Elston Howard	1961
1977–93	.561	Mike Piazza	1993		.585	Chris Hoiles	1993
	.561	Rich Wilkins	1993				
1994–	**.638**	**Mike Piazza**	**1997**		.545	Sandy Alomar	1997

	National League				American League	
	RECORD	**NAME**	**YEAR**	**RECORD**	**NAME**	**YEAR**
Hits *(Minimum 100 Games as Catcher After 1892)*						
1871–75	136	Deacon White	1875—NA			
1876–92	133	Buck Ewing	1889	148	Jack O'Connor	1890
Other:	134	Connie Mack	1890—PL			
1893–1900	179	Deacon McGuire	1895	146	Wilbert Robinson	1894
1901–19	146	Johnny Kling	1903	133	Oscar Stanage	1911
Other:	146	Ted Easterly	1914—FL	133	Hank Severeid	1917
1920–41	173	Spud Davis	1933	176	Bill Dickey	1937
1942–60	164	Roy Campanella	1951	192	Yogi Berra	1950
1961–76	193	Ted Simmons	1975	190	Thurman Munson	1975
1977–93	175	Gary Carter	1984	183	Thurman Munson	1977
				183	Thurman Munson	1978
1994–	**201**	**Mike Piazza**	**1997**	192	Ivan Rodriguez	1996
Total Bases *(Minimum 100 Games as Catcher After 1920)*						
1871–75	168	Deacon White	1875—NA			
1876–92	194	Buck Ewing	1889	230	Jocko Milligan	1891
1893–1900	255	Deacon McGuire	1895	184	John Grim	1894
1901–19	207	Johnny Kling	1903	170	Steve O'Neill	1919
Other:	207	Art Wilson	1914—FL			
1920–41	320	Gabby Hartnett	1930	302	Bill Dickey	1937
1942–60	317	Roy Campanella	1953	318	Yogi Berra	1950
1961–76	**355**	**Johnny Bench**	**1970**	266	Thurman Munson	1976
1977–93	307	Mike Piazza	1993	292	Lance Parrish	1983
1994–	**355**	**Mike Piazza**	**1997**	332	Ivan Rodriguez	1996
Doubles *(Minimum 100 Games as Catcher After 1920)*						
1871–75	23	Deacon White	1875—NA			
1876–92	34	Charlie Bennett	1883	35	Jocko Milligan	1891
1893–1900	30	Deacon McGuire	1895	27	John Grim	1894
1901–19	29	Johnny Kling	1903	35	Steve O'Neill	1919
Other:	31	Art Wilson	1914—FL			
1920–41	37	Babe Phelps	1937	42	Mickey Cochrane	1930
1942–60	33	Roy Campanella	1951	30	Yogi Berra	1950
	33	Stan Lopata	1956			
1961–76	40	Johnny Bench	1968	34	Buck Rodgers	1962
1977–93	42	Terry Kennedy	1982	42	Lance Parrish	1983
1994–	38	Mike Piazza	1998	**47**	**Ivan Rodriguez**	**1996**

	National League			American League	
RECORD	**NAME**	**YEAR**	**RECORD**	**NAME**	**YEAR**

Triples (Minimum 100 Games as Catcher After 1920)

Period	RECORD	NAME	YEAR	RECORD	NAME	YEAR
1871–75	7	Deacon White	1874—NA			
1876–92	**20**	**Buck Ewing**	**1884**	10	Jack O'Connor	1890
1893–1900	13	Duke Farrell	1893	12	Duke Farrell	1894
1901–19	13	Johnny Kling	1902	9	Ray Schalk	1916
Other:	12	Ted Easterly	1914—FL			
1920–41	9	Gabby Hartnett	1928	12	Mickey Cochrane	1928
1942–60	8	Walker Cooper	1947	10	Yogi Berra	1948
	8	Bruce Edwards	1947			
1961–76	13	Tim McCarver	1966	9	Carlton Fisk	1972
1977–93	6	Benito Santiago	1993	10	Darrell Porter	1979
1994–	8	Joe Girardi	1995	4	Ivan Rodriguez	1997/1998
				4	Joe Girardi	1998

Home Runs (Minimum 100 Games as Catcher After 1920)

Period	RECORD	NAME	YEAR	RECORD	NAME	YEAR
1871–75	3	Deacon White	1873—NA			
1876–92	10	Buck Ewing	1883	12	Jocko Milligan	1889
1893–1900	17	Jack Clements	1893	13	Jack Clements	1895
1901–19	7	Pat Moran	1903	6	Boileryard Clarke	1902
Other:	10	Art Wilson	1914—FL			
1920–41	37	Gabby Hartnett	1930	29	Bill Dickey	1937
1942–60	41	Roy Campanella	1953	30	Yogi Berra	1952
				30	Yogi Berra	1956
				30	Gus Triandos	1958
1961–76	45	Johnny Bench	1970*	28	Elston Howard	1963
1977–93	35	Mike Piazza	1993	37	Carlton Fisk	1985
1994–	**42**	**Todd Hundley**	**1996**	35	Terry Steinbach	1996

* Bench hit home runs at other positions, so Hundley is regarded as the record holder.

RBI (Minimum 100 Games as Catcher After 1920)

Period	RECORD	NAME	YEAR	RECORD	NAME	YEAR
1871–75	66	Deacon White	1873—NA			
1876–92	87	Buck Ewing	1889	106	Jocko Milligan	1891
1893–1900	100	Farmer Vaughn	1893	98	Wilbert Robinson	1894
1901–19	71	Larry McLean	1910	57	Wilbert Robinson	1902
Other:	67	Ted Easterly	1914—FL	57	Hank Severeid	1917
1920–41	122	Gabby Hartnett	1930	133	Bill Dickey	1937
1942–60	142	Roy Campanella	1953	125	Yogi Berra	1954
1961–76	**148**	**Johnny Bench**	**1970**	105	Thurman Munson	1976
1977–93	112	Mike Piazza	1993	114	Lance Parrish	1983
1994–	124	Mike Piazza	1997	100	Terry Steinbach	1996

	National League				American League	
RECORD	**NAME**	**YEAR**	**RECORD**	**NAME**	**YEAR**

Runs *(Minimum 100 Games as Catcher After 1920)*

1871–75	79	Deacon White	1873—NA			
1876–92	91	Buck Ewing	1889	92	Fred Carroll	1886
Other:	98	Buck Ewing	1890—PL			
1893–1900	89	Deacon McGuire	1895	81	Lave Cross	1893
1901–19	70	Roger Bresnahan	1908	58	Boileryard Clarke	1901
Other:	78	Art Wilson	1914—FL			
1920–41	84	Gabby Hartnett	1930	**118**	**Mickey Cochrane**	**1932**
1942–60	103	Roy Campanella	1953	116	Yogi Berra	1950
1961–76	108	Johnny Bench	1974	83	Thurman Munson	1975
				83	Gene Tenace	1975
1977–93	91	Gary Carter	1982	106	Carlton Fisk	1977
1994–	104	Mike Piazza	1997	116	Ivan Rodriguez	1996

Walks *(Minimum 100 Games as Catcher After 1920)*

1871–75	14	Fergy Malone	1873—NA			
1876–92	85	Fred Carroll	1889*	38	Jack O'Connor	1890
1893–1900	52	Klondike Douglass	1897	46	Wilbert Robinson	1894
1901–19	83	Roger Bresnahan	1908	62	Ray Schalk	1915
1920–41	79	Bob O'Farrell	1922	106	Mickey Cochrane	1933
1942–60	104	Wes Westrum	1950	75	Aaron Robinson	1950
1961–76	109	Dick Dietz	1970	106	Gene Tenace	1975
1977–93	125	Gene Tenace	1977	**121**	**Darrell Porter**	**1979****
1994–	83	Todd Hundley	1997	69	Mike Stanley	1996

* Carroll played only 43 games at catcher, less than half his total of 91 games.

** Porter is considered the record holder because Tenace also played other positions in 1977.

OBP *(Minimum 100 Games as Catcher After 1920)*

1871–75	.435	Cal McVey	1871—NA			
1876–92	.486	Fred Carroll	1889*	.397	Jocko Milligan	1891
1893–1900	.421	Wilbert Robinson	1894	.403	Klondike Douglass	1897
1901–19	.441	Chief Meyers	1912	.366	Ray Schalk	1915
1920–41	.439	Bob O'Farrell	1922	**.459**	**Mickey Cochrane**	**1933**
1942–60	.402	Roy Campanella	1955	.391	Sherm Lollar	1950
1961–76	.430	Dick Dietz	1970	.398	Gene Tenace	1975
1977–93	.410	Ted Simmons	1977	.429	Darrell Porter	1979
1994–	.431	Mike Piazza	1997	.384	Mike Stanley	1996

* Carroll played only 43 games at catcher, less than half his total of 91 games.

	National League				American League	
	RECORD	**NAME**	**YEAR**	**RECORD**	**NAME**	**YEAR**
Stolen Bases *(Minimum 100 Games as Catcher After 1920)*						
1871–75	20	Mike McGeary	1871—NA			
1876–92	**53**	**Buck Ewing**	**1888**	33	Wilbert Robinson	1886
1893–1900	40	Jack Doyle	1893*	20	Mike Grady	1898/1899*
1901–19	23	Johnny Kling	1902/1903	30	Ray Schalk	1916
1920–41	13	Jimmie Wilson	1927	16	Frankie Pytlak	1937
1942–60	11	Johnny Roseboro	1958	10	Red Wilson	1958
1961–76	13	Johnny Bench	1976	14	Thurman Munson	1976
1977–93	25	John Stearns	1978	36	John Wathan	1982
1994–	26	Jason Kendall	1998	9	Ivan Rodriguez	1998

* Doyle was a catcher in only 48 of the 82 games he played in 1893; Grady also caught only about half the time in 1898 and 1899.

Note: In the 1876–92 era, men who appear under the American League column are the American Association record holders. In the 1893–1900 era, men who appear under the American League column are the runners-up to the National League record holders. Players who performed at more than one position in their record season are considered the record holders at the position where they played the most games. All-time leaders among catchers are in **bold**.

Versatile Virtuosos

1. **In 1879, Mike Dorgan of Syracuse, an outfielder by trade, also played every infield position and both caught and pitched. Because all of Dorgan's gardening occurred in right field, he failed to become the first ML'er to play all nine positions in the same season. That distinction thereupon fell to a turn-of-the-century virtuoso who got into 100 games for the only time in his career the year he performed his famous first. Name him.**

   A) Between 1896 and 1903, he played 418 games in the bigs, 147 in the outfield.
   B) He finished with the 1903 Tigers as a backup shortstop-catcher.
   C) He debuted with Cleveland in 1896 and was 3–4 as a pitcher in 1898.
   D) His ultimate jack-of-all-trades season came with the worst team of all time.
   E) His 1899 Spiders teammates called him "Sport."

2. **Hal Jeffcoat (1948–59) is the most recent player to qualify for both an ERA crown and a batting title during the course of his career. Can you name the only four big league performers who hurled 500 innings in a season and collected 500 at bats in another season?**

   A) Only one of the four is in the Hall of Fame.
   B) All four did it before 1900, but three were still active in the mid-1890s.
   C) Only one of the four logged a 500-inning season for an AA team.
   D) The only man gone by the mid-1890s owns the season record for losses.
   E) The last man to do it later managed an infamous AL flag winner.

Pitched 500 Innings and Compiled 500 ABs in a Season

NAME	500 IP	500 ABS
Monte Ward	1879	1887
John Coleman	1883	1886
Dave Foutz	1886	1888
Kid Gleason	1890	1896

Pitched 400 Innings and Compiled 400 ABs in a Season

NAME	400 IP	400 ABS
Jim Whitney	1881	1883
Elmer Smith	1887	1892

Note: Seasons listed are the first in which the player logged the requisite IP or ABs; several did it more than one time.

3. **Stationed at third base in his big league debut in 1965, he dropped a routine pop fly in the ninth inning that nearly cost the Twins their season opener against the defending-champion Yankees. Banished to the minors a few days later, he missed playing on the first Minnesota flag winner. But he returned the following year as a middle infielder and spent a decade as a regular at one time or another at almost every position except catcher and pitcher without ever again getting a whiff of a World Series cut. Whose career are we describing?**
   A) In 1968 he pulled off the quintessential jack-of-all-trades stunt when he played every position for the Twins.
   B) In 1967 he garnered the only first-place MVP vote that did not go to Yaz.
   C) His 1972 season with the Twins was the only one when he occupied the same post all year—the outfield.
   D) In 1975, after DH'ing for most of the season, he played 2B for the A's in his last LCS appearance.
   E) He and the AL leader in hits the year Ted Williams topped the .400 barrier share the same initials.

4. **What Hall of Famer debuted as a second sacker in 1888, fielded .830 as a shortstop for a Players League entry nicknamed the Infants, won two batting titles as an outfielder, and played first base all of the 1900 season?**
   A) He was born in the city he called home in the Players League.
   B) His .346 career BA was the highest in history when he played his last game.
   C) He has the highest career BA of any player eligible for the Hall of Fame who died while still active.
   D) Like him, all four of his brothers who also played in the majors were born in Cleveland.
   E) He was the first right-handed hitter to compile three .400 seasons.

5. **Who played the hot corner for the first Buffalo big league entry, was at second base for the first Detroit team to play in a World Series (19th century), and manned left field for the one and only Players League champ?**
   A) His forename was Abram, but he went by a nickname short for his middle name.
   B) His primary position was second base, as was the primary position of a New York Giants performer in the same era with the same last name.
   C) He led the PL in RBI.
   D) He was one of Buffalo's famous "Big Four."
   E) They called him "Old True Blue."

6. **Name the only man to play on three world champs at three different positions.**
   A) The three world champs all represented the same franchise.
   B) He was a member of five world champs altogether.
   C) In 1960, his finale, he returned to third base, his original post.
   D) He was the first player from his team to be selected Rookie of the Year.
   E) He played short for the team that lost Game Seven in a World Series to Johnny Podres and second for the team that lost Game Seven in a Series to Lew Burdette.

7. **The first man in the 20th century to win a loop home run crown in a season when he caught at least 25 games started the All-Star Game at third base the year he did it. Who is he?**
   A) He played 121 games that season at yet another position.
   B) The following year, he hit 41 homers for another AL team that gave him his largest dose of outfield duty.
   C) He had a 1.52 ERA and a perfect 1–0 record in 10 big league mound outings.
   D) He played on the 1929 world champs.
   E) His normal spot was 1B, where he saw duty during his two 50-homer seasons.

8. **Who played mainly first base in his first full ML season, was mainly an outfielder two years later when he won his first batting title, and played every inning of the two World Series in which he participated at yet a third position?**
    A) In 1899 he played 75 games at 3B, 61 in the outfield, 7 at 2B, and 4 at 1B.
    B) His primary position was none of the positions he played in 1899.
    C) The only position he never played was catcher.
    D) He is a member of the 3,000-hit club.
    E) Most authorities consider him the best shortstop ever.

9. **Who is the only man to play every game of a seven-game World Series at a position he'd never played in the majors until just a few days before the fall classic?**
    A) During the regular season that year, he played 130 games in the outfield and 15 at 1B but didn't play either position in the World Series.
    B) During 1971–73, all 435 games he played in the field were as a gardener.
    C) His entire 15-year ML career was spent with Detroit.
    D) He was the Tigers' World Series shortstop the year they rallied from a 3–1 deficit in games to cop the big prize.
    E) He and the Red Sox regular backstopper in 1996 share the same initials and the same last name.

10. **He hit .332 as a rookie third baseman; four years later, he batted .317 while playing mostly at second base; at yet a third position—first base—he was a league leader at various times during his 18-year Hall of Fame career in batting, home runs, and RBI. Who is he?**
    A) His brother Joe also played in the majors.
    B) He played in two 19th century World Series.
    C) He's the only lefty thrower to be a regular at three different positions, none of which was an outfield post.
    D) He played with several teams but is best remembered with the New York Giants.
    E) Babe Ruth broke his record for the most career home runs (138) in 1921.

Evolution of Career HR Record

NAME	YEARS	HRS	RECORD	TOTAL
Levi Meyerle	1871–84	10	1871	4
Fred Treacey	1871–76	7	1871	4
Lip Pike	1871–87	20	1872	7
Charley Jones	1876–88	56	1880	21
Harry Stovey	1880–93	122	1885	50
Roger Connor	1880–97	138	1894	123
Babe Ruth	1914–35	714	1921	139
Hank Aaron	1954–76	755	1974	715

Note: Since 1876. Record denotes the year each man became the new record holder; total denotes the number the new record holder needed to break the old mark. Pike, Treacey, and Meyerle tied for the 1871 NA home run crown and began the 1872 season as co-record-holders; Pike assumed sole ownership of the lead when he again led the NA in dingers in 1872 with six, putting him four ahead of Treacey.

11. **Who is the only big leaguer to win a bat title and also play at least one full season as a regular (100 or more games) at three different positions including catcher?**
    - A) In his top offensive season as a backstopper, he hit .321 with 109 RBI.
    - B) He had 101 RBI in 159 games in his first year as a first sacker.
    - C) He celebrated his first year as a third sacker by winning the NL bat title.
    - D) He joined his older brother on the Milwaukee Braves in 1960.
    - E) His first taste of World Series action came in 1996, the first year he donned the uniform of an AL team.

12. **Name the only pitcher in the 20th century to hurl a no-hitter for a certain team and be stationed at a different position the next time that team took part in a no-no.**
    - A) He led the AL in pinch hits in its inaugural ML season.
    - B) His 99 career wins are the most of any post-1893 ML'er who made as many as 900 hits.
    - C) He is the only man in the 20th century to play two different positions for full seasons while serving as a player-manager.
    - D) His six-year gap between his 10th and 11th seasons is the longest of any man who returned to the majors as a regular after departing as a regular.
    - E) He jumped to the AL in 1901 from Chicago, NL, and spent the rest of his playing career with the ChiSox.

13. **Who won a Rookie of the Year Award as a third baseman, fanned a career-high 161 times as an outfielder, and was an MVP selection as a first baseman?**
    - A) The year he won an MVP Award, he was one of three brothers in the majors.
    - B) He led the NL in SA in 1966.
    - C) He saw postseason action with his original team in 1976.
    - D) His .534 career SA is the highest of anyone since expansion who is eligible for the Hall of Fame but has yet to be tapped.
    - E) He was a rookie in 1964 with the Phillies.

14. **He played every position but the outfield the year he led the UA in free passes. The following year, he was primarily an outfielder for the first St. Louis team to win a major league pennant. A year later he was stationed at second base for the only undisputed world champ representing the AA. Who is he?**
    - A) In 1888 he scored 111 runs on just 105 hits.
    - B) He holds the pre-1889 season record for the most walks.
    - C) Between 1887 and 1890, he compiled 427 walks and just 400 hits.
    - D) Like Bill Terry, his real first name was William, but he was known by a nickname that was the middle name of another Terry who pitched for the Red Sox during World War II.
    - E) He has the most career steals of any player with his last name—even Jackie.

15. **Who led the AL in hits three times as a shortstop, scored more than 110 runs in each of his three seasons at third base, and played regularly at second the last year he took part in more than 100 games?**
    - A) He posted a .307 career BA in 10 seasons, all spent in the AL.
    - B) His second big league season came four years after his first.
    - C) In his second season, he participated in his only World Series.
    - D) In 1963 he piloted the same AL team for which he'd debuted 21 years earlier.
    - E) He was somewhat unfairly labeled a "goat" in his lone World Series in 1946.

16. **Craig Biggio is the only man in ML history to have a 100-game season at second base after having a 100-game season as a catcher. Who is the only man to convert to catching after having a 100-game season at shortstop?**
    A) In his sophomore season, he played 154 games at shortstop and hit .251 for a National League cellar dweller.
    B) After playing 25 games during the season as a backup catcher for a National League flag winner, he cracked a pinch double off Joe Page in his lone postseason AB.
    C) In his final ML season, he was fourth on his team's catching depth chart behind Roy Campanella, Gil Hodges, and Bruce Edwards.
    D) He was the first man to manage a major league team based in a city south of Nashville.
    E) In 1947, his lone taste of postseason action, he played against a rookie third baseman whose first name and initials were the same as his.

Players Who Were Both Regular Catchers and Middle Infielders

NAME	YEARS	G/C	G/INF
Mike McGeary	1871–82	94	370
Jake Rowe	1879–90	298	657
Tom Daly	1887–1903	306	1069
Craig Biggio	1988–	427	1044

17. **Who is the only man to be a loop leader in assists for two consecutive years at two different infield positions?**
    A) He led all first sackers in his loop the first year and all second sackers the next.
    B) He is the only man in ML history to hit .175 over a two-year span in which he had at least 800 ABs.
    C) His rookie season with Louisville in 1876 was his only year at 1B.
    D) He is the only man to play for ML teams in Louisville in the 1870s, the 1880s, and the 1890s.
    E) He and the catcher who saw the most postseason action for the 1996 world champs share the same first name and the same initials.

18. **He led the NL in doubles in 1931 as a third baseman, paced the NL in at bats in both 1925 and 1926 as a second baseman, and was the Cubs regular shortstop in 1924, the first year he appeared in 100 ML games.**
    A) In 1927 he compiled 647 ABs while playing three different positions.
    B) His 154 career thefts are the most by anyone between 1920 and World War II who never led a major league in steals.
    C) At 36, he was the oldest regular on the 1931 world champs.
    D) His real first name and initials are the same as those of the only Hall of Fame position player to date who homered in his first ML plate appearance.
    E) He has the same nickname and initials as the first pilot to win world titles with teams in both major leagues.

19. He was the only man to be a regular on Cincinnati teams in both the AA and the NL in the 19th century and yet never be a teammate of Bid McPhee's. He was furthermore the only man to play 1,400 games in the majors and just once play as many as 100 games in a season at one position. What immortal are we describing?

A) In 1900, the year after McPhee retired and officially the last year of the 19th century, none of the Cincinnati regulars dated back to 1889, the last year Cincinnati was in the AA.

B) From the 1882 team, Cincinnati's first in the AA, only McPhee was still on the club when it switched to the NL in 1890.

C) The man who was never a teammate of McPhee's was a regular on Cincinnati ML teams 12 years apart.

D) He was the first man to lead his league in doubles while playing primarily at SS and also the first batting titlist since 1876 to catch more games that year for his team than anyone else on the roster.

E) He and Nap Lajoie are the only two Hall of Famers to manage ML teams that were nicknamed for them.

Many nineteenth century performers were skilled enough to play virtually every position on the diamond, but very few could play all of them well. King Kelly ranked high among that select few. The pitcher's box was probably the only place where Kelly failed to excel.

20. **A number of men have played 100 games in a season at three different positions, but precious few have done it during their first five full seasons in the majors. The most recent addition to this select group joined in 1993. Who is he?**

    A)   He was 3-for-6 in his ML debut in 1988, all as a pinch hitter.

    B)   He led the NL in doubles in 1990.

    C)   In his lone full AL season to date, he played third base for the Royals.

    D)   In 1993, his first season as a full-time first sacker, he hiked his career BA 12 points from .278 to .290.

    E)   In 1997 he joined an even more select group when he became only the third member of the four-position list after serving all season as the Phils' regular left fielder.

Regulars at Multiple Positions, Since 1876

Four Positions

NAME	YEARS	POSITIONS
Denis Menke	1962–74	SS (841), 3B (420), 2B (233), 1B (162)
Pete Rose	1963–86	OF (1327), 1B (948), 3B (634), 2B (628)
Gregg Jefferies	1988–	OF (366), 1B (357), 2B (330), 3B (271)

Three Positions

NAME	YEARS	POSITIONS
Hardy Richardson	1879–92	2B (585), OF (544), 3B (178)
Monte Ward	1878–94	SS (826), 2B (491), P (291)
Buck Ewing	1880–97	C (636), 1B (253), OF (235)
Charlie Bassett	1884–92	2B (559), 3B (240), SS (112)
George Davis	1890–1909	SS (1378), 3B (530), OF (303)
Jim Canavan	1891–97	OF (215), 2B (205), SS (117)
Nixey Callahan	1894–1913	OF (489), P (195), 3B (110)
Bobby Wallace	1894–1918	SS (1823), 3B (427), P (57)
Barry McCormick	1895–1904	3B (411), 2B (314), SS (265)
Bill Keister	1896–1903	SS (215), 2B (214), OF (167)
Wid Conroy	1901–11	3B (667), SS (350), OF (298)
Jim Delahanty	1901–15	2B (567), 3B (295), OF (188)
Buck Herzog	1908–20	2B (488), 3B (472), SS (458)
Frank O'Rourke	1912–31	3B (598), SS (289), 2B (220)
Buddy Myer	1924–41	2B (1340), SS (237), 3B (219)
Eric McNair	1929–42	SS (669), 2B (289), 3B (220)
Jimmy Brown	1937–46	2B (392), 3B (273), SS (235)
Frankie Gustine	1939–50	2B (551), 3B (383), SS (303)
Billy Goodman	1947–62	2B (624), 1B (406), 3B (330)
Ray Boone	1948–60	3B (510), SS (464), 1B (285)
Gil McDougald	1951–60	2B (599), 3B (508), SS (284)
Pete Runnels	1951–64	1B (644), 2B (642), SS (463)
Harmon Killebrew	1954–75	1B (969), 3B (792), OF (470)
Deron Johnson	1960–76	1B (875), 3B (332), OF (254)
Joe Torre	1960–77	C (903), 1B (787), 3B (515)

Three Positions

NAME	YEARS	POSITIONS
Don Buford	1963–72	OF (555), 2B (392), 3B (352)
Dick Allen	1963–77	1B (807), 3B (652), OF (256)
Don Money	1968–83	3B (1025), 2B (192), SS (165)
Toby Harrah	1969–86	3B (1099), SS (813), 2B (244)
Dan Meyer	1974–85	1B (469), OF (326), 3B (157)
Hubie Brooks	1980–94	OF (582), 3B (576), SS (371)
Tony Phillips	1982–	OF (723), 3B (426), SS (293)*

* Phillips through 1998 has also played 711 games at second base, but his high there for a season is only 88, 12 games short of the minimum number needed to qualify as a regular.

Note: Minimum 100 games in a season at a position or 150 innings as a pitcher to qualify. Men active prior to 1887 when a 140-game schedule was first adopted had seasons at each listed position when they played at least three-quarters of their team's games; positions are listed in order of most appearances (games played in parentheses).

POSTSEASON AND ALL-STAR ACTION

- ◆ ALL-STAR APPETIZERS
- ◆ LEAGUE CHAMPIONSHIP SERIES LORE

- ◆ SEVENTH-GAME STARTERS
- ◆ FALL CLASSICS: 1871—1941
- ◆ FALL CLASSICS: 1942—98

All-Star Appetizers

1. *Hal Chase never played in an All-Star Game because he left the majors 14 years before the annual event was introduced in 1933. Many baseball pundits of Chase's time nevertheless put him at first base on their all-time all-star teams. He's also at first base on the all-time all-star team (seen below). Do you know what one unique characteristic he and all the other team members share?*

1B	Hal Chase	C	Mike Hines	Sub	Herman Reich
2B	Kid Mohler	C	Fergy Malone	Sub	Brian Hunter
3B	Hick Carpenter	P	Johnny Cooney	Sub	John Cassidy
SS	Jimmy Macullar	P	Rube Bressler	Sub	Al Nixon
LF	Rickey Henderson	P	Sandy Koufax	Sub	Elmer Foster
CF	Jimmy Ryan	P	Ferdie Schupp	DH	David McCarty
RF	Cleon Jones	P	Woodie Fryman	PH	R C Stevens

2. **What three features do all the members of this all-time All-Star team have in common? 1B—George Sisler; 2B—Nap Lajoie; 3B—Luke Appling; SS—Ernie Banks; LF—Ralph Kiner; CF—Harry Heilmann; RF—Elmer Flick; C—Rick Ferrell; P—Ted Lyons; Player-Manager—Bobby Wallace.**
   A) Yep, all are in the Hall of Fame.
   B) True, all of them played most of their careers in this century.
   C) It'll help to remember that Appling and Lyons were teammates for many years.
   D) If not for 1948, Lou Boudreau might have been this squad's player-manager.
   E) If you're still struggling with the third common denominator, ponder when Appling and Kiner could have faced each other except in All-Star competition.

3. **Of the 16 franchises represented in the first All-Star Game at Comiskey Park in 1933, which was the last to have one of its players homer in All-Star competition?**
   A) Though it finished just sixth in 1933, the team had two of its league's eight starting position players in the first All-Star Game, and between them the pair collected three of their side's nine hits.
   B) In 1934 the team's lone All-Star participant became the first player to collect three hits in a midsummer classic.
   C) In the dramatic 1941 game, two southpaws participated from this team, including Eddie Smith, the winning hurler.
   D) The team's home park hosted the first All-Star Game in 1933.
   E) In 1996 the team acquired a new career home run record holder who'd poked its first All-Star Game homer a year earlier.

4. **What is the only scheduled site of an All-Star Game that was scratched because it was no longer a major league park by the time the game was held?**
   A) Crosley Field replaced the site as the host park the year in question.
   B) The site hosted the fourth All-Star Game in 1936.
   C) The team that played at this site had previously played at the oldest park in the majors, known as South End Grounds.
   D) The site had a section in right field known as "The Jury Box."
   E) The site hosted the first game of the 1948 World Series.

5. **Who was the first man to pilot both an American League and a National League team in an All-Star Game?**
   A) His two All-Star dugout assignments came 12 years apart.
   B) His first All-Star dugout assignment resulted in a win at Cleveland, and his second in a loss at Milwaukee.
   C) Ten years after he did it, in the same midsummer classic Dick Williams and Sparky Anderson became the second and third men to pilot All-Star clubs in both leagues.
   D) He played in the 1948 World Series against a team he later managed.
   E) He was selected Rookie of the Year the last year just one award was given.

6. **Only one man to date homered in his lone All-Star plate appearance. Do you know who he is?**
   A) He started in left field for the NL, homered in the first inning, and exited the next inning after crashing into the outfield wall.
   B) He later won several PCL home run crowns.
   C) His three-run blast triggered a 4–0 NL win in 1940.
   D) He was a Boston Brave when he made his lone All-Star appearance.
   E) His initials are the same as those of the only pitcher to hurl a perfect game on the final day of a season.

7. **Ironically, the first man to hit a pinch homer in All-Star play collected zero four-baggers that year in 133 regular-season games. Who is he?**
   - A)   The previous year he played a key role in his team's World Series loss.
   - B)   He debuted with the 1937 Cardinals.
   - C)   A catcher, he batted for Claude Passeau, and his blast accounted for the NL's only run in the 1942 All-Star clash.
   - D)   He was later temporarily banned for jumping to the Mexican League.
   - E)   His first name was Arnold, but he was known by the same nickname as the AL bat champ the year he jumped South of the Border.

8. **Who was the first man to play for both leagues in an All-Star Game?**
   - A)   His first appearance came the year after he helped his team win a six-game World Series.
   - B)   His second appearance came 11 years later as a pinch hitter for Warren Spahn.
   - C)   He is coholder of the AL record for the most consecutive wins in a season.
   - D)   He was famous for once saying during a radio interview, "How'm I doing, Edna?" (Edna was his wife.)
   - E)   His first name was Linwood, but even Edna called him "Schoolboy."

First 10 All-Stars Selected to Play for Both Leagues

RANK	POS.	NAME	1ST LEAGUE	2ND LEAGUE
1	P	Schoolboy Rowe	AL, 1936	NL, 1947
2	P	Johnny Sain	NL, 1947	AL, 1953
	1B	Johnny Mize	NL, 1939	AL, 1953
4	P	Jim Wilson	NL, 1954	AL, 1956
5	P	Hoyt Wilhelm	NL, 1953	AL, 1959
6	P	Gerry Staley	NL, 1952	AL, 1960
7	2B	Johnny Temple	NL, 1956	AL, 1961
	P	Luis Arroyo	NL, 1955	AL, 1961
9	P	Jim Bunning	AL, 1957	NL, 1964
10	OF	Frank Robinson	NL, 1956	AL, 1966

9. **The only performer in either the AL or the NL starting lineup in the 1934 All-Star Game who failed to make the Hall of Fame went 0-for-2 that day. Who is he?**
   - A)   He started in center field for the NL.
   - B)   Two years later, although he was the lone All-Star selection from his team, he failed to appear in the game even though it was played at his home park.
   - C)   He has the most plate appearances (18) of anyone who played in more than one World Series without ever getting a hit or a walk in fall action.
   - D)   He led the NL in homers and RBI in 1935.
   - E)   He still shares the NL record for the most home runs by a rookie.

10. **Name the first man to represent both Canadian ML teams in All-Star play.**
   - A)   He represented the Expos in 1973 and the Blue Jays in their inaugural season.
   - B)   He made his big league debut prior to expansion.
   - C)   He is among the few men who played 1,000 games at two different positions.
   - D)   He played in four World Series with the same NL team prior to the beginning of division play.
   - E)   He was a San Francisco Giants broadcaster in the early 1990s.

11. **The first rookie to play in an All-Star Game went 0-for-5 and made an error. Who is this later-to-be Hall of Famer?**
    A) He went all the way in right field for the AL.
    B) The game was staged at Braves Field.
    C) Beginning in his rookie year, he played every inning of every All-Star Game for a record seven straight seasons.
    D) Beginning in his rookie year, he played in four straight World Series.
    E) After his rookie year, he occupied center field in all of his remaining All-Star appearances.

12. **On just one occasion have two mound teammates each collected a win in All-Star competition in the same season. Name this lucky pair.**
    A) The NL won both All-Star Games that year.
    B) The first game was played in Kansas City, and the second at Yankee Stadium.
    C) The two mound mates were both right-handers on the NL flag winner that year.
    D) Five years earlier, one of the two had led the NL in ERA and gone a remarkable 14–9 for a last-place team.
    E) A third member of the team's mound crew, Roy Face, worked 1.2 scoreless innings in relief in the first All-Star Game at Kansas City, giving his team 7.1 scoreless innings in midsummer competition that year.

13. **Who is the lone rookie to win both an All-Star Game and a World Series game in the same season?**
    A) His rookie Series win came at Brooklyn's expense.
    B) He won 12 games for the most recent Washington team to play .500 ball.
    C) His manager that year in Washington was the same pilot he served as a rookie.
    D) As a rook he trailed only Allie Reynolds in wins among Yankees starters.
    E) His last name is the same as the name of the stadium that is currently home to the other New York ML team.

Pitchers Winning All-Star and World Series Games in the Same Season

NAME	TEAM	YEAR
Lefty Gomez	NY, AL	1937
Lefty Gomez	NY, AL	1938
Paul Derringer	Cin, NL	1940
Spec Shea	NY, AL	1947
Vern Law	Pit, NL	1960
Sandy Koufax	LA, NL	1965

14. **In 1998, Juan Gonzalez had a record 101 RBI at the All-Star break. What slugger failed to be selected to his loop's All-Star squad even though he had 100 RBI at the break?**
    A) He won his fourth and last RBI crown when he was 35.
    B) Although he didn't make the All-Star squad, he played on a World Championship team that fall.
    C) The previous year, he had led the AL with 63 doubles.
    D) He lost out to Gehrig and Foxx the year he failed to make the All-Star cut.
    E) He hit 58 homers in 1938.

15. **For a long time, the AL reigned supreme by a wide margin in midsummer competition between the two loops. What year did the NL first surpass its junior in All-Star wins?**
    A) The game was the first All-Star contest played in a certain Midwestern state.
    B) Milt Pappas started for the AL that year and lasted only one inning.
    C) Sam McDowell took the loss for the AL when he surrendered a single run in the top of the seventh.
    D) Ron Santo drove in the winning tally in the NL's 6–5 win at Minnesota's park.
    E) The park that same season hosted its first World Series game.

16. **Ever since the second All-Star Game in 1934, the two opposing squads have traditionally been managed by the helmsmen of the two World Series combatants the previous year. Yet, there have been two All-Star Game managers who never piloted a World Series entry. Who are they?**
    A) One replaced a manager who was fired after losing a seven-game World Series.
    B) The other replaced a manager who resigned after winning a seven-game Series.
    C) One was replaced as Orioles skipper by Lum Harris near the end of the season in which he piloted his only All-Star squad.
    D) The other lost a seven-game ALCS after leading 3–1 in games 20 years after he piloted his only All-Star squad.
    E) The pair managed a combined 38 years in the bigs without ever winning a flag.

17. **What Hall of Famer played on the losing team in All-Star competition a record 15 times in his 18 midsummer appearances?**
    A) One of his 18 appearances was the 1962 tie game.
    B) He last appeared on All-Star day in 1974.
    C) All of his midsummer appearances were as a member of the same team.
    D) He won the AL MVP Award in 1964.
    E) He was selected to the All-Star squad each time as a third baseman.

18. **Who are the only two pitchers to start and win an All-Star Game played in their home parks?**
    A) They did it 44 years apart.
    B) Neither played on a pennant winner that year.
    C) One did it the year after he surrendered a home run that ended his team's most serious pennant bid to date.
    D) The first pitcher to do it accomplished something else that year that no other pitcher in major league history has ever done, although Ewell Blackwell came close in 1947.
    E) The parks were in Montreal and Cincinnati.

19. **Only once has a starting All-Star Game infield all come from the same team. What team is it?**
    A) The team won the World Championship that year.
    B) The team's third sacker won his loop's MVP Award that year.
    C) The shortstop had won his loop's MVP Award four years earlier.
    D) The second baseman replaced injured Bill Mazeroski, the NL's top vote-getter that year at second base.
    E) The first baseman was later NL president.

20. **The lone All-Star Game played on Sunday was staged on the Sabbath for a special reason. What was it?**
    A) It was played at Cleveland and won by the NL, 5–4.
    B) Like every All-Star Game in recent memory, it was a night game.
    C) Gary Carter was the MVP of the contest.
    D) The game was played on August 9, the latest date in All-Star history.
    E) The contest was the first game of major league baseball in some ten weeks.

21. **What pitcher had 18 wins, the most in history at the All-Star break, and yet, amazingly, was not selected to his loop's squad that year?**
    A) The AL could have used him, as it lost 7–1 at Kansas City that year.
    B) Along with his 18 wins, he had 14 losses at the break, which was part of the reason he wasn't selected.
    C) He set a post-Deadball season record for the most starts the previous year.
    D) He is the most recent hurler to start both ends of a doubleheader.
    E) In 1973, the year he had 18 wins at the break, he finished at 24–20.

22. **In 1997, Jacobs Field hosted both the All-Star Game and a World Series game, but it will probably eventually host another All-Star contest. What two parks also hosted a World Series game in the one and only year they hosted an All-Star Game?**
    A) One park has since been replaced by a new facility.
    B) The other park was abandoned when its tenant moved.
    C) The two All-Star contests came 16 years apart.
    D) The hosts of the first of the two All-Star contests hosted a World Series game in each of the two seasons involved, albeit in a different city each time.
    E) One team now plays in a "Dome" and the other in a "Ravine."

First Player to Win Two All-Star MVPs
Willie Mays, 1963 and 1968

First All-Star MVP on a Losing Team
AL Brooks Robinson, 1966
NL None

Franchises Extant from 1962–98 That Have Never Had an All-Star MVP
New York Yankees, St. Louis, Houston, Detroit

Franchise with the Most Different All-Star MVPs
Cincinnati—5: Tony Perez, 1967; Joe Morgan, 1972; George Foster, 1976; Ken Griffey, 1980; Dave Concepcion, 1982

Most Consecutive All-Star Appearances in Starting Lineup
AL Cal Ripken, 15 (1984–98)
NL Willie Mays, 14 (1955–68)

First All-Star MVP from an Expansion Team
AL Leon Wagner, Los Angeles Angels, 1962
NL Jon Matlack, New York Mets, 1975

First Player to Win All-Star MVP and Cy Young Awards in the Same Year
AL Roger Clemens, 1986
NL None

First Player to Win All-Star MVP and League MVP in the Same Year
NL Maury Wills, 1962
AL Roger Clemens, 1986

League Championship Series Lore

1. The League Championship Series has been with us only since 1969, not long enough to produce near the number of famous feats linked to the World Series. Yet, LCSes have already sired many great moments. For one, the only man to tag three homers in a losing cause in a postseason game did it in an LCS fray. Who is he?

    A) He is also the only leadoff hitter to tag three dingers in a postseason game.
    B) His three homers came in successive plate appearances off Catfish Hunter.
    C) His .738 career LCS SA leads all players with at least 50 LCS ABs.
    D) He needed four LCS appearances before he finally got into his first Series.
    E) His 300+ career home runs and 3,000+ hits all came with the same AL club.

2. What outfielder's sole day in the limelight in his six-year career came when he tied an LCS record by scoring four runs in his one and only postseason game?

    A) He went 3-for-4 in the game and drove in three runs as a replacement for injured Ben Oglivie.
    B) His effort in Game Four of the 1982 ALCS helped Milwaukee tie matters at 2-all.
    C) He spent his whole career with Milwaukee as a sub gardener, ending in 1985.
    D) He and the man who threw the last pitch in the 1976 ALCS share the same first name.
    E) His initials match those of the hurler who threw a 4–0 shutout and notched 14 Ks in a 1983 ALCS contest.

3. Who is the lone hurler to win as many as two postseason games after going winless the entire regular season?

    A) His first win of the season came on a day that began with his team down 3 games to 1 in an LCS.
    B) His second win of the season put his team up 2–0 in games in a World Series it ultimately lost.
    C) His finale with the 1991 Royals produced a 5.98 ERA in 33 relief stints.
    D) He was 0–2 in 40 games for Boston during the regular season in 1986 but 2–0 in postseason action.
    E) He and the most recent righty to win three games in a World Series for an AL team share the same initials.

4. What team saw its pennant hopes dashed when it lost the last game of an LCS, 2–1, even though its hill staff held the opposition to only one hit that day?

    A) The team's starter was working on a no-hitter when he was pulled in the fifth inning after giving up nine walks.
    B) The game's winning run came on Reggie Jackson's seventh-inning double, scoring Sal Bando.
    C) The team had lost the previous game of the ALCS, 1–0, to Vida Blue.
    D) The team scored six of its seven runs in that year's ALCS in Game One, two of them coming on Bobby Grich's two-run homer.
    E) Mike Cuellar, the pitcher who was yanked in Game Four of that year's ALCS while working on a no-hitter, posted his team's only win when he took the opener, 6–3.

5. **Who set an LCS record (since tied) when he scored eight runs despite compiling just five hits, one walk, and a .161 batting average in the seven-game fray?**
   A) That fall, he played on his second flag winner but in only his first Series.
   B) An injury prevented him from participating in what ought to have been his first Series 11 years earlier.
   C) His team defeated Oakland in the ALCS in his rookie year.
   D) Prior to 1998 he was the most recent man to collect 400 total bases in a season.
   E) He played left field for a team that's lost in seven games in each of its last four World Series appearances.

6. **What Hall of Famer appeared in a record 45 LCS games during his career?**
   A) He also appeared in 27 World Series games and five divisional play-off games, for an all-time-record 77 postseason appearances.
   B) The first pitcher he faced in postseason play was Dave McNally.
   C) His 45 LCS games were spread among three AL teams.
   D) His final LCS appearance came in 1986.
   E) He also holds a share of the record for the most home runs in a World Series game, with three.

7. **What pitcher went 0-7 in seven LCS starts to set an LCS record for the most losses without a win?**
   A) He averaged less than five innings in his seven starts, with a 5.45 ERA.
   B) He was 7–8 as a rookie with the Cardinals in 1970.
   C) He went 1–1 in World Series action to escape also having the record for the most career postseason losses without a win.
   D) He lost the opener of the 1974 NLCS to Los Angeles, the same team for which he made his last postseason start 11 years later.
   E) He is the only southpaw to date to collect 200 career wins without ever having a 20-win season.

Most Career Postseason Losses Without a Win

RANK	NAME	YEARS	DIV.	LCS	WS	TOTAL
1	Doyle Alexander	1973/76/85/87	–	4	1	5
2	Ed Figueroa	1976–78	–	2	2	4
	Ed Summers	1908–09	–	–	4	4
	Bill Sherdel	1926/28	–	–	4	4
	Don Newcombe	1949/55–56	–	–	4	4
	Dwight Gooden	1986/88/97–98	0	2	2	4
7	Freddie Fitzsimmons	1933/36/41	–	–	3	3
	Al Downing	1963–64/74	–	–	3	3
	Lefty Williams	1917/19	–	–	3	3
	Charlie Root	1929/32/35/38	–	–	3	3
	Pat Malone	1929/32/36	–	–	3	3
	Eddie Watt	1969–71	–	–	3	3
	Calvin Schiraldi	1986	–	1	2	3

8. **Whose record did Dave Stewart break in 1990 when he won his fifth LCS game without a loss?**
   A) The first two of his four LCS wins without a loss came in relief.
   B) He gave his team a seemingly prohibitive 2–0 lead when he won Game Two of the 1982 ALCS.
   C) Though he pitched 15 years in the majors (1971–85) mostly as a starter, frequent injuries helped stop him from ever working 200 innings in a season.
   D) He won both an LCS and a World Series game as a 21-year-old rookie.
   E) His rookie season was also the first year that a World Series game was played at night.

9. **What franchise career-wins leader's 28 postseason strikeouts are the most by a pitcher who never participated in a World Series?**
   A) His five postseason starts and 31.2 postseason innings also are the most by any pitcher who never participated in a World Series.
   B) He led the AL twice in innings pitched and once in ERA.
   C) In 1998 he tried, for the first time in six years, to add to his record of 174 career wins for a certain AL franchise.
   D) He lost to Dave Stewart in his last postseason appearance.
   E) He and his Game Seven opponent in 1985 were the first two hurlers to make three starts in an LCS.

10. **In 14 LCS games over a three-year span, who hit .386 to establish the present record for the highest career batting average among men with at least 50 LCS ABs?**
    A) Over the same span he hit just .238 in 14 World Series games.
    B) In his final LCS, he gave way to a defensive replacement in all four games.
    C) He finished in 1984 with 1,660 hits and a .295 BA.
    D) He faced Dennis Leonard in his last LCS plate appearance.
    E) In 1980 he set a new Rangers club record when he had 210 hits.

		Highest Career BA, LCS (Minimum 50 ABs)				
RANK	**NAME**	**TEAM**	**YEARS**	**ABS**	**HITS**	**BA**
1	Mickey Rivers	NY, AL	1976–78	57	22	.386
2	Pete Rose	Cin/Phi, NL	1970/72–73/75–76/80/83	118	45	.381
3	Dusty Baker	LA, NL	1977–78/81/83	62	23	.371
4	Steve Garvey	LA/SD, NL	1974/77–78/81/84	90	32	.356
5	Ozzie Smith	StL, NL	1982/85/87	57	20	.351
6	Brooks Robinson	Bal, AL	1969–71/73-74	69	24	.348
7	George Brett	KC, AL	1976–78/80/84–85	103	35	.340
8	Thurman Munson	NY, AL	1976–78	62	21	.339
9	Tony Fernandez	Tor/Cle, AL	1985/89/93/97	80	27	.338
10	Bill Russell	LA, NL	1974/77–78/81/83	83	28	.337

11. **Who collected both the first shutout and the first complete-game win in an LCS?**
    A) He needed 11 innings to bag the first complete-game win in an LCS.
    B) He was last seen in an Expos uniform.
    C) Curt Motton's pinch single made him a 1–0 victor in Game Two of the 1969 ALCS.
    D) He outdueled Vida Blue, 5–3, in Game One of the 1971 ALCS.
    E) His 181 wins are an Orioles' franchise record for a southpaw.

12. **Can you name the first hurler to notch a win two days in a row in an LCS?**
    A) His two wins brought his team back from a 2–1 deficit in games in a best-of-five LCS.
    B) Both of his wins came on the road.
    C) His 5.1-inning stint in Game Four of the 1977 ALCS was the longest scoreless relief skein in LCS play to that point.
    D) He won a Cy Young Award while with the Yankees.
    E) He coauthored *The Bronx Zoo.*

13. **What former Rookie of the Year was the first man to be selected an LCS MVP for a losing team?**
    A) He hit .611 for a team that bowed in five games.
    B) His .517 LCS career BA is the highest among players with 25 or more LCS at bats.
    C) His 300th career home run came with the 1989 Tigers.
    D) He was the MVP in the 1982 ALCS.
    E) In 1983 he hit the first grand slam in All-Star Game history.

14. **Who is the only man to be named an LCS MVP with two different teams?**
    A) They're the only two teams for which he played in his 19-year career.
    B) He collected 200 or more hits six times in his career.
    C) His two LCS MVP prizes came six years apart for teams that both lost the World Series.
    D) A broken finger ended his consecutive-games-played streak in 1983.
    E) He left his original team in 1983 to play for a club located in the same state.

15. **What 300-game winner's only postseason win was the result of a seven-inning relief stint in an LCS?**
    A) He survived a two-run homer by Orlando Cepeda to notch his only postseason win, 7–4.
    B) He beat Pat Jarvis to clinch his team's first pennant ever.
    C) He hurled only 89.1 innings during the regular season that year but bagged 92 strikeouts.
    D) His first postseason start, in the 1979 ALCS, resulted in no decision for him.
    E) His only other postseason decision was a loss with Houston in a 1981 Division Playoff Series.

Most LCS Wins, Career, 300-Game Winner

RANK	NAME	LCSes	W
1	Steve Carlton	5	4
	Don Sutton	5	4
3	Tom Seaver	3	2
4	Nolan Ryan	4	1
	Gaylord Perry	1	1
6	Phil Niekro	2	0

16. **The only team to lose a best-of-seven postseason match despite getting perfect work (no losses) from its starting pitchers fell in an LCS. What club is it?**
    A) The team also set a record by losing four one-run games.
    B) Two of its four losses came in extra-inning clashes.
    C) It fell victim in the first ALCS to pit two brothers against each other who were both regular position players for their respective teams.
    D) It lost Game Three of that year's ALCS on a controversial steal of home.
    E) Scott Kamieniecki posted the team's last postseason win that year.

17. Name the only starting pitcher to lose three games in a best-of-seven postseason match.

- A) Originally the property of the White Sox, in 1984 he was dealt for Roy Smalley.
- B) His first seven big league wins came with the Yankees in 1986.
- C) He lost Games One, Four, and Seven of an LCS.
- D) He stood to win Game Seven when he held a 2–0 lead going into the bottom of the ninth.
- E) He led the NL with 18 losses in 1993 after joining Houston as a free agent.

LCS Leaders: 1969–98

			Batting				Pitching		
		BA	NAME	TEAM	ERA		NAME	TEAM	W–L
1969	NL	.538	Art Shamsky	New York	2.57		Tom Seaver	New York	1–0
	AL	.500	Brooks Robinson	Baltimore	0.00		Dave McNally	Baltimore	1–0
1970	NL	.500	Willie Stargell	Pittsburgh	0.00		Gary Nolan	Cincinnati	1–0
	AL	.583	Brooks Robinson	Baltimore	1.00		Dave McNally	Baltimore	1–0
1971	NL	.438	Bob Robertson	Pittsburgh	1.00		Bob Johnson	Pittsburgh	1–0
	AL	.429	Don Buford	Baltimore	1.00		Mike Cuellar	Baltimore	1–0
1972	NL	.450	Pete Rose	Cincinnati	1.00		Ross Grimsley	Cincinnati	1–0
	AL	.381	Matty Alou	Oakland	0.00		Blue Moon Odom	Oakland	2–0
1973	NL	.381	Pete Rose	Cincinnati	1.62		Tom Seaver	New York	1–1
	AL	.357	Andy Etchebarren	Baltimore	0.82		Ken Holtzman	Oakland	1–0
1974	NL	.400	Willie Stargell	Pittsburgh	0.53		Don Sutton	Los Angeles	2–0
	AL	.333	Ray Fosse	Oakland	0.00		Vida Blue	Oakland	1–0
					0.00		Ken Holtzman	Oakland	1–0
1975	NL	.500	Richie Zisk	Pittsburgh	3.00		Don Gullett	Cincinnati	1–0
	AL	.500	Sal Bando	Oakland	0.00		Luis Tiant	Boston	1–0
1976	NL	.778	Jay Johnstone	Philadelphia	1.18		Don Gullett	Cincinnati	1–0
	AL	.524	Chris Chambliss	New York	1.93		Paul Splittorff	Kansas City	1–0
1977	NL	.357	Dusty Baker	Los Angeles	0.66		Tommy John	Los Angeles	1–0
		.357	Richie Hebner	Philadelphia					
	AL	.444	Hal McRae	Kansas City	0.96		Sparky Lyle	New York	2–0
1978	NL	.467	Dusty Baker	Los Angeles	0.00		Tommy John	Los Angeles	1–0
	AL	.462	Reggie Jackson	New York	1.13		Ron Guidry	New York	1–0

Willie Stargell in 1979 became the oldest MVP winner to date. That same season, he became the oldest man to lead all NLCS performers in batting. Stargell was also the top batsman in his first taste of NLCS action nine years earlier when his Pirates fell to Cincinnati in three straight games despite his .500 BA.

			Batting				Pitching		
		BA	NAME	TEAM	ERA		NAME	TEAM	W–L
1979	NL	.455	Willie Stargell	Pittsburgh	1.00		Bert Blyleven	Pittsburgh	1–0
	AL	.417	Eddie Murray	Baltimore	0.00		Scott McGregor	Baltimore	1–0
1980	NL	.526	Terry Puhl	Houston	0.00		Joe Niekro	Houston	0–0
	AL	.545	Frank White	Kansas City	2.00		Larry Gura	Kansas City	1–0
1981	NL	.438	Gary Carter	Montreal	0.00		Burt Hooton	Los Angeles	2–0
	AL	.500	Jerry Mumphrey	New York	1.08		Matt Keough	Oakland	0–1
		.500	Graig Nettles	New York					
1982	NL	.556	Darrell Porter	St. Louis	0.00		Bob Forsch	St. Louis	1–0
		.556	Ozzie Smith	St. Louis					
	AL	.611	Fred Lynn	California	1.93		Bruce Kison	California	1–0
1983	NL	.467	Mike Schmidt	Philadelphia	0.66		Steve Carlton	Philadelphia	2–0
	AL	.400	Cal Ripken	Baltimore	0.00		Mike Boddicker	Baltimore	1–0
1984	NL	.400	Steve Garvey	San Diego	1.13		Ed Whitson	San Diego	1–0
	AL	.417	Kirk Gibson	Detroit	0.00		Milt Wilcox	Detroit	1–0
1985	NL	.435	Ozzie Smith	St. Louis	1.88		Fernando Valenzuela	Los Angeles	1–0
	AL	.348	George Brett	Kansas City	0.00		Danny Jackson	Kansas City	1–0
1986	NL	.304	Lenny Dykstra	New York	0.50		Mike Scott	Houston	2–0
	AL	.455	Bob Boone	California	0.84		John Candelaria	California	1–1
1987	NL	.417	Jeffrey Leonard	San Francisco	0.60		Dave Dravecky	San Francisco	1–1
	AL	.412	Tom Brunansky	Minnesota	4.05		Bert Blyleven	Minnesota	2–0
1988	NL	.364	Mike Scioscia	Los Angeles	1.09		Orel Hershiser	Los Angeles	1–0
	AL	.385	Wade Boggs	Boston	1.35		Dave Stewart	Oakland	1–0
1989	NL	.650	Will Clark	San Francisco	3.65		Mike Bielecki	Chicago	0–1
	AL	.400	Rickey Henderson	Oakland	2.81		Dave Stewart	Oakland	2–0
1990	NL	.471	Paul O'Neill	Cincinnati	1.65		Doug Drabek	Pittsburgh	1–1
	AL	.438	Carney Lansford	Oakland	1.13		Dave Stewart	Oakland	2–0
		.438	Wade Boggs	Boston					
1991	NL	.414	Jay Bell	Pittsburgh	0.00		Steve Avery	Atlanta	2–0
	AL	.474	Roberto Alomar	Toronto	0.00		David West	Minnesota	1–0
1992	NL	.438	Gary Redus	Pittsburgh	2.66		John Smoltz	Atlanta	2–0
	AL	.440	Harold Baines	Oakland	2.08		Juan Guzman	Toronto	2–0
1993	NL	.435	Fred McGriff	Atlanta	1.69		Curt Schilling	Philadelphia	0–0
	AL	.444	Devon White	Toronto	1.00		Wilson Alvarez	Chicago	1–0
		.444	Tim Raines	Chicago					
1994	None								
1995	NL	.438	Chipper Jones	Atlanta	1.26		Pete Schourek	Cincinnati	0–1
		.438	Fred McGriff	Atlanta					
	AL	.458	Kenny Lofton	Cleveland	1.29		Orel Hershiser	Cleveland	2–0
1996	NL	.542	Javier Lopez	Atlanta	1.20		John Smoltz	Atlanta	2–0
	AL	.474	Bernie Williams	New York	2.38		Scott Erickson	Baltimore	0–1
1997	NL	.500	Keith Lockhart	Atlanta	0.00		Danny Neagle	Atlanta	1–0
	AL	.360	Brady Anderson	Baltimore	0.60		Mike Mussina	Baltimore	0–0
1998	NL	.333	Steve Finley	San Diego	0.90		Sterling Hitchcock	San Diego	1–0
		.333	Carlos Hernandez	San Diego					
	AL	.440	Omar Vizquel	Cleveland	1.00		Bartolo Colon	Cleveland	1–0

Note: Minimum of three plate appearances per game to qualify as a batting leader.

Seventh-Game Starters

1. **Every World Series manager hopes to have his staff ace on tap in the event the affair goes the limit, but often it doesn't work out that way. Many Game Seven starters have been relatively obscure figures. The only hurler to post a Game Seven shutout in his sole World Series start was one such fellow. Who is he?**

   A)   The final score of his shutout win was 9–0.

   B)   He was aided by Bill Skowron's grand slam in his critical win.

   C)   As a rookie in 1955, he made two Series relief appearances for the loser.

   D)   In four of his first five ML seasons, he won 8 games, and in the other season he won 18.

   E)   His initials match those of the 1950 NL MVP.

Pitchers Throwing Shutouts in Their Only World Series Starts

NAME	TEAM	YEAR	WS GAME
Bill James	Bos, NL	1914	2
Jimmy Ring	Cin, NL	1919	4
Duster Mails	Cle, NL	1920	6
Earl Whitehill	Was, AL	1933	3
Ernie White	StL, NL	1942	3
Gene Bearden	Cle, AL	1948	3
Clem Labine	Bro, NL	1956	6
Johnny Kucks	NY, AL	1956	7
Wally Bunker	Bal, AL	1966	3

2. **This one will curl your hair. Who started Game Seven for the only Washington team to win a World Series?**

   A)   His 18 career wins are the fewest of any World Series Game Seven starter to date.

   B)   He was relieved in the first inning of his Game Seven start by southpaw George Mogridge after facing just two batters.

   C)   A right-hander, he got the call in an effort to induce Giants manager John McGraw to stack his lineup with left-handed hitters.

   D)   His real first name was Warren, but he was known by the same nickname as one of the Three Stooges.

   E)   His initials are the same as those of a Braves backup catcher in 1994–95.

Fewest Career Wins, World Series Game Seven Starter

RANK	NAME	TEAM	YEAR	W
1	Curly Ogden	Was, AL	1924	18
2	Joe Black	Bro, NL	1952	30
3	Hal Gregg	Bro, NL	1947	40
4	Johnny Kucks	NY, AL	1956	54
5	Joe Magrane	StL, NL	1987	57
6	Hugh Bedient	Bos, AL	1912	59
7	Dave Ferriss	Bos, AL	1946	65
8	Don Larsen	NY, AL	1957	81
	Don Larsen	NY, AL	1958	81
10	Blue Moon Odom	Oak, AL	1972	84

Note: Retired pitchers only.

3. **The first hurler to win both Game One and Game Seven of a World Series never won another postseason game after that season. Who is he?**
   A) In that same Series, he also won Game Five.
   B) His line for 28 innings of work in two Series that came 16 years apart shows three wins and a 1.29 ERA.
   C) He was a rookie the year he garnered his Game Seven triumph.
   D) In the 1997 World Series, Jaret Wright threatened to become the first rookie since our man to post a Game Seven triumph in a starting role.
   E) He was the first outstanding player nicknamed "Babe."

4. **Though the finale of a best-of-seven Series, owing to a tie it was officially the eighth contest when what final-game starter was lifted for pinch hitter Olaf Henriksen in the bottom of the seventh with his team trailing 1–0?**
   A) He had earlier won Game Five, 2–1.
   B) His mound opponent in both Game Five and the finale was Christy Mathewson.
   C) He won 20 games as a Red Sox rookie in 1912.
   D) He had the same first name as the loser in the key game of the 1941 Series.
   E) His initials are the same as those of the current holder of the record for the most consecutive games hit safely in fall play.

5. **What starter received no decision for his effort in the first ever winner-take-all Game Seven that pitted two hurlers who had already posted two wins without a loss in that Series?**
   A) He lasted just 0.1 innings, the quickest exit by a Game Seven starter for a National League team.
   B) Two years later, in his only other Series, he suffered his lone fall loss.
   C) He was the first hurler who stood to win three games in a seven-game World Series despite not pitching in the opener.
   D) He and Ray Kremer collected all their team's wins in the 1925 Series.
   E) He and Raschi had the same first name.

6. In 1968, Mickey Lolich became the second and last man to date to bag three complete-game wins in a best-of-seven World Series despite not getting the call to start Game One. Who was the first man to do what Lolich did?

 A) He worked Game Seven on two days' rest because the staff ace, who was slated to start, took sick.

 B) After giving up a run in the third inning of his first start, he then held the opposition scoreless for 24 consecutive innings in that Series.

 C) The following year, he was touched for a run in the first inning of his first Series start against the same opponents, but went on to win, 13–5.

 D) He is the lone hurler to toss four straight complete-game Series wins against the New York Yankees.

 E) His 5–0 Game Seven shutout brought the Braves their only World Championship rings in Milwaukee.

Pitchers with Three Complete-Game Wins in a Best-of-Seven World Series

NAME	TEAM	YEAR
Christy Mathewson	NY, NL	1905
Babe Adams	Pit, NL	1909
Jack Coombs	Phi, AL	1910
Lew Burdette	Mil, NL	1957
Bob Gibson	StL, NL	1967
Mickey Lolich	Det, AL	1968

Note: Bill Dinneen (1903), Deacon Phillippe (1903), and Stan Coveleski (1920) all earned three complete-game wins in a best-of-nine World Series; Harry Brecheen won two complete games and one game in relief in the 1946 Series, and Red Faber did likewise in the 1917 Series; Joe Wood won three games in the 1912 Series but went the distance in only two of them.

7. Prior to 1955 when Johnny Podres bested Tommy Byrne to give the Dodgers their first World Championship, who was the only Yankees hurler to lose Game Seven of a best-of-seven fall fray?

 A) He left after six frames, trailing 3–2, which proved to be the final score.

 B) He won Game Four in the same World Series when he received a record three home runs from a teammate in his support.

 C) Bubbles Hargrave won the NL batting title that year.

 D) He was beaten in the finale by Jesse Haines, with help from Pete Alexander.

 E) He was relieved in Game Seven by fellow Hall of Famer Herb Pennock.

8. Bill Hallahan came out of the pen to nail the final out in what Hall of Famer's lone Game Seven win?

 A) He and Hallahan combined for all of his team's wins in that World Series.

 B) His first Series, 11 years earlier, saw him win Game Two to knot a best-of-nine affair at 1–all.

 C) His first name is shared by no other big leaguer to date.

 D) He is the oldest hurler since 1920 to win 25 games in a season.

 E) He was the last Series hurler legally permitted to throw spitballs.

9. Who drew Dizzy Dean as his hill opponent in his one and only Game Seven start?

A) Earlier in that same World Series, he bested Tex Carleton, 10–4.

B) His 4.42 career ERA is the highest of all retired hurlers who compiled 125 or more wins.

C) He topped the AL in hits allowed in his 1942 finale with the Browns.

D) His .563 winning percentage is seventh on the all-time list of pitchers with at least 200 decisions who totaled more career walks than strikeouts.

E) He was known for his unorthodox submarine delivery.

Highest Career Winning Percentage, More Walks than Ks (Minimum 200 Decisions)

RANK	NAME	YEARS	W–L	Ks	WALKS	WIN. PCT.
1	Nig Cuppy	1892–1901	162–98	504	609	.623
2	Rip Sewell	1932–49	143–97	636	748	.596
3	General Crowder	1926–36	167–115	799	800	.592
4	Dutch Ruether	1917–27	137–95	708	739	.591
5	Eddie Rommel	1920–32	171–119	599	724	.590
6	Guy Bush	1923–45	176–136	850	859	.564
7	Eldon Auker	1933–42	130–101	594	706	.563
8	Harry Gumbert	1935–50	143–113	709	721	.559
9	Frank Killen	1891–1900	164–131	725	822	.556
10	Earl Whitehill	1923–39	218–185	1350	1431	.541

10. Looking for his third World Series win, what Game Seven starter instead incurred his first fall loss when he gave up the winning run on a sac fly by Billy Myers?

A) Seven years later, in his second and last Series, he was kayoed by a six-run Brooklyn rally in the second inning of a Game Three start.

B) In Game One in his first Series, he beat Paul Derringer, the same hurler who edged him 2–1 in the finale.

C) He is the most recent 20-game winner to have an ERA above 5.00.

D) Although he won more than 200 games, his two fall appearances came in virtually the only two seasons in which he pitched for decent teams.

E) Few knew his real first name was Louis, but everyone knew who "Bobo" was.

11. Who has the distinction of being the most recent Cubs hurler both to win and to lose a World Series game?

A) He beat Dizzy two days before he lost to Hal in 1945's Game Seven.

B) He is one of the handful of hurlers to win 20 games in a season divided between two major leagues.

C) He was the last hurler to collect four decisions in a postseason affair.

D) He broke in with the Yankees.

E) His initials match those of the most recent NL shortstop to amass 100 RBI in a season.

12. **Who stood to win Game Seven in the first postseason fray in 28 years that involved a Boston team until he wilted in the eighth inning while holding a 3–1 lead?**
    A) Though he saw action in three World Series, he never collected a Series win.
    B) He finished with the 1959 Kansas City A's at age 43.
    C) His lone 20-win season came in 1951 with a seventh-place team.
    D) His first name sounds the same as the last name of a Giants outfielder who went 0-for-21 in the 1911 Series.
    E) He had the same initials as the Yankees second sacker in the 1996 Series.

13. **After giving up just one run in a seven-inning relief stint in Game Four, what moundsman earned a start against Spec Shea in Game Seven of his only World Series and took the 5–2 loss?**
    A) He was just 4–5 that season with a 5.87 ERA.
    B) He topped the NL in walks in both 1944 and 1945.
    C) His Series start was his last appearance in a Brooklyn uniform.
    D) His initials match those of a former AL home run champ who was finishing his career in the NL that same season.
    E) He has the same last name as the only 20th century lefty to bag 20 wins in each of his first three seasons.

Fewest Wins, Season, World Series Game Seven Starter

RANK	NAME	TEAM	YEAR	W
1	Hal Gregg	Bro, NL	1947	4
2	Jaret Wright	Cle, AL	1997	8
3	Curly Ogden	Was, AL	1924	9
	Don Larsen	NY, AL	1958	9
	Bob Turley	NY, AL	1960	9
	Joe Magrane	StL, NL	1987	9
7	Don Larsen	NY, AL	1957	10
8	Al Leiter	Fla, NL	1997	11
9	Jack Billingham	Cin, NL	1972	12
	Jim Bibby	Pit, NL	1979	12

14. **When Bob Gibson dueled with a certain AL'er one October 12, it marked the first time in 42 years that Game Seven pitted two starters looking for their third wins. Who was Gibson's mound foe that day?**
    A) He lasted six innings and left trailing 6–1.
    B) His two wins came over Dick Hughes and Steve Carlton.
    C) He was the only Red Sox starter to log a win in the 1967 World Series.
    D) A skiing accident short-circuited his mound career.
    E) He and the youngest NL regular in this century share the same initials.

15. **Who is the only A's starter—Philadelphia, Kansas City, or Oakland—to capture a win in Game Seven of a World Series?**
    - A) Both his first and his last career wins came with the Cubs.
    - B) He beat a fellow southpaw 5–2 to earn his Game Seven triumph.
    - C) He was the most recent pitcher to homer in a Series game.
    - D) In 1967 he was 9–0 when his season was ended early by a military call-up.
    - E) He was a member of six pennant-winning teams during the 1970s but appeared in only three World Series.

16. **Shooting for his third win in a World Series one year, who took a 3–0 lead into the bottom of the sixth in Game Seven and emerged with no decision?**
    - A) He left at the end of six innings with the count knotted 3–3.
    - B) He threw lefty, as did the Series Game Seven winner the following year.
    - C) In Game One, he beat Ron Darling, his opponent in Game Seven.
    - D) Two days prior to his Game Seven start, he'd already been voted the Series MVP but lost the honor when his team suffered a stunning extra-inning loss in Game Six.
    - E) He entered the 1998 season with the distinction of being the most recent pitcher to garner a postseason win in a Boston uniform.

17. **In 1997, Florida's Al Leiter became only the second hurler to make more than one start in a World Series without registering a decision. The first man to do it posted a 1.26 overall Series ERA, including a perfect 0.00 in a Game Seven start. Who is he?**
    - A) He exited in the bottom of the eighth of a game tied 0–0 in his Game Seven start.
    - B) Four days earlier, he had exited in the top of the eighth of a 2–2 tie that his team ultimately won 3–2.
    - C) The following year, he finally notched his first decision in four Series starts when he beat Jack Morris in Game Five.
    - D) Morris was also his mound opponent in Game Seven the year before.
    - E) He won his first Cy Young Award in 1996.

A year after authoring the only perfect game in World Series history, Don Larsen got the nod in Game Seven of the 1957 classic despite having only 10 regular-season wins. The next year, Larsen tied a then-existing AL record when he again was given the ball by Casey Stengel in Game Seven of the 1958 fall classic after notching just nine regular-season wins.

Game Seven Winners

YEAR	PITCHER	TEAM	W/SERIES
1909	Babe Adams	Pit, NL	3
1912	Joe Wood	Bos, AL	3
1924	Walter Johnson	Was, AL	1*
1925	Ray Kremer	Pit, NL	2*
1926	Jesse Haines	StL, NL	2
1931	Burleigh Grimes	StL, NL	2
1934	Dizzy Dean	StL, NL	2
1940	Paul Derringer	Cin, NL	2
1945	Hal Newhouser	Det, AL	2
1946	Harry Brecheen	StL, NL	3*
1947	Joe Page	NY, AL	1*
1952	Allie Reynolds	NY, AL	2*
1955	Johnny Podres	Bro, NL	2
1956	Johnny Kucks	NY, AL	1
1957	Lew Burdette	Mil, NL	3
1958	Bob Turley	NY, AL	2*
1960	Harvey Haddix	Pit, NL	2*
1962	Ralph Terry	NY, AL	2
1964	Bob Gibson	StL, NL	2
1965	Sandy Koufax	LA, NL	2
1967	Bob Gibson	StL, NL	3
1968	Mickey Lolich	Det, AL	3
1971	Steve Blass	Pit, NL	2
1972	Catfish Hunter	Oak, AL	2*
1973	Ken Holtzman	Oak, AL	2
1975	Clay Carroll	Cin, NL	1*
1979	Grant Jackson	Pit, NL	1*
1982	Joaquin Andujar	StL, NL	2
1985	Bret Saberhagen	KC, AL	2
1986	Roger McDowell	NY, NL	1*
1987	Frank Viola	Min, AL	2
1991	Jack Morris	Min, AL	2
1997	Jay Powell	Fla, NL	1*

* Won Game Seven in a relief role.

Fall Classics: 1871–1941

1. The first World Series played to completion that pitted the rival champions in two major leagues occurred in 1884. The 1997 fall classic marked the 100th such competition. Since major league baseball is loath to acknowledge that the game existed in the 19th century, there was no official recognition of that milestone. But we're free to celebrate it as we please. It's our first pleasure to introduce one of our favorite unsung fall heroes—the only pitcher to hurl a complete-game win in the finale of two consecutive World Series! Who is he?

   A) He was a 20-game winner both years.
   B) He won 184 games, all in the NL.
   C) His last ML appearance came in the 1929 World Series.
   D) He was a member of the only NL team to win four consecutive flags.
   E) His two successive final-game Series wins came in 1921–22.

2. Who was the first man to play for both an American League and a National League World Series entry?

   A) He played for a Series loser on both occasions.
   B) He was a catcher.
   C) His two Series appearances came three years apart.
   D) He caught George Mullin in his first Series game and Three Finger Brown in his second.
   E) He and a Kansas City A's southpaw who worked 205 innings as a rookie in 1961 but then never won another game in the majors share the same name.

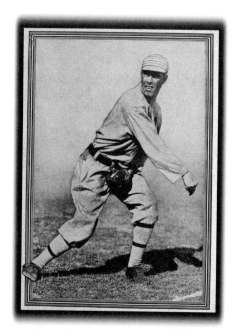

Jack Coombs owns many World Series firsts. On October 20, 1910, he was the first pitcher to collect three hits in a 20th century fall contest, in the process of beating the Cubs, 12–5. Six years later, Coombs became the first pitcher to start a game in an autumn classic for both an American League and a National League team.

First 10 20th Century World Series Participants with Both AL and NL Teams

RANK	NAME	1ST TEAM	2ND TEAM
1	Jimmy Archer	1907 Det, AL	1910 Chi, NL
2	Jack Coombs	1910 Phi, AL	1916 Bro, NL
3	Stuffy McInnis	1911 Phi, AL	1925 Pit, NL
4	Dutch Ruether	1919 Cin, NL	1925 Was, AL
5	Joe Harris	1925 Was, AL	1927 Pit, NL
6	Mark Koenig	1926 NY, AL	1932 Chi, NL
7	Leo Durocher	1928 NY, AL	1934 StL, NL
8	Pat Malone	1929 Chi, NL	1936 NY, AL
9	Tony Lazzeri	1926 NY, AL	1938 Chi, NL
10	Al Simmons	1929 Phi, AL	1939 Cin, NL

Note: Tim Keefe (New York, AA, 1884; New York, NL, 1888) was the first WS participant with teams in two different major leagues. Several members of the 1889–90 Brooklyn team that jumped from the AA to the NL after the 1889 season tied for the honor of being the first to match Keefe's feat. Keefe was also the first Series participant with two different teams; no 19th century performers appeared in postseason play with more than two teams.

3. **Name the first man to see World Series action with three different teams.**
   A) He was also the first to appear in Series action with three losing teams.
   B) His last days in the majors were served as a backup to Lou Gehrig.
   C) His first days in the majors were served as a backup to Fred Tenney.
   D) His last Series appearance was in 1918.
   E) In his first full ML game, he made a mental error that marked him for life.

4. **Many think the first man to appear in fall classics with three different AL teams ought to be in the Hall of Fame, but he's not. Who is he?**
   A) His first and last World Series came 10 years apart.
   B) He owned 2 of the top 10 season BAs by an AL switch-hitter prior to Mickey Mantle's arrival.
   C) He is one of several men who were World Series teammates of the Babe on both the Yankees and the Red Sox.
   D) He was a catcher, and so was his brother.
   E) He was the first man to homer from both sides of the plate in the same game.

First 10 World Series Participants with Three Different Teams

RANK	NAME	1ST TEAM	2ND TEAM	3RD TEAM
1	Fred Merkle	1911–13 NY, NL	1916 Bro, NL	1918 Chi, NL
2	Wally Schang	1913–14 Phi, AL	1918 Bos, AL	1921–23 NY, AL
3	Joe Bush	1913–14 Phi, AL	1918 Bos, AL	1922–23 NY, AL
4	Stuffy McInnis	1911, 1913–14 Phi, AL	1918 Bos, AL	1925 Pit, NL
5	Dutch Ruether	1919 Cin, NL	1925 Was, AL	1926 NY, AL
6	Heinie Groh	1919 Cin, NL	1922–24 NY, NL	1927 Pit, NL
7	Earl Smith	1921–22 NY, NL	1925, 1927 Pit, NL	1928 StL, NL
8	Burleigh Grimes	1920 Bro, NL	1930–31 StL, NL	1932 Chi, NL
9	Mark Koenig	1926–28 NY, AL	1932 Chi, NL	1936 NY, NL
10	Paul Derringer	1931 StL, NL	1939–40 Cin, NL	1945 Chi, NL

5. **What was the first World Series in which all the games were played in stadiums constructed entirely of steel and concrete?**

- A) The losing team rebuilt its home park that year.
- B) The winning team had opened a new home park two years earlier.
- C) The losing team's old park was destroyed by a fire early that season.
- D) The two teams met again in a Series two years later with the same result.
- E) The teams were managed by men who rank 1-2 in career pilot wins.

6. **The first World Series featuring teams that were both managed by men who sat on the bench in street clothes was a first in many ways. When was it?**

- A) Neither manager ever played in the majors.
- B) Neither manager's team still had a major league franchise four years later.
- C) One was the first to pilot Series entrants in two different major leagues.
- D) The other owns the record for the most different teams managed, with seven.
- E) It was the first World Series between two rival ML pennant winners to be played to completion.

7. **What was the first 20th century World Series featuring teams that were both managed by men who sat on the bench in street clothes?**

- A) Both had previously played the same position in the majors.
- B) It was the first World Series in the 20th century to last only four games.
- C) The position the two pilots played was catcher.
- D) The winning pilot was nicknamed "The Miracle Man."
- E) The losing pilot was nicknamed "The Tall Tactician."

8. **Who made the most 20th century World Series starts of any pitcher who never toed the rubber in a fall classic for the New York Yankees, the New York–San Francisco Giants, or the Brooklyn–Los Angeles Dodgers?**

- A) He was 6–4 in his 10 Series starts.
- B) All 10 starts came for the same team.
- C) He won 17 games as a 19-year-old rookie in 1903.
- D) He was beaten in his last Series start in 1914.
- E) He has the most Series wins of any pitcher of American Indian ancestry.

Most 20th Century Series Starts—
None for Yankees, Giants, or Dodgers

RANK	NAME	WS APPEARANCES	TEAMS	STARTS
1	Chief Bender	1905, 1910–11, 1913–14	Phi, AL	10
2	Bob Gibson	1964, 1967–68	StL, NL	9
3	George Earnshaw	1929–31	Phi, AL	8
	Jim Palmer	1966, 1969–71, 1979, 1983	Bal, AL	8
5	Mordecai Brown	1906–08, 1910	Chi, NL	7
	Paul Derringer	1931, 1939–40, 1945	StL, NL, Cin, NL, Chi, NL	7
	Dave McNally	1966, 1969–71	Bal, AL	7
	Ken Holtzman	1972–74	Oak, AL	7
	Gary Nolan	1970, 1972, 1975–76	Cin, NL	7
	Jack Morris	1984, 1991, 1992	Det, AL, Min, AL, Tor, AL	7
	Tom Glavine	1991–92, 1995–96	Atl, NL	7
	John Smoltz	1991–92, 1995–96	Atl, NL	7

Note: Dave Stewart made eight WS starts for Oakland and Toronto but is excluded because he appeared in the 1981 Series twice in relief for the Dodgers.

9. **At age 35, George Whiteman became the 1918 World Series hero after the Red Sox rescued him from the minors late in the season and he hit .250 in fall play. But what 30-year-old Cubs second sacker still languishes in obscurity despite also being salvaged from the minors late in the 1918 season and then proceeding to lead all participants in the 1918 Series with a .389 batting average?**

   A) In 1916 he became the next-to-last ML'er to field under .900 in more than 100 games when he posted an .898 FA as the Philadelphia A's regular third sacker.

   B) His finale was 1920 when he served as the Braves second sacker for most of the season.

   C) He and the A's top catcher prior to Mickey Cochrane share the same initials.

   D) He and his keystone partner in the 1918 World Series had the same first name.

   E) His last name is the same as the shortened last name of Ollie, the outfielder who led the first Cleveland AL team in runs.

10. **In his first World Series, he won three games; in his second fall classic, he played right field in Game One and scored two of his team's three runs, including the winning tally. Who is he?**

   A) His two Series appearances came seven years apart with two different teams.

   B) In 1921 he set an all-time season record for the most RBI in fewer than 200 ABs.

   C) He died in 1985 at age 95.

   D) He has the same nickname as the owner of the highest season BA by a catcher in 100 or more games since the close of World War II.

   E) He is a coholder of the AL season record for the most consecutive hill wins.

Evolution of Season Record for Most RBI with Fewer than 200 ABs

NAME	TEAM	YEAR	ABS	RBI
Rynie Wolters	NY, NA	1871	138	44
Jack Clements	Phi, NL	1896	184	45
Joe Harris	Cle, AL	1919	184	46
Joe Wood	Cle, AL	1921	194	60

11. Which of these 1890s Boston Beaneaters stars was the only one to appear on a team roster of players eligible for a 20th century World Series: Hugh Duffy, Herman Long, Fred Tenney, Kid Nichols, Bobby Lowe, Ted Lewis, or Jack Stivetts?

A) Though eligible for a Series, he saw no action in it.

B) His lone Series came in his final ML season.

C) He played on the first Detroit AL team to see postseason action.

D) He has the all-time record for the lowest season BA (.207) by a second baseman in 500 ABs.

E) He was the first man to hit four homers in a major league game.

12. Which of these 1890s Orioles stars was the only one to appear on a team roster of players eligible for a 20th century World Series: Willie Keeler, Bill Hoffer, John McGraw, Hughie Jennings, Dan McGann, Joe Kelley, or Wilbert Robinson?

A) He is the only one of the aforementioned Orioles stars who was managed by another of the aforementioned Orioles stars in the last season of his career.

B) He is the only one of the aforementioned Orioles stars who failed to see postseason action in the 19th century.

C) He is the only one of the aforementioned Orioles stars to be a switch-hitter.

D) He is the only one of the aforementioned Orioles stars to be primarily a first baseman.

E) He is the only one of the aforementioned Orioles stars to play on a pennant winner under John McGraw.

13. Name the first hurler to win a World Series game for both an American League and a National League team.

A) A Cubs hurler was the second man to do it.

B) Prior to Hank Borowy in 1945, only one other man had ever done it.

C) The first hurler to do it was a perfect 5–0 in World Series action.

D) His last Series start earned Brooklyn's first 20th century postseason win.

E) He scored 31 runs for the 1911 A's to set an AL season record for pitchers.

Most Career Postseason Wins Without a Loss

NAME	YEARS	DIV.	LCS	WS	TOTAL
Lefty Gomez	1932, 1936–39	0	0	6	6
Jack Coombs	1910–11, 1916	0	0	5	5
Herb Pennock	1914, 1923, 1926–27, 1932	0	0	5	5
Monte Pearson	1936–39	0	0	4	4
Jerry Koosman	1969, 1973, 1983	0	0	4	4
Tim Belcher	1988, 1993	0	3	1	4
Rawly Eastwick	1975–76, 1978	0	2	2	4

14. **When Orel Hershiser slapped three hits en route to painting a 6–0 shutout in Game Two of the 1988 fall classic, he became the sixth hurler to date to collect three bingles in a 20th century Series contest. Who had been the last previous hillman to match Hershiser's feat?**

   A) It was last done prior to 1988 in the first year the present Series format was introduced, with the initial two games and the final two games played in the "home" team's park and the visitors hosting the middle three games.

   B) It was done by a lefty who had to go overtime to win a Series opener, 4–3.

   C) The man he beat that day has the record for the most 20th century career wins.

   D) His team ultimately lost the Series in seven games, with the pivotal win going to his mound opponent in Game One.

   E) He's the only pitcher to nail complete-game wins in the finales of two consecutive Series.

Pitchers Compiling Three Hits in a 20th Century World Series Game

NAME	TEAM	YEAR	WS GAME	RESULT
Jack Coombs	Phi, AL	1910	3	W 12–5
Sea Lion Hall	Bos, AL	1912	7	L 11–4
Rube Foster	Bos, AL	1915	2	W 2–1
Dutch Ruether	Cin, NL	1919	1	W 9–1
Art Nehf	NY, NL	1924	1	W 4–3
Orel Hershiser	LA, NL	1988	2	W 6–0

Note: Nehf's game went 12 innings. Hall worked the last eight innings in relief of Joe Wood, who took the loss.

15. **Who was the first man to play on an American League and a National League World Championship team?**

   A) He was also the first man to play on World Championship teams with three different franchises.

   B) One of the franchises has not won a World Championship since he was last a member of it.

   C) In his final Series game, he was 2-for-4 against Walter Johnson.

   D) In his first Series game, he was a defensive replacement for Harry Davis.

   E) He began the 1918 season at third base but returned to his regular position, first base, in time to help his team win its last World Championship to date.

First 10 Members of Championship Teams in Both Leagues

RANK	NAME	1ST TEAM	2ND TEAM
1	Stuffy McInnis	1911 Phi, AL	1925 Pit, NL
2	Leo Durocher	1928 NY, AL	1934 StL, NL
3	Johnny Hopp	1942 StL, NL	1950 NY, AL
4	Enos Slaughter	1942 StL, NL	1956 NY, AL
5	Murry Dickson	1946 StL, NL	1958 NY, AL
6	Bill Skowron	1956 NY, AL	1963 LA, NL
7	Roger Maris	1961 NY, AL	1967 StL, NL
8	Don McMahon	1957 Mil, NL	1968 Det, AL
	Eddie Mathews	1957 Mil, NL	1968 Det, AL
	Dick Tracewski	1963 LA, NL	1968 Det, AL

16. **Who was the first manager with no big league playing experience to pilot a World Series entry in the 20th century?**
    A) His team won a six-game Series.
    B) He piloted the lone pitcher to register four decisions and three wins in a Series that went fewer than seven games.
    C) His team finished third in 1915, his rookie year as a pilot, after he replaced Nixey Callahan at its helm.
    D) He was later a longtime president of the PCL.
    E) His nickname was "Pants."

17. **Who is the only man to play in every World Series game that involved the Washington Senators?**
    A) There were 19 such games, and in 1925 his 19 triples tied a Senators' club record.
    B) He is the only AL'er to appear in five World Series prior to 1964 without ever playing for the Yankees, the Red Sox, or the Athletics.
    C) His 329 total bases in 1925 are the Senators' team record.
    D) He's in the Hall of Fame.
    E) His real first name was Leon, but he was better known by the same nickname as the first hurler to log more than 10 complete games and 300 saves in his career.

18. **Florida's Game One Series starter in 1997, Livan Hernandez, had just nine regular-season wins. The only hurler with fewer than nine wins named to start a Series opener set the mark more than half a century earlier. Who is he?**
    A) His Game One start resulted in his 167th career win, counting both regular-season and postseason action.
    B) He was the last Federal League product to start a World Series game.
    C) In 1923 he won 20 games for a last-place team.
    D) His lone Series start came six years after Mule Watson had been the first Game One starter to post fewer than 10 regular-season wins.
    E) His Game One Series start in 1929 resulted in his last ML win.

Game One World Series Starters with Fewest Regular-Season Wins

RANK	NAME	TEAM	YEAR	W
1	Howard Ehmke	Phi, AL	1929	7
2	Mule Watson	NY, NL	1923	9
	General Crowder	Det, AL	1934	9
	Denny Galehouse	StL, AL	1944	9
	Joe Magrane	StL, NL	1987	9
	Livan Hernandez	Fla, NL	1997	9
7	Rube Marquard	Bro, NL	1920	10
	Dave Koslo	NY, NL	1951	10
9	Roger Craig	LA, NL	1959	11
	Don Gullett	Cin, NL	1976	11
	Bob Walk	Phi, NL	1980	11

Note: The abbreviated 1981 strike season is excluded.

19. **Who is the only man to lead all Series participants in at bats despite compiling a .000 batting average?**
   - A) He was 0-for-17 in a four-game Series that his team lost.
   - B) The left fielder for his team, who had been the NL home run champ four years earlier, was 0-for-15.
   - C) Charlie Keller was the leading hitter in that World Series.
   - D) He and Keller were teammates eight years later.
   - E) He played second base for the losing team in the 1939 fall classic.

20. **What immortal finished his career prior to 1941 with a .361 career World Series batting average to lead all men with 100 at bats in Series action?**
   - A) He also had a .731 SA in Series action.
   - B) All of his World Series at bats came with the same team.
   - C) He played on the winning team in every World Series appearance but his first.
   - D) His .361 Series BA is 21 points higher than his career regular-season BA.
   - E) Only in 1938, his final Series, did he fail to tag an extra-base hit.

Players with a .300 Career World Series BA (Minimum 100 ABs)

RANK	NAME	TEAM	YEARS	ABS	HITS	WS BA
1	Lou Gehrig	NY, AL	1926–28/32/36–38	119	43	.361
2	Eddie Collins	Phi/Chi, AL	1910–11/13–14/17/19	128	42	.328
3	Babe Ruth	Bos/NY, AL	1914–15/18/21–23/26–28/32	129	42	.326
4	Steve Garvey	LA/SD, NL	1974/77–78/81/84	113	36	.319
5	Bobby Richardson	NY, AL	1957–58/61–64	131	40	.305

World Series Batting Leaders

	BA	NAME	TEAM	RBI	NAME	TEAM
19th Century						
1884	.444	Jerry Denny	Pro, NL	2	Done by four men	Pro, NL
	.444	Jack Farrell	Pro, NL			
	.444	Barney Gilligan	Pro, NL			
1885	.423	Cap Anson	Chi, NL	Unavailable		
1886	.400	Tip O'Neill	StL, AA	5	Tip O'Neill	StL, AA
				5	Bob Caruthers	StL, AA
				5	Bill Gleason	StL, AA
1887	.362	Sam Thompson	Det, NL	9	Charlie Bennett	Det, NL
1888	.400	Jocko Milligan	StL, AA	12	Art Whitney	NY, NL
1889	.417	Monte Ward	NY, NL	12	Roger Connor	NY, NL
1890	.471	Patsy Donovan	Bro, NL	8	Jimmy Wolf	Lou, AA

	BA	NAME	TEAM	RBI	NAME	TEAM
20th Century						
1903	.367	Jimmy Sebring	Pit, NL	7	Tommy Leach	Pit, NL
				7	Hobe Ferris	Bos, NL
1904	No World Series					
1905	.316	Mike Donlin	NY, NL	4	Dan McGann	NY, NL
1906	.333	George Rohe	Chi, AL	6	George Davis	Chi, AL
	.333	Jiggs Donahue	Chi, AL			
1907	.471	Harry Steinfeldt	Chi, NL	4	Jimmy Slagle	Chi, NL
1908	.421	Frank Chance	Chi, NL	5	Joe Tinker	Chi, NL
1909	.346	Jim Delahanty	Det, AL	7	Fred Clarke	Pit, NL
1910	.429	Eddie Collins	Phi, AL	8	Danny Murphy	Phi, AL
1911	.375	Frank Baker	Phi, AL	5	Frank Baker	Phi, AL
				5	Harry Davis	Phi, AL
1912	.400	Buck Herzog	NY, NL	5	Red Murray	NY, NL
1913	.450	Frank Baker	Phi, AL	7	Frank Baker	Phi, AL
1914	.545	Hank Gowdy	Bos, NL	3	Hank Gowdy	Bos, NL
				3	Rabbit Maranville	Bos, NL
1915	.444	Duffy Lewis	Bos, AL	6	Fred Luderus	Phi, NL
1916	.353	Duffy Lewis	Bos, AL	6	Larry Gardner	Bos, AL
1917	.500	Dave Robertson	NY, NL	5	Benny Kauff	NY, NL
				5	Chick Gandil	Chi, AL
1918	.389	Charlie Pick	Chi, NL	2	Done by five men	Chi, NL/Bos, AL
1919	.375	Joe Jackson	Chi, AL	8	Pat Duncan	Cin, NL
1920	.333	Steve O'Neill	Cle, AL	6	Elmer Smith	Cle, AL
	.333	Charlie Jamieson	Cle, AL			
	.333	Zack Wheat	Bro, NL			
1921	.364	Frank Snyder	NY, NL	7	Irish Meusel	NY, NL
1922	.474	Heinie Groh	NY, NL	7	Irish Meusel	NY, NL
1923	.417	Aaron Ward	NY, AL	8	Bob Meusel	NY, AL
1924	.385	Joe Judge	Was, AL	7	Bucky Harris	Was, AL
				7	Goose Goslin	Was, AL
1925	.458	Max Carey	Pit, NL	6	Joe Harris	Was, AL
				6	Kiki Cuyler	Pit, NL
1926	.417	Tommy Thevenow	StL, NL	6	Les Bell	StL, NL
1927	.500	Mark Koenig	NY, AL	7	Babe Ruth	NY, AL
1928	.625	Babe Ruth	NY, AL	9	Lou Gehrig	NY, AL
1929	.471	Hack Wilson	Chi, NL	6	Mule Haas	Phi, AL
1930	.364	Al Simmons	Phi, AL	5	Jimmy Dykes	Phi, AL
1931	.500	Pepper Martin	StL, NL	8	Al Simmons	Phi, AL
1932	.529	Lou Gehrig	NY, AL	8	Lou Gehrig	NY, AL
1933	.389	Mel Ott	NY, NL	4	Mel Ott	NY, NL
				4	Fred Schulte	Was, AL
1934	.379	Joe Medwick	StL, NL	7	Hank Greenberg	Det, AL
	.379	Charlie Gehringer	Det, AL			
1935	.385	Pete Fox	Det, AL	6	Billy Herman	Chi, NL

	BA	NAME	TEAM	RBI	NAME	TEAM
1936	.455	Jake Powell	NY, AL	7	Tony Lazzeri	NY, AL
1937	.400	Tony Lazzeri	NY, AL	6	George Selkirk	NY, AL
1938	.471	Stan Hack	Chi, NL	6	Frankie Crosetti	NY, AL
				6	Joe Gordon	NY, AL
1939	.438	Charlie Keller	NY, AL	6	Charlie Keller	NY, AL
1940	.370	Billy Werber	Cin, NL	6	Jimmy Ripple	Cin, NL
				6	Pinky Higgins	Det, AL
				6	Hank Greenberg	Det, AL
1941	.500	Joe Gordon	NY, AL	5	Joe Gordon	NY, AL
				5	Charlie Keller	NY, AL
1942	.381	Phil Rizzuto	NY, AL	5	Charlie Keller	NY, AL
				5	Whitey Kurowski	StL, NL
1943	.357	Marty Marion	StL, NL	4	Bill Dickey	NY, AL
1944	.438	George McQuinn	StL, AL	5	George McQuinn	StL, AL
1945	.423	Phil Cavarretta	Chi, NL	8	Bill Nicholson	Chi, NL
1946	.412	Harry Walker	StL, NL	6	Harry Walker	StL, NL
1947	.500	Johnny Lindell	NY, AL	7	Johnny Lindell	NY, AL
1948	.389	Earl Torgeson	Bos, NL	5	Jim Hegan	Cle, AL
				5	Bob Elliott	Bos, NL
1949	.500	Bobby Brown	NY, AL	5	Bobby Brown	NY, AL
1950	.429	Granny Hamner	Phi, NL	3	Jerry Coleman	NY, AL
	.429	Gene Woodling	NY, AL			
1951	.458	Monte Irvin	NY, NL	7	Gil McDougald	NY, AL
1952	.348	Gene Woodling	NY, AL	8	Duke Snider	Bro, NL
1953	.500	Billy Martin	NY, AL	8	Billy Martin	NY, AL
1954	.500	Vic Wertz	Cle, AL	7	Dusty Rhodes	NY, NL
1955	.417	Yogi Berra	NY, AL	7	Duke Snider	Bro, NL
1956	.360	Yogi Berra	NY, AL	10	Yogi Berra	NY, AL
1957	.393	Hank Aaron	Mil, NL	7	Hank Aaron	Mil, NL
1958	.412	Bill Bruton	Mil, NL	7	Bill Skowron	NY, AL
1959	.391	Ted Kluszewski	Chi, AL	10	Ted Kluszewski	Chi, AL
	.391	Gil Hodges	LA, NL			
1960	.400	Mickey Mantle	NY, AL	12	Bobby Richardson	NY, AL
1961	.391	Bobby Richardson	NY, AL	7	Hector Lopez	NY, AL
1962	.368	Jose Pagan	SF, NL	5	Chuck Hiller	SF, NL
				5	Roger Maris	NY, AL
1963	.400	Tommy Davis	LA, NL	3	Willie Davis	LA, NL
				3	Johnny Roseboro	LA, NL
				3	Bill Skowron	LA, NL
1964	.478	Tim McCarver	StL, NL	8	Mickey Mantle	NY, AL
1965	.379	Ron Fairly	LA, NL	6	Ron Fairly	LA, NL
1966	.357	Boog Powell	Bal, AL	3	Frank Robinson	Bal, AL
1967	.414	Lou Brock	StL, NL	7	Roger Maris	StL, NL

	BA	NAME	TEAM	RBI	NAME	TEAM
1968	.464	Lou Brock	StL, NL	8	Al Kaline	Det, AL
				8	Jim Northrup	Det, AL
1969	.400	Ron Swoboda	NY, NL	4	Donn Clendenon	NY, NL
1970	.474	Paul Blair	Bal, AL	8	Lee May	Cin, NL
1971	.414	Roberto Clemente	Pit, NL	5	Bob Robertson	Pit, NL
				5	Brooks Robinson	Bal, AL
1972	.435	Tony Perez	Cin, NL	9	Gene Tenace	Oak, AL
1973	.423	Rusty Staub	NY, NL	6	Rusty Staub	NY, NL
				6	Reggie Jackson	Oak, AL
1974	.381	Steve Garvey	LA, NL	4	Joe Rudi	Oak, AL
1975	.370	Pete Rose	Cin, NL	7	Tony Perez	Cin, NL
1976	.533	Johnny Bench	Cin, NL	6	Johnny Bench	Cin, NL
1977	.450	Reggie Jackson	NY, AL	8	Reggie Jackson	NY, AL
1978	.438	Brian Doyle	NY, AL	8	Reggie Jackson	NY, AL
1979	.500	Phil Garner	Pit, NL	7	Willie Stargell	Pit, NL
1980	.478	Amos Otis	KC, AL	8	Willie Aikens	KC, AL
1981	.438	Lou Piniella	NY, AL	7	Pedro Guerrero	LA, NL
				7	Bob Watson	NY, AL
1982	.414	Robin Yount	Mil, AL	8	Keith Hernandez	StL, NL
1983	.385	Rick Dempsey	Bal, AL	3	Rich Dauer	Bal, AL
	.385	John Lowenstein	Bal, AL	3	Eddie Murray	Bal, AL
1984	.450	Alan Trammell	Det, AL	7	Kirk Gibson	Det, AL
1985	.370	George Brett	KC, AL	6	Frank White	KC, AL
1986	.433	Marty Barrett	Bos, AL	9	Dwight Evans	Bos, AL
1987	.412	Steve Lombardozzi	Min, AL	7	Dan Gladden	Min, AL
1988	.368	Mickey Hatcher	LA, NL	5	Mickey Hatcher	LA, NL
				5	Jose Canseco	Oak, AL
1989	.474	Rickey Henderson	Oak, AL	7	Terry Steinbach	Oak, AL
1990	.750	Billy Hatcher	Cin, NL	5	Chris Sabo	Cin, NL
				5	Eric Davis	Cin, NL
1991	.417	Mark Lemke	Atl, NL	6	David Justice	Atl, NL
1992	.533	Deion Sanders	Atl, NL	5	Lonnie Smith	Atl, NL
1993	.500	Paul Molitor	Tor, AL	9	Tony Fernandez	Tor, AL
1994	No World Series					
1995	.360	Marquis Grissom	Atl, NL	5	David Justice	Atl, NL
1996	.444	Marquis Grissom	Atl, NL	6	Fred McGriff	Atl, NL
				6	Andruw Jones	Atl, NL
1997	.389	Darren Daulton	Fla, NL	9	Moises Alou	Fla, NL
1998	.500	Tony Gwynn	SD, NL	6	Scott Brosius	NY, AL

Note: Minimum three plate appearances per game to qualify as batting leader.

Fall Classics: 1942–98

1. **The first man to lead the majors in hitting in both the regular season and the postseason also owns the highest World Series batting average by a regular-season major league batting leader. To what three-time Series participant do these two significant distinctions belong?**

    A) He was just 19 when he played in his first postseason game.

    B) He spent his entire 22-year career with teams located in the same city.

    C) He was fired as his team's player-manager prior to the 1954 season when he stated flatly that his club was too weak to win the NL pennant.

    D) He led the NL in hits the year before he won his lone batting title.

    E) His magical season came in 1945 with the Cubs.

Highest World Series BA, Regular-Season BA Leader

RANK	NAME	TEAM	YEAR	RS BA	WS BA
1	Phil Cavarretta	Chi, NL	1945	.355	.423
2	Tommy Davis	LA, NL	1963	.326	.400
3	George Brett	KC, AL	1980	.390	.375
4	Al Simmons	Phi, AL	1931	.390	.333
	Carl Furillo	Bro, NL	1953	.344	.333
6	Joe DiMaggio	NY, AL	1939	.381	.313
7	Wade Boggs	Bos, AL	1986	.357	.290
8	Willie Mays	NY, NL	1954	.345	.286
9	Stan Musial	StL, NL	1943	.357	.278
10	Tony Gwynn	SD, NL	1984	.351	.263

Note: Cavarretta and Davis led all Series participants in batting.

2. **Pat Malone was the first man to appear in a World Series for teams in both major leagues and play under the same manager on each occasion—Joe McCarthy, in 1929 and 1936. Only one man has since matched Malone's unusual postseason feat. Can you name this postexpansion performer?**

    A) Like Malone, he was a pitcher.

    B) Like Malone, he was on a losing NL team in his first Series and a winning AL team in his second.

    C) He played for the first man to pilot a Series winner in each league.

    D) In 1983 he narrowly missed hurling a perfect game when Jerry Hairston stroked a pinch single off him with two out in the ninth.

    E) He started and won Game Three of the 1984 World Series for Sparky.

3. **Frank Bancroft, Providence's manager in 1884, is the only pilot of a 19th century World Series entrant never to lose a game in fall play. However, three managers have logged a perfect 1.000 winning percentage in 20th century World Series play through 1998. Who are they?**
   A) One was the first pilot to win a World Series in four straight games.
   B) Two of the three piloted clubs that swept an A's team.
   C) The third played in more Series games that any other man who managed a team that swept a fall clash.
   D) Each of the three managed a club that was a long shot to win the Series, let alone in a sweep.
   E) The three pilots beat teams managed by Connie Mack, Walter Alston, and Tony LaRussa, respectively.

4. **As you'd expect, the only man to participate in all 44 World Series games between the Brooklyn Dodgers and the New York Yankees is a Hall of Famer. Name him.**
   A) In his first World Series at bat, he faced Red Ruffing.
   B) In his last World Series at bat, he faced Johnny Kucks.
   C) His second of two Series homers came in 1952 off Ray Scarborough in Scarborough's lone postseason appearance.
   D) In his first Series, he outhit a fellow rookie star at his position, .200 to .111.
   E) He's the Dodgers all-time all-star shortstop.

Players in the Most World Series Games Between the New York Yankees and Brooklyn Dodgers

RANK	NAME	TEAM	YEARS	GAMES
1	Pee Wee Reese	Brooklyn	1941/47/49/52–53/55–56	44
2	Jackie Robinson	Brooklyn	1947/49/52–53/55–56	38
3	Phil Rizzuto	New York	1941/47/49/52–53/55	37
	Yogi Berra	New York	1947/49/52–53/55–56	37
5	Carl Furillo	Brooklyn	1947/49/52–53/55–56	36
6	Duke Snider	Brooklyn	1949/52–53/55–56	32
	Gil Hodges	Brooklyn	1949/52–53/55–56	32
	Roy Campanella	Brooklyn	1949/52–53/55–56	32
9	Hank Bauer	New York	1949/52–53/55–56	29
10	Gil McDougald	New York	1952-53/55-56	27
	Billy Martin	New York	1952–53/55–56	27

5. **In 1947, while the Giants were slugging a National League–record 221 homers (since broken), the Dodgers hit a mere 83 and added just 1 in the seven-game World Series. Who hit the lone Brooklyn dinger, an unmemorable solo shot, in that otherwise unforgettable Series?**
   A) It came in Game Two and had little bearing on the final result.
   B) Its claimant debuted with the Yankees in 1931.
   C) Though his Series homer mattered little, his brother once notched a Series-winning RBI.
   D) His Series homer was his last four-bagger in Brooklyn garb.
   E) He was nicknamed "The People's Choice."

6. **What is the only team since World War II without a single man on its Series roster who had previously played in a fall classic?**

    A) The team's pilot had pitched one inning in a Series 21 years earlier.

    B) Just one man with previous Series experience—Willie Jones—played for the team at any point that season.

    C) The team lost the Series in five games.

    D) The team featured a rookie catcher and a rookie nine-game winner who never pitched again in the majors after working the final inning of the final World Series game in a relief role.

    E) The team's right fielder had been the NL Rookie of the Year five years earlier and was the AL MVP five years later.

7. **In 1969, the New York Mets' World Series roster listed only one man who had postseason experience. Who was he?**

    A) He debuted with the 1962 Indians.

    B) His previous World Series action came against the Yankees.

    C) He led the NL in relief wins in 1964, the year he first saw Series action.

    D) He topped the Miracle Mets with 13 saves.

    E) He and the post-1893 record holder for the most runs scored by a rookie share the same initials.

8. **After driving in just 26 runs in 460 regular-season at bats, who had 12 ribbies in Series action that year?**

    A) Two years later, he set a new franchise record (since broken) when he collected 209 regular-season hits.

    B) He is one of only four players who compiled 600 ABs in their final ML seasons.

    C) His last 30 ABs the year he drove in 38 runs total came in a seven-game World Series that his team lost.

    D) His 99 runs in 1962 are the most by an AL second baseman during the 1961–76 era.

    E) His 12 RBI in 1960 are a World Series record.

Players Compiling 600 ABs in Their Final Seasons

NAME	TEAM	YEAR	BA	AB
Buck Weaver	Chi, AL	1920	.331	629
Joe Gedeon	StL, AL	1920	.292	606
Tony Lupien	Chi, AL	1948	.246	617
Bobby Richardson	NY, AL	1966	.251	610

9. **To date, only one man has seen Series action with four different teams. His first appearance came in his rookie year. Who is he?**

    A) He was the first man to face a Kansas City Royals pitcher in a Series game.

    B) He was also the first man ever to bat for the Royals in Game Seven of a Series.

    C) He is the current record holder for the most career World Series home runs by a member of the Atlanta Braves franchise.

    D) He led the NL in runs as a member of the last Cardinals World Championship team to date.

    E) As a Phils frosh in 1980, he became the only 20th century rookie ever to collect 100 hits in fewer than 300 ABs.

10. Rookie Johnny Beazley of the Cardinals was the star of the 1942 World Series, leading all hurlers with a 2.50 ERA and two complete-game wins. Rookie Series batting leaders have been few and far between. In 1939, Charlie Keller of the Yankees became the only frosh to lead all Series combatants in both batting and RBI when he hit a rookie-record .438. Keller's frosh record has since been tied by whom?

A) His record-tying .438 BA came in a six-game fray and led all Series participants.

B) As a frosh, he hit just .192 during the regular season.

C) His rookie BA turned out to be his high-water mark in a four-year career.

D) His lone Series opportunity was created by an injury to Willie Randolph.

E) His brother Denny played the same position in fall play for a rival AL team three years prior to his unlikely Series feat.

RANK	NAME	TEAM	YEAR	ABS	RBI	BA
\multicolumn{7}{c}{**Rookies Batting .300 in a World Series**}
1	Charlie Keller	NY, AL	1939	16	6	.438
	Brian Doyle	NY, AL	1978	16	2	.438
3	Lloyd Waner	Pit, NL	1927	15	0	.400
	Joe Gordon	NY, AL	1938	15	6	.400
5	Jimmy Sebring	Pit, NL	1903	30	5	.367
6	Joe DiMaggio	NY, AL	1936	26	3	.346
7	Freddy Lindstrom	NY, NL	1924	30	4	.333
8	Tom Tresh	NY, AL	1962	28	4	.321
9	Mike McCormick	Cin, NL	1940	29	2	.310
10	Harry Taylor	Lou, AA	1890	30	2	.300
	Billy Johnson	NY, AL	1943	20	3	.300

Note: Minimum 15 ABs. Sebring's rookie status in 1903 is debatable.

Charlie Keller, seen here scoring, led all hitters with his .438 BA in the 1939 World Series. His performance gave him a piece of the WS record for the highest BA by a rookie. Do you know with whom he's tied?

11. **Who is the only player to participate in all six World Series to date involving the Baltimore Orioles?**

    A) He scored his first postseason run in Game Three of the 1970 ALCS.

    B) He scored his first World Series run in Game Four of the 1971 Series.

    C) He was 0-for-4 in his only two Series games in 1979 and was removed on both occasions for a pinch hitter.

    D) He beat Steve Carlton in relief in his last Series appearance.

    E) He holds the Orioles' franchise record for the most career wins.

12. **Among the many disparate and distinguished records a certain pitcher holds is the mark for the longest span of time between his first and his second World Series starts. Who is he?**

    A) He also holds the record for the longest span of time between his first and his second LCS starts.

    B) The year of his first postseason start, he was 15–16, the only season he notched as many as 30 decisions.

    C) He is one of very few men to win 100 games in two different major leagues.

    D) He is the only man to win 100 games in two different major leagues but never win 20 games in a season.

    E) In 1998 he broke Juan Marichal's record for the most career wins by a Latino hurler.

Longest Span of Time Between First and Second World Series Starts

RANK	NAME	TEAM	YEARS	SPAN
1	Dennis Martinez	Bal, AL/Cle, AL	1979/1995	16
2	Steve Carlton	StL, NL/Phi, NL	1967/1980	13
3	Warren Spahn	Bos, NL/Mil, NL	1948/1957	9
4	Freddie Fitzsimmons	NY, NL/Bro, NL	1933/1941	8
	Bert Blyleven	Pit, NL/Min, AL	1979/1987	8
	Rick Reuschel	NY, AL/SF, NL	1981/1989	8
7	Bob Shawkey	Phi, AL/NY, AL	1914/1921	7
	Bob Welch	LA, NL/Oak, AL	1981/1988	7

13. **The only man to date to homer in his lone World Series plate appearance was not a pinch hitter—far from it. In fact, he hit just 12 regular-season taters in more than 1,500 at bats. Who is he?**

    A) His Series mound victim would go on to capture a share of the NL Rookie of the Year Award that season.

    B) His team was a Series sweep victim.

    C) His .203 career BA is the lowest of any man with at least 1,000 career ABs who homered in Series play.

    D) He hit .250 as the Yankees regular shortstop in 1974.

    E) He and the most recent NL'er to win a Triple Crown share the same initials.

14. Although a member of four pennant-winning teams during the 1970s, what performer never saw a single moment of World Series action?

  A) He also never played in an LCS.

  B) He and Arndt Jorgens have a lot in common.

  C) He played with the same team from 1970 through 1977 but was not on his team's Series roster in its first fall appearance in the 1970s.

  D) In eight seasons as Johnny Bench's little-used backup, he posted a .187 BA with a high of .248 in 1976.

  E) He later played for and managed the Mariners.

Most World Series Games Without Ever Seeing Action

RANK	NAME	TEAM	YEARS	GAMES
1	Arndt Jorgens	NY, AL	1932, 1936–39	23
2	Alex Gaston	NY, NL	1921–23	19
3	Bill Plummer	Cin, NL	1972, 1975–76	16
4	Joe Glenn	NY, AL	1936–38	15
5	Joe Jenkins	Chi, AL	1917, 1919	14
6	Heinie Schuble	Det, AL	1934–35	13
7	Cy Perkins	Phi, AL	1929–30	11
	Jack Saltzgaver	NY, AL	1936–37	11
	Don Heffner	NY, AL	1936–37	11
	Jeff Torborg	LA, NL	1965–66	11

Note: Pitchers excluded.

15. In his lone World Series, what 23-year veteran played right field for the loser but led all participants with 11 hits, a .423 batting average, and 16 total bases?

  A) In the NLCS that year he collected just three hits, but all were home runs.

  B) He led his team that season with 76 RBI.

  C) He is the only player to collect 500 hits with four different teams.

  D) The team for which he played in his lone World Series was the first flag winner in ML history without a 20-game winner, a .300 hitter, or a player with 100 RBI.

  E) In 1983–84 he collected 42 pinch hits for the same NL team with which he saw his only postseason action.

16. Several pitchers have won three games in a best-of-seven World Series, but only one has lost three. Who is he?

  A) Prior to the Series in which he gained immortality, he had a 3–12 career record.

  B) He debuted with the 1978 Cards.

  C) His last ML appearance was a two-inning relief stint in the 1987 Series.

  D) His three Series losses came in less than four innings of work.

  E) His team's fourth loss in that Series was sustained by Ron Guidry.

Pitchers with Three Losses in a World Series			
NAME	**TEAM**	**YEAR**	**TEAM RESULT**
Adonis Terry	Bro, AA	1889	L 6–3
Lefty Williams	Chi, AL	1919	L 5–3
George Frazier	NY, AL	1981	L 4–2

Note: The 1887 and the 1888 World Series, which went 15 and 11 games, respectively, are excluded because the last few games in each were exhibition contests.

17. Who is the only man to date to play in three consecutive World Series with three different teams?
   A) They were his only three Series appearances.
   B) His final Series at bat was also his last career AB.
   C) Prior to his three Series appearances, he played on four ALCS losers.
   D) He never played in the field in a World Series game.
   E) He was the AL MVP in 1979.

18. Name the lone pitcher to win at least one game in five straight World Series.
   A) All five wins came with the same team.
   B) He was 11–12 as a 28-year-old rookie with Cleveland in 1943.
   C) He died in 1994.
   D) One year during his skein, he tossed two no-hitters.
   E) His nickname was "The Chief."

19. Who had the lowest regular-season winning percentage of any pitcher chosen as the Game One World Series starter for his team?
   A) He was the first Game One starter since Denny Galehouse in 1944 to have a sub-.500 regular-season winning percentage.
   B) His .448 winning percentage (13–16) broke General Crowder's record for the lowest mark by a Game One starter.
   C) He was the only pitcher to make two World Series starts the year he posted a record-low winning percentage by a Game One starter.
   D) He got the win in the first World Series game played west of the Rockies.
   E) In 1968, his last full season, he collected eight shutouts but only 14 wins.

Game One World Series Starters with the Lowest Regular-Season Winning Percentage

RANK	NAME	TEAM	YEAR	W–L	PCT.
1	Don Drysdale	LA, NL	1966	13–16	.448
2	General Crowder	Det, AL	1934	9–11	.450
3	Jon Matlack	NY, NL	1973	14–16	.467
4	Denny Galehouse	StL, AL	1944	9–10	.474
5	Dave Koslo	NY, NL	1951	10–9	.526
6	Ken Holtzman	Oak, AL	1974	19–17	.528
7	Charlie Leibrandt	Atl, NL	1991	15–13	.536
8	Danny Jackson	KC, AL	1985	14–12	.538
9	Mule Watson	NY, NL	1923	9–7	.563
	Joe Magrane	StL, NL	1987	9–7	.563

20. What pitcher twice led all World Series participants in ERA in the process of compiling a 0.36 career Series ERA to top all men who have hurled at least 20 innings in fall classics?

- A) He finished with the 1980 BoSox, four years after his last Series appearance.
- B) He debuted with a perfect 3–0 record in 50 games for the Dodgers in 1968.
- C) He led the NL in starts in 1973.
- D) He gave up his only earned run in 25.1 innings in the 1975 World Series.
- E) Though never a 20-game winner, he twice won 19 for the Reds.

World Series Pitching Leaders

	WINS	NAME	TEAM	ERA	NAME	TEAM
19th Century						
1884	3	Hoss Radbourn	Pro, NL	0.00	Hoss Radbourn	Pro, NL
1885	3	Jim McCormick	Chi, NL	0.61	Dave Foutz	StL, AA
1886	2	Bob Caruthers	StL, AA	2.01	John Clarkson	Chi, NL
	2	John Clarkson	Chi, NL			
1887	4	Lady Baldwin	Det, NL	1.50	Lady Baldwin	Det, NL
	4	Charlie Getzein	Det, NL			
	4	Bob Caruthers	StL, NL			
1888	4	Tim Keefe	NY, NL	0.51	Tim Keefe	NY, NL
1889	4	Cannonball Crane	NY, NL	1.17	Hank O'Day	NY, NL
1890	2	Tom Lovett	Bro, NL	1.35	Red Ehret	Lou, AA
	2	Red Ehret	Lou, AA			
20th Century						
1903	3	Bill Dinneen	Bos, AL	1.59	Cy Young	Bos, AL
	3	Deacon Phillippe	Pit, NL			
1904	No World Series					
1905	3	Christy Mathewson	NY, NL	0.00	Christy Mathewson	NY, NL

	WINS	NAME	TEAM	ERA	NAME	TEAM
1906	2	Ed Walsh	Chi, AL	1.00	Nick Altrock	Chi, AL
1907	1	Done by four men	Chi, NL	0.00	Mordecai Brown	Chi, NL
1908	2	Orval Overall	Chi, NL	0.00	Mordecai Brown	Chi, NL
	2	Mordecai Brown	Chi, NL			
1909	3	Babe Adams	Pit, NL	1.33	Babe Adams	Pit, NL
1910	3	Jack Coombs	Phi, AL	1.93	Chief Bender	Phi, AL
1911	2	Chief Bender	Phi, AL	1.04	Chief Bender	Phi, AL
1912	3	Smokey Joe Wood	Bos, AL	0.50	Hugh Bedient	Bos, AL
				0.50	Rube Marquard	NY, NL
1913	2	Chief Bender	Phi, AL	0.95	Eddie Plank	Phi, AL
				0.95	Christy Mathewson	NY, NL
1914	2	Bill James	Bos, NL	0.00	Bill James	Bos, NL
	2	Dick Rudolph	Bos, NL			
1915	2	Rube Foster	Bos, AL	1.00	Dutch Leonard	Bos, AL
1916	2	Ernie Shore	Bos, AL	0.64	Babe Ruth	Bos, AL
1917	3	Red Faber	Chi, AL	0.00	Rube Benton	NY, NL
1918	2	Carl Mays	Bos, AL	1.00	Hippo Vaughn	Chi, NL
	2	Babe Ruth	Bos, AL			
1919	2	Hod Eller	Cin, NL	0.64	Jimmy Ring	Cin, NL
	2	Dickie Kerr	Chi, AL			
1920	3	Stan Coveleski	Cle, AL	0.00	Duster Mails	Cle, AL
1921	2	Phil Douglas	NY, NL	0.00	Waite Hoyt	NY, AL
	2	Jesse Barnes	NY, NL			
	2	Waite Hoyt	NY, AL			
1922	1	Done by four men	NY, NL	0.00	Jack Scott	NY, NL
1923	2	Herb Pennock	NY, AL	0.90	Sam Jones	NY, AL
1924	2	Tom Zachary	Was, AL	1.83	Art Nehf	NY, NL
1925	2	Remy Kremer	Pit, NL	2.08	Walter Johnson	Was, AL
	2	Vic Aldridge	Pit, NL			
	2	Walter Johnson	Was, NL			
1926	2	Pete Alexander	StL, NL	0.89	Pete Alexander	StL, NL
	2	Jesse Haines	StL, NL			
	2	Herb Pennock	NY, AL			
1927	1	Done by four men	NY, AL	0.84	Wilcy Moore	NY, AL
1928	2	Waite Hoyt	NY, AL	1.50	Waite Hoyt	NY, AL
1929	1	Done by five men	NY, AL/Chi, NL	0.82	Guy Bush	Chi, NL
1930	2	George Earnshaw	Phi, AL	0.72	George Earnshaw	Phi, AL
	2	Lefty Grove	Phi, AL			
1931	2	Bill Hallahan	StL, NL	0.49	Bill Hallahan	StL, NL
	2	Burleigh Grimes	StL, NL			
	2	Lefty Grove	Phi, AL			
1932	1	Done by four men	NY, AL	1.00	Lefty Gomez	NY, AL
1933	2	Carl Hubbell	NY, NL	0.00	Carl Hubbell	NY, NL
1934	2	Paul Dean	StL, NL	1.00	Paul Dean	StL, NL
	2	Dizzy Dean	StL, NL			

	WINS	NAME	TEAM	ERA	NAME	TEAM
1935	2	Tommy Bridges	Det, AL	0.54	Lon Warneke	Chi, NL
	2	Lon Warneke	Chi, NL			
1936	2	Lefty Gomez	NY, AL	2.00	Monte Pearson	NY, AL
1937	2	Lefty Gomez	NY, AL	1.00	Red Ruffing	NY, AL
1938	2	Red Ruffing	NY, AL	1.00	Monte Pearson	NY, AL
1939	1	Done by four men	NY, AL	0.00	Monte Pearson	NY, AL
1940	2	Bucky Walters	Cin, NL	0.79	Johnny Gorsica	Det, AL
	2	Paul Derringer	Cin, NL			
	2	Bobo Newsom	Det, AL			
1941	1	Done by five men	NY, AL/Bro, NL	1.00	Ernie Bonham	NY, AL
				1.00	Marius Russo	NY, AL
				1.00	Red Ruffing	NY, AL
1942	2	Johnny Beazley	StL, NL	0.00	Ernie White	StL, NL
1943	2	Spud Chandler	NY, AL	0.00	Marius Russo	NY, AL
1944	1	Done by six men	StL, NL/StL, AL	0.00	Jack Kramer	StL, AL
1945	2	Hal Newhouser	Det, AL	0.66	Dizzy Trout	Det, AL
	2	Hank Borowy	Chi, NL			
1946	3	Harry Brecheen	StL, NL	0.00	Joe Dobson	Bos, AL
1947	2	Spec Shea	NY, AL	0.87	Hugh Casey	Bro, NL
	2	Hugh Casey	Bro, NL			
1948	2	Bob Lemon	Cle, AL	0.00	Gene Bearden	Cle, AL
1949	1	Done by five men	NY, AL/Bro, NL	0.00	Allie Reynolds	NY, AL
1950	1	Done by four men	NY, AL	0.00	Vic Raschi	NY, AL
1951	2	Ed Lopat	NY, AL	0.50	Ed Lopat	NY, AL
1952	2	Allie Reynolds	NY, AL	1.59	Vic Raschi	NY, AL
	2	Vic Raschi	NY, AL			
1953	1	Done by six men	NY, AL/Bro, NL	2.00	Ed Lopat	NY, AL
1954	1	Done by four men	NY, NL	0.84	Johnny Antonelli	NY, NL
1955	2	Johnny Podres	Bro, NL	1.00	Johnny Podres	Bro, NL
1956	1	Done by seven men	NY, AL/Bro, NL	0.00	Clem Labine	Bro, NL
1957	3	Lew Burdette	Mil, NL	0.67	Lew Burdette	Mil, NL
1958	2	Bob Turley	NY, AL	0.96	Don Larsen	NY, AL
	2	Warren Spahn	Mil, NL			
1959	2	Larry Sherry	LA, NL	0.71	Larry Sherry	LA, NL
1960	2	Vern Law	Pit, NL	0.00	Whitey Ford	NY, AL
	2	Harvey Haddix	Pit, NL			
	2	Whitey Ford	NY, AL			
1961	2	Whitey Ford	NY, AL	0.00	Whitey Ford	NY, AL
1962	2	Ralph Terry	NY, AL	1.80	Ralph Terry	NY, AL
1963	2	Sandy Koufax	LA, NL	0.00	Don Drysdale	LA, NL
1964	2	Bob Gibson	StL, NL	1.56	Jim Bouton	NY, AL
	2	Jim Bouton	NY, AL			
1965	2	Sandy Koufax	LA, NL	0.38	Sandy Koufax	LA, NL
	2	Mudcat Grant	Min, AL			

	WINS	NAME	TEAM	ERA	NAME	TEAM
1966	1	Done by four men	Bal, AL	0.00	Wally Bunker	Bal, AL
				0.00	Jim Palmer	Bal, AL
1967	3	Bob Gibson	StL, NL	1.00	Bob Gibson	StL, NL
1968	3	Mickey Lolich	Det, AL	1.67	Mickey Lolich	Det, AL
				1.67	Bob Gibson	StL, NL
1969	2	Jerry Koosman	NY, NL	1.13	Mike Cuellar	Bal, AL
1970	1	Done by five men	Bal, AL/Cin, NL	0.00	Clay Carroll	Cin, NL
1971	2	Steve Blass	Pit, NL	0.00	Nelson Briles	Pit, NL
	2	Dave McNally	Bal, AL			
1972	2	Catfish Hunter	Oak, AL	0.00	Jack Billingham	Cin, NL
	2	Ross Grimsley	Cin, NL			
1973	2	Ken Holtzman	Oak, AL	0.66	Rollie Fingers	Oak, AL
1974	1	Done by five men	Oak, AL/LA, NL	1.00	Mike Marshall	LA, NL
1975	2	Rawly Eastwick	Cin, NL	1.00	Jack Billingham	Cin, NL
	2	Luis Tiant	Bos, AL			
1976	1	Done by four men	Cin, NL	1.23	Don Gullett	Cin, NL (7 inn.)
1977	2	Mike Torrez	NY, AL	2.50	Mike Torrez	NY, AL
1978	1	Done by six men	NY, AL/LA, NL	1.00	Ron Guidry	NY, AL
1979	1	Done by seven men	Pit, NL/Bal, AL	1.80	Bert Blyleven	Pit, NL
1980	2	Steve Carlton	Phi, NL	2.19	Larry Gura	KC, AL
1981	1	Done by six men	LA, NL/NY, AL	0.69	Tommy John	NY, AL
1982	2	Joaquin Andujar	StL, NL	1.35	Joaquin Andujar	StL, NL
	2	Mike Caldwell	Mil, AL			
1983	1	Done by five men	Bal, AL/Phi, NL	1.06	Scott McGregor	Bal, AL
1984	2	Jack Morris	Det, AL	0.75	Andy Hawkins	SD, NL
1985	2	Bret Saberhagen	KC, AL	0.50	Bret Saberhagen	KC, NL
	2	John Tudor	StL, NL			
1986	2	Bruce Hurst	Bos, AL	1.53	Ron Darling	NY, NL
1987	2	Frank Viola	Min, NL	2.77	Bert Blyleven	Min, AL
1988	2	Orel Hershiser	LA, NL	1.00	Orel Hershiser	LA, NL
1989	2	Dave Stewart	Oak, AL	1.69	Dave Stewart	Oak, AL
	2	Mike Moore	Oak, AL			
1990	2	Jose Rijo	Cin, NL	0.59	Jose Rijo	Cin, NL
1991	2	Jack Morris	Min, AL	1.17	Jack Morris	Min, AL
1992	2	Jimmy Key	Tor, AL	1.00	Jimmy Key	Tor, AL
	2	Duane Ward	Tor, AL			
1993	1	Done by six men	Tor, AL/Phi, NL	3.52	Curt Schilling	Phi, NL
1994		No World Series				
1995	2	Tom Glavine	Atl, NL	1.29	Tom Glavine	Atl, NL
1996	1	Done by six men	NY, AL/Atl, NL	0.64	John Smoltz	Atl, NL
1997	2	Livan Hernandez	Fla, NL	1.54	Chad Ogea	Cle, AL
	2	Chad Ogea	Cle, AL			
1998	1	Done by four men	NY, AL	4.40	Kevin Brown	SD, NL

Note: Minimum nine innings for ERA leaders except in 1976 when no pitchers worked as many as nine innings; where ties in ERA exist, the leader is the pitcher who worked the most innings.

THE TEAMS

◆ **TEAM TIME: 1871—1919**

◆ **TEAM TIME: 1920—98**

◆ **DISTINGUISHED DOORMATS**

TEAM TIME: 1871–1919

1. **The 1984 Tigers rocketed out of the starting gate to the fastest getaway at the quarter pole of any team in AL or NL history when they banked 35 wins in their first 40 games. But Detroit later came back to the pack in the AL East and allowed Toronto to make a race of it for a while. By winning 33 of its first 40 games, what early 20th century juggernaut bolted so far in front of the pack that it finished 27.5 games ahead of its closest rival, to establish the record for the widest margin of victory in the predivision era?**

    A)   The juggernaut's closest rival was Brooklyn.

    B)   In 1998 the Yankees became the third team to tie the juggernaut's 20th century record for the best start after 81 games.

    C)   The club's top pitcher was Jack Chesbro with 28 wins.

    D)   Chesbro never took part in postseason action—nor did his team that year.

    E)   Honus Wagner led the team in RBI with 91.

Best Start Since 1901 Through 81 Games

RANK	TEAM	YEAR	W–L	GA
1	Pit, NL	1902	61–20	16
	Chi, NL	1907	61–20	12
	NY, NL	1912	61–20	10.5
	NY, AL	1998	61–20	12
5	Phi, AL	1929	59–22	8.5
	Bro, NL	1952	59–22	7.5
7	NY, NL	1904	58–23	8
	Pit, NL	1909	58–23	5
	Phi, AL	1913	58–23	9
	NY, AL	1928	58–23	10.5
	NY, AL	1939	58–23	7
	Bro, NL	1942	58–23	7.5
	StL, NL	1944	58–23	13
	Cin, NL	1970	58–23	9.5

Note: GA denotes games ahead of the second-place team after 81 games.

2. **Since 1890, just one team has finished in the second division despite having two 25-game winners. What Deadball Era nine earned this dubious distinction?**
    A) Both hurlers are in the Hall of Fame.
    B) The team's .536 winning percentage (81–70) is a record high for a fifth-place team in an eight-club league.
    C) It happened in the last season prior to 1994 when there was no World Series.
    D) The two 25-game winners were the first two lefties to make the majors and later make the Hall of Fame.
    E) The team also had a third Hall of Fame hurler in Chief Bender.

3. **Since expansion, it's become fairly common for a team to win a pennant without a .300-hitting regular. Prior to the end of World War II, though, only 10 teams triumphed without at least one .300+ starter. What was the first team to do it?**
    A) Third baseman Ezra Sutton tied for the team lead in home runs with one.
    B) Centerfielder Jim O'Rourke led the team in hitting with a .278 mark.
    C) The team used only 10 players all year, an all-time record low.
    D) The team's lone substitute, Harry Schafer, got into just two games.
    E) It was the last pennant winner Harry Wright managed.

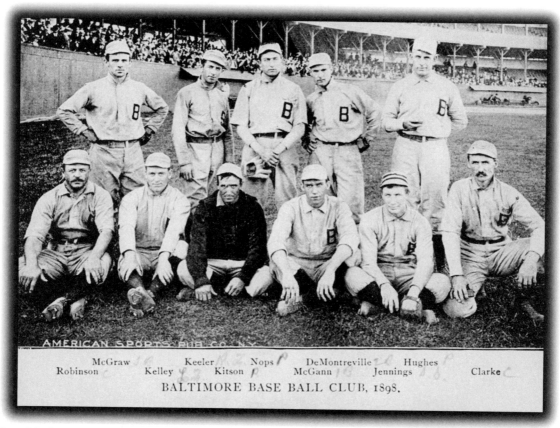

Dan McGann and the rest of the 1898 Baltimore Orioles. That year, McGann's .301 BA ranked just sixth on the second-place Orioles. In 1904, six years later, in the throes of the Deadball Era, his .286 BA led John McGraw's first flag winner, the 1904 New York Giants.

First 10 Pennant Winners Without a .300 Hitter

RANK	TEAM	YEAR	TOP HITTER	BA
1	Bos, NL	1878	Jim O'Rourke	.278
2	StL, AA	1885	Curt Welch	.271
3	Bos, NL	1891	Herman Long	.282
4	NY, NL	1904	Dan McGann	.286
	Bos, AL	1904	Chick Stahl	.295
6	Phi, AL	1905	Harry Davis	.284
7	Chi, AL	1906	George Davis	.277
8	Chi, NL	1907	Frank Chance	.293
9	NY, AL	1943	Billy Johnson	.280
10	Det, AL	1945	Eddie Mayo	.285

Note: Includes only teams without a .300 hitter who qualified for the bat title. The 1885 St. Louis Browns, for one, had Tip O'Neill, who hit .350 before he was disabled in mid-season by a broken leg. Conversely, Babe Ruth hit .300 on the nose for the 1918 Red Sox with just barely enough ABs to win the SA crown.

4. **What team once prompted a franchise shift in a rival league when it led the majors in attendance with 379,988 despite finishing a lackluster fourth?**

   A) The team was managed by its right fielder, who hit .294, seven points below his career average.

   B) The team finished 14½ games behind the first Pittsburgh entry to win a major league pennant.

   C) The team did not finish as high as fourth again for more than a decade.

   D) The team's robust attendance figure despite its mediocre performance invited instant competition for its market.

   E) The franchise shift removed a team from a city that finished next to last in the majors in attendance only to lead the majors in attendance 52 years later the next time it housed a major league team.

5. **What Deadball Era team set a new 20th century record (since broken) for the most homers in its home park just three years after it failed to hit a single four-bagger at home?**

   A) Two years after hitting 48 home blasts to set a new 20th century mark, the team hit 51 taters at home in 1913 to set a 20th century standard that would last until Ruth came to the Yankees.

   B) The team's top slugger the year it hit no homers at home was Kitty Bransfield with three four-baggers.

   C) The year the team set a new mark with 48 blasts at home, Bransfield's replacement, Fred Luderus, hit 16 taters.

   D) The year the team hit no homers at home, the Cubs won their last World Championship to date.

   E) In 1913 the team's top slugger, Gavvy Cravath, set a new 20th century season record with 19 home runs.

6. **Name the last AL team with a sub-.300 slugging average (.287) by working the clue that it was led by rightfielder Doc Cook with a .326 mark.**

   A) Three years later, in Honus Wagner's final season, Pittsburgh became the last ML team to slug below .300, finishing at .298.

   B) Cook's running mate in left field, Roy Hartzell, had a .306 SA.

   C) The team's center fielder at the end of the season, Birdie Cree, began the year in the minors with the Baltimore Orioles.

   D) Six years later, the team became the first in AL history to post a .420+ SA.

   E) The team was run the last two weeks of the season by the youngest pilot in the 20th century.

Lowest Season SA, Team (Minimum 100 Games)

RANK	TEAM	LEAGUE	YEAR	BA	SA
1	Baltimore Orioles	AA	1886	.204	.258
2	Chicago White Sox	AL	1910	.211	.261
3	Pittsburgh Alleghenys	AA	1884	.211	.268
4	St. Louis Maroons	NL	1885	.221	.270
5	Washington Nationals	NL	1888	.208	.271
	Chicago White Sox	AL	1908	.224	.271
7	Providence Grays	NL	1885	.220	.272
8	Boston Braves	NL	1909	.223	.274
	St. Louis Browns	AL	1910	.218	.274
10	Chicago White Sox	AL	1909	.221	.275
	Washington Senators	AL	1909	.223	.275

Note: 1884 was the first season in which the schedule exceeded 100 games; previously there were many sub-.300 team slugging averages. The all-time record by a team playing a full schedule belongs to the 1882 Baltimore Orioles of the AA with a .254 SA and just 88 extra-base hits in 74 games.

7. What Deadball Era team was second in its loop in batting average and fourth in runs, yet posted a dismal .291 winning percentage, largely due to a staff ERA that was 1.22 runs worse than any other team in the majors?

A) Buster Brown's 4.29 ERA was the team's best.

B) The team gave up a 20th-century-record 352 runs more than the next most generous team in its loop.

C) The team was managed by its first baseman, then in the last season of his 17-year NL career.

D) The team's right fielder had 192 hits that season, the most by any NL outfielder during the decade of the 1910s.

E) Lefty Tyler, the team's winning percentage leader at 7–10, was the only player of significance still with the team when it won the NL pennant three years later.

Highest Staff ERA in the Major Leagues by the Widest Margin

RANK	TEAM	LEAGUE	YEAR	ERA	2ND HIGH.	MARGIN
1	St. Louis	NL	1897	6.21	4.67	1.54
2	Philadelphia	NL	1930	6.71	5.24	1.47
3	Cleveland	NL	1899	6.37	4.93	1.44
4	Boston	NL	1911	5.08	3.86	1.22
5	Philadelphia	NL	1921	5.34	4.21	1.13
6	St. Louis	AL	1937	6.00	5.05	.95
7	Cincinnati	NL	1877	4.19	3.37	.82
8	Detroit	AL	1996	6.38	5.59	.79
9	Philadelphia	NL	1916	3.92	3.14	.78
10	St. Louis	NL	1913	4.23	3.46	.77

8. **In 1890, Louisville won the AA pennant after bringing up the rear in 1889. Prior to the 1991 Atlanta Braves and Minnesota Twins, what team came the closest in this century to matching Louisville's feat of going from "worst to first"?**
   A) The team finished last with Three Finger Brown as both its pilot for most of the season and its most effective hurler at 12–6.
   B) The following year, the team was piloted by a man who had won a World Championship nine years earlier.
   C) The team would not have had an opportunity to vie for the World Championship even if it had succeeded in going from "worst to first."
   D) In existence only two seasons, the team was led in ABs both years by rightfielder John Tobin.
   E) The team lost the 1915 Federal League pennant by a single percentage point, the smallest margin in ML history.

9. **What NL team playing a 112-game schedule won more games than a later-day NL flag winner playing a 162-game schedule and yet failed to claim a pennant?**
   A) The team's 85 wins and .759 winning percentage earned only second place.
   B) The team was based in the same city where a National League team later won a pennant with two fewer wins on a 162-game schedule.
   C) The team's manager had won a pennant in a different ML the previous year.
   D) The team's second baseman, Joe Gerhardt, hit .155 while playing every inning of every game.
   E) The team's two Hall of Fame hurlers, Tim Keefe and Mickey Welch, won 76 games between them.

10. **Name the only two teams in ML history to finish 20 or more games in arrears despite posting a .600+ winning percentage.**
    A) One finished at .632, and the other at .608.
    B) Amazingly, both teams were also-rans in the same loop in the same year.
    C) The fourth-place team in their loop that season was led by Hugh Duffy and set a negative NL mark for a first-division club when it finished 11 games below .500.
    D) The first-place team in their loop that season set the all-time ML record for wins with 116.
    E) The first-place team and the two also-rans claimed every NL pennant between 1901 and 1913.

Lowest Winning Percentage for a First-Division Team (1876–1968)

RANK	TEAM	YEAR	W	L	WIN. PCT.
1	Bos, AL	1954	69	85	.448
2	Phi, NL	1906	71	82	.464
3	Chi, NL	1915	73	80	.477
4	Bos, NL	1900	66	72	.478
5	Pro, NL	1885	53	57	.482
6	Cle, AL	1961	78	83	.484
7	Was, AL	1928	75	79	.487
	Det, AL	1941	75	79	.487
	Cle, AL	1941	75	79	.487
	Cle, AL	1942	75	79	.487
	Chi, NL	1944	75	79	.487
	Bos, NL	1949	75	79	.487
	Phi, NL	1954	75	79	.487

Note: Prior to 1876, so few teams completed their schedules that a first-division finish meant little. In 1969 the major leagues split into two divisions. Detroit and Cleveland tied for fourth in the AL in 1941. In 1942 the Indians became the only team ever to finish in the first division two years in a row with a sub-.500 mark.

11. What was the first major league team to lose 100 games in a season?

A)   The team was the first to finish with a winning percentage below .200 (.196) and play at least 100 games.

B)   The team holds the record for the most losses in a season (111) in a major league other than the NL or the AL.

C)   Two of the team's pitchers, Guy Hecker and Toad Ramsey, were a combined 6–29 after winning 64 games between them just three years earlier.

D)   The team lost a record 26 straight games.

E)   In 1890 the team became the first to go from "worst to first."

12. What was the only year that a major league had three teams based in Ohio?

A)   None of the three teams was based in Cleveland.

B)   One of the three teams was managed by a local worthy named Gus Schmelz.

C)   One of the three teams had won the loop's first pennant two years earlier.

D)   One of the three teams employed the first two African American players in ML history that year.

E)   It was the season that featured the first "World's Series" between the pennant winners of two rival major leagues.

13. Counting National Association clubs, which of these states was the last to showcase a major league team: Minnesota, Wisconsin, Indiana, Kentucky, Virginia, Delaware, Connecticut, Iowa, or New Jersey?

A)   Charlie Ganzel was the only team member still in the majors 10 years later.

B)   The city the team called home never again had a major league team bear its name.

C)   The state did not have a major league team again until 77 years later.

D)   The state's first representative was the only major league team that never played a home game.

E)   The state's first ML representative and its "sister" city were responsible for the nickname of the next ML team to represent the state.

14. When the Cubs bagged 116 wins in 1906, what team's ML record for victories did they break?

A)   The team did not see postseason action despite winning 106 games.

B)   Although the team set a new record for wins, it fell 48 points short of the 20th century record at that time for the highest winning percentage.

C)   The team declined an invitation to a postseason match.

D)   The team finished 20 games behind the Cubs in 1906 despite posting 96 wins.

E)   The team won its first pennant in the 20th century the year it set the old mark of 106 victories.

15. What team failed to hit a single four-bagger at home the same season that its second baseman hit one of most historic dingers in the annals of its loop?

A)   The second sacker accounted for 6 of the team's 12 homers that year, all on the road.

B)   The previous year, as a minor leaguer with Toledo, the second sacker had set a new professional baseball record for doubles with 71.

C)   His historic home run came in Chicago off John Skopec.

D)   His name was Erve Beck.

E)   His historic home run was the first in AL history.

16. **In its final year of existence, a certain team made the 1996 Colorado Rockies look like road titans when it became the only ML club ever to play above .500 at home and below .250 on the road. What team was it?**
    A) The team finished last despite scoring 715 runs, second in its loop only to the flag winner.
    B) Leftfielder Kip Selbach led the team in batting at .320.
    C) Second baseman Jimmy Williams led the team in both homers, with eight, and RBI, with 83.
    D) Joe McGinnity led the team in wins with 13 even though he finished the season in another league.
    E) The team's manager at the beginning of the season, John McGraw, also finished the year in another league.

17. **Despite not being spawned until 1903, the Yankees hold the team record for the most home runs since 1901. The first homer by a New York AL team member came on May 11, 1903, off Detroit's George Mullin. Who hit it?**
    A) He hit only two other homers that season yet finished tied for second on the club, two behind leader Herm McFarland.
    B) He tied for the club lead in homers in 1904 but nevertheless lost his job the following season to Hal Chase.
    C) His 16 triples as Cincinnati's first baseman in 1907 led the NL.
    D) His brother had earlier been a big league catcher, and his nephew later played for Washington.
    E) His initials are the same as those of the Reds rookie outfielder who rapped 100 RBI in 1953.

18. **Only two pitchers have ever lost 30 games in a season with teams that posted a winning record. One was Cincinnati's Will White, who hurled a record 680 innings in 1878 when the schedule called for just 84 games. The other tosser did it for a third-place team after the schedule was lengthened to 140 games. What team is it?**
    A) That third-place finish was the initial time in the team's six-year existence that it crept into its loop's first division.
    B) The team's big loser that year joined with its big winner to give the club the third-most victories in AA history by a pair of teammates.
    C) The team featured a rookie first sacker who was the first switch-hitter to collect as many as 140 hits in a season.
    D) The team's big winner that year set the all-time record for the most victories in a season by a southpaw.
    E) The team was based in an eastern city that was without ML ball at one point for more than 50 years.

Most Wins by Two Teammates, Season (Pre-1893)

RANK	NAMES	TEAM	YEAR	W
1	Hoss Radbourn (60) & Charlie Sweeney (17)	Pro, NL	1884	77
2	Mickey Welch (44) & Tim Keefe (32)	NY, NL	1885	76
3	Tim Keefe (42) & Mickey Welch (33)	NY, NL	1886	75
4	Tim Keefe (37) & Jack Lynch (37)	NY, AA	1884	74
5	John Clarkson (53) & Jim McCormick (20)	Chi, NL	1885	73
	Bob Caruthers (40) & Dave Foutz (33)	StL, AA	1885	73
7	Lady Baldwin (42) & Charlie Getzein (30)	Det, NL	1886	72
8	Charlie Buffinton (48) & Jim Whitney (23)	Bos, NL	1884	71
	Dave Foutz (41) & Bob Caruthers (30)	StL, AA	1886	71
	Matt Kilroy (46) & Phenomenal Smith (25)	Bal, AA	1887	71

19. **What are the only two ML teams (some purists maintain there are three) that won pennants every year they were in existence?**

    A) The 1884 St. Louis Maroons don't qualify because the franchise transferred from the UA to the NL in 1885.

    B) One of the teams won a flag after 1901, the only year it was in existence.

    C) The reason some purists say there were three teams is that a team once won back-to-back flags in two different MLs under a similar ownership but with a substantially different cast of players on each occasion.

    D) The leagues in which the two (or three) teams won pennants were the Federal League, the Players League, and the American Association.

    E) King Kelly, Arthur Irwin, and Bill Phillips piloted the only two (or three) teams to win pennants every year they were in existence.

20. **The Yankees set a 20th century record for the highest winning percentage for a decade with a .637 mark during the 1930s. Name the pre-1920 team whose record the Yankees broke and the decade in which the old record was achieved.**

    A) The Yankees won an amazing 972 games during the 1930s but would have fallen short of the record if they had won just 2 fewer games.

    B) The team whose record the Yankees broke never finished below third during its record-setting decade.

    C) The team still has the 20th century NL record for the highest winning percentage during a specific decade.

    D) The team won its first-ever pennant during its record-setting decade.

    E) The team was managed for the entire decade by Fred Clarke.

21. **The 1914 Boston Braves are renowned for leaping from last place in the NL as late as July 16th to the pennant, largely owing to a dazzling 61–16 finishing kick in the last half of the season. What team played .714 ball in its final 77 games (55–22) and yet failed to gain a single percentage point in the second half of a 154-game season on the eventual flag winner?**

    A) The team began its 55–22 skein in second place 6½ games back and ended in second place 6½ games back when its chief rival also went 55–22 down the stretch.

    B) The team featured a Hall of Famer who led the NL in both wins and saves.

    C) The team lost out to a club that had gone 55–20 in its first 75 games.

    D) Solly Hofman, with a .285 BA, was the team's top hitter.

    E) Fred Clarke managed the NL flag winner that year.

22. **Several teams have posted winning records despite having two 20-game losers, but only once has a team finished as high as second despite having two hurlers who each dropped at least 20 decisions. What team is it?**

    A) The team played .584 ball, the highest mark in history at that point by a team representing a certain present-day NL city.

    B) The team featured a loop coleader in wins with 41.

    C) The team's loss leader with 21 was on his way that year to setting a record for the most pitching losses in a particular decade, in his case the 1880s.

    D) The team played in a different ML the following year but kept the same manager, Hustling Horace Phillips.

    E) The team's ace set an all-time record that year for the most shutouts by a southpaw.

Teams with Winning Records That Had Two 20-Game Losers

TEAM	YEAR	W–L RECORD	20-GAME LOSERS
Det, NL	1882	42–41	George Derby (20) & Stump Weidman (20)
Lou, AA	1884	52–45	Guy Hecker (25) & Sam Weaver (20)
Buf, NL	1884	64–47	Pud Galvin (22) & Bill Serad (20)
Phi, NL	1885	56–54	Ed Daily (23) & Charlie Ferguson (20)
Pit, AA	1886	80–57	Pud Galvin (21) & Ed Morris (20)
NY, NL	1886	75–44	Mickey Welch (22) & Tim Keefe (20)
Bal, AA	1889	70–65	Matt Kilroy (25) & Frank Foreman (21)
Tol, AA	1890	68–64	Egyptian Healy (21) & Ed Cushman (21)
Chi, PL	1890	75–62	Mark Baldwin (24) & Silver King (22)
Phi, AA	1891	73–66	Icebox Chamberlain (23) & Gus Weyhing (20)
Pit, NL	1892	80–73	Mark Baldwin (27) & Red Ehret (20)
NY, NL	1893	68–64	Amos Rusie (21) & Mark Baldwin (20)
Bal, AL	1901	68–65	Harry Howell (21) & Joe McGinnity (20)

TEAM TIME: 1920–98

1. **The 1949 season was strange. Loads of unique records were set on all fronts. In 1949 a certain team not only set a new ML mark for the highest fielding average (.983) that's since been eclipsed but also won 18 of 19 extra-inning games, a record for overtime success that still stands. What team are we describing?**

   A) In 1949 the team played only .526 ball in games of regulation length.
   B) Al Benton led the team in saves with 10.
   C) The team's infield unit included two former AL batting titlists.
   D) One of the former batting titlists was also the team's manager in 1949.
   E) The team was the defending world champion in 1949.

2. **What postexpansion team lost 105 games even though its top loser suffered only 13 defeats to tie the record for the fewest losses by a leader on a 100-game loser?**

   A) The following year, the team experienced a near-record 29-game improvement.
   B) The following year, for the first time in franchise history, one of the team's players won the AL MVP Award.
   C) The team's leading loser was Jim Merritt.
   D) The team's leading winner, with nine, was also named Jim, and his brother played in the NBA after starring at UCLA.
   E) The team fired Whitey Herzog during the season and hired Billy Martin.

Fewest Losses, Loss Leader on a 100-Game Loser

RANK	TEAM	YEAR	W–L	LEADER
1	StL, AL	1953	54–100	Duane Pillette & Harry Brecheen (13)
	Tex, AL	1973	57–105	Jim Merritt (13)
	Fla, NL	1998	54–108	Brian Meadows (13)
4	Phi, NL	1941	43–111	Tom Hughes & Ike Pearson (14)
	StL, AL	1951	52–102	Duane Pillette (14)
	Tex, AL	1972	54–100	Rich Hand (14)
	Min, AL	1982	60–102	Brad Havens (14)
	Det, AL	1996	53–109	Felipe Lira (14)
9	Was, AL	1964	62–100	Buster Narum (15)
	Sea, AL	1978	56–104	Glenn Abbott (15)
	Bal, AL	1988	54–107	Jay Tibbs & Jose Bautista (15)
	SD, NL	1993	61–101	Andy Benes (15)

Note: The 1941 Phils had a record seven pitchers who lost in double figures—Hughes, Pearson, Cy Blanton (13), Lee Grissom (13), Si Johnson (12), Johnny Podgajny (12), and Lefty Hoerst (10), with Boom Boom Beck (1–9) nearly making it eight.

3. **In 1995 the Rockies tied for the NL's top home winning percentage in their first year at Coors Field. The previous year, the Indians led the AL in home winning percentage in their initial season at Jacobs Field. Prior to 1994, what was the last team to top its loop in home winning percentage in its first year at a new park?**

   A) Not the Orioles, which, ironically, led the AL in road winning percentage in their first year at Camden Yards.

   B) The 1923 Yankees were the last AL team to do it prior to 1994.

   C) The last NL team to do it did not open its new park that year until June 30.

   D) The team lost its first game in its new park to Atlanta, 8–2, but went on to win the NL flag for its rookie manager.

   E) That year the team lost the last World Series that featured all day games.

4. **What team fell one game short of equaling the 1932 Yankees' record for going through an entire season without being shut out when it was blanked on the final day of the 1979 campaign?**

   A) The pitcher who topped the team, 5–0, earned both his 20th win and a shutout despite allowing nine hits.

   B) That pitcher was the most recent Mets hurler to lose 20 games in a season.

   C) The team's hill staff tied for the AL lead in shutouts in 1979, and Mike Caldwell was its individual leader with four.

   D) Sixto Lezcano led the team with a .573 SA.

   E) George Bamberger managed the team to second place in the AL East in 1979.

5. **The 1965 Dodgers won a World Championship despite hitting just 78 homers, the fewest in the majors, but another club that hit a mere 67 homers, also the fewest in the majors, won a more recent World Championship. What team is it?**

   A) The team's right fielder hit 19 homers, more than a quarter of its total.

   B) The team's regular shortstop, second baseman, and third baseman collected just four homers among them.

   C) The team's top two pitchers won only 15 games apiece.

   D) Second on the club in homers with 12 was catcher Darrell Porter.

   E) The team's last loop home run leader prior to 1998 was Johnny Mize, back in 1940.

Fewest HRs, World Championship Team (Since 1923)

RANK	TEAM	YEAR	BA	SA	HRS
1	Was, AL	1924	.294	.387	22
2	StL, NL	1931	.286	.411	60
	StL, NL	1942	.266	.379	60
4	StL, NL	1982	.264	.364	67
5	Det, AL	1945	.256	.361	77
6	Pit, NL	1925	.307	.449	78
	LA, NL	1965	.245	.335	78
8	StL, NL	1946	.265	.381	81
9	NY, NL	1933	.263	.381	82
10	Cin, NL	1940	.266	.379	89

Note: 1923 was the year the Yankees first demonstrated that the long ball can win championships. Los Angeles (NL) hit 82 homers in the strike-abbreviated 1981 season.

6. **The first team to draw 1 million in attendance was the 1920 New York Yankees, and 26 years later, the Bombers also became the first ML team to pull 2 million in a season. What was the first NL team to crack the 1 million barrier?**

    A) It finished fourth that year.

    B) It had not won a pennant for nine years when it hit the 1 million mark.

    C) It had finished in the cellar two years earlier for the first time in franchise history.

    D) It has not led the NL in attendance since 1938.

    E) The club was managed by the same man who was replaced as Yankees skipper in 1946, the year they became the first team ever to top 2 million.

Each Team's First 1 Milllion Attendance Season

RANK	TEAM	YEAR	ATTENDANCE	PARK
1	New York Yankees	1920	1,289,422	Polo Grounds
2	Detroit Tigers	1924	1,015,136	Navin Field
3	Chicago Cubs	1927	1,159,168	Wrigley Field
4	Brooklyn Dodgers	1930	1,097,329	Ebbets Fields
5	New York Giants	1945	1,016,468	Polo Grounds
6	Boston Red Sox	1946	1,416,944	Fenway Park
	St. Louis Cardinals	1946	1,061,807	Sportsman's Park
	Cleveland Indians	1946	1,057,289	Cleveland Stadium
	Philadelphia Phillies	1946	1,045,247	Shibe Park
	Washington Senators	1946	1,027,216	Griffith Stadium
11	Pittsburgh Pirates	1947	1,283,531	Forbes Field
	Boston Braves	1947	1,277,361	Braves Field
13	Chicago White Sox	1951	1,328,234	Comiskey Park I
14	Baltimore Orioles	1954	1,060,901	Memorial Stadium
15	Kansas City Athletics	1955	1,393,054	Municipal Stadium
16	Cincinnati Reds	1956	1,125,928	Crosley Field

Note: Including only the 16 franchises extant in 1901. Navin Field is the forerunner of Tiger Stadium. Cleveland also played some home games in League Park in 1946. Baltimore (née St. Louis) and Kansas City (née Philadelphia) both pulled 1 million for the first time in franchise history in their initial seasons in new digs. But many relocated and expansion teams failed to crack 1 million their inaugural years—the expansion Washington Senators, for one, never topped 1 million in their 12-year history before moving to Texas. Actually the only relocated and expansion teams that did, apart from Baltimore and the Kansas City A's, were the Milwaukee Braves (1953), Montreal (1969), and the six most recent additions: Seattle and Toronto in 1977, Colorado and Florida in 1993, and Arizona and Tampa Bay in 1998.

7. **What team played its season opener on the road for a record 60 straight years?**

    A) The team opened at home in six of its first seven years in the NL.

    B) The team was the last in the majors to play a Sunday home game.

    C) The team was the only club ever to win the final game of a seven-game World Series on the road after winning the Series lid-lifter at home.

    D) Fred Haney managed the team when it opened at home for the first time in the 20th century.

    E) Forbes Field hosted the team's first home season lid-lifter since 1893.

8. **Only 11 teams have notched 100 wins in a season without having a 20-game winner. Ironically, the co-record-holder for the most wins by a club lacking a 20-game winner tied the 1941 Yankees' record for the fewest wins (15) by a staff leader on a 100-game winner. What team is it?**

   A)   The team set another record when it posted back-to-back 100-win seasons without a 20-game winner.

   B)   In its second straight 100-win season, it again tied the 1941 Yankees' record when its staff leader collected only 15 wins.

   C)   The team is also the only club to win consecutive World Championships without having a pitcher in either season who won more than 15 games.

   D)   The team had two 20-game winners—Slim Sallee and Hod Eller—the year it won its first World Championship.

   E)   Gary Nolan tied for the team lead in wins the first year and led the team outright the following season.

Teams Winning 100 Games Without a 20-Game Winner

YEAR	TEAM	W–L	TOP WINNER
1998	Hou, NL	102–60	Shane Reynolds (19)
1995	Cle, AL	100–44	Charles Nagy & Dennis Martinez (16)
1986	NY, NL	108–54	Bob Ojeda (18)
1984	Det, AL	104–58	Jack Morris (19)
1976	Cin, NL	102–60	Gary Nolan (15)
1975	Cin, NL	108–54	Jack Billingham, Don Gullett & Gary Nolan (15)
1967	StL, NL	101–60	Dick Hughes (16)
1942	Bro, NL	104–50	Whit Wyatt (19)
1941	NY, AL	101–53	Lefty Gomez & Red Ruffing (15)
1931	StL, NL	101–53	Bill Hallahan (19)
1915	Bos, AL	101–50	Rube Foster & Ernie Shore (19)

Note: Teams are listed in reverse chronological order.

9. **What team in a 10-club league was sixth in runs scored, third in homers, fifth in ERA, third in fewest walks allowed, fifth in runs allowed, seventh in batting average, and seventh in fielding average, yet finished last?**

   A)   The team started the year with a pilot who'd skippered a world champ two years earlier.

   B)   The team numbered three former AL MVPs among its eight regulars.

   C)   The team's hill staff included three former or future 20-game winners.

   D)   The manager who led the team for the last five months of the season had previously never finished anywhere but first.

   E)   Thirty-nine years earlier, the team had set an AL record for a 154-game season when it led the junior loop every single day of the 1927 campaign.

10. **What was the most recent team to win two-thirds of its games and fail to qualify for postseason play?**

   A)   The team finished eight games back, the most ever by a club that topped 100 wins.

   B)   Irv Noren, at .319, was the team's top hitter.

   C)   The team had the only pitcher to win 20 games in less than 200 innings.

   D)   The team lost the flag to the only club to be swept in a World Series after winning more than two-thirds of its games during the regular season.

   E)   Despite winning 103 games, the team's manager, Casey Stengel, was denied a pennant for the only time in a 10-year span.

Highest Season Winning Percentage, Non-Pennant Winner

RANK	TEAM	YEAR	W–L	PCT.	FINISH
1	NY, NL	1885	85–27	.759	2nd
2	Det, NL	1886	87–36	.707	2nd
3	StL, NL	1876	45–19	.703	3rd
4	Bal, NL	1897	90–40	.692	2nd
5	Har, NL	1876	47–21	.691	2nd
6	Chi, NL	1909	104–49	.680	2nd
7	Phi, NA	1873	36–17	.679	2nd
8	Bro, NL	1942	104–50	.675	2nd
9	NY, AL	1954	103–51	.669	2nd
10	Bos, NA	1871	20–10	.667	2nd
	StL, AA	1889	90–45	.667	2nd
	NY, NL	1894	88–44	.667	2nd

11. Believe it or not, a team in an eight-club circuit once finished 42 games out of first and 25 games behind the third-place crew and yet earned a cut of first-division money. What team was so rewarded for its ineptness?

A) Its .448 winning percentage is a record low by a first-division finisher.

B) Its manager had piloted a world champion six years earlier.

C) The manager used Milt Bolling most of the year at the same position he'd played during his own career.

D) The same team the manager had previously piloted to a World Series win finished 42 games ahead of his .448 first-division club.

E) The .448 fourth-place team featured the only man besides Mickey Mantle in 1962 to lead his league in walks and SA despite collecting fewer than 400 ABs in a season when a full schedule was played.

Fewest ABs, Season, Leader in Walks

RANK	NAME	TEAM	YEAR	WALKS	ABS
1	Jack Clark	SD, NL	1990	104	334
2	Mickey Mantle	NY, AL	1962	122	377
3	Ted Williams	Bos, AL	1954	136	386
4	John McGraw	Bal, NL	1899	124	399
5	Jack Clark	StL, NL	1987	136	419
	Roy Thomas	Phi, NL	1907	83	419
7	Gene Tenace	SD, NL	1977	125	435
8	Jack Crooks	StL, NL	1892	136	445
9	Jim Wynn	StL, NL	1976	127	449
	Roger Bresnahan	NY, NL	1908	83	449

Note: Minimum 154-game season.

12. **Name the only city to be represented by a team in every major league given birth since 1876 except the American League.**

    A) Ban Johnson's threat to put an AL team in this city helped force the NL to bargain for peace with his upstart league.

    B) The city's Union Association team was transferred there from Chicago.

    C) The Federal League team was nicknamed the Rebels.

    D) The city's American Association franchise was originally based in the neighboring town of Allegheny.

    E) The NL team received its nickname for "pirating" second baseman Lou Bierbauer from the AA.

13. **What post-1920 NL team finished a strong second despite having in its starting rotation the losingest pitcher in the 20th century on a club with a winning record?**

    A) The team's big loser accounted for 35 percent of its 68 losses.

    B) The team's big winner was a Hall of Fame lefty with a 25–13 record that was nearly the reverse of its big loser's 13–23.

    C) The team's keystone combo was Sammy Bohne and Ike Caveney.

    D) The team had won its first NL flag three years earlier and did not win a second for another 17 years.

    E) The team was runner-up to John McGraw's last world champ.

Dolf Luque is the answer to two questions guaranteed to win just about every bar bet. What hurler compiled the most career wins in the majors of any ex–Negro leaguer? What hurler compiled the most losses in a season of anyone in this century who played on a winning team?

14. Name the only team to play above .400 on the road and below .300 at home in the same season.

A) The team was managed by a man who had played against it in the World Series nine years earlier.

B) In 1939 the team logged a 20th century record-low .234 home winning percentage.

C) Reliever Marlin Stuart led the team in wins with eight.

D) The team's franchise entered the 1999 season never having played another regular-season or postseason game since in the city that housed it that year.

E) The team's only Hall of Famer was Satchel Paige.

Worst Home Record, Season (Since 1901)

RANK	TEAM	YEAR	HOME W–L	PCT.
1	StL, AL	1939	18–59	.234
2	Bos, NL	1911	19–54	.260
3	Phi, AL	1915	20–55	.267
	Phi, NL	1923	20–55	.267
5	NY, NL	1962	22–58	.275
6	Phi, NL	1945	22–55	.286
	KC, AL	1956	22–55	.286
	Phi, NL	1961	22–55	.286
9	Bos, AL	1906	22–54	.289
10	Mon, NL	1969	24–57	.296

Note: In the 19th century, usually for monetary reasons, good teams often played many more games at home than bad teams, rendering home-road records less than meaningful in many cases; the classic example is the 1899 Cleveland Spiders, which played only 42 games at home and 112 on the road.

15. What team's four regular infielders set a Lively Ball record (post–1920) for offensive anemia when they collected just five home runs and 116 RBI among them?

A) The three regular infielders with more than 400 ABs hit .185, .212, and .215, respectively.

B) Kirby Farrell, the team's backup first baseman, had 0 homers and just 21 RBI in 280 ABs.

C) Rookie rightfielder Chuck Workman led the team in RBI with 61.

D) Connie Ryan was the team's lone infielder to tally more than 34 runs.

E) The team began the season under Casey Stengel and finished under Bob Coleman.

16. The ML team record for the most consecutive years improving in winning percentage is six. What post-1920 team holds the mark?

A) Oddly, the team's only flag during that span did not come in the sixth year.

B) Its manager at the beginning of the six-year span was Burleigh Grimes.

C) In the first year of the span, the team's catcher, Babe Phelps, hit .367, the highest BA in the 20th century by a receiver in 100 or more games.

D) In the sixth year of the span, the team became the most recent NL entry to win two-thirds of its games and fail to qualify for postseason play.

E) The team's manager at the close of the span was Leo Durocher.

17. What was the first team with three players who each hit 30 or more homers?

    A)   The club leader was also the NL leader that year, with 43 homers.

    B)   Second on the club, with 32 homers, was that year's NL batting title winner.

    C)   The club's first baseman completed the trio by cracking 31 homers.

    D)   The club finished fifth that year under Burt Shotton.

    E)   The club's crosstown rival won the World Series that year, beating the only NL pennant winner managed by Joe McCarthy.

RANK	TEAM	YEAR	TRIO
	First 10 Teams with Three 30-Homer Men		
1	Phi, NL	1929	Klein (43), O'Doul (32) & Hurst (31)
2	NY, AL	1941	Keller (33), Henrich (31) & DiMaggio (30)
3	NY, NL	1947	Mize (51), Marshall (36) & Cooper (35)
4	Bro, NL	1950	Hodges (32), Snider (31) & Campanella (31)
5	Bro, NL	1953	Snider (42), Campanella (41) & Hodges (31)
6	Cin, NL	1956	Robinson (38), Post (36) & Kluszewski (35)
7	Was, AL	1959	Killebrew (42), Lemon (33) & Allison (30)
8	Mil, NL	1960	Adcock (35), Aaron (34) & Mathews (32)
9	SF, NL	1963	McCovey (44), Mays (35) & Cepeda (34)
	Min, AL	1963	Killebrew (45), Allison (35) & Hall (33)

18. The 1914 Yankees, with 251 thefts, became the last AL team for several decades to swipe 250 or more bases. What are the only two AL teams to steal as many as 250 bases in a season since 1914?

    A)   One club got 31 steals from Larry Lintz, who was used almost exclusively as a pinch runner, and the other club was led in steals by a rookie shortstop.

    B)   The shortstop on Lintz's club stole exactly as many bases (54) as the rookie shortstop on the other club.

    C)   The frosh shortstop won the AL Rookie of the Year Award.

    D)   The other shortstop, Bert Campaneris, helped his club to set a new AL-record 341 steals.

    E)   Phil Garner played second base on one of the teams and later managed the other.

19. What team set an all-time record when its relief corps earned 40 of its wins?

    A)   The team won the NL pennant that year by a 13-game margin.

    B)   The team set another all-time record when no fewer than 10 of its pitchers worked more than 70 innings and notched at least seven decisions apiece.

    C)   The previous year, the team's relief corps had won a then-record 38 games, led by a Rookie of the Year who notched 14 of his 15 wins as a fireman.

    D)   That year the team suffered its sixth straight 20th century World Series loss.

    E)   The team's lone 20-game winner, Carl Erskine, was a perfect 1–0 in relief.

1953 Brooklyn Dodgers Relief Corps

NAME	G/R	W/R	L/R	SAVES
Clem Labine	30	10	4	7
Ben Wade	32	7	5	3
Joe Black	31	6	2	5
Bob Milliken	27	5	2	2
Jim Hughes	48	4	3	9
Johnny Podres	15	4	0	0
Billy Loes	7	3	1	0
Carl Erskine	6	1	0	3
Russ Meyer	2	0	1	0
Glen Mickens	2	0	0	0
Preacher Roe	1	0	0	0
	201	40	18	29

20. **In 1997 the California Angels became the Anaheim Angels and thereby moved into second place in alphabetical order on the all-time team list. Name the only city to field a major league team since 1871 that ranks ahead of Anaheim on this list.**
    - A) The team introduced the second man to play 1,000 ML games at shortstop.
    - B) It also introduced the only man to sire a son who both played in the majors and refereed an NFL title game.
    - C) It lost its inaugural game to the St. Louis Maroons.
    - D) It was nicknamed the Mountain Citys.
    - E) It was one of three teams in the UA that year from Pennsylvania that folded before the end of the season.

21. **In the process of leading the NL in runs in 1998, the Astros became the first senior loop team since 1953 with four players who scored 100 runs and only the third NL team in this century to have more than three of its performers score in triple digits. The first such NL club, like the Astros, saw postseason action. What team is it?**
    - A) A Hall of Fame outfielder from the Pirates led the NL in tallies that year.
    - B) The Pirates also led the NL in runs that year with 837 despite finishing fourth.
    - C) The team with four triple-digit scorers was led in tallies by its Hall of Fame first sacker with 123.
    - D) The team's switch-hitting second sacker also scored in triple digits and later made the Hall of Fame.
    - E) The team was swept in the World Series by the last club Miller Huggins piloted in postseason play.

First Team with Three Players Who Scored 100 Runs in a Season

	TEAM/YEAR	NAMES
NL	Chicago 1884	Kelly 120, Dalrymple 111, Anson 108, Pfeffer 105, Gore 104
AA	New York 1884	Nelson 114, Esterbrook 110, Brady 102
	Cincinnati 1884	C. Jones 117, Reilly 114, McPhee 107
NL (since 1901)		
	Philadelphia 1901	Flick 111, Delahanty 106, Thomas 102
	Pittsburgh 1901	Beaumont 118, Clarke 118, Wagner 100
AL	Boston 1901	Collins 109, Stahl 106, Dowd 104

First Team with Four Players Who Scored 100 Runs in a Season

	TEAM/YEAR	NAMES
NL	Chicago 1884	Kelly 120, Dalrymple 111, Anson 108, Pfeffer 105, Gore 104
AA	St. Louis 1887	O'Neill 167, Latham 165, Comiskey 139, Gleason 135, Robinson 102
NL (since 1901)		
	St. Louis 1928	Bottomley 123, Douthit 111, Frisch 107, Hafey 101
AL	Detroit 1921	Cobb 124, Heilmann 114, Veach 110, Blue 103

First Team with Five Players Who Scored 100 Runs in a Season

	TEAM/YEAR	NAMES
NL	Chicago 1884	Kelly 120, Dalrymple 111, Anson 108, Pfeffer 105, Gore 104
AA	St. Louis 1887	O'Neill 167, Latham 165, Comiskey 139, Gleason 135, Robinson 102
PL	Boston 1890	Brown 146, Stovey 142, Richardson 126, Brouthers 117, Nash 103
NL (since 1901)		
	Brooklyn 1953	Snider 132, Gilliam 125, Robinson 109, Reese 108, Campanella 103, Hodges 101
AL	Philadelphia 1929	Foxx 123, Haas 115, Simmons 114, Cochrane 113, Bishop 102

First Team with Six Players Who Scored 100 Runs in a Season

	TEAM/YEAR	NAMES
NL	Boston 1894	Duffy 160, Lowe 158, Long 136, Nash 132, Bannon 130, McCarthy 118, Tucker 112
	Baltimore 1894	Keeler 165, Kelley 165, McGraw 156, Brouthers 137, Brodie 134, Jennings 134
NL (since 1901)		
	Brooklyn 1953	Snider 132, Gilliam 125, Robinson 109, Reese 108, Campanella 103, Hodges 101
AL	New York 1931	Gehrig 163, Ruth 149, Combs 120, Chapman 120, Sewell 102, Lary 100

Only Team with Seven Players Who Scored 100 Runs in a Season

	TEAM/YEAR	NAMES
NL	Boston 1894	Duffy 160, Lowe 158, Long 136, Nash 132, Bannon 130, McCarthy 118, Tucker 112

Distinguished Doormats

The 1889 Louisville Colonels, the first team to lose 100 games in a season. Top: Dan Shannon, Farmer Vaughn, interim manager Brown, John Galligan, and Jimmy Wolf. Seated: John Ewing, Farmer Weaver, Scott Stratton, Red Ehret, and Ed Flanagan. How bad were these Louisvilles? So awful that they could manage only three wins in 40 tries against Brooklyn and St. Louis, the top two teams in the AA in 1889. The following year, however, the Colonels went the opposite route of the 1997–98 Florida Marlins—they became the first team to go from "worst to first."

1. **Pennant winners get practically all the ink. You can count on the fingers of one hand the books that take even a cursory look at some of the most interesting teams in history—cellar dwellers. To eliminate debate, we deem cellar dwellers teams that compile the worst record in their leagues, whether they be 6-, 8-, 10-, 12-, or 14-team circuits. In other words, teams that bring up the rear only in their divisions are not true doormats. From every angle, though, Philadelphia has endured more doormats than any other city even though it's been a one-team town since 1955. What city is Philadelphia's antithesis in that it owns the record for the longest continuous skein of years with at least one big league team before its denizens had to tolerate their first doormat?**

   A) The city was represented in the majors continuously for nearly half a century before one of its teams finished last for the first time.

   B) Just a year later, the city's other ML representative also suffered its first cellar finish.

   C) Ironically, the city had its first doormat the same year that Washington boasted its only World Championship team.

   D) The city is the only one with two ML representatives every season since 1901.

   E) The city housed both the first NL and the first AL pennant winners.

2. **Washington was long known pejoratively for being first in war, first in peace, and last in the American League, but the nation's capital had already had far more than its share of bad ML teams before the AL was formed. Including Washington's pre-1900 representatives in the UA, the AA, and the NL, what was the first Washington club to play .500 ball for a full season?**

   A) The UA team had the worst record of any UA club that played a full schedule.

   B) Washington's two AA teams both were doormats, and its NL teams never broke .500 and suffered more cellar finishes than any other NL city in the 19th century.

   C) The AL Senators broke .500 for the first time eight years after the club became the first in the 20th century to play sub-.250 ball for a 154-game span.

   D) The first Washington team to win more than half its games finished 30 games over .500 when Walter Johnson and Bob Groom combined for 56 wins.

   E) The Red Sox that season were victorious for the only time in their history in a Series that went the limit.

Teams Playing Sub-.250 Ball for a 154-Game Span (Since 1901)

RANK	TEAM	SPAN	W	L	PCT.
1	Phi, AL	8/7/15–8/8/16	29	125	.188
2	Was, AL	9/18/03–10/3/04	37	117	.240
	Phi, AL	7/5/19–7/6/20	37	117	.240
	Phi, NL	7/27/27–7/28/28	37	117	.240
	Bos, NL	4/21/35–4/19/36	37	117	.240
6	StL, NL	7/27/06–7/31/07	38	116	.24675
7	NY, NL	4/11/62–4/10/63	40	122	.24691

3. **The AL record for the most wins by a doormat belongs to what club that featured two relievers who were a combined 15–6 while the rest of its staff was 55–83?**

   A) The team finished last by a mere half game.

   B) The team played a 162-game schedule.

   C) The team finished 10th, half a game behind the Red Sox.

   D) The team's top rookie was reliever Dooley Womack at 7–3 with a club-best 2.64 ERA, and Steve Hamilton (8–3) was its leading lefty bullpenner.

   E) It was the first time in 41 years that the team finished in the second division, let alone the cellar.

4. **What NL team set the current all-time record for the most wins by a doormat when it posted 72 triumphs in 162 decisions?**

   A) It's one of a very few doormats to top its loop in pitching strikeouts.

   B) It trailed the loop flag winner by just 25 games, the smallest deficit of any cellar dweller since the 162-game schedule was adopted.

   C) It played nearly .500 ball in its final 101 games after the 1947 NL bat champ took over its reins.

   D) The following year its sister expansion team became the first expansion club to win a flag.

   E) The team's all-time leader in pitching wins first managed it in 1997.

5. **In 1887 both the NL and the AA adopted a 140-game schedule. The record since then for the fewest losses by a doormat is 78. What team set the mark?**

    A)   Team member Piano Legs Hickman set a post-1893 record for third sackers when he committed 86 errors.
    B)   The team was owned by Andrew Freedman.
    C)   Buck Ewing managed the team at the start of the year, but after shortstop George Davis took the reins, the club won 39 of its last 76 games (.513).
    D)   The team was the first from the nation's largest city to be a doormat.
    E)   The team offered Christy Mathewson his first taste of big league action.

6. **What doormat in an eight-club loop would have finished in the first division if it had won just four more games?**

    A)   The team's .454 winning percentage is the highest ever by a doormat.
    B)   Jeff Tesreau led the team in wins with 19.
    C)   The team featured the first bat titlist in history from a doormat.
    D)   The team trailed the pennant-winning Philadelphia Phillies by just 21 games, a record for proximity to the top by a doormat.
    E)   It was the only time John McGraw finished last when he piloted a team for a full season.

7. **What club boasted the highest winning percentage by a doormat since World War II, only to finish in the basement again the following year?**

    A)   The team finished just 23 games behind first-place Milwaukee.
    B)   The team had the NL batting leader that year.
    C)   Harry Anderson led the team in homers with 23.
    D)   The team still had the same two mound aces that had sparked it to a pennant eight years earlier.
    E)   The two aces were Robin Roberts and Curt Simmons.

The 10 Best Last-Place Teams

RANK	TEAM	LEAGUE	YEAR	W	L	PCT.
1	New York	NL	1915	69	83	.454
2	Philadelphia	NL	1958	69	85	.448
3	Houston	NL	1968	72	90	.444
4	Chicago	NL	1925	68	86	.442
5	New York	AL	1966	70	89	.440
6	New York	NL	1900	60	78	.435
7	Chicago	AL	1924	66	87	.431
8	California	AL	1974	68	94	.420
	New York	NL	1983	68	94	.420
	Oakland	AL	1993	68	94	.420
	Chicago	NL	1997	68	94	.420
	Philadelphia	NL	1997	68	94	.420

Note: The Cubs and Phils tied for last in 1997. Prior to 1900, the record for the best winning percentage by a doormat belonged to Pittsburgh, NL, 1891 (55–80, .407).

8. **What team posted the worst winning percentage in history over a two-year span (.233, 67–221) and, needless to say, finished a sorry last on both occasions?**
   A) Tim Hurst, a longtime NL umpire, managed the team the second year.
   B) The following year, after dumping Hurst, the team improved to 84–67 when it pirated many stars from a rival team by a method that's now illegal.
   C) In 1897 the team became a doormat for the first time in franchise history when it finished a record 23 games behind 11th-place Louisville.
   D) In 1897 the team's top hurler, Red Donahue, set a post-1893 record for losses with 35.
   E) Chris Von Der Ahe owned the team during most of its two-year reign as the game's all-time-worst club.

9. **What are the only three cellar dwellers since 1876 that led the majors in pitcher Ks in seasons when there were at least two big leagues?**
   A) The first doormat to do it featured a rookie southpaw who that year set the all-time season K record.
   B) The first two seasons when this rare feat was achieved came 97 years apart; the third season saw the lowest league-leading BA by a switch-hitter to date.
   C) The second doormat to lead the majors in Ks amazingly did not have a single hurler among the top dozen in Ks in its loop, and club leader Jim Beattie had just 132 Ks.
   D) Billy Barnie managed the first team, and Rene Lachemann piloted the second club for the first half of the season.
   E) The team that won the pennant in the loop where Lachemann's team finished last bore the same name as the team that Barnie piloted to a cellar finish.

Evolution of Team Record for Most Pitching Ks by a Doormat, Season

TEAM	LEAGUE	YEAR	KS	LEADER
Detroit	NL	1884	488	Dupee Shaw (142)
Baltimore	AA	1886	805	Matt Kilroy (513)
Chicago	NL	1957	859	Dick Drott & Moe Drabowsky (170)
Kansas City	AL	1964	966	Orlando Pena (184)
Kansas City	AL	1967	990	Catfish Hunter (196)
Houston	NL	1968	1021	Dave Giusti (186)
Houston	NL	1991	1033	Pete Harnisch (172)
Philadelphia	NL	1997	1209	Curt Schilling (319)

Note: Since 1884, the first year pitchers were permitted to throw overhand.

10. **Which of the eight original AL teams was the last to suffer its first cellar finish, and in what year did it occur?**
   A) Only the presence of the crumbling Baltimore Orioles kept the team from finishing last in 1902 when its 1901 rookie ace slipped to 6–12.
   B) Its first cellar finish came just two years after it won 95 games and vied with the Yankees and BoSox for the AL flag until the last weekend of the season.
   C) Johnny Groth led the team in hitting, and Ted Gray in wins, the year of its initial last-place finish.
   D) The 1996 edition broke this team's old franchise record for losses with 104.
   E) Bobby Shantz was the AL MVP the season the team first was a loop doormat.

First Cellar Finish (Since 1901)

TEAM	LEAGUE	YEAR	PRE-1901
Cincinnati Reds	NL	1901	None
New York Giants	NL	1902	1900
Washington Senators	AL	1902	
St. Louis Cardinals	NL	1903	1897
Philadelphia Phillies	NL	1904	1883
Brooklyn Dodgers	NL	1905	None
St. Louis Browns	AL	1905	
Boston Red Sox	AL	1906	
Boston Braves	NL	1906	None
New York Yankees	AL	1908	
Cleveland Indians	AL	1914	
Philadelphia Athletics	AL	1915	
Pittsburgh Pirates	NL	1917	1891
Chicago White Sox	AL	1924	
Chicago Cubs	NL	1925	None
Detroit Tigers	AL	1952	

Note: 16 teams extant in 1901; Milwaukee, the Browns' predecessor, occupied the AL cellar in 1901; Baltimore, the Yankees' predecessor, claimed the AL cellar in 1902.

11. During the postexpansion predivision era (1961–68), what was the only expansion team that did not endure at least one cellar finish?

A) Its closest brush with the cellar came in 1963 when it finished ninth, albeit 14.5 games up on the doormat.
B) Its first cellar finish did not come until 1974.
C) The franchise entered the 1999 season still in search of its first pennant.
D) The franchise was the first expansion team to break .500 in a season.
E) The franchise changed its name for the second time in 1997.

12. The 1998 Florida Marlins suffered the ignominy of becoming the first defending world champion to post the worst record in the majors the following year. What team had previously been the only pennant winner in ML history to go from "first to worst"?

A) The 1993 Oakland A's don't qualify despite tying for the best record in the AL in 1992 because they failed to win the pennant, losing the ALCS to Toronto.
B) The only previous team to do it went from winning the pennant by 8.5 games to finishing 58.5 games off the pace.
C) Dissension and a tightwad front office combined to rob the team of four Hall of Famers, including Eddie Collins and Home Run Baker.
D) The team's first tumble into the cellar launched a record string of seven straight basement finishes, all under the same manager.
E) The team was the original ancestor of the Oakland A's.

13. **What was the first ML team to drop all the way to the basement just two years after winning a pennant?**
    A)   The team did not see postseason action the year it won the pennant.
    B)   The team's center fielder replaced its third baseman as player-manager the year it plummeted to last.
    C)   The team's basement finish helped produce Cy Young's only 20-loss season.
    D)   The team finished last despite posting a BA nine points higher than that year's world champion, which had the worst BA in its loop.
    E)   The team's player-manager committed suicide during spring training the following year.

14. **What team finished last despite being loaded with all of these assets? A 300-game winner. Two other hurlers who'd also been teammates the previous year when they were the top two winners in their league. A Hall of Fame first baseman. A second sacker who was one of the most ballyhooed off-season acquisitions in history. Two managers who won seven pennants between them. And a left fielder, then in his 10th season, who owned the highest career batting average in the game at the time.**
    A)   The two loop win leaders had been teammates the previous year on a different club in a different league.
    B)   The 300-game winner never pitched on a pennant winner.
    C)   The two managers included a man who made the Hall of Fame as a pilot and the lone man to win back-to-back flags with the same team in two different leagues.
    D)   The second sacker was instrumental in the team's gaining its present nickname.
    E)   The left fielder two years earlier had been on the first ML team to lose 100 games.

15. **Name the only team to date that competed for at least 20 seasons in a major circuit between 1871 and 1998 without ever posting the worst record in its loop.**
    A)   The team currently is the only club in history to qualify for postseason play with a sub-.500 record.
    B)   In the team's maiden season, Jim Rooker led it in losses with 16.
    C)   The team once finished just a game out of the cellar in its division despite posting a plus-.500 record.
    D)   The team's first manager was Joe Gordon.
    E)   The team finished as the doormat in its division for the first time in 1996 and then brought up the rear again in 1997.

16. **Over the 15-year span 1947–61, three teams took turns occupying the NL cellar, with each enduring at least three bottom finishes. What are the three teams, and which was the only one that did not also win a pennant during that period?**
    A)   In 1961, the last season that the NL was an eight-club circuit, the trio finished sixth, seventh, and eighth.
    B)   The two pennant winners between 1947 and 1961 shared the NL basement in 1947.
    C)   The non-pennant winner never finished above .500 during that 15-year span.
    D)   The two flag winners brought up the rear in their respective divisions in 1996.
    E)   Danny Murtaugh, Phil Cavarretta, and Eddie Sawyer each managed one of the three teams for a substantial period during the span.

17. What team set a futility record when it logged the lowest winning percentage in its league during each of the first six seasons in which it had a major league franchise?

    A)   In the team's inaugural season, reliever Jack Baldschun (7–2) was its only hurler with a winning record.

    B)   In its seventh season the team still finished 20 games below .500 under John McNamara.

    C)   The team's first .300-hitting regular was Cito Gaston.

    D)   The team's first above-.500 finish came in 1978 under Roger Craig.

    E)   The team's first 20-game winner was Randy Jones.

18. What is the only NL team in this century to win less than 25 percent of its games?

    A)   The club finished 61.5 games back of the pennant-winning Cubs.

    B)   The club had the NL home run and RBI king that season.

    C)   The club's hill leader, Fred Frankhouse, was 11–15 while the rest of its staff went 27–100.

    D)   One team member became the only man in ML history to retire during a season when he hit three home runs in a game.

    E)   Some 18 years later the club became the first since 1903 to relocate.

19. What team had the longest skein of consecutive doormat finishes in the AL since the end of the Deadball Era?

    A)   It was managed in two seasons during the skein by the only man ever to lead it to two consecutive World Championships.

    B)   It finished in the AL basement six straight years, 1925–30.

    C)   It was the AL doormat nine times in an 11-year span beginning in 1922.

    D)   It had been the AL doormat just once prior to that 11-year span.

    E)   It hasn't finished in the AL basement since the end of that 11-year span.

Each Present Team's Longest Span Between Cellar Finishes

SPAN	TEAM	YEARS SPANNED
86	Los Angeles Dodgers	1906–91
79	St. Louis Cardinals	1919–current
66	Boston Red Sox	1933–current
54	Cleveland Indians	1915–68
53	New York Yankees	1913–65
51	Detroit Tigers	1901–51
48	Chicago Cubs	1876–1923
47	Cincinnati Reds	1935–81
44	Baltimore Orioles	1954–87
41	Atlanta Braves	1936–76
39	Pittsburgh Pirates	1956–84
37	San Francisco Giants	1947–83
35	Philadelphia Phillies	1961–95
34	Minnesota Twins	1910–43
30	Kansas City Royals	1969–current
25	Oakland A's	1968–92
25	Texas Rangers	1974–current
23	Chicago White Sox	1901–23
22	Montreal Expos	1977–current
19	California Angels	1975–93
15	Houston Astros	1976–90
14	Milwaukee Brewers	1970–83
13	Toronto Blue Jays	1982–94
12	San Diego Padres	1975–86
10	New York Mets	1968–77
6	Seattle Mariners	1993–current
6	Colorado Rockies	1993–current
5	Florida Marlins	1993–97
1	Arizona Diamond Backs	1998
0	Tampa Bay Devil Rays	None

Note: Last-place finish constitutes having the worst record in the league.

HONORS AND AWARDS

- ◆ **COOPERSTOWN CONUNDRUMS**
- ◆ **HYPOTHETICAL CY YOUNG WINNERS**
- ◆ **MVP MAINSPRINGS**
- ◆ **FABLED FROSH**

Cooperstown Conundrums

1. **There are no obscure Hall of Famers. Many of us know more about the residents of baseball's pantheon than we do about some of our own family members. Yet, there's plenty, too, that we don't know and perhaps the Cooperstown folks don't either. Nowhere, for instance, on a certain Hall of Famer's plaque is it mentioned that he's the only enshrinee to play in both the NL and the AL before he was old enough to vote. What Cooperstown denizen merits that accolade?**

   A)   He won more than 200 games at a time when 21 was still the legal voting age.
   B)   His youthful nickname was "Schoolboy."
   C)   He broke in under John McGraw and pitched his finale under Burleigh Grimes.
   D)   He was later a Cincinnati broadcaster.
   E)   He was a staff bulwark on the 1927 Yankees.

First 10 Hall of Famers to Play in Both the NL and the AL After 1903

RANK	NAME	1ST LEAGUE	2ND LEAGUE
1	Willie Keeler	AL, 1904	NL, 1910
2	Cy Young	AL, 1904	NL, 1911
3	Frank Chance	NL, 1904	AL, 1913
4	Dazzy Vance	NL, 1915	AL, 1915
5	Ed Walsh	AL, 1904	NL, 1917
	Bobby Wallace	AL, 1904	NL, 1917
7	Waite Hoyt	NL, 1918	AL, 1919
8	Johnny Evers	NL, 1904	AL, 1922
9	Zack Wheat	NL, 1909	AL, 1927
10	George Sisler	AL, 1915	NL, 1928

Note: 1903 brought a peace agreement ending the rampant league-jumping that induced many future HOF'ers like Ed Delahanty, Jimmy Collins, Sam Crawford, and Jack Chesbro to leap from the NL to the AL. Keeler, Young, and Wallace also made the leap but returned to the NL for their final innings.

2. **Nowhere, either, is it stated that a certain pair holds the record for participating in the most victorious games by two Hall of Fame batterymates. Who are they?**

   A)   They were batterymates in 177 winning games.
   B)   They played together on two back-to-back pennant winners.
   C)   Their enshrinement ceremonies occurred 27 years apart.
   D)   The catcher was inducted in 1946, but the pitcher had to endure the longest induction wait of any 300-game winner.
   E)   Their first winning game as batterymates came in 1880, and their last in 1891.

3. Among the omissions on his Cooperstown plaque are: As a frosh he succeeded in just 15 of 42 steal attempts. His soph year, he hit .212 and collected only 120 total bases in 142 games. In 1920 he went homerless in more than 600 at bats. Yet he made the Hall of Fame solely for his playing accomplishments. Who is he?

A) Not surprisingly, he was a shortstop.

B) He played in the 1915 World Series.

C) He is the only switch-hitting position player in Cooperstown solely for his playing accomplishments despite a sub-.280 career BA.

D) He was a member of the Giants dynasty in the early 1920s.

E) His nickname was "Beauty."

Highest Career BA, Switch-Hitting Hall of Fame Position Player

RANK	NAME	YEARS	ABS	HITS	BA
1	Frankie Frisch	1919–37	9112	2880	.316
2	Mickey Mantle	1951–68	8102	2415	.298
3	George Davis	1890–1909	9031	2660	.295
4	Red Schoendienst	1945–63	8479	2449	.289
5	Max Carey	1910–29	9363	2665	.285
6	Dave Bancroft	1915–30	7182	2004	.279
7	Miller Huggins	1904–16	5558	1474	.265
8	Bill McKechnie	1907–20	1822	427	.234

4. The record for the longest span by a pitcher between his first and last World Series appearance is 18 years. What HOF southpaw's plaque might mention that he holds this mark?

A) He died in 1948 of a heart attack.

B) He was a Red Sox exec at the time of his death.

C) His first taste of fall action came in 1914.

D) All of his 240 wins came in the AL.

E) He was 19–8 with the 1927 Yankees.

Most Years Between First and Last World Series Appearances

RANK	NAME	WS	1ST	LAST	SPAN
1	Willie Mays	4	1951	1973	22
2	Herb Pennock	5	1914	1932	18
3	Babe Ruth	10	1915	1932	17
	Jim Kaat	2	1965	1982	17
	Jim Palmer	4	1966	1983	17
6	Babe Adams	2	1909	1925	16
	Enos Slaughter	5	1942	1958	16
	Yogi Berra	14	1947	1963	16
	Steve Carlton	4	1967	1983	16
10	Joe DiMaggio	10	1936	1951	15
	Pee Wee Reese	7	1941	1956	15
	Hal McRae	4	1970	1985	15

5. **What HOF'er was Heywood Broun depicting when he wrote: "His career typifies the heights to which dramatic talent may carry a man in America if only he has the foresight not to go on the stage."**
   - A) He never played a game in either the majors or the minors.
   - B) His middle name is the same as the last name of a hurler who threw a no-hitter for Columbus in 1884.
   - C) He died around the same time as FDR and was sometimes compared to him.
   - D) His death helped open the door for Jackie Robinson to play in the majors.
   - E) Friends called him "Ken," but most knew him as "Judge."

6. **Which Cooperstown denizen missed the first 17 games of his rookie year when he was burned by a diathermy lamp while treating a sore instep but recovered in ample time to be the first frosh selected to appear in an All-Star Game starting lineup?**
   - A) He started his first All-Star Game for an AL team.
   - B) He played left field during his rookie year.
   - C) He drove to his first big league spring training camp with Frankie Crosetti and Tony Lazzeri.
   - D) He holds the PCL record for the most consecutive games hit safely.
   - E) He retired after the 1951 World Series.

7. **Name the 'Famer whose plaque neglects to tell us that he was held hitless in his last ML game by lefty Joe Krakauskas.**
   - A) The game took place on the last day of April in a certain year.
   - B) Krakauskas was 11–17 for Washington that year.
   - C) It was Mickey Vernon's rookie season with Washington.
   - D) The HOF'er benched himself in his team's next game versus Detroit.
   - E) It was his team's first game in nearly 14 years without him in the lineup.

8. **Whose plaque omits mentioning that he and Ernie Lombardi were the only HOF'ers to play for Cincinnati in either the 1939 or the 1940 World Series?**
   - A) The 1939 Series was his fourth but first in the NL.
   - B) Al Kaline made No. 6 famous in Detroit, but in 1936, our man became the first future HOF'er to wear No. 6 for the Bengals.
   - C) In 1933 he hit .331 with 200 hits for the White Sox.
   - D) He lost the AL bat crown in 1927 despite hitting .392.
   - E) All six of his postseason homers came with the Philadelphia A's.

9. **You may know that Juan Marichal was the most recent man to hurl a shutout in his ML debut and later make the Hall of Fame, but whose plaque ignores the fact that he was the first man to do it?**
   - A) He debuted with Washington in the NL.
   - B) Eight years after his debut, he played in his first 20th century World Series.
   - C) He later managed the Cardinals, the same team he whitewashed in his debut.
   - D) His first taste of Series play came in 1905.
   - E) He made the HOF for his work as a catcher.

10. **Who is the only eligible HOF candidate to spend his entire career of 20 or more seasons with the same big league team and be virtually certain now that he'll never be rewarded with a plaque in Cooperstown?**
   - A) His team never won a pennant during his long sojourn with it.
   - B) The year after his retirement, his team won a pennant and he got a World Series cut as its pitching coach.
   - C) He won more than 200 games.
   - D) He threw the first pitch in the inaugural game at Cleveland Stadium in 1932.
   - E) It gets "easier" knowing he was a Tribe coach in 1948.

11. Whose plaque fails to credit him with being the only 'Famer to play against two different teams on the day he made his big league debut?

    A)   He played against both Cleveland and Louisville on September 10, 1899, his first day in the majors.

    B)   His Cincinnati team hosted Cleveland in an A.M. game and Louisville in a P.M. contest.

    C)   He played most of his career in the AL.

    D)   He later faced several members of Louisville's 1899 team in a World Series.

    E)   In the P.M. game, he poked the first of his record 311 career triples.

12. What HOF'er was the first man to manage pennant winners for at least part of a season in both major leagues in the 20th century?

    A)   Joe McCarthy was the first to do it for a full season in both leagues.

    B)   Before becoming a pilot, he was on NL flag winners in two different cities.

    C)   He took over the Giants briefly in the 1924 season for an ailing John McGraw.

    D)   He and McGraw were teammates for many years in the 1890s.

    E)   He and Ralph Houk are the only two men to win pennants in each of their first three seasons as pilots.

13. Who is the only HOF'er to lose 20 games in his rookie season since overhand pitching was legalized in 1884?

    A)   Mickey Welch, Candy Cummings, and Pud Galvin are the only other 'Famers who lost 20 or more games in their first full seasons.

    B)   All of his 368 decisions in the majors came with the same team.

    C)   He won two games in the 1926 World Series.

    D)   He was the last player the Cardinals purchased from a minor league team for some 25 years.

    E)   His nickname was "Pop."

Most Losses, Rookie Year, Hall of Famer

RANK	NAME	TEAM	YEAR	W	L
1	Mickey Welch	Tro, NL	1880	34	30
2	Pud Galvin	Buf, NL	1879	37	27
3	Candy Cummings	NY, NA	1872	33	20
	Jesse Haines	StL, NL	1920	13	20
5	Kid Nichols	Bos, NL	1890	27	19
6	Red Ruffing	Bos, AL	1925	9	18
7	Joe McGinnity	Bal, NL	1899	28	17
	Christy Mathewson	NY, NL	1901	20	17
9	Burleigh Grimes	Pit, NL	1917	3	16
10	Dizzy Dean	StL, NL	1932	18	15

Note: Haines, Ruffing, Mathewson, Grimes, and Dean appeared in the majors prior to their rookie years, but all were rookies according to the modern rookie rule, and even Galvin is viewed as a rookie by the many authorities who refuse to recognize the National Association, where he pitched briefly in 1875, as a major league.

Red Ruffing endured the poorest rookie season ever by a future Hall of Fame pitcher who debuted in the AL when he went 9–18 for the 1925 Red Sox. Only one other future Hall of Fame hurler in this century has suffered more than 18 rookie losses. Do you know who it is?

14. Many 'Famers had brothers who also played in the majors. But only one had a brother who preceded him in the majors by more than 10 years. Who is he?

    A)   The youngest of seven boys, he made his big league debut 15 years after his oldest brother played in the majors.

    B)   His brother played under Connie Mack in 1908.

    C)   As a rookie, he played in the same outfield with Ty Cobb and Harry Heilmann; in his final season, he played with the Waner brothers.

    D)   He won his lone AL batting crown in 1926 when he hit .378 for Detroit.

    E)   He and the 1912 NL bat king share the same nickname.

15. What HOF'er played under the name Mickey King in his first pro season?

    A)   Mickey was his self-coined nickname, but fans knew him by another nickname that he loathed.

    B)   His .38 differential between his .324 career BA and his .362 career OBP is the smallest of any HOF'er who won a home run crown.

    C)   He began and ended his ML career with the Cardinals.

    D)   He won a Triple Crown.

    E)   He was removed from the seventh game of the 1934 World Series for his own safety.

Smallest Differential Between Career BA and OBP, Hall of Famer

RANK	NAME	YEARS	BA	OBP	DIFF.
1	Lloyd Waner	1927–45	.316	.353	37
2	Joe Medwick	1932–48	.324	.362	38
3	George Sisler	1915–30	.340	.379	39
4	Freddy Lindstrom	1924–36	.311	.351	40
5	Nap Lajoie	1896–1916	.338	.380	42
	Pie Traynor	1920–37	.320	.362	42
7	George Kelly	1915–32	.297	.342	45
	Roberto Clemente	1955–72	.317	.362	45
9	Joe Tinker	1902–16	.262	.308	46
	Travis Jackson	1922–36	.291	.337	46
	Al Simmons	1924–44	.334	.380	46
	Edd Roush	1913–31	.323	.369	46

Note: Limited to HOF position players who were selected for their playing accomplishments and whose careers began after 1889 when the four-balls-is-a-walk rule was first enacted.

16. Reading his plaque carefully should give you the clue that he's the only HOF pitcher who won 200 games in both the minors and the majors.

A) He had fewer than 30 wins in the minors at the time he made his ML debut.

B) He is one of four hurlers in this century to have 25-win seasons in two different major leagues.

C) His last job in the majors was as a coach for Brooklyn in 1926 under Wilbert Robinson, his catcher in 1901 and part of the 1902 season.

D) He was the NL's top winner in 1900 in his only year with Brooklyn.

E) He and Matty won four games between them in the 1905 World Series.

17. Whose plaque omits that he's the only 'Famer to be a league leader in both home runs and winning percentage as a minor leaguer but never lead a major circuit in either department?

A) He led the Western Association in home runs and the Florida State League in winning percentage.

B) The only batter he faced as a pitcher in the majors was Frank Baumholtz.

C) He played in four World Series in his first four full ML seasons and then never again played in a postseason game.

D) An arm injury wrecked his mound career after the 1940 season.

E) He holds the ML record for the most career home runs by anyone who was never a loop leader in homers.

18. What HOF'er was denied a chance to be the youngest home run champ in ML history when he was intentionally walked five times in his final game of the season?

A) He would also have been the youngest catcher in ML history if he had debuted at his boyhood position.

B) In his final active season, he hit no home runs for a team that set a league season home run record that has since been tied but never broken.

C) His 42 home runs in 1929 were a personal high.

D) He lost the homer crown in 1929 to Chuck Klein but later won or shared six of them.

E) He was the first man to club 500 home runs while spending his entire career with the same team.

19. Who is the only HOF'er to spend part of a summer in the minors in midcareer after he'd won all three legs of the Triple Crown (albeit not all in the same season)?

    A) He hit 5 homers in the minors and 25 in the majors the year he divided the season between the two.

    B) At the time of his death in 1994, he was second only to Dolph Camilli as the oldest living former ML home run champ.

    C) He won two legs of a Triple Crown in 1939, missing only in RBI.

    D) His last ML turn at bat came in the 1953 World Series, which marked his fifth straight fall appearance.

    E) He held the Cardinals' season home run record prior to 1998.

20. The info on what man's plaque makes it apparent that he's the only HOF'er to play for Detroit teams in two different major leagues?

    A) He made his ML debut in 1885, replacing Gene Moriarity after Moriarity crashed into the right-field wall chasing a fly.

    B) He was a teammate of Ty Cobb in Cobb's first full big league season.

    C) He was 46 years old the year he played with Cobb and hadn't appeared in the majors in eight seasons.

    D) It was his season RBI record that Hack Wilson broke.

    E) In 1894 he was one of the Phillies trio of .400-hitting outfielders.

21. What 'Famer played shortstop his first season in the show but retired with the record for the most career games played at another position?

    A) His record for the most games played at a certain position was broken in 1960 by a member of the Detroit Tigers.

    B) The record later belonged to another man who finished his career with Detroit in 1968.

    C) Prior to this HOF'er, the record had belonged to Lave Cross.

    D) Hick Carpenter was the first to play 1,000 games in the majors at this 'Famer's primary position.

    E) This 'Famer played his entire career with the same team, as did the current record holder for the most games played at his position.

Most Career Games at One Position After Debuting at a Different Position

RANK	NAME	POS.	GAMES	1ST POS.	GAMES
1	Graig Nettles	3B	2412	OF	73
2	Sam Rice	OF	2270	P	9
3	Babe Ruth	OF	2241	P	163
4	Buddy Bell	3B	2183	OF	136
5	Bill Dahlen	SS	2132	3B	223
6	Charlie Grimm	1B	2129	OF	9
7	Wade Boggs	3B	2073	1B	63
8	Steve Garvey	1B	2061	3B	191
9	Cap Anson	1B	2056	3B	118
10	Jesse Burkett	OF	2053	P	23

Note: The record for the most games at another position after debuting as a catcher belongs to HOF'er Jimmie Foxx with 1,919 games at first base.

22. What HOF'er's plaque helps peg him as the youngest man ever to play in a World Series game?

A)   His first Series game came when he was 10 weeks shy of his 19th birthday.

B)   His .40 differential between his .311 career BA and his career .351 on-base percentage is the smallest of any third baseman in Cooperstown.

C)   His second and last fall appearance 11 years later came with a different NL team at a different position.

D)   He holds the 20th century NL season record for the highest BA by a third baseman.

E)   He and Ross Youngs are the only nonpitchers in the HOF who played their last ML games before their 31st birthdays.

23. After enjoying the services of a multitude of future HOF'ers for most of his tenure with the Yankees, Joe McCarthy had only one future 'Famer on his roster when he opened his final full season at the Bombers' helm in 1945. Whose plaque reveals that he's the one?

A)   Red Ruffing did not join the team until later in the 1945 season after he was released from military duty.

B)   The HOF'er with the Yankees at the start of the 1945 season appeared in only one game.

C)   It was his last ML appearance after many years in the NL.

D)   The 'Famer made his 3,000th hit in 1942 as a member of the Braves.

E)   His first hit came with the 1926 Pirates.

24. Whose plaque gives it away that he's the only HOF'er to collect 100 wins and 2,000 hits in the majors?

A)   His 165 career wins are the most of any hurler who never won a game in the majors after his 25th birthday.

B)   His first wife was Helen Dauvray, a popular actress of her day.

C)   In 1892 he was both part owner of the New York Giants and Brooklyn's player-manager.

D)   He played shortstop for the 1888–89 world champs.

E)   He was the prime mover and shaker in the Players League.

25. What HOF'er's plaque fails to note that he holds the 20th century record for the fewest total bases by a batting title winner in a nonstrike season?

A)   Bill Madlock's 149 total bases in the 1981 strike season were 9 fewer than the previous record of 158.

B)   The 'Famer was the most recent man to win a National League bat title without hitting a home run.

C)   He and his brother were teammates from 1915 to 1919.

D)   He played in two World Series with Brooklyn.

E)   He's the only 'Famer whose first or last name begins with Z.

Rod Carew won a postexpansion AL-record seven batting titles. In 1972 he also set a new all-time record for the fewest total bases by a bat title winner with at least 500 at bats when he had just 27 extra-base hits and became the most recent bat titlist to go the full season without hitting a home run.

Fewest TBs, Season, Batting Crown Winner

RANK	NAME	TEAM	YEAR	BA	TBS
1	Zack Wheat	Bro, NL	1918	.335	158
2	Ed Swartwood	Pit, AA	1883	.357	196
3	Ferris Fain	Phi, AL	1951	.344	200
4	Billy Goodman	Bos, AL	1950	.354	203
	Rod Carew	Min, AL	1972	.318	203
6	Jake Daubert	Bro, NL	1914	.329	205
7	Pete Runnels	Bos, AL	1960	.320	208
8	Bill Madlock	Pit, NL	1983	.323	210
9	Rod Carew	Min, AL	1969	.332	214
10	Jake Daubert	Bro, NL	1913	.350	215

Note: Minimum 400 ABs; Wheat's 1918 season was abbreviated by World War I.

26. **Who was the first future HOF hurler to engage in a mound duel against his brother in the majors?**
    A) The two brothers were teammates briefly with Boston in 1892.
    B) A third brother also pitched in the majors.
    C) In 1893 the 'Famer and his brother became the first siblings to win in double figures in the NL.
    D) In 1889 the 'Famer collected nearly 60 percent of his team's victories.
    E) He is the only pitcher in ML history to win 50 games in his first full season.

27. **Name the only HOF'er with at least 1,000 career RBI and 100 homers who never played any other position in the majors but catcher.**
    A) Mickey Cochrane played one game in the outfield.
    B) Ernie Lombardi never played anywhere but catcher but had only 990 RBI.
    C) He was the second man to don the mask in 1,700 games in the AL.
    D) His brother also never played any other position but catcher in the majors.
    E) His brother also spent his entire ML career with the same AL team, albeit a different one from his.

Most Games Played, Career, Catcher as Only Defensive Position

RANK	NAME	YEARS	G/C
1	Ray Schalk	1912–29	1726
2	Bill Dickey	1920–46	1706
3	Jim Hegan	1941–60	1629
4	Ernie Lombardi	1931–47	1542
5	Mike Scioscia	1980–92	1395
6	Johnny Edwards	1961–74	1392
7	Gus Mancuso	1928–45	1360
8	Bob O'Farrell	1915–35	1338
9	Del Rice	1945–61	1249
10	Walker Cooper	1940–57	1223

28. **Careful reading of this 'Famer's plaque will help you to figure out that he's the only shortstop in the 20th century to receive a full loser's share of World Series money for a team in both the NL and the AL.**
    A) He later received a full winner's share of Series money for an AL team but not as a player.
    B) In his first Series he rode the bench in all four games.
    C) His second Series came six years later and went five games.
    D) He once held the record for the most home runs in a season by a shortstop.
    E) In the only Series in which he appeared as a player, he also served as a manager.

29. **What HOF'er pitched for both Connie Mack and Miller Huggins but made two other 'Famers with dugout service the beneficiaries of all five of his 20-win seasons?**
    A) His last career win came for Hug's last flag winner.
    B) Both of his Series losses came against Pittsburgh.
    C) His first Series win came against Brooklyn.
    D) His brother had three 20-win seasons before he had his first.
    E) He and his brother kept their pact never to oppose each other in a major league game.

30. **Who is the only HOF'er whose first and last ML at bats came with Chicago teams in two different major leagues?**
    A) Not Joe Tinker; his first and last at bats both came with the Cubs.
    B) He was the first man to manage both the Cubs and the White Sox.
    C) His uncle bore the same last name and also played in the majors, last with the 1884 Washington Unions.
    D) He had an MVP season with a team based elsewhere than Chicago.
    E) He was the first second baseman with under 2,000 career hits to make the HOF.

31. **What HOF'er banged 33 home runs but scored just 70 runs in more than 800 plate appearances in his last two ML seasons?**
    A) In 1956 he had 20 home runs but just six doubles.
    B) In 1950 he hit 31 home runs but scored just 70 runs.
    C) In a 10-season career, all with the same team, he averaged 24.2 homers a year.
    D) Despite his low run totals in many seasons, he once held the NL season record for the most runs scored by a player at his position.
    E) He was Brooklyn's greatest catcher.

32. **Who made the HOF exclusively for his playing achievements despite sporting an 0–7 career record as a pitcher and a .198 career batting average after his first four ML seasons?**
    A) He was an outfielder for most of his career.
    B) In 1892 he hit .242 for Boston and had a .883 FA in 152 games.
    C) In 1890 he was the runner-up for the AA batting title.
    D) He and John McGraw are the only two men to score 1,000 career runs on fewer than 1,500 hits.
    E) He was one of "The Heavenly Twins."

33. **Who is the only 'Famer to collect World Series money as a member of a Cardinals team that won a seven-game Series and as a member of a team that beat the Cardinals in a seven-game Series?**
    A) Though he got a postseason cut for the AL team that beat the Cardinals in seven, he was ineligible for the Series.
    B) He was traded to another NL team after his only 20-win season with the Cardinals.
    C) He won two games in the 1980 Series.
    D) He's in the 300-win club.
    E) He holds the record for the most career Ks by a lefty.

34. Who hurled winning games for the most different ML teams of any HOF'er?
- A) He posted wins with five different AL teams and three different NL teams.
- B) In 1981 with Atlanta, he led the NL in most hits allowed.
- C) In 1974 with Cleveland, he led the AL in starts.
- D) His brother once led the AL in wins while hurling for Cleveland.
- E) He won Cy Young honors in both leagues.

35. Name the only HOF hurler to post season double-figure win totals with St. Louis teams in two different major leagues.
- A) Three Finger Brown is a terrific guess, but he won only nine games for the Cards in 1903, thereby missing the cutoff here by just one win.
- B) Our man, like Brown, was active only in the 20th century.
- C) He won 21 games in 1915 for a St. Louis team that lost a pennant by the smallest margin in ML history.
- D) Gettysburg was his alma mater.
- E) Most of his 300+ career wins came with the A's.

36. Whose plaque shies away from proclaiming that he's the only outfielder or first baseman in the HOF who was never a league leader in a single offensive department, including at bats, walks and stolen bases?
- A) In 1918 he came the closest to breaking through when he was second in the AL in triples and third in both walks and runs.
- B) In 1921 he posted his top BA when he hit .327 for the White Sox.
- C) He and a three-time AL bat king in the 1920s who never played in a postseason game share the same initials and first name.
- D) He played on four World Championship teams in the 1910s.
- E) He was one of the two members of the Red Sox great outfield in the 1910s to make the HOF.

37. Nowhere on his plaque is it stated that he owns the lowest career batting average of any 'Famer who played either first base or the outfield exclusively.
- A) He is the only 'Famer who had as many as five seasons in which he hit under .240 with 300 or more at bats.
- B) He is the lone 'Famer who had a sub-.200 season in midcareer.
- C) His career-high BA of .2996 came the year he played in his eighth ALCS.
- D) His first homer came in a Kansas City A's uniform, and his last in an Oakland A's uniform.
- E) He had more career strikeouts than any other hitter in ML history.

Lowest Career BA, Hall of Fame Outfielder or First Baseman

RANK	NAME	YEARS	SA	BA
1	Reggie Jackson	1967–87	.490	.262
2	Willie McCovey	1959–80	.515	.270
3	Ralph Kiner	1946–55	.548	.279
4	Harry Hooper	1909–25	.387	.281
5	Willie Stargell	1962–82	.529	.282
6	Max Carey	1910–29	.386	.2846
7	Carl Yastrzemski	1961–83	.462	.2852
8	Tommy McCarthy	1884–96	.376	.292
9	Lou Brock	1961–79	.410	.293
10	Frank Robinson	1956–76	.537	.294

Note: BAs are carried out to four decimal points where ties would otherwise exist.

38. What HOF'er acquired his nickname while working at a state mental hospital in Middletown, New York, in the mid-1890s?

A) He is the only HOF'er who pitched prior to 1939 in the town where the Hall resides.

B) His first double-digit win season in the majors came as a teammate of Wagner, and his last big league appearance came as a teammate of Speaker.

C) He had the most wins in a season of any man who played under Clark Griffith.

D) He is one of the select three hurlers who had 25-win seasons in both the NL and the AL after 1900.

E) His nickname was "Happy Jack."

39. Who are the only two HOF pitchers active in the 20th century to play a full nine innings as teammates in the same no-hit game?

A) A HOF shortstop also played for the team that day.

B) The no-hitter was tossed against the Yankees.

C) The author of the no-hitter also threw two others in his career.

D) The other HOF pitcher also threw a no-hitter later in his career but played center field the day he appeared in his first no-no.

E) The shortstop won the 1944 AL batting crown.

40. Who is the only HOF'er to play for as many as 7 of the 16 teams in existence between 1903 and 1952 but never play for a team based in the cities of St. Louis and New York?

A) He also never played for a team based in Cleveland or Pittsburgh.

B) Nor did he ever play for a National League team based in Chicago or Philadelphia.

C) He hit just one home run with the Boston Red Sox but played nearly a full season with the Boston Braves.

D) His last fall appearance came with Cinci in his lone season with the Reds.

E) He made his first and his last ML hits as a member of the Philadelphia A's.

41. Only one HOF'er had a 20-year career in the majors and also played at least 10 seasons in the minors. Who is he?

    A)   He is the lone 'Famer born in Connecticut who debuted with a major league team in his home state.

    B)   He is the lone 'Famer who managed a 19th century ML team based in Washington.

    C)   He is the lone Hall of Famer to play a full nine-inning game in the majors after his 50th birthday.

    D)   He was the first HOF'er who had both a brother and a son who also played in the majors.

    E)   He was the only member of Boston's NA dynasty (1872–75) to still be active in the majors when the 60'6" pitching distance was established.

42. What HOF'er won his 200th game in his home park in his final start of the year in front of only 526 fans, the smallest crowd in the park's history to that point?

    A)   All of his career wins to that point had come with the same AL team.

    B)   His 200th win was his last with his original team.

    C)   His final win came in relief with the 1954 Indians.

    D)   He holds the 1942–60 era record for the most wins in a season.

    E)   He is the most recent AL southpaw to win more than 25 games in a season.

43. Name the only HOF'er with a brother who played 20 seasons in the majors.

    A)   His brother isn't in the Hall.

    B)   A third brother also played briefly in the majors with the Cubs.

    C)   Teammates for many years, in 1927 he and his brother hit just one home run between them in 1,039 at bats.

    D)   The non-HOF'er managed the 1944 AL champs.

    E)   The 'Famer was the hardest batter in history to strike out.

44. What HOF'er slipped from a .618 career winning percentage to .597 when he went 13–29 in his last two seasons?

    A)   The year prior to his sudden decline, his .767 winning percentage (23–7) had tied his career high.

    B)   His last manager in the bigs was Herman Franks.

    C)   He is the only 'Famer to win ERA crowns in three different decades.

    D)   He went 4–12 for the Mets in 1965 before joining San Francisco, where he finished his career.

    E)   He and Dick Rudolph are tied for the most career wins in the 20th century by a Boston Braves hurler.

45. Who is the only 20th century position player to make the HOF despite boasting a sub-.200 career batting average after his first 400 at bats in the majors?

    A)   He finished with a .267 career BA.

    B)   Eighteen of his first 90 hits in the majors were home runs.

    C)   He had a .714 SA in his first World Series and a .050 SA in his second, three years later.

    D)   He has the most career home runs of any 'Famer who never played so much as a single game in the outfield.

    E)   After hitting just .196 as a rookie in 1973, he led the NL in homers and RBI the following year.

Hypothetical Cy Young Winners

1. **Of the three most prestigious individual honors a player can garner, the Cy Young Award was the last to be created. Consequently, all of the moundsmen featured here never won a Cy Young Award for the simple reason that they were born too early. Had the award existed prior to 1956, all of them almost certainly would have won the top pitching prize at least once, including Cy Young himself. In 1904, Young became the oldest man ever to win 25 games when he snared 26 wins at age 37. Only three pitchers since 1904 have enjoyed 25-win seasons after celebrating their 35th birthdays. One was George McConnell for the Chicago Federal League champs in 1915. The second to do it was hypothetical Cy Young winner Eddie Cicotte in 1919. What other hypothetical Cy Young claimant did it subsequent to 1919 or the end of the Deadball Era?**

   A) He turned 35 in August of the year he did it.

   B) He had four previous 20-win seasons, the first in 1920.

   C) He lived to age 92, the longest of any pitcher currently in the Hall of Fame except for Stan Coveleski.

   D) His 25-win season came with the Pirates in 1928.

   E) He was the last active ML'er legally allowed to throw a spitter.

2. **The holder of several interesting and unsung records, this hypothetical Cy Young winner's most significant one is that his 158 career victories lead all pitchers who celebrated their 30th birthdays before making their ML debuts.**

   A) Not Dazzy Vance, who didn't win his first game till he was nearly 31 but absorbed four losses before he turned 30.

   B) He won 19 games as a rookie, topped the NL in hill appearances, and is rated the top senior-loop pitcher for that year by *Total Baseball*.

   C) His last win came in 1945.

   D) He started and lost the opening game of the 1941 World Series.

   E) In 1939 he set a record for the most decisions in under 250 innings (38) and became the most recent pitcher to hit .380+ in 75 ABs. That same year, an A's reliever with the same initials as his became the last AL hurler to hit .350+.

.350 BA, Season, Pitchers

RANK	NAME	TEAM	YEAR	ABS	HITS	BA
1	Walter Johnson	Was, AL	1925	97	42	.433
2	Jack Bentley	NY, NL	1923	89	38	.427
3	Curt Davis	StL, NL	1939	105	40	.381
4	Red Ruffing	Bos, AL	1930	110	40	.364
5	George Uhle	Cle, AL	1923	144	52	.3611
6	Ad Gumbert	Bro, NL	1895	97	35	.3607
7	Don Newcombe	Bro, NL	1955	117	42	.359
8	Bert Inks	Bal/Lou, NL	1894	84	30	.357
9	Lynn Nelson	Phi, AL	1937	113	40	.354
10	Erv Brame	Pit, NL	1930	116	41	.353
11	Ted Breitenstein	Cin, NL	1899	105	37	.352
12	Chubby Dean	Phi, AL	1939	77	27	.3506
13	Dutch Ruether	Bro, NL	1921	97	34	.3505
14	Catfish Hunter	Oak, AL	1971	103	36	.350

Note: Minimum 75 ABs. Maximum five games at other positions. Orel Hershiser just missed qualifying in 1993 when he hit .356 in 73 ABs for the Dodgers. BAs are carried out to four decimal points where ties would otherwise exist.

3. **Forty-game winners were relatively common until 1889 when three strikes and four balls became a permanent rule and ended experimentation with the ball-strike ratio. Since that rule change, only five pitchers have won as many as 40 games in a season. Name this quintet of hypothetical Cy Young winners.**
   A) Only three of the five are in the Hall of Fame.
   B) Three won fewer than 200 games, including two of the Hall of Famers.
   C) Two of the five dueled in the final game of the only 19th century World Series won outright by an AA team.
   D) Three of their last names begin with the same letter.
   E) The quintet pitched for the Boston Beaneaters, the Brooklyn Bridegrooms, the Chicago Colts, the New York Highlanders, and the Chicago White Sox, respectively, the years they hit 40 or more wins.

4. **Babe Ruth owned a mountain of records when he retired in 1935. Among the least known is that his .671 career winning percentage was the highest to that point among southpaws with at least 100 decisions. What hypothetical Cy Young winner's .640 career winning percentage did Ruth better to set a new record?**
   A) His first win came with Milwaukee of the UA, his last with Buffalo of the PL.
   B) He was 13–10 when he played on his only flag winner in 1887.
   C) His quixotic nickname was the result of his abstemious habits.
   D) He and a White Sox rookie starter in 1996 share the same last name.
   E) His "Cy Young" came the year he set the NL record for wins by a lefty.

Most Wins, Season, by a Left-Hander

RANK	NAME	TEAM	YEAR	W
1	Matt Kilroy	Bal, AA	1887	46
2	Lady Baldwin	Det, NL	1886	42
3	Ed Morris	Pit, AA	1896	41
4	Ed Morris	Pit, AA	1885	39
5	Toad Ramsey	Lou, AA	1886	38
6	Toad Ramsey	Lou, AA	1887	37
7	Frank Killen	Pit, NL	1893	36
8	Ed Morris	Col, AA	1884	34
	Elmer Smith	Cin, AA	1887	34
10	Lee Richmond	Wor, NL	1880	32

Note: The post-1901 NL season record is 27 wins, shared by Sandy Koufax (1966) and Steve Carlton (1972).

5. **Most 19th century pitchers peaked at a young age and then burned out prematurely from overwork. As a result, no fewer than five pre-1901 200-game winners failed to collect a victory after their 30th birthdays. One was Al Spalding. Can you name the other four of these 19th century hypothetical Cy Young winners?**

   A) None collected a win in the 20th century.
   B) Three of them debuted with the same team.
   C) The top winner of the five had 245 victories and posted his last triumph when he was just 27.
   D) In 1890 four of the five pitched for the St. Louis Browns, the New York Giants, the Chicago Pirates, and the Brooklyn Bridegrooms, and the fifth was part owner of the Chicago Colts.
   E) Two of the four were outstanding hitters, one of the four was nicknamed the "Hoosier Thunderbolt," and the fourth man was born Charles Koenig.

6. **What hypothetical Cy Young winner toed the rubber in 10 ML campaigns, never had a losing season, won his last eight career decisions and at one point was undefeated over a 14-year stretch?**

   A) He was a perfect 3–0 in World Series action.
   B) Seventeen years before he made his last ML start, he led the AL in shutouts.
   C) He defeated Bob Kline on October 1, 1933, in his last ML mound appearance.
   D) After pacing the AL with 35 CGs in 1917, he made only 38 more starts.
   E) He probably would have made the Hall of Fame if he'd continued pitching full-time, but he made it anyway, chiefly for his 714 career home runs.

7. **Several hurling stalwarts have led the majors in wins one season and losses the next or vice versa. Just one man, however, topped the majors in wins one year, in losses the next, and then in wins again the following year. What 200-game winner and Cy Young worthy put together this one-of-a-kind string?**

   A) He pitched in two World Series during that three-year span.
   B) His first win came with Detroit in 1905.
   C) He collected 208 career wins and would have been good for more, but a certain nonplaying Hall of Famer decreed otherwise.
   D) His 19 losses in 1918 tied Scott Perry for both the AL and the ML lead.
   E) Since the 154-game schedule was adopted in 1904, his 29 wins in 1919 are the most by any pitcher in a season when the schedule was curtailed.

8. **Denny McLain, the last 30-game winner to date, won 31 games while making just 41 starts in 1968, meaning his ratio of triumphs to starts is a remarkable .76. What hypothetical Cy Young recipient is the only 30-game winner in ML history to register a ratio of triumphs to starts of above 1.00%?**

    A) The previous year he'd been 28–5 in 32 starts with an AL-leading nine saves.

    B) He was 31–4 in just 30 starts in his magic year.

    C) He hurled with his left arm.

    D) He holds the 1920–41 era AL season record for most wins.

    E) His manager for most of his career was Connie Mack.

9. **Greg Maddux currently leads all pitchers in wins in the decade of the 1990s and seems certain to hold the top spot when the century ends. By dint of collecting the most victories in the 1890s, what two-time hypothetical Cy Young winner led all active hurlers in wins at the close of the last century?**

    A) No, not Cy himself, though he was close.

    B) His 297 wins in the 1890s are the most ever by a hurler in a specific decade.

    C) He debuted in 1890, the same year as Cy Young.

    D) In 1904 he became the most recent player-manager also to be a 20-game winner.

    E) His nickname was "Kid."

Most Wins Each Decade

DECADE	NAME	WINS
1870s	Al Spalding	252
1880s	Mickey Welch	285
1890s	Kid Nichols	297
1900s	Christy Mathewson	236
1910s	Walter Johnson	265
1920s	Burleigh Grimes	190
1930s	Lefty Grove	199
1940s	Hal Newhouser	170
1950s	Warren Spahn	202
1960s	Juan Marichal	191
1970s	Jim Palmer	186
1980s	Jack Morris	162
1990s	Greg Maddux	157

Note: Spalding's NA wins are included.

10. **Only one Hall of Famer to date has both tossed a perfect game and notched 300 victories. Name this immortal whose career predated the Cy Young Award.**

    A) His mound opponent in his perfecto was Rube Waddell.

    B) He was the first man to pitch in both a Temple Cup Series and a 20th century World Series.

    C) He was the first man to win 50 games after his 40th birthday.

    D) He is the only hurler to toss a perfecto and win 400 games.

    E) The perfecto was one of his record number of career wins.

Most Wins After Age 40

RANK	NAME	YEARS	40TH YEAR	WINS
1	Phil Niekro	1964–87	1979	121
2	Jack Quinn	1909–33	1923	109
3	Cy Young	1890–1911	1907	75
	Warren Spahn	1942–65	1961	75
5	Red Faber	1914–33	1928	68
	Gaylord Perry	1962–83	1978	68
7	Charlie Hough	1970–94	1988	67
8	Nolan Ryan	1966–93	1987	61
	Tommy John	1963–89	1983	61
10	Hoyt Wilhelm	1952–72	1963	54

Note: Wins after January 1, year of 40th birthday.

11. Hank Aaron needed more than 2,200 games to reach 500 homers; what hypothetical Cy Young winner surrendered 505 homers in just 676 games?

A)   He was touched for his last homer in Cubs garb.

B)   In his lone World Series start, he surrendered a homer to Joe DiMaggio.

C)   He both hit and surrendered his first career homer in 1948.

D)   His 22 losses in 1957 are the most since 1922 by a hurler on a team that finished at .500 or better.

E)   He compiled the most wins in a season of any NL pitcher since World War II.

Highest Career Ratio of HRs Surrendered per Game

RANK	NAME	YEARS	GAMES	HRs	RATIO
1	Catfish Hunter	1965–79	500	374	.748
2	Robin Roberts	1948–66	676	505	.747
3	Don Newcombe	1949–60	344	252	.733
4	Fergie Jenkins	1965–83	664	484	.729
5	Jack Morris	1977–94	549	389	.70856
6	Bill Gullickson	1979–94	398	282	.70854
7	Frank Tanana	1973–93	638	448	.7021
8	Frank Viola	1982–96	421	294	.6983
9	Earl Wilson	1959–70	338	236	.6982
10	Floyd Bannister	1977–92	431	291	.68

Note: Retired pitchers only; minimum 2,000 innings and 250 games. Tom Browning, 1984–95, was touched for 236 homers in just 302 appearances (.78) but hurled only 1,921 innings.

12. **Several men have won 20 games in a season split between two leagues. No one has won 20 games in a season in two different loops. What hypothetical Cy Young winner came the closest in 1884 when he won 19 games in one circuit and 21 in another?**
    A) His 14 straight wins at one point in the 1884 season would have been a record had Hoss Radbourn not embarked on an 18-game win skein at roughly the same time.
    B) He had 252 career wins by the time he was 30.
    C) In 1880 he set an all-time record for the most wins (45) by a pitcher wearing a Cleveland ML uniform.
    D) His 262 career wins are the most by any pitcher born in Scotland.
    E) He has the same last name as the 1967 NL Cy Young winner.

Pitchers Winning 10 Games in a Season in Two Different Leagues

NAME	YEAR	LEAGUES	TOTAL WINS
Billy Taylor	1884	UA (25)/AA (18)	43
Charlie Sweeney	1884	NL (17)/UA (24)	41
Jim McCormick	1884	NL (19)/UA (21)	40
Hank Borowy	1945	AL (10)/NL (11)	21

13. **What hurler is deemed a hypothetical Cy Young winner by many authorities even though he's best known for leading the AL in losses a record four times—on each occasion in the uniform of a different team?**
    A) He was 16–20 as a Browns rookie in 1934.
    B) In 1941 he lost 20 games for Detroit after leading the Tigers to the AL flag the previous year and earning a hypothetical Cy Young.
    C) He is the most recent 200-game winner to retire with more losses than wins.
    D) He has the record for the highest ERA by a 20-game winner—5.08 in 1938.
    E) He was nicknamed "Bobo" because he called everyone else that.

Highest Season ERA, 20-Game Winner

RANK	NAME	TEAM	YEAR	W	ERA
1	Bobo Newsom	StL, AL	1938	20	5.08
2	Ray Kremer	Pit, NL	1930	20	5.02
3	Clark Griffith	Chi, NL	1894	21	4.9247
4	Kid Carsey	Phi, NL	1895	24	4.9163
5	Brickyard Kennedy	Bro, NL	1894	24	4.9159
6	Jack Stivetts	Bos, NL	1894	26	4.90
7	Kid Carsey	Phi, NL	1893	20	4.81
8	Adonis Terry	Chi, NL	1895	21	4.80
9	Ted Breitenstein	StL, NL	1894	27	4.7884
10	Jack Taylor	Phi, NL	1896	20	4.7883

Note: ERAs are carried out to four decimal points where ties would otherwise exist.

14. **Hall of Famers hold just about all of the positive career and season pitching records, but some also own negative records that will almost certainly never be surpassed. At age 29, what Hall of Famer lost a 20th-century-record 29 games five years after he began the century with a season worthy of a Cy Young Award?**

  A) He also owns the 20th century record for the most losses in two consecutive seasons (54).

  B) He debuted in 1898 by winning 24 games for the Boston Beaneaters.

  C) His only World Series appearance came in 1909.

  D) Prior to 1995 he and Jack Powell were the only two hurlers to collect as many as 248 wins between 1893 and expansion and not make the Hall of Fame.

  E) He set a 20th century NL record in 1902 when he notched 45 complete games.

15. **Arguably the most incredible hill season in history belongs to the lone man to top his league in both walks and lowest opponents' on-base percentage since the 60'6" distance was established. Sounds impossible, but he did it. Who was this one-of-a-kind hypothetical Cy Young winner?**

  A) Bob Feller came about as close as any pitcher in the 20th century to doing it in 1941 when he led the AL in OOBP and was third in walks.

  B) The perpetrator of this amazing feat pitched for a second-place team.

  C) Largely owing to his contribution, his team set an all-time record for beating the league ERA by the widest margin.

  D) His seemingly impossible year came in 1894.

  E) His nickname was the "Hoosier Thunderbolt."

Widest Margin Between Team and League ERAs

RANK	TEAM	YEAR	ERA	LEAGUE ERA	MARGIN
1	NY, NL	1894	3.83	5.32	1.49
2	Pro, NL	1884	1.61	2.98	1.37
3	NY, AL	1939	3.31	4.62	1.31
4	Atl, NL	1998	3.06	4.36	1.30
5	Lou, AA	1890	2.57	3.86	1.29
6	NY, NL	1885	1.72	2.82	1.10
7	StL, UA	1884	1.96	3.05	1.09
8	StL, AA	1883	2.23	3.30	1.07
	Lou, AA	1884	2.17	3.24	1.07
	Cle, AL	1948	3.22	4.29	1.07

16. **Name the Hall of Famer who never won a Cy Young Award but might have won the honor with a record three different teams if it had existed when he was active.**

  A) His first hypothetical Cy Young came when he set a new modern rookie K mark in his frosh season.

  B) He's the first 40-year-old on our list to bag a hypothetical Cy Young.

  C) He never won a game in the AL.

  D) He was the first future 300-game winner to lose time while active to military service.

  E) He has the most career wins of any hurler named for a former U.S. president.

Hypothetical Cy Young Award Winners

YEAR	WINNER	TEAM	LEAGUE
1871	Rynie Wolters	New York Mutual	NA
1872	Al Spalding	Boston	NA
1873	Al Spalding	Boston	NA
1874	Bobby Mathews	New York Mutual	NA
1875	Al Spalding	Boston	NA
1876	George Bradley	St. Louis	NL
1877	Tommy Bond	Boston	NL
1878	Tommy Bond	Boston	NL
1879	Will White	Cincinnati	NL
1880	Jim McCormick	Cleveland	NL
1881	Larry Corcoran	Chicago	NL
1882	Jim McCormick	Cleveland	NL
	Will White	Cincinnati	AA
1883	Hoss Radbourn	Providence	NL
	Will White	Cincinnati	AA

Kid Nichols earned back-to-back hypothetical Cy Young honors in 1897–98. Nichols was arguably the game's top hurler in the 1890s, save perhaps for the man for whom the honor is named.

YEAR	WINNER	TEAM	LEAGUE
1884	Hoss Radbourn	Providence	NL
	Guy Hecker	Louisville	AA
	Jim McCormick	Cincinnati	UA
1885	John Clarkson	Chicago	NL
	Ed Morris	Pittsburgh	AA
1886	Lady Baldwin	Detroit	NL
	Toad Ramsey	Louisville	AA
1887	John Clarkson	Chicago	NL
	Matt Kilroy	Baltimore	AA
1888	Tim Keefe	New York	NL
	Silver King	St. Louis	AA
1889	John Clarkson	Boston	NL
	Jesse Duryea	Cincinnati	AA
1890	Bill Hutchison	Chicago	NL
	Sadie McMahon	Philadelphia/Baltimore	AA
	Silver King	Chicago	PL
1891	Bill Hutchison	Chicago	NL
	Jack Stivetts	St. Louis	AA
1892	Cy Young	Cleveland	NL
1893	Amos Rusie	New York	NL
1894	Amos Rusie	New York	NL
1895	Pink Hawley	Pittsburgh	NL
1896	Cy Young	Cleveland	NL
1897	Kid Nichols	Boston	NL
1898	Kid Nichols	Boston	NL
1899	Cy Young	St. Louis	NL
1900	Joe McGinnity	Brooklyn	NL
1901	Vic Willis	Boston	NL
	Cy Young	Boston	AL
1902	Noodles Hahn	Cincinnati	NL
	Cy Young	Boston	AL
1903	Joe McGinnity	New York	NL
	Cy Young	Boston	AL
1904	Joe McGinnity	New York	NL
	Jack Chesbro	New York	AL
1905	Christy Mathewson	New York	NL
	Rube Waddell	Philadelphia	AL
1906	Three Finger Brown	Chicago	NL
	Al Orth	New York	AL
1907	Three Finger Brown	Chicago	NL
	Ed Walsh	Chicago	AL
1908	Christy Mathewson	New York	NL
	Ed Walsh	Chicago	AL
1909	Three Finger Brown	Chicago	NL
	Frank Smith	Chicago	AL

YEAR	WINNER	TEAM	LEAGUE
1910	Christy Mathewson	New York	NL
	Jack Coombs	Philadelphia	AL
1911	Pete Alexander	Philadelphia	NL
	Ed Walsh	Chicago	AL
1912	Christy Mathewson	New York	NL
	Walter Johnson	Washington	AL
1913	Christy Mathewson	New York	NL
	Walter Johnson	Washington	AL
1914	Bill James	Boston	NL
	Walter Johnson	Washington	AL
	Claude Hendrix	Chicago	FL
1915	Pete Alexander	Philadelphia	NL
	Walter Johnson	Washington	AL
	George McConnell	Chicago	FL
1916	Pete Alexander	Philadelphia	NL
	Babe Ruth	Boston	AL
1917	Pete Alexander	Philadelphia	NL
	Eddie Cicotte	Chicago	AL
1918	Hippo Vaughn	Chicago	NL
	Walter Johnson	Washington	AL
1919	Hippo Vaughn	Chicago	NL
	Walter Johnson	Washington	AL
1920	Pete Alexander	Chicago	NL
	Stan Coveleski	Cleveland	AL
1921	Burleigh Grimes	Brooklyn	NL
	Red Faber	Chicago	AL
1922	Wilbur Cooper	Pittsburgh	NL
	Urban Shocker	St. Louis	AL
1923	Dolf Luque	Cincinnati	NL
	George Uhle	Cleveland	AL
1924	Dazzy Vance	Brooklyn	NL
	Walter Johnson	Washington	AL
1925	Dolf Luque	Cincinnati	NL
	Walter Johnson	Washington	AL
1926	Ray Kremer	Pittsburgh	NL
	George Uhle	Cleveland	AL
1927	Pete Alexander	St. Louis	NL
	Wilcy Moore	New York	AL
1928	Burleigh Grimes	Pittsburgh	NL
	Lefty Grove	Philadelphia	AL
1929	Pat Malone	Chicago	NL
	Lefty Grove	Philadelphia	AL
1930	Dazzy Vance	Brooklyn	NL
	Lefty Grove	Philadelphia	AL

YEAR	WINNER	TEAM	LEAGUE
1931	Ed Brandt	Boston	NL
	Lefty Grove	Philadelphia	AL
1932	Lon Warneke	Chicago	NL
	Lefty Grove	Philadelphia	AL
1933	Carl Hubbell	New York	NL
	Mel Harder	Cleveland	AL
1934	Curt Davis	Philadelphia	NL
	Mel Harder	Cleveland	AL
1935	Dizzy Dean	St. Louis	NL
	Wes Ferrell	Boston	AL
1936	Carl Hubbell	New York	NL
	Johnny Allen	Cleveland	AL
1937	Jim Turner	Boston	NL
	Lefty Gomez	New York	AL
1938	Bill Lee	Chicago	NL
	Red Ruffing	New York	AL
1939	Bucky Walters	Cincinnati	NL
	Bob Feller	Cleveland	AL
1940	Bucky Walters	Cincinnati	NL
	Bobo Newsom	Detroit	AL
1941	Whit Wyatt	Brooklyn	NL
	Bob Feller	Cleveland	AL
1942	Mort Cooper	St. Louis	NL
	Tiny Bonham	New York	AL
1943	Rip Sewell	Pittsburgh	NL
	Spud Chandler	New York	AL
1944	Bucky Walters	Cincinnati	NL
	Hal Newhouser	Detroit	AL
1945	Claude Passeau	Chicago	NL
	Hal Newhouser	Detroit	AL
1946	Howie Pollet	St. Louis	NL
	Hal Newhouser	Detroit	AL
1947	Ewell Blackwell	Cincinnati	NL
	Bob Feller	Cleveland	AL
1948	Johnny Sain	Boston	NL
	Bob Lemon	Cleveland	AL
1949	Howie Pollet	St. Louis	NL
	Mel Parnell	Boston	AL
1950	Sal Maglie	New York	NL
	Bob Lemon	Cleveland	AL
1951	Sal Maglie	New York	NL
	Ed Lopat	New York	AL
1952	Robin Roberts	Philadelphia	NL
	Bobby Shantz	Philadelphia	AL

YEAR	WINNER	TEAM	LEAGUE
1953	Warren Spahn	Milwaukee	NL
	Virgil Trucks	St. Louis/Chicago	AL
1954	Johnny Antonelli	New York	NL
	Bob Lemon	Cleveland	AL
1955	Robin Roberts	Philadelphia	NL
	Billy Pierce	Chicago	AL
1956	Herb Score	Cleveland	AL
1957	Jim Bunning	Detroit	AL
1958	Warren Spahn	Milwaukee	NL
1959	Sam Jones	San Francisco	NL
1960	Gerry Staley	Chicago	AL
1961	Warren Spahn	Milwaukee	NL
1962	Camilo Pascual	Minnesota	AL
1963	Camilo Pascual	Minnesota	AL
1964	Larry Jackson	Chicago	NL
1965	Sam McDowell	Cleveland	AL

Note: During 1956–65 only one award was given each year; the hypothetical winners were from the league in which no pitcher won a real Cy Young honor that season.

MVP Mainsprings

1. **Pittsburgh's dynamic duo of Barry Bonds and Bobby Bonilla finished 1-2 in the NL MVP derby in 1990, marking the most recent season that teammates have been voted the top two players in their loop. What is the most recent season that three members of the same team finished 1-2-3 in a loop MVP race?**

    A)   The team won the World Championship that year.
    B)   Three members of the loop runner-up that year finished 4-5-6 in the MVP race.
    C)   All the top three MVP teammates that year won an AL MVP award at some point.
    D)   That season's MVP also won the Triple Crown.
    E)   The previous season, the AL MVP, for the last time to date, was awarded to a shortstop who hit under .300.

Teammates Finishing 1-2-3 in a League MVP Race		
NAMES	**TEAM**	**YEAR**
Frank Robinson, Brooks Robinson & Boog Powell	Bal, AL	1966
Nellie Fox, Luis Aparicio & Early Wynn	Chi, AL	1959
Dolph Camilli, Pete Reiser & Whit Wyatt	Bro, NL	1941
Johnny Evers, Rabbit Maranville & Bill James	Bos, NL	1914

The Miracle Braves were the first team to own the top three finishes in MVP balloting. Johnny Evers, Rabbit Maranville, and Bill James were 1-2-3 in the contest to choose the 1914 Chalmers Award winner.

2. **MVP Awards were first given on an annual basis in both major leagues by the Baseball Writers' Association of America (BBWAA) in 1931. Prior to then, the two leagues had distributed their own MVP Awards, albeit irregularly, commencing in 1910. Who was the first ex–MVP winner to die while still an active player?**
   A)   Not Gehrig, but like Gehrig he was a first baseman.
   B)   In 1917 he collected 122 hits but just 140 total bases.
   C)   He died of surgical complications following his 15th season in the majors.
   D)   His MVP (Chalmers Award) came after he won his first of two straight bat crowns.
   E)   He and the 1947 AL MVP share the same initials.

3. **Who made the best showing ever by a St. Louis Brown in a BBWAA MVP election?**
   A)   He finished second, the best finish to date by a member of an AL doormat.
   B)   A White Sox frosh who failed to win the AL Rookie of the Year Award finished fourth in the MVP balloting that season.
   C)   Ken Wood led the Browns in homers that year.
   D)   Our man accounted for more than 38 percent of the Browns' wins that year.
   E)   He and Baltimore's Hall of Fame pilot in the 1890s share the same first name.

4. **Name the only player who finished ninth or better in MVP balloting in every season during World War II (1942–45).**
   A)   Lou Boudreau missed out when he ranked 10th in the 1942 AL MVP race and 10th again in 1943.
   B)   He played the same position as Boudreau.
   C)   He was nearly traded for Boudreau after the 1947 season.
   D)   He is the lone St. Louis Brownie to finish among the top 10 in MVP balloting four years in a row.
   E)   His 159 RBI in 1949 are the season record for the most ribbies by a shortstop.

5. **Prior to 1994 when first sackers Jeff Bagwell and Frank Thomas both copped MVP honors, what is the most recent season that two infielders who played the same position were the MVPs in both leagues?**
   A)   One was an MVP runner-up four years earlier when he won his first bat title.
   B)   The other man won back-to-back MVP Awards.
   C)   The two opposed each other in the fall classic the year they both collected MVP hardware.
   D)   They played the same position as the two MVP winners in 1964.
   E)   The year it last happened prior to 1994 was 1980.

6. **In 1975, Red Sox rookies Fred Lynn and Jim Rice finished first and third, respectively, in MVP balloting, but other BoSox also garnered votes. What was the lone season that two rookies bagged all the MVP votes received by members of the Red Sox?**
   A)   Neither man ever again got a single MVP vote.
   B)   One was voted the AL Rookie of the Year that season, and the other finished tied for fourth in the frosh balloting.
   C)   One won 15 games as a rookie, and the other hit .259 in 158 games.
   D)   Both their last names begin with the same three letters.
   E)   One shares the same initials and the same last name with the most recent Phillies hurler to fashion a complete-game win in a World Series.

7. **Roger Maris's 61 homers in 1961 overrode his .269 batting average in the eyes of most voters and enabled him to claim his second straight MVP Award. Who is the only MVP-winning position player to win the top prize despite hitting less than .269?**

   A) He played on a flag winner.
   B) He also owns the record for the lowest slugging average by an MVP winner.
   C) His keystone partner the year he won was Emil Verban.
   D) He topped Bill Nicholson by just one point in the balloting the year he won.
   E) His nickname was "Slats."

Season Batting Worsts by MVP-Winning Position Players

| | National League | | | | American League | | | |
	RECORD	NAME	TEAM	YEAR	RECORD	NAME	TEAM	YEAR
Batting Average	.267	Marty Marion	StL	1944	.269	Roger Maris	NY	1961
Slugging Average	.362	Marty Marion	StL	1944	.389	Nellie Fox	Chi	1959
OBP	.324	Marty Marion	StL	1944	.322	Zoilo Versalles	Min	1965
Home Runs	2	Dick Groat	Pit	1960	2	Nellie Fox	Chi	1959
RBI	48	Maury Wills	LA	1962	66	Phil Rizzuto	NY	1950
Hits	119	Willie Stargell	Pit	1979	140	Elston Howard	NY	1963
Runs	50	Marty Marion	StL	1944	75	Elston Howard	NY	1963
Doubles	13	Maury Wills	LA	1962	19	Roger Maris	NY	1961
Triples	0	Orlando Cepeda	StL	1967	0	Jose Canseco	Oak	1988
	0	Willie Stargell	Pit	1979				
Total Bases	183	Marty Marion	StL	1944	243	Nellie Fox	Chi	1959
Bases on Balls	31	Steve Garvey	LA	1974	35	Elston Howard	NY	1963
Stolen Bases	0	Ernie Lombardi	Cin	1938	0	Ted Williams	Bos	1946

Note: 1981 and 1994 strike seasons excluded. Lombardi and Williams were the first MVPs in their respective leagues with no steals; there have since been others.

8. **What was the only season to date that three pitchers finished among the top four vote-getters in an MVP race?**

   A) It was the lone season that two rookie pitchers ranked among the top four MVP candidates in a major loop.
   B) One of the rookie pitchers is in the Hall of Fame, and the other was selected his loop's Rookie of the Year that season.
   C) The third pitcher among the top four finishers won only two fewer games that year than the two rookies combined.
   D) The two rookies won 15 games apiece, mainly in relief.
   E) The three hurlers lost the top prize to the first member of a second-division team to snag an MVP Award.

9. **Who was the first man to win both an MVP Award and the World Series MVP prize in the same season?**

   A) It was his only MVP Award, but he later won another Series MVP.
   B) He won six major awards during his career, including his two Series MVPs.
   C) His team swept the Series that year, beating a club that was heavily favored.
   D) He was a perfect 3-for-3 that year in winning major awards for which he was eligible.
   E) He holds the 20th century record for the most wins by a pitcher in his final big league season.

10. **Who is the only man to sweep all three top player awards—MVP, LCS MVP, and World Series MVP—in the same season?**

    A) It was the only season that he won a major award of any sort.

    B) He led his team to a come-from-behind World Series triumph in seven games.

    C) He is the oldest man to be selected a World Series MVP.

    D) He was the catalyst that season on a team that called itself "The Family."

    E) He holds the Pirates' career home run record.

Evolution of Record for Oldest League MVP

NAME	TEAM	YEAR	AGE
Wildfire Schulte	Chicago, NL	1911	29
Johnny Evers	Chicago, NL	1914	33
Dazzy Vance	Brooklyn, NL	1924	33
Gabby Hartnett	Chicago, NL	1935	35
Spud Chandler	New York, AL	1943	36
Willie Stargell	Pittsburgh, NL	1979	39

Note: Age as of December 31 of year selected MVP. Vance's birthday came earlier in the year, making him older than Evers.

11. **In 1933, his lone season as a full-time regular, Giants shortstop Blondy Ryan finished ninth in the NL MVP voting despite hitting just .238 with a .259 OBP. What hurler of the same vintage as Ryan went on to have a lackluster 16–21 career record with a 4.48 ERA and just one save after nearly finishing among the top 10 as a rookie in a BBWAA MVP election?**

    A) He finished 11th in the balloting in 1932.

    B) In 1932 he was a 21-year-old NL frosh.

    C) His 14–7 mark helped the Braves reach .500 in 1932.

    D) His initials are the same as those of Cleveland's third sacker in the first decade of the 20th century.

    E) He and the only M.D. and former ballplayer to become an American League president shared the same name at birth.

12. **Which of the eight NL teams extant when the first BBWAA MVP trophies were awarded in 1931 went the longest before one of its players won the top prize?**

    A) A Hall of Famer from the team was the MVP runner-up in 1934.

    B) Another 'Famer from the team was third in the MVP race in both 1935 and 1938.

    C) The team's top vote-getter the year before it garnered its first MVP trophy was a relief pitcher.

    D) A shortstop bagged the team's first BBWAA MVP Award the year it won its first pennant in more than 30 years.

    E) The team entered the 1999 season still in search of its first Rookie of the Year Award winner.

First BBWAA MVP Winner, Teams Extant in 1931

TEAM	1ST WINNER	YEAR
St. Louis, NL	Frankie Frisch	1931
Philadelphia, AL	Lefty Grove	1931
Philadelphia, NL	Chuck Klein	1932
New York, NL	Carl Hubbell	1933
Detroit, AL	Mickey Cochrane	1934
Chicago, NL	Gabby Hartnett	1935
New York, AL	Lou Gehrig	1936
Cincinnati, NL	Ernie Lombardi	1938
Boston, AL	Jimmie Foxx	1938
Brooklyn, NL	Dolph Camilli	1941
Boston, NL	Bob Elliott	1947
Cleveland, AL	Lou Boudreau	1948
Chicago, AL	Nellie Fox	1959
Pittsburgh, NL	Dick Groat	1960

Note: Two of the 16 teams extant in 1931, the Washington Senators and the St. Louis Browns, never had a BBWAA MVP winner before they moved to Minnesota and Baltimore, respectively.

13. **No two brothers have both won MVP honors. What sibs came the closest thus far to being the first to do it?**
    A)   One won the top prize one year, and the other was later a runner-up.
    B)   They're the only pair of brothers who both finished among the top five in a loop MVP race.
    C)   They were teammates during the years they vied for MVP honors.
    D)   They're the only batterymates to finish among the top five in a National League MVP derby.
    E)   They were the main battery for the Cards' three successive flag winners in 1942–44.

14. **What team has had the most MVP winners in years when it failed to win a pennant?**
    A)   Including Chalmers Awards and league awards, the team has had nine MVP recipients, but only two played on flag winners.
    B)   The team's first MVP recipient beat out Christy Mathewson.
    C)   The team's only MVP recipient in the 1980s set a record that season for the most home runs by a player in his first year with a new team.
    D)   The team is the only club to have a loop MVP in a season in which it finished last in its division.
    E)   The team is the only club to own a shortstop who won back-to-back MVP honors.

15. **Bob O'Farrell in 1926 and Mickey Cochrane in 1928 were the first NL and AL catchers, respectively, to cop MVP honors. Prior to 1926, each loop had just one backstopper who'd finished as high as third in an MVP vote. Who are the two "well-received" receivers?**
    A)   The NL candidate finished among the top five twice in the race for a new Chalmers.
    B)   The AL honoree is the lone catcher to receive votes for both a Chalmers Award and a league award.
    C)   The AL'er is in the Hall of Fame.
    D)   The NL'er in 1911 fell one hit short of being the first catcher in major league history to win a batting title.
    E)   The pair would have met in the 1917 World Series if the NL'er had still been active with his 1911 team.

16. **The 1968 season is the only campaign when pitchers copped MVP honors in both leagues. What are the only two seasons to date that catchers took both top prizes?**
    A) The seasons came four years apart.
    B) The two winning receivers faced each other in fall play on the second occasion.
    C) During the five-year span under consideration here, Al Rosen was the lone AL MVP winner who was not a batteryman.
    D) The same two backstoppers were involved on both occasions.
    E) The two backstoppers first opposed each other in the 1949 Series.

17. **In 1995, Mo Vaughn became the second BoSox first sacker since 1938 to cop an MVP Award. What is the only team that can claim three MVP-winning gateway guardians since 1938?**
    A) One of the trio won top honors at two different positions.
    B) The lone righty hitter of the three won his second NL RBI crown the year he bagged his MVP prize.
    C) All three played on World Championship teams with the club.
    D) Two of the three won batting titles the year they bagged MVP honors as first basemen.
    E) One of the trio is the only member of his team to tie for the NL's top award.

18. **What pitcher found himself voted an MVP runner-up after he began the season as a mop-up man for a team in another major league?**
    A) He began the season as a bullpenner with Cleveland.
    B) He lost the MVP that year to a teammate.
    C) His teammate also won the Cy Young Award that year.
    D) That same year, he became the only man ever to pitch a complete game in a World Series in which he received absolute zero offensive support—not so much as a single base runner, let alone a run.
    E) They called him "The Barber."

Repeat MVP Winners		
POS.	**NAME**	**YEARS**
1B	Jimmie Foxx	1932–33
1B	Frank Thomas	1993–94
2B	Joe Morgan	1975–76
3B	Mike Schmidt	1980–81
SS	Ernie Banks	1958–59
OF	Mickey Mantle	1956–57
OF	Roger Maris	1960–61
OF	Dale Murphy	1982–83
OF	Barry Bonds	1992–93
C	Yogi Berra	1954–55
P	Hal Newhouser	1944–45

Note: Prior to Bonds's repeat win in 1993, there were exactly nine
repeat winners, and they formed a perfect all-star team—
one catcher, one pitcher, one at each infield position, and
three outfielders.

Fabled Frosh

1. **In 1975, Fred Lynn became the first big leaguer to cop both the Rookie of the Year and MVP Awards in the same year. Lynn remains the only frosh to be so honored, but in his second season, the Boston phenom was nailed by the sophomore jinx and failed to receive a single MVP vote. Who is the lone man to beat the sophomore jinx so thoroughly that he won a Rookie of the Year Award followed by an MVP Award in his second season?**

   A) He beat out a Twins first sacker for the rookie honor.
   B) He narrowly edged out a teammate to win his first MVP Award.
   C) He won a second MVP Award nearly 10 years later.
   D) Eddie Murray was the teammate he nosed out to cop his first MVP prize.
   E) The night the number 2,191 appeared in mammoth lights at Camden Yards, he set a significant new ML record.

2. **After tying for third in the NL ROY vote with a .242 batting average, who made mincemeat of the sophomore jinx when he hit .302 with 47 homers and 135 RBI while setting the pre-1998 NL record for the most total bases by a player at his position?**

   A) He was last seen in action in the 1968 World Series.
   B) He later managed the team for whom he played most of his career.
   C) He's the holder of many NL season slugging records for men at his position.
   D) 1952 was his rookie year.
   E) He was the last member of the Boston Braves to receive a ROY Award vote.

3. **The youngest big league regular (100 or more games) was just 17 the summer of his rookie year. Who is he?**

   A) He was born on November 26, 1866.
   B) He starred for the winning team in the 1889 World Series.
   C) The year he debuted, a 17-year-old third baseman named Pat Callahan hit .260 in 61 games for Indianapolis of the AA and then was never seen again.
   D) He hit .208 for the Boston Unions as a 17-year-old frosh outfielder in 1884.
   E) His first name and initials are the same as those of the regular catcher for the last NL world champ from the state of California.

Teenage Regulars, Season (Minimum 100 Games)

NAME	TEAM	YEAR	AGE	GAMES
Bob Kennedy	Chi, AL	1940	19*	154
Rusty Staub	Hou, NL	1963	19	150
Robin Yount	Mil, AL	1975	19*	147
Phil Cavarretta	Chi, NL	1935	18	146
Buddy Lewis	Was, AL	1936	19*	143
Al Kaline	Det, AL	1954	19*	138
George Davis	Cle, NL	1890	19*	136
Will Smalley	Cle, NL	1890	19	136
Cass Michaels	Chi, AL	1945	19	129
Ken Griffey Jr.	Sea, AL	1989	19*	127
Mel Ott	NY, NL	1928	19	124
Phil Cavarretta	Chi, NL	1936	19*	124
Sibby Sisti	Bos, NL	1940	19*	123
Les Mann	Bos, NL	1913	19*	120
Jose Oquendo	NY, NL	1983	19*	120
Ed Kranepool	NY, NL	1964	19*	119
Chubby Dean	Phi, AL	1936	19*	111
Tony Conigliaro	Bos, AL	1964	19	111
Milt Scott	Det, NL	1884	18	110
Robin Yount	Mil, AL	1974	18	107
Mike Slattery	Bos, UA	1884	17	106
Johnny Lush	Phi, NL	1904	18	106
Jimmy Sheckard	Bro, NL	1898	19*	105
Freddy Lindstrom	NY, NL	1925	19*	104
Monte Ward	Pro, NL	1879	19	83
Jack Glasscock	Cle, NL	1879	19*	80
Lew Brown	Bos, NL	1876	18	45
Lew Brown	Bos, NL	1877	19	58

* Celebrated 20th birthday after July 1.

Note: Ward, Glasscock, and Brown played more than the equivalent of 100 games
as rookies; the schedule called for far fewer than 100 games in the 1870s.
Davis and Smalley made the 1890 Cleveland Spiders the only team in history
with two teenage regulars.

4. Who was the first Rookie of the Year to start so poorly the following season that he was banished to the minors for a refresher course?

A) To earn the AL rookie prize, he had to beat out a future Hall of Fame pitcher who posted a .900 winning percentage.

B) Third in the AL rookie balloting the season he won was Chico Carrasquel.

C) Al Rosen might have denied him the frosh prize but was ruled ineligible for it.

D) Whitey Ford, with a 9–1 record, was the AL rookie runner-up to him in 1950.

E) His 144 RBI missed the all-time rookie record by one.

5. Who won Rookie of the Year honors when he hit .306 as a frosh but then had to wait five seasons before he again played enough to qualify for a batting title?

A)   He was last seen with the 1965 Senators.

B)   As a rookie, he played in the same outfield with Dick Kokos and Stan Spence.

C)   He led the White Sox in homers in both 1960 and 1961.

D)   In 1957 he became the first Senator to top the AL in both homers and RBI.

E)   He was the first AL'er to receive a ROY Award.

First ROY Award Winner, Each Current Club

TEAM	LEAGUE	1ST WINNER	YEAR
Brooklyn—Los Angeles	NL	Jackie Robinson	1947
Boston—Milwaukee—Atlanta	NL	Alvin Dark	1948
St. Louis—Baltimore	AL	Roy Sievers	1949
Boston	AL	Walt Dropo	1950
New York—San Francisco Giants	NL	Willie Mays	1951
New York Yankees	AL	Gil McDougald	1951
Philadelphia—Kansas City—Oakland	AL	Harry Byrd	1952
Detroit	AL	Harvey Kuenn	1953
St. Louis	NL	Wally Moon	1954
Cleveland	AL	Herb Score	1955
Cincinnati	NL	Frank Robinson	1956
Chicago	AL	Luis Aparicio	1956
Philadelphia	NL	Jack Sanford	1957
Washington—Minnesota	AL	Albie Pearson	1958
Chicago	NL	Billy Williams	1961
New York Mets	NL	Tom Seaver	1967
Kansas City Royals	AL	Lou Piniella	1969
Montreal	NL	Carl Morton	1970
Washington—Texas	AL	Mike Hargrove	1974
San Diego	NL	Butch Metzger	1976
Toronto	AL	Alfredo Griffin	1979
Seattle	AL	Alvin Davis	1984
Houston	NL	Jeff Bagwell	1991
Milwaukee	AL	Pat Listach	1992
Los Angeles—California—Anaheim	NL	Tim Salmon	1993

None to date: Pittsburgh, Florida, Colorado, and Arizona (NL); Tampa Bay (AL).

6. **Several pitchers have fizzled after winning ROY honors, but only one position player never again put in a full season as a regular after copping the top frosh prize. Who is he?**

    A)   He hit 23 homers and had 87 RBI as a rookie.

    B)   Like another rookie star, Herb Score, he was felled by injuries.

    C)   Also like Score, he won rookie honors in a Cleveland uniform.

    D)   He was probably the flakiest ROY ever.

    E)   His nickname was "Super Joe."

7. **What rookie topped the AL in stolen bases, collected 13 more RBI than any other AL frosh, outhit the next-best AL frosh batter by 20 points, and yet finished second in his loop's rookie voting to the man he outhit by 20 points?**

    A)   Frosh honors in the AL that year went to a third sacker on the world champs.

    B)   He hit over .300 eight times, last with the 1960 White Sox.

    C)   His final ML game was in 1980.

    D)   His first ML game came with Cleveland in 1949.

    E)   He has the most career hits of any player whose first name is Saturnino.

Dick Howser, the shortstop on the "Overlooked" Rookie All-Star team. He scored 108 runs in 1961 for the last-place Kansas City A's but lost the top rookie honor to Don Schwall.

The "Overlooked" Rookie All-Star Team

POS.	NAME	TEAM	YEAR	RUNS	RBI	BA
1B	Todd Helton	Col, NL	1998	78	97	.315
2B	Juan Samuel	Phi, NL	1984	105	69	.272
3B	Kevin Seitzer	KC, AL	1987	105	83	.323
SS	Dick Howser	KC, AL	1961	108	45	.280
LF	Minnie Minoso	Cle/Chi, AL	1951	112	74	.324
CF	Richie Ashburn	Phi, AL	1948	78	40	.333
RF	Jim Rice	Bos, AL	1975	92	102	.309
C	Jason Kendall	Pit, NL	1996	54	42	.300
Sub	Tim Raines	Mon, NL	1981	61	37	.304
Sub	Mitchell Page	Oak, AL	1977	85	77	.307
Sub	Pete Ward	Chi, AL	1963	80	84	.295
Sub	Jim Finigan	Phi, AL	1954	57	51	.302

POS.	NAME	TEAM	YEAR	IP	W	ERA
P	Larry Jansen	NY, NL	1947	248	21	3.16
P	Gene Bearden	Cle, AL	1948	230	20	2.43
P	Alex Kellner	Phi, AL	1949	245	20	3.75
P	Tom Browning	Cin, NL	1985	261.1	20	3.55
P	Jerry Koosman	NY, NL	1968	263.2	19	2.08

8. Whose .313 batting average and .538 slugging average are both records among 20th century rookie regulars who played only one season in the majors?

A) He began as a pitcher with Oakland of the PCL.

B) He holds many minor league career records.

C) In his lone ML season, he was a teammate of Chuck Klein.

D) He was a 32-year-old switch-hitter with the Phils in his lone ML season.

E) He and Pete Bavasi's father share the same nickname.

Highest BA by a One-Year Wonder (Minimum 400 ABs)

RANK	NAME	TEAM	YEAR	ABS	SA	BA
1	Harry Moore	Was, UA	1884	461	.414	.336
2	Buzz Arlett	Phi, NL	1931	418	.538	.313
3	Irv Waldron	Mil/Was, AL	1901	590	.378	.311
4	Ernie Sulik	Phi, NL	1936	404	.386	.287
5	Buddy Blair	Phi, AL	1942	484	.397	.279
6	Charlie Hamburg	Lou, AA	1890	485	.344	.272
7	Dutch Schleibner	Bro/NL, StL/AL	1923	520	.362	.271
8	Moon Mullen	Phi, NL	1944	464	.304	.267
9	Hector Rodriguez	Chi, AL	1952	407	.307	.2654
10	Larry Murphy	Was, AA	1891	400	.325	.2650

Note: Limited to men who played only one ML season.

9. What rookie in 1955 was fourth in the AL in homers and knocked home 93 runs but never again put in a full season as a regular performer?

    A)   A first sacker, he topped the AL in KS as a frosh.

    B)   He lost his job to Mickey Vernon in 1956.

    C)   His 27 frosh homers are the most of anyone whose lone 20-homer season was his first.

    D)   His last initial is the same as that of an AL home run champ during the 1950s.

    E)   He and the 1961 AL batting champ share the same first name.

Players with 20 HRs, Rookie Year Only

NAME	TEAM	YEAR	C/HRS	R/HRS
Norm Zauchin	Bos, AL	1955	50	27
Ken Hunt	LA, AL	1961	33	25
Roy Foster	Cle, AL	1970	45	23
Joe Charboneau	Cle, AL	1980	29	23
Don Lenhardt	StL, AL	1950	61	22
Sam Bowens	Bal, AL	1964	45	22
Dave Hostetler	Tex, AL	1982	37	22
Ray Jablonski	StL, NL	1953	83	21
Bernie Carbo	Cin, NL	1970	96	21
Mitchell Page	Oak, AL	1977	72	21

Note: Limited to retired players. C/HRs denotes career home runs; R/HRs denotes rookie home runs.

10. Who is the lone manager to win a flag in his rookie year as a pilot and then be fired before the completion of the following season?

    A)   He never played in the majors.

    B)   After he was fired, his former team went on to take part in postseason action under its new skipper.

    C)   He later piloted another team to a division title.

    D)   Dick Howser replaced him in his sophomore year as a pilot.

    E)   He led the Cubs to their first post–World War II postseason appearance.

11. The lone rookie in the 20th century who both won and lost 20 games in his maiden season finished with just 62 wins. Who is he?

    A)   He was only 4–8 with the 1910 White Sox, but all four wins were shutouts to tie an all-time record for the most wins in a season, all of them shutouts.

    B)   He led the NL in starts, complete games, and innings in both his rookie and his sophomore seasons.

    C)   He's the only 20th century hurler to lose 20 games in each of his first three seasons.

    D)   He was a member of the only pitching staff to feature four 20-game losers two years in a row.

    E)   Because his last name was the same as that of one of the era's top hurlers, he was called "____ the Second."

Irv Young, the last man to be both a 20-game winner and a 20-game loser as a frosh. His 378 innings in 1905 are a 20th century yearling record.

Fewest Career Wins, Rookie 20-Game Winner (Since 1901)

RANK	NAME	TEAM	YEAR	R/W	C/W
1	Henry Schmidt	Bro, NL	1903	22	22
2	Johnny Beazley	StL, NL	1942	21	31
3	Roscoe Miller	Det, AL	1901	23	39
4	Lou Fette	Bos, NL	1937	20	41
	Scott Perry	Phi, AL	1918	21	41
6	Gene Bearden	Cle, AL	1948	20	45
7	King Cole	Chi, NL	1910	20	55
8	Hugh Bedient	Bos, AL	1912	20	60
9	Bob Grim	NY, AL	1954	20	61
10	Irv Young	Bos, NL	1905	20	62

Note: R/W denotes rookie wins; C/W denotes career wins.

12. The only two seasons that both ROY Award winners were ultimately selected for the Hall of Fame came 11 years apart. Name all four rookie award winners.

A) The four winners played shortstop, outfield, second base, and pitcher.

B) None of the four played on a pennant winner as a rookie.

C) All but the shortstop later won either an MVP or a Cy Young Award.

D) The shortstop and the outfielder were later teammates, and the pitcher and the second baseman faced each other in 1985 in the AL.

E) The second baseman finished his career at first base, and the outfielder finished his as a manager-DH.

13. **Who is the only rookie in this century to win more than 40 percent of his team's games?**
- A) The team finished in the AL basement.
- B) The team's rookie ace won more games than its next three biggest winners (Vean Gregg, Mule Watson, and Willie Adams) combined.
- C) His 21 wins were only two behind Walter Johnson, the AL win leader that year.
- D) A world crisis ended the season that year on Labor Day.
- E) He and the brothers who broke the Clarksons' record for the most career wins by siblings share the same last name.

14. **What rookie southpaw was the most recent hurler to make his ML debut as an Opening Day starter?**
- A) He lost to Brooklyn, 11–4, on April 23, 1943.
- B) His last ML start came with the 1948 Browns.
- C) He was 10–19 with the Phils as a frosh in 1943.
- D) His initials are the same as those of a man who shared the AL ROY Award in 1979.
- E) The name that follows his in *The Baseball Encyclopedia* belongs to the lone rookie ever to go 0–12 in his only ML season.

15. **At one time the AL record holder for the highest batting average by a rookie, he later led another AL team in total bases while posting a slugging average that was 42 points below his frosh batting average! Who is he?**
- A) He holds the all-time record for the fewest total bases (133) by a team leader in total bases in a season when a full schedule of 154 or more games was played.
- B) His 133 TBs were 12 more than runner-up Rollie Zeider accumulated.
- C) He led the first 20th century world champion in runs and hits.
- D) Traded to "The Hitless Wonders" in time to appear in the 1906 World Series, he finished his career in a White Sox uniform.
- E) His first name and initials match those of the record holder for the lowest SA by a man with at least 2,000 career hits and a .300 BA.

Fewest TBs, Season, by a Team Leader in TBs

RANK	NAME	TEAM	YEAR	TBS
1	Patsy Dougherty	Chi, AL	1910	133
2	Jerry Remy	Cal, AL	1976	152
3	Tommie Agee	NY, NL	1972	158
4	Fielder Jones	Chi, AL	1908	162
5	Ted Ford	Tex, AL	1972	164
6	Ginger Beaumont	Bos, NL	1908	165
7	Bob Unglaub	Was, AL	1909	168
8	Bob Ganley	Was, AL	1908	171
9	Buck Herzog	Cin, NL	1914	173
10	Vern Duncan	Bal, FL	1915	174

Note: Includes only teams that played at least a 154-game schedule.

16. Name the hurler who never threw another pitch in the majors after he was chosen the NL hill Rookie of the Year by *The Sporting News*.

A) His nine frosh wins in 1961 are the most since expansion by a pitcher who played only one season in the majors.

B) He began spring training in his lone ML season as a nonroster player.

C) He has the same name as an AL player who hit 25 homers in 1961, his lone big league season as a regular.

D) He played on the NL champs in 1961, and his AL counterpart was on the Angels.

E) He and the NL ROY in 1962 share both the same first name and the same initials.

Most Wins by a One-Year Wonder

RANK	NAME	TEAM	YEAR	IP	W
1	Jocko Flynn	Chi, NL	1886	257	23
2	Henry Schmidt	Bro, NL	1903	301	22
3	Fred Smith	Tol, AA	1890	286	19
	Park Swartzel	KC, AA	1889	410.1	19
5	John Keefe	Syr, AA	1890	352.1	17
6	Fleury Sullivan	Pit, AA	1884	441	16
7	Perry Werden	StL, UA	1884	141.1	12
	Bob Hart	StL, AA	1890	201	12
	Doc Landis	Phi/Bal, AA	1882	358	12
	Erv Lange	Chi, FL	1914	190	12
	Max Fiske	Chi, FL	1914	198	12

Note: Limited to men who served as pitchers in only one ML season.

17. Who are the only two 20th century pitchers to hurl as many as 700 innings in their first two ML seasons combined?

A) Both won 20 games as rookies.

B) Both hurled fewer than 1,500 innings in the majors.

C) They pitched against each other in 1905 when one of them was a rookie.

D) The other man was a rookie teammate of the only hurler in the 20th century to win 20 games in his one and only ML season.

E) One man's last name is shared by the all-time record holder for the most consecutive losses, and the other man's last name is shared by the only hurler to throw a no-hitter in his first ML game.

Most Innings Pitched in Rookie Season (Since 1893)

RANK	NAME	TEAM	YEAR	W–L	IP
1	Sam Leever	Pit, NL	1899	21–23	379
2	Irv Young	Bos, NL	1905	20–21	378
3	Pete Alexander	Phi, NL	1911	28–13	367
4	Joe McGinnity	Bal, NL	1899	28–16	366.1
5	Bill Carrick	NY, NL	1899	16–27	361.2
6	George McQuillan	Phi, NL	1908	23–17	359.2
7	Stoney McGlynn	StL, NL	1907	14–25	352.1
8	Chick Fraser	Lou, NL	1896	12–27	349.1
9	Oscar Jones	Bro, NL	1903	19–14	324.1
10	Still Bill Hill	Lou, NL	1896	9–28	319.2

18. **Name the four ROY winners whose first ML games came with teams other than those whose uniforms they wore when they won their awards.**

    A)   Three of them played with Cleveland before winning ROY honors with other AL teams.

    B)   The fourth won the top rookie honor with Cleveland after debuting in the NL.

    C)   One of the four tied for first prize in the 1979 AL rookie sweepstakes.

    D)   Two were outfielders, one was a shortstop, and the lone man of the four who was still active in 1999 is a catcher.

    E)   The shortstop and the two outfielders won rookie honors with the Blue Jays, the White Sox, and the Royals, respectively.

19. **George Watkins is generally recognized as the record holder for the highest batting average by a rookie, even though he had fewer than 400 at bats when he hit .373 with the 1930 Cardinals. Joe Jackson, on the other hand, was not considered a rookie in 1911 when he hit .408 because he'd previously played in a handful of games. Among NL or AL freshmen with at least 400 at bats who are unequivocally considered rookies, who has the all-time highest batting average?**

    A)   He took Charlie Irwin's third-base job as a rookie.

    B)   Pirates third sacker Jimmy Williams fell three points short of the all-time rookie record when he hit .355 in 1899.

    C)   The all-time rookie mark was set in 1895.

    D)   The rookie record holder switched to first base in 1898 when Cap Anson finally gave up the job.

    E)   The rookie record holder's initials are the same as those of the 19th century's greatest catcher.

Highest BA by a Rookie (Minimum 400 ABs)

RANK	NAME	TEAM	YEAR	ABS	BA
1	Benny Kauff	Ind, FL	1914	571	.370
2	Bill Everitt	Chi, NL	1895	550	.358
3	Jimmy Williams	Pit, NL	1899	617	.3549
4	Lloyd Waner	Pit, NL	1927	629	.3545
5	Kiki Cuyler	Pit, NL	1924	466	.3541
6	Chick Stahl	Bos, NL	1897	469	.3539
7	Ginger Beaumont	Pit, NL	1899	437	.3524
8	Hack Miller	Chi, NL	1922	466	.3519
9	Dale Alexander	Det, AL	1929	626	.343
10	Patsy Dougherty	Bos, AL	1902	438	.342

Note: Includes only men with 400 ABs who are unequivocally considered rookies; among those eliminated are Joe Jackson (.408 in 1911), Dave Orr (.354 in 1884), and Pete Browning (.378 in only 288 ABs in 1882). BAs are carried out to four decimal points where ties would otherwise exist.

20. **Who holds both the AL record for the most total chances and the preexpansion record for the most at bats by a rookie second sacker?**
    A) He tallied 102 runs on 191 hits as a Cleveland frosh.
    B) His keystone partner in his rookie year was Joe Sewell.
    C) After playing 154 games as a frosh, he played only 90 more games in the bigs.
    D) His initials are the same as those of the AL record holder for the most total chances in a season by an outfielder.
    E) His last name and the last name of the Pirates regular second sacker during 1988–92 are spelled the same but pronounced differently.

Players Scoring 100 Runs in Their Rookie Year Only

NAME	TEAM	YEAR	C/R	R/R
Ted Scheffler	Roc, AA	1890	128	111
Dale Alexander	Det, AL	1929	369	110
Kevin Seitzer	KC, AL	1987	739	105
Ike Davis	Chi, AL	1925	110	105
Jim Burns	KC, AA	1889	131	103
Irv Waldron	Mil/Was, AL	1901	102	102
Carl Lind	Cle, AL	1928	131	102
Hersh Martin	Phi, NL	1937	331	102
Walt Dropo	Bos, AL	1950	478	101
John Farrell	Was, AL	1901	329	100
Kiddo Davis	Phi, NL	1932	281	100

Note: Scheffler and Ike Davis are not unequivocally considered rookies. C/R denotes career runs; R/R denotes rookie runs.

21. **What rookie set the current post-1920 NL record for the lowest slugging average by a .300-hitting outfielder with at least 400 at bats when his 125 safeties in 1940 produced just 148 total bases?**
    A) He also had a record-low .326 OBP to go with his .356 SA after logging just 13 walks.
    B) He played on pennant winners in three different NL cities in the 1940s.
    C) He finished with Washington in 1951, hitting .288 in 81 games.
    D) He and the first sacker on his first pennant winner in 1940 had the same last name but were not related.
    E) The first sacker who shared his last name also played with him on his next pennant winner, the 1948 Boston Braves.

22. **Name the rookie third sacker who led his loop in runs in the process of hitting .318 for a team that fell one game short of winning the pennant.**
    A) He never played in a World Series.
    B) He never had a season in which he totaled more RBI than strikeouts.
    C) He won an MVP Award with an AL team.
    D) He was the most recent rookie to lead the NL in runs.
    E) As a rookie in 1964, he bore the same nickname as a Hall of Fame outfielder who debuted with his 1964 team 16 years earlier.

Rookies Leading in Runs

NAME	TEAM	YEAR	BA	RUNS
Ed Swartwood	Pit, AA	1882	.329	86
Lloyd Waner	Pit, NL	1927	.355	133
Frank Robinson	Cin, NL	1956	.290	122
Dick Allen	Phi, NL	1964	.318	125
Tony Oliva	Min, AL	1964	.323	109
Fred Lynn	Bos, AL	1975	.331	103

23. **In his rookie year he tallied 72 runs and hit .284, mostly as a third baseman; moved to second the following year, he never again scored more than 45 runs in a season although he played regularly for eight more years. Who is he?**
    A) He finished his 14-year career with the 1977 Red Sox.
    B) In his lone World Series he was managed by one of the few rookie pilots to take their team to a pennant.
    C) He played third base in his first full season but swapped posts the next season with a teammate who had won a ROY Award as a second baseman.
    D) He won a ROY Award in 1966.
    E) He scored just 42 runs in 150 games for the 1970 NL flag winner.

Fewest Runs per At Bat, Career (Minimum 4,000 ABs)

RANK	NAME	YEARS	RUNS	ABS	R/AB
1	Ken Reitz	1972–82	366	4777	.077
2	Frank Snyder	1912–27	331	4229	.078
3	Jerry Grote	1963–81	352	4339	.081
4	Tommy Helms	1964–77	414	4997	.083
	Red Dooin	1902–16	333	4004	.083
6	Mickey Doolan	1905–18	513	5977	.086
	Gus Mancuso	1928–45	386	4505	.086
8	Bob Aspromonte	1956–71	386	4369	.088
9	Ivey Wingo	1911–29	362	4003	.090
10	Ed Brinkman	1961–75	550	6045	.091

24. **Though his name is found in few record books, who is the true holder of the all-time record for the most shutouts by a rookie pitcher?**

A) George Bradley is officially credited with the record (16 in 1876), but Bradley's first major league season was really 1875, when he pitched for St. Louis in the National Association.

B) The true record holder had nine shutouts as a frosh in 1881.

C) He won 29 games in 1881 for the first Detroit team in major league history.

D) His initials are the same as those of the NL loss leader in 1906 with 26.

E) Old-time Detroit fans thought of him every time they doffed their hats.

Evolution of AL Rookie HR Record

NAME	TEAM	YEAR	HRS
Socks Seybold	Philadelphia	1901	8
Duffy Lewis	Boston	1910	8
Bob Meusel	New York	1920	11
Earl Sheely	Chicago	1921	11
Ike Boone	Boston	1924	13
Lou Gehrig	New York	1925	20
Dale Alexander	Detroit	1929	25
Hal Trosky	Cleveland	1934	35
Rudy York	Detroit	1937	35
Al Rosen	Cleveland	1950	37
Mark McGwire	Oakland	1987	49

Evolution of NL Rookie HR Record

NAME	TEAM	YEAR	HRS
Charley Jones	Cincinnati	1876	4
Dan Brouthers	Troy	1879	4
John O'Rourke	Boston	1879	6
Harry Stovey	Worcester	1880	6
Mike Muldoon	Cleveland	1882	6
Frank Meinke	Detroit	1884	6
Sam Thompson	Detroit	1885	7
Billy O'Brien	Washington	1887	19
Buck Freeman	Washington	1899	25
Del Bissonette	Brooklyn	1928	25
Wally Berger	Boston	1930	38
Frank Robinson	Cincinnati	1956	38

Evolution of AL Rookie RBI Record

NAME	TEAM	YEAR	RBI
Socks Seybold	Philadelphia	1901	90
Ping Bodie	Chicago	1911	97
Al Simmons	Philadelphia	1924	102
Tony Lazzeri	New York	1926	114
Dale Alexander	Detroit	1929	137
Hal Trosky	Cleveland	1934	142
Ted Williams	Boston	1939	145

Evolution of NL Rookie RBI Record

NAME	TEAM	YEAR	RBI
John Morrill	Boston	1876	26
Russ McKelvey	Indianapolis	1878	36
John O'Rourke	Boston	1879	62
Alex McKinnon	New York	1884	73
Marty Sullivan	Chicago	1887	77
Bill Lange	Chicago	1893	88
Jimmy Bannon	Boston	1894	114
Buck Freeman	Washington	1899	122

Note: The 20th century NL record belongs to Wally Berger of Boston with 119 RBI in 1930.

Era Rookie Season Pitching Record Holders

	National League			American League		
	RECORD	NAME	YEAR	RECORD	NAME	YEAR
Innings						
1872–75	535.2	George Bradley	1875—NA			
1876–92	**590.2**	**Lee Richmond**	**1880**	583	Matt Kilroy	1886
1893–1900	379	Sam Leever	1899	366.1	Joe McGinnity	1899
1901–19	378	Irv Young	1905	332.1	Scott Perry	1918
1920–41	302	Jesse Haines	1920	274.2	Herm Pillette	1922
1942–60	313	Bill Voiselle	1944	264.2	Boo Ferriss	1945
1961–76	284.2	Carl Morton	1970	268.2	Frank Tanana	1974
1977–93	261.1	Tom Browning	1985	265.2	Roger Erickson	1978
1994–	217	Matt Morris	1997	203.2	Jason Dickson	1997
Games						
1872–75	60	George Bradley	1875—NA			
1876–92	74	Lee Richmond	1880	68	Matt Kilroy	1886
1893–1900	51	Sam Leever	1899	50	Win Mercer	1894
1901–19	48	George McQuillan	1908	52	Reb Russell	1913
	48	Pete Alexander	1911			
1920–41	53	Orville Jorgens	1935	55	Jim Walkup	1935
1942–60	71	Hoyt Wilhelm	1952	54	Jack Crimian	1956
1961–76	74	Dan McGinn	1969	69	Bob Lee	1965
				69	Bill Kelso	1967
1977–93	78	Tim Burke	1985	80	Mitch Williams	1986
1994–	72	Rich Loiselle	1997	**88**	**Sean Runyan**	**1998**
Wins						
1872–75	33	Candy Cummings	1872—NA			
	33	George Bradley	1875—NA			
1876–92	**43**	**Larry Corcoran**	**1880**	34	Ed Morris	1884
1893–1900	31	Bill Hoffer	1895	28	Joe McGinnity	1899
1901–19	28	Pete Alexander	1911	26	Russ Ford	1910
1920–41	20	Cliff Melton	1937	22	Monte Weaver	1932
	20	Lou Fette	1937			
	20	Jim Turner	1937			
1942–60	21	Johnny Beazley	1942	21	Boo Ferriss	1945
	21	Bill Voiselle	1944			
	21	Larry Jansen	1947			
1961–76	19	Jerry Koosman	1968	19	Gary Peters	1963
				19	Wally Bunker	1964
				19	Mark Fidrych	1976
1977–93	20	Tom Browning	1985	17	Mark Langston	1984
				17	Tom Gordon	1989
				17	Dave Fleming	1992
1994–	13	Done by four men		14	Rolando Arrojo	1998

	National League				American League		
	RECORD	**NAME**	**YEAR**		**RECORD**	**NAME**	**YEAR**
Winning Percentage (Minimum 15 Wins)							
1872–75	.623	Candy Cummings	1872—NA				
1876–92	.793	Jocko Flynn	1886		.727	Silver King	1887
1893–1900	.838	Bill Hoffer	1895		.769	Jerry Nops	1897
1901–19	.833	King Cole	1910		.813	Russ Ford	1910
1920–41	**.842**	**Emil Yde**	**1924**		.810	Johnny Allen	1932
1942–60	.833	Hoyt Wilhelm	1952		.789	Hank Borowy	1942
1961–76	.727	Dick Hughes	1967		.792	Wally Bunker	1964
1977–93	.690	Tom Browning	1985		.696	Ron Guidry	1977
1994–	.684	Hideo Nomo	1995*		.571	Andy Pettitte	1995*

* Nomo and Pettitte had fewer than 15 wins but are exempted because 1995 was a strike-shortened season.

	National League				American League		
Losses							
1872–75	32	Tommy Bond	1874—NA				
1876–92	**48**	**John Coleman**	**1883**		41	Larry McKeon	1884
1893–1900	28	Still Bill Hill	1896		27	Chick Fraser	1896
					27	Bill Carrick	1899
1901–19	25	Harry McIntyre	1905		26	Bob Groom	1909
	25	Stoney McGlynn	1907				
1920–41	21	Ed Brandt	1928		20	Bobo Newsom	1934
1942–60	20	Nate Andrews	1943		20	Bill Wight	1948
	20	Sam Jones	1955				
1961–76	20	Al Jackson	1962		19	Frank Tanana	1974
	20	Clay Kirby	1969				
1977–93	18	Bob Shirley	1977		19	Rick Langford	1977
1994–	13	Osvaldo Fernandez	1996		14	Brad Radke	1995
	13	Brian Meadows	1998				

	National League				American League		
Strikeouts							
1872–75	60	George Bradley	1875—NA				
1876–92	268	Larry Corcoran	1880		**513**	**Matt Kilroy**	**1886**
1893–1900	160	Vic Willis	1898		145	Noodles Hahn	1899
1901–19	227	Pete Alexander	1911		209	Russ Ford	1910
1920–41	191	Dizzy Dean	1932		135	Bobo Newsom	1934
1942–60	185	Sam Jones	1955		245	Herb Score	1955
1961–76	215	John Montefusco	1975		206	Bob Johnson	1970
1977–93	276	Dwight Gooden	1984		204	Mark Langston	1984
1994–	236	Hideo Nomo	1995		152	Rolando Arrojo	1998

	National League			American League		
RECORD		**NAME**	**YEAR**	**RECORD**	**NAME**	**YEAR**
Walks						
1872–75	30	Candy Cummings	1872—NA			
1876–92	184	Tom Vickery	1890	**205**	**Mike Morrison**	**1887**
1893–1900	166	Chick Fraser	1896	155	Still Bill Hill	1896
1901–19	147	Orval Overall	1905	168	Elmer Myers	1916
1920–41	123	Kirby Higbe	1939	149	Bobo Newsom	1934
1942–60	198	Sam Jones	1955	154	Herb Score	1955
1961–76	125	Carl Morton	1970	127	Jim Hughes	1975
1977–93	136	Ron Darling	1984	143	Bobby Witt	1986
1994–	87	Alan Benes	1996	86	Steve Sparks	1995
ERA						
1872–75	2.03	Tommy Bond	1874—NA			
1876–92	**0.86**	**Tim Keefe**	**1880**	1.21	Denny Driscoll	1882
1893–1900	2.68	Noodles Hahn	1899	2.68	Joe McGinnity	1899
1901–19	1.42	Ed Reulbach	1905	1.39	Harry Krause	1909
1920–41	2.24	Elmer Riddle	1941	2.28	Wilcy Moore	1927
1942–60	2.13	Johnny Beazley	1942	2.29	Mickey Haefner	1943
1961–76	2.08	Jerry Koosman	1968	2.05	Stan Bahnsen	1968
1977–93	2.48	Fernando Valenzuela	1981	2.76	Kevin Appier	1990
1994–	2.54	Hideo Nomo	1995	3.56	Rolando Arrojo	1998
Games Started						
1872–75	60	George Bradley	1875—NA			
1876–92	**66**	**Lee Richmond**	**1880**	**66**	**Matt Kilroy**	**1886**
1893–1900	43	Bill Carrick	1899	41	Joe McGinnity	1899
1901–19	42	George McQuillan	1908	36	Reb Russell	1913
				36	Scott Perry	1918
1920–41	37	Jesse Haines	1920	37	Herm Pillette	1922
1942–60	41	Bill Voiselle	1944	33	Arnie Portocarrero	1954
1961–76	37	Carl Morton	1970	37	Steve Busby	1973
1977–93	38	Tom Browning	1985	37	Paul Thormodsgard	1977
				37	Roger Erickson	1978
1994–	33	Matt Morris	1997	32	Jason Dickson	1997
				32	Rolando Arrojo	1998

| | National League | | | American League | |
RECORD	NAME	YEAR	RECORD	NAME	YEAR
Complete Games					
1872–75	57	George Bradley	1875—NA		
1876–92	64	Mickey Welch	1880	**66**	**Matt Kilroy**
1893–1900	40	Bill Carrick	1899	39	Jack Taylor
1901–19	41	Irv Young	1905	35	Roscoe Miller
1920–41	24	Jim Turner	1937	21	Charlie Robertson
1942–60	24	Bill Voiselle	1944	26	Boo Ferriss
1961–76	18	Tom Seaver	1967	24	Mark Fidrych
1977–93	11	Fernando Valenzuela	1981	16	Dave Rozema
1994–	6	Ismael Valdez	1995	3	Done by three men
Shutouts					
1872–75	5	George Bradley	1875—NA		
1876–92	**9**	**George Derby**	**1881**	5	Tony Mullane
				5	Matt Kilroy
1893–1900	6	Wiley Piatt	1898	5	Jim Hughes
1901–19	7	Done by three men		8	Russ Ford
				8	Reb Russell
1920–41	5	Done by four men		4	Done by five men
1942–60	6	Ewell Blackwell	1946	6	Gene Bearden
	6	Harvey Haddix	1953		
1961–76	7	Jerry Koosman	1968	4	Done by nine men
1977–93	8	Fernando Valenzuela	1981	5	Ron Guidry
				5	Mike Boddicker
1994–	3	Hideo Nomo	1995	2	Rolando Arrojo
Saves					
1872–75	1	Frank Heifer	1875—NA	1	Pud Galvin
1876–92	3	Lee Richmond	1880	4	Herb Goodall
1893–1900	3	Win Mercer	1894	3	Ernie Beam
	3	Sam Leever	1899		
1901–19	7	George Ferguson	1906	7	Carl Mays
1920–41	9	Bob Bowman	1939	15	Firpo Marberry
1942–60	16	Jack Meyer	1955	20	Ryne Duren
1961–76	22	Rawly Eastwick	1975	24	Dick Radatz
1977–93	**36**	**Todd Worrell**	**1986**	27	Gregg Olson
1994–	30	Kerry Ligtenberg	1998	17	Darren Hall

Additional American League YEAR values:
- Matt Kilroy (Complete Games) 1886
- Tony Mullane 1882, Matt Kilroy 1886, Jim Hughes 1898, Russ Ford 1910, Reb Russell 1913, Gene Bearden 1948, Ron Guidry 1977, Mike Boddicker 1983, Rolando Arrojo 1998
- Pud Galvin 1875—NA, Herb Goodall 1890, Ernie Beam 1895, Carl Mays 1915, Firpo Marberry 1924, Ryne Duren 1958, Dick Radatz 1962, Gregg Olson 1989, Darren Hall 1994

Era Rookie Season Batting Record Holders

	National League			American League		
	RECORD	**NAME**	**YEAR**	**RECORD**	**NAME**	**YEAR**
At Bats						
1872–75	268	Nat Hicks	1872—NA			
1876–92	574	Jimmy Cooney	1890	579	Jim Burns	1889
1893–1900	617	Jimmy Williams	1899	599	Jimmy Slagle	1899
1901–19	606	Zack Wheat	1910	632	George Stone	1905
1920–41	656	Billy Herman	1932	650	Carl Lind	1928
1942–60	635	Wally Moon	1954	679	Harvey Kuenn	1953
1961–76	661	Ken Hubbs	1962	672	Tony Oliva	1964
1977–93	**701**	**Juan Samuel**	**1984**	641	Kevin Seitzer	1987
1994–	641	Tony Womack	1997	684	Nomar Garciaparra	1997
Batting Average						
1872–75	.359	Tim Murnane	1872—NA			
1876–92	.354	Abner Dalrymple	1878	.378	Pete Browning	1882
1893–1900	.358	Bill Everitt	1895	.355	Jimmy Williams	1899
1901–19	.317	Jim Viox	1913	**.408**	**Joe Jackson**	**1911**
Other:	.370	Benny Kauff	1914—FL			
1920–41	.355	Lloyd Waner	1927*	.343	Dale Alexander	1929
1942–60	.333	Richie Ashburn	1948	.331	Johnny Pesky	1942
1961–76	.330	Rico Carty	1964	.331	Fred Lynn	1975
1977–93	.318	Mike Piazza	1993	.323	Kevin Seitzer	1987
1994–	.315	Todd Helton	1998	.314	Derek Jeter	1996

* George Watkins (.373 in 1930) qualified for the NL batting crown in his time but fell short of 400 at bats.

	National League			American League		
Slugging Average						
1872–75	.400	Frank McCarton	1872—NA			
1876–92	.521	John O'Rourke	1879	.539	Dave Orr	1884
1893–1900	.563	Buck Freeman	1899	.546	Tom McCreery	1896
1901–19	.446	Tom Long	1915	.590	Joe Jackson	1911
Other:	.534	Benny Kauff	1914—FL			
1920–41	.614	Wally Berger	1930*	.609	Ted Williams	1939*
1942–60	.556	Frank Robinson	1956	.583	Walt Dropo	1950
1961–76	.557	Dick Allen	1964	.566	Fred Lynn	1975
1977–93	.561	Mike Piazza	1993	**.618**	**Mark McGwire**	**1987**
1994–	.516	Raul Mondesi	1994	.534	Nomar Garciaparra	1997

* George Watkins (.621 in 1930) and Rudy York (.651 in 1937) qualified for the NL and AL slugging crowns, respectively, in their time but lacked the necessary plate appearances under the modern rule.

	RECORD	National League NAME	YEAR	RECORD	American League NAME	YEAR
Hits						
1872–75	82	Nat Hicks	1872—NA			
1876–92	156	Jimmy Cooney	1890	181	Bug Holliday	1889
1893–1900	219	Jimmy Williams	1899	197	Bill Everitt	1895
1901–19	173	George Burns	1913	**233**	**Joe Jackson**	**1911**
Other:	211	Benny Kauff	1914—FL			
1920–41	223	Lloyd Waner	1927	215	Dale Alexander	1929
1942–60	205	Vada Pinson	1959	209	Harvey Kuenn	1953
1961–76	201	Dick Allen	1964	217	Tony Oliva	1964
1977–93	191	Juan Samuel	1984	207	Kevin Seitzer	1987
1994–	178	Tony Womack	1997	209	Nomar Garciaparra	1997
Total Bases						
1872–75	98	Nat Hicks	1872—NA			
1876–92	223	Billy O'Brien	1887	280	Bug Holliday	1889
1893–1900	331	Buck Freeman	1899	328	Jimmy Williams	1899
1901–19	247	Harry Lumley	1904	327	Joe Jackson	1911
Other:	305	Benny Kauff	1914—FL			
1920–41	342	Johnny Frederick	1929	**374**	**Hal Trosky**	**1934**
1942–60	330	Vada Pinson	1959	326	Walt Dropo	1950
1961–76	352	Dick Allen	1964	**374**	**Tony Oliva**	**1964**
1977–93	310	Juan Samuel	1984	344	Mark McGwire	1987
1994–	281	Todd Helton	1998	365	Nomar Garciaparra	1997
Doubles						
1872–75	12	Nat Hicks	1872—NA			
1876–92	31	Charlie Eden	1879	39	Sam Barkley	1884
1893–1900	33	Bill Hassamaer	1894	30	Chick Stahl	1897
1901–19	37	George Burns	1913	45	Joe Jackson	1911
Other:	44	Benny Kauff	1914—FL			
1920–41	**52**	**Johnny Frederick**	**1929**	45	Roy Johnson	1929
1942–60	47	Vada Pinson	1959	38	Dick Wakefield	1943
1961–76	40	Johnny Bench	1968	47	Fred Lynn	1975
1977–93	41	Warren Cromartie	1977	35	Tim Salmon	1993
1994–	44	Brad Fullmer	1998	44	Nomar Garciaparra	1997

		National League			American League	
	RECORD	**NAME**	**YEAR**	**RECORD**	**NAME**	**YEAR**
Triples						
1872–75	5	Jack Remsen	1872—NA			
1876–92	16	Marty Sullivan	1887	18	Jim Canavan	1891
1893–1900	**27**	**Jimmy Williams**	**1899**	25	Buck Freeman	1899
1901–19	25	Tom Long	1915	19	Joe Cassidy	1904
				19	Frank Baker	1909
				19	Joe Jackson	1911
1920–41	22	Paul Waner	1926	18	Jeff Heath	1938
1942–60	17	Jim Gilliam	1953	14	Minnie Minoso	1951
1961–76	13	Dick Allen	1964	14	Jake Wood	1961
1977–93	19	Juan Samuel	1984	10	Done by four men	
1994–	12	Dave Dellucci	1998	11	Nomar Garciaparra	1997
Home Runs						
1872–75	3	Count Gedney	1872—NA	3	Jimmy Hallinan	1875—NA
1876–92	19	Billy O'Brien	1887	19	Bug Holliday	1889
1893–1900	25	Buck Freeman	1899	13	Jimmy Bannon	1894
1901–19	12	Tim Jordan	1906	8	Socks Seybold	1901
				8	Duffy Lewis	1910
1920–41	38	Wally Berger	1930	35	Hal Trosky	1934
				35	Rudy York	1937
1942–60	38	Frank Robinson	1956	37	Al Rosen	1950
1961–76	33	Earl Williams	1971	33	Jimmie Hall	1963
1977–93	35	Mike Piazza	1993	**49**	**Mark McGwire**	**1987**
1994–	25	Todd Helton	1998	30	Nomar Garciaparra	1997
RBI						
1872–75	33	Nat Hicks	1872—NA			
1876–92	77	Marty Sullivan	1887	112	Dave Orr	1884
1893–1900	122	Buck Freeman	1899	116	Jimmy Williams	1899
1901–19	91	Kitty Bransfield	1901	97	Ping Bodie	1911
Other:	95	Benny Kauff	1914—FL			
1920–41	119	Wally Berger	1930	145	**Ted Williams**	**1939**
1942–60	112	Ray Jablonski	1953	144	Walt Dropo	1950
1961–76	99	Willie Montanez	1971	105	Fred Lynn	1975
1977–93	112	Mike Piazza	1993	118	Mark McGwire	1987
1994–	97	Todd Helton	1998	98	Nomar Garciaparra	1997

	National League			American League		
	RECORD	**NAME**	**YEAR**	**RECORD**	**NAME**	**YEAR**
Runs						
1872–75	55	Nat Hicks	1872—NA			
1876–92	114	Jimmy Cooney	1890	**142**	**Mike Griffin**	**1887**
	114	Bill Dahlen	1890			
Other:	121	Bill Joyce	1890—PL			
1893–1900	137	Roy Thomas	1899	130	Jimmy Bannon	1894
1901–19	98	Lefty Davis	1901	126	Joe Jackson	1911
Other:	120	Benny Kauff	1914—FL			
1920–41	133	Lloyd Waner	1927	132	Joe DiMaggio	1936
1942–60	131	Vada Pinson	1959	112	Minnie Minoso	1951
1961–76	125	Dick Allen	1964	109	Tony Oliva	1964
1977–93	107	Vince Coleman	1985	105	Kevin Seitzer	1987
1994–	93	Scott Rolen	1997	122	Nomar Garciaparra	1997
Walks						
1872–75	9	Bill Harbidge	1875—NA			
1876–92	87	Bob Allen	1890	96	Jack Crooks	1890
Other:	**123**	**Bill Joyce**	**1890—PL**			
1893–1900	115	Roy Thomas	1899	86	Elmer Flick	1898
1901–19	88	Miller Huggins	1904	95	Morrie Rath	1912
1920–41	82	Heinie Sand	1923	107	Ted Williams	1939
1942–60	100	Jim Gilliam	1953	106	Les Fleming	1942
1961–76	97	Joe Morgan	1965	92	Dick Howser	1961
1977–93	86	Bill Doran	1983	97	Alvin Davis	1977
1994–	80	Quilvio Veras	1995	85	Ben Grieve	1998
OBP						
1872–75	.359	Tim Murnane	1872—NA			
1876–92	.387	Steve Brodie	1890	.434	Cupid Childs	1890
1893–1900	.457	Roy Thomas	1899	.430	Elmer Flick	1898
1901–19	.440	Fred Snodgrass	1910	**.468**	**Joe Jackson**	**1911**
Other:	.447	Benny Kauff	1914—FL			
1920–41	.413	Paul Waner	1926	.447	Charlie Keller	1939
1942–60	.410	Richie Ashburn	1948	.422	Minnie Minoso	1951
1961–76	.383	Dick Allen	1964	.405	Fred Lynn	1975
1977–93	.391	Jeff Bagwell	1991	.407	Mitchell Page	1977
1994–	.386	Quilvio Veras	1995	.393	Bob Hamelin	1994

	National League			American League		
	RECORD	**NAME**	**YEAR**	**RECORD**	**NAME**	**YEAR**
Stolen Bases						
1872–75	7	Tom Barlow	1872—NA			
1876–92	82	Dummy Hoy	1888	94	Mike Griffin	1887
1893–1900	55	Emmett Heidrick	1899	47	Done by three men	
1901–19	57	Hap Myers	1913	53	Donie Bush	1909
Other:	75	Benny Kauff	1914—FL			
1920–41	43	George Grantham	1923	24	Bill Hunnefield	1926
1942–60	35	Sam Jethroe	1950	31	Minnie Minoso	1951
1961–76	69	Larry Lintz	1973	40	Pat Kelly	1969
1977–93	**110**	**Vince Coleman**	**1985**	66	Kenny Lofton	1992
1994–	60	Tony Womack	1997	26	Randy Winn	1998

* Men listed under the American League column in the 1876–92 era are the American Association record holders. Men listed under the American League column in the 1893–1900 era compiled the second-highest NL season totals in that era.

Note: NA rookie records begin in 1872 because, in effect, everyone was a rookie in 1871. Rookie status for hitters requires both fewer than 50 games and one plate appearance per game prior to a player's first full season according to the schedule length in effect at the time. Rookie status for pitchers requires both less than 25 games and 50 innings pitched prior to a pitcher's first full season. Note that the application of a universal rookie standard throughout history results in the citation of many hitherto unrecognized all-time rookie record holders, with Joe Jackson the leading example, as well as deeming some men rookies even though they previously spent significant time on ML rosters but played little. All-time leaders among rookies are in **bold**.

HISTORIAN'S CORNER

◆ **THE CHANGING GAME**
◆ **FAMOUS FIRSTS**
◆ **FAMOUS LASTS**

The Changing Game

1. Test your knowledge of how and why baseball has evolved into the game we know today. To start, after the National League was formed in 1876, just two ML teams posted .300 season batting averages prior to 1893. On the first occasion, the chief contributor to his team's .337 mark compiled many of his hits via a method that forced a permanent rule change to be implemented the following year. On the second occasion, owing to a rule in effect for only that one year, the chief contributor to his team's .307 average actually had a higher mark (as did his team) than the one with which he is currently credited. First, why is 1893 the demarcation point? Next, name the two pre-1893 teams that hit .300+, the two years in which they topped the barrier, the two players chiefly responsible for their respective teams' .300+ marks, and the two rules that were revised after the two seasons cited here.

2. In 1908, the depth of the Deadball Era, big league teams on an average compiled six triples and 16 stolen bases for every home run they hit. That sort of ratio persisted for many years. What was the first year that the total number of home runs hit in the majors exceeded the total numbers of both triples and stolen bases?
   - A) The Reds led the majors that year with 134 steals, and the White Sox topped the AL with 106.
   - B) The pennant-winning Cubs were last in the majors in triples with 46.
   - C) The Phillies collected 102 more home runs than triples and led the majors in batting, OBP, and SA.
   - D) Charlie Gehringer topped the AL in both triples and stolen bases.
   - E) It was the last season to date that the A's and Cubs met in fall play.

3. The 1884 season brought three major leagues and a record number of errors as the three circuits conspired to commit 14,555 bobbles. Against that, there were only 1,756 double plays turned in the majors that season. Not until the close of World War II did the number of double plays begin to rival the number of errors. In what year did double plays exceed errors in both the NL and the AL for the first time?
   - A) The 1989 season was the most recent one in which errors exceeded double plays in one league—the NL.
   - B) The two pennant winners in 1989 finished fourth and fifth, respectively, under Hall of Fame managers the first year that double plays outstripped errors in both leagues.
   - C) Cleveland led the majors in fielding that year, thanks largely to its crack keystone combo.
   - D) Both members of Cleveland's keystone combo managed the Tribe at some point.
   - E) It was the last season that Bill Bevens and Al Gionfriddo appeared in ML box scores.

4. What was the most historically significant feature of the 1950 World Series?
   - A) No one at the time could have realized the historical significance of the 1950 Series.
   - B) The 1950 Series' most significant feature was a last occurrence rather than a first occurrence.
   - C) The feature was not true of the 1949 Series.
   - D) The 1947 Series marked a significant first that has been true of every fall classic since— except in 1950.
   - E) What was true of the 1950 Series was also true of every ML postseason affair prior to 1947.

5. **Thanks largely to Babe Ruth, the 1920 Yankees were the first AL team to collect more home runs than stolen bases. What was the first NL team to match the 1920 Yankees' feat?**

A) The team had a dip in stolen bases rather than the sort of sharp increase in homers that occurred once the Yankees acquired Babe Ruth.

B) The team led the NL with 88 homers and was last in steals with 66 after swiping 100 bases a year earlier.

C) Despite having the most home runs in the NL, the team tallied the fewest runs, in part because it collected the fewest walks and the most strikeouts.

D) The team finished last for the third year in a row and was led in homers by Cy Williams with 18.

E) Six years earlier, the team won its only pennant prior to 1950.

First Year with More HRs than Stolen Bases

TEAM	YEAR	HRs	SBs
New York Yankees	1920	115	64
Philadelphia Phillies	1921	88	66
Philadelphia Athletics	1921	82	69
St. Louis Cardinals	1922	107	73
St. Louis Browns	1923	82	64
New York Giants	1924	95	82
Brooklyn Dodgers	1924	72	34
Chicago Cubs	1927	74	65
Detroit Tigers	1929	110	95
Pittsburgh Pirates	1930	86	76
Cincinnati Reds	1930	74	48
Cleveland Indians	1930	72	51
Boston Red Sox	1930	47	42
Boston Braves	1932	63	36
Washington Senators	1934	51	47
Chicago White Sox	1934	71	36

Note: The 16 teams extant in 1920. In 1933 the White Sox had both 43 homers and 43 steals.

6. **Because no National Association team in 1871, the loop's fledgling season, played more than 35 games, no pitchers suffered as many as 20 defeats. What was the next ML season when there were no 20-game losers?**

A) Bob Steele and Earl Moore tied for the NL lead in losses that year with 19.

B) The AL loss leader that year with 19 is the record holder for the most losses by a non-300-game winner.

C) Jack Coombs and Pete Alexander tied for the ML win lead that year with 28.

D) The Braves and the Browns each lost 107 games and finished last.

E) Home Run Baker acquired his nickname in the World Series that year.

7. **The point of the preceding question is that 20-game losers once were more frequent than no-hit games. Nowadays they're even more rare than a perfect game. What was the last season to date that both the NL and the AL had a 20-game loser?**

    A)   The AL loss leader, with 21, had previously won 3 games in a World Series.

    B)   Three hurlers tied for the NL loss lead with 22.

    C)   One of the NL co-leaders in losses won a Cy Young Award two years later.

    D)   For the first time since 1883, a pitcher that year had more hill appearances than any ML team had wins.

    E)   The season was the last to date that the same team won the last official game of the season for the third year in a row.

8. **In a similar vein, five-man pitching rotations are the vogue now. But time was that teams customarily used three- and even two-man rotations. What was the first ML team to employ a four-man pitching rotation so religiously for a full season that all four hurlers were involved in at least 20 decisions?**

    A)   One of the four hurlers won more than 300 games.

    B)   The team finished next to last and disbanded at the end of the season.

    C)   The city that housed the team never again had a representative in either the NL or the AL.

    D)   The year was 1885.

    E)   The team in 1885 had a quartet of stars known as "The Big Four," none of them pitchers.

First 10 Four-Man Rotations (Minimum 20 Decisions Each Member)

RANK	TEAM	YEAR	PITCHERS
1	Buf, NL	1885	Galvin, Serad, Conway, Wood
2	Phi, AA	1886	Atkinson, Mathews, Hart, Kennedy
3	Was, NL	1887	Whitney, O'Day, Gilmore, Shaw
	Bro, AA	1887	Porter, Terry, Harkins, Toole
5	Phi, NL	1888	Buffinton, Casey, Sanders, Gleason
	Ind, NL	1888	Boyle, Healy, Shreve, Burdick
	Lou, AA	1888	Ramsey, Stratton, Hecker, Chamberlain, Ewing
8	Chi, NL	1889	Hutchison, Tener, Dwyer, Gumbert
	Cle, NL	1889	O'Brien, Beatin, Bakely, Gruber
	Cin, AA	1889	Duryea, Viau, Mullane, Smith

Note: Pitchers are listed in order of decisions. Philadelphia in 1888 was the first winning team (69–61) with a four-man rotation. That same year, Louisville used the first five-man rotation, largely owing to the lack of a staff ace; the team finished 44–87. Chicago in 1889 had the first four-man rotation when all four bore such an equal load that their W–L records were nearly identical: Hutchison 16–17, Dwyer 16–13, Gumbert 16–13, and Tener 15–15.

9. **In 1884 what ML pitcher would have been credited with whiffing 19 batters in a game but for a scoring rule in his time that has since been rescinded?**

    A)   He was denied a 19th K when his catcher missed a third strike, allowing the batter to reach first and rescinding the K, according to the scoring rules then.

    B)   His catcher was rookie Bill Krieg of the Chicago Browns.

    C)   His 28 wins that year were split among three different teams, all of which were gone forever from the majors by the following spring.

    D)   His first name was Hugh, but he was known by a famous nickname.

    E)   His nickname stemmed from a disability that prevented him from wearing a fielder's glove.

10. **The most recent team to average fewer than three batter strikeouts per game won a World Championship that year. What team is it?**
    A) The team's catcher fanned just 12 times in 597 ABs.
    B) The team's hill staff led the AL in K's with 712, but Cleveland had the individual leader in Bob Lemon.
    C) The team's center fielder led the AL in SA in his next-to-last ML season.
    D) Sub outfielder Cliff Mapes led the team with 61 Ks.
    E) The Phillies won their first flag in 35 years that season.

11. **What was the last team to strike out fewer than 500 times in a season?**
    A) The club's shortstop, with 55, was the only man who had more than 38 Ks.
    B) The K leader in the club's loop that year was a rookie third sacker who had 115 Ks to go with 25 homers.
    C) The club's left fielder, Peanuts Lowrey, fanned just 13 times.
    D) Vinegar Bend Mizell led the club's hill staff in Ks with 146.
    E) It was the last year in which the 16 teams extant at the time had represented the same cities they had represented since 1903.

Each Team's Last Year with Fewer than 500 Batter Strikeouts

TEAM	YEAR	FINISH	Ks
St. Louis Cardinals	1952	3rd	479
New York Yankees	1950	1st	463
Detroit Tigers	1950	2nd	480
Philadelphia Athletics	1950	Last	493
Cincinnati Reds	1950	6th	497
Washington Senators	1949	Last	495
Boston Braves	1946	4th	468
Brooklyn Dodgers	1945	3rd	434
New York Giants	1945	5th	467
Chicago Cubs	1945	1st	462
Pittsburgh Pirates	1945	4th	480
Chicago White Sox	1945	6th	467
Philadelphia Phillies	1942	Last	488
Boston Red Sox	1938	2nd	463
Cleveland Indians	1936	5th	470
St. Louis Browns	1929	4th	431

Note: The 16 teams extant in 1952; teams are listed in reverse chronological order.

12. **What hurler held the ML record for the most strikeouts in a season before overhand pitching was first allowed by a major circuit?**
    A) The schedule still called for fewer than 100 games when a HOF'er set the preoverhand mark of 361 whiffs.
    B) His league continued to ban overhand tosses the year after he set his record.
    C) The year he set the preoverhand whiff mark he, Hoss Radbourn, and Pud Galvin became the last men prior to Mike Marshall in 1974 to appear in more games as pitchers than any team in the majors had wins.
    D) He won a pitching Triple Crown with the Big Apple's first NL flag winner.
    E) In 1890 the Players League ball was made by his Manhattan sporting goods firm and had his name on it.

13. **What twirler easily had the best strikeout ratio in the majors the only year batters were given four strikes?**
    A) He K'd an average of 5.7 batters per nine innings and had 118 more strikeouts than John Clarkson, who had the second-most Ks in the majors that year.
    B) His 37 wins that year are the sixth-most in history by a southpaw.
    C) The previous year he had fallen just 14 Ks short of the total that still stands as the all-time season K record.
    D) He holds the record for the most career wins (114) by a pitcher who never played in the NL or AL.
    E) He also holds the record for the most wins by a pitcher nicknamed "Toad."

Top K Ratios in 1887 Under the Four-Strike Rule

RANK	NAME	TEAM	KS	IP	RATIO
1	Toad Ramsey	Lou, AA	355	561	5.70
2	Mike Morrison	Cle, AA	158	316.2	4.49
3	Mark Baldwin	Chi, NL	164	334	4.42
4	Frank Gilmore	Was, NL	114	234.2	4.37
5	Charlie Buffinton	Phi, NL	160	332.1	4.33
6	George Van Haltren	Chi, NL	76	161	4.25
7	John Clarkson	Chi, NL	237	523	4.08
8	Adonis Terry	Bro, AA	138	318	3.91
9	Charlie Ferguson	Phi, NL	125	297.1	3.78
10	Phenomenal Smith	Bal, AA	206	491.1	3.77

14. **Despite losing an all-time-record 134 contests, the 1899 Cleveland Spiders' hill staff logged 138 complete games. What team's mound corps was the first to total fewer than 100 complete games in a season subsequent to 1886 when both the NL and the AA began playing a 126-game schedule?**
    A) The team had just 88 CGs, 25 fewer than any other ML club that year.
    B) The team's manager finished tied for second in his loop in saves with three.
    C) Al Orth was the only member of the team's starting rotation to complete more than two-thirds of his starts.
    D) The team finished sixth after being in the AL pennant race until the final day of the season the previous year.
    E) The team unveiled a flashy new first sacker named Hal Chase.

Thornton Lee, the leader of the 1941 Chicago White Sox hill staff. The 1941 White Sox were the last team to log 100 complete games. Led by lefty ace Lee's 30 route-going efforts, the Sox finished a surprising third that year, albeit 24 games behind the World Champion Yankees.

Each Team's Most Recent Season with 100 Complete Games

TEAM	YEAR	CGS	LEADER
Chicago White Sox	1941	106	Thornton Lee (30)
New York Yankees	1923	101	Joe Bush (22)
Boston Red Sox	1918	105	Carl Mays (30)
Boston Braves	1917	105	Jesse Barnes (27)
Philadelphia Phillies	1917	102	Pete Alexander (34)
St. Louis Browns	1913	104	George Baumgardner (22)
Detroit Tigers	1912	107	Ed Willett (24)
Washington Senators	1911	106	Walter Johnson (36)
Philadelphia Athletics	1910	123	Jack Coombs (35)
Brooklyn Dodgers	1910	103	Nap Rucker (27)
Chicago Cubs	1910	100	Three Finger Brown (27)
Cleveland Indians	1909	110	Cy Young (30)
New York Giants	1909	105	Christy Mathewson (26)
Cincinnati Reds	1908	110	Bob Ewing (23)
Pittsburgh Pirates	1908	100	Vic Willis (25)
St. Louis Cardinals	1907	127	Stoney McGlynn (33)

Note: The 16 teams extant in 1941, the last time a team compiled 100 CGs. The 1913 Browns were the last cellar dweller to notch 100 CGs.

15. **What was the first hill staff to complete fewer than half of its starts?**
    A) The team finished third despite notching just 75 CGs in 152 efforts.
    B) It was the first year that half or more of the 16 ML teams failed to receive CGs from their pitchers at least two-thirds of the time—and also the first year in which a World Series game was played in a stadium built of concrete and steel.
    C) Of the team's 75 CGs, a club-high 17 of them came from a pitcher who also established a new season save record that year.
    D) The team was managed by Fred Lake and was led in TBs by a 21-year-old center fielder from Texas.
    E) Both Ty Cobb and Honus Wagner played in their last World Series that season.

16. **The first mound crew to total more saves than complete games led the majors that year in ERA as well as saves. What team did they pitch for?**
    A) The 1945 Phils, in the process of finishing last, were the first ML team to register nearly as many saves (26) as CGs (31).
    B) The first team to notch more saves than CGs finished the opposite of last, winning a major-league-high 98 games.
    C) Bob Grim, the team leader with 19 saves, also led the ML in saves that year.
    D) The team lost the World Series to a club that paced the ML that year with 60 CGs.
    E) Of those 60 CGs, a major-league-high 18 came from the top southpaw winner of all-time.

17. **What was the most recent year (and possibly the last time ever) that a team's mound staff logged more complete games than saves?**
    A) The 1990 Dodgers nearly became the most recent team when they had the exact same number of CGs (29) as they had saves.
    B) The first season that no team registered as many CGs as saves followed the most recent season that a team had more CGs than saves.
    C) The Cubs were the most recent team with more CGs than saves in the NL, and the Rangers were likewise in the AL.
    D) The Cubs and the Rangers both had more CGs than saves in the same season; it was also the most recent season that two pitchers collected as many as 15 CGs.
    E) One of the CG leaders set the current record for the most consecutive shutout innings that same season.

18. **In the Deadball Era a stolen base was worth far more than it is now. Runners accordingly took more risks, and it was not uncommon for a team to be successful in fewer than half of its theft attempts. Nowadays it is extremely rare. The 1994 New York Mets are the only such team thus far in the 1990s, but the Mets attempted only 61 steals. What was the most recent team with at least 100 steal attempts to have a success rate below 50 percent?**
    A) The team finished last in its division, in part because its base runners were nabbed 57 times in 109 steal attempts and in part because it finished last in its loop in home runs.
    B) The team had won a pennant two years earlier and led the majors in home runs.
    C) The team's worst base thief, its left fielder, was caught in all six of his attempts four years after he'd been an AL coleader in home runs.
    D) The team was piloted by Rene Lachemann.
    E) Shortstop Robin Yount, who succeeded in 14 of 18 attempts, was the team's lone competent base thief.

10 Most Recent Teams with a Sub-.500 Stolen-Base Success Rate

RANK	TEAM	YEAR	SBS	CS	PCT.
1	NY, NL	1994	25	26	49
2	Mil, AL	1984	52	57	48
3	Tor, AL	1980	67	72	48
4	Tor, AL	1978	28	52	35
5	Cle, AL	1973	60	68	47
	Pit, NL	1973	23	30	43
7	Cle, AL	1972	49	53	48
	Phi, NL	1972	42	50	46
9	Det, AL	1971	35	43	45
10	Cle, AL	1970	· 25	36	41
	Det, AL	1970	29	30	49

Note: The 1978 Blue Jays had the lowest success rate since 1958 when Washington (22-for-63) also finished at 35 percent. A year earlier, Washington posted just a 25 percent success rate (13-for-51), an all-time record low. The 1971 Tigers are the most recent team with a winning record (91–71) to be successful in fewer than half of its attempts. In 1971 the Indians swiped 57 bases in 94 attempts, avoiding what otherwise would have been an unprecedented four-year skein (1970–73) with a sub-.500 success rate.

Famous Firsts

1. **The perpetrators of significant baseball "Firsts" often gain immortality solely for their isolated feats. Candy Cummings, reputedly the inventor of the curveball, is one who made the Hall of Fame largely on the basis of his debatable discovery. Walter Johnson, the first performer in ML history to spend an entire career of 20 or more seasons with the same team, is a very different sort. The first man to match Johnson's feat, like Walter, is a legitimate Hall of Famer. Who is he?**

   A) He pitched on two flag winners but played in only one World Series.
   B) He led the AL in saves as a rookie in 1914.
   C) He is the only hurler to log four decisions in a World Series that went fewer than seven games.
   D) He is the only spitballer to have a 25-win season in the AL after the pitch was banned.
   E) His first name was Urban, but they called him "Red."

Mel Harder, the only man to spend his entire ML career of 20 or more seasons with the same team and not make the Hall of Fame. George Brett and Robin Yount, the two most recent members to join this select list, were both tapped in 1999, the first year they were eligible.

20-Year Men with Only One Team

RANK	NAME	TEAM	YEARS	TOTAL YEARS
1	Walter Johnson	Was, AL	1907–27	21
2	Red Faber	Chi, AL	1914–33	20
3	Mel Ott	NY, NL	1926–47	22
4	Mel Harder	Cle, AL	1928–47	20
5	Luke Appling	Chi, AL	1930–50	21
6	Bob Feller	Cle, AL	1936–56	21
7	Ted Williams	Bos, AL	1939–60	22
8	Stan Musial	StL, NL	1941–63	23
9	Al Kaline	Det, AL	1953–74	22
10	Brooks Robinson	Bal, AL	1955–77	23
11	Willie Stargell	Pit, NL	1962–82	21
12	Carl Yastrzemski	Bos, AL	1961–83	23
13	George Brett	KC, AL	1973–93	21
14	Robin Yount	Mil, AL	1974–93	20

Note: Includes credit for seasons lost to military service: Feller 3, Williams 3, Appling 1, and Musial 1.

2. **What city was represented by teams that played in both the first and the 100,000th big league games?**
    A) The city was without a major league team in 1885–86.
    B) The city has had a major league team continuously since 1901.
    C) The city's first representative in three different major circuits was called the Blues.
    D) The city had a team in the PL known as the Infants and a later-day AL team that was dubbed the Cry Babies.
    E) The city is nicknamed the Forest City.

3. **What man's dossier includes all these "Famous Firsts": the losing pitcher in the first ML game, the first ML strikeout king, and the first man to manage a Pittsburgh ML team?**
    A) He was replaced as Pittsburgh manager in 1883 by Ormund Butler, a booking agent on the side for Buffalo Bill Cody.
    B) He notched a National Association–leading 33 Ks in 1871.
    C) His entire big league career was spent with the Forest City club.
    D) His initials are also the same as those of the rookie who led the A's in losses their last year in Philly.
    E) His initials are also the same as those of the pint-size 1958 AL Rookie of the Year.

4. **When Larry Doby pinch-hit for Bryan Stephens on July 5, 1947, and thereupon became the first African American to play in an AL game, what White Sox hurler earned a historical footnote by fanning him?**
    A) He debuted with the Reds in 1945.
    B) His final K came with the 1953 Tigers.
    C) His nickname was "Irish."
    D) His initials are the same as those of the NL ERA leader in 1944 who was called "the Wild Elk of the Wassatch."
    E) His initials are also the same as those of the Padres shortstop who collected just 12 RBI in 549 ABs as a rookie in 1971.

5. **The first African American player to homer in his first ML at bat, on August 26, 1947, never hit another four-bagger in the show. Who is he?**
   - A) He was only the second African American to have an opportunity to homer in his first at bat in a National League game.
   - B) He was the first African American to pitch in a major league game.
   - C) All nine of his career wins came with the 1950 Dodgers.
   - D) He appeared in the 1947 World Series but not as a pitcher.
   - E) He had the same last name as the Mariners' top winner in 1989.

6. **Name the only man to play in both the first Temple Cup Series (1894) and the first 20th century World Series (1903).**
   - A) He was the lone RBI leader prior to the establishment of the 60'6" pitching distance to play in a 20th century World Series.
   - B) He debuted with Chicago in 1888.
   - C) In 1891 he became the second switch-hitter to win a loop home run crown.
   - D) He had an unparalleled record skein at one point in his career when he played 100 or more games six years in a row with six different teams.
   - E) At the time he retired, he held the career record for pinch hits.

Players in both a Temple Cup Series and 20th Century World Series

NAME	YEARS	TCS	WS
Duke Farrell	1888–1905	1894	1903
George Davis	1890–1909	1894	1906
Cy Young	1890–1911	1895–96	1903
Jimmy Collins	1895–1908	1897	1903
Chick Stahl	1897–1906	1897	1903

7. **John McGraw, considered by many observers to be the greatest manager ever, is associated most closely with the New York Giants. His first game at the Giants' helm was spoiled, however, by the owner of the 20th century NL record for the most defeats by a pitcher in his lone big league season. Name the otherwise luckless hurler who beat the Giants 4–3 on July 19, 1902, McGraw's first day as their pilot.**
   - A) He played under Bill Shettsline in his lone big-time season.
   - B) He later pitched in the PCL.
   - C) His 18 losses were second on his team to Doc White's 20.
   - D) His first name was Herman, but they called him "Ham."
   - E) He also holds the record for the most losses in a season by a pitcher whose last name begins with I.

Most Losses by a One-Year Wonder

RANK	NAME	TEAM	YEAR	L
1	George Cobb	Bal, NL	1892	37
2	Fleury Sullivan	Pit, AA	1884	35
3	Doc Landis	Phi/Bal, AA	1882	28
4	Park Swartzel	KC, AA	1889	27
5	Dory Dean	Cin, NL	1876	26
6	John Keefe	Syr, AA	1890	24
7	Charlie McCullough	Bro/Syr, AA	1890	23
8	Charlie Knepper	Cle, NL	1899	22
9	Alex Voss	Was/KC, UA	1884	20
	Hank Keupper	StL, FL	1914	20

Note: Keupper holds the 20th century record and Ham Iburg the 20th century NL record with 18 losses for the 1902 Phils; the AL record belongs to Orie Arntzen with 13 losses for Philadelphia in 1943.

8. **He was the first man to score 150 or more runs in back-to-back seasons. He is the only man to play beside Davy Force and Al Bridwell in a major league game. The first man as well to play 1,500 games at third base in the majors, he died at age 92. Who is he?**

A) In 1884 he hit .274, and the only other big leaguer in history to share his last name hit .169 that same season for Louisville in 308 ABs.

B) He was the first infielder to swipe 100 bases in back-to-back years.

C) He made his rep as a volatile base coach for one of the game's first dynasties.

D) He both played and managed under Chris Von Der Ahe.

E) He was nicknamed "The Freshest Man on Earth."

First Men to Play 1,500 Games, Each Position

NAME	YEARS	POS	G/POS.	1500TH
Cap Anson	1871–1897	1B	2058	1892
Jack Glasscock	1879–1895	SS	1638	1893
Bid McPhee	1882–1899	2B	2126	1894
Arlie Latham	1880–1909	3B	1571	1895
Tom Brown	1882–1898	OF	1783	1895
Deacon McGuire	1884–1912	C	1611	1905

Note: The most remarkable thing about this list is that Anson is the only one of these "Famous First" achievers in the Hall of Fame.

9. Who was the first documented major leaguer to fan 100 times in a season?

   A) In 1890 he achieved another "Famous First" when he became the first member of a last-place team to collect 100 RBI in a season.

   B) He fanned 104 times the first year the NL allowed overhand pitching.

   C) He was the shortstop on the first Boston ML pennant winner who was not managed by Harry Wright.

   D) In 1887 he posted a .522 SA, the highest by a shortstop in the 1876–92 era.

   E) He has the same first name and same initials as the first rookie hurler to lead the NL in losses, with 31 in 1878.

First 10 Players to Whiff 100 Times in a Season

RANK	NAME	TEAM	YEAR	KS
1	Sam Wise	Bos, NL	1884	104
2	Danny Moeller	Was, AL	1913	103
3	Gus Williams	StL, AL	1914	120
4	Bruce Campbell	Chi/StL, AL	1932	104
5	Harlond Clift	StL, AL	1934	100
6	Dolph Camilli	Phi, NL	1935	113
7	Jimmie Foxx	Bos, AL	1936	119
8	Vince DiMaggio	Bos, NL	1937	111
	Frankie Crosetti	NY, AL	1937	105
	Hank Greenberg	Det, AL	1937	101

10. Name the first man to play in a 20th century World Series and later ump in one.

   A) He umped in several World Series, first in 1921.

   B) He also managed in the majors but never handled a flag winner.

   C) He played in the 1909 World Series.

   D) He manned third base for Ty's team.

   E) He and Sherlock Holmes's arch nemesis have something in common.

11. Who was the first man to pilot a team to a World Series win without having played in the majors himself?

   A) He was also the first man to pilot seven different teams.

   B) He piloted NL entries in three cities that haven't had teams in the senior circuit since 1889.

   C) He skippered the winning team in the very first World Series.

   D) He and the NL home run champ in 1910 shared the same initials.

   E) His last name is the same as that of a Hall of Fame shortstop.

12. Who was the first pitcher to notch a "save" in a World Series game?

   A) He retired just one batter, Jake Daubert, on a hard shot to short with the bases loaded to save a win for Ernie Shore.

   B) He led the AL in saves as a rookie in 1915.

   C) He took the only loss for the winner of the 1916 World Series.

   D) He is the most recent BoSox hurler to win the final game of a World Series.

   E) His name and Ray Chapman's are forever linked.

13. **Who was the first member of a 20th century expansion team to lead either the NL or the AL in a batting or pitching department?**
    A) He was 2-for-11 as a pinch hitter with the 1955 White Sox.
    B) He was 0–2 with an 8.19 ERA as a Braves rookie in 1950.
    C) He and Luis Tiant were Cleveland's only 20-game winners during the 1960s.
    D) He paced the AL in ERA in 1961 for the expansion Senators.
    E) His initials are the same as those of the pre-1988 record holder for the most consecutive shutout innings pitched.

14. **Nowadays it's common for a pitcher to make 20 or more starts in a season without completing any of them. Prior to expansion, however, it had never been done. Do you know who the first hurler was to perform this dubious achievement?**
    A) He was 4–13 for an expansion team, with zero complete games in 21 starts.
    B) The previous year he hurled in an All-Star Game.
    C) He debuted with the most recent Chicago team to play in the final game of a major league season.
    D) He and the winning-percentage leader in the National Association's inaugural season have the same last name.
    E) He led the Angels with 12 wins in their inaugural season.

15. **In 1958, Stu Miller took the NL ERA crown with just six wins and four complete games, but more than half of Miller's 41 appearances that year were in relief. Who was the first starting pitcher to win an ERA crown with both fewer than 10 wins and fewer than 10 complete games?**
    A) His 9–6 mark and meager total of five CGs in 1978 were largely due to his team's failure to score for him, forcing his frequent removal for a pinch hitter.
    B) He won his ERA crown toiling for a cellar dweller led in wins by Nino Espinosa with 11.
    C) After winning 14 games in 1979, he received an enormous multiyear contract to keep him from testing his worth on the free-agent market.
    D) His manager the year he won his ERA crown piloted the 1996 World Champs.
    E) Like early-day star Charlie Sweeney, he was felled prematurely by wing trouble, and he shared something else with Sweeney—the same initials.

Fewest Combined Wins and Complete Games, ERA Leader

RANK	NAME	TEAM	YEAR	W	CGS	TOTAL
1	Nolan Ryan	Hou, NL	1987	8	0	8
2	Joe Magrane	StL, NL	1988	5	4	9
3	Stu Miller	SF, NL	1958	6	4	10
4	Diego Segui	Oak, AL	1970	10	3	13
	Bill Swift	SF, NL	1992	10	3	13
6	Craig Swan	NY, NL	1978	9	5	14
	Danny Darwin	Hou, NL	1990	11	3	14
8	Hoyt Wilhelm	NY, NL	1952	15	0	15
	Juan Guzman	Tor, AL	1996	11	4	15
10	Scott Garrelts	SF, NL	1989	14	2	16

Note: The 1981 and 1994 strike seasons are excluded. Wilhelm was the first ERA crown winner who was exclusively a reliever the year he won.

16. Who was the first hurler in ML history to win a game prior to age 20 and after age 40?

A) His inaugural win came in 1912 at age 18.

B) His last win came with the 1934 Red Sox.

C) He was a perfect 5–0 in postseason action.

D) He currently ranks seventh in career wins by a switch-hitter, with 240.

E) He ranks first on the all-time list in career wins by a switch-hitter who threw exclusively with his left arm.

Most Career Wins by a Switch-Hitter

RANK	NAME	YEARS	THREW	W
1	Kid Nichols	1890–1906	R	361
2	Early Wynn	1939–63	R	300
3	Robin Roberts	1948–66	R	286
4	Tony Mullane	1881–94	Both	284
5	Ted Lyons	1923–46	R	260
6	Red Faber	1914–33	R	254
7	Herb Pennock	1912–34	L	240
8	Mickey Lolich	1963–79	L	217
9	Jim Perry	1959–75	R	215
10	Vida Blue	1969–86	L	209

17. Who was the first pitcher to win a pennant-clinching game on the final day of the season?

A) He beat Cleveland's Henry Gruber on October 5 of a certain year.

B) He's been in the Hall of Fame since 1964.

C) Had he lost that day, another Hall of Famer could have won the pennant for Boston by beating Pud Galvin.

D) His win over Gruber gave him 28 victories, tied for second in the NL that year but, amazingly, 21 wins shy of the leader, John Clarkson.

E) The following year, his sporting goods firm manufactured a ball with his name on it that was used by the Players League.

18. In 1884, Abner Dalrymple became the first player in history to collect 20 home runs with fewer than 20 walks when he slapped 22 dingers while garnering just 14 free passes. Nowadays this dubious achievement is relatively common. A couple of men like Tony Armas have even done it more than once. But after Dalrymple's "First" in 1884, it was 73 years before anyone matched his feat. Like Dalrymple, he was an outfielder. Can you name him?

A) That same year, another outfielder in his league rapped 21 homers with just 29 walks for a World Championship team.

B) Four years earlier, he hammered 15 homers as a rookie center fielder.

C) In 1953 he had a rookie teammate who snagged 112 RBI on just a .268 BA.

D) He and his fellow rookie whiz in 1953 shared the same ethnicity.

E) His first name was Eldon, but they called him "Rip."

19. Major league baseball excludes National Association feats from its official records. Assuming this judgment is correct (and many do not, including me), who was the first man to net 1,000 ML hits?

A)   Cap Anson is everyone's natural guess, but actually another early-day star bagged his 1,000th hit just a few days before Anson did.

B)   It happened in 1884 and was done by an ex-teammate of Anson in 1876–77.

C)   He led the NL in doubles in 1884 for the third time in his career.

D)   In 1884 he also played in the first sanctioned NL-versus-AA World Series.

E)   He was the first man to win back-to-back NL batting crowns.

First 10 Men to Collect 1,000 Hits (Since 1876)

RANK	NAME	TEAM	1000TH
1	Paul Hines	Pro, NL	1884
2	Cap Anson	Chi, NL	1884
3	Jim O'Rourke	Buf, NL	1884
4	Deacon White	Buf, NL	1885
5	Joe Start	Pro, NL	1885
6	Ezra Sutton	Bos, NL	1886
7	Abner Dalrymple	Chi, NL	1886
8	King Kelly	Chi, NL	1886
9	John Morrill	Bos, NL	1886
10	Hardy Richardson	Det, NL	1887

Note: Players are listed in the order they achieved their 1,000th hit.

20. Again excluding National Association achievements, who was the first pitcher to compile 200 ML wins?

A)   Tommy Bond in 1878 became the first to reach 100 and looked certain to be the first to hit 200 when he had 180 at age 24 after the 1880 season, but someone else beat him to the mark.

B)   His 200th win came in Cincinnati livery.

C)   His 200th win came in the 1884 season and preceded by only a few weeks the 200th win by another pitcher with a Cincinnati team in a different league and the 200th win by still another pitcher in yet a third league.

D)   In 1880 he and one of the other first three hurlers to rack up 200 career wins became the first two twirlers to have both 40-win and 40-loss seasons in their careers.

E)   He collected 210 wins before his 30th birthday but finished with just 229 when he quit after going 1–2 with Cincinnati in 1886.

First 10 Pitchers to Collect 200 Wins (Since 1876)

RANK	NAME	TEAM	200TH
1	Will White	Cin, AA	1884
2	Pud Galvin	Buf, NL	1884
3	Jim McCormick	Cin, UA	1884
4	Hoss Radbourn	Pro, NL	1885
5	Mickey Welch	NY, NL	1886
6	Tim Keefe	NY, NL	1887
7	John Clarkson	Bos, NL	1889
8	Tony Mullane	Cin, AA	1889
9	Charlie Buffinton	Phi, PL	1890
10	Bob Caruthers	Bro, NL	1891

Note: Pitchers are listed in the order they achieved their 200th win.

21. Cy Young, as you'd expect, was the first pitcher to win 200 games in the AL. Who was the second to do it?

A) His 200th win came late in the 1910 season.

B) He never led the AL in wins—or losses, for that matter.

C) His 284 career wins are still the record for a certain AL franchise.

D) He alone collected his 300th win in the Federal League.

E) His 69 career shutouts are still the most by a southpaw.

First 10 Pitchers to Collect 200 Wins in the AL

RANK	NAME	TEAM	200TH
1	Cy Young	Cleveland	1909
2	Eddie Plank	Philadelphia	1910
3	George Mullin	Detroit	1912
4	Walter Johnson	Washington	1915
5	Eddie Cicotte	Chicago	1920
6	Hooks Dauss	Detroit	1925
7	Stan Coveleski	Washington	1926
8	Red Faber	Chicago	1926
9	Herb Pennock	New York	1929
10	Jack Quinn	Philadelphia	1930

22. Like Cy Young, Nap Lajoie profited from the fact that he was in the AL at its inception in 1901 and thereby became the first to achieve 2,000 hits in AL action. Who was the second man to accomplish that feat?

A) No, not Ty Cobb; Cobb was the third.

B) In his 15-year sojourn in the AL, he never led the junior loop in hits, batting, or slugging.

C) He topped the AL in RBI on three occasions.

D) His first and last AL hits came with the same team that the most recent AL shortstop to compile 2,000 hits played for his entire career.

E) His 2,000th hit in the AL came in 1913, the same year that he led the AL in triples for the fourth of what would be a record six times.

First 10 Men to Compile 2,000 Hits in the AL

RANK	NAME	YEARS	HITS	TEAM	2000TH
1	Nap Lajoie	1901–16	2521	Cleveland	1912
2	Sam Crawford	1903–17	2466	Detroit	1913
3	Ty Cobb	1905–28	4189	Detroit	1915
4	Tris Speaker	1907–28	3514	Cleveland	1919
5	Eddie Collins	1906–30	3312	Chicago	1920
6	Clyde Milan	1907–22	2100	Washington	1921
7	Harry Hooper	1909–25	2466	Chicago	1922
8	Bobby Veach	1912–25	2063	Boston	1924
9	George Sisler	1915–28	2307	St. Louis	1926
10	Harry Heilmann	1914–29	2499	Detroit	1927

Famous Lasts

1. The last player or team to perform an exceptional feat can be as significant as the first to do it but seldom is as highly esteemed. World Series firsts and lasts are a prime example. The first World Series game involving the ancestral teams of the New York Giants and the Brooklyn Dodgers found them pitted against each other on October 18, 1889. Five future Hall of Famers participated in that contest. The only man to appear in the last World Series games played by both the New York Giants and the Brooklyn Dodgers is not in the Hall of Fame and never will be. Can you name him?
    - A) He was on the losing side in the last World Series game ever played at Cleveland Municipal Stadium.
    - B) He was the last batter Babe Pinelli rang up on strikes prior to his retirement as a major league umpire.
    - C) He is the last Tribe player to date to lead the AL in both hits and triples.
    - D) He is the last man to date to tag as many as 23 triples in a season.
    - E) Both his last ML plate appearance and his last World Series plate appearance came on the same day against Johnny Kucks.

2. What pitcher made his first ML start for the losingest team in history and his last ML start for the winningest team in history?
    - A) His final starting assignment on June 6, 1906, was his lone appearance with the Cubs after coming to them from Cincinnati; he was forced to leave the game in the first inning when his hand was injured by a line drive.
    - B) He had two 23-win seasons in a brief eight-year career.
    - C) His real first name was Charles, but he went by Jack.
    - D) His last name matches that of the Senators lefty who led the AL with 21 losses in 1919.
    - E) His initials match those of a teammate of his in 1899 who was the last hurler to lose 30 games in a season.

3. A certain catcher's last ML at bat assured that he would hit .000 for the losingest team in the 20th century. Eight years earlier, his final at bat of the year assured that he would hit .500 for the winningest team in AL history prior to 1998. Who is he?
    - A) He hit .361 in 11 games in his first taste of big league action in 1948.
    - B) He played in the Mets' first game in 1962 but was released soon thereafter.
    - C) He was the Tigers regular receiver in 1951–52.
    - D) Named Myron after his father, he called himself Joe.
    - E) He and the ex–Ole Miss quarterback who was the Yankees regular backstopper in 1967–68 share the same initials.

4. By 1919, Babe Ruth had homered in seven of the eight AL parks in use at the time. What was the last junior-circuit park that he conquered with a home run?

A) The park housed a player who once tied the Babe for an AL home run crown.
B) The park's predecessor was home to the only man ever to win four straight home run crowns without making the Hall of Fame.
C) The park housed the 1951 AL home run champ.
D) It housed the second player in AL history to collect 50 homers in a season.
E) It housed a record seven straight cellar dwellers.

5. Ted Williams is the lone member of the *Cooperstown* 500 who homered in his last ML at bat. Who surrendered Ted's 521st and last career home run in 1960?

A) He went 12–11 with the 1960 O's, marking his only winning year in the majors.
B) In 1961 he surrendered Roger's record-tying 60th home run.
C) He was the most recent Mets pitcher to lead the NL twice in losses.
D) He and a current Mariners hurler who's ranked among the 10 worst-hitting pitchers of all-time (minimum 200 career ABs) share the same initials.
E) His nickname was "Fat Jack."

The All-Time Worst-Hitting Pitchers (Minimum 200 ABs)

RANK	NAME	YEARS	ABS	HITS	BA
1	Ron Herbel	1963–71	206	6	.029
2	Don Carman	1983–92	209	12	.057
3	Mark Clark	1991–	240	14	.058
4	Dean Chance	1961–71	662	44	.066
5	Clem Labine	1950–62	227	17	.075
6	Jeff Fassero	1991–	210	16	.076
7	Dick Drago	1969–81	274	21	.077
8	Bill Hands	1965–75	472	37	.078
9	Lee Stange	1961–70	305	24	.079
10	Bruce Ruffin	1986–96	294	24	.082

6. What hurler's last ML win came in the game that showcased the most heated denouement ever to a batting title race?

A) A teammate of his that year was Steve Brye.
B) His manager when he won his last game was Gene Mauch.
C) The last hit he surrendered in his final win was a specious inside-the-park homer by George Brett that Hal McRae still contends robbed him of the 1976 AL bat crown.
D) He and a Dodgers reliever in the early 1950s share the same name.
E) He and the first pitcher in ML history to hurl shutout wins in each of his first two starts share the same name.

7. **Joe DiMaggio collected 30 home runs while compiling fewer strikeouts than home runs five years in a row (1937–41). DiMag had a sixth such season in 1948. Since World War II, only Johnny Mize, Yogi Berra, and Ted Kluszewski have had more than one such season, and since 1956, no one at all has done it. Mize and Kluszewski were first basemen, and Berra was a catcher. Who is the last outfielder to date, and the only one subsequent to DiMag in 1948, to hit at least 30 homers in a season and compile fewer strikeouts than four-baggers?**

   A) In his big season, he had 36 homers and just 32 Ks.
   B) A year later, in 1951, he had 30 homers and fewer than 40 Ks.
   C) He logged 110 RBI for the most recent Cubs' pennant winner.
   D) He saw Series action with three different NL teams between 1945 and 1958.
   E) He and the Cubs outfielder who fanned 135 times in his first full season in 1966 share the same initials.

30 HRs and Fewer Ks than HRs, Season (Since 1945)

NAME	TEAM	YEAR	HRS	KS
Johnny Mize	NY, NL	1947	51	42
Willard Marshall	NY, NL	1947	36	30
Johnny Mize	NY, NL	1948	40	37
Joe DiMaggio	NY, AL	1948	39	30
Stan Musial	StL, NL	1948	39	34
Andy Pafko	Chi, NL	1950	36	32
Yogi Berra	NY, AL	1952	30	24
Ted Kluszewski	Cin, NL	1953	40	34
Ted Kluszewski	Cin, NL	1954	49	35
Ted Kluszewski	Cin, NL	1955	47	40
Ted Kluszewski	Cin, NL	1956	35	31
Yogi Berra	NY, AL	1956	30	29

8. **Name the only pitcher whose last two big league wins came on the same day.**

   A) He won both ends of a twin bill in relief against the Milwaukee Braves.
   B) His final two victories came on May 12, 1962.
   C) He set an all-time record when his last 19 career decisions in 1962–63 were all defeats.
   D) His initials are the same as those of a macabre cartoonist.
   E) He and the first switch-hitter to lead the AL in steals (39 in 1906) share the same last name.

9. **Who holds the record for the longest span of time between his last and his next-to-last ML hits?**

   A) He collected his last hit as a pinch hitter 21 years after he made his next-to-last hit while playing short for the Cardinals.
   B) His first ML game was in 1904, and his last in 1934 while he was coaching for the Browns.
   C) In 11 World Series games with Detroit, he hit just .103.
   D) He and the Dodgers southpaw who won 20 in 1969 and fell just four victories short of 200 share the same initials.
   E) He wasn't related to the woman whose cow was accused of starting a famous fire.

10. **His lone claim to fame is that he was the starting pitcher for the Philadelphia A's on October 1, 1950, in the last game managed by Connie Mack. Who is he?**
    - A) He was a 30-year-old rookie at the time.
    - B) He collected his first career win in Connie's last game.
    - C) He bagged only four more career wins, all in relief.
    - D) His initials and first name are the same as those of the winner of the seventh game of the 1956 World Series.
    - E) Those who do the daily "*Jumble*" in their favorite newspaper will be out "a buck" if they miss this one.

11. **What member of the Top 20 list in career batting average came within one hundredth of a point of hiking his average a point in his last big league game?**
    - A) He went 2-for-2 with a walk in his finale on September 30, 1894.
    - B) In his coda appearance, he played right field for Brooklyn in the second game of a closing-day doubleheader.
    - C) The twin bill was played in Louisville.
    - D) He began the day with a .34122 career BA and finished it at .34149.
    - E) He was the first rookie to win a major league batting crown.

12. **Who is the only man to win a major award—MVP, Cy Young, or Rookie of the Year—in his last season in the bigs?**
    - A) It was not his first major award.
    - B) He batted .076 in the last season in which he had 100 or more ABs.
    - C) He was a dual award winner one year in the 1960s for a world champ.
    - D) He achieved nearly 59 percent of his total career wins in his final four ML seasons.
    - E) He holds the NL record for the most wins by a pitcher in his last season.

13. **What "Famous Last" do Billy Hunter, Lou Limmer, Eddie Mathews, Gail Harris, and Randy Jackson have in common?**
    - A) Hunter was the second on this list to join the club.
    - B) Limmer joined in 1954.
    - C) Mathews was the group's first new member since 1915.
    - D) The group added four new members in 1891 and also four new members in 1899.
    - E) The four new members in 1899 came from teams based in Washington, Cleveland, Baltimore, and Louisville.

14. **Just three days after coming within one out of tossing the first no-hitter in World Series history, Bill Bevens made his last ML appearance when he combined with Joe Page to hold Brooklyn scoreless in the last seven innings of the 1947 World Series finale. The first pitcher whose last ML appearance came in the final game of a 20th century World Series is not nearly as well known as Bevens, but the Series is even more famous than the 1947 classic.**
    - A) His 15 wins for the Browns in 1914 were a personal high.
    - B) He was never seen again by a major league audience after he relieved Lefty Williams in the finale of the 1919 Series.
    - C) Known as "Big Bill," in 1919 he became the first hurler ever to play for three AL clubs in the same season.
    - D) He and the rookie third sacker on Joe McCarthy's last World Championship team share the same initials.
    - E) He had the same name as a pitcher who won 11 more games in 1914 than he did.

15. Who was the last AL ERA qualifier to hit .300 in a season before the DH rule went into effect?

    A)   Boston's Sonny Siebert led all hurlers that year with six home runs.

    B)   His .350 BA was the first .300 season since 1947 by an AL pitcher with at least 100 ABs.

    C)   He hit .350 in 103 ABs for a division winner in 1971.

    D)   He's in the Hall of Fame.

    E)   He supplanted Don Larsen as the best hitter since Monte Ward to throw a perfect game.

Last 10 AL Pitchers to Bat .300 in a Season (Minimum 100 ABs)

NAME	TEAM	YEAR	ABS	HITS	BA
Catfish Hunter	Oakland	1971	103	36	.350
Fred Hutchinson	Detroit	1947	106	32	.302
Red Ruffing	New York	1939	114	35	.307
Lynn Nelson	Philadelphia	1937	113	40	.354
Wes Ferrell	Boston	1935	150	52	.347
Red Ruffing	New York	1935	109	37	.339
Schoolboy Rowe	Detroit	1935	109	34	.312
Johnny Marcum	Philadelphia	1935	119	37	.311
Schoolboy Rowe	Detroit	1934	109	33	.303
Red Ruffing	New York	1932	124	38	.306

The Yankees second sacker pictured here evades a sliding Harvey Kuenn to turn a double play in this moment of action in a 1953 AL game. Later that same year, our mystery Yankee was one of the last four infielders allowed to leave his glove on the field in a major league game. Note the glove belonging to a Detroit player on the grass behind second base.

16. **Who were the last four infielders permitted to leave their gloves on the playing field in a major league game?**

    A) One is in the Hall of Fame; one was a Rookie of the Year two years earlier; one was a defensive replacement playing his last game with a World Championship team; and the fourth later managed that team to a World Championship.
    B) The defensive replacement shared first base with Lou Limmer for the last AL team in Philadelphia.
    C) The winning pitcher that day notched his seventh World Series victory against only two losses.
    D) The second baseman picked up his glove to start the ninth inning that day knowing he was the first player to make 12 hits in a six-game World Series.
    E) Their opponents that day were on the losing end of a World Series for a record seventh straight time.

17. **Burleigh Grimes was the last pitcher to win a game in both the NL and the AL who was licensed to throw a spitball and also the last spitballer to win 20 games in a season. Who was the last legal spitballer to post a 20-win season in the AL?**

    A) He led the junior loop in winning percentage and ERA the year he did it.
    B) He was the only exempted spitballer to win 20 or more games for two different AL teams after the pitch was outlawed.
    C) He won his 200th game in 1926 with Washington.
    D) He was the only spitballer to win three games in a World Series after the pitch was outlawed.
    E) He's one of the three exempted spitballers who are in the Hall of Fame.

20-Win Seasons by Spitballers After Pitch Was Outlawed

NAME	TEAM	YEAR	W
Stan Coveleski	Cle, AL	1920	24
Red Faber	Chi, AL	1920	23
Burleigh Grimes	Bro, NL	1920	23
Ray Caldwell	Cle, AL	1920	20
Urban Shocker	StL, AL	1920	20
Bill Doak	StL, NL	1920	20
Urban Shocker	StL, AL	1921	27
Red Faber	Chi, AL	1921	27
Stan Coveleski	Cle, AL	1921	25
Burleigh Grimes	Bro, NL	1921	22
Urban Shocker	StL, AL	1922	24
Red Faber	Chi, AL	1922	21
Burleigh Grimes	Bro, NL	1923	21
Urban Shocker	StL, AL	1923	20
Burleigh Grimes	Bro, NL	1924	22
Stan Coveleski	Was, AL	1925	20
Burleigh Grimes	Pit, NL	1928	25

18. The last man to pitch two complete games on the same day is also the oldest hurler to do it in this century. Who is he?

- A) Emil Levsen was the last to hurl two CG-game wins in a doubleheader but not the last to achieve two CGs in a twin bill.
- B) In 1927, the year this Phils righty became the last to pitch both ends of a doubleheader to completion, he led the NL in losses and mound appearances.
- C) An outstanding hitter for a moundsman, he posted an even .300 BA over his last nine seasons in the majors.
- D) He fashioned a four-hit shutout win for the Giants in the 1922 World Series.
- E) He and the '50s pop singer who recorded "Burning Bridges" share the same name.

19. Bumpus Jones is not only the first and thus far only pitcher to throw a no-hitter in his first ML game, he is also responsible for two "Famous Last" achievements. What are they?

- A) His Famous First and two Famous Last achievements all came on the same day.
- B) The date of his no-hitter—October 15, 1892—is very significant.
- C) In his next ML game, Jones was shelled—as were many other pitchers that year.
- D) In 1984, Mike Witt more than matched one of Jones's "last" achievements.
- E) Jones's other "last" achievement can never be matched as long as the geometry of the playing field remains as it is now.

20. Rube Waddell is thus far the only pitcher to win both a National League and an American League ERA crown after January 1, 1900. He was also the last pitcher to win a major league strikeout crown while laboring under a certain handicap. What was it?

- A) The year he won his first AL whiff crown, Vic Willis, his NL counterpart, did not labor under the same handicap.
- B) The year he won his first AL whiff crown, the NL outstripped its junior in Ks for the last time until 1916—14 years later.
- C) The year after he won his first AL whiff crown, the NL and AL made peace and agreed to play under the same set of rules.
- D) A National League rule that was implemented in 1901 was a big reason that pitchers in the senior loop posted far more Ks in both 1901 and 1902 than AL hurlers.
- E) The rule was designed to curb hitters like Willie Keeler and Roy Thomas who excelled at poking pitches foul until they got one they liked.

21. In 1951 a pitcher for the first time had to hurl a minimum of one inning for every game his team played to qualify for an ERA crown—i.e., 154 innings on the old 154-game schedule. Previously the rule required a moundsman to pitch at least 10 complete games and a minimum of 100 innings to qualify. No pitchers who are now considered to have won an ERA crown under the old rule would have been ineligible under the new one. One man, however, was both the first and last hurler now accepted as the winner of an ERA crown prior to 1951 even though he failed to meet the requirement of 10 complete games. Who is he?

- A) He won his crown in his rookie year despite tossing just six complete games.
- B) He pitched on a world champ as a rookie.
- C) He led the AL in saves as well as ERA as a rookie.
- D) He fell just one victory short of becoming the AL's first 30-year-old rookie 20-game winner.
- E) He hurled for the 1927 Yankees as a frosh.

MISCELLANEOUS

- ◆ **LIKE FATHER, LIKE SON**
- ◆ **FAMOUS BROTHER ACTS**
- ◆ **ETHNIC ESOTERICA**
- ◆ **DYNAMIC DUOS**
- ◆ **COMMON DENOMINATORS**
- ◆ **PREMIER PILOTS**
- ◆ **MEN IN BLUE**

- ◆ **EARLY EXITS**
- ◆ **THE NAME'S THE SAME**
- ◆ **THIRTY OUTSTANDING ACHIEVEMENTS YOU WON'T FIND IN STANDARD BASEBALL RECORD BOOKS**

Like Father, Like Son

1. **More sons of former major leaguers are playing in the show now than ever before. In 1989 the Griffeys became the first father and son to play in the same season, but more such combinations are sure to follow. Prior to expansion, the only father and son ever to play in the same decade were Earle Brucker and his son Earle Jr., who both were active in the 1940s. The Bruckers are a footnote in the father-and-son lexicon, but 24 years after a certain father's sizzling season at the plate narrowly missed bringing a certain city its first flag in this century, his son played on a World Championship team in that same city. Who are this famous father and son?**

   A) The son was on a National League flag winner in another city four years later.
   B) The son's younger brother later pitched for the Red Sox and Senators.
   C) The son's first flag winner beat the BoSox in the World Series.
   D) The son once hit a three-run homer on the final day of the season to give a team in another NL city the pennant.
   E) The father was the first man to make the Hall of Fame after spending most of his career with the AL St. Louis Browns.

2. **In 1993, Barry Bonds became the first second-generation performer to lead the same league (the NL) in homers that his father had led in batter strikeouts. What son paced the White Sox in losses 37 years after his father topped the AL in wins?**

   A) Ed Walsh and son are a fine guess but a wrong one.
   B) The father died in 1972 and missed seeing his son pitch in the majors.
   C) The son won a game for the Cubs in the 1984 NLCS.
   D) The father was part of a tandem that won a post-1920 preexpansion season-record 56 games by two teammates.
   E) The father had the same nickname as the NL's most recent 30-game winner.

3. **Name the first African American ML'er to sire a son who also made the show.**
   A) He caught briefly for the White Sox after years in the Negro leagues and died in 1997.
   B) In 1951 he became the first African American catcher in the AL.
   C) He had the good fortune to have not one but two sons who played ML ball.
   D) The younger son led the AL three times in pinch hits.
   E) He and the only third sacker to collect 2,000 hits and post a career .300 BA with the Cubs share the same initials.

4. **No father-and-son duo have ever served as pitchers simultaneously on the same team in the majors, but several such pairs have played together in the minors. What former ML pitcher played with his son in 1929 on the San Francisco Seals in the PCL?**

   A) In 1917 he had an execrable 6–19 record for the Pirates despite a fine 2.81 ERA.

   B) Four of his nine wins with the 1918 Phillies were shutouts.

   C) His last two ML wins came with the 1927 White Sox, but his previous 48 career wins all came in the NL with four different teams.

   D) His initials are the same as those of the pitcher who surrendered Babe Ruth's first professional home run in 1914.

   E) His last name is the same as that of the Philadelphia A's second sacker in 1954 who was nicknamed "Spook."

5. **Name the only Cy Young Award winner to date with either a father or a son who played in the majors.**

   A) It was a son of a Cy Young–winning father, and he debuted with his father's old team.

   B) The father hurled his first ML game when he was 20 and his last at age 37.

   C) As a rookie in 1950, the father was on the same mound staff as Murry Dickson and Cliff Chambers.

   D) Father and son have the same initials and were both born in Idaho.

   E) Ernie Broglio and Warren Spahn both won more games than the father the year he received Cy Young honors, but his team won the NL flag.

Major Award Winners with Big League Fathers or Sons

NAME	AWARD	YEAR	RELATIVE
Eddie Collins Sr.	MVP	1914	Eddie Jr. (son)
George Sisler	MVP	1922	Dick & Dave (sons)
Yogi Berra	MVP	1951/54/55	Dale (son)
Vern Law	Cy Young	1960	Vance (son)
Tom Tresh	Rookie	1962	Mike (father)
Maury Wills	MVP	1962	Bump (son)
Cal Ripken Jr.	Rookie/MVP	1982/83	Cal Sr. (father—manager)
Sandy Alomar Jr.	Rookie	1990	Sandy Sr. (father)
Barry Bonds	MVP	1990/92/93	Bobby (father)
Ken Griffey Jr.	MVP	1997	Ken Sr. (father)

6. **A certain catcher set a World Series 0-for record (since broken) when he went 0-for-21 and fanned nine times. Thirty-four years later, his son, then a backstopper with the Tigers, went 2-for-13 in his only Series and in the process made the pair the first father and son each to appear in a fall classic. Who are they?**

   A) In 1936 the son hit .351 as Cleveland's top receiver.

   B) The two were the first father and son who both had solid big league careers.

   C) Both the father and the son were teammates of Red Faber's.

   D) The father hit .214 as the regular catcher for "The Hitless Wonders."

   E) The father and son both have the same initials as the father of a backup catcher who last played with the 1991 Indians and whose first name is Joel.

Fathers and Sons Each Playing in a World Series

NAMES	FATHER	SON
Billy Sullivan Sr. & Jr.	Chi, AL 1906	Det, AL 1940
Ernie & Don Johnson	NY, AL 1923	Chi, NL 1945
Jim & Mike Hegan	Cle, AL 1948	NY, AL 1964
Ray & Bob Boone	Cle, AL 1948	Phi, NL 1980
Bob & Terry Kennedy	Cle, AL 1948	SD, NL 1984
Julian & Stan Javier	StL, NL 1964	Oak, AL 1988
Mel & Todd Stottlemyre	NY, AL 1964	Tor, AL 1992
Pedro & Pedro Borbon	Cin, NL 1972	Atl, NL 1995
Felipe & Moises Alou	SF, NL 1962	Fla, NL 1997

Note: First Series appearances only; several pairs played in more than one.

7. **Twenty-two years after his father led the AL in starts, what son duplicated the feat while pitching for the same team?**
    A) The son's only World Series experience was with the 1946 Red Sox.
    B) The father pitched in a World Series for the team they shared in common.
    C) The father was nicknamed "Sarge."
    D) The father was the first pitcher to homer in a 20th century World Series.
    E) The father was the last preexpansion AL righty to win 30 games.

8. **Who were the first father and son each to play in an All-Star Game?**
    A) The father appeared first in the 1953 spectacle, and the son first appeared 20 years later.
    B) Both the father and the son carried the first name of David.
    C) The father led the NL in triples in 1951, and the son led the AL in ABs in 1979.
    D) The pair currently hold the record for the most combined career hits of any father and son in ML history.
    E) The father lived just long enough to see his son's son in 1995 make him the progenitor of only the second three-generation family in ML history.

9. **Who currently has the record for the most ML games played by the son of a Hall of Fame father?**
    A) The son's 853rd and last game came with the Astros in 1987.
    B) The son held the Pirates shortstop post from 1982 to 1984.
    C) The son was born two months after the father caught the final pitch in one of the most memorable World Series games of all time.
    D) The son has the same first name as the man who fanned on that final pitch.
    E) The son played under his father briefly in 1985.

Most ML Games Played by the Son of a Hall of Famer

RANK	NAME	YEARS	GAMES	FATHER
1	Dale Berra	1977–87	853	Yogi Berra
2	Dick Sisler	1946–53	799	George Sisler
3	Earl Averill	1956–63	449	Earl Averill
4	Dave Sisler	1956–62	247	George Sisler
5	Eddie Collins Jr.	1939–42	132	Eddie Collins
6	Ed Walsh	1928–32	79	Ed Walsh
7	Queenie O'Rourke	1908	34	Jim O'Rourke
8	Earle Mack	1910–14	5	Connie Mack

10. Who were the first father and son each to collect a hit in World Series play?

A) The son did it 12 years before the son of one of the father's World Series teammates got his first Series hit.

B) The father was a catcher, and so was the son of the father's teammate.

C) The son was a backup first baseman for most of his career.

D) The son's first Series hit came in 1972 while he was playing for the A's.

E) The father was the AL's best defensive catcher in the early 1950s.

11. As a Dodger, Tom Paciorek played in a certain father's last big league game on October 1, 1972, with Cincinnati. Twelve years later, then with the White Sox, Paciorek also played in the son's first ML game on April 15, 1984, with the Yankees. Who are this father-and-son combo?

A) The father originally belonged to the Pirates but was traded because he played the same position as Maz.

B) The son is a switch-hitting outfielder.

C) The father played on two World Championship teams in the 1960s, and the son played on the 1989 world champs.

D) The son was born in 1964, the year Dad played on his first world champ.

E) The son was San Francisco's regular center fielder in 1996 before injuries marred his season.

12. Who is the lone receiver to catch both a Hall of Fame hurler and his son in the majors?

A) He caught the son just once, in his 1,755th and final game with a certain AL club.

B) Hours before catching his old batterymate's son, the backstopper resigned as his club's manager.

C) The backstopper is also in the Hall of Fame.

D) When the backstopper caught him, the son was making his ML debut on July 4, 1928, for the White Sox.

E) The father's 1.82 career ERA is the lowest in ML history.

13. Who are the only father and son each to play in a perfect game?

A) Both played behind a perfect game hurler, but only the son played behind a victorious perfect game hurler.

B) The father played 19 seasons in the majors.

C) Both had career batting averages below .230.

D) The son played in the only perfecto to occur on the final day of a season.

E) The father played short behind Haddix the night Harvey went overtime in a vain effort to win his perfecto.

14. **Name the first father and son each to score a run in World Series action.**
    A)   The father scored when he ran for Bullet Joe Bush in the final game of the 1923 World Series.
    B)   The son scored the Cubs' very first tally in the 1945 Series.
    C)   The father was the White Sox regular shortstop in 1921–22 before becoming a utility infielder with the Yankees.
    D)   The son was a 32-year-old rookie second sacker with the Cubs in 1944.
    E)   The father had the same name as the hurler who made the most relief appearances for the Braves in the 1950s.

15. **What father and his two sons combined for an abysmal .134 career batting average as pinch hitters with just 22 hits in 164 pinch at bats?**
    A)   The father was 1-for-10 as a pinch hitter with the Miracle Braves.
    B)   The elder son led the NL in pinch ABs in 1947, his big league coda.
    C)   The younger son held the Giants first base job for most of the 1950 season and hit .220.
    D)   The father was a successful manager for many years in the minors.
    E)   Their last name is the same as the first name of the man who piloted the 1969 world champs.

16. **Thornton and Don Lee are well known as the only father-and-son mound duo who each faced Ted Williams in regular or postseason action. What family hill duo featured a father who was a teammate of Ted in All-Star competition and a son who played under him while he managed?**
    A)   The father's only All-Star selection came in 1948.
    B)   The son won his first two major league starts with Washington in 1965 when he was just 18 years old.
    C)   The son was a 20-game winner in the AL both before and after the DH rule came into being.
    D)   They are the only father-son duo who played under both Connie Mack and Ted Williams; the father of course played for Mack and the son for Williams.
    E)   They share the same last name with the hurler who holds the all-time record for the most losses in a season.

Gus Bell retired in 1964 with the NL season record for the fewest runs (59) by a man with 100 RBI. His career totals have since been incremented by son Buddy and grandson David, making the Bells the number-one family in several key offensive departments.

Father-Son Combined Career Records

	RECORD	FATHER-SON
		Batting
Games	4146	Buddy (2405) & Gus (1741) Bell
At Bats	15473	Buddy (8995) & Gus (6478) Bell
Batting Average	.325	George (.340) & Dick (.276) Sisler
Slugging Average	.512	Barry (.556) & Bobby (.471) Bonds
Hits	4337	Buddy (2514) & Gus (1823) Bell
Total Bases	6538	Buddy (3654) & Gus (2884) Bell
Doubles	746	Pete (746) & Pete (0) Rose
Triples	192	George (164) & Dick (28) Sisler
Home Runs	743	Barry (411) & Bobby (332) Bonds
RBI	2240	Barry (1216) & Bobby (1024) Bonds
Runs	2722	Barry (1364) & Bobby (1258) Bonds
Stolen Bases	906	Bobby (461) & Barry (445) Bonds
Strikeouts	2807	Bobby (1757) & Barry (1050) Bonds
Walks	2271	Barry (1357) & Bobby (914) Bonds
		Pitching
Games	822	Dizzy (521) & Steve (301) Trout
Wins	287	Mel (164) & Todd (123) Stottlemyre
Losses	253	Dizzy (161) & Steve (92) Trout
Innings	4637.1	Mel (2661.2) & Todd (1975.2) Stottlemyre
Strikeouts	2522	Todd (1265) & Mel (1257) Stottlemyre
Walks	1624	Dizzy (1046) & Steve (578) Trout
Games Started	656	Mel (356) & Todd (300) Stottlemyre
Complete Games	265	Ed (250) & Ed (15) Walsh
ERA	2.20	Ed (1.82) & Ed (5.57) Walsh
Shutouts	44	Mel (40) & Todd (4) Stottlemyre
Saves	83	Pedro (80) & Pedro (3) Borbon
Winning Pct.	.579	Ed (.607) & Ed (.314) Walsh

Father-Son Combined Season Records

	RECORD	FATHER-SON
		Batting
Games	322	Maury (165/1962) & Bump (157/1978) Wills
At Bats	1289	Buddy (670/1979) & Gus (619/1954) Bell
Batting Average	.362	George (.420/1922) & Dick (.296/1950) Sisler
Slugging Average	.597	Barry (.677/1993) & Bobby (.530/1973) Bonds
Hits	412	George (257/1920) & Dick (155/1950) Sisler
Total Bases	706	Barry (365/1992) & Bobby (341/1973) Bonds
Doubles	92	Hal (54/1977) & Brian (38/1995) McRae
Triples	24	George (18/thrice) & Dick (6/twice) Sisler
Home Runs	85	Barry (46/1993) & Bobby (39/1973) Bonds
RBI	244	Barry (129/1996) & Bobby (115/1977) Bonds
Runs	260	Bobby (131/1973) & Barry (129/1993) Bonds
Stolen Bases	156	Maury (104/1962) & Bump (52/1978) Wills
Strikeouts	291	Bobby (189/1970) & Barry (102/1986) Bonds
Walks	246	Barry (151/1996) & Bobby (95/1974) Bonds
Fewest Ks	52	Dick (38/1949) & George (14/1922) Sisler
		Pitching
Games	92	Jim (49/1917) & Jim (43/1938) Bagby
Wins	48	Jim (31/1920) & Jim (17/1942-43) Bagby
Losses	37	Mel (20/1966) & Todd (17/1990) Stottlemyre
Innings	612.2	Jim (339.2/1920) & Jim (273/1943) Bagby
Strikeouts	360	Todd (205/1995) & Mel (155/1965) Stottlemyre
Walks	285	Joe (158/1974) & Joe (127/1949) Coleman
Games Started	74	Jim (38/1920) & Jim (35/1942) Bagby
Complete Games	46	Jim (30/1920) & Jim (16/1942–43) Bagby
ERA	2.42	Jim (1.96/1917) & Jim (2.96/1942) Bagby
Shutouts	12	Jim (8/1917) & Jim (4/1942) Bagby
Saves	20	Pedro (18/1977) & Pedro (2/1995) Borbon
Winning Pct.	.696	Jim (31–12/1920) & Jim (17–9/1942) Bagby

Note: Limited to only a father and one son—the most productive son if there are more than one. Includes only families that received a full-season contribution from each member—i.e., sufficient ABs to qualify for a batting title or sufficient innings to qualify for an ERA crown. Each family member's total is in parentheses, with the larger contributor listed first.

Famous Brother Acts

1. **The three DiMaggio brothers were active simultaneously in the 1930s and 1940s. In 1963 the three Alou brothers all played in the same outfield on occasion for the San Francisco Giants. The three Wright Brothers—Harry, George, and Sam—were the first trio of brothers all to be active in the same season when Sam debuted with New Haven in the National Association in 1875. What three brothers were the most recent trio of siblings all to play in the majors in the same season?**

    A)   It happened in 1977.

    B)   Two of the brothers played with the Cardinals in 1973.

    C)   The eldest of the trio was the last to play in the majors, finishing in 1988.

    D)   The three were all born in Arroyo, Puerto Rico.

    E)   Tommy, the middle brother, played only 7 games in the majors, but Jose, the eldest, played 2,353.

2. **Someday Glenn Hoffman, brother of Padres bullpen ace Trevor, may join the select group of managers who have skippered their brothers in the majors. The first to do so was Harry Wright, way back in 1871. What Hall of Famer piloted his brother while acting as player-manager of the New York Players League entry in 1890?**

    A)   The 'Famer's brother led the NL in winning percentage and ERA in 1891.

    B)   The two sibs hailed from Cinci, and the elder last played for the 1897 Reds.

    C)   The 'Famer debuted with Troy in 1880.

    D)   Though mainly a catcher during his career, the 'Famer played every position at one time or another.

    E)   For years it was wrongly believed that the 'Famer's middle name was Buckingham.

Managers Who Piloted Their Brothers

NAME	TEAM	YEAR	BROTHER
Harry Wright	Boston, NA	1871–75	George
Harry Wright	Boston, NL	1876	Sam
Harry Wright	Boston, NL	1876–78, 1880–81	George
Deacon White	Cincinnati, NL	1879	Will
Harry Wright	Providence, NL	1882	George
Arthur Irwin	Washington, NL	1889	John
Buck Ewing	New York, PL	1890	John
Arthur Irwin	Boston, AA	1891	John
Patsy Tebeau	Cleveland, NL	1895	White Wings

White Wings Tebeau, the most recent ML'er to be managed by his brother. Tebeau was piloted by his elder sibling Patsy in 1895, his final big league season.

3. What three siblings followed in the footsteps of Harry, George, and Sam Wright and became the second trio of brothers to play in the majors?

    A) They formed the outfield trio for Albany's minor league team in 1881.

    B) Two of trio were ML teammates but for just one game, with Syracuse in 1879.

    C) There was an ill-advised campaign to award the eldest brother the AA bat crown in 1883 when he hit .402 for St. Louis, albeit in just 28 games.

    D) Their first names were Mike, Tom, and John.

    E) Their last names are followed in *The Baseball Encyclopedia* by an ex-Braves utility man who stroked 30 homers but collected just 64 RBI for the 1964 Red Sox.

4. One member of this undeservedly obscure sib pair was a 30-game winner who won his last ML game before his 23rd birthday; the other member hurled 33 complete games in his finale and finished among his loop's Top 10 in ERA. Name them.

    A) One brother debuted with the last Buffalo team to be a member of the NL, and the other with the first ML team from Brooklyn.

    B) Both finished their ML careers in 1889, with Kansas City and Pittsburgh, respectively.

    C) The Pittsburgh finisher won 30 games a year earlier with Detroit at age 21.

    D) The pair had the same last name as the second brother battery in AA history.

    E) Though their last name is common, no ML performer has borne it since 1948, when a shortstop whose first name was Jack last saw duty with the Giants as Buddy Kerr's understudy after previously being Lou Boudreau's understudy in Cleveland.

5. Bet a cold one you don't recall the pair of brothers who shared the Pittsburgh third-base job in 1955.

    A) The older brother did little in the majors but was a star in the PCL.

    B) An ankle injury shortened the younger brother's career in 1962 at age 28, although he played as a part-timer until 1966.

    C) The younger brother had his career year with the 1961 NL champs.

    D) The pair has the same first names as those of the AL's 1949 batting champ and top rookie winner in 1948.

    E) Both sibs have the same first and last initials as the 1977 NL homer king.

6. **The Ripkens are the longest-running sibling keystone combo in ML history. What brothers gave the Tigers the second longest-running sib keystone combo in 1958?**
   A) The elder brother earlier had been the Red Sox regular shortstop.
   B) The younger brother became a Detroit regular the same year as Al Kaline.
   C) The younger brother was later dealt to the Braves for Bill Bruton.
   D) The younger brother was still platooning at second base for the Braves when the team moved to Atlanta. .
   E) The elder sib has the same initials as Seattle's main third sacker in 1995.

Sibling Keystone Combos		
BROTHERS	**TEAM**	**YEAR**
George & Sam Wright	Bos, NL	1876
Barney & Frank McLaughlin	KC, UA	1884
Harry & John Gilbert	Pit, NL	1890
Garvin & Granny Hamner	Phi, NL	1945
Eddie & Johnny O'Brien	Pit, NL	1953/55–56
Frank & Milt Bolling	Det, AL	1958
Billy & Cal Ripken	Bal, AL	1987–92/96

Note: The O'Briens are the only twins to form a keystone combo.

7. **These two brothers faced off against each other in several mound duels, but their most memorable one came when the younger beat the elder 4–3 and hit a home run off him, the only blast of his long ML career. Who are they?**
   A) The older brother's first ML homer came in 1968.
   B) Both brothers pitched in both the NL and the AL.
   C) Neither brother peaked as a pitcher until he hit 30.
   D) These two brothers hold many important sibling mound records.
   E) The elder brother won more than 300 games.

8. **Though they were the first pair of siblings to each play on a pennant winner in the 20th century, only one of them participated in a World Series. Who are they?**
   A) The elder brother played on three flag winners after 1900, but none of his teams saw postseason action.
   B) The younger brother hit a weak .220 in 1,089 games, mostly as a third baseman.
   C) The elder brother hit .256 in 506 games, most of them as a pitcher, and was a 20-game winner six times.
   D) The younger brother was a member of "The Hitless Wonders."
   E) The elder sib and the pilot of the 1996 world champs share the same initials.

9. **What 20-game winner in 1977 got relief help on several occasions from his brother, who made a staff-high 69 appearances?**
   A) Between them, they won 230 games, 214 of them by the younger sib.
   B) The younger sib almost won 20 again with another NL team in 1988.
   C) On August 21, 1975, they became the only two brothers ever to hurl a combined ML shutout.
   D) Their team in 1977 was the Cubs.
   E) The younger brother was nicknamed "Big Daddy."

10. **In 1936 he and his brother combined for 197 hits. His brother had all 197 of them, however, while he went hitless in 35 at bats to set a season record for the most at bats without a hit by a player other than a pitcher. Can you name this pair?**

   A) The elder brother's 0-for-35 season came with the 1936 Pirates.

   B) That same season, his younger brother led the AL in ABs.

   C) The younger brother led both the Red Sox and the AL in pinch hits in 1939.

   D) The younger brother and the 1929 AL batting champ share the same first name and initials.

   E) Their first names match those of Cleveland's player-manager and top pinch hitter the last year to date that the Tribe won a World Championship.

Most ABs Without a Hit, Season, Non-Pitcher

RANK	NAME	TEAM	YEAR	POS.	ABS
1	Hal Finney	Pit, NL	1936	C	35
2	Larry Littleton	Cle, AL	1981	OF	23
3	Ed Whiting	Was, NL	1886	C	21
4	Cliff Carroll	Pit, NL	1888	OF	20
	Fred Tauby	Phi, NL	1937	OF	20
	Kevin Elster	NY, AL	1994	SS	20
7	John Kenney	Atl, NA	1872	2B	19
	Harry Redmond	Bro, NL	1909	2B	19
	Chuck Harmon	Cin/StL, NL	1956	OF	19
	Ron Hansen	Bal, AL	1958	SS	19
	Bill Plummer	Cin, NL	1971	C	19

11. **In 1933 a certain pair of brothers combined to fan just 28 times in 1,118 at bats while posting a .294 combined batting average. Who are they?**

   A) Amazingly, in 1933, another pair of brothers fanned 28 times in 998 ABs while hitting a combined .269.

   B) The pair that hit a combined .294 were teammates in 1933.

   C) The elder brother won two batting titles.

   D) They hold many sib season batting records, including most hits and most runs.

   E) Both are in the Hall of Fame.

12. **The Cincinnati Reds achieved a first in the final game of the 1998 season when their starting infield consisted of two sets of brothers, Barry and Steve Larkin and Aaron and Bret Boone. But despite the many pairs of brothers now active in the majors, the Reds, along with 29 other ML teams, lacked a sibling battery in 1998. What was the last brother battery to start a big league game together?**

   A) It happened in a National League game on September 10, 1959.

   B) The pitching half made his only career start, going seven innings for the Reds in a 5–3 loss to the Cubs.

   C) The catcher was a longtime NL backstopper, mostly for the Reds and Giants.

   D) The catcher has the same initials as the only shortstop to win back-to-back MVP awards.

   E) The brothers had the same last name as a vaunted Pittsburgh Bonus Baby in the early 1960s whose last ML at bat came with the 1978 Red Sox.

13. **The most recent brother battery to appear in a big league game worked together on June 28, 1962, for just two innings. Who are they?**

    A) They never formed a starting battery in a big league game.
    B) One brother was a reliever in 1962, and the other backed up Johnny Roseboro.
    C) The catching half of the duo was later a longtime coach under Roger Craig.
    D) The pitching half was the MVP in the 1959 World Series.
    E) The Series MVP and the player who appeared in a record four World Series with four different teams between 1980 and 1991 have the same initials.

14. **Name the only brother battery to debut in their team's first big league game.**

    A) They were also the first brother battery in a certain major league and only the second brother battery in ML history.
    B) The second brother battery in their team's league was Bill and Dick Conway of the 1886 Baltimore Orioles.
    C) Their team was a late-season replacement for the first post-1876 Washington ML entry.
    D) Their last name is the same as that of the third baseman on "Murderers' Row."
    E) They have the same first names as the 20-game winner and the regular shortstop on the 1963 Red Sox.

Chronological List of Brother Batteries

RANK	NAMES	TEAM	YEAR
1	Will & Deacon White	Cin, NL	1878
2	Ed & Bill Dugan	Vir, AA	1884
3	Pete & Fred Wood	Buf, NL	1885
4	Dick & Bill Conway	Bal, AA	1886
5	John & Buck Ewing	NY, PL	1890
6	Mike & Jack O'Neill	StL, NL	1902
7	Homer & Tommy Thompson	NY, AL	1912
8	Lefty & Fred Tyler	Bos, NL	1914
9	Milt & Alex Gaston	Bos, AL	1929
10	Wes & Rick Ferrell	Bos, AL	1934
11	Mort & Walker Cooper	StL, NL	1940
12	Elmer & John Riddle	Cin, NL	1941
13	Bobby & Billy Shantz	Phi, AL	1954
14	Jim & Ed Bailey	Cin, NL	1959
15	Larry & Norm Sherry	LA, NL	1959

Note: The team listed is the one with which the two brothers first played together; several brother batteries played for more than one team.

15. **The Aarons hold the sib record for the most home runs, but Hank accounted for 755 of the family's 768 blasts. Who is the only pair of brothers to pole more than 400 home runs between them with each contributing at least 150 to the family total?**
    A) They had a third brother who failed to homer in 111 ML games.
    B) The third brother was a pitcher, and the other two brothers played the same infield position.
    C) The pitching brother and the brother with the most career homers in the family both debuted with the Cardinals.
    D) One of the brothers won an MVP Award.
    E) The two who played the same position faced each other in the 1964 postseason.

16. **Name the first duo of brothers each to win 20 games in the same season.**
    A) One brother co-led the AL in wins in his sophomore season with 18.
    B) The younger brother is the lone Cy Young winner to date for the team with which his brother debuted.
    C) The elder brother was traded by his original team for Sam McDowell.
    D) They once held the record for the most career wins by a sibling pair.
    E) They are the only duo of brothers to each win a Cy Young Award.

Brother Combined Season Records

	RECORD	BROTHERS
		Batting
Games	311	Cal (161) & Billy (150) Ripken, 1988
At Bats	1258	Lloyd (662) & Paul (596) Waner, 1929
Batting Average	.367	Paul (.380) & Lloyd (.355) Waner, 1927
Slugging Average	.545	Emil (.548) & Bob (.542) Meusel, 1925
Hits	450	Paul (227) & Lloyd (223) Waner, 1927
Total Bases	621	Bob (338) & Emil (283) Meusel, 1925
Doubles	89	Paul (62) & Lloyd (27) Waner, 1932
Triples	35	Lloyd (20) & Paul (15) Waner, 1929
Home Runs	54	Bob (33) & Emil (21) Meusel, 1925
	54	Tony (36) & Billy (18) Conigliaro, 1970
RBI	249	Bob (136) & Emil (113) Meusel, 1925
Runs	266	Lloyd (135) & Paul (131) Waner, 1929
Stolen Bases	58	Roberto (55) & Sandy (3) Alomar, 1993
Strikeouts	221	Lee (125) & Carlos (96) May, 1970
Walks	168	Dom (101) & Joe (67) DiMaggio, 1948
Fewest Ks	28	Paul (20) & Lloyd (8) Waner, 1933*

* Joe and Luke Sewell also had only 28 Ks in 1933 but with 120 fewer at bats.

	RECORD	BROTHERS
		Pitching
Games	125	Todd (65) & Tim (60) Worrell, 1997
Wins	49	Dizzy (30) & Paul (19) Dean, 1934
Losses	32	Phil (18) & Joe (14) Niekro, 1978
Innings	605.2	Phil (342) & Joe (263.2) Niekro, 1979
Strikeouts	382	Gaylord (214) & Jim (168) Perry, 1970
Walks	228	Phil (164) & Joe (64) Niekro, 1977
Games Started	82	Phil (44) & Joe (38) Niekro, 1979
Complete Games	48	Dizzy (29) & Paul (19) Dean, 1935
ERA	2.59	Harry (1.97) & Stan (3.41) Coveleski, 1916
Shutouts	12	Dizzy (7) & Paul (5) Dean, 1934
Saves	45	Todd (44) & Tim (1) Worrell, 1996
Winning Pct.	.731	Dizzy (.811) & Paul (.633) Dean, 1934

Note: Best two brothers, eliminating trios like the DiMaggios and the Alous who would otherwise dominate almost every department. Each brother's total is in parentheses, with the larger contributor listed first. Batting and slugging average leaders must both have enough ABs to qualify for a batting title.

10 Best Batter-Pitcher Brother Combinations, Season

RANK	BROTHERS	YEAR	1st Brother			2nd Brother	
			BA	HRS	RBI	W–L	ERA
1	Walker & Mort Cooper*	1943	.318	9	81	21–8	2.30
2	Walker & Mort Cooper*	1944	.317	13	72	22–7	2.46
3	Rick & Wes Ferrell*	1935	.301	3	61	25–14	3.52 (.347 BA)
4	Deacon & Will White*	1879	.330	1	52	43–31	1.99
5	Rick & Wes Ferrell	1932	.315	2	65	23–13	3.66
6	Deacon & Will White*	1878	.314	0	29	30–21	1.79
7	Deacon & Will White	1884	.325	5	74	34–18	3.32
8	Walker & Mort Cooper*	1942	.281	7	65	22–7	1.78
9	Rick & Wes Ferrell	1931	.306	3	57	22–12	3.75
10	Buck & John Ewing*	1890	.338	8	72	18–12	4.24

* Batterymates that year.

Ethnic Esoterica

1. **The first African American to score a run in a big league game was not Jackie Robinson but Moses Walker, way back in 1884. However, Robinson was the first African American to make the Hall of Fame. Do you know who currently owns the most career wins of any American-born non-Caucasian pitcher who will have to be selected by the Veterans' Committee in order to join Robinson in Cooperstown?**

    A) He won loop strikeout crowns with two different teams.
    B) His 182 career wins all came in the AL.
    C) He led the AL in Ks, shutouts, and ERA at age 37, which was also the only year he won 20 games.
    D) A Native American, he won his first K crown as a Tribe rookie in 1943.
    E) Cleveland traded him to the Yankees in 1947 for Joe Gordon.

2. **Japanese league graduate Hideo Nomo finished the 1998 season with 49 career victories. Only two American-born hurlers with big league experience have posted more wins in Japanese leagues than Nomo's current ML total. One is Kip Gross. Who is the other?**

    A) He won an even 100 games in Japan.
    B) His final win in Japan came seven years after he logged his one and only ML win for that year's AL World Series representative.
    C) His lone ML win came in relief for Al Lopez's last flag winner.
    D) His last name is very similar to that of the man who replaced Lopez at the White Sox helm in 1966.
    E) His initials match those of the winner of the 1996 NL Cy Young Award.

3. **In 1996, Rafael Palmiero shattered the record for the most walks by a Latin-born player, formerly shared by Roberto Alomar and Carmelo Martinez. Prior to 1985, when Martinez walked 87 times for the Padres, who held the season record for the most free passes by a Latino?**

    A) Born in Cuba, he collected 86 walks at age 33 to break fellow Cuban Bobby Estalella's old record of 85.
    B) His first big league walk came with Cleveland in 1949.
    C) He collected his final big league walk in 1964 at age 41.
    D) In 1960 he led the AL in hits with 184, his career high.
    E) He led the AL in triples and stolen bases as a rookie in 1951 but lost his loop's top rookie honor to a player with the same last initial.

Most Walks by a Latino/Hispanic Player, Season

RANK	NAME	TEAM	YEAR	WALKS
1	Rafael Palmiero	Bal, AL	1996	95
2	Roberto Alomar	Bal, AL	1996	90
3	Jose Offerman	KC, AL	1998	89
4	Roberto Alomar	Tor, AL	1992	87
	Carmelo Martinez	SD, NL	1985	87
6	Minnie Minoso	Chi, AL	1956	86
7	Manny Ramirez	Cle, AL	1996	85
	Bobby Estalella	Was, AL	1942	85
9	Bob Abreu	Phi, NL	1998	84
	Quilvio Veras	SD, NL	1998	84

Note: Limited to players born south of the U.S. border.

4. Name the first two African Americans to play against each other in a big league game.
- A) Later they also faced each other in a World Series game.
- B) Both debuted at 2B, but each made his mark at another position.
- C) Neither man ever played for Brooklyn.
- D) Their World Series meeting occurred in 1954.
- E) In 1947, the year they first faced each other, they played for Cleveland and the St. Louis Browns.

5. In 1951, Don Newcombe became the first African American to win 20 games in a season. Who was the first African American to do the same in the AL?
- A) He debuted with Cleveland.
- B) The first time he was traded, it was for Jack Kralick.
- C) His last name is the same as that of a Civil War general.
- D) His first postseason action came in 1965.
- E) They called him "Mudcat."

First 10 African American 20-Game Winners

RANK	NAME	TEAM	YEAR	W–L
1	Don Newcombe	Bro, NL	1951	20–9
2	Sam Jones	SF, NL	1959	21–15
3	Bob Gibson	StL, NL	1965	20–12
	Mudcat Grant	Min, AL	1965	21–7
5	Fergie Jenkins	Chi, NL	1967	20–13
	Earl Wilson	Det, AL	1967	22–11
7	Al Downing	LA, NL	1971	20–9
	Vida Blue	Oak, AL	1971	24–9
9	J. R. Richard	Hou, NL	1976	20–15
10	Mike Norris	Oak, AL	1980	22–9

Mudcat Grant, the first African American hurler to log a 20-win season in the AL. Grant was 21–7 with the 1965 Minnesota Twins.

6. **Of the 16 franchises extant in 1947 when the majors were permanently integrated, which was the last to give an African American suffcient playing time that he logged enough plate appearances to qualify for a batting title?**

    A)   The team's first African American regular was a rookie second baseman whose name was not Pumpsie Green.

    B)   He set a record as a rookie for the most ABs (663) by a man with only one season when he collected 400 ABs.

    C)   His frosh season was an expansion year in his league.

    D)   He helped his team to win 100 games for only the third time in its history.

    E)   He led the AL in triples and batter Ks as a frosh 49 years after a man with the same last name paced the AL with 34 wins and an .872 winning percentage.

7. **What was the first season that an African American or black Latino pitcher led each major league in ERA?**

    A)   Both hurlers also led their loops in shutouts with a combined total of 22.

    B)   Both hurlers posted the lowest ERAs in their loops since expansion.

    C)   Both hurlers won more than 200 games.

    D)   The season that both were ERA leaders featured the last 30-game winner.

    E)   In 1975 one of the pair went 3–10 in his final season, while the other hurled two complete-game wins in his only World Series.

8. **Who was the first African American or black Latino player to be selected the AL Rookie of the Year?**

    A)   The NL's top rookie that year was African American.

    B)   The only vote he did not receive as the AL's top rookie went to Wally Bunker.

    C)   Jimmie Hall, a teammate of his, finished third in the AL rookie balloting the previous year.

    D)   He played his entire career under his brother's name.

    E)   He was the first rookie in this century to win a batting title.

9. **The first African American pitcher to receive a vote for an AL MVP Award is a Hall of Famer. Who is he?**
    - A) A pitcher was selected the AL MVP that year.
    - B) He received 12 votes, tying him with Vic Raschi and Jackie Jensen.
    - C) The previous year, another pitcher on his team had finished second in the AL MVP balloting.
    - D) He was the first African American pitcher to hurl in a World Series game.
    - E) He was 40-something when he made his big league debut.

10. **Name the first non-Caucasian player to make the Hall of Fame.**
    - A) Jackie Robinson is the standard guess, but it's wrong.
    - B) Our man was inducted while Jackie was still an active player.
    - C) Our man was the first non-Caucasian to win a World Series game.
    - D) He was inducted into the Hall of Fame two years after the manager he played under for most of his career piloted his last ML game.
    - E) There have been many players nicknamed "Chief," but he's the only one in the Hall of Fame.

11. **By 1956, Jackie Robinson, Roy Campanella, Willie Mays, and Don Newcombe had won MVP Awards in the NL. Meanwhile no African American as yet had won an AL MVP Award, and only two had finished among the top three in the balloting. Who are they?**
    - A) They were teammates prior to the 1956 season.
    - B) Harry Simpson, the AL's top African American MVP vote-getter in 1956, had also been a teammate of theirs earlier in the decade.
    - C) Both played for the White Sox in the late 1950s, but they were never teammates on the White Sox.
    - D) One was a rookie in 1947, and the other was a rookie in 1954.
    - E) The 1947 rookie finished second in the balloting in 1954, and the 1954 rookie finished third in 1955.

12. **In 1961, African Americans and black Latinos claimed the top four spots in the NL MVP race and seven of the top nine spots. Who was the lone African American or black Latino player to finish among the top nine in the AL MVP contest that year?**
    - A) He finished ninth with 30 votes.
    - B) He had been the first African American batting title qualifier on his team two years earlier.
    - C) He had only the fifth-highest MVP vote total on his team in 1961.
    - D) He alone caught both Ryne Duren and Jim Lonborg in postseason play.
    - E) In 1963 he became the first African American to win an AL MVP Award.

13. **Don Newcombe won the first Cy Young Award in 1956. How long was it before an AL African American pitcher received even a single vote for the top mound honor?**
    - A) The first African American to earn a Cy Young vote in the AL pitched on a division winner.
    - B) It was his first full season in the majors.
    - C) He was not only the first African American hurler to get a vote but also the first to win the AL's top pitching prize.
    - D) He owns the most career wins of any African American eligible for the Hall of Fame but not yet enshrined.
    - E) He is also the answer to the question: Who is the only African American switch-hitter to win an AL MVP Award?

Most Career Wins: African American, Latino, Native American Non-HOF'ers

RANK	NAME	YEARS	WINS
1	Luis Tiant	1964–82	229
2	Vida Blue	1969–86	209
3	Dolf Luque	1914–35	194
4	Mike Cuellar	1959–77	185
5	Allie Reynolds	1943–54	183
6	Camilo Pascual	1954–71	174
7	Rudy May	1965–83	152
8	Don Newcombe	1949–60	149
9	Mudcat Grant	1958–71	145
10	Dock Ellis	1968–79	138

Note: Limited to pitchers eligible for enshrinement.

14. **Negro League great Martin DiHugo is the only Hall of Famer who is also enshrined in the Cuban and Mexican baseball halls of fame. Only one performer currently in both the Cuban and Mexican baseball halls of fame is eligible for Cooperstown solely on the basis of his ML achievements. Who is he?**

   A)   His best showing in a Hall of Fame ballot came in 1958 when he received 15 votes.

   B)   He was the first man to collect a win in both a Negro League and a major league contest.

   C)   His performance against Washington in the 1933 World Series at age 43 induced Senators owner Clark Griffith to redouble his scouting efforts in Cuba.

   D)   Nicknamed "The Pride of Havana," he died in the Cuban capital in 1957.

   E)   His glittering performance in 1923 for Cinci made him the NL hypothetical Cy Young winner that year.

15. **In 1969, Rod Carew was rightly awarded the AL batting title even though he was a few short of the requisite number of plate appearances because his average exceeded the runner-up's by 23 points. What African American star would have won his lone batting crown if Carew had been ruled ineligible?**

   A)   His .309 mark would have edged out Tony Oliva by a fraction of a point.

   B)   He led the NL in OBP in 1977.

   C)   His first taste of postseason action came in 1967.

   D)   He collected the last of his 2,020 hits with the 1982 Giants.

   E)   He played against another African American star with the same first name in both the 1977 and the 1978 World Series.

16. **Don Newcombe owns the season record for the most wins (27) by an African American hurler. Who owns the equivalent record for a Latino hurler?**

   A)   He also won 27 games in his big season.

   B)   He was the first hurler in ML history to win a game prior to age 30 and yet post more career wins after his 40th birthday than he owned at age 30.

   C)   All his 194 career wins came in the NL.

   D)   He holds the post–Deadball Era record for the most losses in a season (23) by a pitcher on a winning team.

   E)   In 1923 he topped Cincinnati and the NL with 27 wins and a 1.93 ERA.

Most Wins, Season, African American, Latino, Native American Pitcher

RANK	NAME	TEAM	YEAR	W
1	Dolf Luque	Cin, NL	1923	27
	Don Newcombe	Bro, NL	1956	27
3	Juan Marichal	SF, NL	1968	26
4	Juan Marichal	SF, NL	1963	25
	Juan Marichal	SF, NL	1966	25
	Fergie Jenkins	Tex, AL	1974	25
7	Vida Blue	Oak, AL	1971	24
	Fergie Jenkins	Chi, NL	1971	24
	Doc Gooden	NY, NL	1985	24
10	Chief Bender	Phi, AL	1910	23
	Bob Gibson	StL, NL	1970	23

17. In 1921, Dolf Luque became the first Cuban-born hurler to win a major league shutout crown. Who was the first hurler born in Puerto Rico to make the same claim?

A) He was the only pitcher in the 1940s to log his first career win with the Cubs and his last with the ChiSox.

B) He died in Mexico in 1952 at age 35.

C) The park occupied by the first San Juan team to be a member of the International League was named after him.

D) His 18 wins in 1943 led all NL hurlers who were on second-division teams.

E) His initials match those of the most recent Cubs hurler both to win and lose a World Series game.

18. Which expansion franchise went the longest before it had an African American pitcher in its starting rotation (at least 15 starts in a season)?

A) The Astros went the longest in the NL, waiting until 1967 when Don Wilson joined their rotation.

B) Seattle would be a winning guess if Odell Jones hadn't made 19 starts in 1979.

C) The team's first African American starter was a former Cy Young winner.

D) The team installed its first African American starter two years after it won its first pennant.

E) The team's other main starters that year were Larry Gura, Dennis Leonard, and Paul Splittorff.

19. In 1954, Gene Baker and Ernie Banks formed the first regular African American keystone combo in the NL. Who formed the first African American pair to play at least 100 games each at short and second for an AL team?

A) In 1961, when African American second sacker Jake Wood teamed with Latino shortstop Chico Fernandez for the Tigers, the AL still had not had an African American keystone combo.

B) Zoilo Versalles and Rod Carew formed the AL's first black Latino keystone pair for the 1967 Twins; that same year, African American second sacker Horace Clarke teamed with black Latino shortstop Ruben Amaro for the Yankees.

C) The second-base half of the first AL African American keystone pair was born in 1950 in Greenville, Mississippi, and the shortstop in 1953 in Stringtown, Oklahoma.

D) The pair played for a world champ the first year they each performed in at least 100 games.

E) The two share the same last initial, and the second baseman collected more than 2,000 hits, all while wearing the same uniform.

First African American or
Black Latino Batting Title and ERA Qualifiers

	Batting		Pitching	
	NAME	**YEAR**	**NAME**	**YEAR**
American League				
Baltimore	Bob Boyd	1957	Connie Johnson	1956
Boston	Willie Tasby	1960	Earl Wilson	1962
Los Angeles/California/Anaheim	Leon Wagner	1961	Marcelino Lopez	1965
Chicago	Minnie Minoso	1951	Juan Pizarro	1961
Cleveland	Larry Doby	1948	Mudcat Grant	1958
Detroit	Jake Wood	1961	Earl Wilson	1966
Kansas City	Joe Foy	1969	Vida Blue	1982
	Pat Kelly	1969		
Seattle/Milwaukee	Tommy Harper	1969	Ray Burris	1985
	Tommy Davis	1969		
Washington/Minnesota	Carlos Paula	1954	Mudcat Grant	1964
New York	Elston Howard	1959	Al Downing	1963
Philadelphia/Kansas City/Oakland	Vic Power	1954	Norm Bass	1961
Washington/Texas	Willie Tasby	1961	Bennie Daniels	1961
National League				
Boston/Milwaukee/Atlanta	Sam Jethroe	1950	Pascual Perez	1983
Chicago	Ernie Banks	1954	Sam Jones	1955
	Gene Baker	1954		
Cincinnati	Frank Robinson	1956	Brooks Lawrence	1956
Houston	Ramon Mejias	1962	Don Wilson	1967
	Walt Bond	1964		
Brooklyn/Los Angeles	Jackie Robinson	1947	Don Newcombe	1949
Montreal	Coco Laboy	1969	Ray Burris	1981
	Mack Jones	1969		
New York	Charlie Neal	1962	Al Jackson	1962
Philadelphia	Tony Taylor	1960	Grant Jackson	1969
	Pancho Herrera	1960		
Pittsburgh	Curt Roberts	1954	Al McBean	1962
			Earl Francis	1962
St. Louis	Curt Flood	1958	Brooks Lawrence	1954
San Diego	Nate Colbert	1969	Juan Eichelberger	1981
	Ollie Brown	1969		
New York/San Francisco	Hank Thompson	1950	Ruben Gomez	1953

Note: Limited to franchises extant prior to 1977.

Dynamic Duos

1. **Babe Ruth and Lou Gehrig will always be indelibly linked. Many other dynamic duos are not nearly so well remembered, often because the significant connection between them has never before been highlighted. For instance: Two pitchers were voted into the Hall of Fame solely for their hill accomplishments. Each won more than 240 ML games. Both were born in the same year. Both spent most of their careers not only in the same league but also with the same team. Yet, they never hurled against one another, nor were they ever teammates. What's more, the younger of the two won his last ML game before the elder won his first. Impossible? Nope. Who is this apparently inseparable but in actuality very disparate duo of early-day mound greats?**
   - A) Their year of birth was 1871.
   - B) The elder split his two 20th century World Series decisions despite having a perfect 0.00 ERA in fall competition.
   - C) The younger debuted with his hometown Indianapolis NL team.
   - D) The younger won his last game in 1898 and the elder won his first in 1899.
   - E) They both spent most of their careers in a New York Giants uni.

2. **What two ex-AL stars were a sometimes mound duo for the 1945 Phils 13 years after each had paced the junior circuit in a major offensive department?**
   - A) One of the pair topped the AL in stolen bases in 1932.
   - B) When not pitching for the Phils in 1945, the other member of the pair often played 1B, his normal position.
   - C) The former stolen-base king also managed the Phils in 1945.
   - D) The pitcher–first sacker is in the Hall of Fame.
   - E) The 1945 Phils manager has the same initials as the first AL hurler subsequent to expansion to work enough innings solely in relief to qualify for an ERA crown.

3. **Name the first post-1876 teammates to finish 1-2 in a loop bat race.**
   - A) They played for the first pennant winner in a city that has not had a major league team in more than 100 years.
   - B) The number-one finisher is now recognized to be the first Triple Crown winner.
   - C) The team featured a Hall of Fame shortstop serving in his lone year as a manager.
   - D) The number-two finisher's first and last ML games came 32 years apart.
   - E) The number-one finisher's initials match those of the co-record-holder for the most consecutive hits.

4. **Who composed the first duo of teammates to win 20 games apiece in a season?**
   - A) Between them, they netted 64 of their pennant winner's 67 victories.
   - B) One of the pair that season had an .875 winning percentage, the 19th century high by a 20-game winner.
   - C) The other pair member was the first hurler to toss three no-no's.
   - D) They had the same first names as the pilot and the top winner on the 1957 Cards.
   - E) The hurler with the same first name as the 1957 Cards pilot also had the same first name and initials as the Astros reliever who led the NL in saves in 1969.

5. **Just four middle infielders in ML history have posted .300 career batting averages with 1,500 hits and not made the Hall of Fame. The four oddly enough formed two noted keystone duos. One duo comprised a man who won an AL batting title on the last day of a season and a man who was once a bat title runner-up to a .400 hitter. The other duo was the first keystone pair to play side by side for at least eight full seasons. Who are they?**

   A) The bat crown winner beat out Joe Vosmik.
   B) Vosmik played most of his career in the same city as the other keystone duo.
   C) One duo played together in the 1890s, and the other in the 1930s.
   D) The second sackers in the two duos were nicknamed Buddy and Cupid.
   E) Their shortstop sidekicks were called Cecil and Ed.

Highest Career BA, Middle Infielder, Non–Hall of Famer

RANK	NAME	YEARS	ABS	HITS	BA
1	Cecil Travis	1933–47	4914	1544	.314
2	Cupid Childs	1888–1901	5618	1720	.306
3	Buddy Myer	1925–41	7038	2131	.303
4	Ed McKean	1887–99	6890	2083	.30232
5	George Grantham	1922–34	4989	1508	.30226
6	Hardy Richardson	1879–92	5642	1688	.299
7	Del Pratt	1912–34	6826	1996	.292
8	Pete Runnels	1951–64	6373	1854	.291
9	Jack Glasscock	1879–95	7030	2040	.2902
10	Larry Doyle	1907–20	6509	1887	.2899

Note: Minimum 1,500 career hits; the leading casualty of this qualifier is Johnny Pesky (.307 with 1,455 hits). Grantham, Richardson, and Runnels were not pure middle infielders but played more games at one or both middle infield posts than anywhere else; Harvey Kuenn (.303), on the other hand, is excluded because he played more games in the outfield than at short.

6. **What great batting feat forever linked George Turbeville and Red Bullock?**

   A) The event occurred on May 24, 1936, at Shibe Park.
   B) The pair pitched for the A's that day against the Yankees.
   C) They were the victims of the first ML'er to slug two grand-slam homers in the same game.
   D) The man who victimized them set another AL record that day that still stands.
   E) Mark Whiten and Jim Bottomley are the NL coholders of the same record.

7. **Jim McCormick died before Solly Hemus was even born, but he and Solly are the only two men in history to share a most interesting accomplishment. What is it?**

   A) They're linked by something both did while in the NL.
   B) They're linked by something both did as managers.
   C) They're the only men to manage at least two full seasons in the NL and do this.
   D) The closest any AL manager has ever come to matching their achievement was John McGraw, who did the same thing for a season and a half.
   E) McCormick managed Cleveland in 1879–80 and part of the 1882 season but would have left Hemus as the only man to accomplish this feat had he managed in 1883.

8. **When they collected 267 RBI between them for a pennant winner, what duo became the first pair of NL teammates each to achieve 100 ribbies?**

    A)   That same year, no fewer than four teammates on a team in a rival ML collected 100 RBI apiece!

    B)   The two NL'ers played for the lone ML pennant winner managed by Bill Watkins.

    C)   Both are in the Hall of Fame.

    D)   Both hit lefty and had career BAs above .330.

    E)   Their dual 100-RBI seasons came with the 1887 Detroit Wolverines.

Pre-1893 Teammates Each with 100 RBI, Season

NAMES	TEAM	YEAR
Tip O'Neill (123), Curt Welch (108), Dave Foutz (108) & Charlie Comiskey (103)	StL, AA	1887
Sam Thompson (166) & Dan Brouthers (101)	Det, NL	1887
Pete Browning (118) & Chicken Wolf (102)	Lou, AA	1887
Roger Connor (130) & Danny Richardson (100)	NY, NL	1889
Harry Stovey (119) & Lou Bierbauer (105)	Phi, AA	1889
Dave Foutz (113) & Oyster Burns (100)	Bro, AA	1889
Tip O'Neill (110) & Charlie Comiskey (102)	StL, AA	1889
Jim O'Rourke (115) & Roger Connor (103)	NY, PL	1890
Duke Farrell (110), Hugh Duffy (110) & Dan Brouthers (109)	Bos, AA	1891

9. **What distinctive accomplishment that can never be duplicated did Spec Shea and Gene Bearden achieve?**

    A)   Their achievements came one year apart.

    B)   In 1949 it became impossible for anyone ever again to do what they did.

    C)   Shea was the first AL'er ever do to what he did.

    D)   In 1948, Bearden became the second and last AL'er to do what Shea had first done a year earlier.

    E)   Derek Jeter received the award in 1996 that ought to have been Bearden's 48 years earlier.

10. **In what way are Babe Herman and Frankie Hayes permanently linked?**

    A)   Their corresponding achievements came approximately four years apart.

    B)   Herman's feat came at Crosley Field and Hayes's at Shibe Park.

    C)   Hayes made Cleveland his victim in the first game of its type in AL history.

    D)   Bobby Doerr, in 1942, was the first to do what Hayes did in an All-Star Game.

    E)   Herman's feat came some six weeks after the first game of its type in ML history had been played, also at Crosley Field.

11. **Name the first 20th century keystone duo each to homer in double figures.**

   A)   Both are in the Hall of Fame.

   B)   The season they did it, another player established a new season home run record that lasted 34 years.

   C)   The first and third basemen in the duo's infield are also Hall of Famers.

   D)   The keystoners both homered in double figures 33 years after Bobby Lowe and Herman Long became the first pair of keystoners ever to do it.

   E)   The keystoners both had unusual first names, but the first and third sacker were named George and Freddy, respectively.

HERMAN C. LONG, Shortstop,
BOSTON, 1900.
(Copyrighted by E. Chickering, Boston.)

Herman Long, one-half of the first keystone duo each to homer in double figures. Long joined with second-base partner Bobby Lowe to produce 29 homers for Boston in 1894. Six years later, he became the first shortstop to win a home run crown.

First 10 Keystone Duos Each to Homer in Double Figures, Season

RANK	NAMES	TEAM	YEAR
1	Bobby Lowe (17) & Herman Long (12)	Bos, NL	1894
2	Rogers Hornsby (26) & Travis Jackson (14)	NY, NL	1927
3	Tony Cuccinello (12) & Glenn Wright (10)	Bro, NL	1932
4	Tony Lazzeri (14) & Frankie Crosetti (11)	NY, AL	1934
5	Frankie Crosetti (15) & Tony Lazzeri (14)	NY, AL	1936
6	Tony Lazzeri (14) & Frankie Crosetti (11)	NY, AL	1937
	Joe Cronin (18) & Boob McNair (12)	Bos, AL	1937
8	Joe Gordon (28) & Frankie Crosetti (10)	NY, AL	1939
	Joe Cronin (19) & Bobby Doerr (12)	Bos, AL	1939
10	Joe Cronin (24) & Bobby Doerr (22)	Bos, AL	1940

12. What dynamic duo holds the AL season record for the most wins by two teammates?

A) Between them, they won 64 games.

B) One of the duo won more than 200 games but lost more games than he won.

C) They were managed by Clark Griffith.

D) Their team lost the pennant on the last day of the season when one of the duo wild-pitched home the winning run in the game that decided the pennant.

E) Both had the same first name.

Most Wins, Season, Two Teammates (Post-1893)

RANK	NAMES	TEAM	YEAR	W
1	Amos Rusie (36) & Jouett Meekin (33)	NY, NL	1894	69
2	Joe McGinnity (35) & Christy Mathewson (33)	NY, NL	1904	68
3	Jack Chesbro (41) & Jack Powell (23)	NY, AL	1904	64
4	Cy Young (35) & Nig Cuppy (26)	Cle, NL	1895	61
	Joe McGinnity (31) & Christy Mathewson (30)	NY, NL	1903	61
6	Christy Mathewson (37) & Hooks Wiltse (23)	NY, NL	1908	60
7	Ed Walsh (40) & Doc White (18)	Chi, AL	1908	58
	Kid Nichols (32) & Jack Stivetts (26)	Bos, NL	1894	58
9	Kid Nichols (31) & Fred Klobedanz (26)	Bos, NL	1897	57
	Kid Nichols (31) & Ted Lewis (26)	Bos, NL	1898	57

13. What hill duo has the postexpansion AL season record for the most wins by a lefty-righty teammate tandem?

- A) They also nailed all four of their team's wins in the World Series that year.
- B) Their postexpansion AL teammate duo record of 48 wins was broken in 1990.
- C) Another lefty-righty duo had led the team to its last previous world title 23 years earlier.
- D) The lefty hit the only home run of his ML career in his first World Series plate appearance.
- E) The right-hander that year became the most recent 30-game winner.

Most Wins, Season, Two Teammates (Post-1960)

RANK	NAMES	TEAM	YEAR	W
1	Bob Welch (27) & Dave Stewart (22)	Oak, AL	1990	49
	Sandy Koufax (26) & Don Drysdale (23)	LA, NL	1965	49
3	Denny McLain (31) & Mickey Lolich (17)	Det, AL	1968	48
	Mike Cuellar (24) & Dave McNally (24)	Bal, AL	1970	48
5	La Marr Hoyt (24) & Richard Dotson (22)	Chi, AL	1983	46
6	Whitey Ford (24) & Jim Bouton (21)	NY, AL	1963	45
	Vida Blue (24) & Catfish Hunter (21)	Oak, AL	1971	45
	Mickey Lolich (25) & Joe Coleman (20)	Det, AL	1971	45
	Wilbur Wood (24) & Stan Bahnsen (21)	Chi, AL	1972	45
	Ron Guidry (25) & Ed Figueroa (20)	NY, AL	1978	45
	Steve Stone (25) & Scott McGregor (20)	Bal, AL	1980	45

14. Dirty Jack Doyle and Larry McLean were both Irish through and through, but they share another much more distinctive claim to fame. What is it?

- A) McLean made his mark at age 19 in his ML debut on April 26, 1901.
- B) Doyle's feat, which is much better known, came on June 7, 1892.
- C) McLean was not only the first man in AL history to do what he did successfully but also the first even to try to do it.
- D) Prior to Doyle, several players had tried unsuccessfully to do what he did.
- E) John Vander Wal currently excels at what they were first to do.

15. Tony Cloninger and Vic Raschi were both right-handers, and both were 20-game winners. What much more distinctive feat do they share?

- A) Cloninger's feat is more famous, but Raschi's is less likely to be surpassed.
- B) Cloninger fell one short of Harry Staley's all-time NL record on July 3, 1966, and Raschi put his name in the AL record book on August 4, 1953.
- C) Raschi's feat is made even more remarkable by the fact that he had no home runs in 1953.
- D) Exactly 14 percent of Raschi's career total of 50 RBI came in one game.
- E) Another Yankee has the AL mark for all players that Raschi owns for pitchers.

Most RBI, Game, Each Position

NAME	POS	TEAM	DATE	RBI
Mark Whiten	RF	StL, NL	September 7, 1993	12
Jim Bottomley	1B	StL, NL	September 16, 1924	12
Wilbert Robinson	C	Bal, NL	June 10, 1892	11
Tony Lazzeri	2B	NY, AL	May 24, 1936	11
Harry Staley	P	Bos, NL	June 1, 1893	10
Fred Lynn	CF	Bos, AL	June 18, 1975	10
Nomar Garciaparra	SS	Bos, AL	May 10, 1999	10
Heinie Zimmerman	3B	Chi, NL	June 11, 1911	9
Jim Tabor	3B	Bos, AL	July 4, 1939	9
Roy Howell	3B	Tor, AL	September 10, 1977	9
Johnny Rizzo	LF	Pit, NL	May 30, 1939	9
Chris James	LF	Cle, AL	May 6, 1991	9
Mike Greenwell	LF	Bos, AL	September 2, 1996	9

16. Harry Heilmann and Jeff Heath were the first two men in ML history to accomplish what feat?

A) Heilmann was with Cinci when he became the first man to scale this height.

B) Johnny Mize was the third man to do what they did.

C) The feat that Heilmann, Heath, and Mize achieved grew much more common after 1959, when a certain restriction was lifted.

D) Heath equaled Heilmann's feat in 1948, his first season in the NL.

E) Babe Ruth might have been the second man in history to scale this height if he had finished out the 1935 season with the Boston Braves.

17. Wade Boggs and Cal Ripken became a dynamic duo when they shared what unparalleled feat in common as minor leaguers?

A) The feat occurred in 1981.

B) Ripken was playing for Rochester at the time, and Boggs for Pawtucket.

C) Ripken played a lot of third base in the minors.

D) Ripken played an *awful* lot of third base at one point in 1981.

E) The third sackers who share the same unparalleled feat in the majors did it in 1920 in a game between the Boston Braves and Brooklyn.

Common Denominators

1. **The main link among Lefty Grove, Dizzy Dean, and Denny McLain is that they're the only 30-game winners since the end of the Deadball Era. Featured here are teams and players who share an equally distinctive connection. First off: the 1946 Indians, the 1954 Yankees, the 1958 Red Sox, and the 1953 Cardinals.**

    A) The 1946 St. Louis Browns also belong in this group of teams.
    B) So do the 1948 New York Giants.
    C) In 1954 Tom Alston joined the Cards.
    D) Pumpsie Green made the 1959 Red Sox the last major league team to do what the 1884 Toledo Blue Stockings had been the first team to do.
    E) Every major league team between 1885 and 1947 lacked an ingredient that the 1884 Toledo and the 1947 Brooklyn teams both possessed.

2. **Lee Richmond, Howard Ehmke, Ned Garver, Nolan Ryan, Scott Perry, and Matt Kilroy.**

    A) Ryan joined this club in 1974.
    B) Dave Fleming made a bid to join in 1992 before finishing with 17 wins.
    C) Jeff Tesreau fell just one win short of gaining membership in 1915.
    D) Garver joined the club in 1951.
    E) Richmond was the club's charter member.

20-Game Winners for Doormats

NAME	TEAM	YEAR	W–L
Lee Richmond	Wor, NL	1881	25–26
Hardie Henderson	Bal, AA	1885	25–35
Matt Kilroy	Bal, AA	1886	29–34
Mark Baldwin	Pit, AA	1891	22–28
Sadie McMahon	Bal, AA	1892	20–35
Noodles Hahn	Cin, NL	1901	22–19
Scott Perry	Phi, AL	1918	20–19
Howard Ehmke	Bos, AL	1923	20–17
Sloppy Thurston	Chi, AL	1924	20–14
Ned Garver	StL, AL	1951	20–12
Steve Carlton	Phi, NL	1972	27–10
Nolan Ryan	Cal, AL	1974	22–16

Note: Doormats are teams with the worst W–L record in their leagues. McMahon's win total is disputed; some sources credit him with only 19 wins.

3. Don Newcombe, Denny Galehouse, Doc White, Jim Palmer, Mike Torrez, and Christy Mathewson.
- A) Doc White was 18–12 on the morning of the day he joined this club.
- B) Galehouse made the club in his last ML start.
- C) White and Mathewson are the only two men to make the club in the same year.
- D) Ralph Branca was the first man to make this club for his work in relief.
- E) Mark Langston joined up in 1995.

4. Duffy Lewis, Forrest Cady, Del Gainor, and Olaf Henriksen.
- A) Lewis was the club's charter member.
- B) Lewis founded the club on July 14, 1914.
- C) The club only has four members—Lewis, Cady, Gainor, and Henriksen.
- D) All four made it for something they did with the Red Sox in the midteens.
- E) No new Red Sox players could possibly have joined this club after 1919.

5. Harvey Kuenn, George Kell, and Al Kaline share three key items in common apart from the fact that their last games begin with K. What are they?
- A) Right, they won batting crowns.
- B) True, they were with Detroit when they won their batting crowns.
- C) Carney Lansford also shares the third distinction they have in common.
- D) So do Alex Rodriguez and Edgar Martinez.
- E) Harry Heilmann shares all three distinctions they have in common.

6. Tommy Bond, Willie McGill, Jumbo McGinnis, and Larry McKeon.
- A) Bob Feller fell short in his bid to join this club in 1938.
- B) In 1971, Bert Blyleven came as close to gaining membership as anyone has in recent years.
- C) Bond made the club for work he did in the National Association.
- D) McKeon bid to make the club in 1884 and then made it in 1885.
- E) McGill is the club's youngest member—and that's going some!

7. Reb Russell, Cannonball Morris, Tom Browning, Alex Kellner, Kid Nichols, and Leon Viau.
- A) Jesse Duryea and Mickey Hughes are also members.
- B) Curt Davis fell one win short of membership.
- C) Irv Young joined in 1905.
- D) Gene Bearden joined in 1948.
- E) Browning was the most recent pitcher to earn membership.

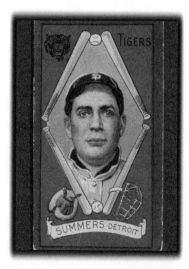

Ed Summers, the most recent Detroit Tiger to win 20 games as a frosh. His 24 wins in 1908 are also the AL mark for the most victories by a rookie who never again cracked the 20-win circle.

NAME	TEAM	YEAR	W–L
Tom Browning	Cin, NL	1985	20–9
Bob Grim	NY, AL	1954	20–6
Harvey Haddix	StL, NL	1953	20–9
Alex Kellner	Phi/KC/Oak, AL	1949	20–12
Gene Bearden	Cle, AL	1948	20–7
Larry Jansen	NY/SF, NL	1947	21–5
Dave Ferriss	Bos, AL	1945	21–10
Jim Turner	Bos/Mil/Atl, NL	1937	20–11
Lou Fette	Bos/Mil/Atl, NL	1937	20–10
Reb Russell	Chi, AL	1913	22–16
Larry Cheney	Chi, NL	1912	26–10
Pete Alexander	Phi, NL	1911	28–13
Ed Summers	Det, AL	1908	24–12
Henry Schmidt	Bro/LA, NL	1903	22–13
Sam Leever	Pit, NL	1899	21–23

Most Recent Rookie 20-Game Winner, Each Present Team

Note: None: Washington/Minnesota, AL, St. Louis/Baltimore, AL, and all expansion teams. Some authorities don't consider Leever or Nick Maddox (1908) rookies; if that is the case, Pittsburgh has never had a rookie 20-game winner.

8. Tim Raines, Mickey Mantle, Pete Rose, Willie Wilson, Willie McGee, and Terry Pendleton.

    A)   For many years Tommy Tucker was the club's only member.

    B)   Red Schoendienst narrowly missed earning membership in 1953.

    C)   Schoendienst's failed bid made Rose the first member from the NL.

    D)   Carlos Baerga could one day become a member.

    E)   So too could the 1996 NL MVP.

9. Ed Swartwood, Dan Brouthers, Chicken Wolf, Dave Orr, and Tommy Tucker.

    A)   Swartwood was the club's second member.

    B)   For years, Harry Stovey was considered a member, but he no longer is.

    C)   Orr died long before anyone realized he belonged in this club.

    D)   Brouthers is the only member in the Hall of Fame.

    E)   Pete Browning was the club's charter member.

10. Nap Lajoie, Ossie Vitt, Patsy Tebeau, Joe Gordon, and Lee Fohl.

    A)   Fohl is the only one to hold membership in two clubs for the same reason.

    B)   Tebeau was the club's charter member.

    C)   Al Lopez was also in the club until he was expelled in 1954.

    D)   The club's doors have been shut ever since Gordon joined in 1959.

    E)   Mike Hargrove can no longer ever become a member.

11. **Dale Alexander, Richie Ashburn, Larry Doyle, Edgar Martinez, and Tony Gwynn.**
    A) There are no 19th century players in the club.
    B) Doc Miller missed being the club's charter member only because he had one too many ABs.
    C) Doyle is the club's charter member.
    D) Alexander is the club's first AL member and also is its only present member who split the season that qualified him for membership between two teams.
    E) In 1996, Jim Eisenreich's BA qualified him, but he fell about 100 plate appearances short of eligibility for membership.

12. **Bill Melton, Nap Lajoie, Buck Freeman, Sam Crawford, and Jesse Barfield.**
    A) Sam Thompson attained membership in 1889.
    B) Ken Williams became a member in 1922.
    C) Tommy Leach was all that prevented Ralph Kiner's membership after Kiner's rookie year.
    D) The Kansas City Royals still have an empty seat at the table of this club.
    E) Wally Pipp is a member, and as a result, Babe Ruth is not.

First League HR Leader, Each Present Club

TEAM	BORN	NAME	HRS	YEAR
Boston-Milwaukee-Atlanta Braves	1876 (NL)	Charley Jones	9	1879
St. Louis Cardinals	1882 (AA)	Oscar Walker	7	1882
New York-San Francisco Giants	1883 (NL)	Buck Ewing	10	1883
Chicago Cubs	1876 (NL)	Ned Williamson	27	1884
Cincinnati Reds	1882 (AA)	Long John Reilly	11	1884
Philadelphia Phillies	1883 (NL)	Sam Thompson	20	1889
Philadelphia-Kansas City-Oakland A's	1901 (AL)	Nap Lajoie	14	1901
Pittsburgh Pirates	1882 (AA)	Tommy Leach	6	1902
Brooklyn-Los Angeles Dodgers	1884 (AA)	Jimmy Sheckard	9	1903
Boston Red Sox	1901 (AL)	Buck Freeman	13	1903
Detroit Tigers	1901 (AL)	Sam Crawford	7	1908
Cleveland Indians	1901 (AL)	Braggo Roth	7	1915
Baltimore-New York Yankees	1901 (AL)	Wally Pipp	12	1916
Milwaukee-St. Louis-Baltimore Orioles	1901 (AL)	Ken Williams	39	1922
Washington-Minnesota Twins	1901 (AL)	Roy Sievers	42	1957
Washington-Texas Rangers	1961 (AL)	Frank Howard	44	1968
Chicago White Sox	1901 (AL)	Bill Melton	33	1971
Seattle-Milwaukee Brewers	1969 (AL)	George Scott	36	1975
Los Angeles-California-Anaheim Angels	1961 (AL)	Bobby Grich	22	1981
New York Mets	1962 (NL)	Dave Kingman	37	1982
Toronto Blue Jays	1977 (AL)	Jesse Barfield	40	1986
Seattle Mariners	1977 (AL)	Ken Griffey Jr.	40	1994
Colorado Rockies	1993 (NL)	Dante Bichette	40	1995

Note: None to date: Kansas City, Florida, Arizona, and Tampa Bay. Roth hit three of his seven homers with Chicago, AL, before being traded to Cleveland.

13. Pete Alexander, Dizzy Dean, Jimmy Piersall, Jackie Robinson, and Ty Cobb.

- A) Christy Mathewson would seem a natural for this club but strangely is not a member.
- B) Nor are Cy Young and Walter Johnson members.
- C) But Jim Thorpe is a member.
- D) Babe Ruth is the club's most prolific member.
- E) Lou Gehrig is probably the club's most memorable member.

14. Waite Hoyt, Harry Heilmann, Ralph Kiner, Herb Score, George Kell, and Ron Fairly.

- A) Mike Shannon is also a member.
- B) Shannon's teammate, Tim McCarver, is an even more renowned member.
- C) Sandy Koufax was a member for a time.
- D) Jack Graney is the club's charter member.
- E) Kell and Al Kaline are both members and current club partners.

15. Willie Mays, Vic Power, Jim Kaat, Eddie Mathews, and Don Larsen.

- A) Kaat was the only club member still active in the majors in the 1980s.
- B) Johnny Roseboro is also a club member—as is Fred Stanley on the basis of his rookie year in 1969.
- C) Had Hank Aaron debuted with the Braves two years earlier, he, and not Mathews, would be a club member.
- D) Mathews is the club's charter member.
- E) Kaat is the club's representative from the original Washington Senators, while Toby Harrah is its representative from the expansion Senators.

16. Harry Barton, Pat Donahue, Paddy Livingston, Wickey McAvoy, and Joe Palmisano.

- A) Palmisano was the last man to gain membership.
- B) If it had been up to Lefty Grove, Palmisano would have lost his membership eligibility.
- C) Palmisano would have been happy to lose his eligibility.
- D) Pepper Martin was the reason Grove wanted Palmisano to lose his eligibility.
- E) The club's members all played the same position as Mickey Cochrane and Jack Lapp.

17. Tom Pagnozzi, Earnest Riles, Kurt Bevacqua, Keith Moreland, Kurt Abbott, and Lee Lacy.

- A) All are in the club for something they accomplished with NL teams.
- B) Dan Driessen was the first to do what they did, but he's not in the club.
- C) Prior to 1976 the club couldn't possibly have existed.
- D) The club took in no new members in 1995 or 1996.
- E) Pagnozzi and Abbott are the only aforementioned club members who might one day lose their membership.

18. Rube Marquard, Dickie Kerr, Herb Pennock, Lon Warneke, Mike Caldwell, Hugh Casey, and Whitey Ford.

- A) Ford is the only man to earn membership to this club on two separate occasions.
- B) Warneke is perhaps the club's most distinguished member.
- C) Had Walter Johnson been removed when he tired in the 1925 World Series finale, he might have become a member.
- D) Tim Wakefield in 1992 became the most recent hurler to earn membership in the LCS branch of this club.
- E) Chad Ogea in 1997 became this esteemed club's newest member.

2-0 Pitchers with World Series Losers

NAME	TEAM	YEAR	IP	ERA
Rube Marquard	NY, NL	1911	18	0.50
Dickie Kerr	Chi, AL	1919	19	1.42
Herb Pennock	NY, AL	1926	22	1.23
Lon Warneke	Chi, NL	1935	16.2	0.54
Hugh Casey	Bro, NL	1947	10.1	0.87
Whitey Ford	NY, AL	1955	17	2.12
Whitey Ford	NY, AL	1960	18	0.00
Jim Bouton	NY, AL	1964	17.1	1.56
Luis Tiant	Bos, AL	1975	25	3.60
Mike Caldwell	Mil, AL	1982	17.2	2.04
Bruce Hurst	Bos, AL	1986	23	1.96
Chad Ogea	Cle, AL	1997	11.2	1.54

Note: Warneke is the only pitcher to win two games for a losing team in a World Series that went fewer than seven games.

19. **The 1903 Boston Pilgrims, 1910 Philadelphia A's, 1915 Boston Red Sox, 1920 Cleveland Indians, and 1921 New York Giants.**
    A) Many teams have earned membership to this club since 1921.
    B) The 1992 Blue Jays belong here, as do the 1981 Dodgers.
    C) The 1886 St. Louis Browns were this club's first team members.
    D) Cleveland began each of its five World Series appearances with the same result but earned membership only in 1920 and 1948.
    E) The Yankees were admitted to the club in 1996.

20. **The 1909 Detroit Tigers, 1926 New York Yankees, 1934 Detroit Tigers, 1945 Chicago Cubs, and 1952 Brooklyn Dodgers.**
    A) The 1909 Tigers are the club's charter member.
    B) The 1986 BoSox own one of the criteria for membership but lack the second.
    C) The 1987 Twins escaped becoming members.
    D) The 1957–58 New York Yankees and Milwaukee Braves took turns making each other members.
    E) The 1991 Twins are the most recent team even to have an opportunity to join this club.

21. **Sandy Koufax, Marty Pattin, Mace Brown, Brickyard Kennedy, and Nap Rucker.**
    A) Kennedy was the first to achieve membership in this club in the 20th century.
    B) Paul Lindblad became one of the club's most obscure members in 1978.
    C) Rucker earned entry in 1916.
    D) Bill Bevens is in some ways the club's most distinguished member.
    E) Koufax is the only hurler who earned membership after winning 20 games during the regular season.

22. Spec Shea, Gene Bearden, Johnny Beazley, Livan Hernandez, Jeff Tesreau, and Wilcy Moore.

    A)   King Cole failed in his bid to join the club on October 22, 1910.

    B)   Hugh Bedient joined on October 12, 1912.

    C)   Les Straker was unsuccessful in two bids to join the club in 1987.

    D)   Gene Bearden joined the club for his work in Game Three of the 1948 World Series.

    E)   Babe Adams is the club's charter member, and Hernandez and Jaret Wright are its most recent additions.

23. Ellis Kinder, Roger Wolff, Curt Davis, Ray Kremer, and George McConnell.

    A)   Stoney McGlynn might have become a member if he'd played for a better team in 1907.

    B)   Kinder became a member in 1949.

    C)   Kremer is the club's most prolific member.

    D)   Connie Marrero was eminently eligible for membership but twice fell nine wins short of making it.

    E)   There were no club members in the 19th century, but Bill Hutchison came the closest to meeting the standards for eligibility.

24. Dick Barrett, George Cobb, Pete Dowling, Gordon Rhodes, and Doyle Alexander.

    A)   Cobb belongs to another select club with a similar criterion for membership.

    B)   Larry McKeon prevented Fleury Sullivan from becoming a member.

    C)   Dowling is the only man to pitch for two different teams the year he became a member.

    D)   Alexander, like most of this club's members, was aided in his bid for membership by the fact that he toiled for a doormat.

    E)   Jim Abbott lost potential membership for his work in the 1996 season when he returned to the majors in 1998.

25. John Ewing, Henry Schmidt, Jocko Flynn, Toad Ramsey, Henry Boyle, Charlie Ferguson, Bill Sweeney, and Harry Salisbury.

    A)   Flynn's credentials for membership are disputed by some.

    B)   Sweeney had double the necessary minimum number for entry into this club.

    C)   Ferguson was the club's only member to achieve unequivocal membership the year his name was put up for it.

    D)   Hank O'Day is also a club member for his work with the 1890 New York Players League entry.

    E)   Sandy Koufax also became a member by choice.

26. Lou Fette, Jesse Duryea, Alex Kellner, Irv Young, Bob Grim, Tom Vickery, Tom Browning, and King Cole.

    A)   Duryea is the club's most prodigious member.

    B)   A teammate of Fette's, Jim Turner, is also a member.

    C)   In 1988, Browning nearly lost his qualification for membership, but now it's extremely doubtful he ever will.

    D)   Jocko Flynn is also a member of this club.

    E)   Gene Bearden became a member in 1948, although he couldn't know it then.

Most Wins, 20-Game Winner, Rookie Year Only

RANK	NAME	TEAM	YEAR	WINS
1	Jesse Duryea	Cin, AA	1889	32
2	George Derby	Det, NL	1881	29
3	Ed Daily	Phi, NL	1885	26
4	Gus Krock	Chi, NL	1888	25
	Mickey Hughes	Bro, AA	1888	25
6	Ed Summers	Det, AL	1908	24
	Tom Vickery	Phi, NL	1890	24
8	Bill Wise	Was, UA	1884	23
	Jocko Flynn	Chi, NL	1886	23
	Roscoe Miller	Det, NL	1901	23
	George McQuillan	Phi, NL	1908	23

Premier Pilots

1. **Joe McCarthy holds a swarm of managerial records. Among them is the mark for piloting the most games of anyone who was never a big league player. Prior to McCarthy, the record belonged to Frank Selee. But while many authorities credit Selee with being the first man to serve as a major league pilot for 10 full seasons without ever having played in the majors himself, the distinction belongs to another man. Who actually was the first to do it?**

   A) As a rookie skipper at age 34, he guided his hometown team to a near pennant only to see it disband at the end of the season.
   B) In his second pilot's job, he worked under Henry Lucas.
   C) He is the only man in ML history to skipper three different Ohio-based teams.
   D) His trademark item was his flaming red beard.
   E) He and the Milwaukee first sacker who paced the AL in both homers and RBI in 1975 share the same initials.

	Most Games, Manager Who Was Never a ML Player		
RANK	**NAME**	**YEARS**	**GAMES**
1	Joe McCarthy	1926–50	3487
2	Earl Weaver	1968–86	2541
3	John McNamara	1969–96	2417
4	Frank Selee	1890–1905	2180
5	Jim Leyland	1986–	2039
6	Dave Bristol	1966–80	1424
7	Gus Schmelz	1884–97	1357
8	Danny Ozark	1973–84	1161
9	Jim Mutrie	1883–91	1114
10	Al Buckenberger	1889–1904	1043

2. **Among men at the reins for at least 300 ML games, roughly equivalent to two full seasons, who owns the highest winning percentage (.521, 174–160) without ever having piloted a first division team?**

   A) He made the Hall of Fame as a player.
   B) He was later an executive with the Red Sox.
   C) He managed a team with which he had previously played in two World Series.
   D) He succeeded another Hall of Fame second sacker as a pilot in 1924.
   E) Red Faber pitched for him five years after both Faber and he played on their last pennant winner.

3. Whose .595 (179–122) winning percentage is the highest of anyone at the reins of a big league team or teams for 300 games without ever winning a pennant?

A) Ossie Vitt is second to him with a .570 winning percentage.

B) He won a loop home run crown the season he first became a manager.

C) With 42 games left in the season, he replaced Arthur Irwin at the reins of a team that was 17 games below .500 and spurred it to a 28–14 finishing kick.

D) He holds the all-time rookie record for the most walks collected.

E) In 1894 he became the last man to score 100 runs in fewer than 100 games when he posted 103 tallies for Washington in just 99 contests.

Managers with the Highest Winning Percentage and No Pennants (Minimum 300 Games)

RANK	NAME	YEARS	W–L	PCT.
1	Bill Joyce	1896–98	179–122	.595
2	Ossie Vitt	1938–40	262–198	.570
3	Monte Ward	1880/84/90–94	412–320	.563
4	Patsy Tebeau	1890–1900	726–583	.555
5	Buck Ewing	1890/95–1900	489–395	.553
6	Walter Johnson	1929–35	529–432	.5504
7	Nap Lajoie	1905–09	377–309	.5496
8	Bill Shettsline	1898–1902	367–303	.548
9	George Gibson	1920–22/25/32–34	413–344	.546
10	Eddie Kasko	1970–73	345–295	.539

Note: Percentage carried out to four decimal points where ties would otherwise exist.

4. Bill Joyce's record as a manager becomes all the more impressive when it's noted that he also leads all pilots who were primarily third basemen as players in career winning percentage. Only 11 ex–third basemen were successful enough as pilots to do better than break even in as many as 300 games. Of the 11, just 4 collected 1,000 wins and posted a .500+ record. Three of them are Braves guru Bobby Cox and Hall of Famers John McGraw and Bill McKechnie. Who is the fourth?

A) He departed with 1,008 wins and a .509 winning percentage.

B) He debuted as a player with the 1925 Reds and finished with the 1933 Giants.

C) He also played pro football in the 1920s with the Chicago Staleys.

D) He died of a heart attack while at the helm of the 1966 Tigers.

E) He was the first pilot since Bill McGunnigle to win back-to-back pennants with Brooklyn.

.500+ Winning Percentage as Manager, Former Third Basemen (Minimum 300 Games)

RANK	NAME	GAMES	W–L	PCT.
1	Bill Joyce	316	179–122	.595
2	John McGraw	4769	2763–1948	.586
3	Ossie Vitt	462	262–198	.570
4	Bobby Cox	2565	1418–1145	.553
5	Jimmy Collins	842	455–376	.548
6	Pie Traynor	868	457–406	.530
7	Bill McKechnie	3647	1896–1723	.524
8	Billy Hitchcock	535	274–261	.512
9	Chuck Dressen	1990	1008–973	.509
10	Don Zimmer	1744	885–858	.508
11	Pinky Higgins	1119	560–556	.502

5. What pitcher labored six years in the majors under six different managers, including five future Hall of Famers and Hank O'Day, who arguably should also be in the Hall?

A) In 1913, his rookie year, he was 13–5 for the Cubs with a stellar 2.31 ERA.

B) He spent five seasons with the Cubs and his finale with the Cardinals.

C) His HOF pilots were Frank Chance, Johnny Evers, Roger Bresnahan, Joe Tinker, and Miller Huggins.

D) His initials are the same as those of the record holder for the most consecutive games played prior to 1893.

E) His last name and that of the White Sox top winner in the 1950s are pronounced the same but spelled differently.

6. Who finished the season as the manager of the first club in history to post a winning percentage below .200 on a schedule of at least 100 games and then piloted the same club all of the following year when it played .667 ball?

A) He owns the lowest career winning percentage of any 19th century manager who served at least five full seasons as a helmsman.

B) He managed the first Detroit ML club to finish in the basement.

C) He piloted the only ML team that was incontrovertibly proved to have dumped a pennant race.

D) He skippered the first team to vault from the cellar to a pennant.

E) He and the most recent man to pilot a Boston team that won 100 games in a season share the same initials.

Managers with the Lowest Career Winning Percentage (Minimum 800 Games)

RANK	NAME	YEARS	W–L	PCT.
1	Preston Gomez	1969–72/74–75/80	346–529	.395
2	Jimmie Wilson	1934–38/41–44	493–735	.401
3	Jack Chapman	1876–78/82–85/89–92	350–501	.411
4	Harry Craft	1957–59/61–64	360–485	.426
5	Dan Howley	1927–32	397–524	.431
6	Del Crandall	1972–75/83–84	364–469	.437
7	Patsy Donovan	1897/99/1901–04/06–08/10–11	684–879	.4378
8	Rene Lachemann	1981–84/93–96	428–549	.4381
9	Billy Barnie	1883–94/97–98	632–810	.4383
10	Tom Loftus	1884/88–91/1900–03	454–580	.439

5. McClelian.
6. Proesser.
7. Keas.
8. Loftus, Mgr.

JOSEPH HALL. Photo., Brooklyn, N.Y.

9. Faatz, Capt.
10. Howe.
11. Zimmer.
12. Albert.

CLEVELAND BALL CLUB, 1888.

Manager Tom Loftus and his 1888 Cleveland Blues. Loftus was both Hoss Radbourn's and Ed Delahanty's last manager in the majors. He nevertheless posted one of the lowest career winning percentages of anyone who acted as a major league pilot in 1,000 or more games.

7. **Name the only full-term ML manager in 1889 who jumped to the Players League the following year.**
   A) His club was the preseason favorite for the PL flag.
   B) Only in 1894, his last season as a pilot, did he lead a team that finished below .500.
   C) He later owned a major league team based in the same city where he managed in 1890.
   D) He and Ralph Houk are the only two men to pilot a major league pennant winner in each of their first four full seasons as a manager.
   E) His nicknames were "Commie" and "The Old Roman."

8. **Who is the only pilot to win 100 games two years in a row without ever leading a pennant winner?**
   A) He never played in the majors.
   B) His most recent ML dugout job came with the 1984 Giants.
   C) He won three consecutive division titles.
   D) His first 100-game winner lost the LCS to the most recent NL team to win two consecutive World Series.
   E) He is the only ML pilot whose last name is that of a U.S. mountain range.

Managers Winning 100 Games in a Season but Never a Pennant

NAME	TEAM	YEAR	WINS
Bob Scheffing	Det, AL	1961	101
Danny Ozark	Phi, NL	1976	101
Danny Ozark	Phi, NL	1977	101
Dusty Baker	SF, NL	1993	103
Larry Dierker	Hou, NL	1998	100

Note: Baker and Dierker are active managers and may yet win one.

9. **Many pilots have lost 100 games more than once, but just one was at the helm of teams in two different major leagues that each tasted defeat 100 times. Name him.**
   A) He lost 111 games in his first year as an AL helmsman and 104 in his first year as a National League skipper.
   B) He narrowly missed winning three consecutive pennants in his last three seasons as a helmsman.
   C) His .352 BA as a rookie is the highest frosh BA by anyone who later managed a World Championship team.
   D) Roy Hartsfield is the most recent man to pilot three straight cellar finishers in the AL; our man held the same distinction among NL managers until Preston Gomez superseded him in 1971.
   E) He and Walter Alston are the only managers who both beat and lost to the Yankees in a seven-game World Series.

10. **Who is the only man to pilot teams in four different major leagues?**
    A) He played only nine ML games, the last with the 1883 St. Louis Browns.
    B) He replaced Jimmy Williams at the helm of the Cleveland Blues in the middle of the 1888 season.
    C) He had Cincinnati at the top of the NL on July 4 in 1890.
    D) He was Ed Delahanty's last manager in the bigs.
    E) His initials are the same as those of the most recent pilot to win two World Championships with the same NL team.

11. **Name the only member of the A's $100,000 infield who never managed in the majors.**

    A)   None of the game's most famous infield quartet ever won a pennant, but the shortstop piloted a second-place club in his only year as a helmsman.

    B)   The second baseman is the only man to pilot two consecutive second-division finishers that played .500+ ball in his only two full seasons as a helmsman.

    C)   The only member of the quartet to play on World Championship teams in three different cities piloted the cellar-dwelling Phillies in 1927, his only season as a big league manager.

    D)   The only nonmanager of the four is also the only one of the four to play on a pennant winner in his final season.

    E)   The only nonmanager of the four is the lone third baseman active prior to 1920 who made the Hall of Fame solely on the basis of his playing credentials.

12. **Who was the only playing member of the 1927 Yankees to manage in the majors?**

    A)   He was also the only member whose service with the Yankees was long enough to reach back to the days when Bill Donovan piloted them.

    B)   The 1927 season was his last as a player.

    C)   His four 20-win seasons lead all Yankees pitchers not in the Hall of Fame.

    D)   He preceded Joe McCarthy as the Yankees skipper.

    E)   He and the man who piloted the first Brooklyn Dodgers team to participate in a best-of-seven World Series that went the full seven games share the same initials.

13. **What gardener was the first man to play under arguably the two most famous managers in history, John McGraw and Connie Mack?**

    A)   He joined the Orioles early in the 1899 season, McGraw's first as a helmsman, and later played on Mack's 1901 A's.

    B)   A lawyer after his playing days were over, he was instrumental in organizing an early players' union.

    C)   He holds the 20th century record for the most stolen bases (44) by a player in his final ML season.

    D)   He led the AL in runs scored in 1902.

    E)   He and the most recent 40-game winner to manage at least one full season in the majors share the same initials and have very similar names.

14. **Who is the only preexpansion manager to win four pennants in the 20th century and not make the Hall of Fame?**

    A)   He led the NL in triples in 1919.

    B)   His first and last flag winners came just seven years apart.

    C)   He played on flag winners under both John McGraw and Rogers Hornsby.

    D)   He piloted the winner of the last World Series to be played entirely in the same park.

    E)   His last postseason game as a pilot was also the last postseason game played in Braves Field.

Most Pennants Won in the 20th Century

RANK	NAME	YEARS	PENNANTS
1	Casey Stengel	25	10
2	John McGraw	33	9
3	Connie Mack	53	8
4	Walter Alston	23	7
5	Miller Huggins	17	6
	Sparky Anderson	26	6
7	Frank Chance	11	4
	Billy Southworth	13	4
	Bobby Cox	17	4
	Earl Weaver	17	4
	Fred Clarke	19	4
	Dick Williams	21	4
	Tom Lasorda	21	4
	Bill McKechnie	25	4

15. Since Babe Ruth joined the Yankees in 1920, who is the only Bombers skipper who never sat in the home-team dugout in a regular season game at Yankee Stadium?

A) Although he never occupied the visitors' dugout at Yankee Stadium as a pilot either, he occupied it one fall as a player.

B) He piloted a division winner in his first year as a helmsman but never again came as close to managing a World Series entrant.

C) His .519 career winning percentage is currently the best of any man who managed 10 seasons in the majors without ever handling a pennant winner.

D) At one point in his managerial career, he piloted the same team for which he played in his lone World Series.

E) He and Billy Martin are the only two men since 1923 to pilot the Yankees at a home park other than Yankee Stadium.

16. Name the only man who twice won a World Championship in his first year at the helm of a team.

A) Just three times in his 29 seasons as a manager did he skipper a team that finished higher than third place.

B) In his final season as a pilot, his 1956 Tigers tied the AL record for the top winning percentage (.532) by a second-division team in an eight-club league.

C) Pat Moran is the only other manager to win a pennant in his first year with two different clubs, but Moran won a World Championship with only one of them—Cincinnati in 1919.

D) He's in the Hall of Fame as a manager despite winning just one pennant in his last 27 seasons as a big league helmsman.

E) Nicknamed "The Boy Wonder," he won a World Championship in his rookie year as a pilot and his second one 23 years later.

17. **Who was the first man to see his former charges win a pennant under his replacement after he was relieved of his team's managerial reins during the season?**

   A) A player-manager, he continued to play second base for his former club after he was removed as its skipper.

   B) He led the NL in RBI the season he was removed in midstream.

   C) His name is not Rogers Hornsby—his feat actually occurred some 30 years before Hornsby made his big league debut.

   D) In 1888 he set a record for the lowest season BA by an infielder or outfielder with 300 at bats when he hit .142 while splitting the season between Boston (NL) and Brooklyn (AA).

   E) Nicknamed "Black Jack," he was replaced as Boston's skipper in 1883 by a man nicknamed "Honest John."

Lowest Season BA by an Infielder or Outfielder (Minimum 300 ABs)

RANK	NAME	TEAM	YEAR	POS.	AB	HITS	BA
1	Jack Burdock	Bos/NL, Bro/AA	1888	2B	325	46	.1415
2	Sam Crane	Det/StL, NL	1886	2B	301	46	.1528
3	Joe Gerhardt	NY, NL	1885	2B	399	62	.1554
4	Jim Canavan	Chi, NL	1892	2B	439	73	.1663
5	Dave Roberts	SD, NL	1974	3B	318	53	.1666
6	Charlie Bastian	Phi, NL	1885	SS	389	65	.1671
7	Willie Kuehne	Lou/StL/Cin, NL	1892	3B	339	57	.1681
8	Juice Latham	Lou, AA	1884	1B	308	52	.1688
9	George McBride	StL, NL	1906	SS	313	53	.1693
10	Ben Conroy	Phi, AA	1890	SS	404	69	.1708

Note: Conroy's .1708 BA barely made the list. Deron Johnson hit .1709 in 1974 (60 for 351), and George Scott hit .1714 in 1968 (60 for 350). Infielders and outfielders who also pitched at least 100 innings that same season are excluded.

18. **Casey Stengel managed without distinction for years before he took over the Yankees and was acclaimed a genius. Who is the only man to play for him both before and after he became a genius?**

   A) He fanned just 20 times in 774 career at bats.

   B) In 1947 he hit .346, had 18 RBI, and struck out only once.

   C) As a rookie in 1942, he was 4–7 in 40 hill appearances under Stengel.

   D) In 1952, again under Stengel, he had three pinch hits and 11 wins.

   E) He won the opener of the 1948 World Series, 1–0.

19. **Who was the only man Connie Mack managed for a full season with two different ML teams?**

   A) He played on Connie's first World Series entry in 1905.

   B) He and Harry Davis were teammates for all of the 1905 season, but Davis had previously played only part of a season under Mack when Mack piloted Pittsburgh.

   C) He was Connie's regular shortstop in 1895.

   D) His .189 BA in 1904 is the all-time season low by a player with 500 ABs.

   E) He and the third baseman on Mack's first World Series entrant had the same last name but were not related.

20. **Just 1 of the 28 men at the controls of ML teams when the game's longest strike ended in 1995 at that time held an all-time season record in either a batting or pitching department for a franchise in existence since 1901. He has since lost that distinction. Who is he?**

    A) After his first two seasons in the majors, he was 7-for-18 as a pinch hitter, but he then went just 11-for-62 in pinch roles over the remainder of his career.

    B) His .323 BA as a rookie was a personal high and brought him his loop's top frosh honor.

    C) In 1978 he led the AL with 107 walks even though he hit just .251.

    D) At the beginning of the 1995 season, he was at the helm of the same club for which he set an all-time season record in 1980.

    E) His franchise record fell in 1996 to Jim Thome.

21. **Tommy Lasorda is the most recent former pitcher to pilot a flag winner—the 1988 Dodgers—but even though Lasorda played with the Dodgers, he never won a game for them. Name the only three 20th century managers who won pennants with teams for which they also won at least one game as a pitcher.**

    A) One is the only pitcher player-manager to win a flag in the 20th century.

    B) The other two won flags for NL clubs after World War II.

    C) The second man to do it won his final ML game for the first Mound City pennant winner in this century.

    D) The third man to do it won his final ML game for the team that seemed certain to be the first Phillies flag winner since 1950.

    E) One of the three managed in the majors in 1901, one managed in the first year after World War II, and the third managed as late as 1996.

22. **Commencing with 1884, the first season that two ML winners played a postseason clash to completion, who was the first man to pilot three different franchises in postseason play?**

    A) Grady Hatton was a rookie third sacker on the last ML team he managed.

    B) He was the last ex–Federal League pilot to skipper a major league team.

    C) He is in the Hall of Fame.

    D) Some authorities think he should also be credited with at least being the copilot of yet a fourth different franchise to make it into a World Series—Cleveland in 1948.

    E) His first World Championship came in 1925, and his last in 1940.

Most Managerial Wins, Career

RANK	NAME	YEARS	WINS
1	Connie Mack	53	3731
2	John McGraw	33	2763
3	Sparky Anderson	26	2194
4	Bucky Harris	29	2157
5	Joe McCarthy	24	2125
6	Walter Alston	23	2040
7	Leo Durocher	24	2008
8	Casey Stengel	25	1905
9	Gene Mauch	26	1902
10	Bill McKechnie	25	1896

Most Managerial Losses, Career

RANK	NAME	YEARS	LOSSES
1	Connie Mack	53	3948
2	Bucky Harris	29	2218
3	Gene Mauch	26	2037
4	John McGraw	33	1948
5	Casey Stengel	25	1842
6	Sparky Anderson	26	1834
7	Leo Durocher	24	1709
8	Walter Alston	23	1613
9	Jimmy Dykes	21	1541
10	Ralph Houk	20	1531

Men in Blue

1. **Not long ago, most major league umpires began their baseball careers as players. At least it doesn't seem so long ago, and yet it actually is a while back. Name the only big league umpire whose playing career was both long enough and recent enough to enable him to earn a major league pension as a player.**

    A)   His last season as a National League umpire was 1973.

    B)   Twelve years before he debuted as a man in blue, he won 18 games as a rookie.

    C)   His first season as a National League umpire was 1957.

    D)   He was on the 1946 world champs but saw no action in the Series.

    E)   He has the same initials as the first sacker on the first Pittsburgh pennant winner who also later became a National League umpire.

2. **Who was the first former player to ump in the majors for at least 20 years?**

    A)   He wore a rug.

    B)   He joined the NL umpiring staff in 1891 and remained in blue until 1924.

    C)   In 1884 he became the first Canadian-born hurler to enjoy a 20-win season in the majors when he bagged 32 victories for Baltimore of the AA.

    D)   He and the 1947 NL MVP share the same initials and first name.

    E)   He worked the bases in the famous "Merkle" game.

3. **The only man to pitch in a 19th century World Series game and ump in a 20th century World Series game is linked forever historically to the first former player to ump in the majors for 20 years or longer. Who is he?**

    A)   He faced the Brooklyn Bridegrooms in World Series action.

    B)   He and Tony Mullane accounted for all of Toledo's wins in his rookie season.

    C)   He won 22 games for New York in the Players League in his big league finale.

    D)   He managed the Cubs the last year Tinker and Evers were their keystone combo.

    E)   He worked the plate in the famous "Merkle" game.

4. **When he umped 2,541 consecutive ML games over a 16-and-a-half-year stretch, he set an all-time endurance record for men in blue. Can you name him?**

    A)   He began his umpiring career in the Tri-State League in 1913 at age 17.

    B)   He joined the AL staff in 1925 and remained a junior loop arbiter until 1954.

    C)   He and the Browns regular left fielder in 1929 share the same last name.

    D)   He and the holder of the all-time record for the most ML games umpired share the same first name.

    E)   Prior to Nester Chylak he was the most recent AL umpire to make the Hall of Fame.

5. **Bill Klem worked a record five consecutive World Series between 1911 and 1915. No other umpire has ever appeared in more than two straight World Series. The first man in blue to officiate two fall classics in a row worked the 1907–08 Cubs-Tigers battles. Who is he?**
   - A) He debuted as an arbiter in the Players League in 1890 and worked only one year (1892) as a regular NL umpire before joining the AL staff in 1901.
   - B) In 1890 he publicly proclaimed he'd heard hearing- and speech-impaired outfielder Dummy Hoy speak during a tense moment in a Players League game.
   - C) He was the ump who made a famous decision to stop a game in 1892 because the sun was too bright.
   - D) His initials are the same as those of the Dodgers outfielder in 1989 who had 12 home runs but just 25 RBI and a .183 BA in 108 games.
   - E) He and the left fielder on the only Kansas City team to win a World Series have the same last name.

6. **Who was the only member of the 1927 Yankees to ump a World Series game?**
   - A) He worked the last World Series to be played entirely in one park.
   - B) Bill McKinley replaced him as an AL umpire in 1946.
   - C) His 102nd and final career hill win came with the 1933 Red Sox.
   - D) He topped the AL in wins with 24 in 1928.
   - E) His initials and first name are the same as those of the pre-1893 record holder for the most consecutive ML games played.

7. **After being nearly banned from the game for slugging an umpire, what one-time NL batting champ later himself became a man in blue?**
   - A) He was suspended for decking umpire Bill Finneran in 1911.
   - B) His suspension probably cost him the 1911 NL RBI crown.
   - C) He won two legs of a Triple Crown in 1910 when he led the NL in batting and RBI.
   - D) An epileptic, he died just a few months after he was hired as a National League arbiter in 1928.
   - E) His 1,176 career RBI are the most of any Deadball Era player who's not in the Hall of Fame.

8. **What umpire helped Babe Ruth become the first man to hit three home runs in a World Series game when he gave the Bambino what amounted to an extra strike?**
   - A) He ruled that Ruth had been victimized by a quick pitch with two strikes and refused to ring him up on a called third.
   - B) Bill Sherdel was the Cards hurler who quick-pitched the Babe in the 1928 Series.
   - C) The ump's coda in his 17-year NL career was the finale of the 1936 Series.
   - D) His initials are the same as those of the Cubs hurler who tossed a one-hitter in the 1945 Series.
   - E) He and the game's all-time leading winner share the same first name.

9. **What pitcher did plate umpire Harry Wendelstedt put in the record book when he refused to give Giants catcher Dick Dietz his base after Dietz was hit by a pitch?**
   - A) The game took place in Dodger Stadium.
   - B) The game occurred in 1968.
   - C) Wendelstedt's ruling cost the Giants a run.
   - D) The run the Giants lost proved to be very significant and not just in the outcome of the game.
   - E) The pitcher lost his spot in the record book to Orel Hershiser in 1988.

10. **Who is the only man to ump a World Series game and coach a Stanley Cup champ?**
    A)   He coached the 1938 Blackhawks, the last Chicago Stanley Cup champion prior to expansion.
    B)   In 1937 he umped in his first World Series.
    C)   He was a member of the NL umpiring staff from 1933 to 1954.
    D)   His initials are the same as those of one of the coholders of the record for the most errors in a season (122).
    E)   He has the same last name as the Cubs rookie second sacker who teamed with Joey Amalfitano to replace the ill-fated Ken Hubbs in 1964.

11. **Name the first umpire to work a big league game wearing specs.**
    A)   He first wore cheaters in an AL game on April 18, 1956.
    B)   He umped his first game in the AL in 1938 some six years after he pitched his last game in the majors.
    C)   He was rewarded with his last ML win after working a record 17 innings in relief against Cleveland.
    D)   All 171 of his career wins came in the same AL uniform.
    E)   He was 12–2 with the 1929 World Champs.

12. **What NL umpire made his big league debut as a pitcher, finished his playing career as a catcher, and worked as a college football coach in the off-season?**
    A)   He coached Bo McMillan.
    B)   He joined the NL umpiring staff in 1917 and remained until 1939.
    C)   He tutored grid squads at Texas A&M, Carlisle, and Bucknell, among other institutions.
    D)   He gained most of his renown for coaching the Centre College team that upset Harvard 6–0 in 1921.
    E)   He and the only man to hit into an unassisted triple play in a postseason game share the same initials.

13. **Who played on the losing side in arguably the most ignominious World Series sweep ever and later umped in arguably the most shocking World Series sweep ever?**
    A)   He was 2–1 in three World Series starts.
    B)   His two Series appearances as a player came four years apart and both saw him pitch on the losing side.
    C)   His lone Series as an umpire came 19 years after he last pitched in a fall classic.
    D)   His first taste of Series action came in Babe Ruth's last fall appearance.
    E)   He was nicknamed "The Arkansas Hummingbird."

14. **Whose hiring as a National League umpire in 1922 did John McGraw violently protest because he'd had a vicious fight with McGraw during his playing days?**
    A)   He battled McGraw in 1906.
    B)   He was a Phils rookie infielder at the time he fought with McGraw.
    C)   He died at the beginning of the 1923 season while still a member of the NL's officiating crew.
    D)   His real first name was Leopold, but he preferred to be called Paul.
    E)   His initials are the same as those of the Detroit outfielder whose two-run homer in Game Three of the 1987 ALCS averted a sweep.

15. Who became the first umpire to eject a pitcher expressly for throwing a spitball when he tossed Browns hurler Nels Potter out of a game in 1944?

  A) He had 20/10 vision, the best of any man ever to be a major league arbiter.
  B) Ironically, his career was interrupted in 1951 by eye problems.
  C) He was the most physically imposing umpire of his day.
  D) He was elected to the Hall of Fame in 1976, a year prior to his death.
  E) He had previously been enshrined in the Pro Football Hall of Fame.

16. What umpire was behind the plate in both the longest day game by time and the longest night game by time in ML history that was not suspended and finished later?

  A) He was the plate ump in the second game of a twin bill at Shea Stadium on May 31, 1964, between the Giants and the Mets that lasted seven hours and 23 minutes before the Giants won 8–6 in 23 innings.
  B) Ten years later, on September 11, 1974, he found himself behind the plate again at Shea when the Cards defeated the Mets 4–3 in 25 innings, the longest night game in history, excluding the suspended game in 1984 between the White Sox and Brewers.
  C) He also worked the plate in the first NL perfect game in the 20th century.
  D) One of the last umpires who'd had a lengthy career as a player, he joined the NL staff in June 1957 after some 13 seasons as a minor league first baseman.
  E) His initials are the same as those of the White Sox first sacker who compiled 103 RBI on just three home runs in 1924.

Sherry Magee, almost certainly the most talented offensive performer who later became a full-time umpire in the majors. He holds practically every major career batting record among arbiters who were former players.

Career Record Holders Among Players Who Became Umpires

Batting	National League RECORD	NAME	American League RECORD	NAME
Games	2087	Sherry Magee	2383	Bobby Wallace
At Bats	7441	Sherry Magee	8618	Bobby Wallace
Batting Average	.311	Bug Holliday	.282	Bob Caruthers
Slugging Average	.448	Bug Holliday	.400	Bob Caruthers
Hits	2169	Sherry Magee	2309	Bobby Wallace
Total Bases	3175	Sherry Magee	3088	Bobby Wallace
Doubles	425	Sherry Magee	391	Bobby Wallace
Triples	166	Sherry Magee	143	Bobby Wallace
Home Runs	83	Sherry Magee	34	Bobby Wallace
RBI	1176	Sherry Magee	1121	Bobby Wallace
Runs	1521	Tom Brown	1057	Bobby Wallace
OBP	.376	Bug Holliday	.391	Bob Caruthers
Stolen Bases	739	Arlie Latham	248	George Moriarty
Strikeouts	383	Billy Nash	129	George Pipgras
Walks	803	Billy Nash	774	Bobby Wallace
Pitching				
Games	445	Lon Warneke	500	Eddie Rommel
Wins	204	Al Orth	218	Bob Caruthers
Losses	189	Al Orth	177	Bill Dinneen
Innings	3354.2	Al Orth	3074	Bill Dinneen
Strikeouts	1140	Lon Warneke	1736	Ed Walsh
Walks	1064	Bert Cunningham	829	Bill Dinneen
Games Started	394	Al Orth	352	Bill Dinneen
Complete Games	324	Al Orth	306	Bill Dinneen
ERA	3.18	Lon Warneke	1.82	Ed Walsh
Shutouts	31	Al Orth	57	Ed Walsh
Saves	13	Lon Warneke	34	Ed Walsh
Winning Pct.	.613	Lon Warneke	.688	Bob Caruthers

Notes: Includes only regular umpires after 1901 in either the AL or the NL.

Early Exits

1. **Ray Chapman is the lone man to die as a direct and immediate result of an injury sustained on the playing field in a major league game, but many other performers also died prematurely and, in some cases, tragically. The unusually grim circumstances surrounding the death of a certain early-day catcher received more publicity than the demise of any other player in history to that point. Notwithstanding all the attention the press devoted to his demise, only two members of the baseball community—Connie Mack and Billy Hamilton—attended his funeral. Who is he?**

   A) His brother, soon to be a big leaguer, was also at his funeral.
   B) His brother was also a catcher.
   C) He killed his wife and children in January 1900 before taking his own life.
   D) His initials match those of the Orioles shortstop during the 1970s.
   E) He and his brother Bill aren't related to Candace and Edgar.

Some 79 years after his fatal beaning, Ray Chapman remains the only man to die as a direct result of an injury sustained in a major league game. Chapman is also still the only regular performer on a team bound for a World Championship to die when his club was in the midst of a pennant fight.

2. **Name the only batting crown winner to die during a season when he was defending his title.**
   - A)   His last manager in the majors was Tom Loftus.
   - B)   He never played in a 20th century World Series, but one of his brothers did.
   - C)   He was the only righty batter to hit .400 twice prior to 1901.
   - D)   Until 1923 he held the Senators' club record for the highest BA in a season.
   - E)   He is the only man to win batting titles in both the NL and the AL.

3. **What outstanding all-around performer had 99 career wins before age 25, only to die just days after his 25th birthday?**
   - A)   He was the first switch-hitter to win 20 games and hit .300 in the same year.
   - B)   He holds the season record for the most RBI by anyone with fewer than 300 ABs.
   - C)   In 1886 he went 30–9 for the Phillies and topped the NL with a 1.98 ERA.
   - D)   He and the game's first switch-hitter of note share the same last name.
   - E)   His initials match those of the player most responsible for free agency.

4. **Who is the only man to log a 20-win season in the majors and die before his 25th birthday?**
   - A)   At one point in his career, he played for three teams in three different leagues that were all based in the same city.
   - B)   His finale came with the first Boston team to win a pennant with Hugh Duffy in its lineup.
   - C)   His 20-win season came in a Cleveland uniform.
   - D)   He and a contemporary player with the same nickname and last name died less than a year apart.
   - E)   His namesake was a Brooklyn outfielder prior to his death.

Earliest Exit, 20-Game Winner

RANK	NAME	TEAM	20/W	AGE/DEATH
1	Darby O'Brien	Cle, NL	1889	24
2	Charlie Ferguson	Phi, NL	1884	25
3	Jack Taylor	Phi, NL	1894	26
4	Kid Madden	Bos, NL	1887	28
	Win Mercer	Was, NL	1896	28
	Doc McJames	Bal, NL	1898	28
7	Ed Daily	Phi, NL	1885	29
	Pat Luby	Chi, NL	1890	29
	King Cole	Chi, NL	1910	29
10	John Ewing	NY, NL	1891	31
	Addie Joss	Cle, AL	1905	31

Note: 20/W is the first 20-win season; several players had more than one.

5. **Do you know the only future Hall of Fame hurler to die while still active?**
   - A)   He expired on the eve of the 1911 season.
   - B)   His passing caused his Cleveland teammates to threaten to go on strike if they were made to play their season opener instead of attending his funeral.
   - C)   Prior to 1920 he held the season record for wins by a Cleveland AL hurler.
   - D)   He has the second-best career ERA of any pitcher in history.
   - E)   He threw a perfect game in the heat of the 1908 pennant race.

Most Wins, Career, Pitchers Dying While Active

RANK	NAME	YEARS	AGE/DEATH	W
1	Urban Shocker	1916–28	38	187
2	Addie Joss	1902–10	31	160
3	Win Mercer	1894–1902	28	131
4	Jack Taylor	1891–99	27	120
5	Hal Carlson	1917–30	38	114
6	Don Wilson	1966–74	29	104
7	Tiny Bonham	1940–49	36	103
8	Charlie Ferguson	1884–87	25	99
9	Doc McJames	1895–1901	28	79
10	Bob Moose	1967–76	29	76

Note: Pitchers who died either during their last ML seasons or over the off-season immediately pursuant.

6. Who was shot to death in a bar fight less than four months after he threw the final pitch tossed by a member of the Seattle Pilots?

- A) He worked the final inning in relief in the Pilots' finale on October 2, 1969.
- B) He was slain in the same Puerto Rican town where he was born.
- C) He had the same nickname as Brooklyn's rookie 20-game winner in 1888.
- D) His initials match those of the AL leader in saves and hill appearances in 1960.
- E) His last name matches that of the second sacker for the 1971 NL West champs.

7. A dune-buggy accident took the life of what relief ace on New Year's Day, 1977?

- A) He led the Brewers in saves in 1976 despite not being acquired until June.
- B) He debuted as a starter with the 1967 Mets.
- C) He was of Italian stock.
- D) In 1971 he bagged 12 saves and a 1.99 ERA in 53 pen appearances for the Mets.
- E) His initials match those of the Cubs regular first sacker during 1952–56.

8. What postexpansion outfielder who sported a .311 career batting average was shot to death late in his fourth ML season?

- A) He was on a road trip to Chicago at the time.
- B) He was slain in 1978.
- C) He had joined the Angels just that season as a free agent.
- D) In 1977 he hit .336 for the Twins and scored 104 runs.
- E) His initials match those of the Phillies shortstop at the time of his death.

9. Name the BoSox hurler who was murdered during spring training in 1932 at a fish fry given in his honor.

- A) He was stabbed to death in an argument with a gas station owner.
- B) He had the same name as a star southpaw in the 1880s.
- C) He came within one win in 1928 of logging 20 victories for a cellar team.
- D) He also came within one win in 1928 of being the only rookie since the end of the Deadball Era to win 20 games for a doormat.
- E) His initials match those of the Indians main DH in 1995.

10. **What budding star died less than two years after he slapped 19 triples to set an AL rookie record that still stands?**
    A) He played short for the Senators.
    B) He died just prior to the 1906 season.
    C) Even though his last name is fairly common, there has not been another big leaguer with it since he died.
    D) His last name is shared by the only man from a major league team representing Hartford to be a batting title runner-up.
    E) His initials match those of the man whose bat abruptly ended the 1993 World Series.

Earliest Exits, Leaders in Major Batting Departments

	NAME	TEAM	YEAR	AGE/DEATH
Triples	Joe Cassidy	Was, AL	1905	23
RBI	Jim Nealon	Pit, NL	1905	25
Walks	Jim Fogarty	Phi, NL	1887	27
Stolen Bases	Jim Fogarty	Phi, NL	1889	27
Runs	Hub Collins	Bro, NL	1890	28
Doubles	Hub Collins	Lou/Bro, AA	1888	28
Strikeouts	Ross Youngs	NY, NL	1918	30
OBP	Yank Robinson	StL, AA	1888	34
Batting Average	Ed Delahanty	Phi, NL	1899	35
Total Bases	Ed Delahanty	Phi, NL	1893	35
Home Runs	Ed Delahanty	Phi, NL	1893	35
	Oscar Walker	StL, AA	1882	35
Slugging Average	Ed Delahanty	Phi, NL	1892	35
Hits	Ed Delahanty	Phi, NL	1899	35

Note: Year is the first year a player led his league; Delahanty was a leader on more than one occasion in several departments.

11. **Who was the only Rookie of the Year winner to die before his 25th birthday?**
    A) He led the NL in batting strikeouts as a frosh.
    B) He died like another Rookie of the Year, Thurman Munson, did—in a private plane crash.
    C) He was a second baseman.
    D) Ernie Banks was one of his teammates.
    E) He had the same first name and initials as a Reds rookie starter who debuted the same year he did but never pitched again in the bigs after that season.

Award-Winners Dying While Still Active

NAME	AWARD	DIED	AGE/DEATH
Jake Daubert	MVP	1924	40
Ken Hubbs	Rookie	1964	22
Roberto Clemente	MVP, WS MVP	1972	38
Thurman Munson	Rookie, MVP	1979	32

12. **Name the only ML manager to commit suicide during his tenure as a helmsman.**

    A) Win Mercer isn't the man because he had not yet begun his duties as Detroit's manager when he killed himself prior to the 1902 season.

    B) Our man batted against Mercer many times near the end of the 19th century.

    C) Also an active player at the time of his death, he did himself in by drinking carbolic acid during spring training.

    D) He played on the winning team in the first 20th century World Series.

    E) He and the pinch hitter who walked to spoil Milt Pappas's bid for a perfect game have the same last name.

13. **The first hurler to throw two no-hitters for an expansion team died while he was still active. Who is he?**

    A) His 1975 death by carbon monoxide poisoning was ruled accidental.

    B) He died in the city where he played his entire nine-year major league career.

    C) He won in double figures for eight straight years between 1967 and 1974.

    D) At the time of his death, he was second only to Larry Dierker in career wins by an Astro.

    E) His initials match those of the Jays reliever who won two games in the 1992 World Series.

14. **What hurler died in an auto accident in 1976 on his 29th birthday while driving to a party being held in his honor?**

    A) He spent his entire 10-year career with the same NL team.

    B) He sported a glittering 14–3 mark as a starter in 1969 in 19 starts.

    C) In 1976, his final season, he was 3–9 with 10 saves.

    D) His wild pitch abruptly ended the 1972 NLCS.

    E) His initials match those of a Red Sox 20-game winner in 1963.

15. **He and Lou Gehrig are the only position players in the Hall of Fame who died from ailments that forced them to quit the game prematurely.**

    A) He topped the NL in whiffs as a rookie in 1918.

    B) He led the NL in runs in 1923.

    C) He died of Bright's disease when he was just 30 years old.

    D) John McGraw adored him.

    E) Robin Yount in 1999 removed a certain Hall of Fame distinction from him.

16. **He played nine years in the majors; 12 of his 18 career homers came as a rookie in a league that had ML status just one season; in 1893, his final campaign, he hit .452 in 15 games as a pitcher-outfielder; three years later, tormented by an unhappy love affair, he committed suicide. Whose career are we describing?**

    A) He debuted with Boston in the Union Association.

    B) He is the only ERA leader who also nearly won a home run crown.

    C) He was a member of the 1888 and 1889 NL flag winners.

    D) He had the same nickname as the all-time season record holder for the most shutouts by a southpaw.

    E) The initials of his real first name and last name match those of a Hall of Fame second baseman.

17. **Born in the same city as Pete Browning, like Pete he broke in with his hometown team. Traded to Brooklyn late in the 1888 season, he topped the AA that year in doubles and paced the NL in runs two years later. He died of typhoid fever in 1892 just a few days after playing in his final big league game. Who is he?**
    A) In 1891 he was nearly killed in a collision with teammate Oyster Burns while chasing a pop fly.
    B) The city of his birth was Louisville.
    C) He was moved from the outfield to 2B after being traded to Brooklyn in 1888.
    D) His initials match those of an infamous first baseman.
    E) He was known by a nickname derived from his first name of Hubert.

18. **What rookie showed rare speed for a first sacker, leading his team in triples with eight and finishing second on the club in stolen bases, only to die early in his sophomore season of a pulmonary embolism?**
    A) As a rookie, he was a member of arguably the worst first-division team in history.
    B) He pursued a career in baseball even though he was an All-American in another sport.
    C) He looked to be the BoSox first sacker for years to come prior to his untimely death.
    D) He was an All-American quarterback in college.
    E) He was nicknamed "The Golden Greek."

Best Performance in Final Full Season Prior to Death

| | National League | | | | American League | | | |
	RECORD	NAME	TEAM	YEAR	RECORD	NAME	TEAM	YEAR
Batting								
At Bats	574	Austin McHenry	StL	1921	617	Thurman Munson	NY	1978
Batting Average	.350	Austin McHenry	StL	1921	.376	Ed Delahanty	Was	1902
Slugging Average	.531	Austin McHenry	StL	1921	.590	Ed Delahanty	Was	1902
Hits	201	Austin McHenry	StL	1921	199	Lyman Bostock	Min	1977
Total Bases	305	Austin McHenry	StL	1921	301	Lyman Bostock	Min	1977
Doubles	37	Austin McHenry	StL	1921	43	Ed Delahanty	Was	1902
Triples	12	Jim Doyle	Chi	1911	14	Ed Delahanty	Was	1902
Home Runs	17	Austin McHenry	StL	1921	14	Lyman Bostock	Min	1977
RBI	102	Austin McHenry	StL	1921	93	Ed Delahanty	Was	1902
Runs	92	Austin McHenry	StL	1921	104	Lyman Bostock	Min	1977
OBP	.393	Austin McHenry	StL	1921	.453	Ed Delahanty	Was	1902
Stolen Bases	57	Darby O'Brien	Bro	1892	23	Joe Cassidy	Was	1905
Strikeouts	63	Hub Collins	Bro	1891	70	Thurman Munson	NY	1978
Walks	59	Hub Collins	Bro	1891	62	Ed Delahanty	Was	1902

		National League				American League		
	RECORD	**NAME**	**TEAM**	**YEAR**	**RECORD**	**NAME**	**TEAM**	**YEAR**
Pitching								
Games	53	Bob Moose	Pit	1976	72	Steve Olin	Cle	1992
Wins	22	Charlie Ferguson	Phi	1887	18	Urban Shocker	NY	1927
Losses	13	Don Wilson	Hou	1974	18	Win Mercer	Det	1902
Innings	297.1	Charlie Ferguson	Phi	1887	281.2	Win Mercer	Det	1902
Strikeouts	125	Charlie Ferguson	Phi	1887	47	Steve Olin	Cle	1992
Walks	100	Don Wilson	Hou	1974	80	Win Mercer	Det	1902
Games Started	33	Charlie Ferguson	Phi	1887	33	Win Mercer	Det	1902
Complete Games	31	Charlie Ferguson	Phi	1887	28	Win Mercer	Det	1902
ERA	3.00	Charlie Ferguson	Phi	1887	2.84	Urban Shocker	NY	1927
Shutouts	4	Don Wilson	Hou	1974	4	Win Mercer	Det	1902
Saves	10	Bob Moose	Pit	1976	29	Steve Olin	Cle	1972
Winning Pct.	.688	Charlie Ferguson	Phi	1887	.750	Urban Shocker	NY	1927

Note: Includes only men who died within 12 months after their last full ML seasons; Shocker died in September 1928 after pitching two innings earlier that year. The record for the most bases on balls by a pitcher who died immediately following his final season belongs to Darby O'Brien, who gave up 127 walks for Boston of the AA in 1891.

The Name's the Same

1. Nomar Garciaparra is a baseball rarity in that no other player in big league history has shared either his first or last name. Conversely, the record holders for the most career wins by a pitcher in a Washington uniform; the most career pinch home runs; and the most home runs in a season by anyone who played at least 100 games at second base all share the same last name— Johnson. How about some more "name's-the-samers"? The outfielder who's the most recent Caucasian player to steal as many as 70 bases in a season; the only outfielder in ML history to compile fewer than 750 runs and fewer than 750 RBI in more than 6,000 at bats; and the outfielder who led the NL with 148 runs in 1890 despite hitting just .278.

RANK	NAME	YEARS	ABS	RUNS	RBI	TOTAL
	Fewest Combined Runs and RBI, Outfielder, Career, (Minimum 6,000 ABs)					
1	Paul Blair	1964–80	6042	776	620	1396
2	Dode Paskert	1907–21	6017	868	577	1445
3	Shano Collins	1910–25	6390	747	709	1456
4	Bill Bruton	1953–64	6056	937	545	1482
5	Curt Flood	1956–71	6357	851	636	1487
6	Dave Philley	1941–62	6296	789	729	1518
7	Garry Maddox	1972–86	6331	777	754	1531
8	Tommy Harper	1962–76	6269	972	567	1539
9	Charlie Jamieson	1915–32	6560	1062	552	1614
10	Clyde Milan	1907–22	7359	1004	617	1621

2. The shortstop who was the first man to play 100 or more games in each of his first three seasons with three different teams in three different major leagues; the first man to log three no-hitters; and the first Tigers rookie to lead the AL in pinch hits.

3. An AL batting champ with Boston; a National League leader in triples with Cincinnati; and the first Milwaukee ML team's gateway guardian.

4. The AL leader in pinch hits in 1936; the NL leader in losses in 1883; and the current owner of the top career pinch-hit batting average among retired players with at least 100 pinch at bats.

5. An ex–University of Michigan football star who was born in Ann Arbor and played for Detroit's 1984 flag winner; the NL leader in runs in 1913 at age 35; and the outfielder who was the Giants weakest-hitting regular in 1929 at .290.

6. The first sacker who led Cleveland with 94 walks in 1932; the only player to reach base on a walk for a team that came out a loser in a nine-inning perfect game; and the only rookie to lead either the NL or the AL in walks.

Rookies Leading the League in Walks

NAME	TEAM	YEAR	BA	W
Ed Pinkham	Chi, NA	1871	.263	18
Jack Gleason	StL, AA	1882	.254	27
Yank Robinson	Bal, UA	1884	.267	37
Bill Joyce	Bro, PL	1890	.252	123
Al Wickland	Chi, FL	1914	.276	81
Joe Morgan	Hou, NL	1965	.271	97

Note: Wickland's rookie credentials are debatable. If they're accepted, it means that every ML circuit since 1871 except the NL and the AL was led in walks by a rookie in its fledgling season.

7. The AL doubles leader in 1979; an AL triples coleader in 1956; and the AL Hall of Famer who hit .269 in 1949 but had a .556 slugging average.

Highest SA, Season, Pitcher

RANK	NAME	TEAM	YEAR	ABS	BA	TBS	SA
1	Don Newcombe	Bro, NL	1955	117	.359	74	.632
2	Wes Ferrell	Cle, AL	1931	116	.319	72	.621
3	Red Ruffing	Bos/NY, AL	1930	110	.364	64	.582
4	Walter Johnson	Was, AL	1925	97	.433	56	.577
5	Jack Bentley	NY, NL	1923	89	.427	51	.573
6	Bob Lemon	Cle, AL	1949	108	.269	60	.556
7	Wes Ferrell	Bos, AL	1935	150	.347	80	.533
8	Claude Hendrix	Chi, NL	1912	121	.322	64	.529
9	Doc Crandall	NY, NL	1910	73	.342	38	.521
10	Don Drysdale	LA, NL	1965	130	.300	66	.508

Note: Minimum 70 ABs; maximum five games at other positions.

8. A star pitcher on the first White Sox world champs; the regular third sacker on the first Tigers world champs; and a key performer on the first Dodgers team to lose a World Championship to the Yankees.

9. The first man to whiff 175 times in a season; the most recent Cub to lead the NL in home runs, runs, and RBI in the same season; and the Pirates outfielder who hit .360 in 99 games in 1920 and led the NL in pinch hits.

10. The next Pirate after Ralph Kiner to hit 30 homers in a season; the first Brewer to hit 40 homers in a season; and the first Phillies regular to hit no homers in a 154-game season.

11. The BoSox regular shortstop in 1915 who hit .201; the BoSox first-sack regular in 1968 who hit .171; and the Baltimore first-sack regular in 1886 who hit .190.

12. The Senators top hitter in 1936; the Browns top hitter in 1906; and the Senator who in 1954 became the only man to win an All-Star Game without throwing a pitch.

13. The Braves outfielder who hit .200 in 130 games in 1915; the third sacker with the Senators and Browns who hit .196 in 144 games in 1904; and the Mets shortstop who hit .193 in 119 games in 1963.

14. The Phils leading hitter in 1967; the only NL catcher to collect 400 at bats in 1924; and the Rangers only two-time home run crown winner.

15. Careful—here's a "name's-the-same" foursome! The most recent first sacker to win more than one AL RBI crown; the most recently retired player with a .500+ career slugging average who never played any position but catcher; the most recent pitcher to notch 25 complete games seven years in a row; and the most recent pitcher to win 20 games for a National League pennant winner three years in a row.

16. The AL runs leader in 1918; the AL stolen-base leader in 1931; and the last member of the Philadelphia A's to hit .300 with at least 20 home runs and 100 RBI.

17. The O's outfielder who swiped 53 bases in 1992; the Phils outfielder who led the NL in batter Ks in 1958; and the Pirates rookie outfielder who had 85 hits and 80 walks in 1907.

18. The first NL bat champ who played first base; the only NL first baseman in the 1960s to score 100 runs three years in a row; and the switch-hitting AL outfielder who in 1975 played the only seven games at first base that he served there in his 15-year career.

19. The Tigers hurler who led the AL in wild pitches in 1920; the Dodgers chucker who topped the NL in saves in 1935; and the Royals righty who paced the AL in shutouts in 1979.

20. The pinch hitter who spoiled Milt Pappas's bid for a perfect game with a two-out walk in the ninth inning; the outfielder who holds the Braves' franchise record for the highest batting average by a rookie; and the first man to win an AL home run crown and then not play a single game in the majors the following season.

21. The 23-game winner for the Pittsburgh Rebels (FL) in 1915; the Cleveland reliever who had a .000 winning percentage in 47 appearances in 1967; and the Yankees rookie who had an .810 winning percentage in 33 appearances in 1932.

22. The lefty who won 23 games for a UA team in his last full ML season; the lefty who won 18 games for the White Sox in his last full ML season; and the lefty who had a 1.69 ERA in 165 innings for the Senators in his first full ML season.

23. The AL loss leader with Boston in 1924; the NL loss leader with Boston in 1909; and the Phillies stalwart who was the only hurler to have a 30-win season with fewer than 10 losses at the pre-1893 pitching distance.

Most Wins, Season, Fewer than 10 Losses

RANK	NAME	TEAM	YEAR	WIN. PCT.	L	W
1	Walter Johnson	Was, AL	1913	.837	7	36
2	Joe McGinnity	NY, NL	1904	.814	8	35
3	Joe Wood	Bos, AL	1912	.872	5	34
4	Jouett Meekin	NY, NL	1894	.786	9	33
5	Lefty Grove	Phi, AL	1931	.886	4	31
	Bill Hoffer	Bal, NL	1895	.838	6	31
	Denny McLain	Det, AL	1968	.838	6	31
	Christy Mathewson	NY, NL	1905	.775	9	31
	Jack Coombs	Phi, AL	1910	.775	9	31
10	Dizzy Dean	StL, NL	1934	.811	7	30
	Charlie Ferguson	Phi, NL	1886	.769	9	30

24. The Browns pitcher who suffered 24 losses in just 258 innings in 1931; the Tigers hurler who tied for the AL lead in losses in 1951 despite working only 197.1 innings; and the Senators hurler who lost 51 games in his three-year career while pitching just 568 innings.

At the time of his retirement in 1979, Roy White held the record for the most career home runs (160) by a switch-hitter who was never a league leader in four-baggers. He is also one-third of the answer to a question in this section.

25. The rookie St. Louis Browns right-hander who compiled no shutouts in 27 starts in 1886; the veteran Washington right-hander who posted no shutouts in 30 starts in 1950; and the Phils rookie right-hander who logged no shutouts in 26 starts in 1983.

26. The 1942 AL leader in batter Ks; the third sacker who clouted 30 home runs with just 39 Ks in 1948; and the hurler who compiled 167 Ks in just 158 innings in 1991.

27. The Angels' home run leader in 1962; Louisville's home run leader in 1898; and the Red Sox shortstop who hit just one homer in 153 games in 1908.

28. The only rookie to be a 30-game loser despite posting an ERA below 2.00; the only rookie to be a 20-game winner for a Washington ML team despite posting an ERA above 4.00; and the only rookie with at least 500 at bats in both his debut and his coda seasons to log a batting average in his finale (.331) that was more than 100 points higher than his frosh performance (.224).

29. The catcher who at age 33 logged a complete-game shutout in his lone mound appearance; the rookie outfielder who hurled a five-inning relief stint in a 19th century World Series game; and the pitcher whose first career home run was also the first four-bagger by a National League hurler in a 20th century Series game.

30. The Phils pitcher who won 19 games as a 30-year-old rookie; the Browns pitcher who won 18 games in his first full season at age 30; and the 30-year-old rookie pitcher who was the only Cub to have a winning record (11–7) in 1954.

31. The future Hall of Famer who scored 98 runs as a rookie in 1890 for the Cleveland Spiders; the rookie outfielder who scored 100 runs in 1932 for the Phillies; and the rookie gardener who scored 98 runs in 1901 split between Brooklyn and Pittsburgh.

32. The outfielder who hit .194 in 123 games with a flag winner and played with five different teams in his six ML seasons; the outfielder who in his second ML season was traded by a flag winner for a Hall of Fame pitcher and had played every position including DH by his sixth ML campaign; and the outfielder in one game in 1929 who played 594 games at another position and never was on a flag winner in 21 seasons, all spent with one team.

Lowest BA, Season, Regular on Pennant Winner (Minimum 350 ABs)

RANK	NAME	TEAM	YEAR	POS.	ABS	BA
1	Lee Tannehill	Chi, AL	1906	3B	378	.183
2	Jack Boyle	StL, AA	1887	C	350	.189
3	Eddie Kennedy	NY, AA	1884	OF	378	.190
4	Germany Smith	Bro, NL	1890	SS	481	.191
5	Harry Lyons	StL, AA	1888	OF	499	.194
6	Paul Radford	NY, AA	1884	OF	355	.197
7	Skeeter Webb	Det, AL	1945	SS	407	.199
8	Don Wert	Det, AL	1968	3B	536	.200
9	Everett Scott	Bos, AL	1915	SS	359	.201
10	Swede Risberg	Chi, AL	1917	SS	474	.203

33. The rookie who was denied a bat crown despite having his league's highest batting average and meeting all the qualifying criteria at the time; the rookie who was the first 20th century frosh at his position to collect 100 RBI; and the rookie who had the second-most wins on the Boston Braves in 1945 despite not making his big league debut until July 29.

34. A 33-game loser as a rookie with Syracuse's only NL entry; a Cleveland hurler who lost 40 games that same season; and a southpaw who won 22 games and the Cy Young Award 88 years later.

35. The coholder of the AL record for the most shutouts by a rookie; the ML record holder for the fewest wins by a pitcher in 2,000 career innings; and the only pitcher to notch 40 saves in one season and lead his league in losses in another.

36. An AL Rookie of the Year who collected just 31 RBI in 624 at bats; an AL rookie first sacker who had just 20 RBI in 467 at bats; and an AA rookie in 1887 who compiled 94 RBI in 532 at bats and set the all-time frosh record for runs scored.

Fewest RBI, Season, First Baseman (Minimum 400 ABs)

RANK	NAME	TEAM	YEAR	ABS	BA	RBI
1	Ivy Griffin	Phi, AL	1921	467	.238	20
	Joe Agler	Buf, FL	1914	463	.272	20
3	Fred Tenney	Bos, NL	1901	451	.278	22
4	Fred Tenney	Bos, NL	1907	554	.273	26
5	Wes Parker	LA, NL	1968	468	.239	27
	Buddy Hassett	Bos, NL	1940	458	.234	27
	Chuck Stevens	StL, AL	1946	432	.248	27
8	Fred Tenney	Bos, NL	1905	549	.288	28
	Fred Tenney	Bos, NL	1906	544	.283	28
10	Bayard Sharpe	Bos, NL	1910	439	.239	29

37. The NL triples leader in 1909; the AL triples leader in 1949; and the only man to hit into an unassisted triple play in a World Series game.

38. A Kansas City outfielder who was a league leader in triples with just 15 fewer triples than RBI in 637 at bats; a league leader in triples from Pittsburgh who had six more triples than he had doubles and home runs combined; and a league leader in RBI who had 123 more RBI for the Cubs that year than he had career triples.

Smallest Difference Between Triples and RBI, Season

RANK	NAME	TEAM	YEAR	3BS	RBI	DIFF.
1	Emmett Seery	Ind, NL	1887	15	28	13
2	Joe Cassidy	Was, AL	1904	19	33	14
	Max Carey	Pit, NL	1914	17	31	14
4	Willie Wilson	KC, AL	1997	15	30	15
5	Bid McPhee	Cin, NL	1920	15	32	17
	Carson Bigbee	Pit, NL	1920	15	32	17
7	Bris Lord	Phi, AL	1910	18	37	19
8	Harry Wolter	NY, AL	1911	15	36	21
	Whitey Witt	Phi, AL	1916	15	36	21
10	Willie Wilson	KC, AL	1985	21	43	22
	Bid McPhee	Cin, NL	1891	16	38	22

Note: Minimum 400 ABs and 15 triples.

Thirty Outstanding Achievements You Won't Find in Standard Baseball Record Books

1. Even if you go all the way back to 1871, you will find that just once in big league history has a man finished in the top five in his loop in batting average, slugging average, and on-base percentage despite hitting under .300, posting a sub-.400 OBP, and compiling fewer than 200 total bases. Obviously this never-before-documented achievement happened in a year when hitting was suppressed. But what year? And who did it?

    A) He played for a last-place team, and it was his last full year in the majors.
    B) He was 17th in the AL in total bases that year with 196.
    C) At one time, he held the season record for the most walks by a Latino player.
    D) He was banned from the majors for nearly four full seasons after he jumped to the Mexican League in 1946.
    E) His grandson made his ML debut with the Phillies in 1996 and had a three-homer game in 1997.

2. Buddy Bradford was a prototypal player in the 1970s, perennially looking as if he had oodles of talent but never actually doing anything very well. His fielding stats were mediocre, his stolen-base percentage was poor, and he posted a .226 career batting average, dismal for an outfielder. Nevertheless, Bradford received so many chances to blossom that he eked out 11 seasons in the majors. What turn-of-the-century performer was Bradford's antithesis, prematurely disappearing from the show after the 1903 season at age 29, the owner of a truly eerie record for hitting .300+ with 400 or more at bats for five straight years with five different teams?

    A) In his seven ML seasons, he never played the same position—let alone with the same team—two years in a row.
    B) He was dropped by the Phils after he paced them in RBI and hit .320 in 1903.
    C) He fielded an AL-record low .851 as Baltimore's shortstop in 1901.
    D) His nickname was "Wagon Tongue."
    E) His initials are the same as those of the only Federal League bat titlist.

3. **In 1996, Jim Eisenreich set a very underpublicized record when for the fourth consecutive season, he hit .300 and played in at least 100 games but collected fewer than 400 at bats. Who is the only other outfielder or infielder to equal Eisenreich's feat as many as three years in a row?**

A) After his three-year skein, he had a season later in his career when he hit .364 in 112 games but with just 283 at bats.

B) He played both his first and last games in Philadelphia garb 21 years apart.

C) In the final year of his record string, he fanned just 13 times in 383 ABs, but another player that same season with the same initials collected a mere 12 Ks in 417 ABs and hit his only career homer in more than 3,000 plate appearances.

D) He holds the season record for the most walks by a pinch hitter.

E) He's the only big leaguer born in Ribnik, Czechoslovakia.

Chief Meyers in 1911–13 became the first man to hit .300 three years in a row in 100 games with fewer than 400 at bats. It has since been done only four other times, most recently by Jim Eisenreich.

.300 BA in 100 Games with Fewer than 400 ABs, Three or More Consecutive Years

NAME	POS	YEARS
Jim Eisenreich	OF	1993–96
Elmer Valo	OF	1946–48
Ernie Lombardi	C	1935–37
Shanty Hogan	C	1929–31
Chief Meyers	C	1911–13

4. **The first man to compile 600 at bats in a season was also the only man to play in both the lone no-hit game in the Players League and the last no-hit game at the 50' pitching distance. Odd and intriguing as these record feats are, he's much better known for several other unusual achievements in his long career. Who is he?**

   A) He first topped 600 ABs in 1887 for a pennant winner.
   B) Two years earlier, for the same team, he had just 100 hits in 486 ABs for a .206 BA.
   C) His first name was Walter, but he played under a nickname derived from his middle name, which is the same as the name of a famous cemetery.
   D) He scored 1,478 career runs, the last one coming with the 1909 Giants.
   E) He holds the pre-1901 record for the most games at third base.

5. **Although trades were infrequent in the 19th century, most players changed teams and even leagues several times during their careers. Who set the 19th century record for fidelity when he retired in 1899 after spending his entire career of 13 seasons as a regular with the same team in the same major league?**

   A) As a rookie in 1887, he abandoned his right field post five times to chuck a few innings in relief but then never left the garden again in his career.
   B) He played on a flag winner in his second and third seasons and then never played on another.
   C) We'll be quiet while you think.
   D) He led the NL in SA in 1890 and again in 1891 and is among the elite handful of 19th century performers who collected 100 career homers.
   E) He and the Detroit catcher who amassed 122 walks and 137 whiffs in 1992 share the same initials.

10 Consecutive Years with the Same Team and League, 19th Century

NAME	TEAM	YEARS	SEASONS
Cap Anson	Chi, NL	1876–97	22
Jack Clements	Phi, NL	1885–97	13
Mike Tiernan	NY, NL	1887–99	13
Tom Burns	Chi, NL	1880–91	12
Herman Long	Bos, NL	1890–1900	11
Bobby Lowe	Bos, NL	1890–1900	11
Kid Nichols	Bos, NL	1890–1900	11
Silver Flint	Chi, NL	1879–89	11
Chief Zimmer	Cle, NL	1889–98	10
Ed McKean	Cle, NL	1889–98	10
Bid McPhee	Cin, NL	1890–99	10
Chicken Wolf	Lou, AA	1882–91	10
Mickey Welch	NY, NL	1883–92	10
Ed Delahanty	Phi, NL	1891–1900	10
Sam Thompson	Phi, NL	1889–98	10

Note: Clements also played for Philadelphia part of the 1884 season.
     Zimmer also played for Cleveland part of the 1899 season.

6. **Excluding pitchers and catchers, only one man played 10 years in the 19th century without ever participating in as many as 100 games in a season. Who is he?**
   A) He played 11 seasons, all after the schedule had been hiked to 126+ games.
   B) His most active year was 1893, when he played 94 games for Brooklyn.
   C) His 708 career games were split about equally between the infield and the outfield.
   D) He is the lone man to play with Washington's 1886–89 NL franchise for all four seasons that it was extant.
   E) His initials and first name match those of the Hall of Famer whose son hit a three-run homer to win a pennant.

7. **Connie Mack managed the Philadelphia A's from their first day in the AL through 1950, five years before they moved to Kansas City. Who owns the record for the most games played in Philadelphia A's livery without ever being piloted by Mack?**
   A) Morrie Martin, with 111 games, holds the record for a pitcher.
   B) Our man was originally owned by the Indians but debuted with the White Sox.
   C) He set a new ChiSox season home run record (since broken) in his lone full year in Chicago.
   D) He was the last member of the Philadelphia A's to win a home run crown.
   E) He was nicknamed for the title character of the only nationally syndicated comic strip in the 1940s and '50s that featured a three-sport pro athlete.

8. **To date, only one pitcher has finished with as many as 150 career wins despite hurling fewer than 2,000 innings. Who he is?**
   A) In his 87 relief appearances, he was just 11–16 in bullpen decisions.
   B) The last four of his 1,967.1 career innings came with the St. Louis Browns.
   C) His career record as a starter is 139–67.
   D) He is the most recent hurler to top his league in both complete games and saves in the same season.
   E) He and his brother combined for exactly 200 career wins in 2,854.2 innings.

Most Career Wins with Fewer than 2,000 Innings Pitched

RANK	NAME	YEARS	IP	W
1	Dizzy Dean	1930–41/47	1967.1	150
2	Dave Foutz	1884–94	1997.1	147
3	Ray Kremer	1924–33	1954.2	143
4	Johnny Allen	1932–44	1950.1	142
5	Jim Maloney	1960–71	1849	134
	Pat Malone	1928–37	1915	134
	Gerry Staley	1947–61	1981.2	134
8	Harry Brecheen	1940/43–53	1907.2	133
9	Vic Raschi	1946–55	1819	132
10	Denny McLain	1963–72	1886	131

9. **Several players have performed for three or more different teams in a season. Some have even been lucky enough to perform for more than one flag or division winner. Their antithesis is the middle infielder who hit .128 in 45 games the year he became the only man in history to play for three ML teams that all lost 100 or more games. Can you name him?**

   A) The previous year, in his final campaign as a regular, he hit .217.

   B) His .222 career BA ranks him among the 10 worst hitters of all time with 3,000 ABs, and his .128 season ranks 23rd on the all-time worst list for nonpitchers with at least 100 plate appearances.

   C) In 1985 he played for every division cellar dweller except the Rangers.

   D) A shortstop, he began the 1985 season with the Giants, the team with which he spent almost his entire career.

   E) The first name he used when he signed autographs is spelled the same as the true first name of the manager of the 1997 NL West division winner.

Lowest Season BA by a Nonpitcher, 100 Plate Appearances

RANK	NAME	TEAM	YEAR	ABS	HITS	BA
1	Sandy Nava	Pro, NL	1884	116	11	.095
2	Mike Jordan	Pit, NL	1890	125	12	.096
3	Ben Egan	Cle, AL	1915	120	13	.108
4	Jose Gonzalez	LA/Pit, NL/Cle, AL	1991	117	13	.111
5	John Humphries	NY, NL	1883	107	12	.112
6	Gracie Pierce	Col, AA/NY, NL	1883	103	12	.117
7	Dwain Anderson	StL/SD, NL	1973	124	15	.121
8	George Baker	StL, NL	1885	131	16	.1221
9	Frank O'Rourke	Bos, NL	1912	196	24	.1224
10	Mike Benjamin	SF, NL	1991	106	13	.123

10. **In 1937 the Boston Bees pitching staff featured two rookie 20-game winners, Jim Turner and Lou Fette. The Bees are the only team in this century to produce two such frosh hurlers, but they don't hold the AL or NL team record for the most wins by rookie pitchers. The pennant-winning 1952 Dodgers do with 51 victories. The only other club since 1920 to receive more than 45 wins from frosh hurlers was far from being a flag winner. What team is it?**

   A) The 1986 Texas Rangers, with 45 frosh wins, led by Ed Correa and Mike Witt, fell just 2 victories short of the post-1920 record of 47.

   B) The team also holds the post-1920 record for the most frosh losses with 57.

   C) Frosh hurlers logged 47 of the team's 68 wins and 109 of its 154 starts three years after three veteran hurlers had accounted for 72 of its 107 wins.

   D) Joe Cascarella, Johnny Marcum, and Bill Dietrich were the only team members to win in double digits and also three of the team's five rookies to post at least one win.

   E) It was the only team managed by Connie Mack to finish as high as fifth between Dizzy Dean's finest season and his final ML appearance.

Teams Receiving the Most Wins from Rookie Hurlers, Season

RANK	TEAM	YEAR	W	ROOKIE PITCHERS
1	Chi, FL	1914	53	Lange (12), Fiske (12), Johnson (9), Watson (9), McGuire (5), Prendergast (5) & Black (1)
2	Phi, AA	1887	51	Weyhing (26) & Seward (25)
	Bro, NL	1952	51	Black (15), Loes (13), Wade (11), Rutherford (7), Hughes (2), Moore (1), Lehman (1) & Landrum (1)
4	Cle, AL	1911	49	Gregg (23), Krapp (13), Blanding (7), West (3), James (2) & Yingling (1)
5	Chi, NL	1889	48	Hutchison (16), Gumbert (16) & Dwyer (16)
6	Phi, AL	1934	47	Marcum (14), Cascarella (12), Dietrich (11), Benton (7) & Caster (3)
7	Chi, NL	1880	46	Corcoran (43), Poorman (2) & Guth (1)
8	Tex, AL	1986	45	Correa (12), Witt (11), Guzman (9), Williams (8), Mohoric (2), Loynd (2) & Brown (1)
	NY, AL	1910	45	Ford (26), Vaughn (13), Fisher (5) & Caldwell (1)
10	Bro, NL	1903	44	Schmidt (22), Jones (19) & Thatcher (3)
	Bos, NL	1937	44	Turner (20), Fette (20) & Hutchings (4)

11. **When Tommie Agee led the Mets in hits with just 96 in 1972, how long had it been since a major league team played a full schedule without having a man who compiled 100 hits?**

   A) The 1972 Mets are the only ML team in the 20th century to do it in a nonstrike year.

   B) The 1972 Mets are the only ML team playing more than 80 games to do it.

   C) The last ML loop to play a schedule calling for 80 or fewer games was led in hits by Hick Carpenter with 120.

   D) Carpenter played for the loop's initial flag winner that year.

   E) That year, two of the loop's six teams—Baltimore and Philadelphia—lacked a player with 100 hits.

12. **In 1997, Eddie Murray set a new record for the most career games (3,025) by a man who played with as many as five different teams. Who owns the converse record for the fewest career games (27) by a man who played with five or more teams?**

   A) He was later a convict hero in a thwarted prison break.

   B) In five consecutive major league seasons, he played for five different teams and in just 27 games, 9 fewer than Hank Schreiber who likewise played minimally for five different teams over the course of five seasons.

   C) His 27 games are 4 more than Art Veltman's record low for a player with five or more major league seasons.

   D) His real first name was Clifford, but the initials of his nickname and last name match those of the Twins catcher who homered in his first major league game in the same 1981 contest in which two other Twins also debuted with homers.

   E) His nickname was "Tacks."

Fewest Career Games

	GAMES	NAME	YEARS
5 or More ML Seasons	23	Art Veltman	1926–34
6 or More ML Seasons	23	Art Veltman	1926–34
7 or More ML Seasons	98	Johnny Riddle	1930–48
8 or More ML Seasons	102	Ken Silvestri	1939–51
9 or More ML Seasons	140	Matt Sinatro	1981–92
10 or More ML Seasons	140	Matt Sinatro	1981–92

13. **George Shoch was the first man to play 10 years in the majors and compile 2,500 plate appearances without ever having enough plate appearances in a season, by today's rule, to be eligible for a batting title. Who was the first man to total 3,000 career plate appearances without ever having enough plate appearances in a season to qualify for a bat crown?**
    A) His last plate appearance came in the 1966 World Series.
    B) He hit .303 with 17 homers for the 1963 Phils.
    C) His iffy glove work kept him from ever winning a regular outfield post.
    D) In 1958 he hit .330 and whacked 24 homers and 74 RBI in just 90 games.
    E) He was a Dodgers teammate in 1966 of an outfielder with the same initials who looked as if he too might collect 3,000 plate appearances without ever qualifying for a bat crown before he broke through in 1973 to hit .295 in 145 games.

14. **What catcher owns the all-time record for the longest ML career by a position player without ever seeing action in as many as 100 games in a season?**
    A) He played 18 seasons in the bigs between 1916 and 1933 and caught about an equal number of games in both the NL and the AL.
    B) He debuted with the worst team in AL history and was never on a flag winner.
    C) His top season was 1928, when he hit .302 in 96 games with the Reds.
    D) He's the only receiver to work no-hit games with three different teams.
    E) His initials are the same as those of the first black player on the Philadelphia A's to qualify for a batting crown.

15. **What ex–Long Island University star has the record for the longest ML career by an infielder or an outfielder who never played as many as 100 games in a season?**
    A) He debuted with the team the Miracle Mets surprised in the World Series.
    B) He finished with the last team Bill Virdon managed for a full season.
    C) His most active season in his 15-year career was 1972, when he played 97 games and collected 247 at bats for the Orioles.
    D) His 108 career pinch hits currently put him eighth on the all-time list.
    E) He and the preexpansion record holder for the most seasons playing 100 or more games share the same initials.

Most Seasons by a Non-Batteryman with No 100-Game Season (Since 1887)

RANK	NAME	YEARS	MOST GAMES	SEASONS
1	Terry Crowley	1969–83	97	15
2	Lou Klimchock	1958–70	90	12
	Harry Spilman	1978–89	83	12
4	Bob Heise	1967–77	95	11
	Domingo Ramos	1978–90	98	11
6	George Shoch	1887–97	94	10
	Mike McNally	1915–25	93	10
	Sammy Esposito	1952–63	98	10
	Jim Beauchamp	1963–73	77	10
	Terry Harmon	1967–77	87	10
	John Vukovich	1970–81	74	10
	Benny Ayala	1974–85	76	10
	Luis Aguayo	1980–89	99	10
	Carmen Castillo	1982–91	94	10

Note: Shoch also had one pre-1887 season of fewer than 100 games. McNally was the first to have 10 sub-100-game seasons after the 154-game schedule was adopted in 1904. Vukovich played 277 career games and had a .161 BA; both are record lows for a non-batteryman with 10 seasons.

16. **In 1912, when Pittsburgh hit 129 triples to set a still-standing 20th century team record, what other new team record (since broken) did the Pirates set that contributed just as heavily to their surprising second-place finish in the NL?**

    A)   Their record-low figure of 169 for a 154-game season lasted until 1921, when the Cubs shaved the mark to 161.

    B)   Honus Wagner logged 32 of the record-low 169, the most of any club member.

    C)   In 1912 the Pirates also led the NL in fewest runs allowed with 565, thanks largely to their record low of 169 somethings.

    D)   In 1912 the Philadelphia A's led the AL in the same department with a loop-low figure of 263.

    E)   Chief Wilson's .961 fielding average was 11 points below the team's new record mark of .972.

17. **The only man to play for Cleveland ML teams in both the American Association and the American League saw action in the fewest ML games (389) of any position player who debuted before the four-ball walk rule was introduced and finished his career after the foul-strike rule became universal. Who is he?**

    A)   He is also one of the only three men to play for Detroit ML teams in both the NL and the AL.

    B)   The lone year he got into 100 games was served at shortstop for the only team to play a full season in a preexisting major league and finish in the first division in the lone year it was extant.

    C)   The team was Toledo in the AA in 1890.

    D)   He and Erve Beck formed Cleveland's first keystone combo in the AL.

    E)   His initials are the same as those of a utility infielder nicknamed "Chicken" on the last team prior to 1993 to win back-to-back World Championships.

18. **What slugger currently holds the record for the most career home runs by a player who failed to hit any dingers with his original ML team?**
    A) He batted .176 in 23 games in 1983 with his original club.
    B) He paced the AL in RBI in his second full ML season.
    C) In 1990 he compiled 115 RBI on a .232 BA.
    D) He hit his 371st career homer in 1997 after hitting none with the Cubs, his original team.
    E) He is best remembered for his most recent postseason dinger in 1993.

19. **Babe Ruth easily holds the record for the most home runs compiled by a player after leaving his original ML team, clobbering 665 dingers subsequent to his departure from the Red Sox. Among retired players, who is second to the Babe with 378 circuit clouts after saying goodbye to his original team?**
    A) He led the NL in pinch-hit at bats the year he broke Norm Cash's old record of 373 homers after leaving the White Sox.
    B) His last dinger came with the 1988 Expos.
    C) He saw World Series action with teams in both leagues but never with the Twins, his original team.
    D) The vast majority of his career home runs came with the same club that Ruth made the beneficiary of most of his dingers.
    E) He holds the Yankees record for the most career homers by a third sacker.

20. **Johnny Mostil owns the record for the fewest career RBI (372) by a player with 1,000 hits and a .300 career batting average. But Mostil played in just 972 games and had barely more than 1,000 hits. Among 1,000-gamers with 1,000 hits and a .300 career batting average, who has the fewest RBI?**
    A) He had a .312 career BA in 1,170 games but just 397 RBI.
    B) In his final season as a regular, he hit .326 for the A's and scored 95 runs but went homerless in 515 ABs.
    C) In 1940, his soph season, he led the AL in triples with 19 and shared the lead in hits with 200.
    D) In his final big league season in 1953, he was a teammate of the man who is second to him on the Top 10 list.
    E) In 1946 he was the only AL regular whom Bob Feller was unable to fan and later was a teammate of Feller's in his final three big league seasons, 1951–53.

Fewest RBI with a .300 Career BA, 1,000 Hits and 1,000 Games

RANK	NAME	YEARS	HITS	BA	RBI
1	Barney McCosky	1939–53	1301	.312	397
2	Dale Mitchell	1946–56	1244	.312	403
3	Johnny Pesky	1942–54	1455	.307	404
4	Ralph Garr	1968–80	1562	.306	408
5	Matty Alou	1960–74	1777	.307	427
6	Charlie Jamieson	1915–32	1990	.303	552
7	Taffy Wright	1938–49	1115	.311	553
8	Jack Tobin	1914–27	1906	.309	581
9	Bob Fothergill	1922–33	1064	.325	582
10	Richie Ashburn	1948–62	2574	.308	586
	Rube Bressler	1914–32	1170	.301	586

21. **Three leagues have been accorded major status for at least 10 seasons by historians. They are: the National League, American League, and American Association. Many men have played in two of those three circuits, and some 19th century performers even lasted long enough to play in all three. But only one man played in the AA and the AL without ever playing in the NL. Who is he?**

    A) His two ML managers were Billy Barnie and Frank Dwyer.

    B) He played eight games with Baltimore in 1891 (AA), then disappeared from the majors until 1902 when he played eight games with Detroit (AL).

    C) He and the Pittsburgh third sacker who was dealt to Milwaukee after he swatted .294 in his first full ML season in 1953 share the same last name.

    D) He and the last player to be banned for life after attempting to bribe an opponent share the same initials and same last name.

    E) His first name matches that of the man with the most career wins of any NL manager.

22. **What Hall of Famer is currently the unlikely owner of the season record for the fewest runs scored by an outfielder with 500 or more at bats?**

    A) He set the record as a rookie when he collected just 42 tallies in 504 ABs.

    B) He scored 1,622 runs in 22 seasons.

    C) He was a 19-year-old Bonus Baby the year he set the mark for the fewest runs by an outfielder in 500 or more ABs.

    D) He collected his 3,007th and final hit in his last season.

    E) The year after he set his negative runs record, he established the record for being the youngest man ever to win a major league batting title.

Fewest Runs Scored, Minimum 500 ABs, Season, Each Position

POS.	NAME	TEAM	YEAR	ABS	BA	RUNS
SS	Leo Cardenas	Cal, AL	1972	551	.223	25
1B	Earl Sheely	Bos, NL	1931	538	.273	30
2B	Billy Gardner	Bal, AL	1958	560	.225	32
3B	Hobe Ferris	StL, AL	1909	556	.216	36
	Billy Purtell	Chi/Bos, AL	1910	536	.226	36
C	Shanty Hogan	NY, NL	1932	502	.287	36
RF	Al Kaline	Det, AL	1954	504	.276	42
CF	Joe Kelly	Pit, NL	1914	508	.222	47
LF	Howie Shanks	Was, AL	1914	500	.224	44

23. **Only in recent years has it become relatively common for a player to compile 2,000 hits with a sub-.300 career batting average. Who was the first 2,000-hit man to retire with a batting average that fell below .300?**

    A) His last big league at bat came in 1894.

    B) Of his 2,140 career hits, 193 came with the 1893 Giants.

    C) He led the NL twice in stolen bases.

    D) He played his first ML game in 1878 at age 18.

    E) He is the only 2,000-hit man who also bagged at least 100 wins.

Evolution of Record for Lowest Career BA with 2,000 Hits

NAME	YEARS	HITS	BA
Deacon White	1871–90	2066	.312
Paul Hines	1872–91	2135	.302
Monte Ward	1878–94	2105	.275
Bid McPhee	1882–99	2250	.271
Tommy Corcoran	1890–1907	2251	.25579
Graig Nettles	1967–88	2225	.248

24. **Seven 19th century players performed in the Union Association, the American Association, the National League, and the Players League, but only two put in a full season in each of the four major leagues extant between 1876 and the close of the 19th century. Hence the two are the all-time co-record-holders for playing at least one full season in the most different major leagues. Who are they?**

A) One was a pitcher, and the other was an outfielder.

B) The gardener hit under .230 in consecutive years for Indianapolis in 1887–88.

C) The pitcher is the only man to have four seasons in four different major leagues in which he hurled at least 300 innings.

D) The pitcher toiled for Cleveland teams in three different major leagues in three consecutive years, and the outfielder's last name is almost identical to that of the only Tribe player to lead the AL in batter Ks three years in a row.

E) Both of their first names begin with E, and one has the second-most career hits and the other the most career wins among players with their respective first names.

25. **In 1971, Roger Metzger became the first man ever to lead a major circuit in an extra-base-hit department with a sub-.300 slugging average when he co-led the NL with 11 triples while slugging just .299. Who currently owns the record for the lowest season slugging average by a leader in an extra-base-hit department?**

A) He slugged .293 and collected just 26 extra-base hits the lone year he topped the NL in three-baggers.

B) He collected the last of his 504 career hits with the 1982 Yankees.

C) All three of his career home runs came in 1979 with the NL East runner-up.

D) He hit .167 for the losing side in the 1980 NLCS the same year he topped the senior loop with 13 triples.

E) He and Carew have the same first name.

26. **What rookie in 1955 set the current all-time record for the most at bats in a season without putting the ball in play?**

A) In 12 games as a frosh, he collected 12 ABs and fanned all 12 times.

B) In his final season, he compiled 57 whiffs in 118 ABs.

C) He batted right and threw left, but few noticed which way he batted.

D) His left arm took him to the Hall of Fame even though he fanned 386 times in 776 career ABs.

E) He has both the highest percentage of batter Ks per pitcher faced and the highest percentage of pitcher Ks per batter faced of anyone whose last name begins with K.

27. **Excluding pitchers and Johnny Cooney (a pitcher for nearly half his career), who holds the record for the fewest career games played among men who spent at least 20 years in the majors?**
    A) He played 1,454 games spread over 21 seasons.
    B) He played 100 games in a season for the last time in 1898 when he hit .249 for Cleveland while dividing his time between first base and catcher.
    C) He played for a St. Louis amateur team called the Peach Pies as a youth, leading to one of his nicknames.
    D) He was unofficially banned from the majors for his part as St. Louis Browns manager in trying to throw the 1910 AL batting race Nap Lajoie's way.
    E) He and a coholder of the record for hurling the longest complete game in history share the same initials.

28. **Lou Brock currently has the record for the most career games (2,616) by a position player with fewer than 20 seasons in the majors, but Brock's career started after the schedule grew to 162 games. Who holds the record for the most career games played by a man with fewer than 20 seasons in the majors before the schedule became 162 games?**
    A) He played 2,517 games in 19 seasons, including 61 in his finale in 1917.
    B) After leaving the majors in 1917, he played several more years in the PCL and eventually died in Hollywood at age 88.
    C) In 1914–15, he played 313 games and led the AL in RBI both seasons.
    D) He was the first man in the 20th century to lead both the NL and the AL in triples.
    E) His 311 career triples are the record for which he's best known.

29. **The first ML'er to retire with 1,000 career hits and a sub-.250 batting average was on flag winners in two different NL cities in his first two seasons. Who is he?**
    A) He has another odd record—he is the only man in ML history to be a regular for eight straight seasons with eight different teams.
    B) In his second season he hit .197 as the regular right fielder for the first team to win a 19th century World Series.
    C) His offensive high came in 1890 when he rapped .292 for Cleveland of the PL.
    D) In 1891 he played shortstop and helped the Boston Reds win the last AA flag.
    E) He was named after one of our greatest patriots.

30. **Who ended a 14-year ML career in the mid-1990s as the new owner of the all-time record for the most at bats by a man who retired with fewer than 1,000 career hits?**
    A) The previous 20th century record holder was Roger Metzger with 4,201 ABs.
    B) Both his first and his 985th and last hits came with the same AL team.
    C) In 1988 he compiled a career-high 126 hits in 527 ABs.
    D) In 1986, his only postseason exposure, he hit .300 for the ALCS loser.
    E) He and his father hold the record for the lowest combined career BA (.229) by a father and son with at least 6,000 combined ABs.

Most Career ABs with Fewer than 1,000 Hits

RANK	NAME	YEARS	BA	HITS	ABS
1	Dick Schofield	1983–96	.230	989	4299
2	Willie Kuehne	1883–92	.232	996	4284
3	Pop Smith	1880–91	.222	941	4238
4	Roger Metzger	1970–80	.231	972	4201
5	Rabbit Warstler	1930–40	.229	935	4088
6	Rick Cerone	1975–92	.245	998	4069
7	Mal Kittridge	1890–99, 1901–06	.219	882	4027
8	Woodie Held	1954–69	.240	963	4019
9	Dick Green	1963–74	.240	960	4007
10	Red Dooin	1902–16	.240	961	4004

ANSWERS

Answers

The Elite 3,000

1. Worsts

Lowest Batting Average	Dave Winfield .283
Lowest Slugging Average	Pete Rose .409
Fewest Total Bases	Rod Carew 3998
Fewest Home Runs	Eddie Collins 47
Lowest OBP	Lou Brock .344
Fewest RBI	Lou Brock 900
Fewest Runs	Roberto Clemente 1416
Fewest Triples	Eddie Murray 35
Fewest Walks	Nap Lajoie 516
Most Strikeouts	Lou Brock 1730
Fewest Stolen Bases	Roberto Clemente 83

2. Robin Yount, George Brett, Rod Carew, and Roberto Clemente

3. Nap Lajoie

4. Al Kaline, Carl Yastrzemski, Roberto Clemente, Robin Yount, George Brett, and Stan Musial

5. Carl Yastrzemski

6. Eddie Collins, Dave Winfield, Robin Yount, Eddie Murray, and Lou Brock

7. Paul Waner

8. Cap Anson and Nap Lajoie, 1896

9. Ty Cobb and Eddie Collins; Tris Speaker

10. Paul "Big Poison" Waner

11. Honus Wagner, 1903

12. Tris Speaker

13. Luke Appling and Ted Williams

14. Roger Connor

15. Willie Mays

The Cooperstown 500

1. Worsts

Lowest Batting Average	Harmon Killebrew .256
Lowest Slugging Average	Eddie Murray .476
Fewest Total Bases	Harmon Killebrew 4143
Lowest Home Run Ratio	Mel Ott 5.4
Lowest OBP	Ernie Banks .333
Fewest Hits	Harmon Killebrew 2086
Fewest RBI	Eddie Mathews 1453
Fewest Runs	Willie McCovey 1229
Fewest Walks	Ernie Banks 763
Most Strikeouts	Reggie Jackson 2597
Fewest Stolen Bases	Harmon Killebrew 19

2. Jimmie Foxx

3. Frank Robinson: Cincinnati, Baltimore, Los Angeles, California, and Cleveland

4. Pittsburgh, Chicago White Sox, and St. Louis Cardinals

5. Harmon Killebrew

6. Jimmie Foxx

7. Willie Mays and Willie McCovey, Hank Aaron and Eddie Mathews, Ted Williams and Jimmie Foxx

8. Mel Ott

9. Jimmie Foxx versus Burleigh Grimes

10. Ted Williams and Willie Mays

11. Gavvy Cravath

12. Jimmie Foxx and Lefty Grove, 1940 Boston Red Sox

13. Eddie Mathews; Detroit; Boston Braves; Braves franchise; Houston 1967

14. Jimmie Foxx

Hallowed Hitsmiths

1. Rogers Hornsby and Sam Rice
2. Joe Jackson and Tuck Turner
3. Al Simmons (.363), Rogers Hornsby (.361), and Chuck Klein (.360)
4. Rabbit Warstler
5. Gil Coan; Gordy Coleman
6. Tommy Holmes in 1945
7. Donie Bush
8. Tom Brown
9. Red Ruffing
10. Tris Speaker
11. Frank McCormick
12. Hal McRae
13. Terry Forster; Tony Fernandez
14. Buck Freeman; Bill Freehan
15. Doc Cramer
16. Maury Wills, 1962
17. Eddie Lake; Eddie Mayo
18. Felipe Alou, 1968; son Moises; Montreal
19. Matty Alou, 1966–69
20. Jesus Alou; Jerry Adair

On the Double

1. George Brett
2. Ruppert Jones, 1981, 34 doubles and 99 hits; Jake Ruppert
3. Baby Doll Jacobson, 1926, 51 doubles and 62 runs
4. Sonny Jackson; Shoeless Joe Jackson
5. Ken Reitz; Heinie Reitz
6. Willie Keeler
7. Bobby Byrne; Charlie Byrne; Barry Bonds
8. Willie Mays, 18 in 1954
9. Harmon Killebrew, 11 doubles and 49 homers in 1964
10. Enos Slaughter (52), Joe Medwick (48), and Johnny Mize (44)
11. George Burns (64) and Tris Speaker (52)

12. Shano Collins; Eddie Collins
13. AL, 1966–74; Zoilo Versalles and Fred Lynn
14. Harry Taylor; Hal Trosky
15. Goat Anderson; John Anderson
16. Edgar Martinez, 1995
17. Billy Herman

Triple Threats

1. Harry Stovey
2. Sam Rice
3. Kiki Cuyler
4. Casey Stengel, 1922
5. Mike Mitchell; Dale Mitchell
6. Bid McPhee
7. Duke Farrell
8. Bill Madlock
9. Don Mattingly
10. Joe Kelley; King Kelly
11. Jerry Denny; Jim Donnelly
12. Dale Mitchell
13. Roger Metzger; Butch Metzger
14. Harry Davis
15. Phils, 1947, Harry Walker
16. Craig Worthington; Al Worthington
17. Joe Jackson

Tater Titans

1. 1947 Pittsburgh Pirates, Ralph Kiner and Hank Greenberg; Pat Seerey
2. Luscious "Luke" Easter; Lucius "Luke" Appling
3. Johnny Miller; Joe Medwick; Bing Miller
4. Dave Kingman, 1982
5. Phil Todt; Patsy Tebeau
6. Charlie Keller; Clyde King
7. Frank Howard
8. 1898 Cleveland Spiders; Ed McKean; Jesse Burkett; Louis Sockalexis; Cy Young
9. Dan Brouthers and Hardy Richardson
10. Chuck Klein, 1928 and 1938; Charlie Keller

11. Hack Wilson (56) and Gabby Hartnett (37), 1930 Cubs; Wally Berger

12. Rudy York

13. Tony Armas; Tommie Aaron

14. Rogers Hornsby

15. Gavvy Cravath

16. Rocky Colavito

17. Eddie Yost

18. Briggs Stadium (formerly Navin Field); Hank Greenberg

19. Rabbit Maranville

20. Johnny Mize, 1947, 51 homers and 42 Ks

21. Bob Meusel, 1925

Brilliant Bat Titlists

1. Snuffy Stirnweiss, 1945

2. Mickey Mantle, 1956–57

3. Babe Ruth; Boston, AL, and Boston, NL

4. Tip O'Neill, 1887–88, born in Canada

5. Sportsman's Park, 1910; Jack O'Connor

6. Billy Goodman

7. Alex Johnson

8. Rod Carew; Cesar Tovar was his 1971 teammate

9. Dale Alexander; Doyle Alexander

10. Willie Keeler

11. Mike Donlin

12. Jake Daubert and Ferris Fain

13. Pete Runnels and Carl Yastrzemski

14. Honus Wagner, Roberto Clemente, and Dave Parker

15. Tony Cuccinello, 1945; Johnny Dickshot; Tony Conigliaro

16. Will Clark, 1989; Carney Lansford was the A's third sacker

17. 1948, Lou Boudreau (2) and Dale Mitchell (3)

18. Jack Clements

19. Pete Browning

20. Lou Boudreau, 1944, followed Luke Appling, 1943, making two consecutive shortstop batting crown winners; Nap Lajoie and Tris Speaker were the other future Hall of Fame player-managers

21. Billy Hamilton; Dan Brouthers in 1892

22. Stan Musial versus Frank Baumholtz on September 28, 1952

23. Richie Ashburn, 1958; Ted Williams had a .462 OBP to Ashburn's .441

RBI Rulers

1. Rudy York, 1937, 115 hits and 103 RBI; Frank Thomas, 1953, 116 hits and 102 RBI; Roy Sievers, 1954, 119 hits and 102 RBI; Phil Plantier, 1993, 111 hits and 100 RBI; Joe Carter, 1994, 118 hits and 103 RBI

2. Jim Gentile

3. Hack Wilson

4. Mark McGwire and Paul Sorrento

5. 1930 Phillies, Chuck Klein and Pinky Whitney

6. Gus Bell, 1959, and Vic Wertz, 1960; Gus Zernial and Vic Power

7. Fred Tenney; Frank Tanana

8. Heinie Reitz and Hughie Jennings

9. Hubie Brooks

10. Gorman Thomas

11. Jimmy Bannon; Johnny Blanchard

12. Maury Wills, Willie Wilson, and Larry Bowa

13. George Grantham; Gary Gaetti

14. Wally Berger, 1935

15. Vern Stephens

16. Lloyd Waner; Matty Alou; Paul Waner

17. Beals Becker; Bruce Bochy

18. Ron Northey

19. Joe Gordon, Ken Keltner, and Lou Boudreau, 1948 Indians, with Eddie Robinson at first base; Walt Dropo, Vern Stephens, and Bobby Doerr, 1950 Red Sox

20. Lou Boudreau, 1948

21. Dixie Walker, 8–124 in 1945 and 9–116 in 1946; Bob Elliott in 1943 and 1945 was the next-to-last to do it twice in his career; Harry Walker

22. Jocko Milligan and Farmer Vaughn

Silver Sluggers

1. Dick Allen
2. Jack Fournier
3. Joe Kelley
4. Carl Yastrzemski
5. Patsy Donovan
6. John Anderson; Brady Anderson
7. Mel Ott, 1936
8. Rogers Hornsby
9. Willie Stargell
10. Bob Johnson; brother Roy
11. Dan Brouthers
12. Ted Williams, 1954
13. Zack Wheat
14. Hal Lanier; father Max; Herman Long
15. Robin Yount, 1982
16. Carlton Fisk, 1972
17. 1904, Honus Wagner and Nap Lajoie
18. John Tobin; Jim Tobin
19. Johnny Mize
20. Dan Brouthers

Speed Merchants

1. Bob Dillinger; John Dillinger
2. Art Devlin; Jim Devlin
3. Danny Murtaugh, 1941
4. Frank Isbell
5. Ron LeFlore; Rudy Law, 77 in 1983
6. Bob Bescher; Barry Bonds
7. Sam Mertes; Sam McDowell
8. Russ Nixon; *Nixon*
9. Don Mattingly, 1986
10. Herb Washington; Claudell Washington
11. Sam Jethroe
12. Eddie Collins
13. Jackie Jensen
14. Dave Philley
15. Stan Hack

16. Dave Collins; Eddie Collins
17. Pepper Martin
18. Nap Lajoie

Super Scorers

1. Tip O'Neill and Arlie Latham, 1887 St. Louis Browns
2. Red Rolfe
3. Chuck Klein
4. Johnny Mostil; Joe Medwick
5. Rickey Henderson and George Burns
6. Yank Robinson; Tom Brown
7. Max Bishop; Lefty Grove and Connie Mack
8. Earl Torgeson; Earl Averill; Snohomish, Washington
9. Cal Ripken, 1983; brother Billy
10. Dick McAuliffe; Ray Oyler
11. Yogi Berra
12. Dick Higham
13. Dick Stuart
14. Brooks Robinson
15. Bid McPhee
16. Bill Madlock
17. 1891; Billy Hamilton and Tom Brown
18. Tim Raines
19. Gus Williams; George Weiss; Ted Williams
20. Miller Huggins
21. Dick Howser
22. George Case, 1943
23. Wee Willie Keeler, tied in 1899 with 140
24. Solly Hemus; Sollie Hofman; Stan Hack
25. Harlond Clift at third base with the 1936 St. Louis Browns; Red Rolfe; Rogers Hornsby; Hal Chase

Walk Wizards

1. Mickey Mantle, Ted Williams, and Hank Greenberg
2. Eddie Yost
3. Wade Boggs

4. Max Bishop, 117 runs and 111 hits in 1930; Moe Berg

5. Mike Hargrove

6. Wes Westrum; Wes Covington

7. Whitey Witt trailed Babe Ruth; Willie Wilson; Mike Witt

8. Eddie Yost

9. Darrell Evans; 1973 Braves; Hank Aaron and Davey Johnson were his 40-homer teammates with the 1973 Braves

10. Joe Morgan

11. Topper Rigney; Bill Rigney

12. George Burns

13. 1976–78 Yankees; Mickey Rivers; Willie Randolph

14. Samuel James Tilden "Jimmy" Sheckard

15. Jack Crooks; Jimmy Collins

16. Bob Elliott; Jackie Robinson

17. Roy Cullenbine; Roy Hughes; Roy Campanella

18. Jim Wynn, .207 in 1976

19. Pittsburgh

20. Lenny Dykstra

21. Yank Robinson; Bill White

BothWay Bammers

1. Max Carey

2. George Davis

3. Billy Rogell; Bobby Richardson

4. John Anderson

5. Tom McCreery, July 12, 1897; Terry Moore

6. Jim Gilliam (3B), Maury Wills (SS), Jim Lefebvre (2B), and Wes Parker (1B)

7. 1902 White Sox: Tom Daly, George Davis, and Sammy Strang

8. Bob Ferguson

9. Buck Weaver

10. Ripper Collins

11. Willie McGee

12. Frankie Frisch

13. Roy Cullenbine

14. Kid Gleason; George Davis was his keystone partner in 1897

15. Danny Moeller in 1913; Don Money

16. Mark Koenig

In a Pinch

1. Jose Morales

2. Bob Lemon

3. George Mullin

4. Dave Philley; Darrell Porter

5. Ham Hyatt; Harry Hooper; Harry Heilmann

6. Ira Thomas

7. Earl Averill

8. Bob Fothergill

9. Pat Mullin; Paul Molitor; George Mullin

10. Vic Wertz

11. Gordy Coleman; George Crowe

12. Ed Kranepool

13. Henry Cotto; Harry Craft, 1939–40

14. Red Lucas

15. Greg Gross; George Grantham

16. Chuck Essegian; Cecil Espy

17. Frank Snyder; Pop Snyder

18. Clint Courtney

19. Ivan Murrell; Ivan "Ike" Delock

20. Russ Snyder; Riggs Stephenson; Frank Snyder

21. Cy Williams; Ken Williams

22. Bob Cerv

23. Jerry Lynch; Jose Lind; Jack Lynch

The Choice 300

1.   Worsts

Highest ERA	Early Wynn 3.54
Most Walks	Nolan Ryan 2795
Fewest Strikeouts	Pud Galvin 1799
Most Hits per 9 Innings	Pud Galvin 9.6
Lowest Winning Percentage	Nolan Ryan .526
Fewest Shutouts	Hoss Radbourn 34
Fewest Complete Games	Don Sutton 178
Most Losses	Cy Young 315
Fewest 20-Win Seasons	Don Sutton 1
Highest Opponents' OBP	Early Wynn .321

2. Pud Galvin

3. Gaylord Perry and Phil Niekro

4. Eddie Plank

5. Cy Young, John Clarkson, Steve Carlton, Phil Niekro, Gaylord Perry, and Early Wynn

6. Early Wynn

7. Hoss Radbourn, John Clarkson, Cy Young, Warren Spahn, Phil Niekro, and Kid Nichols; Young leads all righties in wins and Spahn leads all lefties

8. Detroit

9. Tony Mullane; Moses Walker in 1884

10. Mickey Welch; Tim Keefe was his teammate; Bob Welch

11. Don Sutton

12. Steve Carlton

13. Grover Cleveland "Pete" Alexander

14. Cy Young

15. Mickey Welch; Troy, New York

16. John Clarkson

17. Red Ruffing and Ted Lyons

18. Lefty Grove

Strikeout Stories

1. 1961 Dodgers: Sandy Koufax, Don Drysdale, and Stan Williams

2. 1967 Twins: Dean Chance (220), Jim Kaat (211), and Dave Boswell (204)

3. Camilo Pascual, 1961–63, Minnesota; brother Carlos

4. Urban Shocker

5. Jim Bunning (Rube Waddell led the NL in 1900 before the AL earned major league status)

6. Hippo Vaughn

7. Noodles Hahn, 1899–1901

8. Joe Bowman, 1945 Reds; Johnny Vander Meer; Jim Bouton

9. Phil Marchildon; Paul Minner

10. 1921 Giants, 357 Ks in 153 games, led by Art Nehf with 67

11. Tom Hughes, 1902 Orioles; Tex Hughson

12. The Reds; Red Lucas (40 in 220), Eppa Rixey (10 in 94), Benny Frey (12 in 132), and Ray Kolp (28 in 150); Donie Bush

13. Bill Beckman, 20 in 155.1 innings in 1939; 1942 Cardinals; Bo Belinsky; Rod Beck

14. Slim Sallee in 1919

15. Jerry Koosman; Jose DeLeon

16. Terry Felton; Terry Forster

17. 1924 Indians: Stan Coveleski, George Uhle, Joe Shaute, and Sherry Smith; Tris Speaker

18. Allie Reynolds; he, Bender, and Yellowhorse were Native Americans

19. Bob Veale; Bill Virdon

20. Dodgers, 1921–28, Grimes and Dazzy Vance; Angels, 1972–79, Nolan Ryan and Frank Tanana

21. Lefty Grove

22. Bob Turley; Jack Chesbro in 1904

23. Dazzy Vance, 1924; Burleigh Grimes; Dolf Luque; Rogers Hornsby

24. Tom Hughes

25. Smokey Joe Wood

26. John Clarkson

Kings of the Hill: 1871–1919

1. Jim Whitney

2. 1884 Cincinnati Outlaw Reds: Dick Burns, Jim McCormick, and George Bradley

3. 1886 New York Mets; Jack Lynch was the third

4. Matt Kilroy; set the all-time season K record as a rookie; brother Mike

5. George Mullin

6. Bill Hutchison

7. Jim McCormick, 1886, Chicago; Jack McDowell

8. Chief Bender

9. King Cole, 1910; Alex Cole

10. Noodles Hahn, Cincinnati, 1901

11. 1916 A's: Elmer Myers, Joe Bush, and Jack Nabors

12. Washington, NL, 1889; Alex Ferson (19–19) was its break-even pitcher

13. Larry McKeon, 1884, Indianapolis, AA (41), and John Coleman, 1883, 48 with Philadelphia, NL

14. Sam Leever; 1899 Pirates

15. Fred Goldsmith, 1880; Fred Gladding

16. Al Maul; Andy Messersmith

17. Jim Hughey, 16 straight for the 1899 Spiders

18. Tom Seaton; Tom Seaver

19. Lee Meadows

20. Happy Townsend

21. Bill Bailey; Ed Bailey, 28 in 1956

22. Billy Taylor; Bob Tewksbury

23. Les German; Larry Gura

24. Red Ames; Rick Aguilera

25. Pete Schneider; Paul Splittorff

26. Johnny Lush; Johnny Lindell

27. Chick Fraser; Chuck Finley

28. Toad Ramsey

Kings of the Hill: 1920–98

1. Bob Turley, 13 losses in 1955

2. Tracy Stallard; Craig Anderson lost 17 in 1962; Jack Fisher and Roger Craig were the last two 24-game losers

3. Mark Langston

4. Carl Mays; his pitch killed Ray Chapman

5. Sam McDowell

6. Freddie Fitzsimmons, 217 wins and 870 Ks

7. Larry Jaster; Larry Jackson, 1964

8. "Bullet" Joe Bush, 1922; "Bullet" Joe Rogan

9. Bob Grim; Scott Erickson; and John Smiley

10. Storm Davis, 1989 A's, 169.1 innings; Johnny Sturm

11. Allie Reynolds

12. Tom Zachary

13. Fergie Jenkins

14. Johnny Allen

15. Rick Honeycutt

16. Marlin Stuart; Mike Smithson

17. Freddie Fitzsimmons

18. Luis Aloma; Luis Arroyo

19. Rich Robertson; Charlie Robertson

20. Bob Welch

21. Robin Roberts and Denny McLain

Precious Pen Men

1. Joe Berry; Juan Berenguer

2. Bob Osborn; Bob Ojeda

3. Hugh Casey

4. Garland Braxton; Ginger Beaumont; Wayne Garland

5. Bob Veale

6. Todd Worrell; brother Tim

7. Dick "The Monster" Radatz

8. Kid Nichols

9. Charlie Hough

10. Charley Hall; Charlie Hough

11. Lindy McDaniel

12. Ellis Kinder

13. Clem Labine

14. (Selva) Lew Burdette

15. Goose Gossage

16. Joe Page and Luis Arroyo; Yogi Berra; Johnny Sain

17. Wilbur Wood

18. Ed Walsh, 40 of his 195 wins in 1908

No-No's and Perfectos

1. Jim Bunning, 1958 Tigers and 1964 Phils; his perfecto came on Father's Day

2. Jim Maloney, 1965; Reds

3. Milwaukee Braves

4. Ossee Schreckengost (Schreck); Rube Waddell was the pitcher he caught

5. Harry Hooper; Ernie Shore was the other pitcher

6. Nick Maddox, 1907, in Pittsburgh

7. Jack Morris and Ken Forsch, whose brother Bob had earlier thrown a no-hitter, making them the first pair of no-no siblings

8. Bobby Burke; Britt Burns; Tim Burke

9. Doc Amole; Mike Meola; Don Aase

10. Ted Breitenstein

11. Byron Browne and Don Young

12. George Estock; Cliff Chambers; George Earnshaw; socket

13. Jeff Tesreau

14. Dummy Hoy, teammate of Ted Breitenstein in 1891; versus Bill Hawke in 1893 and versus Earl Moore in 1901

15. Jim O'Rourke

16. Sal Maglie, 1956

17. The Phillies; Johnny Lush in 1906 and Jim Bunning in 1964

18. Sam Kimber; Sandy Koufax

Wondrous Wild Men

1. Dick Weik, 1949; Dick Welteroth; Duane Ward

2. Willie McGill; Wilcy Moore

3. Tommy Byrne; Tom Browning

4. Bruno Haas, with the 1915 A's, which gave up 827 walks; Brian Harvey

5. Giants; Bill George and Henry Mathewson, brother of Christy; Amos Rusie; Sam Jones in 1959

6. Phil Knell; Pete Kilduff

7. David Cone

8. Sam Jones, 1959

9. Babe Ruth, 1916

10. Herm Wehmeier; Herman Wedemeyer; Hoyt Wilhelm

11. Lefty Grove, 1925

12. George Uhle, 1926; George Burns

13. Chick Fraser, 31 hit batsmen in 1901 and 149 walks in 1905; Chuck Finley

14. Mike Torrez

15. Bobo Newsom

16. Brickyard Kennedy

17. Nolan Ryan

18. Gus Weyhing; brother John

Gold Glove Gems

1. Bill Mazeroski

2. Jack Doyle; George Davis; Jim Derrington; Jimmy Dykes

3. Elmer Smith

4. Claude Ritchey; Charles "Hoss" Radbourn

5. Mike Griffin; Tommy Tucker; 1887 Baltimore Orioles

6. Bobby Wine; Bill White

7. A's; Jimmy Walsh, Amos Strunk, and Rube Oldring

8. Herman Reich; Harold Reynolds

9. Lou Stringer; Lenn Sakata

10. Eddie Miller; Rick Miller; Eddie Murray

11. 1977 Reds

12. Joe and Luke Sewell

13. Billy Herman and Billy Jurges, 1935 Cubs; Phil Cavarretta

14. Ned Williamson; Cap Anson, Tom Burns, and Fred Pfeffer were the other three Chicago infielders from 1883 through 1889

15. Sam Mertes; Stan Musial

16. Heinie Majeski; Heinie Groh

17. Pat Moran

18. John "Jiggs" Donahue; Joe DiMaggio

19. Wally Gerber

20. Vic Power

Gateway Guardians

1. Stuffy McInnis and Jake Daubert

2. George Kelly, 1921; Gene Kelly

3. Lu Blue

4. Cecil Cooper

5. George Scott and Tony Bartirome; Tony Gwynn; George C. Scott

6. Joe Quinn; Jack Quinn

7. Dave Foutz

8. Dave Orr

9. Deacon White, 1877; brother Will

10. Hal Chase

11. Tommy Tucker

12. Candy LaChance

13. Cap Anson, 1883 (Steve Brady of the New York Mets also went homerless in 1883 while dividing his time between first base and the outfield.)

14. Zeke Bonura

15. Keith Hernandez

16. Earl Sheely; son Earl; Eddie Stanky

17. Nap Lajoie and Ed Delahanty

Crackerjack Keystoners

1. Bill Mazeroski; Buddy Myer

2. Dots Miller; Honus Wagner; Don Money

3. Eddie Collins; son Eddie

4. Dick Green; Don Gullett

5. Mark Lemke; Mike Lum

6. Juan Samuel

7. Joe Gordon

8. Danny Murphy; Dale Murphy

9. Del Pratt; St. Louis Browns; Rogers Hornsby; Dick Porter

10. Snuffy Stirnweiss, 1945 wartime season; Bobby Grich, 1981 strike season

11. Charlie Gehringer

12. Frank Isbell; Cecil Isbell

13. Billy Herman; Babe Herman; Roger Hornsby was the future Hall of Famer

14. Ryne Sandberg

15. Bobby Lowe, 1894

16. Bill Sweeney; Charlie Sweeney

Hot Corner Highlights

1. Hick Carpenter

2. Graig Nettles; Greg Maddux

3. Al Rosen

4. Red Rolfe; 1952 Tigers; Frankie Crosetti, 137 runs in 1936

5. Chuck Workman

6. Pepper Martin, 1933

7. Jimmy Austin

8. Frank "Home Run" Baker

9. Tommy Leach; Al Reach

10. Billy Nash; Bob Nieman

11. Jimmy Dykes

12. Chris Brown; Bobby Brown

13. The Phillies: Mike Schmidt, Lave Cross, and Pinky Whitney

14. John Castino; Jimmy Collins

15. Pie Traynor; Cy Young

16. Lafayette "Lave" Cross

17. Larry Gardner

18. Buddy Bell; Toby Harrah; father Gus

Stellar Shortstops

1. Luis Aparicio

2. Pittsburgh: Honus Wagner, Arky Vaughan, Joe Cronin, and Rabbit Maranville

3. Travis Jackson, Ernie Banks, and Eddie Miller; Eddie Mathews, 1952

4. Toby Harrah

5. Larry Bowa

6. Frankie Crosetti

7. 1884 Detroit

8. Dick Howser, 1961

9. Jack Glasscock

10. Joe Cronin; Clark Griffith was his father-in-law

11. Rabbit Maranville

12. Glenn Wright; George Wright

13. John Gochnaur; Jack Glasscock

14. Herman Long

15. Bill Dahlen

16. Garry Templeton; Gorman Thomas

17. Tommy Corcoran; Terry Crowley; Larry Corcoran

Grand Gardeners

1. Paul Hines

2. Lou Brock

3. Willie Keeler

4. Jimmy Barrett; Red Barrett; Jay Bell

5. Tommy Holmes

6. Gene Stephens; Vern Stephens

7. Kip Selbach; Kevin Seitzer

8. George Selkirk

9. 1908 Cubs: Wildfire Schulte, Jimmy Slagle, and Jimmy Sheckard; 1906 White Sox: Bill O'Neill, Fielder Jones, Ed Hahn, and Patsy Dougherty

10. Jim Lillie; Jim Levey; Bob Lilly

11. 1921 Tigers: Ty Cobb, Bobby Veach, and Harry Heilmann; 1921 Yankees; 1961 Yankees: Roger Maris and Mickey Mantle

12. 1980 Indians; Super Joe Charboneau; Miguel Dilone

13. Gavvy Cravath

14. Roy Thomas; Robby Thompson

15. Ben Chapman

16. Charlie Jamieson; Chipper Jones

17. Tommy Davis

18. Don Baylor

19. Cliff Heathcote; Chick Hafey

20. Doc Miller; Dots Miller

21. Irish Meusel; brother Bob

22. Chick Hafey

Regal Receivers

1. Doc Bushong, 1886 St. Louis Browns, AA

2. Deacon McGuire, Washington, 1895

3. Connie Mack, Buffalo, PL, 1890

4. Chief Zimmer, Cleveland, 1890

5. Bill Rariden, 1914–15 Indianapolis and Newark, FL, and 1916 New York Giants, NL

6. Eddie Ainsmith, 1917 and 1919 AL and 1922 NL

7. Jack O'Connor, 1890, .324 with Columbus

8. Frankie Hayes, Philadelphia A's, 1945

9. Yogi Berra, New York Yankees, 1951, 1954, and 1955

10. 1883 Boston Beaneaters, NL: lefty Mike Hines split the job with Mert Hackett

11. Spud Davis; Spud Chandler; Jody Davis

12. Gabby Street; Gabby Hartnett

13. Eddie Ainsmith; Ed Albrecht in 1949; Ed Abbaticchio

14. Deacon McGuire

15. Manny Sanguillen, 1969–71; Mike Stanley

16. Rick Ferrell; brother Wes

17. Wally Schang; brother Bobby

18. Andy Seminick

19. Gene Tenace

20. Johnny Bassler; Jim Bouton

21. Bill Freehan; Lance Parrish; Barry Foote

22. Billy Sullivan and son Billy; Jimmy Sheckard

23. Rich Dempsey; Jack Dempsey

24. Jocko Milligan; Buck Ewing

Versatile Virtuosos

1. Sport McAllister, Cleveland in 1899

2. Dave Foutz, John Coleman, Monte Ward, and Kid Gleason

3. Cesar Tovar; Cecil Travis

4. Ed Delahanty; brothers Tom, Frank, Jim, and Joe

5. Hardy Richardson; Danny Richardson

6. Gil McDougald

7. Jimmie Foxx

8. Honus Wagner

9. Mickey Stanley; Mike Stanley

10. Roger Connor

11. Joe Torre; brother Frank

12. Nixey Callahan

13. Dick Allen; brothers Hank and Ron

14. Yank Robinson; Yank Terry

15. Johnny Pesky

16. Bobby Bragan; Bobby Brown

17. Joe Gerhardt, first base in 1876 and second base in 1877; Joe Girardi

18. Earl "Sparky" Adams; Earl Averill; Sparky Anderson

19. King Kelly, 1878–79 Cincinnati Red Stockings, NL, and 1891 Cincinnati Kelly's Killers, AA

20. Gregg Jefferies

All-Star Appetizers

1. All batted right-handed and threw left-handed.

2. All never played on or managed a pennant winner.

3. White Sox; Frank Thomas

4. Braves Field

5. Alvin Dark, 1963 and 1975

6. Max West; Mike Witt

7. Mickey Owen, 1942; Mickey Vernon in 1946

8. Schoolboy Rowe, 1936, AL, and 1947, NL

9. Wally Berger; Braves Field, 1936

10. Ron Fairly

11. Joe DiMaggio, 1936

12. Bob Friend and Vern Law, 1960

13. Spec Shea, 1947

14. Hank Greenberg, 1935

15. 1965; Minnesota; Metropolitan Stadium

16. Paul Richards in 1961, replacing fired Yankees manager Casey Stengel, and Gene Mauch in 1965, replacing resigned Cardinals manager Johnny Keane

17. Brooks Robinson

18. Steve Rogers, 1982, and Johnny Vander Meer, 1938, threw back-to-back no-hitters

19. Dick Groat, Ken Boyer, Bill White, and Julian Javier of the 1964 Cards, with Javier replacing Mazeroski

20. It marked the end of the 1981 strike.

21. Wilbur Wood, 1973

22. Ebbets Field in 1949 and Bloomington in 1965

League Championship Series Lore

1. George Brett, three solo homers in Game Three, 1978, lost by Kansas City, 6–5

2. Mark Brouhard; Mark Littell; Mike Boddicker

3. Steve Crawford; Stan Coveleski

4. Baltimore, 1974

5. Jim Rice; Boston

6. Reggie Jackson; Oakland, New York, and California

7. Jerry Reuss

8. Bruce Kison, 1971

9. Dave Stieb; Toronto; Charlie Leibrandt

10. Mickey Rivers

11. Dave McNally

12. Sparky Lyle

13. Fred Lynn

14. Steve Garvey

15. Nolan Ryan

16. 1997 Baltimore Orioles

17. Doug Drabek

Seventh-Game Starters

1. Johnny Kucks; Jim Konstanty

2. Curly Ogden; Charlie O'Brien

3. Babe Adams, 1909

4. Hugh Bedient; Hugh Casey; Hank Bauer

5. Vic Aldridge versus Walter Johnson

6. Lew Burdette

7. Waite Hoyt; Babe Ruth

8. Burleigh Grimes

9. Eldon Auker

10. Bobo Newsom

11. Hank Borowy; Hubie Brooks

12. Murry Dickson; Red Murray; Mariano Duncan

13. Hal Gregg; Hank Greenberg; Vean Gregg

14. Jim Lonborg; Johnny Lush, 1904 Phils

15. Ken Holtzman; Jon Matlack

16. Bruce Hurst; Frank Viola

17. John Smoltz

Fall Classics: 1871–1941

1. Art Nehf

2. Jimmy Archer

3. Fred Merkle, 1911–13 Giants, 1916 Dodgers, and 1918 Cubs; his error was failing to touch second base in a 1908 game

4. Wally Schang, 1913–14 A's, 1918 Red Sox, 1921–23 Yankees; brother Bobby

5. 1911; Shibe Park and the Polo Grounds; Connie Mack and John McGraw

6. 1884; Jim Mutrie and Frank Bancroft

7. 1914; Connie Mack and George Stallings

8. Chief Bender

9. Charlie Pick; Cy Perkins; Charlie Hollocher; Ollie "Pick" Pickering

10. Smokey Joe Wood; Smoky Burgess, .368 in 1954

11. Bobby Lowe, 1907 Tigers

12. Dan McGann, 1905 Giants; Joe Kelley managed him in 1908

13. Jack Coombs

14. Art Nehf, 1924; Walter Johnson was his hill opponent in Game One

15. Stuffy McInnis, 1911 and 1913 A's, 1918 Red Sox, and 1925 Pirates

16. Pants Rowland

17. Goose Goslin; Goose Gossage

18. Howard Ehmke

19. Lonnie Frey, 1939; Wally Berger

20. Lou Gehrig

Fall Classics: 1942–98

1. Phil Cavarretta

2. Milt Wilcox (Sparky Anderson)

3. George Stallings, Hank Bauer, and Lou Piniella

4. Pee Wee Reese; Phil Rizzuto was his fellow rookie in 1941

5. Dixie Walker; brother Harry in 1946

6. 1961 Reds; Fred Hutchinson; Johnny Edwards and Ken Hunt; Frank Robinson

7. Ron Taylor; Roy Thomas

8. Bobby Richardson

9. Lonnie Smith

10. Brian Doyle

11. Jim Palmer

12. Dennis Martinez, 1979 and 1995

13. Jim Mason, off Pat Zachry in Game Three in 1976; Joe Medwick

14. Bill Plummer

15. Rusty Staub, 1973 Mets

16. George Frazier

17. Don Baylor, 1986 Red Sox, 1987 Twins, and 1988 A's

18. Allie Reynolds, 1949–53

19. Don Drysdale

20. Jack Billingham

Team Time: 1871–1919

1. 1902 Pirates

2. 1904 A's, Eddie Plank and Rube Waddell

3. 1878 Boston Red Caps

4. 1901 St. Louis Cardinals; Patsy Donovan; their high attendance induced the Milwaukee AL franchise to move to St Louis in 1902

5. 1911 Phillies

6. 1914 Yankees; Roger Peckinpaugh

7. 1911 Braves

8. 1914–15 St. Louis Terriers in the Federal League; Fielder Jones

9. 1885 New York Giants; Jim Mutrie

10. New York and Pittsburgh; Philadelphia; Chicago; 1906 NL season

11. 1889 Louisville

12. 1884 AA: Columbus, Cincinnati, and Toledo

13. Minnesota; St. Paul Apostles, 1884, after Richmond and Wilmington had also briefly fielded teams in 1884; Minnesota Twins (named for the "Twin Cities")

14. 1904 Giants, played .693 ball, 48 points short of Pittsburgh's .741 in 1902

15. 1901 Cleveland Blues

16. 1902 Baltimore Orioles

17. John Ganzel; brother Charlie and nephew Babe; Jim Greengrass

18. 1887 Baltimore Orioles; Phenomenal Smith (25–30); Matt Kilroy (46–19); Tommy Tucker was the rookie first sacker

19. 1914 Indianapolis Hoosiers, 1890 Boston Reds, 1891 Boston Reds

20. Pittsburgh Pirates, 1900s, .636

21. 1909 Chicago Cubs; Three Finger Brown; Pittsburgh

22. Pittsburgh 1886, Pud Galvin (29–21) and Ed Morris (41–20)

Team Time: 1920–98

1. Cleveland; Lou Boudreau and Mickey Vernon

2. 1973 Texas Rangers; Jeff Burroughs; Jim Bibby and brother Henry

3. 1970 Cincinnati Reds in Riverfront Stadium

4. Milwaukee; Jerry Koosman

5. 1982 Cards

6. 1927 Cubs; Joe McCarthy

7. Pittsburgh, 1894–1953; 1909 World Series

8. 1975-76 Reds

9. 1966 Yankees; Johnny Keane and Ralph Houk were the two managers

10. 1954 Yankees

11. 1954 Red Sox; Lou Boudreau; Ted Williams

12. Pittsburgh

13. 1922 Cincinnati Reds; Dolf Luque; Eppa Rixey

14. 1953 Browns; Marty Marion

15. 1943 Braves; Eddie Joost, Ryan, Whitey Wietelmann, and Johnny McCarthy

16. 1937–42 Dodgers

17. 1929 Phils; Chuck Klein (43), Lefty O'Doul (32), and Don Hurst (31); 1929 Athletics

18. 1976 A's (341) and 1992 Brewers (256); Pat Listach

19. 1953 Brooklyn Dodgers; Joe Black

20. Altoona; Germany Smith; Charlie Berry

21. 1928 Cardinals; Jim Bottomley, Frankie Frisch, Taylor Douthit, and Chick Hafey; Paul Waner

Distinguished Doormats

1. Chicago, with a franchise since 1876, or 48 years—1924 White Sox and 1925 Cubs

2. 1912 Senators

3. 1966 Yankees

4. 1968 Astros; Harry Walker, 1969 Mets; Larry Dierker

5. 1900 New York Giants

6. Larry Doyle; 1915 New York Giants

7. 1958 Phillies; Richie Ashburn

8. 1897–98 St. Louis Browns

9. 1886 Baltimore Orioles, 1983 Seattle Mariners, and 1991 Houston Astros (1975 Angels were not last overall, and 1968 Astros led the NL only while finishing last); Terry Pendleton, .319

10. 1952 Tigers; Roscoe Miller

11. Los Angeles–California–Anaheim Angels

12. 1914–15 Philadelphia A's; Connie Mack

13. 1904–1906 Boston Pilgrims; Jimmy Collins and Chick Stahl

14. 1891 Pittsburgh Pirates: Pud Galvin, Silver King and Mark Baldwin, Jake Beckley, Lou Bierbauer, Ned Hanlon and Bill McGunnigle, and Pete Browning

15. Kansas City Royals

16. Pittsburgh, Chicago, and Philadelphia; Chicago never won

17. San Diego Padres, 1969–74

18. 1935 Boston Braves; Wally Berger; Babe Ruth

19. Red Sox; Bill Carrigan

Cooperstown Conundrums

1. Waite Hoyt

2. Buck Ewing and Mickey Welch; 1888–89 New York Giants

3. Dave Bancroft

4. Herb Pennock, 1914 and 1932

5. Kenesaw Mountain Landis; Frank Mountain

6. Joe DiMaggio

7. Lou Gehrig

8. Al Simmons

9. Roger Bresnahan

10. Mel Harder

11. Sam Crawford

12. Hughie Jennings

13. Jesse Haines

14. Heinie Manush; brother Frank; Heinie Zimmerman

15. Joe "Ducky" Medwick

16. Joe McGinnity

17. Stan Musial

18. Mel Ott

19. Johnny Mize in 1949

20. Sam Thompson

21. Pie Traynor, third base; Eddie Yost; Eddie Mathews; Brooks Robinson

22. Freddy Lindstrom

23. Paul Waner

24. Monte Ward; Providence

25. Zack Wheat; brother Mack

26. John Clarkson; brother Dad; brother Walter

27. Bill Dickey; brother George

28. Joe Cronin

29. Stan Coveleski; Tris Speaker and Bucky Harris; brother Harry

30. Johnny Evers; uncle Tom

31. Roy Campanella

32. Tommy McCarthy

33. Steve Carlton, with the Twins at the end of the 1987 season

34. Gaylord Perry; brother Jim

35. Eddie Plank

36. Harry Hooper; Harry Heilmann; Tris Speaker was his fellow HOF outfielder

37. Reggie Jackson

38. Jack Chesbro

39. Bob Feller and Bob Lemon, April 30, 1946; Lou Boudreau

40. Al Simmons

41. Jim O'Rourke; brother John; son Queenie

42. Hal Newhouser; Briggs Stadium

43. Joe Sewell; brothers Luke and Tommy

44. Warren Spahn

45. Mike Schmidt

Hypothetical Cy Young Winners

1. Burleigh Grimes

2. Curt Davis; Chubby Dean

3. John Clarkson, 1889; Bob Caruthers, 1889; Bill Hutchison, 1890; Jack Chesbro, 1904; Ed Walsh, 1908

4. Lady Baldwin; James Baldwin

5. Amos Rusie, 245, last at 27; Jack Stivetts, 202, last at 29; Silver King, 204, last at 29; and Bob Caruthers, 218, last at 28

6. Babe Ruth

7. Eddie Cicotte, 1917-19; banned in 1920 by Judge Landis

8. Lefty Grove, 1931 A's

9. Kid Nichols

10. Cy Young

11. Robin Roberts

12. Jim McCormick; Mike McCormick

13. Bobo Newsom

14. Vic Willis

15. Amos Rusie

16. Pete Alexander

MVP Mainsprings

1. 1966 Baltimore: Frank Robinson, Brooks Robinson, and Boog Powell; Minnesota; Zoilo Versalles

2. Jake Daubert; Joe DiMaggio

3. Ned Garver, 1951; Ned Hanlon

4. Vern Stephens

5. George Brett and Mike Schmidt

6. Don Schwall and Chuck Schilling, 1961; Curt Schilling

7. Marty Marion

8. 1952: Robin Roberts, Joe Black, and Hoyt Wilhelm; Hank Sauer

9. Sandy Koufax in 1963

10. Willie Stargell, 1979

11. Robert "Bob" Brown; Bill Bradley; Robert "Bobby" Brown

12. Pittsburgh; Dick Groat, 1960

13. Morton and Walker Cooper, 1943

14. Cubs; Wildfire Schulte, 1911; Andre Dawson, 1987, when the Cubs were last in the NL East; Ernie Banks, 1958–59

15. Chief Meyers and Ray Schalk

16. Roy Campanella and Yogi Berra, 1951 and 1955

17. Cardinals: Stan Musial, 1946; Orlando Cepeda, 1967; and Keith Hernandez, 1979

18. Sal Maglie, 1956; Don Newcombe won both major awards

Fabled Frosh

1. Cal Ripken, 1983–84

2. Eddie Mathews

3. Mike Slattery, Boston, UA, 1884; Mike Scioscia

4. Walt Dropo, 1951

5. Roy Sievers

6. Joe Charboneau

7. Saturnino "Minnie" Minoso

8. Buzz Arlett

9. Norm Zauchin; Gus Zernial; Norm Cash

10. Jim Frey, Kansas City, 1980–81

11. Irv Young

12. Luis Aparicio and Frank Robinson, 1956; Tom Seaver and Rod Carew, 1967

13. Scott Perry, 1918 A's; Gaylord and Jim Perry

14. Al Gerheauser; Alfredo Griffin; Steve Gerkin

15. Patsy Dougherty; Patsy Donovan

16. Ken Hunt; Ken Hubbs

17. Irv Young and Oscar Jones; Henry Schmidt, Anthony Young, and Bumpus Jones

18. Lou Piniella, Tommy Agee, Alfredo Griffin, and Sandy Alomar

19. Bill Everitt; Buck Ewing

20. Carl Lind; Chet Lemon; Jose Lind

21. Mike McCormick; Frank McCormick

22. Dick "Richie" Allen; Richie Ashburn

23. Tommy Helms; Sparky Anderson; Pete Rose

24. George Derby; Gus Dorner

The Changing Game

1. Beginning in 1893, .300 team averages became commonplace after the pitching distance was increased to 60'6"; Chicago White Stockings, 1876, Ross Barnes, before the fair-foul rule was abolished; St. Louis Browns, 1887, Tip O'Neill, the lone year that walks were counted as hits

2. 1929

3. 1947; Lou Boudreau and Joe Gordon; Mel Ott managed the Giants and Connie Mack the A's

4. 1950 was the last all-white World Series

5. 1921 Phils

6. 1911; Jack Powell

7. 1974: Mickey Lolich, AL, and Bill Bonham, Randy Jones, and Steve Rogers, NL; Mike Marshall; in 1883, Hoss Radbourn and Pud Galvin appeared in 76 games in the NL and Tim Keefe appeared in 68 in the AA while the A's led the majors with 66 wins; Oakland, 1972–74

8. Buffalo: Pud Galvin, Billy Serad, Pete Conway, and Pete Wood

9. One Arm Daily; Chicago, Pittsburgh, and Washington, all in the UA, were his three teams

10. 1950 Yankees; Yogi Berra; Joe DiMaggio

11. 1952 Cardinals, led by Solly Hemus; Eddie Mathews

12. Tim Keefe; overhand pitching was allowed in the NL in 1884 and in the AA in 1885

13. Toad Ramsey, 1887

14. 1905 New York Highlanders; Clark Griffith

15. 1909 Boston Red Sox; Frank Arellanes; Tris Speaker

16. 1957 Yankees; Milwaukee Braves; Warren Spahn

17. 1988, Danny Jackson and Orel Hershiser, who also set the shutout record

18. 1984 Brewers; Ben Oglivie

Famous Firsts

1. Red Faber
2. Cleveland
3. Al Pratt; Arnie Portocarrero; Albie Pearson
4. Earl Harrist; Ed Heusser; Enzo Hernandez
5. Dan Bankhead; Scott Bankhead
6. Duke Farrell
7. Ham Iburg
8. Arlie Latham; Juice Latham
9. Sam Wise; Sam Weaver
10. George Moriarty
11. Frank Bancroft; Fred Beck; Dave Bancroft
12. Carl Mays
13. Dick Donovan; Don Drysdale
14. Ken McBride in 1964; Dick McBride
15. Craig Swan; Joe Torre
16. Herb Pennock
17. Tim Keefe
18. Rip Repulski; Wes Covington; Ray Jablonski
19. Paul Hines
20. Will White; Jim McCormick; Pud Galvin
21. Eddie Plank; the A's
22. Sam Crawford; Alan Trammell; Detroit

Famous Lasts

1. Dale Mitchell
2. Jack Harper; Harry Harper; Jim Hughey; 1899 Cleveland Spiders
3. Myron "Joe" Ginsberg; 1962 Mets and 1954 Indians; Jake Gibbs
4. Shibe Park in 1919; Tilly Walker; Harry Davis; Gus Zernial; Jimmie Foxx; Columbia Park
5. Jack Fisher; Jeff Fassero
6. Jim Hughes, 1976
7. Andy Pafko in 1950; Adolfo Phillips
8. Craig Anderson; Charles Addams; John Anderson
9. Charlie O'Leary, 21 years; Claude Osteen; Mrs. O'Leary's cow

10. Johnny Kucab; Johnny Kucks
11. Pete Browning
12. Sandy Koufax won the Cy Young in 1966.
13. Each hit the last home run in a major league uniform that was never seen again after that season: Hunter, St. Louis Browns; Limmer, Philadelphia A's; Mathews, Boston Braves; Harris, New York Giants; Jackson, Brooklyn Dodgers
14. Bill James; Billy Johnson, 1943
15. Catfish Hunter, 1971 A's
16. Phil Rizzuto, Don Bollweg, Gil McDougald, and Billy Martin, Game Six of the 1953 Series; Allie Reynolds; Brooklyn Dodgers (The 1954 season was the first that did not allow gloves to be left on the playing field.)
17. Stan Coveleski
18. Jack Scott
19. Jones was the last pitcher to throw a major league no-hitter at the 50' distance and also the first to throw one on the last day of a season; Witt tossed the first perfect game on the last day of a season.
20. Foul balls with fewer than two strikes were counted as strikes in the American League for the first time in 1903.
21. Wilcy Moore

Like Father, Like Son

1. Dick, George, and Dave Sisler
2. Dizzy and Steve Trout; Trout and Hal Newhouser, 56 wins in 1944; Dizzy Dean
3. Sam Hairston, sons Jerry and John; Stan Hack
4. Elmer Jacobs; Ellis Johnson; Spook Jacobs
5. Vern and Vance Law; 1960
6. Billy Sullivan Sr. and Jr.; Bob Skinner
7. Jim Bagby Sr. and Jr.
8. Gus and Buddy Bell and grandson David
9. Dale Berra; Dale Mitchell
10. Jim and Mike Hegan, 1948 and 1972; second were Bob and Terry Kennedy, 1948 and 1984
11. Julian and Stan Javier
12. Ray Schalk; Ed Walsh Sr. and Jr.; the White Sox
13. Dick Schofield and son Dick

14. Ernie Johnson and son Don

15. Larry, Charlie, and Tookie Gilbert;
Gilbert Hodges

16. Joe Coleman and son Joe; John Coleman

Famous Brother Acts

1. Jose, Hector, and Tommy Cruz

2. Buck and John Ewing

3. The Mansells; Felix Mantilla

4. Pete and Jim Conway; Dick and Bill Conway;
Jack Conway

5. Gene and George Freese; George Kell and Gene
Bearden; George Foster

6. Milt and Frank Bolling; Mike Blowers

7. Phil and Joe Niekro

8. Jesse and Lee Tannehill; Joe Torre

9. Rick and Paul Reuschel

10. Hal and Lou Finney; Lew Fonseca; Lou
Boudreau and Hal Peck in 1948

11. Lloyd and Paul Waner; Joe and Luke Sewell
were the other brother pair

12. Jim and Ed Bailey; Ernie Banks; Bob Bailey

13. Norm and Larry Sherry; Lonnie Smith

14. Bill and Ed Dugan with Virginia of the American
Association, 1884; Joe Dugan; Bill
Monbouquette and Ed Bressoud

15. Ken and Clete Boyer, 282 and 162 homers,
and Cloyd

16. The Perrys, 1970: Gaylord, 23–13 for San
Francisco, and Jim, 24–12 for Minnesota

Ethnic Esoterica

1. Allie Reynolds

2. Joe Stanka; Eddie Stanky; John Smoltz

3. Minnie Minoso; Gil McDougald

4. Larry Doby and Hank Thompson

5. Mudcat Grant; Ulysses S. Grant

6. Detroit, 1961, Jake Wood; Smokey Joe Wood

7. 1968, Luis Tiant and Bob Gibson

8. Tony Oliva, 1964; Dick Allen

9. Satchel Paige, 1952

10. Chief Bender

11. Larry Doby; Al Smith

12. Elston Howard

13. 1971, Vida Blue

14. Dolf Luque

15. Reggie Smith; Reggie Jackson

16. Dolf Luque

17. Hi Bithorn; Hank Borowy

18. Royals, 1982, Vida Blue

19. Frank White and U. L. Washington, 1980 Royals

Dynamic Duos

1. Amos Rusie and Joe McGinnity

2. Ben Chapman and Jimmie Foxx; George Wright
was their manager; Bill Campbell in 1976

3. Paul Hines and Jim O'Rourke, Providence 1878;
Pinky Higgins

4. Larry Corcoran and Fred Goldsmith; Larry
Jackson and Fred Hutchinson; Fred Gladding

5. Buddy Myer and Cecil Travis; Cupid Childs and
Ed McKean

6. Tony Lazzeri, 11 RBI in a game

7. They're the only men to manage at least two full
seasons in the NL and never manage against a
New York team.

8. Sam Thompson and Dan Brouthers

9. They were the top AL rookie vote-getters in 1947
and 1948, the only two years that just one
BBWAA Rookie of the Year Award was given.

10. They hit the first NL and AL home runs in a
night game.

11. Rogers Hornsby and Travis Jackson in 1927;
George Kelly and Freddy Lindstrom;
Babe Ruth

12. Jack Chesbro and Jack Powell

13. Denny McLain and Mickey Lolich; broken in
1990 by Bob Welch and Dave Stewart; Hal
Newhouser and Dizzy Trout

14. They are credited with the first NL and AL pinch hits.

15. They hold the 20th century NL and AL records, respectively, for the most RBI in a game by a pitcher; Tony Lazzeri

16. They were the first to homer in every major league park in use during their careers; interleague trading became common in 1959, increasing player movement between leagues.

17. They were the opposing third basemen for Pawtucket and Rochester in the longest game in organized baseball history, 33 innings in 1981. Tony Boeckel and Jimmy Johnston were the opposing third basemen in the 26-inning tie between Boston and Brooklyn in 1920.

Common Denominators

1. They were the last all-white teams for these franchises.

2. All won 20 games for last-place teams.

3. All were losing pitchers in a pennant- or division-deciding game on the final day of a season.

4. All pinch-hit for Babe Ruth.

5. All were right-handed hitting bat crown winners with Detroit.

6. All were 20-game winners before they turned 20.

7. All won 20 games their rookie seasons.

8. Switch-hitters who have won batting titles; Ken Caminiti

9. AA bat crown winners

10. All managed Cleveland teams to second-place finishes but never managed a pennant winner in the majors; Fohl also managed the St. Louis Browns to a second-place finish in 1922.

11. All won batting titles playing for last-place teams.

12. All were the first players to lead their franchise's loop in homers.

13. All had feature films made of their life stories.

14. All became broadcasters after their playing days were over; Kell and Kaline work together with the Tigers.

15. All were the last active players in the majors from teams that relocated.

16. All were backup catchers on A's flag winners under Connie Mack who saw no World Series action; Grove wanted Palmisano to replace Mickey Cochrane, whom he claimed was being stolen blind by Martin.

17. All appeared in World Series play exclusively as DHs for NL teams.

18. Each had a perfect 2–0 record in a World Series with a losing team, Ford in 1955 and again in 1960.

19. All won a World Series after losing the first game.

20. All lost the deciding seventh game of a World Series at home.

21. All were pitchers whose last mound appearances came in a World Series.

22. All started and won World Series games as rookies.

23. All were 20-game winners who didn't start their major league careers until they were past 30.

24. All led their leagues in losses in their final major league seasons.

25. All won 20 in their final major league seasons; Ferguson died; Schmidt and Koufax both quit the majors; Flynn played one game the following season as an outfielder.

26. All won 20 as rookies and never did it again; Duryea won 32, the record for most wins by a rookie who never again won 20 in a season.

Premier Pilots

1. Gus Schmelz; George Scott

2. Eddie Collins; Johnny Evers

3. Bill Joyce

4. Chuck Dressen

5. George Pearce; George Pinkney; Billy Pierce

6. Jack Chapman, Louisville; Joe Cronin, 1946

7. Charlie Comiskey

8. Danny Ozark, 1976–77 Phils

9. Fred Haney

10. Tom Loftus; Tom Lasorda

11. Frank Baker

12. Bob Shawkey; Burt Shotton

13. Dave Fultz, 1899 Orioles and 1901 A's; Dave Foutz

14. Billy Southworth

15. Bill Virdon, 1974–75, when the Yankees used Shea Stadium while Yankee Stadium was being refurbished

16. Bucky Harris, 1924 Washington and 1947 Yankees

17. Jack Burdock; John Morrill

18. Johnny Sain

19. Monte Cross; Lave Cross

20. Mike Hargrove, 111 walks for Cleveland

21. Clark Griffith, Dallas Green, and Eddie Dyer

22. Bill McKechnie

Men in Blue

1. Ken Burkhart; Kitty Bransfield

2. Bob Emslie; Bob Elliott

3. Hank O'Day

4. Bill McGowan; Beauty McGowan; Bill Klem

5. Jack Sheridan; John Shelby; Pat Sheridan

6. George Pipgras, 1944; George Pinkney

7. Sherry Magee

8. Cy Pfirman; Claude Passeau; Cy Young

9. Don Drysdale had his consecutive scoreless innings streak extended when Wendelstedt refused to give Dietz his base and force home a run after Dietz was hit by a pitch with the bases loaded.

10. Bill Stewart; Billy Shindle; Jimmy Stewart

11. Eddie Rommel

12. Charlie Moran; Clarence Mitchell

13. Lon Warneke, 1932 and 1954

14. Paul Sentell; Pat Sheridan

15. Cal Hubbard

16. Ed Sudol; Earl Sheely

Early Exits

1. Marty Bergen; Mark Belanger

2. Ed Delahanty

3. Charlie Ferguson; Bob Ferguson; Curt Flood

4. Darby O'Brien

5. Addie Joss

6. Miguel "Mickey" Fuentes; Mickey Hughes; Mike Fornieles; Tito Fuentes

7. Danny Frisella; Dee Fondy

8. Lyman Bostock; Larry Bowa

9. Ed Morris; Eddie Murray

10. Joe Cassidy; John Cassidy, runner-up for the NL batting title in 1877; Joe Carter

11. Ken Hubbs; Ken Hunt

12. Chick Stahl; Larry Stahl

13. Don Wilson; Duane Ward

14. Bob Moose; Bill Monbouquette

15. Ross Youngs; prior to 1999, the last name in the Hall alphabetically

16. Ed "Cannonball" Crane; Cannonball Morris; Eddie Collins

17. Hub Collins; Hal Chase

18. Harry Agganis

The Name's the Same

1. Dave, Shano, and Hub Collins

2. Tommy, Larry, and Tim Corcoran

3. Billy, Ival, and Jake Goodman

4. Ed, John, and Gordy Coleman

5. Rick, Tommy, and Freddy Leach

6. Eddie, Ray, and Joe Morgan

7. Chet, Jim, and Bob Lemon

8. Frank, Marv, and Mickey Owen

9. Dave, Bill, and Fred Nicholson

10. Frank, Gorman, and Roy Thomas

11. Everett, George, and Milt Scott

12. John, George, and Dean Stone

13. Herb, Charlie, and Al Moran

14. Tony, Mike, and Juan Gonzalez

15. Cecil, Walker, Wilbur, and Mort Cooper

16. Ray, Ben, and Sam Chapman

17. Brady, Harry, and Goat Anderson

18. Deacon, Bill, and Roy White

19. Hubert "Dutch" Leonard, Emil "Dutch" Leonard, and Dennis Leonard

20. Larry, Chick, and Jake Stahl

21. Frank, Bob, and Johnny Allen

22. Dick, Britt, and Sleepy Bill Burns

23. Alex, George, and Charlie Ferguson (30–9 in 1886)

24. Sam, Ted, and Dolly Gray

25. Nat, Sid, and Charlie Hudson

26. Joe, Sid, and Tom Gordon

27. Leon, Honus, and Heinie Wagner

28. Sam, Monte, and Buck Weaver

29. John, Jimmy, and Rosy Ryan

30. Curt, Dixie, and Jim Davis

31. George, Kiddo, and Lefty Davis

32. Harry, Steve, and Ted Lyons; Tom Seaver was traded for Steve Lyons in 1986

33. Taffy, Glenn, and Ed Wright (8–3)

34. Harry, Jim, and Mike McCormick

35. Reb, Jack, and Jeff Russell

36. Alfredo, Ivy, and Mike Griffin

37. Mike, Dale, and Clarence Mitchell

38. Willie, Chief, and Hack Wilson

Thirty Outstanding Achievements You Won't Find in Standard Baseball Record Books

1. Bobby Estalella, 1945; .299 BA, .399 OBP, and .435 SA

2. Bill Keister; Benny Kauff

3. Elmer Valo, 1946–48; Emil Verban

4. Walter Arlington "Arlie" Latham; Arlington National Cemetery

5. "Silent Mike" Tiernan; Mickey Tettleton

6. George Shoch; George Sisler

7. Gus Zernial, 1951–54, 528 games; Ozark Ike

8. Dizzy Dean; brother Paul

9. Johnnie LeMaster; Johnnie "Dusty" Baker

10. 1934 Philadelphia A's; George Caster and Al Benton were the other two rookie hurlers.

11. 90 years; 1882, American Association

12. Tacks Latimer; Tim Laudner

13. Wes Covington; Willie Crawford

14. Val Picinich; Vic Power

15. Terry Crowley; Ty Cobb, 20 seasons

16. 169 errors, the fewest in a season to that point

17. Frank Scheibeck; Fred Stanley; Sam Thompson and Deacon McGuire are the other two men who played for Detroit in both the NL and the AL

18. Joe Carter

19. Graig Nettles

20. Barney McCosky

21. John O'Connell; Danny O'Connell; Jimmy O'Connell; John McGraw

22. Al Kaline

23. Monte Ward

24. Emmett Seery and Enoch "Jersey" Bakely; Pat Seerey

25. Rodney Scott

26. Sandy Koufax

27. Jack "Peach Pie" O'Connor; Joe Oeschger, 26 innings

28. Sam Crawford

29. Paul Revere Radford

30. Dick Schofield